Lecture Notes
in Business Information Processing 515

LNBIP reports state-of-the-art results in areas related to business information systems and industrial application software development – timely, at a high level, and in both printed and electronic form.

The type of material published includes

- Proceedings (published in time for the respective event)
- Postproceedings (consisting of thoroughly revised and/or extended final papers)
- Other edited monographs (such as, for example, project reports or invited volumes)
- Tutorials (coherently integrated collections of lectures given at advanced courses, seminars, schools, etc.)
- Award-winning or exceptional theses

LNBIP is abstracted/indexed in DBLP, EI and Scopus. LNBIP volumes are also submitted for the inclusion in ISI Proceedings.

Yiliu Paul Tu · Maomao Chi
Editors

E-Business

New Challenges and Opportunities for Digital-Enabled Intelligent Future

23rd Wuhan International Conference, WHICEB 2024
Wuhan, China, May 24–26, 2024
Proceedings, Part I

 Springer

Editors
Yiliu Paul Tu (iD)
University of Calgary
Calgary, AB, Canada

Maomao Chi
China University of Geosciences
Wuhan, China

ISSN 1865-1348   ISSN 1865-1356 (electronic)
Lecture Notes in Business Information Processing
ISBN 978-3-031-60263-4   ISBN 978-3-031-60264-1 (eBook)
https://doi.org/10.1007/978-3-031-60264-1

This Springer imprint is published by the registered company Springer Nature Switzerland AG
The registered company address is: Gewerbestrasse 11, 6330 Cham, Switzerland

If disposing of this product, please recycle the paper.

Preface

The 23rd Wuhan International Conference on E-Business (WHICEB), an AIS-affiliated annual conference, took place from May 24 to 26, 2024, in Wuhan, China. The conference hosts were the School of Economics and Management, China University of Geosciences, Wuhan, China, and Baden-Württemberg Cooperative State University Heidenheim, Heidenheim, Germany. The organizers were The Center for International Cooperation in E-Business, China University of Geosciences, Wuhan, China, the School of Information Management, Wuhan University, China, and the College of Business Administration, Ningbo University of Finance & Economics, China. The conference was sponsored by the Association for Information Systems (AIS), the China Association for Information Systems (CNAIS), the China Information Economics Society, and Wuhan University of Communication.

WHICEB is dedicated to advancing scholarly research and fostering networking opportunities within the e-business sector and related fields. Our goal is to catalyze academic inquiry and business innovation by facilitating discussions on e-business, global finance, and the imperative for ongoing innovation. This conference aims to showcase cutting-edge research, solutions, and methodologies that leverage the Internet as a powerful tool for global commerce. The digital age presents a myriad of challenges, from technological hurdles to behavioral adaptations, marketing strategies to data analytics, and concerns over efficacy to security. In recent years, the ABCD Technology—big data, cloud computing, artificial intelligence, and blockchain—has sparked a new wave of innovation across manufacturing, business, education, and personal life sectors. This digital and intelligent transformation is paving the way for a novel digital economy growth model, redefining "Internet Plus" applications, and enabling businesses to reinvent their models from the ground up. In response to this digital and intelligent trend, companies are actively engaging with new challenges, thereby generating numerous research opportunities.

This year's conference theme, "New Challenges and Opportunities for a Digital-Enabled Intelligent Future," is designed to ignite robust academic and corporate engagement by integrating e-business and information technology in our increasingly digital and intelligent landscape, alongside fresh insights and discoveries in service, marketing, and operational management reform. The conference sought to highlight groundbreaking scientific research in fields enabled by artificial intelligence, foster cross-disciplinary studies, and share experiences from various nations and regions. These proceedings encompass 16 tracks and will be indexed appropriately. The selected best papers from the proceedings will be recommended to international academic journals including but not limited to the following: Electronic Commerce Research and Applications, Electronic Markets, Electronic Commerce Research, Internet Research, Journal of Organizational and End User Computing, Journal of Information & Knowledge Management, International Journal of Networking and Virtual Organizations, and Journal of Systems and Information Technology.

The research papers in these proceedings went through a double-blind peer review process. Papers were accepted based upon a clear research methodology and contributions to the knowledge of e-business including but not limited to case studies, experiments, simulations, and surveys. The efforts made by our track chairs in reviewing submissions are really appreciated, which ensures the quality of the proceedings. On behalf of the conference organization, we thank them for their professional diligence. They are: *Xing Wan, Jiangnan Qiu, and Lin Jia*, Advancing Digital Education; Innovations, Challenges, and Opportunities; *Yaobin Lu, Ling Zhao, and Jiang Wu*, Artificial Intelligence & IoT(AIoT) Enabled Business Innovation; *Yi Wang, Yuan Sun, and Si Shi*, Artificial Intelligence and New Ways of Working; *Guoyin Jiang, Xiaodong Feng, and Wenping Liu*, Computing and Complexity in Digital Platforms; *Dongxiao Gu, Jia Li, and Yiming Zhao*, Data Science and Smart Social Governance; *Zhongyun (Phil) Zhou, Yongqiang Sun, and Xiao-Ling Jin*, Digital Enablement and Digital Governance; *Xiaobo (Bob) Xu, Weiyong Zhang, and Fei Ma*, Digital Innovation and Social Impact; *Ping Wang, Xiuyan Shao, and Cong Cao*, Disruptive Technologies and Digital Transformation; *Xiaoling Li, Lu Wang, and Qing Huang*, E-business Strategy & Online Marketing; *Rong Du, Hongpeng Wang, and Peng Wang*, Emerging e-Commerce Initiatives Enabled by Advanced Technologies; *Shaobo Wei, Xiayu Chen, and Hua Liu*, Emerging Technologies and Social Commerce; *Nannan Xi, Hongxiu Li, Juho Hamari, and Juan Chen*, Engaging Technologies; *Zhaohua Deng, Tailai Wu, and Jia Li*, Healthcare Service and IT Management; *Haichao Zheng, Yuxiang Zhao, and Bin Zhu*, Human-Computer/AI Interactions; *Hefu Liu, Meng Chen, and Zhao Cai*, Information Systems and Operations Management; *Zhao Du, Ruoxin Zhou, and Shan Wang*, Transformative Digital Innovations: Education, Sports, and Entertainment.

This year, we received a total of 354 submissions, from which 107 papers successfully secured acceptance for publication. This results in an acceptance rate of approximately 30.79%. Our proceedings are structured across three volumes. Each paper included in these volumes has undergone a rigorous review process, involving a minimum of three double-blind reviews conducted by members of the Program Committee. Again, we express our sincere appreciation to all members of the Program Committee for their invaluable contributions, unwavering support, and dedicated efforts throughout this process.

April 2024

Yiliu Paul Tu
Maomao Chi

Organization

Conference Co-chairs

Jing Zhao   School of Economics and Management, China
University of Geosciences, China

Juergen Seitz   Baden-Württemberg Cooperative State University
Heidenheim, Germany

Doug Vogel   Harbin Institute of Technology, China

Publication Chairs and Proceedings Editors

Yiliu (Paul) Tu   University of Calgary, Canada

Maomao Chi   China University of Geosciences, China

Program Committee

Chairs

Weiguo (Patrick) Fan   University of Iowa, USA

Zhen Zhu   China University of Geosciences, Wuhan, China

Members

Yukun Bao   Huazhong University of Sciences & Technology,
China

Zhao Cai   University of Nottingham Ningbo, China

Cong Cao   Zhejiang University of Technology, China

Juan Chen   Anhui University of Finance and Economics,
China

Meng Chen   Soochow University, China

Xiayu Chen   Hefei University of Technology, China

Xusen Cheng   Renmin University of China, China

Zhaohua Deng   Huazhong University of Sciences & Technology,
China

Rong Du   Xidian University, China

Zhao Du   Beijing Sport University, China

Xiaodong Feng   Sun Yat-sen University, China

Dongxiao Gu	Hefei University of Technology, China
Juho Hamari	Tampere University, Finland
Qing Huang	Chongqing Technology and Business University, China
Zhongyi Hu	Wuhan University, China
Lin Jia	Beijing Institute of Technology, China
Guoyin Jiang	University of Electronic Science and Technology of China
Xiaoling Jin	Shanghai University, China
Hongxiu Li	Tampere University, Finland
Jia Li	East China University of Science and Technology, China
Xiaoling Li	Chongqing University, China
Xixi Li	University of Science and Technology Beijing, China
Hefu Liu	University of Science and Technology of China, China
Hua Liu	Anhui University of Finance and Economics, China
Wenping Liu	Hubei University of Economics, China
Yaobin Lu	Huazhong University of Sciences & Technology, China
Fei Ma	Chang'an University, China
Jian Mou	Pusan National University, South Korea
Jiangnan Qiu	Dalian University of Technology, China
Xiuyan Shao	Southeast University, China
Si Shi	Southwestern University of Finance and Economics, China
Yongqiang Sun	Wuhan University, China
Yuan Sun	Zhejiang Gongshang University, China
Yiliu (Paul) Tu	University of Calgary, Canada
Xing Wan	Nanjing University of Finance & Economics, China
Ping Wang	Central China Normal University, China
Fang Wang	Wilfrid Laurier University, Canada
Hongpeng Wang	Lanzhou University, China
Lu Wang	Zhongnan University of Economics and Law, China
Peng Wang	Northwestern Polytechnical University, China
Shan Wang	University of Saskatchewan, Canada
Yi Wang	Southwestern University of Finance and Economics, China
J. Christopher Westland	University of Illinois at Chicago, USA

Qiang Wei	Tsinghua University, China
Shaobo Wei	University of Science and Technology of China, China
Jiang Wu	Wuhan University, China
Tailai Wu	Huazhong University of Science & Technology, China
Nannan Xi	University of Vaasa, Finland
Huosong Xia	Wuhan Textile University, China
Wenlong Xiao	Chang Gung University, Taiwan RoC
Xiaobo (Bob) Xu	Xi'an Jiaotong-Liverpool University, China
Ying Yang	Hefei University of Technology, China
Jinmei Yin	Nanjing University of Aeronautics and Astronautics, China
Ming Yi	Central China Normal University, China
Shuping Zhao	Hefei University of Technology, China
Yiming Zhao	Wuhan University, China
Yuxiang Zhao	Nanjing University of Science and Technology, China
Haichao Zheng	Southwestern University of Finance and Economics, China
Zhongyun Zhou	Tongji University, China
Ling Zhao	Huazhong University of Sciences & Technology, China
Weiyong Zhang	Old Dominion University, USA
Ruoxin Zhou	University of International Business and Economics, China
Bin Zhu	Oregon State University, USA

Session Chairs

Kanliang Wang	Renmin University, China
Jinghua Xiao	Sun Yat-sen University, China
Rong Du	Xidian University, China
Xiangbin Yan	Guangdong University of Foreign Studies, China
Yi Jiang	China University of Geosciences, China

Organization Committee

Chair

Yao Zhang	China University of Geosciences, Wuhan, China

Secretary-General

Fei Wang	China University of Geosciences, Wuhan, China

Members

Jiang Wu	Wuhan University, China
Shangui Hu	Ningbo University of Finance & Economics, China
Yating Peng	China University of Geosciences, Wuhan, China
Jing Wang	China University of Geosciences, Wuhan, China
Qian Zhao	China University of Geosciences, Wuhan, China

International Advisory Board

Chairs

Joey George	Iowa State University, USA
Robert Kauffman	Copenhagen Business School, Denmark
J. Christopher Westland	University of Illinois at Chicago, USA

Pacific Asian

Patrick Chau	Beijing Normal University-Hong Kong Baptist University United International College (UIC), China
Guoqing Chen	Tsinghua University, China
Wei Kwok Kee	National University of Singapore, Singapore
Feicheng Ma	Wuhan University, China
Jiye Mao	Renmin University, China
Michael D. Myers	University of Auckland, New Zealand
Bernard Tan	National University of Singapore, Singapore
Kanliang Wang	Renmin University, China
Nilmini Wickramasinghe	Deakin University, Australia
Kang Xie	Sun Yat-sen University, China
Qiang Ye	University of Science and Technology of China, China
J. Leon Zhao	City University of Hong Kong, China

Artificial Intelligence and IoT (AIoT) Enabled Business Innovation

Yaobin Lu	Huazhong University of Science & Technology, China
Ling Zhao	Huazhong University of Science & Technology, China
Jiang Wu	Wuhan University, China

Artificial Intelligence and New Ways of Working

Yi Wang	Southwestern University of Finance and Economics, China
Yuan Sun	Zhejiang Gongshang University, China
Si Shi	Southwestern University of Finance and Economics, China
Jindi Fu	Hangzhou Dianzi University, China

Computing and Complexity in Digital Platforms

Guoyin Jiang	University of Electronic Science and Technology of China
Xiaodong Feng	Sun Yat-sen University, China
Wenping Liu	Hubei University of Economics, China

Data Science and Smart Social Governance

Dongxiao Gu	Hefei University of Technology, China
Jia Li	East China University of Science and Technology, China
Yiming Zhao	Wuhan University, China
Ying Yang	Hefei University of Technology, China
Shuping Zhao	Hefei University of Technology, China
Xiaoyu Wang	First Affiliated Hospital of Anhui University of Chinese Medicine, China

Digital Enablement and Digital Governance

Zhongyun (Phil) Zhou	Tongji University, China
Yongqiang Sun	Wuhan University, China
Xiao-Ling Jin	Shanghai University, China
Zhenya "Robin" Tang	University of Northern Colorado, USA
Qun Zhao	Ningbo University, China
Wei Hu	Tongji University, China

Digital Innovation and Social Impact

Xiaobo (Bob) Xu	Xi'an Jiaotong-Liverpool University, China
Weiyong Zhang	Old Dominion University, USA
Fei Ma	Chang'an University, China

Disruptive Technologies and Digital Transformation

Ping Wang	Central China Normal University, China
Xiuyan Shao	Southeast University, China
Cong Cao	Zhejiang University of Technology, China
Peter Shi	Macquarie University, Australia
Yiran Li	Zhejiang University of Technology, China

E-Business Strategy and Online Marketing

Xiaoling Li	Chongqing University, China
Lu Wang	Zhongnan University of Economics and Law, China
Qing Huang	Chongqing Technology and Business University, China

Emerging E-Commerce Initiatives Enabled by Advanced Technologies

Rong Du	Xidian University, China
Hongpeng Wang	Lanzhou University, China
Peng Wang	Northwestern Polytechnical University, China

Emerging Technologies and Social Commerce

Shaobo Wei   Hefei University of Technology, China
Xiayu Chen   Hefei University of Technology, China
Hua Liu   Anhui University, China
Jinmei Yin   Nanjing University of Aeronautics and
                            Astronautics, China

Engaging Technologies

Nannan Xi   Tampere University, Finland
Hongxiu Li   Tampere University, Finland
Juho Hamari   Tampere University, Finland
Juan Chen   Anhui University of Finance and Economics,
                            China

Healthcare Service and IT Management

Zhaohua Deng   Huazhong University of Science & Technology,
                            China
Tailai Wu   Huazhong University of Science & Technology,
                            China
Jia Li   East China University of Science and Technology,
                            China

Human-Computer/AI Interactions

Haichao Zheng   Southwestern University of Finance and
                            Economics, China
Yuxiang Zhao   Nanjing University of Science and Technology,
                            China
Bin Zhu   Oregon State University, China
Bo Xu   Fudan University, China
Kai Li   Nankai University, China

Information Systems and Operations Management

Hefu Liu	University of Science and Technology of China, China
Meng Chen	Soochow University, China
Zhao Cai	University of Nottingham Ningbo, China
Yuting Wang	Shanghai University, China
Liangqing Zhang	Chongqing University, China
Yao Chen	Jiangsu University of Science and Technology, China

Transformative Digital Innovations: Education, Sports, and Entertainment

Zhao Du	Beijing Sport University, China
Ruoxin Zhou	University of International Business and Economics, China
Shan Wang	University of Saskatchewan, Canada
Fang Wang	Wilfrid Laurier University, Canada

Best Paper Award and Journal Publication Committee

Chairs

Yiliu (Paul) Tu	University of Calgary, Canada
Maomao Chi	China University of Geosciences, China

Members

Alain Chong	University of Nottingham Ningbo China, China
Chris Yang	Drexel University, USA
Chris Westland	University of Illinois at Chicago, USA
Doug Vogel	Harbin Institute of Technology, China
Patrick Chau	Beijing Normal University-Hong Kong Baptist University United International College (UIC), China
Jun Wei	University of West Florida, USA
John Qi Dong	Nanyang Technological University, Singapore

Weiguo (Patrick) Fan   University of Iowa, USA
Wen-Lung Shiau   Chang Gung University, Taiwan RoC

Sponsoring Journals (alphabetical order)

Electronic Commerce Research
Electronic Commerce Research and Applications
Electronic Markets-The International Journal on Networked Business
Internet Research
Journal of Database Management
Journal of Organizational and End User Computing
International Journal of Networking and Virtual Organizations
Journal of Systems and Information Technology

Contents – Part I

Contents – Part II

Contents – Part III

Cross-Store Discount or Purchase Subsidy? Promotion Strategy of E-commerce Platforms Based on the Two-Sided Market Theory

Miao Wang, Zhenhua Qu, Zhiyuan Fan, Yifei Liu, and Min Wang[✉]

Nanjing University of Aeronautics and Astronautics, Nanjing 211106,
People's Republic of China
min.wang@nuaa.edu.cn

Abstract. This paper investigates two different promotion strategies of e-commerce platforms, i.e., the cross-store discount strategy and the purchase subsidy strategy. We take the additional utility and the degree of merchant concessions on price under the cross-store discount strategy into account and analyze how they affect platforms' optimal promotion strategy. Result shows that the additional utility is the determining factor of platforms' strategy choice. More precisely, when the two platforms adopt different promotion strategies, only when the additional utility is greater than a certain threshold may adopting the cross-store discount strategy bring more profits, and the threshold of the additional utility depends on promotion costs and the degree of merchant concessions on price. When the two platforms adopt the same promotion strategy, without the consideration of promotion costs, adopting the cross-store discount strategy simultaneously can make the platforms more profitable. In addition, whether a platform should change its promotion strategy depends on the value of the additional utility under the cross-store discount strategy. When the value of that utility is within a certain interval, both the platforms tend to maintain their original promotion strategy.

Keywords: E-commerce · Platform competition · Promotion strategy · Two-sided market

1 Introduction

During the Double 11 shopping festival in China, e-commerce platforms usually come up with various promotion strategies to attract consumers. Online merchants often participate in promotion plans of the platform to achieve higher sales volume. For example, the cross-store discount strategy is a promotion strategy first proposed by Taobao, and it has been widely adopted by e-commerce platforms. Under this strategy, consumers could buy products from different online merchants participating in the promotion activity of the platform, and when the total consumption amount exceeds a certain threshold, they get discounts. For instance, consumers get a 50 RMB price reduction for every 300 RMB they pay. This strategy helps the merchants varying across categories, brands and shops to achieve their sales goals. However, it may have a negative effect on the consumers

Y. P. Tu and M. Chi (Eds.): WHICEB 2024, LNBIP 515, pp. 1–12, 2024.
https://doi.org/10.1007/978-3-031-60264-1_1

whose consumption amount doesn't reach the threshold or are tired of searching for other items on the platform to reach the threshold.

Although the cross-store discount strategy has been adopted by many e-commerce platforms, some other e-commerce platforms such as Pinduoduo opts for a more direct promotion strategy, i.e., the purchase discount strategy. Under this strategy, the e-commerce platform directly subsidizes consumers purchasing products so that consumers need to pay less. Although consumers' direct perception of the promotion strength of the purchase discount strategy is weaker compared to that of the cross-store discount strategy, consumers can get direct discounts in the simplest way, which helps to attract consumers.

Considering the pros and cons of the above two promotion strategies, i.e., the cross-store discount strategy is more budget-friendly and the purchase subsidy strategy is easier to operate, this paper investigates the impact of different promotion strategies on the pricing decisions and profits of e-commerce platforms. Specifically, on the basis of the two-sided market theory, whether and when a promotion strategy outweighs the other strategy will be analyzed.

The rest of this paper is organized as follows. Section 2 presents the literature review. Section 3 describes the model setup. Section 4 presents the equilibrium results of the model, and Sect. 5 analyzes and compares the equilibrium results under the two promotion strategies. Section 6 concludes the paper and provides some managerial implications.

2 Literature Review

There is a number of research that addresses the issue of promotion strategies in the field of e-commerce. Many scholars have studied a variety of promotional strategies. Li et al. [1] explored the effect of hidden-price promotions on consumers' purchase behaviors. Song et al. [2] studied the optimal price strategy for the retailers under the cross-store full-reduction promotion mode with the consideration of speculative consumers. Wang and Zhou [3] explored the impact of e-commerce platform collocation discount activities on the pricing strategies of dual-channel suppliers and retailers, and the results showed that the increases in discounts didn't lead to the increases in profits. Some other scholars have compared different promotional strategies. Zhang et al. [4] constructed two price promotion models of price discounts and cash coupons, and took the merchant's advertisement investment decision into consideration to explore the optimal price promotion strategy of the platform. Wu et al. [5] analyzed trade promotions under demand disruption. Three trade promotion types, i.e., off-invoice, scan-back, and revenue-sharing, were examined, and the optimal promotion decisions were derived for each strategy. Tong et al. [6] built a three-level hierarchical promotion structure and evaluated the impact of different platform promotions on sales and conversion rate.

The above literature examines promotional strategies in a non-competitive context, however, as an important measure to stimulate consumption, the promotion strategy is also an important competitive approach. Li and Zhou [7] examined a sustainable supplier's price discount strategy in a competitive environment. Bauner et al. [8] established a game model between a manufacturer and a retailer owning his own label, and explored the coupon placement strategy when they competed. Huang and Bai [9] examined the context in a supply chain with one leading manufacturer and two competing retailers and studied the cooperative promotion problem in the presence of the promotion reference effect. Shang et al. [10] constructed the consumer demand model of competitive merchants under the decision of points and cash rebate, and studied the optimal pricing and rebate strategies of two competitive merchants. Jiang et al. [11] considered two competing sellers selling on an online marketplace and examined the sellers' promotion choice equilibrium strategy and the optimal rebate value for the sellers and platform operator. Li et al. [12] investigated the role of coupons on pricing and channel competition by introducing a game model that included three coupon issuing patterns in the context of dual-channel supply chain.

To sum up, most of the above studies examined different promotion strategies from the perspective of supply chain structure, while this paper applies the two-sided market theory and the utility theory to explore the optimal promotion strategy for e-commerce platforms. In addition, the above literature only considered the positive effects that the promotion strategies bring about without considering the negative effects that it may simultaneously have on consumers, which have been comprehensively considered by this paper and modelled in consumer's utility so that the impact of this factor on the e-commerce platform's optimal promotion strategy could be analyzed.

3 Models and Assumptions

3.1 Platforms

We assume that there exist two competing e-commerce platforms, 1 and 2, which are horizontally differentiated and located on the two extremes of each of the two Hotelling lines (faced by the consumers and the merchants) [13, 14]. In order to attract more consumers, e-commerce platforms often hold promotion activities. The purchase subsidy strategy enables consumers to buy goods at a lower price, such as the 10 billion subsidy activity of the Pinduoduo, and the amount of the subsidy is usually funded by the platform. Another strategy is the cross-store discount strategy, which means that consumers can consume in different shops and have a certain amount of price reduction when the total amount is greater than a certain threshold, and it has been adopted by many e-commerce platforms such as Taobao, J.D., and Xiaohongshu. This promotion activity is often organized jointly by platforms and merchants, and promotion costs are usually shared between them.

We assume that e-commerce platforms charge merchants' entry fees but don't charge consumers, which corresponds to the practice of most e-commerce platforms. Assuming that platform i's entry price for merchants is p_{si}, and the platform can choose only one promotion strategy. Since we focus on the impact of the two types of promotion strategies from the perspective of consumer's utility, to simplify the analysis, we assume that the costs of implementing promotion strategies are fixed and are respectively c_c and c_p (the subscripts c and p are represented by m). Therefore, the platform i's profit is:

$$l_i = p_{si}n_{si} - c_m \tag{1}$$

3.2 Consumers

Consumers are uniformly distributed along the Hotelling line. Depending on the location on the Hotelling line, a consumer may incur a mismatch cost t per unit of distance traveled. Put differently, t reflects the strength of consumers' brand preferences toward the two platforms. Usually, consumers only choose one platform to purchase a certain sort of products in a single period [15], as such, we assume that consumers are single-homing. In general, the cross-store discount strategy is more budge-friendly, however, when consumers are tired of searching for products in different online stores, this strategy may bring negative effects. Assuming that platform 1 adopts the purchase subsidy strategy and platform 2 adopts the cross-store discount strategy, we express the utility of consumers joining these two platforms as

$$u_{b1} = v_1 + \alpha_b n_{s1} - p_0 - tx \tag{2}$$

$$u_{b2} = v_2 + v_0 + \alpha_b n_{s2} - p_0 - t(1 - x) \tag{3}$$

v_i is the basic utility that consumers getting from purchasing the product, and only depends on the quality of the product itself. Due to the small difference among similar products, we assume that $v_1 = v_2 = v$ [15]. α_b is the network effect of merchants on consumers, and it originates from the inherent characteristics of two-sided platforms. v_0 is the additional utility of joining platform 2; when consumers are willing to search for products in different shops, they can obtain additional utility due to the greater discount. In this case, v_0 is positive. When consumers are unwilling to consolidate orders across different shops, this strategy will bring them negative utility, and in this case v_0 is negative [16]. p_0 is the price of products after the platform adopts promotion strategies. Since we focus on the changes in consumers' utility under different promotion strategies, we assume that p_0 remains unchanged and is an exogenous variable.

3.3 Merchants

Similar to consumers, we assume that merchants are also uniformly distributed on a Hotelling line as the e-commerce platforms are horizontally differentiated from merchants' perspective. Merchants' transportation cost per unit of distance is also given by t, which reflects a match between a merchant and a platform that are independent of the consumer base. In order to simplify the analysis, we assume that merchants are single-homing. In reality, except for large companies and sellers, most of the merchants are small, which are individual merchants and only join one platform. Since the pricing of products is not the focus of this paper and the pricing of similar products on different platforms does not vary significantly, we assume that the original price of products is p, and it is an exogenous variable. When adopting the subsidy strategy, merchants pay no costs and still sell the product at price p. However, when adopting the cross-store discount strategy, merchants have to surrender part of profit to consumers based on the rules set by the platform. To simplify the analysis, we use price discounts to denote merchants' concessions on profit and assume that they sell the products at the price θp

$(1 > \theta > 0)$, the smaller θ is, the greater the concession is. The utilities of merchants joining these two platforms are:

$$u_{s1} = \alpha_s n_{b1} + n_{b1}p - p_{s1} - ty \tag{4}$$

$$u_{s2} = \alpha_s n_{b2} + n_{b2}\theta p - p_{s2} - t(1 - y) \tag{5}$$

α_s is the network effect of consumers on merchants.

The notations involved in the model is listed in Table 1.

Table 1. Parameter and Decision Variables

Symbol	Definition
v_i	Consumers' intrinsic utility of accessing platform i ($i = 1,2$)
α_j	Network effects of one side on the other side j ($j = $ b,s)
θ	Degree of merchant concessions on price
v_0	Additional utility brought by the cross-store discount strategy
t	Unit misfit cost of consumers and merchants
p_0	Price of products after the platform adopts promotion strategies
p	Original price of products
c_m	Implementation cost of promotion strategy m ($m = $ p,c)
p_{si}	Merchants' entry price set by platform i ($i = 1,2$)
n_{si}	Number of merchants participating in platform i ($i = 1,2$)
n_{bi}	Number of consumers participating in platform i ($i = 1,2$)

4 Equilibrium Results Solving

In this section, we consider different scenarios, i.e., the scenarios where two platforms adopt different strategies and both platforms adopt the purchase subsidy strategy or cross-store discount strategy. Referring to Bakos and Halaburda [17] and for simplicity, we assume $t = 1$. In order to guarantee the existence of the optimal solutions, the parameters need to satisfy the following condition: $p < \frac{2 - 2\alpha_b\alpha_s}{\alpha_b + \theta\alpha_b}$.

The sequence of the game is as follows. On stage 1, platforms announce their promotion strategies simultaneously. On stage 2, the two platforms announce prices simultaneously after observing each other's promotion strategy choices. Lastly, on stage 3, both consumers and merchants make participation decisions.

4.1 Adopting Different Strategies

We denote this scenario with the superscript "PC". The consumers' utility indifference point x satisfies: $u_{b1}^{PC} = u_{b2}^{PC}$. With the assumption of rational expectations, $n_{b1}^{PC} =$

$n_{b1}^{PCe} = x$, $n_{b2}^{PC} = n_{b2}^{PCe} = 1 - x$. Similarly, the merchants' utility indifference point y satisfies: $u_{s1}^{PC} = u_{s2}^{PC}$, and $n_{s1}^{PC} = n_{s1}^{PCe} = y$, $n_{s2}^{PC} = n_{s2}^{PCe} = 1 - y$. On this basis, we obtain the numbers of consumers and merchants participating in the two platforms:

$$n_{b1}^{PC} = \frac{-1 + v_0 + \alpha_b(p\theta + p_{s1} - p_{s2} + \alpha_s)}{-2 + \alpha_b(p + p\theta + 2\alpha_s)} \tag{6}$$

$$n_{b2}^{PC} = \frac{-1 - v_0 + \alpha_b(p - p_{s1} + p_{s2} + \alpha_s)}{-2 + \alpha_b(p + p\theta + 2\alpha_s)} \tag{7}$$

$$n_{s1}^{PC} = \frac{-2 + p(-1 + \theta) + 2p_{s1} - 2p_{s2} + (v_0 + \alpha_b)(p + p\theta + 2\alpha_s)}{-4 + 2\alpha_b(p + p\theta + 2\alpha_s)} \tag{8}$$

$$n_{s2}^{PC} = \frac{-2 + p - p\theta - 2p_{s1} + 2p_{s2} - (v_0 - \alpha_b)(p + p\theta + 2\alpha_s)}{-4 + 2\alpha_b(p + p\theta + 2\alpha_s)} \tag{9}$$

Using backward induction, the entry prices for merchants to join the two platforms are obtained:

$$p_{s1}^{PC} = \frac{6 + p - p\theta - (v_0 + 3\alpha_b)(p + p\theta + 2\alpha_s)}{6} \tag{10}$$

$$p_{s2}^{PC} = \frac{6 - p + p\theta + (v_0 - 3\alpha_b)(p + p\theta + 2\alpha_s)}{6} \tag{11}$$

Proposition 1. $\frac{\partial p_{s1}}{\partial v_0} < 0$, $\frac{\partial p_{s2}}{\partial v_0} > 0$; when $v_0 > -1 - 3\alpha_b$, $\frac{\partial p_{s1}}{\partial \theta} < 0$, when $v_0 < 3\alpha_b - 1$, $\frac{\partial p_{s2}}{\partial \theta} < 0$.

Proposition 1 reflects the trend of the equilibrium pricing for merchants with respect to certain parameters. Platform 1's entry price decreases as v_0 increases, platform 2's entry price increases as v_0 increases. This occurs because when v_0 increases, the utility of consumers participating in platform 2 increases, with the impact of network effects, the number of merchants participating in the platform also increases, and the bargaining power of platform 2 increases. In contrast, platform 1 needs to cut down its price to attract more merchants.

When $v_0 > -1 - 3\alpha_b$, platform 1's entry price decreases as θ increases, and when $v_0 < 3\alpha_b - 1$, platform 2's entry price decreases as θ increases. When v_0 is not very small, the disutility brought by cross-store discount is limited. With the increase of θ, the utility of merchants participating in platform 2 increases, the competitive disadvantage of platform 2 decreases, thus platform 1 can cut down its price to enhance its competitive advantage. When v_0 is not very large, the cross-store discount imposes little positive effect to consumers. Even if θ increases, platform 2 is still at a competitive disadvantage and have to cut down its entry price to attract more merchants.

Substituting Eqs. (10) and (11) into Eqs. (6)–(9) to get the number of consumers and merchants participating in the platform:

$$n_{b1}^{PC} = \frac{-3 + \alpha_b(p + 2p\theta + 3\alpha_s) - v_0(-3 + \alpha_b(p + p\theta + 2\alpha_s))}{3(-2 + p\alpha_b + p\theta\alpha_b + 2\alpha_b\alpha_s)} \tag{12}$$

$$n_{s1}^{PC} = \frac{-6 + p(-1+\theta) + (v_0 + 3\alpha_b)(p + p\theta + 2\alpha_s)}{6(-2 + p\alpha_b + p\theta\alpha_b + 2\alpha_b\alpha_s)} \tag{13}$$

$$n_{b2}^{PC} = \frac{-3 + \alpha_b(p(2+\theta) + 3\alpha_s) + v_0(-3 + \alpha_b(p + p\theta + 2\alpha_s))}{3(-2 + p\alpha_b + p\theta\alpha_b + 2\alpha_b\alpha_s)} \tag{14}$$

$$n_{s2}^{PC} = \frac{-6 + p - p\theta - (v_0 - 3\alpha_b)(p + p\theta + 2\alpha_s)}{6(-2 + p\alpha_b + p\theta\alpha_b + 2\alpha_b\alpha_s)} \tag{15}$$

Then we obtain the profits of the two platforms:

$$l_1^{PC} = \frac{(-6 + p(-1+\theta) + (v_0 + 3\alpha_b)(p + p\theta + 2\alpha_s))^2}{36(2 - \alpha_b(p + p\theta + 2\alpha_s))} - c_p \tag{16}$$

$$l_2^{PC} = \frac{(6 + p(-1+\theta) + (v_0 - 3\alpha_b)(p + p\theta + 2\alpha_s))^2}{36(2 - \alpha_b(p + p\theta + 2\alpha_s))} - c_c \tag{17}$$

Proposition 2. (1) $\frac{\partial n_{b1}}{\partial v_0} < 0$, $\frac{\partial n_{s1}}{\partial v_0} < 0$; $\frac{\partial n_{b2}}{\partial v_0} > 0$, $\frac{\partial n_{s2}}{\partial v_0} > 0$. (2) when $v_0 > -1 + \alpha_b(p + \alpha_s)$, $\frac{\partial n_{b1}}{\partial \theta} < 0$, $\frac{\partial n_{s1}}{\partial \theta} < 0$, $\frac{\partial n_{b2}}{\partial \theta} > 0$, $\frac{\partial n_{s2}}{\partial \theta} > 0$. (3) $\frac{\partial l_1}{\partial v_0} < 0$, $\frac{\partial l_2}{\partial v_0} > 0$.

The first part of Proposition 2 indicates that with the increase of v_0, the number of consumers and merchants participating in platform 1 decreases, while the number of consumers and merchants participating in platform 2 increases. This occurs because v_0 stands for the additional utility brought by the cross-store discount strategy, and thus if v_0 increases, the utility of consumers participating in platform 2 increases, and the number of consumers participating in the platform also increases. With the impact of network effects, the number of merchants participating in the platform also increases. Since both consumers and merchants are single-homing, the number of consumers and merchants participating in platform 1 is subsequently reduced.

The second part of Proposition 2 shows that when $v_0 > -1 + \alpha_b(p + \alpha_s)$, the number of consumers and merchants participating in platform 1 decreases as θ increases, while the number of those participating in platform 2 increases as θ increases. When v_0 is greater than this threshold, the disutility brought by cross-store discount is limited, and the number of consumers participating in the platform is not greatly affected by it. As θ increases, the utility of merchants participating in platform 2 increases, thus the number of merchants also increases. Under the influence of network effects, the number of consumers also increases. Correspondingly, the number of consumers and merchants participating in platform 1 decreases since both of them are single-homing.

The last part of Proposition 2 demonstrates that regardless of whether v_0 is positive or negative, the profit of platform 1 decreases as v_0 increases, while the profit of platform 2 increases as v_0 increases. As v_0 increases, the number of merchants participating in platform 2 increases, and the entry price also increases, therefore, the profit of platform 2 increases. The influence of v_0 on platform 1 is opposite to that on platform 2.

4.2 Adopting the Same Strategies

When both platforms adopt a subsidy strategy, we denote this scenario with the superscript "PP". The utility indifference points of both side of users satisfy the following equations:

$$v + \alpha_b n_{s1} - p_0 - x = v + \alpha_b n_{s2} - p_0 - (1 - x) \tag{18}$$

$$\alpha_s n_{b1} + n_{b1} p - p_{s1} - ty = \alpha_s n_{b2} + n_{b2} p - p_{s2} - (1 - y) \tag{19}$$

When both platforms adopt the cross-store discount strategy, we denote this scenario with the superscript "CC". The utility indifference points of both side of users satisfy the following equations:

$$v + v_0 + \alpha_b n_{s1} - p_0 - x = v + v_0 + \alpha_b n_{s2} - p_0 - (1 - x) \tag{20}$$

$$\alpha_s n_{b1} + n_{b1} \theta p - p_{s1} - ty = \alpha_s n_{b2} + n_{b2} \theta p - p_{s2} - (1 - y) \tag{21}$$

Similar to Sect. 4.1, using backward induction, the equilibrium results of these two situations are obtained (Table 2):

Table 2. Equilibrium results

	Purchase Subsidy strategy	Cross-store discount strategy
n_{bi}	$n_{b1}^{PP} = n_{b2}^{PP} = \frac{1}{2}$	$n_{b1}^{CC} = n_{b2}^{CC} = \frac{1}{2}$
n_{si}	$n_{s1}^{PP} = n_{s2}^{PP} = \frac{1}{2}$	$n_{s1}^{CC} = n_{s2}^{CC} = \frac{1}{2}$
p_{si}	$p_{s1}^{PP} = p_{s2}^{PP} = 1 - \alpha_b(p + \alpha_s)$	$p_{s1}^{CC} = p_{s2}^{CC} = 1 - \alpha_b(p\theta + \alpha_s)$
l_i	$l_1^{PP} = l_2^{PP} = \frac{1 - \alpha_b(p + \alpha_s)}{2} - c_p$	$l_1^{CC} = l_2^{CC} = \frac{1 - \alpha_b(p\theta + \alpha_s)}{2} - c_c$

When the two platforms adopt the same strategy, the competition between them is evenly matched, and the equilibrium results of the two platforms are the same. Since the comparison between the two different strategies is the focus of this research, we will only compare platforms' profits in different situations in next section to analyze when a platform is likely to adopt another platform's promotion strategy.

5 Comparison of Equilibrium Results

5.1 Adopting Different Strategies

In the following content, we will compare the equilibrium results in the scenario where the two platforms adopt different strategies and explore which strategy can bring platforms more profits.

Proposition 3: When v_0 is greater than a certain threshold, platform 2 gains more profits.

Proposition 3 is proven that $l_1^{PC} - l_2^{PC} = \frac{p-p\theta-v_0(p+p\theta+2\alpha_s)+3(c_c-c_p)}{3}$, when $v_0 > \frac{p-p\theta+3(c_c-c_p)}{p+p\theta+2\alpha_s}$, the equation is negative. In other words, when v_0 is greater than a certain threshold, platform 2 can obtain more profits. In this situation, the number of merchants participating in platform 2 and the entry price of platform 2 both overwhelm those of platform 1. $n_{s1}^{PC} - n_{s2}^{PC} = \frac{p(-1+\theta)+v_0(p+p\theta+2\alpha_s)}{-6+3\alpha_b(p+p\theta+2\alpha_s)}$, $p_{s1}^{PC} - p_{s2}^{PC} = \frac{p-p\theta-v_0(p+p\theta+2\alpha_s)}{3}$, when $v_0 > \frac{p-p\theta}{p+p\theta+2\alpha_s}$, the two equations are negative simultaneously.

Proposition 3 is explained that when v_0 is large enough, consumers tend to join platform 2, and merchants will also join platform 2 under the influence of network effects. Meanwhile, in order to attract more merchants, platform 1 will cut down its price. With more merchants and the higher price, platform 2 gains more profits.

Corollary 1: When $c_c \geq c_p$, only if v_0 is positive, platforms can gain more profits when adopting the cross-store discount strategy.

It is easily proven that the critical value of the difference between the profits of the two platforms $v_0 = \frac{p-p\theta+3(c_c-c_p)}{p+p\theta+2\alpha_s}$ is positive when $c_c \geq c_p$. Since the merchants have to make concessions on price when platform 2 adopts the cross-store discount strategy, they obtain smaller utility. Only when v_0 is positive, platform 2 can attract more consumers with the advantage of v_0, so as to make up for the loss of utility brought about by the merchants' concessions. And the threshold of v_0 and θ is negatively correlated: the smaller θ is, the bigger v_0 is going to be. Therefore, when adopting the cross-store discount strategy, the platform had better investigate the consumer's attitude towards this strategy in advance and correspondingly adjust the ratio of merchants' concessions. When the majority of consumers have a positive attitude, the adoption of the cross-store discount strategy is more likely to make the platform more profitable.

5.2 Adopting the Same Strategies

In this part, we compare two scenarios where the platforms adopt the same promotion strategy and analyze which strategy is more effective. Additionally, by comparing the equilibrium profits in scenario "PC" with those in scenario "PP" and "CC", we analyze when a platform may change its own promotion strategy and adopt that of its rival platform.

Proposition 4: When the two platforms adopt the same promotion strategies and the implementation costs of the two promotion strategies are the same, adopting the cross-store discount strategy simultaneously can make the platforms more profitable.

Proposition 4 is proven that $l_i^{PP} - l_i^{CC} = \frac{p(-1+\theta)\alpha_b+2(c_c-c_p)}{2}$, when $c_c = c_p$, $l_i^{PP} - l_i^{CC} < 0$ always holds true.

When the two platforms adopt the same promotion strategies, v_0 no longer affects platforms' profits. In scenario "CC", the merchants need to make concessions and the utility they gain is smaller than that in scenario "PP", thus the number of merchants in scenario "CC" will be fewer theoretically. Consequently, the platform will increase the entry price for merchants to gain more profits. Since the consumer market has not changed in both cases, the platform is more profitable in scenario "CC".

Proposition 5: When v_0 is within a certain interval, both platforms tend to maintain their original promotion strategy rather than adopt the other platform's strategy.

Proposition 5 is proven that when $v_0 < v_1$, $l_1^{PC} - l_1^{CC} > 0$; when $v_0 > v_2$, $l_2^{PC} - l_2^{PP} > 0$. Among which $v_1 = \frac{(3(p+p\theta+2\alpha_s)-3\sqrt{2}A+C)(-2+\alpha_b(p+p\theta+2\alpha_s))}{(p+p\theta+2\alpha_s)^2}$, $v_2 = \frac{(-3(p+p\theta+2\alpha_s)+3\sqrt{2}B+C)(-2+\alpha_b(p+p\theta+2\alpha_s))}{(p+p\theta+2\alpha_s)^2}$, and it can be concluded that $v_2 - v_1 < 0$.

$$\left(A = \sqrt{\frac{(p+p\theta+2\alpha_s)^2(-1+2(c_c-c_p)+\alpha_b(p+\alpha_s))}{-2+\alpha_b(p+p\theta+2\alpha_s)}}, B = \sqrt{\frac{(p+p\theta+2\alpha_s)^2(-1+2(c_c-c_p)+\alpha_b(p\theta+\alpha_s))}{-2+\alpha_b(p+p\theta+2\alpha_s)}},\right.$$
$$\left. C = \frac{p(-1+\theta)(p+p\theta+2\alpha_s)}{-2+\alpha_b(p+p\theta+2\alpha_s)}\right)$$

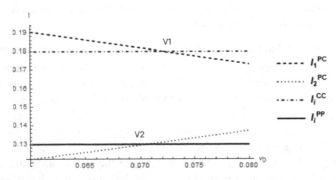

Fig. 1. Platform profit under different scenarios ($\alpha_b = 0.2$; $\alpha_s = 0.2$; $\theta = 0.8$; $p = 2.5$; $c_c = c_p = 0.1$)

Based on Proposition 5, we plot Fig. 1 ($\alpha_b = 0.2$; $\alpha_s = 0.2$; $\theta = 0.8$; $p = 2.5$; $c_c = c_p = 0.1$) to show the trends in platforms' profit with respect to v_0, and it's consistent with Proposition 2 and Proposition 5.

Based on Fig. 1, we plot Fig. 2 to more clearly reflect the optimal promotion strategy of the platforms in different scenarios. The figure shows that when v_0 is lower than a certain threshold, platform 1 tends to maintain the purchase subsidy strategy. When v_0 is greater than a certain threshold, platform 2 tends to maintain the cross-store discount strategy. More precisely, when $v_2 < v_0 < v_1$, both platform 1 and platform 2 will maintain their original promotion strategy. When $v_2 < v_0$, both of them tend to adopt the purchase subsidy strategy. When $v_0 < v_1$, both of them tend to adopt the cross-store discount strategy.

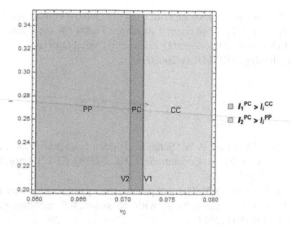

Fig. 2. Optimal promotion strategy ($\alpha_b = 0.2$; $\alpha_s = 0.2$; $\theta = 0.8$; $p = 2.5$; $c_c = c_p = 0.1$)

6   Conclusion

Promotion is an important approach for e-commerce platforms to attract consumers. This paper analyzes the impact of two different promotion strategies on the platforms using the two-sided market theory. We find that the platform's promotion strategy choice is jointly determined by the additional utility and the degree of merchant concessions on price under the cross-store discount strategy. More precisely, when the two platforms adopt different promotion strategies, only when $v_0 > 0$ may adopting the cross-store discount strategy bring more profits, and the threshold of v_0 depends on θ. When the two platforms adopt the same promotion strategy, adopting the cross-store discount strategy simultaneously can make the platforms more profitable.

In addition, we find that whether the platform should change its promotion strategy depends on v_0 the value of v_0. When v_0 is within a certain interval, both platforms tend to maintain their original promotion strategy. When v_0 is greater than the interval, both platforms tend to adopt the cross-store discount strategy. When v_0 is less than the interval, both platforms tend to adopt the purchase subsidy strategy. Consequently, before making the choice of promotion strategies, it's necessary for the platform to investigate the consumers' attitude towards the cross-store discount strategy in advance. When the majority of consumers have a positive attitude, adopting the cross-store discount strategy is more likely to be more profitable. Moreover, the platforms can flexibly adjust the degree of merchant concessions on price based on the analysis of v_0. Lastly, whether a platform should change its promotion strategy depends on the value of the additional utility. When it is below the threshold, platforms should not switch to another promotion strategy even if their rival platforms can make more profits under this strategy.

In the future, we will extend this research in the following directions. First, we assumed that platforms can either adopt the purchase subsidy or cross-store discount strategy. However, an e-commerce platform in reality can adopt a hybrid of the two strategies, which will be considered in the future. In addition, this paper didn't consider the situation where the promotion strategy is provided by merchants, which could be further explored.

Acknowledgement. This work was supported by National Natural Science Foundation of China (No. 72001038) and the Fundamental Research Funds for the Central Universities (No. NJ2023027), Key Laboratory of Intelligent Decision and Digital Operations, Ministry of Industrial and Information Technology (KLADDO-200303).

References

1. Li, W., Hardesty, D.M., Craig, A.W., Song, L.: Hidden price promotions: could retailer price promotions backfire? J. Retail. Consum. Serv. **64**, 102797 (2022). https://doi.org/10.1016/j.jretconser.2021.102797
2. Song, S.J., Peng, W., Zeng, Y.Y.: Optimal pricing strategy of retailers considering speculative customers' add-on items return behavior with cross-store full-reduction promotion. RAIRO-Oper. Res **57**(2), 551–569 (2023)
3. Wang, D.P., Zhou, Y.: Coordination pricing of dual-channel supply chain considering group-purchase discount of e-commerce platforms. J. Syst. Eng. **37**(4), 535–548 (2022). In Chinese
4. Zhang, H., Li, L., Zhu, X.Z., He, X.: Online shopping platform optimal price promotion strategy: price discount or cash coupon. Chin. J. Manage. Sci. **12**, 1–11 (2021). In Chinese
5. Wu, J., Chen, Z., Ji, X.: Sustainable trade promotion decisions under demand disruption in manufacturer-retailer supply chains. Ann. Oper. Res. **290**(1–2), 115–143 (2020)
6. Tong, T.T., Xu, X., Yan, N.N., Xu, J.J.: Impact of different platform promotions on online sales and conversion rate: the role of business model and product line length. Decis. Support. Syst. **156**, 113746 (2022). https://doi.org/10.1016/j.dss.2022.113746
7. Li, Y., Zhou, J.: Sustainable supplier's equilibrium discount strategy under random demand. Sustainability **14**(8), 4802 (2022). https://doi.org/10.3390/su14084802
8. Bauner, C., Jaenicke, E., Wang, E., Wu, P.C.: Couponing strategies in competition between a national brand and a private label product. J. Retail. **95**(1), 57–66 (2019)
9. Huang, Z.S., Bai, P.J.: Dynamic cooperative promotion in the presence of consumer reference effect with competing retailers. J. Retail. Consum. Serv. **60**, 102441 (2021). https://doi.org/10.1016/j.jretconser.2021.102441
10. Shan, Z.J., Huang, H.L., Lin, Q., He, W.X., Chen, B.Y.: Competitive merchant strategy under rebate promotion mode. Syst. Eng. **41**(3), 83–93 (2023). In Chinese
11. Jiang, X., Jia, Z., Wu, L.L.: Sellers promotion competition on the online marketplace. J. Ind. Eng. Eng. Manage. **36**(1), 217–227 (2022). In Chinese
12. Li, Z.H., Yang, W.S., Liu, X.H., Si, Y.Y.: Coupon promotion and its two-stage price intervention on dual-channel supply chain. Comput. Ind. Eng. **145**, 106543 (2020). https://doi.org/10.1016/j.cie.2020.106543
13. Lin, X.G., Zhou, Y.W., Xie, W., Zhong, Y.G., Cao, B.: Pricing and product-bundling strategies for e-commerce platforms with competition. Eur. J. Oper. Res. **283**, 1026–1039 (2020)
14. Feng, N., Chen, J.J., Feng, H.Y., Li, M.Q.: Optimal product selection and pricing strategies for platform vendors under two-sided network effects. Electron. Commer. Res. Appl. **43**, 100990 (2020)
15. Wang, M., Deng, H.H., Leong, K.G.: Innovation investment and subsidy strategy in two-sided market. Inf. Technol. Manage. **24**, 337–351 (2022). https://doi.org/10.1007/s10799-021-00331-x
16. Chatterjee, P., Zhou, B.: Sponsored content advertising in a two-sided market. Manage. Sci. **67**(22), 7560–7574 (2021)
17. Bakos, H.: Platform competition with Multihoming on both sides. Manage. Sci. **66**(12), 5599–5607 (2020)

A Bibliometric Analysis of Location-Based Social Networks and Applications: Research Trends and Future Challenges

Lin Liu[1] and Xiaoyu Yao[2(✉)]

[1] College of Resources and Environment, Anhui Agricultural University, 130 Changjiangxilu, Hefei, Anhui, China
[2] School of Management, University of Science and Technology of China, Jinzhai Road 96, Hefei, Anhui, China
jushenyxy@mail.ustc.edu.cn

Abstract. Location-based social networks (LBSN) have undergone rapid development over the past decade, garnering extensive attention from scholars in various research domains. However, the current status and overarching trends in the field of LBSN and relevant applications remain unclear, and key research hotspots and keywords are yet to be distinctly identified. This bibliometric study delves into the expansive realm of LBSN, uncovering research trends and future challenges. This study aims to address these issues by analyzing 1,099 high-quality articles from the Web of Science database between 2010 and 2023, and the analytical tools are CiteSpace and VOSviewer. The study unveiled pressing challenges confronting LBSN research, such as privacy concerns, the integration of emerging technologies, and the imperative for interdisciplinary collaboration. These challenges present promising opportunities for future exploration and innovation within the LBSN domain. As a roadmap for future research endeavors, this analysis guides researchers to Supporting socially marginalized communities, discovering and preventing of public health issues, and integrating and organizing multimodal geographic information.

Keywords: bibliometric analysis · Location-based social network · Geo-social network · Geo-privacy · smart city

1 Introduction

The latest decade witnessed the soaring development of location-based social networks (LBSNs) [1, 2]. LBSN integrates geographical location information and social interactions with the ubiquity of GPS-equipped intelligent mobile terminals [3]. LBSNs integrate geographical location information and social interactions to provide users with personalized location services and social experiences, fostering information sharing and communication with geographic awareness. Nowadays, LBSNs and corresponding applications, like location-based social media, play a crucial role in e-commerce process by facilitating personalized recommendations, targeted marketing, real-time communication, and online-offline interaction [4] through precise location information and

Y. P. Tu and M. Chi (Eds.): WHICEB 2024, LNBIP 515, pp. 13–23, 2024.
https://doi.org/10.1007/978-3-031-60264-1_2

social interactions, thereby enhancing user experience and data-driven effectiveness of e-commerce operations.

In addition to its successful applications in business, Location-Based Social Networks (LBSN) also provides a unique perspective for research, attracting scholars from various fields around the world. Firstly, LBSN integrates social interaction with geographic spatial information, enabling researchers to delve into user behaviors and relationships within geographical contexts [5]. This comprehensive research approach not only expands our understanding of social networks but also enriches the applications in geographic information science [6] and social network research, injecting new vitality into these domains. Secondly, LBSN emphasizes a personalized and customized research orientation. By analyzing user behavior in specific geographic locations, researchers can gain deeper insights into individual needs, preferences, and social patterns [7]. This refined personalized research not only propels the development of personalized recommendation systems and location-based services but also provides more effective solutions for sectors such as business, social interactions, and health. Furthermore, the research content of LBSN is remarkably diverse, encompassing various domains from geographic location recommendation and social network analysis to urban planning. This diversity allows LBSN to not only meet the academic community's need for in-depth exploration of complex social systems but also offer innovative applications and solutions for industries.

The rapid development of theories and practices related to the location-based social network has not been comprehensively analyzed quantitatively and visually, encompassing aspects such as main research themes, popular keywords, disciplinary distribution and evolution, productive institutions, regional productivity, and their cooperation network. Consequently, there is a need for a comprehensive review to systematically compile the literature on LBSN. To address this, a bibliometric analysis, or science mapping, is employed as an effective approach to illustrate the general state and trajectory of a specific academic field.

In order to enhance the objectivity and comprehensiveness of this review and to identify major research orientations within the LBSNs and applications, a qualitative content analysis was also performed on high-impact articles. This method is widely accepted in contemporary bibliometric research [8]. The primary objective of this article is to uncover the dynamics and trajectory of the literature through a mixed-method approach involving both quantitative bibliometric review and qualitative content analysis.

2   Method

To improve the objectiveness and comprehensiveness of this study, we used a mixed review method that involved both bibliometric analysis and content analysis of the collected articles.

2.1   Research Process

Bibliometric analysis serves as a robust mapping tool for quantitatively evaluating scientific production. In comparison to conventional narrative reviews, bibliometric analysis is considered more objective, offering a more effective demonstration of the dynamics and trajectory within a specific research domain. To augment the comprehensiveness and objectivity of this literature review, a qualitative content analysis was incorporated. This research adhered to a six-stage process (refer to Fig. 1), an extension of previous review studies [8, 9]. This section outlines the first three stages, while the subsequent Sects. (3–5) elaborate on stages 4, 5, and 6, respectively.

2.2 Research Flow

Our study utilized the Web of Science database, chosen for its authoritative standing in academia and comprehensive data relevant to bibliometric analysis. Within the Web of Science, three renowned indexes (SCI-E, SSCI, and A&HCI) were specifically selected to ensure the inclusion of references of high research quality. The search parameters were set to 'English' as the language, and the document type was restricted to 'Article.' Given that the first impactful article on the subject of LBSN was published in 2010, the search timespan was confined to the inclusive period between 2010 and 2023. Additionally, we employed the advanced search function in the Web of Science, incorporating features such as Topic Search (TS) and the Boolean operators 'OR' and 'AND.'

Initially, an exploratory search was conducted to refine the search query. Based on the preliminary findings, additional keywords related to LBSN and its extended themes of geo, spatial, and mobile social network/media were identified. Subsequently, the search query was revised by incorporating these newly identified keywords under relevant categories such as field terms and related terms. To further enhance searching precision, multiple iterations of the search process were carried out, refining the query with each iteration. The search process continued until saturation was reached, and no further relevant keywords could be identified. The final search strategy involved the utilization of the following keywords, specified as TS (Topic) = ("geo-social network*" OR "geosocial media*" OR "geographical Social network*" OR "Location-aware Social Network*" OR "Location-based Social Network*" OR "Spatial Social Network*") AND ("geosocial media" OR "geo-social media" OR "geographical social media" OR "location-aware social media" OR "location-based social media" OR "spatial social media"). This search aimed to retrieve all archived documents containing relevant publications. The selected publications encompassed those with the specified keywords or their close variants (indicated by *), appearing in their titles, abstracts, or keywords. Information, including titles, abstracts, keywords, authors, institutions, and cited references, was downloaded. The bibliographic search yielded a total of 1,099 publications.

3 Results of Bibliometric Analysis

In order to unveil the overall state and dynamics of the LBSN domain, this section presents the results obtained from bibliometric analysis. The analysis was conducted using two widely accepted tools, namely CiteSpace and VOSviewer. Both of these software applications are commonly employed in recent studies for their effectiveness in visualizing and analyzing bibliometric data.

3.1 Publications and Citations Analysis

Figure 2 illustrates the dynamics and trends observed in the collected articles from 2010 to 2023. Both the number of publications and their citations show a consistent increase over time, indicating a growing research interest in the LBSN domain. A general upward trend in publications is evident from 2010 to 2019, with 2019 being the most prolific year with 164 articles published. Before 2013, only a limited number of articles were published, and there was a brief decrease in publications in 2020. This apparent decline may result from the COVID-19 pandemic. During the pandemic, people's mobility has greatly weakened, which means that their geographic location information may become more centralized and stable [10], which may have an impact on LBSN analysis. Despite fluctuations in publication rates, there is a consistent growth in citations, indicating a sustained impact of the publications over time.

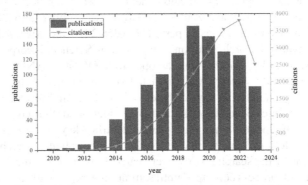

Fig. 1. Volume of publications and citations (2010–2023)

3.2 Productive and Highly Cited Journals

The bibliometric analysis reveals that the 1,099 articles are spread across 340 journals. Table 1 presents the top 10 journals from this list, indicating that 24.02% of the articles are published in these top 10 journals. To bolster the credibility of the study, the Impact Factor (IF) and H-index are utilized as ranking criteria. Both metrics are widely accepted for evaluating scientific production and research productivity [11]. The H-index, which denotes that an author or journal has at most H papers cited at least H times, serves as a crucial indicator for assessing the impact of authors or journals.

Analyzing the top 10 journals in LBSN research reveals interesting insights into the scholarly landscape. As shown in Table 3, the *ISPRS International Journal of Geo Information* leads with a remarkable 58 articles, showcasing prolific contributions to the field. Notably, its citation count of 316 signifies substantial recognition and influence. Despite a moderate Impact Factor (IF) of 3.4, the consistent output and impact distinguish it as a prominent outlet for LBSN research. *IEEE Access* follows closely with 35 articles, surpassing others in citation count (368). This suggests a focused and impactful presence in LBSN literature, reaffirmed by a commendable IF of 3.9. The journal's strategic balance between quantity and influence is evident, making it a noteworthy venue for LBSN scholars. Meanwhile, *IEEE Transactions on Knowledge and Data Engineering*, despite a smaller article count (34), boasts a high citation count of 156, underscoring the journal's emphasis on high-quality research. Its exceptional IF of 8.9 further cements its reputation as a leading journal in the LBSN domain. In the realm of specialized focus, *Neurocomputing*, with 23 articles, achieves a commendable citation count of 67, indicating a dedicated readership. Its IF of 6 positions it as a recognized platform for LBSN research, catering to the intersection of neuroscience and computing. These trends are echoed in other journals like *World Wide Web Internet and Web Information Systems, Information Sciences*, and *ACM Transactions on Intelligent Systems and Technology*. Each journal's unique balance of article output, citation impact, and IF contributes to the rich tapestry of LBSN literature, reflecting the diverse avenues of exploration in this dynamic field (Table 1).

Table 1. Productive and highly cited journals (top 10)

Journal	Number of articles	Citation	IF (2022)	Proportion (Total)
ISPRS International Journal of Geo Information	58	316	3.4	5.27
IEEE Access	35	368	3.9	3.18
IEEE Transactions on Knowledge and Data Engineering	34	156	8.9	3.09
Neurocomputing	23	67	6	2.31
World Wide Web Internet and Web Information Systems	22	102	3.7	2.00
Information Sciences	20	118	8.1	1.82
ACM Transactions on Intelligent Systems and Technology	19	54	5	1.73
International Journal of Geographical Information Science	18	112	5.7	1.64
Transactions in GIS	18	103	2.4	1.64
Electronics	17	67	2.9	1.55
Sub-sum	264	–	–	24.02

3.3 Productive Institutions and Cooperation

In VOSviewer, we conducted a co-authorship analysis based on organizational affil-iations, setting the "Minimum number of documents of an organization" to 10. This configuration revealed 32 interconnected research institutions in the visualization. The depiction shows a notably close collaboration among Chinese and American research institutions, with two prominent research clusters emerging, namely Wuhan University and New York University. Additionally, there are several institutions in other developed regions, including Western Europe (e.g., University of New South Wales) and Singapore (e.g., National University of Singapore). Notably, a institution located in a developing country is the Universidade Federal de Minas Gerais in Brazil. This suggests the impor-tance for institutions in developed regions to consider strengthening collaborations with counterparts situated in other developing countries.

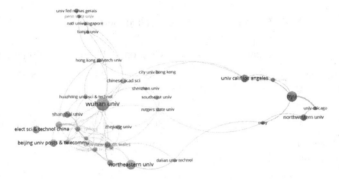

Fig. 2. Institutional cooperation network (VOSviewer)

3.4 Co-occurrence Analysis for Popular Keywords

A total of 3471 keywords were gathered initially. After excluding keywords with co-occurrence frequencies below 25 and eliminating irrelevant terms or interference terms (e.g. LBSN itself), 30 popular keywords were selected for co-occurrence analysis. These keywords were classified into three main streams, namely Recommendation Technology, Service Usage and Behavior Analysis, and Sexual Health, representing the most popular research topics in the LBSN domain.

First, Recommendation Technology includes keywords related to recommenda-tion technology in the geographical context, such as 'location/POI recommendation', 'deep learning', 'data mining', and 'risk'. These keywords highlight the significance of advanced technologies like deep learning in the development of Point of Interest (POI) recommendation systems and the inherent consideration of risk factors in location-based recommendation algorithms [12, 13].

Second, Service Usage and Behavior Analysis comprises keywords associated with the analysis of service usage and behavioral patterns, such as 'Twitter', 'Foursquare', 'pattern', '(human) mobility', and 'behavior'. The co-occurrence of these terms underscores the importance of platforms like Twitter and Foursquare in studying human mobility patterns and behavior, showcasing a growing interest in the intersection of social media data and location-based behavior analysis.

Third, Sexual Health involves keywords related to sexual health research, including 'HIV', 'Men who have Sex with Men' (MSM), 'gay,' and 'risk.' Notably, these keywords reflect a focus on the intersection of location-based data and sexual health, emphasizing key issues such as HIV prevention [14], Pre-Exposure Prophylaxis (PrEP) [15], and the health risk behaviors of specific populations. This stream of medical interdisciplinary research focused on marginalized groups in society, including AIDS patients and sexual minority groups, and helped to safeguard the rights of relevant individuals (Fig. 3).

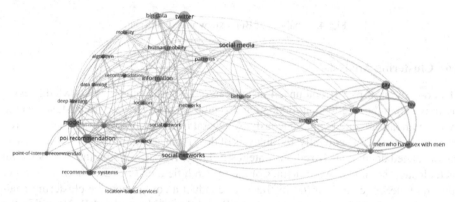

Fig. 3. Co-occurrence network of popular keywords (VOSviewer)

3.5 Burst Analysis of Keywords

The burst analysis of keywords within the domain of LBSN reveals significant trends in research focus and impact over time. Noteworthy bursts include a surge in attention to location-based services during 2014–2015, indicating intensified research efforts in this area. A sustained burst in geosocial network research from 2014 to 2017 underscores the enduring scholarly interest in understanding social interactions within geographical contexts. The burst in location recommendation research during 2015–2016 reflects a concentrated period of substantial contributions and impact in enhancing location-based recommendation systems. Furthermore, topics such as young men, matrix factorization, and men experienced bursts, suggesting extended periods of heightened scholarly attention to these specific themes. The bursts in research on China, sex, and cities during various periods highlight evolving interests within the location-based domain. Of notable significance is the substantial and sustained burst in point of Interest (POI) recommendation research from 2021 to 2023, indicating a highly impactful and actively researched area. These bursts provide valuable insights into the dynamic evolution of research themes, emphasizing both the enduring and emerging focal points within the landscape of location-based services and social networking (Fig. 4).

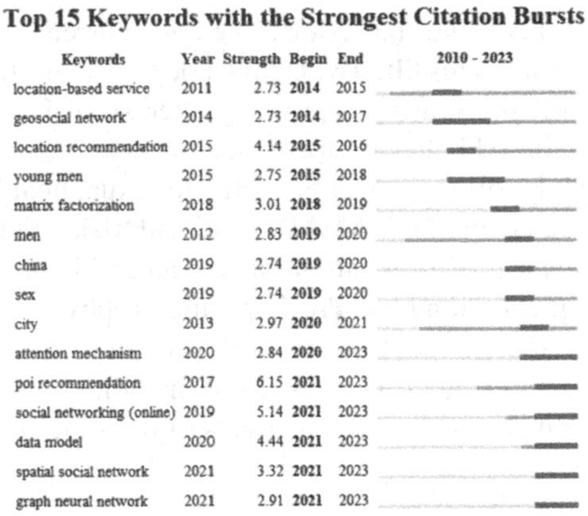

Top 15 Keywords with the Strongest Citation Bursts

Keywords	Year	Strength	Begin	End	2010 - 2023
location-based service	2011	2.73	2014	2015	
geosocial network	2014	2.73	2014	2017	
location recommendation	2015	4.14	2015	2016	
young men	2015	2.75	2015	2018	
matrix factorization	2018	3.01	2018	2019	
men	2012	2.83	2019	2020	
china	2019	2.74	2019	2020	
sex	2019	2.74	2019	2020	
city	2013	2.97	2020	2021	
attention mechanism	2020	2.84	2020	2023	
poi recommendation	2017	6.15	2021	2023	
social networking (online)	2019	5.14	2021	2023	
data model	2020	4.44	2021	2023	
spatial social network	2021	3.32	2021	2023	
graph neural network	2021	2.91	2021	2023	

Fig. 4. Analysis of Burst keywords (CiteSpace)

3.6 Clustering Analysis

The co-citation of papers can unveil insights into the development of knowledge associations within the intellectual foundation. Co-citation refers to the circumstance where two documents are cited simultaneously by several other documents, signifying shared research themes. Consequently, the analysis of document co-citation enables the clustering of related documents based on content similarity. By scrutinizing the papers within each cluster, the fundamental themes of the research field can be identified. This paper employs CiteSpace v.6.1.R6(64-bit)Basic to conduct a comprehensive clustering analysis on the evolving landscape of Location-Based Social Networks (LBSN) within the time span of 2010 to 2023, utilizing data extracted from Web of Science. The selection criteria for clustering include g-index (k = 25), Local Relevance Factor (LRF = 3.0), Lineage Impact Number (LIN BY = 5), and Early Burstiness (e = 1.0). The resulting network consists of 766 nodes and 3202 edges, with a density of 0.0109. The Largest Connected Component (LCC) encompasses 71% of the total nodes. The clustering is characterized by a Modularity Q of 0.7146, Weighted Mean Silhouette S of 0.9012, and a Harmonic Mean (Q, S) of 0.7971.

The clustered results of Ranked Terms under the LBSN (Location-Based Social Network) theme reveal several key thematic clusters, each shedding light on specific research directions and related content. The following provides a logically coherent discussion for each thematic cluster:

Cluster #0: This thematic cluster revolves around the implementation of cutting-edge technologies like temporal convolutional networks and spatial-temporal attention in recommendation systems. The emphasis lies on understanding and incorporating the dimensions of space and time to enhance user interest recommendations.

Cluster #1: Encompassing terms such as "of-interest recommendation" and "location-based social network", this cluster delves into the realm of human trajectory data and interest recommendations. The discussions within this theme explore collaborative filtering-based poi recommendation, context-awareness, tensors, weighted point-of-interests, and personalized models. The overarching goal is to develop recommendation systems adaptable to user interests and locations.

Cluster #2: Focused on "of-interest recommendation" and "location-based social network", this cluster explores successive poi recommendations, social influence, convolution matrix factorization, and deep attentive networks. The integration of deep attentive networks [13] and aggregated temporal tensor factorization models leads to personalized poi recommendations, with a particular emphasis on the role of social influence.

Cluster #3: Centered around "location-based social network" and "cross-domain community detection", this cluster delves into socio-spatial affiliation networks, group colocation behavior, and technological social networks. The study in this cluster investigates overlapping communities and profiling models, utilizing semantic signatures, geocoding, and temporal aspects.

Cluster #4: Focused on "geo-social media" and "social media data", this thematic cluster explores the application of geo-social media data in disaster management and local topics. The research within this theme includes urban crowd detection, lbsn data, case studies, and demographic characteristics.

Cluster #7: Centered on "location-based social network" and "serendipity-oriented personalized trip recommendation model", this cluster highlights personalized and serendipitous trip recommendations. Technologies such as graph embedding representation and online spread contribute to refining trip recommendations.

Cluster #8: This thematic cluster addresses "geo-social network", "untrusted service provider", and "preserving privacy", placing a strong focus on privacy preservation in

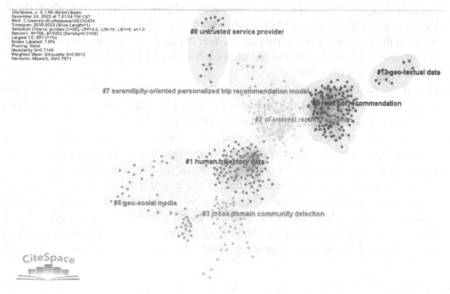

Fig. 5. Clustering Analysis (CiteSpace)

geo-social networks. Concepts such as private badges, curious buddies, and untrusted service providers are explored to safeguard privacy.

Cluster #12: This thematic cluster addresses "rumor detection", "dual-level network" and "geo-textual data stream", placing a focus on utilizing geo-textual data in social networks. Diverse utility of geo-textual data, such as event check-in, real-time site-specific user feedback, and rumor detection, are widely studied.

In summary, these thematic clusters offer profound insights into various directions within LBSN research, spanning from interest recommendations to social network privacy protection. The academic community's rich exploration in this field is evident across diverse aspects, showcasing the multifaceted nature of LBSN research (Fig. 5).

4 Conclusion and Suggestions

The bibliometric analysis conducted on location-based social networks (LBSN) and applications has yielded valuable insights into the evolving landscape of this interdisciplinary field. The identified research clusters, encompassing themes such as recommendation systems, geo-social networks, and privacy preservation, underscore the diverse dimensions of LBSN research. Furthermore, the study identified pressing challenges and opportunities that warrant attention in future LBSN research. Privacy concerns, the integration of emerging technologies, and the need for interdisciplinary collaboration stand out as pivotal areas for exploration. The interdisciplinary nature of LBSN research emphasizes the importance of fostering collaboration across domains to address complex challenges comprehensively. This paper put forward the following suggestions:

(1) Supporting socially marginalized communities. LBSN serves as a platform for building social support networks for socially marginalized groups, such as disabilities, Patients with rare diseases, LGBTQIA, etc. More services can be customized to them on the premise of not infringing on their privacy. This not only helps alleviate potential feelings of loneliness but also contributes to the establishment of more robust social support systems.

(2) Discovering and preventing of public health issues. Leveraging the rich spatial and social data from LBSN can offer insights into patterns of behavior, identifying early signs of physical and mental health challenges in communities. This proactive approach enables the development of targeted interventions and support systems, contributing to the prevention and improved management of public health issues.

(3) Integrating and organizing multimodal geographic information. Exploring the seamless exchange of diverse geographic data types within the network framework can enhance the integration of textual, visual, and sensory information. Geo-textual information has been widely studies but studies on others are limited. This approach fosters a more comprehensive understanding of spatial contexts, opening avenues for innovative applications in navigation, augmented reality, and context-aware services.

Acknowledgement. This research was supported by the National Natural Science Foundation of China under Grant 42171333.

References

1. Hu, S., et al.: Exploring the impacts of mobile devices usage on individual's creativity: a cross-cultural perspective. Int. J. Mobile Commun. **22**, 449–475 (2023)
2. Li, Y., et al.: Customer's reaction to cross-channel integration in omnichannel retailing: the mediating roles of retailer uncertainty, identity attractiveness, and switching costs. Decis. Support. Syst. **109**, 50–60 (2018)
3. Yang, Q., et al.: Self-disclosure in mobile payment applications: common and differential effects of personal and proxy control enhancing mechanisms. Int. J. Inf. Manage. **52**, 102065 (2020)
4. Fang, J., et al.: Retaining customers with in-store mobile usage experience in omni-channel retailing: the moderating effects of product information overload and alternative attractiveness. Electron. Commer. Res. Appl. **46**, 101028 (2021)
5. Trung, H.T., et al.: Learning holistic interactions in LBSNs with high-order, dynamic, and multi-role contexts. IEEE Trans. Knowl. Data Eng.a Eng. **35**, 5002–5016 (2023)
6. Liu, L., Yao, B.: Monitoring vegetation–cover changes based on NDVI dimidiate pixel model,. Trans. Chin. Soc. Agric. Eng. **26**, 230–234 (2010)
7. Liu, Y.W., et al.: Interaction-enhanced and time-aware graph convolutional network for successive point-of-interest recommendation in traveling enterprises. IEEE Trans. Ind. Inf. **19**, 635–643 (2023)
8. Du, H.S., et al.: Bibliometric mapping on sustainable development at the base-of-the-pyramid. J. Clean. Prod. **281**, 125290 (2021)
9. Ma, F., et al.: Research on the organization of user needs information in the big data environment. Electron. Libr. **35**, 36–49 (2017)
10. Zhang, J., et al.: Changes in contact patterns shape the dynamics of the COVID-19 outbreak in China. Science **368**, 1481–1486 (2020)
11. Gu, D., et al.: A case-based reasoning system based on weighted heterogeneous value distance metric for breast cancer diagnosis. Artif. Intell. Med. **77**, 31–47 (2017)
12. Gao, R., et al.: Sentiment Classification of Time-Sync Comments: A Semi-Supervised Hierarchical Deep Learning Method. Eur. J. Oper. Res. **314**, 1159–1173 (2023)
13. Yao, X., Feng, J.: An end to end two-stream framework for station-level bike-sharing flow prediction. Expert Syst. Appl. **247**, 123273 (2024)
14. Torres, T.S., et al.: Awareness of prevention strategies and willingness to use preexposure prophylaxis in Brazilian men who have sex with men using apps for sexual encounters: online cross-sectional study. JMIR Pub. Health Surveill. **4**, 147–161 (2018)
15. Assaf, R.D., et al.: Are men who have sex with men at higher risk for HIV in Latin America more aware of PrEP? PLoS ONE **16**(8), e0255557 (2021)

Pricing and Recycling Decisions in a Closed-Loop Supply Chain with Self-recycling by the Cosmetic Brand Owner

Qi Zhou, Xiaoke Li, Longyu Zhu, Tianxin Wang, and Min Wang[✉]

College of Economics and Management, Nanjing University of Aeronautics and Astronautics, Nanjing 211106, China
min.wang@nuaa.edu.cn

Abstract. To investigate the pricing and recycling decisions of supply chain members when the cosmetic brand owner conducts self-recycling, we consider a closed-loop supply chain consisting of a cosmetic brand owner and a retailer. We first derive the optimal decisions of the supply chain members using the backward induction. Then, we conduct the sensitivity analysis on some critical parameters and compare the brand owner's and the retailer's pricing decisions as well as the market demand for their products. The results show that the cost of production and the cost-saving of the cosmetic brand owner through recycling are related to the decision making of supply chain members. Based on the above study, we provide theoretical support for the cosmetic supply chain members to make more appropriate and profitable decisions.

Keywords: Supply chain management · Pricing · Recycling · Remanufacturing

1 Introduction

With the growth in living standards and the enrichment of the needs of people, all kinds of products are being updated more and more quickly. Meanwhile, in order to enhance brand competitiveness and product attractiveness, brand owners are investing more resources in product packaging. However, the soaring consumption of packaging does not mean the proper disposal of packaging waste. Statistics show that the global waste production in 2019 was 56.3 million tons, up 3.5% year-on-year, while the recycling rate was only 17.4% [1]. Cosmetic packaging waste is an important part of the mass of packaging waste. As one of the fastest-growing industries in emerging economies, the cosmetics industry has developed rapidly in recent years. According to Euromonitor, the cosmetics market size has risen from 483 billion dollars in 2020 to 511 billion dollars in 2021. It's predicted to exceed 716 billion dollars by 2025, and 784.6 billion dollars by 2027. Although the continuous expansion of the market share of cosmetics products can meet the diversified consumer demand for high-quality products and stimulate economic growth, the raw materials of its product packaging are mostly disposable plastic, which

Y. P. Tu and M. Chi (Eds.): WHICEB 2024, LNBIP 515, pp. 24–34, 2024.
https://doi.org/10.1007/978-3-031-60264-1_3

brings great pressure on environmental protection and resource recycling. Suppose the cosmetic packaging waste is not properly treated. In that case, it will not only aggravate the environmental pollution from incineration and landfill, but also cause a waste of resources, and increase production costs and garbage bills of brands, which will harm the rights and interests of consumers and the economic benefits of brands, and ultimately stagnate the improvement of productivity and the development of the green economy. There-fore, how to increase the recycling rate of used cosmetic packaging in the market is crucial to sustainable economic development, and this topic has gradually become a common focus of enterprises, governments, and academics.

Spurred on by the policy of building a resource-saving and environment-friendly society, China began to require cosmetic brands to assume more social responsibilities. On September 2nd, 2021, the General Administration of Market Supervision held a special press conference on the theme of "National Standards for Restricting Excessive Packaging of Commodities for Food and Cosmetics", to guide green production and consumption with the new standards, and to realize the effective supervision of the manufacturing of product packaging. It is far from enough to control the pro-duction of cosmetic packaging alone, and attention should also be paid to its recycling. However, at present, due to the lack of proper theoretical guidance and rich practical experience, this work has not yet made much progress. Therefore, it is necessary to conduct an in-depth study on the packaging recycling strategy of cosmetic brands from the perspective of closed-loop supply chain. This will not only reduce the environmental pollution caused by used packaging and help build a resource-saving and environment-friendly society, but also help to shape the brand image of cosmetic brands, reduce production costs and improve economic efficiency for them, and safeguard the legitimate rights and interests of consumers.

Based on the above background, we conduct a study on the pricing and recycling strategy of a cosmetic brand owner when there is an authorized retailer reselling its products. Specifically, we investigate the following questions:

(1) What are the optimal pricing and recycling decisions for the supply chain members when the cosmetic brand owner conducts self-recycling?
(2) What are the critical parameters that influence the decision-making of supply chain members?

The remainder of this paper is organized as follows. We review the relevant literature in Sect. 2 and describe the model setup in Sect. 3. In Sect. 4, we obtain the equilibrium results and analyze the critical parameters. Section 5 summarizes the main findings of this study and provides some management implications.

2 Literature Review

There are two main literature streams related to this paper: the closed-loop supply chain and the dual-channel supply chain. Firstly, among the studies of the closed-loop supply chain, scholars have carried out in-depth research on different closed-loop supply chains based on their characteristics. Gu et al. explore the optimal pricing strategy of the manu-facturer and the remanufacturer based on a closed-loop supply chain for electric vehicle batteries [2]. Zhen et al. discuss the construction of a green and sustainable closed-loop supply chain network under the condition of demand uncertainty [3]. Zhu et al. investigate the optimal warranty strategies for new and remanufactured products based on the consumer behavior theory [4]. Zhang and Li analyze the impact of manufacturer's fairness concerns and green efficiency on the closed-loop supply chain in four different game scenarios [5]. Gong et al. investigate the optimal decision and performance of supply chain members while considering both recycling patterns and channel power structures [6]. Since the external socio-economic environment is complicated and changeable, the impacts of environmental protection input [7], coupling of logistics and capital flow [8], and governmental policies [9] on the closed-loop supply chain have also been studied. However, few researchers have studied the closed-loop supply chain of cosmetics. With the growth of the beauty industry, there is a pressing need to address the issue of cosmetic packaging waste. Thus, we will conduct our study with such consideration.

Secondly, in the study of the dual-channel supply chain, some scholars have focused on different optimization strategies to maximize the supply chain members' profits. Zhao et al. find that transshipment always benefits the Online-to-Offline supply chain [10]. Matsui explores when a manufacturer should negotiate the whole-sale price with a retailer in order to achieve higher profits [11]. Considering the differences in consumer behavior, some scholars have investigated the impact of consumer preference and rates of consumer returns [12], as well as consumers' behavior of utilizing the retailer's services for free-riding [13], on the dual-channel supply chain. Meanwhile, the pricing decisions of supply chain members have also been examined by many scholars. Xia et al. construct a two-period dual-channel supply chain model to examine the impact of social influences on channel sequence and pricing decisions [14]. Based on the above studies, we found that few researches about the dual-channel supply chain consider the involvement of brand owners in recycling, which prompts us to conduct this study.

To summarize, this paper contributes to theoretical research by considering the characteristics of reverse supply chains for cosmetic packaging. In practice, this paper provides support for supply chain members to make optimal pricing and recycling decisions.

3 Model Setup

We consider a closed-loop supply chain that consists of a cosmetic brand owner and a retailer. Concerning the role of each supply chain member, we assume that the brand owner produces and sells new products through its official stores, which is the direct channel for the product. Meanwhile, the brand owner recycles used empty bottles from consumers and remanufactures new products using the returned bottles. The retailer is authorized by the brand owner to purchase new products from the brand owner at the wholesale price and reprice them for sale to consumers, which is the reselling channel for the product.

3.1 Recycling Quantity and Cost

Analogous to the work by Bakal and Akcali [15] and Huang and Wang [16], the recycling quantity of the brand owner q_r can be considered to be a linear function of the acquisition price p_{Br}, and can be modeled as $q_r = v + \theta p_{Br}$ ($v > 0$ and $\theta > 0$), where v represents the recycling quantity when $p_{Br} = 0$ and θ represents the sensitivity of consumers to the acquisition price.

Since there are costs involved in the recycling process, such as establishing a recycling channel and recycling publicity, in addition to the acquisition price paid for each unit of product, the brand owner also needs to pay a fixed recycling cost. Therefore, the total recycling cost I_B consists of the variable cost $p_{Br}q_r$ and the fixed cost c_0, i.e.,

$$I_B = p_{Br}q_r + c_0 \tag{1}$$

3.2 Demand Functions

As stated in previous literature such as Liu et al. [17] and Ghosh et al. [18], participation in recycling can generate a brand effect for the brand owner, which increases the market demand for its products. Following these studies, we characterize the market demands of the products sold by the supply chain members as follows:

$$D_B = \alpha - p_B + \beta p_R + \gamma \tag{2}$$

$$D_R = \alpha - p_R + \beta p_B \tag{3}$$

3.3 Profit Functions

The profit functions of the brand owner and the retailer are as follows:

$$\Pi_B = (p_B - c_n)D_B + (w - c_n)D_R + q_r(c_n - c_r) - I_B \tag{4}$$

$$\Pi_R = (p_R - w)D_R \tag{5}$$

In Eq. (4), $(p_B - c_n)D_B$ is the brand owner's revenue from selling products directly to consumers, $(w - c_n)D_R$ is the revenue from selling products to the retailer at the wholesale price, $q_r(c_n - c_r)$ is the cost-saving through recycling, and I_B is the cost of recycling. In Eq. (5), $(p_R - w)D_R$ represents the retailer's revenue from selling products to consumers.

Table 1 summarizes the notations in this paper. Note that we use "B" and "R" to denote the brand owner and the retailer, respectively.

Table 1. Notations

Symbol	Description
Decision variables	
p_B	Unit selling price of B
w	Unit wholesale price of B
p_B	Unit acquisition price of B
p_T	Unit selling price of R
Parameters	
c_n	Cost of producing per new product for B
c_r	Cost of producing per remanufacturing product for B
v	Basic recycling quantity
θ	Consumer's sensitivity coefficient to the acquisition price
c_0	Fixed recycling cost
α	Basic market demand
β	Consumer's sensitivity coefficient to the selling price
γ	Brand effect of recycling

3.4 Decision Sequence

A Stacklberg game is applied in describing the relationship between the supply chain members. Based on the practical background, the bargaining power of the brand owner is always greater due to its advantages in channel, technology and customer trust, while the retailer is less powerful. Therefore, the brand owner acts as the leader in this Stacklberg game and is followed by the retailer. The brand owner first determines the selling price in its official stores (p_B), the wholesale price to the authorized retailer (w), and the acquisition price (p_{Br}). The retailer then determines its selling price (p_R) according to the decisions already made by the brand owner. Figure 1 depicts the decision sequence of the supply chain members.

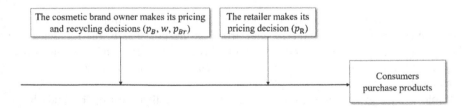

Fig. 1. Decision sequence of the cosmetic supply chain members

4   Model Analysis

In this section, the backward induction is applied to solve the Stackelberg game, and the equilibrium solution is derived. Then we analyze the impact of critical parameters and compare the pricing decisions and the market demands of the cosmetic brand owner and the retailer.

4.1   Equilibrium Results

Based on the decision sequence and realistic background, the optimization problem in our model can be expressed as shown below:

$$max \, \Pi_B(p_B, w, p_{Br})$$

$$s.t. \begin{cases} p_R(p_B, w, p_{Br}) = argmax\{\Pi_R(p_B, w, p_{Br}, p_R)\} \\ p_R \geq w \\ p_B, w, p_{Br} \geq 0 \\ D_B(p_R), D_R(p_R) \geq 0 \end{cases} \quad (6)$$

By applying the backward induction, we solve this optimization problem, and the equilibrium results are summarized in Table 1. Here we use $\Delta_B = c_n - c_r$ to represent the unit cost-saving to the brand owner from participating in recycling. The solution procedure is given in the Appendix (Table 2).

Table 2. Optimal decisions of supply chain members

Symbol	Equilibrium results
p_R	$\frac{(3-\beta)\alpha(1+\beta)+2\beta\gamma+(1+\beta)(1-\beta^2)c_n}{4(1-\beta^2)}$
w	$\frac{\alpha(1+\beta)+\beta\gamma+(1-\beta^2)c_n}{2(1-\beta^2)}$
p_B	$\frac{\alpha(1+\beta)+\gamma+(1-\beta^2)c_n}{2(1-\beta^2)}$
p_{Br}	$\frac{\theta\Delta_B-v}{2\theta}$
Π_R	$\frac{(\alpha-(1-\beta)c_n)^2}{16}$
Π_B	$\frac{\alpha^2(1+\beta)(3+\beta)+4\alpha\gamma(1+\beta)+2\gamma^2}{(1-\beta^2)8} - \frac{c_n(2\alpha(3+\beta)+4\gamma-(1-\beta)(3+\beta)c_n)}{8} +$ $\frac{\theta\Delta_B(2v+\theta\Delta_B)+v^2}{4\theta} - c_0$
D_R	$\frac{\alpha-(1-\beta)c_n}{4}$
D_B	$\frac{\alpha(\beta+2)+2\gamma+(\beta^2+\beta-2)c_n}{4}$

4.2 Impact of Critical Parameters

The influence of critical parameters on the optimal decisions of supply chain members and the market demands for the products sold by them will be explored next. There are two parameters we mainly consider, i.e., the cost of producing new products (c_n), and the cost-saving of the brand owner through recycling (Δ_B).

Proposition 1. The impact of the cost of producing new products includes:

(a) $\frac{\partial p_R}{\partial c_n} > 0$, $\frac{\partial w}{\partial c_n} > 0$, $\frac{\partial p_B}{\partial c_n} > 0$, $\frac{\partial p_{Br}}{\partial c_n} = 0$.

(b) $\frac{\partial D_R}{\partial c_n} < 0$, $\frac{\partial D_B}{\partial c_n} < 0$. If $0 < \alpha < (1-\beta)c_n$, $\frac{\partial \Pi_R}{\partial c_n} > 0$; otherwise $\frac{\partial \Pi_R}{\partial c_n} \le 0$. If $0 < \alpha < (1-\beta)c_n - \frac{2\gamma}{3+\beta}$, $\frac{\partial \Pi_B}{\partial c_n} > 0$; otherwise $\frac{\partial \Pi_B}{\partial c_n} \le 0$.

Proof: $\frac{\partial p_R}{\partial c_n} = \frac{1+\beta}{4} > 0$. $\frac{\partial w}{\partial c_n} = \frac{1}{2} > 0$. $\frac{\partial p_B}{\partial c_n} = \frac{1}{2} > 0$. $\frac{\partial D_R}{\partial c_n} = -\frac{1-\beta}{4} < 0$. $\frac{\partial D_B}{\partial c_n} = -\frac{2-\beta-\beta^2}{4} < 0$. $\frac{\partial \Pi_R}{\partial c_n} = \frac{(1-\beta)((1-\beta)c_n-\alpha)}{8}$. $\frac{\partial \Pi_B}{\partial c_n} = \frac{(3+\beta)((1-\beta)c_n-\alpha)-2\gamma}{4}$. If $0 < \alpha < (1-\beta)c_n$, $\frac{\partial \Pi_R}{\partial c_n} > 0$; otherwise $\frac{\partial \Pi_R}{\partial c_n} \le 0$. If $0 < \alpha < (1-\beta)c_n - \frac{2\gamma}{3+\beta}$, $\frac{\partial \Pi_B}{\partial c_n} > 0$; otherwise $\frac{\partial \Pi_B}{\partial c_n} \le 0$.

Proposition 1 reveals how the supply chain members' optimal response prices, market demands, and profits change with the cost of production. When the unit cost of production increases, it's easy to infer that the brand owner's optimal selling price and wholesale price will increase. At the same time, the optimal selling price of the retailer also increases due to the higher wholesale price. Affected by the increasing selling prices, market demands for the product sold by the brand owner and the retailer decrease. Meanwhile, when the market size is relatively small, the brand owner's and the retailer's profits increase with the cost of producing new products. Market competition is likely to be relatively low in a smaller market, so the brand owner and the retailer are able to obtain higher pricing power to compensate them for the increased cost of producing new products and to make higher profits. However, in a larger market, the increased cost of producing new products may lead to lower profits for the brand owner and the retailer. This is because there are usually more competitors in a larger market, which means that consumers have more choices. The brand owner and the retailer no longer have the higher pricing power to pass on cost increases to consumers, which costs them profits.

Proposition 2. The impact of the cost-saving of the brand owner through recycling includes: $\frac{\partial p_{Br}}{\partial \Delta_B} > 0$, $\frac{\partial \Pi_B}{\partial \Delta_B} > 0$.

Proof: $\frac{\partial p_{Br}}{\partial \Delta_B} = \frac{1}{2} > 0$. $\frac{\partial \Pi_B}{\partial \Delta_B} = \frac{v+\theta\Delta_B}{2} > 0$.

According to Proposition 2, with the increase of Δ_B, the brand owner's acquisition price and profit also increase. As the cost-saving from recycling increases, the brand owner may be willing to reinvest these funds into the development of its reverse supply chain, which means they will pay more to improve recycling systems, expand recycling channels, increase recycling efficiency and price, and even explore new recycling technologies or methods. At the same time, as participation in recycling saves the brand owner's production costs and promotes the brand image, the brand owner's profit will also increase.

4.3 Main Conclusion Comparison

Proposition 3. Comparison of the optimal price of supply chain members, includes: If $c_n > \frac{\alpha(1+\beta)-2\gamma}{(1-\beta)^2}$, $p_B > p_R$; otherwise $p_B \le p_R$.

Proposition 3 shows that the brand owner's optimal price is higher than the retailer's optimal price when the brand owner's production cost is higher than a certain degree. The operating costs of the official stores are usually higher than those of the reselling channel, making the selling price of the official stores relatively high. In addition, there is a brand premium on the product sold in the official stores and the brand owner will provide consumers with a better shopping experience, so as to maintain the image of the product, resulting in a relatively high price. When the brand owner's production cost is lower than a certain degree, the brand owner's optimal price is lower than the retailer's optimal price. The brand owner has the flexibility to control the price of the product in the official stores, so it can choose to attract consumers and enhance market competitiveness by reducing the price of the product under the condition of lower production costs.

Proposition 4. Comparison of the market demand of supply chain members, includes: If $c_n > \frac{\alpha(1+\beta)+2\gamma}{1-\beta^2}$, $D_B > D_R$; otherwise $D_B \le D_R$.

As seen in Proposition 4, the market demand for the product sold by the brand owner in the official stores is higher than the demand for the product sold by the retailer when the brand owner's cost of production is above a certain level, while the reverse applies when brand owner's cost of production is lower than a certain value. Higher production cost usually means that the product's quality is relatively high, so the price of the product is correspondingly higher. With this in mind, consumers will be more willing to purchase through the official stores because they can have a clearer understanding of the value of the product and are willing to pay more for a high-quality product.

5 Conclusion

In this paper, considering the scenario that a cosmetic brand owner recycling the used cosmetics packages by itself, we investigate the pricing and recycling decisions of the brand owner and a retailer in a closed-loop supply chain. We first derive the optimal solutions using the backward induction and then analyze the effects of some critical parameters on the decisions of the supply chain members by conducting the sensitivity analysis. Finally, we compare the cosmetic brand owner's and the retailer's optimal prices, as well as the market demand for their products at the optimal price. We find that an increase in the cost of production can lead to an increase in the optimal prices of the brand owner and the retailer and a decrease in market demand. In addition, the comparison of the brand owner's and the retailer's optimal prices and market demands varies with the cost of production. Furthermore, if the cost-saving of the brand owner through recycling increases, the acquisition price as well as the profit of the brand owner increases. According to the above findings, management implications for brand owners and retailers in closed-loop supply chains are provided as follows:

(1) Management implications for cosmetic brand owners: To stimulate more demand, brand owners should reasonably control their costs of production, such as improving production efficiency, optimizing product design, coordinating supply chains, etc., so as to reduce the price of their products without losing profits. In addition, brand owners should improve their recycling cost-effectiveness, which allows them to make higher profits.

(2) Management implications for retailers: The production cost is a critical parameter that influences retailers' decisions, while the cost-saving of brand owners through recycling also indirectly influences retailers' decisions. Therefore, it's the right choice for retailers to cooperate with brand owners to get relevant information about production costs and recycling strategies so that they can make more appropriate decisions.

There are several further directions for expansion of this research. Firstly, we only consider the scenario of the cosmetic brand owner conducting self-recycling in this paper. In future studies, we may consider the scenario where the cosmetic brand owner cooperates with the retailer to recycle. In addition, in practice, the recycling of cosmetic packaging often involves the participation of third-party recyclers. Thus, we will explore the impact of third-party recyclers' participation in recycling in the future.

Acknowledgement. This work was supported by National Natural Science Foundation of China (No. 72001038) and the Fundamental Research Funds for the Central Universities (No. NJ2023027), Key Laboratory of Intelligent Decision and Digital Operations, Ministry of Industrial and Information Technology (KLADDO-200303).

Appendix

The first and second order derivatives of the retailer's profit function to its pricing decision are derived firstly:

$$\frac{d\Pi_R}{dp_R} = w + \alpha + \beta p_B - 2p_R \tag{A1}$$

$$\frac{d^2\Pi_R}{dp_R} = -2 \tag{A2}$$

Equation (A2) is less than 0, which means that for the retailer's profit function, there exists a maximum value of its price. Solving $\frac{d\Pi_R}{dp_R} = w + \alpha + \beta p_B - 2p_R = 0$, we have the retailer's optimal response function:

$$p_R = \frac{1}{2}(w + \alpha + \beta p_B) \tag{A3}$$

Then, plugging Eq. (A3) into Π_B, and computing the Hessian matrix of the brand owner's profit function of decision variables p_B, w, and p_{Br}, we have.

$$H_1 = \begin{pmatrix} -2 & \beta & 0 \\ \beta & 0 & 0 \\ 0 & 0 & -2\theta \end{pmatrix} \tag{A4}$$

The first and third order principal minors of this Hessian matrix are less than 0, and the second order principal minor is greater than 0. Thus, the Hessian matrix is a negative definite matrix, and the brand owner's profit function is concave and has a unique maximum.

Solving $\frac{\partial \Pi_B}{\partial p_{Br}} = 0$, $\frac{\partial \Pi_B}{\partial w} = 0$, and $\frac{\partial \Pi_B}{\partial p_B} = 0$, respectively, we have $p_{Br} = \frac{\theta \Delta_B - v}{2\theta}$, $w = \frac{1}{2}(\alpha + c_n - \beta c_n + 2\beta p_B)$, and $p_B^* = \frac{\alpha(1+\beta)+\gamma+(1-\beta^2)c_n}{2(1-\beta^2)}$. Plugging p_B^* into p_R and w, we have $p_R^* = \frac{(3-\beta)\alpha(1+\beta)+2\beta\gamma+(1+\beta)(1-\beta^2)c_n}{4(1-\beta^2)}$ and $w^* = \frac{\alpha(1+\beta)+\beta\gamma+(1-\beta^2)c_n}{2(1-\beta^2)}$. Plugging in these best-response decisions, we calculate the brand owner's and the retailer's profits:

$\Pi_B^* = \frac{\alpha^2(1+\beta)(3+\beta)+4\alpha\gamma(1+\beta)+2\gamma^2}{(1-\beta^2)8} - \frac{c_n(2\alpha(3+\beta)+4\gamma-(1-\beta)(3+\beta)c_n)}{8} + \frac{\theta\Delta_B(2v+\theta\Delta_B)+v^2}{4\theta} - c_0$

and $\Pi_R^* = \frac{(\alpha-(1-\beta)c_n)^2}{16}$.

References

1. Cao, X., Qi, X., Wen, H., Zhang, C.: Closed-loop supply chain recycling and pricing decisions considering cost sharing under fairness concerns. J. Syst. Sci. Math. Sci. **42**(12), 3213–3233 (2022). (in Chinese)

2. Gu, X., Ieromonachou, P., Zhou, L., Tseng, M.L.: Developing pricing strategy to optimise total profits in an electric vehicle battery closed loop supply chain. J. Clean. Prod. **203**, 376–385 (2018)

3. Zhen, L., Huang, L., Wang, W.: Green and sustainable closed-loop supply chain network design under uncertainty. J. Clean. Prod. **227**, 1195–1209 (2019)

4. Zhu, X., Yu, L., Li, W.: Warranty period decision and coordination in closed-loop supply chains considering remanufacturing and consumer behavior. Sustainability. **11**(15), 4237 (2019)

5. Zhang, N., Li, B.: Pricing and coordination of green closed-loop supply chain with fairness concerns. IEEE Access. **8**, 224178–224189 (2020)

6. Gong, Y., Chen, M., Zhuang, Y.: Decision-making and performance analysis of closed-loop supply chain under different recycling modes and channel power structures. Sustainability. **11**(22), 6413 (2019)

7. Su, J., Li, C., Zeng, Q., Yang, J., Zhang, J.: A green closed-loop supply chain coordination mechanism based on third-party recycling. Sustainability. **11**(19), 5335 (2019)

8. Duan, W., Ma, H., Xu, D.S.: Analysis of the impact of COVID-19 on the coupling of the material flow and capital flow in a closed-loop supply chain. Adv. Prod. Eng. Manag. **16**(1), 5–22 (2021)

9. Hassanpour, A., Bagherinejad, J., Bashiri, M.: A robust leader-follower approach for closed loop supply chain network design considering returns quality levels. Comput. Ind. Eng. **136**, 293–304 (2019)

10. Zhao, F., Wu, D., Liang, L., Dolgui, A.: Lateral inventory transshipment problem in online-to-offline supply chain. Int. J. Prod. Res. **54**(7), 1951–1963 (2016)

11. Matsui, K.: Optimal bargaining timing of a wholesale price for a manufacturer with a retailer in a dual-channel supply chain. Eur. J. Oper. Res. **287**(1), 225–236 (2020)

12. Radhi, M., Zhang, G.: Pricing policies for a dual-channel retailer with cross-channel returns. Comput. Ind. Eng. **119**, 63–75 (2018)

13. Liu, C., Dan, B., Zhang, X., Zhang, H.: Composite contracts for dual-channel supply chain coordination with the existence of service free riding. J. Theor. Appl. El. Comm. **17**(2), 789–808 (2022)

14. Xia, Y., Li, J., Xia, L.: Launch strategies for luxury fashion products in dual-channel distributions: impacts of social influences. Comput. Ind. Eng. **169**, 108286 (2022)
15. Bakal, I.S., Akcali, E.: Effects of random yield in remanufacturing with price-sensitive supply and demand. Prod. Oper. Manag. **15**(3), 407–420 (2006)
16. Huang, Y., Wang, Z.: Closed-loop supply chain models with product take-back and hybrid remanufacturing under technology licensing. J. Clean. Prod. **142**, 3917–3927 (2017)
17. Liu, Z., Anderson, T.D., Cruz, J.M.: Consumer environmental awareness and competition in two-stage supply chains. Eur. J. Oper. Res. **218**(3), 602–613 (2012)
18. Ghosh, S.K., Seikh, M.R., Chakrabortty, M.: Analyzing a stochastic dual-channel supply chain under consumers' low carbon preferences and cap-and-trade regulation. Comput. Ind. Eng.. Ind. Eng. **149**, 106765 (2020)

Carbon Reduction Effects of Anti-corruption Policies: Evidence from Energy-Intensive Industries

Qi Zhang[1], Yu Feng[1], Jiangxin Niu[1], and Yangyan Shi[2(✉)]

[1] China University of Geosciences (Wuhan), Wuhan, China
[2] Macquarie Business School, Macquarie University, Sydney, NSW, Australia
1781284239@qq.com

Abstract. Against the background of China's "double carbon" target and environmental issues becoming important management matters, energy-intensive industries have received widespread attention as a major source of carbon emission pollutants; at the same time, China is carrying out a sustained and efficient anti-corruption campaign, and energy-intensive industries are mostly state-owned enterprises, and corruption has been a controversial issue. The issue of corruption in energy-intensive industries, which are mostly state-owned enterprises, has also been highly controversial. Faced with the dual dilemma of environmental and political pollution, is there an inevitable link between the anti-corruption campaign in China's energy-intensive industries and the level of carbon emissions? What is the mechanism of influence? To this end, we discuss the impact in this context using a fixed-effects model with panel data of energy-intensive industries from 2007 to 2016. The results show that the anti-corruption campaign significantly reduces the level of carbon emissions in the industry, while on the other hand, green innovation does not play a role in improving the phenomenon of excessive carbon emissions at the technological level.

Keywords: carbon emissions · anti-corruption · green innovation capacity

1 Introduction

Air pollution and climate change are two important issues that threaten the sustainable development of mankind (Ravindra et al., 2019), and concern the common interests of all countries. In order to effectively combat global warming, carbon neutrality has become a consensus among the world's major carbon emitters, with many Western countries introducing policies to ban the use of fossil fuels (Shi et al., 2022), and the introduction of carbon peaking and carbon neutrality targets by various countries all indicate that low-carbon transformation has become a key priority for national development (Ren et al., 2018). According to the BP Statistical Yearbook of World Energy, China's total energy consumption ranked first in the world in 2021, accounting for 26.5% of the world's total energy consumption, and the growing energy consumption and CO_2 emissions have caused China to face enormous international public opinion pressure in international

Y. P. Tu and M. Chi (Eds.): WHICEB 2024, LNBIP 515, pp. 35–47, 2024.
https://doi.org/10.1007/978-3-031-60264-1_4

climate change negotiations (Hao and Liu, 2015). On September 22, 2020, China made a proposal at the 75th United Nations General Assembly to achieve the goal of carbon peaking by 2030 and carbon neutrality by 2060. Exploring the main goals and important paths for China's carbon emissions reduction, the energy-intensive sector has received much attention. The industry is an important source of pollutants in China, and data from the "Carbon Emission Ranking of Listed Companies in China (2022)" show that carbon emissions from the iron and steel sector alone have already amounted to more than 50% of China's greenhouse gas emissions in 2022. Not only that, but because of the industry's state-owned attributes, the issue of corruption within the industry has also attracted the attention of scholars (Guo et al., 2021), and in the face of both environmental pollution and political pollution in the face of both environmental and political pollution, energy-intensive industries must be the focus of emissions reduction and anti-corruption efforts if they are to make a difference in the "carbon neutral and peak carbon" initiative.

In many studies, scholars have pointed out that the increase in environmental degradation is largely related to corruption in government departments (Sulemana and Kpienbaareh, 2020), and Transparency International (TI) has pointed out on the connection between environmental issues and political governance that government corruption is the Transparency International has identified government corruption as a "major culprit" in environmental degradation in relation to the link between environmental issues and political governance.

The pathways through which corruption acts on environmental problems in the existing literature can be developed along two dimensions: direct and indirect. Matthew (2007) argues that the first possible "direct" role is in the direct impact of corruption on environmental regulation and enforcement, where corruption reduces the effectiveness of environmental regulation, affects environmental quality, and leads to environmental degradation; corruption may also affect environmental quality through an "indirect" mechanism (Tran, 2020; Xuan et al., 2021). Corruption may also affect environmental quality through an 'indirect' mechanism, and there is now a wealth of research evidence suggesting that corruption acts as an impediment to economic growth (Tran, 2020; Zhang et al., 2021), while a large body of literature centers on the inverted U-shaped relationship between per capita income and pollution, known as the environmental Kuznets curve. The inverted U-shaped relationship between per capita income and pollution has been developed to argue that there is a link between the economy and environmental pollution (Kaika and Zervas, 2013; Liu, 2022). Based on this, the indirect effect of corruption on the environment can be considered as its effect on income levels, and by affecting income, corruption will therefore indirectly affect environmental quality. Overall, corruption, as one of the important factors affecting the quality of the environment, will also significantly affect the level of carbon emissions in a country.

In this anti-corruption campaign of China, energy-intensive industries have been identified as the main target and have been significantly affected (Chen et al., 2022), therefore, energy-intensive industries are a window to explore whether the anti-corruption campaign can ameliorate excessive GHG emissions by mitigating corruption, and whether green innovation capacity plays a role in it. Based on the industry classification standards issued by the China Securities Regulatory Commission (CSRC), we selected eight energy-intensive industries, to collect 2007–2016[1] panel dataset of listed enterprises in the industries to empirically study the impact of anti-corruption campaign on carbon emissions of Chinese enterprises in energy-intensive industries, and further explore the mechanism of this impact and analyze the role of green innovation capacity of enterprises affected by the anti-corruption campaign in it.

The rest of the paper is organized as follows: Sect. 2 presents the theoretical framework and hypothesis development, Sect. 3 describes the data and the model, Sect. 4 sets out the empirical results and discussion, and Sect. 5 provides a short conclusion.

2 Theoretical Assumptions

The level of carbon emissions is closely related to the regulatory activities of government authorities due to the fact that corrupt governments are willing to allow lobbyists to influence policy decisions, thus reducing the rigidity of policy implementation. For example, Zhang et al. (2016) indicate that, according to rent-seeking theory, corrupt government officials will be more biased towards options where more rent-seeking rents are available and received, and high-emitting firms will thus be more likely to seek political patronage through lobbying or bribing government officials in order to circumvent stringent environmental regimes and regulations, and in this case, corruption reduces the efficiency of the government's environmental regulation, and bribed or malfeasance officials will have sufficient incentives and ability to allow polluting firms to emit excessive pollutants even as they implement strict environmental policies, and thus the rigidity of policy implementation is threatened. In contrast, a widespread anti-corruption campaign improves the transparency of public sector governance, which means that the quality of environmental regulation is improved, and the enforcement of environmental laws and regulations becomes correspondingly stricter, and policies are implemented (Hao et al., 2021); in addition to this, anti-corruption increases the likelihood of corruption being exposed, and on the one hand, rent-seeking behavior is strongly constrained and regulated, and on the other hand, in the event of an increase in risk, the risk of rent-seeking behavior increases. On the other hand, the illegal cost of rent-seeking behavior under increased risk will also increase, all of which make it more difficult for firms to seek political protection and assume the necessary social responsibility for environmental protection and reduce excessive greenhouse gas emissions. The following assumptions are therefore made:

H1: Anti-corruption has a negative contribution to CO_2 emissions.

---

[1] The data for the anti-corruption campaign in this study comes from the China Prosecutorial Yearbook, which is currently updated to 2016, so the cutoff year for the data in this paper is 2016.

Seeking political connections and improving innovation are two alternative ways of growing a firm, and political connections can distort resource allocation and have a crowding-out effect on innovative capacity (Wu et al., 2022). Once corrupt behavior occurs, rent-seeking activities increase transaction costs, reduce R&D capital, and inhibit firms' willingness to engage in technological innovation activities. Anti-corruption campaigns increase the efficiency of resource utilization and reduce the resources needed for firms to collude with government officials, prompting firms to shift their attention from unusual activities such as rent-seeking to strict compliance with environmental regulations, thus leaving more human and financial resources for innovation (Yang et al., 2021). Not only that, but the loss of political advantage in this anti-corruption campaign is a major external shock for firms that previously benefited from their political connections. The loss of political protection in turn prompts firms to adopt proactive environmental strategies, such as increasing R&D investment in innovation, to make up for their lost political competitiveness; in addition to this, green innovation can help firms to build a green brand image and send positive signals of CSR, which in turn can benefit firms by attracting more customers (Tang et al., 2018).

Green innovation contributes to the reduction of carbon dioxide emissions, which scholars such as Song et al. (2018) believe may be due to the fact that green technologies are more accurately targeting environmental protection issues, not only that, but it is expected to increase the level of energy efficiency, so we argue that the overall demand for energy by organizations or sectors becomes less, and that a lower demand for energy implies a lower level of carbon dioxide emissions. Emissions. In addition to this, green innovation is also expected to promote the use of renewable energy. Many studies by scholars have also proved that green innovations are effective in reducing CO_2 emissions, and in a related study in the Organization for Economic Cooperation and Development (OECD) countries, Hashmi and Alam (2019) found that an increase in the number of green patent applications reduces the level of CO_2 emissions in these countries. Similarly, in a related study of the G7 economies, Khan et al. (2020) argue that green innovation capabilities and renewable energy consumption can help reduce consumption-based CO_2 emission levels, and that enhancing environmentally friendly technologies and the use of renewable energy sources can help most of the G7 countries to comply with their emission reduction commitments. Overall, the role of green innovation as a mechanism to reduce CO_2 emissions has been widely explored. Based on the above research, this paper makes the following assumptions:

H2: Increased green innovation capacity enhances the negative contribution of anti-corruption to carbon emissions.

Based on the above analysis, a theoretical framework of the mechanism was designed in order to clearly reveal the relationship between anti-corruption, green innovation and carbon emissions as shown in Fig. 1 below:

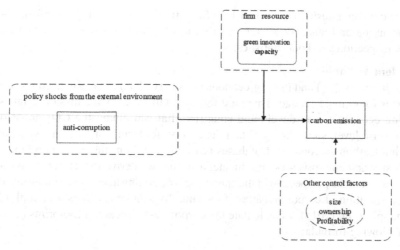

Fig. 1. Theoretical framework

3 Research Design

3.1 Models and Estimation Methods

In order to investigate whether anti-corruption campaigns have an impact on carbon emissions in energy-intensive industries, and whether corporate green innovation capacity plays a moderating role in the process of anti-corruption campaigns affecting carbon emissions, this paper constructs the following model:

$$CO2_{it} = \alpha_0 + \alpha_1 A - COR_t + \alpha_2 \, Controls_{it} + \varepsilon_{i,t} \tag{1}$$

$$CO2_{it} = \beta_0 + \beta_1 A - COR_t + \beta_2 Gre + \beta_3 Gre \times A - COR_t + \beta_4 Controls_{it} + \theta_{i,t} \tag{2}$$

Equation (1) is the main effect of the impact of anti-corruption on carbon emissions, and Eq. (2) is the model after the addition of regulatory variables to the main effect. In the model, i, t denotes the enterprise and year respectively, the explanatory variable CO_2 it is the enterprise's carbon dioxide emissions measurement, the explanatory variable A-COR t is the anti-corruption campaign strength, Gre_{it} is the enterprise's green innovation ability, $Controls_{it}$ is the control variable group.

3.2 Data and Variables

To test our hypotheses, we constructed a longitudinal dataset of Chinese firms in energy-intensive industries listed on the Shanghai and Shenzhen exchanges for the period from 2007 to 2016. Data on firms' financial sex indicators are mainly from the CSMAR database. The main source of data for identifying firms' green innovations is the China Research Data Service Platform (CNRDS). The data calculation basis for enterprise-level CO_2 emissions is taken from the CEADs database (Shan et al., 2018). In addition, there are data on industries from the China Statistical Yearbook, and for information on anti-corruption and integrity we refer to Ren et al. (2021) for measurement based on China's inspection yearbook statistics.

Dependent Variable

Carbon dioxide (CO_2) and other greenhouse gases (GHGs) are recognized by scholars as proxies for climate change. There are few specialized carbon emission databases in emerging economies and developing countries that can obtain the CO_2 emissions at the enterprise level, so we firstly obtain the carbon footprints of each industry through the China Carbon Accounting Databases (CEADs), and on this basis, combined with the industry and enterprise-specific financial status, we derive the carbon emissions of enterprises from the perspective of the enterprise's operating activities. Emissions. Based on the calculation of corporate carbon footprints by scholars such as Wei et al. (2021) and Chapple et al. (2013), we calculate the corporate-level carbon footprints according to the following formula:

$$E_m = F_m \times O_m / O_{i,m}$$

where E_m is the carbon emissions of firm m; F_m is the total carbon emissions of industry i to which company m belongs; O_m is the main business cost of company m; $O_{i,m}$ is the total cost of main business of industry i. In addition, for robustness, we add 1 to the firm-level carbon footprint and then take the logarithm to calculate it.

Independent Variable

In previous empirical studies on anti-corruption, Transparency International's Corruption Perceptions Index (CPI) has been widely used, but Yan et al. (2021) points out that the shortcoming of this type of subjective indicator is that it is unable to measure the true level of corruption in different regions. In order to make the measurement of the indicator more objective, we believe that the increase in the number of investigated officials reflects the increase in the government's anti-corruption efforts, which can directly reflect the changes in China's political environment to a certain extent, so we use the number of government officials investigated each year in China's Inspection Almanac to measure the anti-corruption efforts. To ensure the robustness of the results, we use the logarithm of the number of investigated and sanctioned job crimes to test the empirical model.

Moderating Variables

An enterprise's green innovation capability responds to its efforts to control CO_2 emissions. Some studies focus on innovation investment to measure innovation capacity; however, this method does not effectively test the efficiency of innovation investment into outcomes. Therefore, patents are considered the most appropriate proxy for innovation. The number of patents has been used as a proxy for corporate innovation in the studies of scholars such as Bronzini and Piselli (2016), Hu et al. (2017). The advantage of using the number of patents as a dependent variable is that they can indicate whether an organization is carrying out research and development on technologies related to environmental protection. Patent in China can be categorized into three types: inventions, utility models and designs. Compared with invention patents, utility model patents and design patents represent small and incremental innovations, and have received few patent examinations and relatively low independent innovation capabilities. Therefore, based on the existing research on enterprise innovation, this paper uses the number of green invention patent applications independently obtained by companies in different years to measure the green innovation capability of enterprises according to the data on the green patent application situation of listed companies in the CNRDS data.

Control Variables

After using corporate carbon intensity as the dependent variable, we follow the relevant research to control the following variables. First, we use traditional firm-level financial indicators as control variables. Second, because the strategic management of firms is subject to the constraints of the institutional environment (Mutta kin et al., 2020), we control variables related to the board of directors' level, such as the proportion of independent directors; finally, compared with non-state-owned enterprises, the nature of state-owned enterprises is more special, so we control the nature of corporate ownership. The breakdown of the study variables is shown in Table 1 below:

Table 1. Definition and measurement of variables

variable name		meaning	measure	data sources
dependent variable	CO_2	Carbon dioxide emissions	We measure a company's carbon footprint using the total carbon emissions of the industry in which it operates and the company's costs as a percentage of the total industry costs, taking the natural logarithm in the results of the calculation	CSMAR; the Statistical Yearbook; CEADs database
independent variable	A-cor	Anti-Corruption Efforts	Measured using the natural logarithm of the number of officials investigated and prosecuted for job-related crimes per year	Ren (2021)

(*continued*)

Table 1. (continued)

variable name		meaning	measure	data sources
moderator variable	Gre	Green innovation capacity	We measure the green innovation capacity of listed companies by the number of green patents they independently obtain each year	CNRDS database
control variables	size	Enterprise size	Natural logarithm of total assets	CSMAR
	profit	profitability	Return on assets (net profit to total assets)	
	growth	growth rate	sales growth rate	
	lever	financial leverage	Ratio of total liabilities to total assets	
	IndD	Proportion of independent directors	Proportion of independent directors to the size of the board of directors	
	cash	in cash	Ratio of cash and equivalents to total assets	
	TobinQ	Tobin's Q	Ratio of enterprise market value to total assets	
	RightsNature	Nature of enterprise ownership	The nature of the enterprise is state-owned or non-state-owned	

4 Analysis of Empirical Results

4.1 Correlation Analysis

Table 2 shows the Pearson correlation coefficient matrix of the variables, which is consistent with our hypotheses, and the results show that anti-corruption and CO_2 emissions are strongly correlated.

Table 2. Table of Pearson correlation coefficients of variables

	$\ln\_CO_2$	$\ln\_A\text{-}COR$	size	profit	growth	lever	IndD	cash	TobinQ
$\ln\_CO_2$	1								
$\ln\_A\text{-}COR$	-0.06^*	1							
size	0.65^*	0.08^*	1						
profit	-0.01	-0.10^*	-0.00	1					
growth	0.03	-0.17^*	0.02	0.24^*	1				
lever	0.35^*	-0.07^*	0.43^*	-0.42^*	0.02	1			
IndD	-0.05^*	0.07^*	-0.01	-0.02	-0.00	-0.05^*	1		
cash	0.51^*	0.03^*	0.69^*	0.09^*	0.02	0.13^*	0.03	1	
TobinQ	-0.32^*	0.08^*	-0.47^*	0.14^*	-0.01	-0.32^*	0.03^*	-0.23^*	1

The numbers in the table are the person correlation coefficients between the main variables, * $p < 0.1$, ** $p < 0.05$, *** $p < 0.01$

4.2 Regression Analysis

Based on Eqs. (1) and (2), using a fixed-effects model to test the impact of anti-corruption campaigns on firms' CO_2 emissions, and Table 3 below exhibits the results of the fixed-effects stratified regressions. Model 1 is the baseline model containing only the control variables, Model 2 contains our explanatory variables, and Model 3 is the regression of the moderated model after adding the interaction terms of the moderating variables Green Innovation and Green Innovation.

In Table 3, The regression results show that the regression coefficient of anti-corruption on carbon emissions of energy-intensive firms is negative (-1.318) at the 1% significance level, which suggests that anti-corruption has a significant negative contributing effect on CO_2 emissions, i.e., anti-corruption can effectively suppress excessive CO_2 emissions, which is consistent with our hypothesis H1. The effective implementation of anti-corruption campaign can largely improve the governance level and transparency of the government, political stability is gradually restored, environmental regulation is gradually strengthened, regulatory efficiency is strongly guaranteed, the regulated enterprises cannot avoid the environmental system and regulations that should be complied with by paying bribes, and the distorted environmental protection policies can be effectively implemented and enforced in the anti-corruption campaign.

Model 3 adds the interaction term between anti-corruption campaign and green innovation after decentralization treatment, thus presenting the effect of firms' green innovation level, and the results show that the coefficient of the interaction term is -0.146 and is significant at the 5% level, which indicates that the firms' green innovation level has a significant negative moderating effect on the impact of the anti-corruption campaign on carbon emissions, that is, the firms' green innovation significantly inhibits the anti-corruption campaign's impact on carbon emission reduction, which is contrary to our hypothesis 2, Based on the results of this hypothesis test, we propose the following possible explanations:

Table 3. Regression results for anti-corruption campaigns, carbon emissions, green innovation

Var	ln_CO2MT	ln_CO2MT	ln_CO2MT
	Model 1	Model 2	Model 3
size	0.140^{***}	0.140^{***}	0.140^{***}
	(0.008)	(0.008)	(0.008)
profit	0.303^{***}	0.303^{***}	0.305^{***}
	(0.067)	(0.067)	(0.068)
growth	0.045^{***}	0.045^{***}	0.045^{***}
	(0.007)	(0.007)	(0.007)
lever	0.069^{**}	0.069^{**}	0.074^{**}
	(0.030)	(0.030)	(0.030)
IndD	0.001	0.001	0.001
	(0.001)	(0.001)	(0.001)
cash	0.000^{***}	0.000^{***}	0.000^{***}
	(0.000)	(0.000)	(0.000)
TobinQ	0.017^{***}	0.017^{***}	0.017^{***}
	(0.004)	(0.004)	(0.004)
RightsNature	0.077^{***}	0.077^{***}	0.076^{***}
	(0.025)	(0.025)	(0.025)
Main effects			
ln_COR1		-1.318^{***}	-1.359^{***}
		(0.233)	(0.234)
Two-way Interactions			
c_Gre			1.533^{**}
			(0.765)
ln_COR1 × c_Gre			-0.146^{**}
			(0.073)
_cons	-2.774^{***}	10.951^{***}	11.395^{***}
	(0.181)	(2.337)	(2.356)
N	3063.000	3063.000	3053.000
r2	0.277	0.277	0.278
r2_a	0.158	0.158	0.157
Year	Yes	Yes	Yes

Standard errors in parentheses
$^{*}\ p < 0.1,\ ^{**}\ p < 0.05,\ ^{***}\ p < 0.01$

This may be due to China's unique context of generous "government subsidies" for patent applications, in which the number of patents for green inventions as a measure of green innovation capacity may be flawed because many patents would not have been filed without the generous government subsidies (Jiang et al. 2019); in other words, this context implies that the purpose of many patent applications is profit-driven rather than for the purpose of improving green technologies to achieve carbon reduction and emission reduction;

Secondly, we argue that firms may enhance their technological innovation capacity for the sake of government subsidies and preferential policies, and in this process, firm managers need to obtain political blessings from local officials through "connections", while anti-corruption cuts off "connections" between firms and officials, so in the short term, the fight against corruption may inhibit technological innovation in such firms (Wang et al., 2019);

Finally, in addition to the above reasons, it may be related to the specificity of our chosen industry. Energy is the support and driving force of the economy, especially in China, where the energy industry is largely state-owned (Chen et al., 2021), with a certain degree of "administrative monopoly", in which case the operating losses of these firms are usually borne by both the government and the consumers, and thus do not need to consider too much about efficiency and cost; the willingness to take risks are also usually low (Zhan, 2017). Therefore, even if the anti-corruption campaign removes a number of senior officials from the industry who are engaged in "rent-seeking" activities, it does not change the "inertia" of business managers who tend to be risk-free, and thus does not significantly promote the phenomenon of green innovation activities by enterprises in the industry.

5 Conclusion

Carbon neutrality is increasingly becoming a consensus among countries, and low-carbon transformation has become the key to a country's development. Enterprises are the key subject and main source of carbon emissions, as well as the solution to the carbon emission problem, and their carbon emission levels are affected by various uncertainties at the micro level. Therefore, in this paper, we study how anti-corruption affects the level of their carbon emissions and the moderating role of enterprises' green innovation capacity in this, using a sample of listed enterprises in China's Shanghai and Shenzhen A-shares in energy-consuming industries in the period of 2007–2016. Our findings confirm that the anti-corruption campaign has a significant negative effect on corporate CO_2 emissions, and that the anti-corruption campaign reduces uncertainty in the institutional environment, safeguards the effective implementation of environmental protection policies and the regulatory efforts of local governments, and serves as an effective emission reduction.

From the perspective of theoretical contribution, our findings provide new insights into corporate carbon emission reduction in emerging markets, broaden the scope of existing theories, analyze the impact of anti-corruption policies on carbon emissions and the moderating role of green innovation, and then propose a new perspective for the study of carbon emissions of China's energy enterprises, which achieves a certain degree of theoretical innovation. In addition to providing theoretical contributions, the real-world policy implications of our findings deserve more attention:

From a policy point of view, the deterioration of the environment will also be affected by government supervision, and a weak political system will first reduce the effectiveness of environmental supervision. Therefore, the government should strengthen supervision, institutionalize the anti-corruption for a long time, fundamentally curb the occurrence of corruption, effectively reduce the opportunity for enterprises to seek rent from government officials, and encourage enterprises to seek development by technological innovation. In addition, in the assessment and evaluation of local governments, in addition to the indicators of economic growth, more attention should be paid to the indicators of environmental protection, so as to avoid the local government to pursue economic growth and ignore the irreversible negative impacts and consequences of economic growth for the environment; Finally, the government must strengthen the protection and application of intellectual property rights, and constantly improve the level of intellectual property rights protection, to better protect the achievements of enterprises' innovations.

For enterprises, by promoting anti-corruption campaigns, policymakers can improve the governance system and optimize the market environment, create a fairer and more orderly competitive environment for the healthy development of enterprises, enable managers to abandon the concept of seeking political blessings through economic ties from the source, and enable them to gain access to government resources for innovation, thus encouraging companies to engage in innovative activities and fundamentally improve their own hard power and competitiveness. We are committed to the construction of corporate operational performance and corporate social responsibility, and ultimately help our country to realize the goal of carbon neutrality and carbon peak.

In China's unique context, there are many flaws in the measurement of this indicator of green innovation. Based on the research of scholars, we believe that future research can distinguish corporate innovation into "symbolic innovation" and "substantive innovation", and that the general patent subsidy (e.g., patent subsidy) can be regarded as a kind of innovation. Generally, patent subsidies occur during the application process and within 1 year after the grant, and the patent application process takes about 2 years. If the enterprise abandons the renewal fee 3 years after the patent application (Jiang et al., 2019), it is reasonable to regard the innovation as a "symbolic innovation", and it would be more in line with the actual situation of China if the study is based on this distinction. It will be more in line with China's actual situation and to a certain extent exclude the phenomenon of "symbolic patent" affecting the results too much in patent applications, thus making the conclusions more generalizable.

References

Shi, Y.Y., Feng, Y., Zhang, Q., Shuai, J., Niu, J.: Does China's new energy vehicles supply chain stock market have risk spillovers? from raw material price effect on lithium batteries, Energy, Volume 262, Part A (2023)

Zhou, K.Z., Gao, G.Y., Zhao, H.X.: State ownership and firm innovation in China: an integrated view of institutional and efficiency logics. Adm. Sci. Q. **62**(2), 375–404 (2016)

Yang, Q.-J.: Corporate growth: political affiliation or capacity building? Econ. Res. **46**(10), 54–66+94 (2011)

Zhan, J.V.: Do natural resources breed corruption? Evidence from China. Environ. Resource Econ. **66**(2), 237–259 (2017)

Yang, C., Zhang, W., Sheng, Y., Yang, Z.: Corruption and firm efforts on environmental protection: evidence from a policy shock. Pacific- Basin Finan. J. **65** (2021). https://doi.org/10.1016/j.pac fin.2020.101465

Tang, M., Walsh, G., Lerner, D., Fitza, M.A., Li, Q.: Green innovation, managerial concern and firm performance: an empirical study. Bus. Strat. Environ. **27**(1), 39–51 (2018). https://doi. org/10.1002/bse.1981

Song, M., Wang, S., Sun, J.: Environmental regulations, staff quality, green technology, R&D efficiency, and profit in manufacturing. Technol. Forecast. Soc. Chang. **133**, 1–14 (2018). https://doi.org/10.1016/j.techfore.2018.04.020

Shan et al.: "China CO2 emission accounts 1997–2015. Scientific Data" (2018). https://www.nat ure.com/articles/sdata2017201

Ren, Y.S., Ma, C.Q., Apergis, N., Sharp, B.: Responses of carbon emissions to corruption across Chinese provinces. Energy Econ. **98** (2021). https://doi.org/10.1016/j.eneco.2021.105241

Wei, P., Li, Y.Y., Ren, X.H., Duan, K.: Crude oil price uncertainty and corporate carbon emissions. Environ. Sci. Pollut. Res. **29**(2), 2385–2400 (2021). https://doi.org/10.1007/s11356-021-158 37-8

Jiang, S., He, W., Lu, J.: Innovation as a political strategy: corporate symbolic innovation in the context of transition economy. Nankai Manag. Rev. **22**(02), 104–113 (2019)

Bridging Technostress and Perceived Value: Why Middle-Aged and Elderly People Resist Using Chronic Diseases Management Apps

Ying Zhao[1], Hongyu Liao[1], and Liang Zhou[2(✉)]

[1] School of Public Administration, Sichuan University, Chengdu 610065, China
[2] School of Economics and Management, North China Institute of Science and Technology, Langfang 065201, China
zhouliang_bnu@163.com

Abstract. This paper aims to explore the causes of resistance to using chronic disease management APPs in middle-aged and elderly people. By integrating technostress theory and status quo bias (SQB) theory, a conceptual model was proposed to explore the resistance of information system users. A total of 290 questionnaires were collected in the middle-aged and elderly population, and the CB-Structural Equation Model was used to test the hypotheses. We found that both technology anxiety and perceived value can directly affect the resistance intention, while technology anxiety can also indirectly affect the resistance intention by significantly affecting the perceived value. We also found that switching cost has no significant impact on perceived value. The paramount contribution is the combination of technostress theory and the status quo bias theory in the study of system resistance intention and the in-depth discussion of the functional relationship between the two.

Keywords: Chronic diseases · elderly · Resistance intention · Technology anxiety · Perceived value

1 Introduction

Chronic diseases are the most serious disease that disturbs the middle-aged and elderly groups. With the popularity of smartphones, wearable devices and health record systems, mobile chronic diseases management apps provide new solutions to chronic disease management [1]. Many research results on the mobile information systems also indicate that the long-term chronic disease management intervention programs of APPs are beneficial to the rehabilitation and treatment of patients with chronic diseases [2]. However, in practice, as a group with high incidence of chronic diseases, the middle-aged and elderly are less receptive to this new form of services [3]. Chronic diseases management APPs have encountered great resistance to promotion.

Many researches discussed about why people resist using a new information system and what factors influence people's resisting behavior [4]. They found that the reasons for users adopting and not adopting new technology were significantly different [5]. The

Y. P. Tu and M. Chi (Eds.): WHICEB 2024, LNBIP 515, pp. 48–61, 2024.
https://doi.org/10.1007/978-3-031-60264-1_5

technostress theory [6], often used in work scenarios in organizations, and the perceived value derived from status quo bias theory [7], often used in social media scenarios, are the two main theoretical explanation to users' resisting behavior. However, in marketing and psychology research, function factors, e.g. quality, and affective factors, e.g. feelings, are simultaneously associate to perceived value [8]. As previous research on adoption and resistance to new systems mostly focuses on young people, those of middle-aged and above with the great physical and psychological differences from young people are less addressed. Compared to young people, the middle-aged and elderly people are more vulnerable of using information technology, less familiar with the forms of mobile services, more susceptible to emotional experiences, and pay more attention to health status [9]. So we may find empirical evidence to bridge technostress and perceived value in this context.

This study attempts to explore the resistance intention of the middle-aged and elderly to chronic diseases management APPs. On one hand, we brought two traditional factors of resistance intention, technostress and perceived value, into a research framework for discussion and studied their relationship. On the other hand, we discussed the role in resistance intention played by group characteristics of middle-aged and elderly people.

2   Theoretical Background

2.1   Resistance Behaviors and Technostress Theory

Resistance behavior is defined as explicit or covert actions that prevent the systems from implementing or using or prevent the systems designers from achieving predetermined goals. Most scholars incline to regard the resistance behavior as a psychological state, and it is found that users' resistance is not merely due to the lack of positive factors, as there is possible negative resistance inclination which may be hidden behind the surface of acceptance behaviors [10].

With the middle-aged and elderly people being disadvantaged groups of information technology, and technology being an important factor causing stress [11], the consequences of stress will bring negative effects on individual mentality and behavior, thus leading to users' resistance intention. Technostress is a psychological activity formed under the current technical social environment [11]. For the middle-aged and elderly people, technostress refers to the emotion and experience when dealing with new technology products, which is a modern adaptive disease caused by them inability to deal with new technology properly.

Many researches substantiate the claim that technostress is the negative impact of technology on people's attitude, psychology, cognition, and behavior [11]. The Stressors-Strain-Outcomes framework was proposed to elaborate the process of technostress affecting people's attitude and behavior [12]. This model is derived from the work scene, widely applied to many research fields of information technology and consists of three parts: stressors, strain, and outcomes (Fig. 1). It assumes that stress is the result of perceiving stressors and is the leading variable of the outcome, where "stressors" refer to the environmental stimuli like techno-complexity and techno-insecurity. The mediating variable "strain" refers to physiological and psychological response to stressors, including the bad emotions such as anxiety and fear. "Outcomes" refer to psychological or behavioral consequences caused by long-term tolerance of stress and stress performance, e.g. intention to quit, etc.

Fig. 1. Stressors-Strain-Outcomes framework

There are many types of stressors and strain related to technical stress [6]. Techno-complexity, which describes the complexity associated with ICT (information and communication technology) that makes users feel inadequate in technical capability and urges them to spend time and effort learning and understanding aspects of ICT, and technology anxiety are considered as the stressor and strain in this study, because they are the most commonly mentioned and prominent factors and especially important for elderly [5]. Since the middle-aged and elderly people are not familiar with information technology and losing energy, it is difficult for them to use new technology, and thus they are most likely to perceive Techno-complexity.

2.2 Resistance Behaviors and Status Quo Bias Theory

Researchers believe that users' resistance intention comes from rational decisions made based on comprehensive considerations between the benefits brought by new technologies and the costs of using new technologies [7]. Shang, from the perspective of users, believes that the resistance is caused by the gap between users' desire to maintain the status quo and the change brought by the systems [13]. The SQB theory was proposed by Samuelson and Zeckhauser [14] to explain the behavior that people prefer to maintain the status quo, which explains the phenomenon that individuals tend to maintain the status quo or maintain the previous decision and choose not to act when making new decisions. The theory holds that even if the environment has changed and alternative decision plan appeared, people will carefully compare the benefit and cost of switching to decide whether to transform their status. When switching benefit is larger than switching cost, people will change their status, otherwise, they will maintain the status quo. The perceived value after integrating the switching benefit and switching cost is the key factor for people to decide whether to resist the new information systems or not [10].

Based on the above analysis, from the perspective of technostress theory, it is noted that, according to Stressors-Strain-Outcomes framework, technostress may aggravate users' resistance intention. However, from the perspective of the SQB theory, the perceived value formed after comprehensive consideration of switching costs and switching benefits may reduce users' resistance intention [10]. Then under the combined effects of the above two perspectives, how exactly is the resistance intention formed by middle-aged and elderly users?

Meanwhile, in the previous studies, the role of technostress theory and SQB theory in user resistance behavior was studied separately [4]. However, from the perspective of rational decision-making, there has been plenty historical evidence analyses, behavior observations and experimental data showing that psychological stress beyond a certain level makes people unable to systematically consider all relevant solutions and fail to make rational choices [15]. For the elderly, the low capability to handle technical pressure will affect the judgment on the perceived value of using chronic diseases management APPs. Besides, bad emotions will directly decrease the perceived value in some marketing researches [8]. It is thus a sensible choice for this study to combine technostress theory with SQB theory.

3 Research Model and Hypotheses

3.1 Constructs from SQB

Switching Cost, Switching Benefit and Perceived Value. The switching cost and switching benefit are derived from the SQB theory. Switching cost refers to the negative effect felt by users when they switch from the status quo to new information systems, which consists of transaction cost, uncertain cost, and sunk cost [14]. In this study, the switching cost mainly results from the switching process of patients with chronic disease from using offline medical service resources to using online medical services. Because it takes time and effort to familiarize with a new system, users have to bear a high switching cost, which leads to lower perceived value [16]. Switching benefit is defined as the utility gained after using the new systems [10]. In this study, the switching benefits mainly come from the benefits gained by reducing medical expenses, increasing the efficiency of seeing doctors, strengthening self-health management, etc. These are direct benefits to middle-aged and elderly users of chronic diseases management APPs, which increases their perceived value of the new system. Perceived value of the middle-aged and elderly users are measured by weighing the costs and benefits of change. Therefore, the following hypotheses are proposed:

H1: The perception of product switching cost by middle-aged and elderly patients will negatively affect the perceived value.

H2: The perception of product switching benefits by middle-aged and elderly patients will positively affect the perceived value.

Perceived Value and Resistance Intention. According to the SQB theory, the perceived value is the evaluated result of whether the gained benefit by switching from the status quo to the new state is worth of the cost [10]. When users decide to either keep the status quo or choose a new system, if the perceived value of the change is low, users are more likely to show a higher resistance intention to the implementation of the new system. Conversely, if the perceived value of the change is high, users may incline to reduce their resistance intention to the new system. Since users have a strong tendency to maximize value when making decisions [17], users may be more resistant to changes if the perceived value of changes is low [14]. However, if the perceived value is high and the user feels that the benefit is greater than the cost, it will be easier to accept the change, and the resistance intention to new technologies and products will be reduced. To sum up, the following hypothesis is proposed:

H3: The perceived value of middle-aged and elderly patients negatively affects their resistance intention to products.

3.2   Constructs from Technostress

Technology Complexity and Technology Anxiety. Technology complexity refers to the degree to which an individual does not have to expend effort to use the technology, representing an increase in the mental effort and learning curve required [18]. Numerous studies have confirmed a mutual influence relationship between technology complexity and technostress [11]. In this study, the middle-aged and elderly people have a low degree of mastery of information technology and are sensitive to technical complexity, hence they have a low evaluation of information technology self-efficacy, resulting in their belief of their incapability of using chronic diseases management Apps. Due to the significant influence of individual self-evaluation on the perceived stress level, technostress is generated during the subjects' use of technology, which leads to technology anxiety. Therefore, the following hypothesis is proposed:

H4: Technology complexity positively affects technology anxiety.

Technology Anxiety and Resistance Intention. Technology anxiety is related to the fear or discomfort that people experience when thinking about or actually using technology. It also refers to an individual's fear of the possibility of using technology [4]. People with technology anxiety will weaken their performance and resist using new technologies, as they perceive themselves as inefficient, focus excessively on their shortcomings, and immerse themselves much in thoughts of failure and fear. Yusop and Basar [19] Studies have found that there are quite a few students resisting using online tool Wiki which can support collaborative learning experience, in which case, the personal factors (i.e. anxiety of using the new technologies) are greater resistance factors compared with technical factors (i.e. slow network connection outside the classroom). In this study, although chronic diseases management APPs can improve health management efficiency, due to the physical and cognitive limitations of this group, their deficiencies of information technology capabilities are prominent, technology anxiety is obvious, and it is easy to generate resistance intention. Moreover, Deng et al. [3] also observed this phenomenon in the use of mobile health services. Based on this, the following hypothesis is proposed:

H5: Technology anxiety positively affects resistance intentions of middle-aged and elderly people.

According to existing studies, psychological pressure exceeding a certain intensity can affect the quality of decision-making [15], and individuals under pressure often fail to adhere to the rational choice. As perceived value is the result of a comparison between perceived benefits and perceived costs, individuals' state of being under pressure inevitably affects the process of rational decision-making. Middle-aged and elderly people in the state of technology anxiety could not rationally compare the benefits and costs of using chronic diseases management APPs, thus affecting the judgment of perceived value.

Besides, technology anxiety can be seen as a negative emotion, which are often depicted as unpleasant subjective experiences, imposes additional psychological costs on middle-aged and elderly users, and reduces the perceived value. Some empirical evidences have showed that emotional responses had a significant impact on the perceived value. Some other researches also indicated that negative emotions may prolong the service waiting time perceived by customers, reduce their participation in purchasing, and generate a desire to retreat from the environment [20].

Moreover, anxiety is often regarded as a component of perceived value, for whom, the emotional response is included in the construction of perceived value. For example, Sánchez-Garcia et al. [8] identified six dimensions of perceived value, including four functional values (e.g. product, price), social value, and emotional value. Based on this, the following hypothesis is proposed:

H6: Technology anxiety negatively affects the perceived value of middle-aged and elderly people.

The research model of this study is revealed in Fig. 2 below.

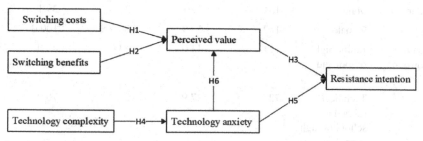

Fig. 2. The influencing factor model of resistance intention of the middle-aged and elderly using chronic diseases management APPs.

4 Methodology and Results

4.1 Participants and Procedure

The subjects of this survey are middle-aged and elderly people who are over 45 years old, can communicate normally, and suffer from chronic diseases (World Health Organization divides the age group over 45 years old into middle-aged and elderly people). Tiaoshanta (TST) Community Health Center and Wangjiang road (WJR) Community Health Center at Chengdu city, China, were the research sites of the field survey. In the beginning, the team members were trained on the survey's purpose and attention. Before the formal data collection, 15 middle-aged and elderly patients with chronic disease were randomly selected from the survey site as the pre-survey objects. The questionnaire was pre-tested and adjusted according to the analysis results.

Considering that middle-aged and elderly patients with chronic disease may have problems in reading or understanding the contents of the questionnaire, or even in physical movements, the whole process is conducted in a "one-to-one" manner, where one investigator faces one survey object at a time. Small gifts were distributed as an incentive measure to the middle-aged and elderly who participated in the survey. A total of 290 questionnaires were collected from the survey, including 19 invalid or missing questionnaires, and 13 questionnaires taken by those aged under 45 being deleted, making a total of 258 valid questionnaires, with a recovery rate of 88.97%.

4.2 Measurement Model

Descriptive statistics are mainly analyzed from demographic variables, self-perceived health status and functional needs. In this questionnaire survey, female subjects accounted for 60.9%, nearly 50% of them were people with junior high school education and below. See Table 1 for details:

Table 1. Descriptive statistics of demographic variables

Basic information	Statistics items	Distribution	Percentage	Effective percentage	Cumulative percentage
Gender	Male	101	39.1	39.1	39.1
	Female	157	60.9	60.9	100.0
Education background	Junior high school and below	111	43.0	43.0	43.0
	Technical secondary school or high school	72	27.9	27.9	70.9
	College degree or above	75	29.1	29.1	100.0
Age	45–49	14	5.4	5.4	5.4
	50–59	31	12.0	12.0	17.4
	60–69	93	36.1	36.1	53.5
	70–79	87	33.7	33.7	87.2
	80 and above	33	12.8	12.8	100
Health condition	very bad (1 point)	4	1.6	1.6	1.6
	Bad (2 points)	29	11.2	11.2	12.8
	general (3 points)	80	31.0	31.0	43.8
	Good (4 points)	100	38.8	38.8	82.6
	Very good (5 points)	45	17.4	17.4	100.0

Our study has six factors: Technology Complexity (UD), Technology Anxiety (TA), Switching Benefits (SB), Switching Costs (SC), Perceived Value (PV), and Resistance intention (RTC). The questionnaire items were designed with reference from a large number of related literature and slightly modified according to the results of the preliminary survey, with high content validity. SPSS 22.0 was used for statistics and the measurement result of sample KMO is 0.956. Meanwhile, the significance value of Bartlett sphericity test is 0.000, which is very suitable for factor analysis.

As we used mature scales to measure all the factors, here we only need to perform Confirmatory Factor Analysis (CFA) to check the validity and reliability. Cronbach's α, Average Variance Extracted (AVE), and Composite Reliability (CR) were calculated to examine the internal consistency reliability and convergent validity. As shown in Table 2, all the Cronbach's α values were higher than 0.7, indicating a high reliability of the scales.

Table 2. Results of standardized item loading, α, CR, and AVE

Construct	Item	Std.factor loading	t-value	Composite reliability (CR)	Average variance extracted (AVE)
Resistance Intention (RTC)	RTC1	0.856	Fixed	0.963	0.897
	RTC2	0.999	26.156		
	RTC3	0.980	25.156		
Switching Costs (SC)	SC1	0.975	Fixed	0.954	0.840
	SC2	0.985	53.231		
	SC3	0.856	25.146		
	SC5	0.842	23.674		
Perceived Value (PV)	PV1	0.982	Fixed	0.954	0.984
	PV2	0.988	45.699		
	PV3	0.961	48.254		
Technology Anxiety (TA)	TA1	0.969	Fixed	0.950	0.826
	TA2	0.966	41.219		
	TA3	0.862	24.366		
	TA4	0.831	21.804		
Switching Benefits (SB)	SB1	0.939	Fixed	0.968	0.793
	SB2	0.808	29.622		
	SB3	0.965	34.637		
	SB4	0.951	32.268		
	SB5	0.904	26.382		
	SB6	0.783	18.155		

(continued)

Table 2. (*continued*)

Construct	Item	Std.factor loading	t-value	Composite reliability (CR)	Average variance extracted (AVE)
	SB7	0.873	23.675		
	SB8	0.885	24.614		
Technology Complexity (UD)	UD1	0.808	Fixed	0.965	0.798
	UD2	0.809	20.160		
	UD3	0.850	23.128		
	UD4	0.918	30.607		
	UD5	0.962	39.618		
	UD6	0.964	39.623		
	UD7	0.926	31.654		

4.3 Hypothesis Testing

In this study, CB - SEM method was used to draw the structural equation model diagram with Amos22.0. Then, the maximum likelihood method was used to estimate parameters and standardize the model. Finally, path analysis was carried out.

Model Fitting Degree Analysis. The measurement results of the model fitness are shown in Table 3. It can be seen that all the fitness indexes have reached the ideal values, indicating that the modified model has a good fit with the sample data.

Table 3. Model fitness checklist for the whole model

Fitness index	Ideal value	Value of this model
Chi-square (CMIN)		622.956
Degrees of freedom (DF)		344
χ^2/df	<3	1.811
GFI	>0.8	0.863
AGFI	>0.8	0.826
SRMR	<0.1	0.0717
CFI	>0.9	0.977
RMSEA	<0.08	0.056
NFI	>0.9	0.950
TLI	>0.9	0.973
IFI	>0.9	0.977

Model Path Coefficient Analysis. After empirical testing and modification, the model and path coefficients are finally obtained, as shown in Fig. 3.

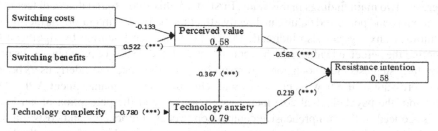

Fig. 3. Model diagram of influencing factors of resistance intention of middle-aged and elderly people using chronic diseases management Apps (unstandardized coefficient).

4.4 Common Method Bias Testing

In measurement, the artificial covariation between predictor variables and benchmark variables caused by the same data source or scorer, the same measurement environment, and the characteristics of the project itself, that is, the common method bias. Control of method factor effect without measurable method adds the common method bias to the structural equation model, which can better test and control the common method bias effect, when the source doesn't need to be identified. Therefore, we add the common method bias latent variable to the model, and compare the fitness of the model before and after adding the variable (Table 4). It can be found that after adding the common method bias latent variable, the chi-square value increased by 31.805, and the RMSEA value increased 0.002, the values of CFI, TLI and IFI didn't change, indicating that after adding the variable, the fitness of the model didn't improve significantly. Thus, there is no significant common method bias in the model.

Table 4. Common method bias test results

	Chi-square	RMSEA	CFI	TLI	IFI
Model without common method bias variable	1227.170	0.096	0.928	0.919	0.928
Model with common method bias variable	1450.708	0.106	0.913	0.903	0.913

5 Discussion and Conclusion

5.1 Discussion of Results

There are two main findings in this study. First of all, this study found that both technology anxiety and perceived value can directly affect the resistance intention; furthermore, technology anxiety can also indirectly affect the resistance intention by significantly affecting the perceived value, which is consistent with the results of previous works [4]. This study suggests the association may result from middle-aged and elderly users being under pressure to use new technologies with chronic diseases management APPs. On one hand, the psychological cost increases obviously, and the perception of net benefit is reduced in the comprehensive comparison process on benefits and costs; on the other hand, technology anxiety can reduce the sequence of users' instantaneous thinking activities, and the benefits brought by chronic diseases management APPs cannot be systematically justified under the influence of cognitive limitation, thus negatively affecting perceived value. This means that the rational comparison process of obtaining perceived value in this study is affected by negative emotions. In the future design and promotion of chronic diseases management APPs, the emotional responses of the middle-aged and elderly should be taken into account to reduce the negative emotions in their use.

Second, this study finds that the switching cost has no significant effect on perceived value. The reason may be that the subject group has a more consistent perception of switching costs. Previous studies have suggested that higher switching costs reduce the perceived value of the net benefit or the change to the user, as the net benefit is assessed by weighing that associated with the changing cost [16]. However, in the scenario of this study, the switching cost of the subject group people is relatively consistent and does not reflect a big change. The objects of this study basically grew up in the 1980s and before when the application of Internet technology was not yet widespread in China. Mobile applications became popular around the year 2010, when the research objects were generally devoted to work and family, had little spared energy for learning, thus could only passively accept the popularization of technology, causing the investment and cost of using chronic diseases management Apps basically the same. According to "The 52nd Statistical Report on China's Internet Development", by June 2023, there were over 400 million middle-aged and elderly Internet users in China, more than half of whom spent more than a quarter of their time on mobile phones, mainly consuming social, news and video contents; the consistency of the middle-aged and elderly population is evident. This shows that the group characteristics of middle-aged and elderly users should be considered to promote perceived value, avoiding unnecessary efforts in reducing the switching costs of using chronic diseases management APPs.

5.2 Theoretical Contribution

This paper contributes theoretically in the following two aspects. First, its paramount contribution is the combination of technostress theory and the status quo bias theory in the study of system resistance intention and the in-depth discussion of the functional relationship between the two. They illustrate the decision-making process of user resistance from two different perspectives: technostress and status quo bias. However, few studies have put the two theories together to explore user resistance of information systems. In this study, we found the negative influence path of technology anxiety on perceived value, thus uncovering the connection between the two theories. This makes up for the current research gap and also further explains the decision-making path. Additionally, it reminds subsequent research on information system resistance intention to consider the influence of negative emotions such as pressure on rational decision-making.

Second, this study enriches the relevant theories of system resistance intention. At present, there is no consistent conclusion on how the benefits of new systems and the barriers to adoption affect users' resistance intention among middle-aged and elderly people. However, in the scenario of this study, switching cost has no significant impact on perceived value resistance intention, indicating that obstacles have little impact compared with benefits. This supports the research on information system resistance intention and broadens the influence mode of users' resistance intention. Among them, the characteristics of middle-aged and elderly people play a decisive role in the formation of the system resistance intention, which reminds follow-up studies on information system resistance to note the influence of the characteristics of the subject group.

5.3 Practical Implications

The empirical study shows that the subject group with chronic diseases give up using mobile Apps services mainly because of technology anxiety. Thus, for those patients with chronic diseases to eventually fit better into the society, they should face the existence of technology anxiety, actively participate in skills training, and gradually adapt to the new health management model.

For those service providers of chronic diseases management APPs, they can reduce the resistance from both management and technology levels. At the management level, they can mainly increase switching benefits to weaken resistance intention and increase the perceived benefits with promotions, incentives, or promotions through the help of their trusted people. Meanwhile at the technology level, as complexity is the main cause of technology anxiety, specific measures can be implemented to reduce the complexity in the following two aspects: (1) Optimize system functions; (2) Optimize system interface and user interaction design. In this study, it was found that patients in the subject group with chronic diseases were easily confused by icons' meanings, missed messages, and forgot the operation steps when using mobile apps, as they are generally prone to have psychology problems caused by technology anxiety. Service providers can take corresponding measures, e.g. design icons in consistence with traditional medical services, and provide user-friendly message reminders such as text or voice prompts, flashing lights, easily recognized sound or vibration, and interface message reminders, etc., to compensate for the defects of people with visual or hearing impairment.

5.4 Limitations and Future Research

Our study has its limitations, which may lead to future research. For the resistance intention of new technologies, this study deeply combines the reasons of the status quo bias theory and the technostress and verifies them in the mobile applications of chronic disease management for middle-aged and elderly people. Future studies can extend the thinking, exploration mode, and conclusion to other scenarios. Besides, this study is only limited to the individual level of user resistance intentions. Future studies can further explore the resistance intentions in the organizational environment. Finally, this study mainly adopts the self-report method to measure technostress. From this perspective, the accuracy can be greatly improved if future studies adopt new technologies such as nuclear magnetic resonance imaging (MRI), EEG, etc.

Acknowledgement. This research was supported by the National Social Science Fund of China under Grant 19BTQ046.

References

1. Mollard, E., Michaud, K.: Self-management of rheumatoid arthritis: mobile applications. Curr. Rheumatol. Rep. **23**(1) (2021)
2. Moses, J.C., Adibi, S., Islam, S.M.S., Wickramasinghe, N., Nguyen, L.: Application of smartphone technologies in disease monitoring: a systematic review. Healthcare **9**(7), 889 (2021)
3. Deng, Z., Mo, X., Liu, S.: Comparison of the middle-aged and older users' adoption of mobile health services in China. Int. J. Med. Inform. **83**(3), 210–224 (2014)
4. Tsai, J., Cheng, M., Tsai, H., Hung, S., Chen, Y.: Acceptance and resistance of telehealth: the perspective of dual-factor concepts in technology adoption. Int. J. Inf. Manage. **49**, 34–44 (2019)
5. Talukder, M.S., Laato, S., Islam, A.K.M.N., Bao, Y.: Continued use intention of wearable health technologies among the elderly: an enablers and inhibitors perspective. Internet Res. **31**(5), 1611–1640 (2021)
6. Tarafdar, M., Tu, Q., Ragu-Nathan, B.S., Ragu-Nathan, T.S.: The impact of technostress on role stress and productivity. J. Manage. Inform. Syst. **24**(1), 301–328 (2007)
7. Lee, K., Joshi, K.: Examining the use of status quo bias perspective in IS research: need for re-conceptualizing and incorporating biases. Inf. Syst. J. **27**(6), 733–752 (2017)
8. Sánchez-Garcia, J., Moliner-Tena, M.A., Callarisa-Fiol, L., Rodriguez-Artola, R.M.: Relationship quality of an establishment and perceived value of a purchase. Serv. Ind. J. **27**(1–2), 151–174 (2007)
9. Pu, B., Peng, H., Xia, S.: Role of emotion and cognition on age differences in the framing effect. Int. J. Aging Human Dev. **85**(3), 305–325 (2017)
10. Kim, H., Kankanhalli, A.: Investigating user resistance to information systems implementation: a status quo bias perspective. MIS Q. **33**(3), 567–582 (2009)
11. Califf, C.B., Sarker, S., Sarker, S.: The bright and dark sides of technostress: a mixed-methods study involving healthcare IT. MIS Q. **44**(2), 809–856 (2020)
12. Teng, L., Liu, D., Luo, J.: Explicating user negative behavior toward social media: an exploratory examination based on stressor-strain-outcome model. Cogn. Technol. Work **24**(1), 183–194 (2022)
13. Shang, S.S.C.: Dual strategy for managing user resistance with business integration systems. Behav. Inf. Technol. **31**(9), 909–925 (2012)
14. Samuelson, W., Zeckhauser, R.: Status quo bias in decision making. J. Risk Uncertain. **1**(1), 7–59 (1988)
15. Phillips-Wren, G., Adya, M.: Decision making under stress: the role of information overload, time pressure, complexity, and uncertainty. J. Decis. Syst. **29**, 213–225 (2020)

16. Chang, Y.: What drives organizations to switch to cloud ERP systems? The impacts of enablers and inhibitors. J. Enterp. Inf. Manag. **33**(3), 600–626 (2020)
17. Hu, B., Liu, Y., Yan, W.: Should I scan my face? The influence of perceived value and trust on Chinese users' intention to use facial recognition payment. Telemat. Inform. **78**, 101951 (2023)
18. Saunders, C., Rutkowski, A.F., Pluyter, J., Spanjers, R.: Health information technologies: from hazardous to the dark side. J. Assoc Inf. Sci. Technol. **67**(7), 1767–1772 (2016)
19. Yusop, F.D., Basar, S.M.M.A.: Resistance towards wiki: implications for designing successful wiki-supported collaborative learning experiences. Univers. Access Inf. Soc. **16**(2), 349–360 (2017)
20. Li, S., Jiang, Y., Cheng, B., Scott, N.: The effect of flight delay on customer loyalty intention: the moderating role of emotion regulation. J. Hosp. Tour. Manag. **47**, 72–83 (2021)

Fresh Food E-commerce Supply Chain Coordination Mechanism Under the Background of New Retail

Xiaolin Li, Qianwei Xiao[✉], and Weichun Xue

Business and Tourism School, Sichuan Agricultural University, Chengdu 611830, China
xiaoqianwei918@163.com

Abstract. In recent years, the rapid development of new retail has promoted the growth of the fresh food e-commerce industry. More and more fresh food e-commerce enterprises are selling their products through platforms similar to JD Daojia, and there are also platform-based, new retail-based operation modes. In this context, it is particularly important to compare the operation modes of fresh food e-commerce and study the coordination mechanisms of fresh food e-commerce supply chains to improve the overall benefits of the supply chain. This paper constructs a dual-channel supply chain consisting of fresh food e-commerce enterprises and fresh food e-commerce platforms. Based on the consideration of the input of fresh preservation efforts, it compares and analyzes the operation modes of platform-based and new retail-based fresh food e-commerce, and studies the coordination problems of platform-based e-commerce supply chains.

Keywords: Fresh Food E-commerce · Fresh-keeping Effort · Coordinating Covenants

1 Introduction

1.1 Background

The concept of "new retail" was first introduced at the "Cloud Conference" in 2016 [1]. It is Alibaba's strategy to transform traditional retail elements such as people, goods, and venues into an information-based and data-driven mode through mobile internet technology. As consumer demand for high-quality products has increased, the traditional fresh food e-commerce mode has become inadequate to meet these needs [2]. From 2016 to 2019, the industry experienced a downturn, resulting in layoffs, bankruptcies, and capital chain ruptures. However, the outbreak of COVID-19 at the end of 2019 led to a surge in online sales of fresh products, which are essential for daily life [3]. This sudden increase in consumer demand has brought about a "rebirth" of the nearly bankrupt fresh food e-commerce industry [4]. Under the new retail mode, fresh food e-commerce enterprises utilize their own channels, technology, and big data advantages to effectively address the coverage radius and variety issues of traditional fresh products, and further meet the needs of consumers for quality differentiation [5]. Consumers can purchase

Y. P. Tu and M. Chi (Eds.): WHICEB 2024, LNBIP 515, pp. 62–73, 2024.
https://doi.org/10.1007/978-3-031-60264-1_6

fresh products in two ways under this new operational mode: the first is to place an order and complete payment on a specialized APP in the new retail environment, after which merchants assign special logistics personnel to distribute the fresh products through self built logistics or third-party logistics companies. The second way is for consumers to visit offline stores to buy products according to their preferences, and then hand them over to professionals in the store for processing and cooking, thereby enhancing the overall shopping experience.

1.2 Research Purpose and Significance

With the continuous growth of new retail formats, the fresh food e-commerce industry is flourishing, and many scholars at home and abroad are conducting academic research in this direction. The vast majority of scholars are studying how to better optimize the fresh food e-commerce supply chain, in order to draw some conclusions that are worth learning from. Among them, the transformation of fresh food e-commerce supply chain channels, coordination among members, and the establishment of contractual relationships to promote supply chain coordination have greatly helped the rapid development of the fresh food e-commerce industry [6]. However, considering the different perceptions and operational modes of different enterprises towards the development of fresh food e-commerce under the new retail environment, and referring to various research methods of fresh food e-commerce supply chains, this article plans to take the new retail environment as the research background, compare and explore the operational modes of the two most popular fresh food e-commerce supply chains in China under certain factors, and design coordination contracts for the less efficient operational modes, In order to further optimize the total revenue of its supply chain.

This article is a study on the coordination mechanism of fresh food e-commerce supply chain considering preservation efforts in the context of new retail. It is based on the deduction of mathematical modes, and then simulates the real operation situation through numerical analysis, ultimately verifying the effectiveness of the contract mode. By considering the optimal pricing, preservation level, and profit of the supply chain under preservation efforts for two common fresh food e-commerce operation modes, we can identify the operation mode with lower efficiency, and design corresponding coordination mechanisms to optimize the overall efficiency of the supply chain.

1.3 Literature Review

In the context of new retail, China's fresh e-commerce industry has undergone a new transformation, gradually forming a pattern of multiple models coexisting. Maruyama et al. [7] explored the factors that Chinese consumers purchase fresh food from traditional and modern retail forms, and further explored the regional differences in consumer shopping behavior, providing substantive suggestions for China's retail transformation and upgrading. Xiyue Xiao [8] discussed the supply chain model of fresh e-commerce under the background of "new retail". He believes that the arrival of the "new retail" era requires fresh e-commerce enterprises to improve their supply chain model, build a complete product supply chain, ensure product quality, improve distribution efficiency, and introduce advanced technology to transform traditional management concepts into consumer demand-based management concepts. Strengthen the concept of fresh supply chain to better promote the improvement of the fresh supply chain.

At present, there are still a lot of relevant studies on the preservation efforts of fresh agricultural products. Considering consumers' requirements for the freshness of fresh agricultural products and their personalized needs for the service of fresh food e-commerce platform, scholars at home and abroad take the preservation efforts of fresh agricultural products provided by supply chain members as the main influencing factor to discuss the coordination of the supply chain of fresh agricultural products. To ensure a balance of interests among decision-makers, Zhang et al. [9] models the time-dependent demand for fresh products and proposes an incentive mechanism to coordinate the new retail fresh products' supply chain; further, it demonstrates that the prices can be significantly decreased with the designed contract, and all the supply chain members can benefit from Pareto improvement. In order to explore the impact of preservation efforts on the inventory and profit of fresh agricultural products, Shuyun Wang et al. [10] established a two-level inventory mode of fresh agricultural products supply chain composed of a supplier and a retailer, so as to maximize the profit of the whole fresh agricultural supply chain and achieve win-win cooperation between the two sides. Jie Ding et al. [11] studied the coordination problem of the dual-channel supply chain dominated by fresh food e-commerce, designed a hybrid contract of cost sharing and fixed compensation to optimize the coordination of the supply chain, and finally conducted a numerical analysis to explore the influence of crossprice and other parameters. Xue Wang [12] established a fresh supply chain system composed of fresh merchants and fresh merchant platforms. An improved combination contract of "commission discount+fresh effort cost sharing" was designed for coordination.

From many academic studies, we find that there is a certain basis for the current research on fresh food e-commerce's fresh preservation effort, and there are also a lot of studies on the coordination mode design of fresh food e-commerce supply chain. However, it is only for the decision of a single fresh food e-commerce supply chain, and it is still rare to design the coordination contract based on the optimal decision of multiple fresh food e-commerce operation modes.

2   Construction of Fresh Food E-commerce Supply Chain Mode

2.1   Mode Hypothesis

Platform-Based Operation Mode. The platform-based operation mode of fresh food e-commerce [13] refers to fresh food sellers utilizing the powerful resource integration capabilities of comprehensive e-commerce platforms such as JD Daojia to provide a trading platform for fresh food sellers and consumers. Build a platform style fresh food e-commerce supply chain consisting of fresh food sellers and consumers as shown in the left figure of Fig. 1, assuming that the fresh food seller is the sole supplier of the entire fresh food supply chain. One sales channel is for the fresh food seller to publish product information through a third-party fresh food e-commerce platform, and the seller provides a proportional commission to the e-commerce platform for selling fresh agricultural products on the platform. Third party e-commerce platforms invest in preservation efforts. Another sales channel is for fresh food sellers to directly use their own offline sales channels to sell products, where consumers pay fees offline. At the same time, suppliers prepare goods and directly ship them to consumers. During the delivery process, fresh food suppliers invest their own preservation efforts.

New Retail-Based Operation Mode. The new retail-based fresh food e-commerce operation mode [14] refers to consumers having the option to browse products online or experience them firsthand in physical stores. Construct a secondary supply chain consisting of fresh food e-commerce enterprises and consumers as shown in the right figure of Fig. 1, assuming that the fresh food e-commerce enterprise is the sole supplier of the entire fresh supply chain. In the context of new retail, fresh food e-commerce enterprises promote their products through self built platforms and offline stores simultaneously. One channel is to use online platforms for promotion and sales of fresh products, with fresh food e-commerce companies investing in preservation efforts. Another sales channel is for fresh food e-commerce enterprises to directly use their offline stores to sell products, while the enterprise directly ships to consumers. During the delivery process, fresh food suppliers invest their own efforts in preserving fresh agricultural products.

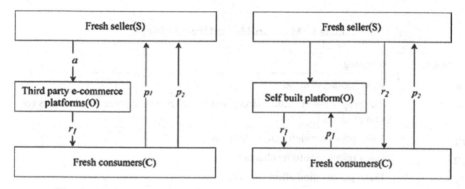

Fig. 1. Platform/New retail fresh food e-commerce supply chain structure

At the same time, combined with the research of existing scholars, this paper makes the following hypotheses:

Hypothesis 1: Considering the investment in preservation efforts, the freshness of fresh products after the investment in preservation technology is:

$$\delta(r_i) = \delta_0 + k_1 r_i \tag{1}$$

Hypothesis 2: Since fresh food e-commerce enterprises and third-party e-commerce platforms need certain cost support when investing in fresh preservation efforts, we further assume that the cost functions of fresh preservation efforts are respectively:

$$c_i = k_r r_i^2 / 2 \tag{2}$$

Hypothesis 3: Consumer demand is mainly determined by product price and freshness. Where the total demand is inversely proportional to the selling price, directly proportional to the relative selling price, and directly proportional to the freshness of the product. There is no difference between basic demand and freshness, and the demand functions of online and offline sales channels in the two modes are constructed as follows:

Online channel demand function:

$$d_1 = m - p_1 + \beta p_2 + \theta \delta(r_1) \tag{3}$$

Offline channel demand function:

$$d_2 = m - p_2 + \beta p_1 + \theta \delta(r_2) \tag{4}$$

Hypothesis 4: The online and offline channels of the two modes of operation are in a perfect information environment, and both the fresh food e-commerce enterprises (fresh food sellers) and the third-party fresh food e-commerce platforms are absolutely rational, with the ultimate goal of maximizing profits.

In order to construct the relevant supply chain structure mode, this paper also sets the main variables and their meanings as shown in Table 1.

Table 1. Main variables and their meanings.

Parameters	Meaning
m	Basic market demand
α	The proportion of commission given by sellers to e-commerce platforms for unit products
p_1	Sales prices through online channels
p_2	Sales prices for offline channels
r_1	Fresh preservation efforts in online channels
r_2	Fresh preservation efforts in offline channels
δ_0	Freshness of fresh agricultural products when they reach consumers without preservation efforts
c_1	The cost of preservation efforts in online channels
c_2	The cost of preservation efforts in offline channels
θ	The freshness demand elasticity of fresh agricultural products
β	Cross price elasticity coefficient between online and offline channels
k_1	The level of impact of preservation efforts on freshness
k_r	The coefficient of impact of preservation efforts on preservation costs
d_1	The demand for online channels
d_2	The demand for offline channels
π_s	Profit of fresh food e-commerce enterprises (fresh food sellers)

(*continued*)

Table 1. (*continued*)

Parameters	Meaning
π_p	Profit of third-party e-commerce platforms
Superscript e	The optimal decision of platform mode
Superscript f	The optimal decision for the new retail mode
Superscript g	The optimal decision under the coordination mode

2.2 Optimal Decisions Under Different Modes of Operation

Platform-Based Operation Mode. Considering that the operation mode of platform based fresh food e-commerce has a decentralized decision-making mode, a decentralized decision-making mode is adopted for the supply chain of platform based fresh food e-commerce [15]. That is, fresh food sellers first determine their online and offline sales prices and the preservation efforts provided by offline sales based on market demand, and then third-party fresh food e-commerce platforms decide the preservation efforts provided by their online sales channels, Finally, the optimal decision for fresh food sellers and third-party e-commerce platforms in a decentralized decision-making order is obtained, as well as the online and offline market demand and profits of fresh food sellers and third-party e-commerce platforms:

$$p_1^e = \frac{k_r(\theta\delta_0 + m)\{[(\beta + 2)\alpha - 2\beta - 2]k_r - k_1^2\theta^2(-1 + \alpha)\}}{(a^2\beta^2 - 4\alpha\beta^2 + 4\beta^2 + 4\alpha - 4)k_r^2 - 4(-1 + \alpha)k_1^2\theta^2(\alpha + 1/2)k_r + 2k_1^4\alpha\theta^4(-1 + \alpha)} \quad (5)$$

$$p_2^e = \frac{k_r(1 - \alpha)(\theta\delta_0 + m)[(\alpha\beta - 2\beta - 2)k_r + 2k_1^2\alpha\theta^2]}{(a^2\beta^2 - 4\alpha\beta^2 + 4\beta^2 + 4\alpha - 4)k_r^2 - 4(-1 + \alpha)k_1^2\theta^2(\alpha + 1/2)k_r + 2k_1^4\alpha\theta^4(-1 + \alpha)} \quad (6)$$

$$r_2^e = \frac{k_r(1 - \alpha)(\theta\delta_0 + m)[(\alpha\beta - 2\beta - 2)k_r + 2k_1^2\alpha\theta^2]\theta}{(a^2\beta^2 - 4\alpha\beta^2 + 4\beta^2 + 4\alpha - 4)k_r^2 - 4(-1 + \alpha)k_1^2\theta^2(\alpha + 1/2)k_r + 2k_1^4\alpha\theta^4(-1 + \alpha)} \quad (7)$$

$$r_1^e = \frac{\alpha\theta k_1(\theta\delta_0 + m)\{[(\beta + 2)\alpha - 2\beta - 2]k_r - k_1^2\theta^2(-1 + \alpha)\}}{(a^2\beta^2 - 4\alpha\beta^2 + 4\beta^2 + 4\alpha - 4)k_r^2 - 4(-1 + \alpha)k_1^2\theta^2(\alpha + 1/2)k_r + 2k_1^4\alpha\theta^4(-1 + \alpha)} \quad (8)$$

$$d_1^e = -\frac{(\theta\delta_0 + m)\{(\beta + 1)[(\beta - 2)\alpha - 2\beta + 2]k_r^2 + \theta^2 k_1^2\left[(\beta + 2)\alpha^2 - \alpha - 1\right]k_r - k_1^4\alpha\theta^4(\alpha - 1)\}}{(a^2\beta^2 - 4\alpha\beta^2 + 4\beta^2 + 4\alpha - 4)k_r^2 - 4(-1 + \alpha)k_1^2\theta^2(\alpha + 1/2)k_r + 2k_1^4\alpha\theta^4(-1 + \alpha)} \quad (9)$$

$$d_2^e = \frac{k_r(\alpha - 1)(\theta\delta_0 + m)\{(\beta + 1)[\alpha\beta - 2\beta + 2]k_r - \theta^2 k_1^2[(\beta + 2)\alpha - \beta]\}}{(a^2\beta^2 - 4\alpha\beta^2 + 4\beta^2 + 4\alpha - 4)k_r^2 - 4(-1 + \alpha)k_1^2\theta^2(\alpha + 1/2)k_r + 2k_1^4\alpha\theta^4(-1 + \alpha)} \quad (10)$$

$$\pi_p^e = -\frac{(\theta\delta_0 + m)^2\left(E_1 k_r - \theta^2(\alpha - 1)k_1^2\right)\alpha\left(E_2 k_r^2 + E_3 k_1^2 k_r - \frac{3k_1^4\alpha\theta^4(\alpha - 1)}{2}\right)k_r}{(a^2\beta^2 - 4\alpha\beta^2 + 4\beta^2 + 4\alpha - 4)k_r^2 - 4(-1 + \alpha)k_1^2\theta^2(\alpha + 1/2)k_r + 2k_1^4\alpha\theta^4(-1 + \alpha)} \quad (11)$$

$$\pi_s^e = -\frac{\left[(\alpha - 2)(\beta + 1)k_r + k_1^2\theta^2(\alpha + 1)/2\right](\theta\delta_0 + m)^2 k_r(\alpha - 1)}{(a^2\beta^2 - 4\alpha\beta^2 + 4\beta^2 + 4\alpha - 4)k_r^2 - 4(-1 + \alpha)k_1^2\theta^2(\alpha + 1/2)k_r + 2k_1^4\alpha\theta^4(-1 + \alpha)} \quad (12)$$

The total profit is:

$$\pi^e = \pi_p^e + \pi_s^e$$
$$= -\frac{(\theta\delta_0 + m)^2 k_r\left[(\beta + 1)E_4k_r^3 + 2k_1^2\theta E_5k_r^2 - k_1^4 E_6(\alpha - 1)\theta^4 k_r + \theta^6 k_1^6\alpha(\alpha - 1)^2(5\alpha/2 + 1)\right]}{(a^2\beta^2 - 4\alpha\beta^2 + 4\beta^2 + 4\alpha - 4)k_r^2 - 4(-1 + \alpha)k_1^2\theta^2(\alpha + 1/2)k_r + 2k_1^4\alpha\theta^4(-1 + \alpha)}$$
$$(13)$$

New Retail-Type Operation Mode. Considering that the new retail style fresh food e-commerce operation mode is a dual channel mode for fresh food e-commerce enterprises to meet market demand, consisting of online channel sales achieved by fresh food e-commerce enterprises through self built e-commerce platforms and offline store channel sales. Therefore, a centralized decision-making mode is adopted for the supply chain of new retail style fresh food e-commerce [15], which means that fresh food e-commerce enterprises and their self built e-commerce platforms belong to the same role for decision-making, Make joint decisions on the sales prices and preservation efforts of the fresh food e-commerce supply chain in a dual channel mode. The optimal decision for fresh food e-commerce enterprises under this decision-making mode is:

$$p_1^f = p_2^f = -\frac{k_r(\theta\delta_0 + m)}{k_1^2\theta^2 + 2\beta k_r - 2k_r} \quad (14)$$

$$r_1^f = r_2^f = -\frac{\theta k_1(\theta\delta_0 + m)}{k_1^2\theta^2 + 2\beta k_r - 2k_r} \quad (15)$$

Online and offline market demand are as follows:

$$d_1^f = d_2^f = \frac{k_r(\beta - 1)(\theta\delta_0 + m)}{(2\beta - 2)k_r + k_1^2\theta^2} \quad (16)$$

The optimal profit is:

$$\pi^f = -\frac{k_r(\theta\delta_0 + m)^2}{(2\beta - 2)k_r + k_1^2\theta^2} \quad (17)$$

From this, we can see that under the operation mode of new retail-based fresh food e-commerce, the optimal price is the same as that of online and offline channels, and the effort level of fresh preservation is the same.

2.3 Optimal Decisions Under Different Modes of Operation

The first two sections respectively solve the optimal decision of the platform-based fresh food e-commerce operation mode and the new retail-based fresh food e-commerce operation mode, and obtain the optimal fresh-keeping effort, optimal pricing, optimal demand and optimal profit of the two modes. This section makes a comparative analysis of the optimal decision of the two modes of operation, so as to draw some conclusions. (1) Compared with the new retail fresh food e-commerce supply chain, the platform fresh food e-commerce supply chain has a loss of offline sales price and a loss of online consumer demand. (2) Compared with the new retail mode, the online and offline fresh preservation efforts of the platform mode are lost. (3) Compared with the new retail mode, the overall profit of the platform mode decreases, which indicates that there is a double marginal effect in the platform fresh food e-commerce supply chain, that is because both the fresh seller and the third-party e-commerce platform take the maximization of their own interests as the premise. Therefore, it is necessary to coordinate and optimize the operation mode of platform fresh food e-commerce.

2.4 Construction of Coordination Mode

Due to the fact that the new retail-based fresh food e-commerce operation mode is a relatively ideal state, while the platform-based fresh food e-commerce operation mode with fresh food sellers as the main body can only rely on the online sales channels of third-party e-commerce platforms, there will be dual marginal effects, which will damage the overall revenue of the supply chain. If we set the total revenue of the platform based fresh food e-commerce supply chain under the new coordination contract to be equal to the total revenue under the new retail mode, and the revenue of fresh food sellers and third-party e-commerce platforms increases simultaneously, that is, achieving Pareto improvement, then as rational supply chain members, they will voluntarily fulfill this contract. Therefore, we assume that fresh food sellers will actively bear a certain proportion of the cost of preservation efforts on third-party e-commerce platforms. At the same time, fresh food sellers will provide a fixed fee to third-party e-commerce platforms to ensure that they can provide a better online sales channel for preservation efforts. The cooperation between fresh food sellers and third-party e-commerce platforms can not only stimulate their enthusiasm, but also adjust their profit levels, continuously optimizing the entire supply chain. At this point, the dual channel decision-making mode corresponding to the platform-based fresh food e-commerce operation mode is:

Profit of the third-party platform under the coordination mode:

$$\pi_p^g = \alpha p_1 d_1 - (1 - \varepsilon)c_1 + F \tag{18}$$

Profit of fresh food sellers under the coordination mode:

$$\pi_s^g = (1 - \alpha)p_1 d_1 + p_2 d_2 - \varepsilon c_1 - c_2 - F \tag{19}$$

And the constraint condition is required:

$$S.t. \begin{cases} \pi_p^g \geq \pi_p^e \\ \pi_s^g \geq \pi_s^e \end{cases} \tag{20}$$

According to the backward solution method, the optimal decision solution of the platform fresh food e-commerce supply chain under the coordination mode can be obtained as follows:

$$\varepsilon = 1 - \alpha \tag{21}$$

There is a fixed cost that enables the coordination of the platform based fresh food e-commerce supply chain, and the value of the fixed cost will be determined by the bargaining power of both coordinating parties. Fresh food sellers and third-party e-commerce platforms can negotiate and adjust the relative proportion of fixed costs, which can encourage both parties to freely allocate and coordinate the increased profits of this supply chain before and after.

$$-\frac{(\theta\delta_0 + m)^2 (E_1 k_r - \theta^2(\alpha - 1)k_1^2)\alpha\left(E_2 k_r^2 + E_3 k_1^2 k_r - \frac{3k_1^4\alpha\theta^4(\alpha-1)}{2}\right)k_r}{(a^2\beta^2 - 4\alpha\beta^2 + 4\beta^2 + 4\alpha - 4)k_r^2 - 4(-1 + \alpha)k_1^2\theta^2(\alpha + 1/2)k_r + 2k_1^4\alpha\theta^4(-1 + \alpha)}$$
$$+ \frac{\alpha k_r(\theta\delta_0 + m)^2}{(4\beta - 4)k_r + 2k_1^2\theta^2} \le F \le \frac{(\alpha - 2)k_r(\theta\delta_0 + m)^2}{(4\beta - 4)k_r + 2k_1^2\theta^2} \tag{22}$$
$$+ \frac{[(\alpha - 2)(\beta + 1)k_r + k_1^2\theta^2(\alpha + 1)/2](\theta\delta_0 + m)^2 k_r(\alpha - 1)}{(a^2\beta^2 - 4\alpha\beta^2 + 4\beta^2 + 4\alpha - 4)k_r^2 - 4(-1 + \alpha)k_1^2\theta^2(\alpha + 1/2)k_r + 2k_1^4\alpha\theta^4(-1 + \alpha)}$$

By coordinating with fresh food sellers to take the initiative to bear the cost of fresh preservation efforts on third-party e-commerce platforms, while ensuring that the platforms provide optimal online sales channels for fresh preservation efforts, fresh food sellers offer a fixed fee to support the quality of fresh preservation efforts. This supply chain coordination mechanism of cost sharing and fixed compensation promotes effective collaboration between fresh food sellers and third-party e-commerce platforms. As a result, it effectively enhances the profits of both parties and elevates the overall profit level of the supply chain to that of the new retail fresh food e-commerce operation mode.

3 Verification of Coordination Mechanism

According to the parameter assignment provided by scholars Ding Jie et al. [11] in their article, assign certain numerical values to the variables involved in the article. The specific parameter values are shown in Table 2, and based on this, a detailed case analysis is conducted on the optimal decision.

Table 2. Parameter values

Variable	m	α	δ_0	θ	β	k_1	k_r
Assignment	100	0.3	1	10	0.3	0.5	100

3.1 Optimal Decision Analysis

In this section, we use Maple software to calculate and obtain the optimal pricing, optimal fresh-keeping level, optimal demand and optimal profit of the two operation modes, as shown in Table 3.

Table 3. Comparison of optimal decision making

Optimal decision	Optimal pricing	Optimal freshness level	Optimal demand	Optimal demand
Platform-based operation mode	$p_1^e = 95.132$	$r_1^e = 1.427$	$d_1^e = 49.177$	$\pi^e = 9946.262$
	$p_2^e = 90.581$	$r_2^e = 4.529$	$d_2^e = 70.604$	
New retail-type operation mode	$p_1^f = 95.652$	$r_1^f = 4.783$	$d_1^f = 66.957$	$\pi^f = 10521.739$
	$p_2^f = 95.652$	$r_2^f = 4.783$	$d_2^f = 66.957$	

From the table, it is apparent that in the platform's fresh operation mode, both the fresh food sellers and the third-party e-commerce platform prioritize their own interests and are reluctant to invest significantly to guarantee the quality of fresh agricultural products. Consequently, even if prices are lowered, they fail to meet consumers' expectations for high-quality fresh agricultural products. This ultimately results in a decline in the overall profit of the supply chain.

3.2 Verification of Coordination Mechanism

When other parameters are determined, we discuss the influence of the coefficient of preservation effort on preservation costs on the upper and lower limits of fixed compensation costs. At the same time, considering the limitations of certain conditions that the equilibrium solution needs to meet in the previous text, in order to ensure the rationality of the final result, the range of the coefficient of preservation effort on preservation costs is set to $50 < k_r < 200$.

From Fig. 2, it is evident that there is an optimal interval for the fixed compensation costs obtained by third-party e-commerce platforms. Additionally, as the impact coefficient continues to increase, the upper limit of fixed compensation costs decreases. This implies that as the impact of preservation efforts on costs increases, fresh food sellers can provide lower fixed compensation costs. As fresh food sellers are important stakeholders, they consider their own interests and respond to market changes when determining compensation costs in order to balance their own losses. Lastly, it was discovered that the lower limit of the fixed compensation fee falls in the negative range within a certain impact coefficient range. This suggests that when fresh food sellers share the cost of freshness preservation efforts on third-party e-commerce platforms, if the sharing ratio sufficiently meets the optimal profit increase of the third-party e-commerce platform, they may not need to provide compensation fees. Consequently, the existence and amount of compensation fees are determined by the bargaining power of both parties.

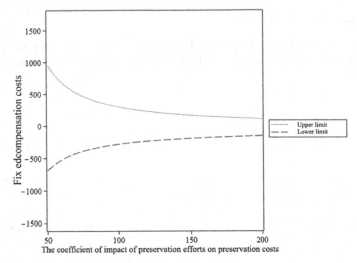

Fig. 2. The impact of changes in k_r on the upper and lower limits of fixed compensation costs

4 Conclusions

Based on the previous scholars' research on the operation mode of the current fresh ecommerce industry, this paper focuses on the optimal decision-making relationship among pricing, demand and profit of the two most popular operation modes of fresh food e-commerce supply chain, and constructs the contract coordination mode for the one with low overall benefit of the supply chain. In order to meet the development needs of fresh food e-commerce industry under the current new retail background, so as to improve the overall profit of the supply chain.

First of all, in the process of studying the new retail mode, it is found that the online and offline sales prices are the same, and the effort level of fresh preservation is the same [16]. This shows that in the context of new retail, fresh food e-commerce enterprises pay equal attention to online and offline sales channels, and do not prefer a single channel. Secondly, in the comparative analysis of the platform mode and the new retail mode of fresh food e-commerce, it is found that under the new retail mode of fresh food e-commerce, fresh food e-commerce enterprises are more sensitive to the perception of consumers' demand for fresh agricultural products, and can respond quickly to ensure consumers' demand for freshness of agricultural products. This shows that fresh food e-commerce enterprises should focus on consumers' demand for freshness of fresh agricultural products and pay attention to the concept of green health, which can bring more benefits. Finally, in the process of optimizing and coordinating the platform mode, it is found that if the fresh food e-commerce enterprises and the third-party e-commerce platform can deeply cooperate and encourage each other, they can effectively coordinate the benefits of both sides, and then improve the overall benefits of the supply chain.

However, this article only designed two typical operation modes of fresh e-commerce supply chain modes that consider preservation efforts in the context of new retail, and constructed a coordination contract mode for the operation mode with lower overall efficiency of the supply chain, ultimately enabling continuous coordination and optimization of the supply chain. Moreover, author has simplified and idealized the construction of the supply chain mode, and have not included important supply chain members such as third-party logistics platforms and suppliers in the mode construction, which makes the mode research in this article lack comprehensive exploration. In future research, suppliers, third-party logistics enterprises, and other members can be introduced into the supply chain to explore more comprehensive and practical supply chain modes. At the same time, platform service level, logistics distribution level, and consumer timeliness of agricultural products can be added to further explore the operation mode of the fresh e-commerce industry.

References

1. Wang, X., Ng, C.T.: New retail versus traditional retail in e-commerce: channel establishment, price competition, and consumer recognition. Ann. Oper. Res. **291**, 921–937 (2020)
2. Liu, Y., Ma, D., Hu, J., et al.: Sales mode selection of fresh food supply chain based on blockchain technology under different channel competition. Comput. Ind. Eng.. Ind. Eng. **162**, 107730 (2021)
3. Guan, G., Liu, D., Zhai, J.: Factors influencing consumer satisfaction of fresh produce E-commerce in the background of COVID-19—a hybrid approach based on LDA-SEM-XGBoost. Sustainability **14**(24), 16392 (2022)
4. Lin, J., Li, T., Guo, J.: Factors influencing consumers' continuous purchase intention on fresh food e-commerce platforms: an organic foods-centric empirical investigation. Electron. Commer. Res. Appl. **50**, 101103 (2021)
5. Sun, Y., Lian, F., Yang, Z.Z.: Optimizing the location of physical shopping centers under the clicks-and-mortar retail mode. Environ. Dev. Sustain. **24**(2), 2288–2314 (2022)
6. Song, Z., He, S., Xu, G.: Decision and coordination of fresh produce three-layer E-commerce supply chain: a new framework. IEEE Access **7**, 30465–30486 (2018)
7. Maruyama, M., Wu, L., Huang, L.: The modernization of fresh food retailing in China: the role of consumers. J. Retail. Consum. Serv. **30**, 33–39 (2016)
8. Xiao, X.: A study on the supply chain model of fresh e-commerce under the background of "New Retail". Small and Medium-Sized Enterprise Management and Technology (first half of the year) (4), 164–165 (2021)
9. Zhang, S., Ding, Q., Rao, Y., et al.: Research on incentive and coordination strategy of fresh products' supply chain with delivery time under new retail (2023). SSRN 4348736
10. Wang, S., Ma, W.: Inventory and coordination optimization of fresh agricultural product based on preservation efforts. J. Highway Transp. Res. Dev. **36**(6), 125–134 (2019). (in Chinese)
11. Ding, J., Li, G., Sun, J.: Consider coordinating the dual channel supply chain of fresh products for preservation efforts. Logist. Technol. **41**(2), 88–95 (2022). (in Chinese)
12. Wang, X.: Coordination of fresh food e-commerce supply chain under asymmetric information on freshness effort level. Chin. Storage Transp. **1**, 116–120 (2021). (in Chinese)
13. Wang, S., Yang, X., Chen, F.: Research on the operation mode of fresh food e-commerce in the Era of "Internet+." Natl. Bus. Inform. **12**, 25–27 (2016). (in Chinese)
14. Ren, G.: Case analysis of Alibaba group's investment in new retail fresh Hema. Enterp. Sci. Technol. Dev. **4**, 196–198 (2021). (in Chinese)
15. Zhang, S., Mei, Y., Bao, Q., et al.: Coordination strategy for a new retail supply chain based on combination contract. Complexity **2021**, 1–13 (2021)
16. Zhao, J., Bin, Z., Jie, M.: Research on cross channel cooperative return strategies for online and offline retailers. Chin. Manag. Sci. **31**(06), 164–173 (2023). (in Chinese)

Research Status, Hot Spots and Frontiers Related to Chinese Banking in the Wave of Digital Transformation: Bibliometric Analysis and Knowledge Graph

Jiangping Wan[(⊠)], Jiahong Lin[(⊠)], and Siting Lin

School of Business Administration, South China University of Technology, WuShan, Guangzhou, Guangdong, China

csjpwan@scut.edu.cn, 202130380544@mail.scut.edu.cn

Abstract. Today, the digital transformation of banks is a hot topic in both theory and practice. In recent years, the number of relevant research results has increased significantly, and the research focus, level and perspective are complicated. So it is necessary to systematically summarize and sort out it, and build a relatively complete knowledge graph to provide support for subsequent research. At the same time, it can provide useful reference for the banking industry and policy makers. In this paper, CiteSpace is used to analyze the literatures of bank digital transformation. Firstly, the research status is analyzed from the aspects of publication trends, institutions and authors. Secondly, through keyword co-occurrence, keyword clustering and keyword burst analysis, the research hotspots and evolution trend are studied. Finally, we construct the knowledge graph of bank digital transformation, and six research topics are identified. In addition, we propose five possible research directions in the future.

Keywords: Banking · Commercial Bank · Digital Transformation · Knowledge Graph · CiteSpace

1 Introduction

Since the implementation of the national "14th Five-Year Plan", all walks of life continue to accelerate the process of digital transformation, the banking industry is in the main position of financial industry in China, with the rapid development of global fintech, the banking industry has ushered in unprecedented opportunities and challenges, the depth and breadth of its digital transformation continues to strengthen. In early 2022, the "FinTech Development Plan (2022–2025)" [1] and the "Guidance on the Digital Transformation of the Banking and Insurance Industry" [2] issued by the People's Bank of China and the Banking and Insurance Regulatory Commission respectively further promoted the pace of digital transformation of China's banks. The development direction of the banking industry in fintech innovation, data capacity building and financial supply-side reform has been clarified. In addition, the COVID-19 pandemic has also played a role in promoting the development of the digital economy, resulting in a sharp rise in the demand for "contactless" services in the financial industry, which has further promoted the digital transformation of banks.

In recent years, researches related to bank digital transformation have also been the focus of academic circles. Studies on how to carry out the digital transformation of banks, the impact and empowerment brought by the digital transformation of banks have emerged in an endless stream. The number of relevant research results has increased significantly, and the research focus, level and perspective are complicated. Therefore, it is necessary to systematically sort out and summarize the existing research results. The main contributions of this study are as follows: (1) There are almost no relevant review in this field in China now, this paper fills the gap and summarizes each subject area and its relationship by constructing a knowledge graph; (2) Systematic integration of scattered research results is helpful for scholars to understand the current research status, hot spots and shortcomings in this field more clearly and comprehensively, so as to provide effective reference for follow-up research; (3) For the banking industry, it can guide them to better understand the necessity, opportunity and challenge of digital transformation, and provide reference value for their thinking about the direction and strategy of digital transformation practice; (4) This paper provides some enlightenment for policy makers to think about how to better and more scientifically promote the digital transformation of banks and avoid the risks in the transformation.

2 Materials and Methods

This paper selects the literatures related to bank digital transformation from the CSSCI database of CNKI, and sets the search keywords to "bank" and "'digital transformation' + 'digital' + 'intellectualization transformation' + 'intellectualization' + 'Internet' + 'financial technology' + 'science and technology finance' + 'big data' + 'artificial intelligence' + 'cloud computing' + 'block chain' + 'Internet of things'". The document type is selected as "CSSCI", and the search time is set to 2000–2023. We manually excluded the following three types of literature: (1) The title, abstract and keywords include keywords related to digital transformation, but the research object has nothing to do with banks; (2) Research on digital transformation of other types of enterprises. (3) The invalid literatures such as duplication, missing key information and research report essence. Then we obtain 857 literatures. CiteSpace is used to convert the exported documents to the recognizable WOS format, and the data are de-processed, finally get 832 records.

CiteSpace software, a visual analysis software developed by Professor Chen Chaomei, is a powerful tool for bibliometric research. It can reveal research hotspots and trends more objectively, scientifically and accurately by presenting co-occurrence visual maps of keywords, countries, institutions and authors, and has the characteristics of diversity, time-sharing and dynamics. So we applied CiteSpace 6.1.6 to analyze the research status of digital transformation of banks from the aspects of the publication trends, institutions and authors. And further analyzed the research hotspots and evolutionary trends through keyword co-occurrence, keyword clustering and keyword burst analysis. Finally, based on the above analysis, the knowledge graph of bank digital transformation is constructed to clarify the logical relationship between the relevant subject areas of bank digital transformation.

3 Research Status Analysis

3.1 Publication Trends and Author Analysis

From 2000 to 2010, research results have been sporadic. The number of published papers increased rapidly from 2013 to 2015, indicating that this field began to attract more and more researchers' attention. In 2021 and 2022, 111 and 112 articles were published respectively, indicating that the research heat in bank digital transformation still maintains a high level. According to the statistics of CiteSpace, Liu MF, the author with the most published papers, has 9 published papers, but no core author group has been formed. There is some cooperation among core authors, indicating the close cooperation among the core authors. But most have not formed a cooperative network.

3.2 Institutions Analysis

The top 10 institutions are all universities, with a total of 111 publications, accounting for 13.3% of the total sample literature, indicating that universities have made certain contributions to this field. The centrality of almost all research institutions is 0, indicating that they still have no obvious influence. There are two relatively large research cooperation networks (Fig. 1), with School of Finance of Renmin University of China and School of Finance of Central University of Finance and Economics as the core nodes respectively. In general, a small number of key institutions have formed a certain cooperation network, but most of the institutions are still relatively low correlation degree, and the cooperation intensity is insufficient.

Fig. 1. Distribution network of research institutions.

4 Analysis of Research Hotspots and Evolutionary Trends

4.1 Co-occurrence Analysis

Figure 2 shows the keyword co-occurrence network diagram, which contains 457 nodes and 513 connections. The network density is 0.0049, and the keyword co-occurrence density is sparse. The top 5 keywords are fintech (187 times), commercial banks (172 times), blockchain (71 times), digital currency (46 times), big data (31 times), and digital currency (46 times). To a certain extent, it reflects that the current research focuses on the digital transformation of commercial banks, the enabling role of fintech (blockchain, big data, etc.) on the digital transformation of banks, and the digital products and services of banks (such as digital currency). There are 32 keywords with centrality greater than 0.1, among which the top 5 are financial technology(0.81), commercial banks(0.55), financial innovation(0.55), blockchain(0.26) and inclusive finance(0.26). The research hotspots reflected are little different from the previous analysis based on word frequency, and also include financial innovation, macro-control, and digital inclusive finance.

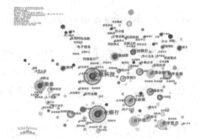

Fig. 2. Keyword co-occurrence network.

Fig. 3. Keyword clustering knowledge map.

4.2 Keyword Cluster Analysis

The knowledge map of keyword clustering (Fig. 3) shows that the value of Modularity Q is 0.8841, which is significantly greater than the value of network modularity evaluation index 0.3, indicating a good clustering effect. The Weighted Mean Silhouette value of

0.8947 indicates that the clustering results have high reliability. The cluster labels are obtained by using the log-likelihood algorithm (LLR) to extract the keywords from the cited literature. Figure 3 shows 16 clusters with nodes greater than 10. Each cluster represents a research topic, and all the literature contained in the cluster forms the research basis of the topic. Relevant information is shown in Table 1. According to the main research content of each cluster, six research topics can be further sorted out, which are commercial banks, fintech, indirect impact, digital products and services, digital business models and digital inclusive finance. Among them, commercial banks are the main body of banking digital transformation; Fintech includes the application of a series of technologies in the financial field, enabling the digital transformation of banks; Indirect impact refers to some indirect impacts on banks brought by fintech in the process of digital transformation. Digital products and services are represented by digital currencies; Digital business model includes network bank, technology bank, open bank and other business models different from traditional banks. Digital inclusive finance is the development and realization of inclusive finance brought about by the digital transformation of banks.

Table 1. Keyword clustering results and research topics

Clusters	Size	Silhouette	Mean (Year)	Thematic Area
#0 Commercial Banks	52	0.998	2018	Commercial Banks
#1 Fintech	41	0.992	2017	Fintech
#2 Big Data	29	1	2016	
#13 Digital finance	14	1	2021	
#15 Information Technology	10	0.951	2014	
#6 Monetary Policy	24	0.959	2014	Indirect Impact
#9 Bank Competition	20	0.982	2021	
#4 Bitcoin	25	0.939	2018	Digital Products and Services
#5 Digital Currency	24	1	2018	
#10 Yu 'e Bao	17	0.941	2015	
#7 Network Finance	24	0.98	2006	Digital Business Model
#8 Data Sharing	22	0.941	2013	
#12 Science and Technology Bank	17	1	2013	
#14 Open Bank	11	1	2020	
#3 Inclusive Finance	28	0.964	2017	Digital Inclusive Finance
#11 Rural Finance	17	0.982	2015	

4.3 Keyword Burst Analysis

Keyword burst detection can reflect the evolution trend of research hotspots in a certain research field within a certain time range, and also help to reveal the current and future hot research topics [3]. In this paper, a total of 20 burst keywords are obtained (Fig. 4).

According to Fig. 4, the research frontier related to the digital transformation of banks has changed over time. "financial innovation" has a high intensity of burst and is the keyword with the longest duration(2003–2017). Financial innovation is a broad concept, and "Internet finance" and "fintech" can be regarded as financial innovation. Financial innovation is not only the driving force but also the background of the digital transformation of banks. In terms of the burst time, "e-commerce" is the earliest(2000), indicating that the research on digital transformation of banks first appeared in the research on e-commerce. In terms of burst intensity, "blockchain" has the highest burst intensity (10.99), and related research mainly focuses on "digital currency" and "supply chain finance". In the past two years and in the future, "digital finance", "risk taking", "profitability" and "bank risk" may be the research hotspots, that is, the impact of digital transformation on bank risk taking, profitability and bank risk.

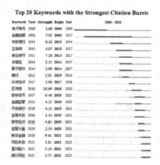

Fig. 4. Keyword burst diagram.

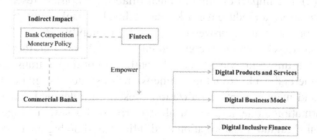

Fig. 5. Knowledge graph of bank digital transformation.

5 Knowledge Graph

The digital transformation of banks is a complicated, pluralistic and long-term process.

A knowledge graph is conducive to better classifying all existing research results, summarizing the main research content and research status within each topic, and further clarifying the relationship between various topics.

Based on the analysis above, this paper constructs a relatively complete knowledge graph for bank digital transformation (Fig. 5). It reflects the key research subject areas and content on the digital transformation of banks, and clarifies the logical relationships between the various research themes. In general, commercial bank is the main body of the research in this field. On the one hand, fintech continues to empower banks and promote its digital transformation [4]; on the other hand, it also exerts indirect impacts on banks through affecting bank competition and monetary policy. In the process of digital transformation continuously enabled by fintech, for banks themselves, the digital transformation of products and services and the digital transformation of business models are two major research topics. As the most important traditional financial institutions, the digital transformation of banks will also bring about the development and gradual realization of digital inclusive finance. Therefore, this paper divides the researches on digital transformation of banks into the following six themes.

5.1 Commercial Banks

Commercial bank is the main research object of banking digital transformation. Fintech, represented by Internet finance, has triggered huge changes in the financial industry, giving birth to new financial products and services such as digital payment, network and big technology credit, etc. It has long been a consensus that traditional commercial banks must promote digital transformation to improve their competitiveness and customer service capabilities. Around commercial banks, scholars mainly carried out research from three perspectives: (1) How to carry out digital transformation? Scholars have conducted relevant studies from the perspectives of strategy, tactics and path selection [5]. (2) The impact of digital transformation. Empirical research shows that digital transformation can reduce the risk bearing level of banks, improve the operating efficiency, and promote the improvement of bank profitability [6, 7]. (3)What are the results of digital transformation of commercial banks? At present, there are not many relevant studies in this field. Xie Xl et al. [8] built a set of digital transformation index system of commercial banks from three dimensions of strategic digitalization, business digitalization and management digitalization. Based on a detailed analysis of banks' digital transformation strategies, Xie et al. [9] proposed a new intelligent evaluation method for banks' digital transformation credibility based on big data analysis.

5.2 Fintech

Fintech can be roughly divided into external fintech and internal fintech, the latter also known as bank fintech, which is specifically manifested in the bank's own investment and development of fintech to achieve the empowerment of banks [10]. This paper refers mainly to the latter. Specifically, scholars pay more attention to the enabling role of bank fintech in the transformation and upgrading of traditional risk management of commercial banks [11], and some have conducted relevant studies on the mechanism and effect of enabling the development of small and micro enterprise credit business of large commercial banks [12], and some have pointed out that bank fintech enables banks to improve the efficiency of liquidity creation and operational efficiency and effectively alleviate bank credit risks [6, 13]. In addition, some scholars pay attention to the way banks promote their own fintech development, and conduct relevant research on the cooperation and innovation between commercial banks and external fintech companies [14]. From the perspective of specific technologies, scholars pay more attention to the application of big data in banking [15].

5.3 Indirect Impact

While banks develop fintech to empower itself, external fintech exerts an indirect impact on commercial banks by intensifying bank competition and influencing monetary policy. In terms of bank competition, Sun XR et al. [16] found that the development of external financial technology would seize the deposit and loan market, thus directly intensifying the competition among banks, forcing banks to innovate credit technology, optimize and adjust the credit term and credit structure, and further increase the risks undertaken by banks. In addition, from the perspective of enterprise growth, some scholars have studied that bank competition can act as a regulatory factor and positively amplify the promoting effect of fintech on the growth of different types of enterprises [17]. In terms of monetary policy, Sheng TX et al. [18] pointed out that when the level of fintech is developed to a certain extent, it will weaken the influence of monetary policy on the liquidity creation ability of banks, and it will have different regulatory effects on banks with different asset and liability structure characteristics. Song QH et al. [19] found that the development of fintech improved the effectiveness of price monetary policy tools such as interest rates, but weakened the role of quantitative monetary policy in regulating bank money supply. In addition, some scholars have studied the impact of the development of Internet finance on the transmission mechanism and transmission effect of monetary policy [20].

5.4 Digital Products and Services

Digital currency is the most widely concerned among the digital products of banks, which can be divided into legal and non-legal digital currency. Some scholars have studied the concept, evolution, related legal issues, global governance and antitrust issues of digital currency. At present, private digital currencies are completely prohibited in China. Scholars mainly focus on Libra, the international private digital currency, and conduct a comprehensive analysis of it from the perspective of economics [21]. They pay attention to the challenges it poses to China's own digital currency regulation, monetary policy and even China's economy and society [22, 23]. For the digital transformation of Chinese banks, digital currency mainly refers to the central bank's legal digital currency. Current researches mainly includes the law and financial regulation of central bank digital currency [24], the driving force of its issuance and the principles to be followed [25]. Song M et al. [26] sorted out and summarized relevant researches on central bank digital currency and prospected possible research directions in the future.

5.5 Digital Business Model

Open banking is a digital banking business model that takes value creation as its open purpose, platform-based business model as its open form, financial data as its open content, and API technology as its open means. The essence of open banking is data sharing and some scholars study open banking based on this [27]. The ultimate goal of open banking is to build an interactive ecosystem that encompasses all participants, and some scholars conduct research from the perspective of open banking ecosystem [28]. The data portability right defined by the General Data Protection Regulation (GDPR) of the European Union is the theoretical basis of open banking [29]. Some scholars have also done relevant studies on the introduction of data portability right [29] and the corresponding regulatory logic [30].

Another digital business model is science and technology banks. Some scholars explored the ways and modes of developing science and technology banks in China by studying the practice cases of science and technology sub-branches [31]. Cui B [32] proposed the "Chinese model" of science and technology bank by comparing and analyzing the difference between the credit basis of financial transactions between science and technology sub-branches and science and technology micro-loan companies. Du YY et al. [33] analyzed the necessity of science and technology bank to replace science and technology branch based on literature research and field investigation, and proposed the idea of establishing science and technology bank.

5.6 Digital Inclusive Finance

The development of inclusive finance is an important part of national strategy. Digital inclusive finance is conducive to promoting the transformation and development of enterprises[34] and can promote the sustainable development of economy [35]. The digital transformation of banks enabled by fintech can help establish a digital financial inclusion model and alleviate or even solve the problem of commercial unsustainability of inclusive finance. In this regard, scholars mainly studied the impact of the development of inclusive finance on the profitability of banks through empirical methods[36], and the promotion effect of the digital transformation of banks on the commercial sustainability of inclusive finance[37]. Lin B et al.[38] proposed that commercial banks should achieve commercial sustainability in the context of digital transformation by building a digital inclusive financial model that is "scenario-based, data-oriented and platform-based". Rural finance is an important part of inclusive finance. Zhu TX et al.[39] combined the digital transformation of small and medium-sized rural banks with the strategy of rural revitalization, proposed the "double-chain linkage" model of financial service supply chain and rural industrial supply chain linkage.

6   Conclusions

By using CiteSpace, this paper analyzes the research status, hotspots and evolutionary trends in bank digital transformation. The main research conclusions are as follows:

Firstly, research popularity continues to rise. Universities have made important contributions to this research field. A few key institutions have formed cooperative networks, but most of the cooperation intensity is weak. The influence of research results is insufficient. The core authors have not yet formed, and the cooperation among authors is not enough. This situation may not be conducive to the sharing of research results, and it will also have a certain impact on the quality of research results, which will have a certain adverse impact on the cohesion and progress of research in this field.

Secondly, the research frontiers of bank digital transformation are constantly changing. At first, researches mainly focused on e-commerce, online banking and financial innovation etc., then shifted to Internet finance, technology banking, shadow banking, real economy etc., and later focused on blockchain and digital currency, financial regulation and regulatory technology, digital economy and finance, and open banking. Recent studies have focused more on banks' risk-taking and profitability.

Thirdly, through the knowledge graph, we summarize six thematic areas: Commercial Banks, Fintech, Indirect Impact, Digital Products and Services, Digital Business Model, Digital Inclusive Finance. Base on that, we further propose five future research hotspots and possible research directions: (1) Bank fintech enables bank risk control. Risk control is the lifeline of banks. It is of great significance to study the enabling effect of bank fintech on risk control. (2) The impact of fintech on monetary policy. Monetary policy has an important function of macro-control, and the development of fintech has impact on different aspects of monetary policy, research on this topic is conducive to promoting the transformation of monetary policy regulation mode and improving its effectiveness. (3) Digital currency. Digital transformation of currency is an inevitable trend, the further study of related issues of digital currency can provide more theoretical guidance for China's central bank legal digital currency issuance and supervision and other work. (4) Digital inclusive finance. The development of inclusive finance is one of the important contents of financial development. It is of great significance to study how banks can empower themselves to build digital inclusive financial models through fintech. (5) Evaluation system of bank digital transformation. Current evaluation system and index are mostly designed for manufacturing industry, which are not entirely applicable to banks. Therefore, the construction of a digital transformation evaluation system specifically for the banking industry may be another direction.

Acknowledgement. This research is supported by Guangzhou key industrial technology project modern industrial technology under Grant 201802010035.

References

1. The People's Bank of China. PBC Releases FinTech Development Plan (2022–2025). http://www.pbc.gov.cn/zhengwugongkai/4081330/4406346/4693549/4470403/index.html. Accessed 11 Nov 2023. (in Chinese)
2. China Banking and Insurance Regulatory Commission. Guidance of the General Office of the China Banking and Insurance Regulatory Commission on the digital transformation of the banking industry. http://www.cbirc.gov.cn/cn/view/pages/governmentDetail.html?docId=1034763&itemId=861&generaltype=1. Accessed 11 Nov 2023. (in Chinese)
3. Zhang, Z., Zhang, N., Jiayi, G.: A systematic literature review of digital transformation of manufacturing enterprises: bibliometric analysis and knowledge framework. In: Yiliu, T., Chi,

M. (eds.) WHICEB 2023. LNBIP, vol. 481, pp. 144–155. Springer, Cham (2023). https://doi. org/10.1007/978-3-031-32302-7_13

4. Zhu, Y., Jin, S.: COVID-19, digital transformation of banks, and operational capabilities of commercial banks. Sustainability **15**(11), 8783 (2023)

5. Xie, Z.C., Zhao, X.L., Liu, Y.: Fin-tech driving and strategic digitization transformation of commercial banks. China Soft Sci. **8**, 184–192 (2018). (in Chinese)

6. Li, Q., Pei, P.: Fintech development of banking department and operating efficiency of commercial banks—empirical test based on text mining. J. Shanxi Univ. Finan. Econ. **43**(11), 42–56 (2021). (in Chinese)

7. Yu, B., Zhou, N., Huo, Y.Q.: The impact of financial technology on the profitability of commercial banks: an empirical test based on the dynamic panel GMM model. South. Finan. (03), 30–39 (2020). (in Chinese)

8. Xie, X.L., Wang, S.H.: Digital transformation of commercial banks in China: Measurement, progress and impact. China Econ. Q. Int. **3**(1), 35–45 (2023). (in Chinese)

9. Xie, C.: Intelligent evaluation method of bank digital transformation credibility based on big data analysis. J. Comput. Methods Sci. Eng. **22**(4), 1349–1359 (2022)

10. He, X.G., Luo, X., Guo, X.B.: Fintech, resource allocation and banking structure. Contemp. Finan. Econ. (06), 54–66 (2023). (in Chinese)

11. Jiang, Z.M., Chen, J.F., Zhang, C.: The empowerment of financial technology on the risk management transformation of commercial banks. Contemp. Econ. Manag. **41**(01), 85–90 (2019). (in Chinese)

12. Zheng, L.J., Han, Q.X., Wang, Z.X.: Fintech, goal compatibility and small and micro credit supply—the micro bank evidence based on the regional questionnaire. Stud. Int. Finan. (03), 50–60 (2023). (in Chinese)

13. Bao, X., Li, W., Li, Q.: Fintech application and bank credit risk—an analysis from the dual perspectives of information asymmetry and internal control. Finan. Forum. **27**(01), 9–18 (2022). (in Chinese)

14. Wu, C.P.: Discussion on joint innovation between commercial banks and fintech companies. New Finan. (02), 54–58 (2018). (in Chinese)

15. Cheng, Z.G., Li, F.R., You, R.: Discussion on personal customer relationship management in commercial banks under the background of big data. Stat. Decis. (07), 165–167 (2016). (in Chinese)

16. Sun, X.R., Wang, K.S., Wang, F.R.: Fin tech, competition and bank credit structure—based on the perspective of small and medium-sized enterprises financing. J. Shanxi Univ. Finan. Econ. **42**(06), 59–72 (2020). (in Chinese)

17. Wang, Y., He, H.Q., Chang, C.H.: FinTech, bank competition and firm growth. Theory Pract. Finan. Econ. **41**(05), 20–27 (2020). (in Chinese)

18. Sheng, T.X., Fan, C.L.: Fintech, bank heterogeneity and liquidity creation effect of monetary policy. Nanjing J. Social Sci. (12), 19–25+42 (2020). (in Chinese)

19. Song, Q.H., Xie, K., Deng, W.: FinTech and monetary policy effectiveness: a comparative study of quantity and price tools. Stud. Int. Finan. (07), 24–35 (2021). (in Chinese)

20. Zhan, M.H., Zhang, C.R., Shen, J.: Development of internet finance and the bank lending transmit channel of monetary policy. Econ. Res. J. **53**(04), 63–76 (2018). (in Chinese)

21. Wu ,T., Guo, J.L.: An economic analysis of facebook's cryptocurrency libra: background, implications, and challenges. Guizhou Soc. Sci. (09), 144–152 (2019). (in Chinese)

22. Yang, D., Ma, Y.: Libra's challenge to china's cryptocurrency regulation and its response. Explor. Free Views (11), 75–85+158+161 (2019). (in Chinese)

23. Qi, Y.D., Chu, X.: The impact of international private digital currency on China's economy and countermeasures. Res. Finan. Econ. Issues (02), 53–61 (2021). (in Chinese)

24. Ke, D.: Study on the legal attributes of central bank digital currency. Sci. Technol. Law (04), 57–65 (2019). (in Chinese)

25. Peng, X.S.: Central bank's digital currency: drivers and principles for issuance. Economist. (10), 51–60 (2021). (in Chinese)
26. Song, M., Xu, R.F.: New research progress on central bank digital currency innovation. Econ. Perspect. (05), 143–160 (2022). (in Chinese)
27. Chen M.: Open banking innovation from the perspective of data sharing mechanism. New Finan. (05), 33–37 (2020). (in Chinese)
28. Ji, C., Ye, J.: The open banking ecosystem: models, challenges, and countermeasures. New Finan. (08), 40–44 (2019). (in Chinese)
29. Xing H.Q.: On the introduction of right to data portability in China—from the perspective of open bank. J. Polit. Sci. Law (02), 14–24 (2020). (in Chinese)
30. Yang, X.K., An, X.M.: Open banking in practice: the right to data portability and the logic behind its supervision. Finan. Econ. Res. 36(02), 132–142 (2021). (in Chinese)
31. Fu J.F., Guo R., Shen W.J., Zhu H.M.: How to develop our country's sci-tech bank?—based on a case study on sci-tech sub-branch of hangzhou bank. Forum Sci. Technol. China (04), 92–97 (2013). (in Chinese
32. Cui, B.: The "Chinese Model" of sci-tech bank—based on the comparison of the sci-tech sub-branch bank and the sci-tech small-loan company. Shanghai Finan. (01), 34–37+117 (2013). (in Chinese)
33. Du, Y.Y., Shu, L.G.: From science and technology branch to science and technology bank – based on literature research and field research. Sci. Technol. Progr. Policy 31(09), 5–10 (2014). (in Chinese)
34. Lee, C.C., Tang, M., Lee, C.C.: Reaping digital dividends: digital inclusive finance and high-quality development of enterprises in China. Telecommun. Policy. 47(2), 102484 (2023)
35. Sun, Y., Tang, X.: The impact of digital inclusive finance on sustainable economic growth in China. Financ. Res. Lett. 50, 103234 (2022)
36. Xie, R.Q., Li, S.Q., Zhang, M.X.: Research on the influence of inclusive finance on the profitability of commercial banks under the background of financial technology. J. Quant. Technol. Econ. 38(08), 145–163 (2021). (in Chinese)
37. Li, J.J., Jiang, S.C.: Bank financial technology and commercial sustainability of inclusive finance—micro evidence of financial enhancement effect. China Econ. Q. 21(03), 889–908 (2021). (in Chinese)
38. Lin, B., Du, Y.Y.: The research of digital transformation to promote financial inclusion business sustainability. New Finan. 09, 42–46 (2020). (in Chinese)
39. Zhu, T.X., Zhang, Y.T.: Rural revitalization enabled by digital transformation of small and medium sized rural banks and double chain linkage model innovation. Front. Econ. China 18(2), 244 (2023)

Pricing Strategy in a Dual-Channel Supply Chain Considering Consortium Blockchain and Cost Information Asymmetry

Qing Fang and QingLing He[(✉)]

School of Management, Wuhan University of Science and Technology, Wuhan 430065, China
1606225894@qq.com

Abstract. For a dual-channel supply chain constructed by a manufacturer and a retailer, the upstream and downstream members of the supply chain are in the condition of cost information asymmetry. In this paper, we explore whether investing in consortium blockchain technology can mitigate the effects of information asymmetry on the supply chain's overall performance. Three stackelberg game models are constructed to discuss the pricing strategies of supply chain members to deal with information asymmetry. The study's findings indicate that supply chain members deal with the impact of information asymmetry on sales volume by reducing prices. Consortium blockchain technology's input is advantageous to the supply chain's overall profit. When the level of consortium blockchain technology's input is low, the retailer should bear the entire cost of the consortium blockchain, conversely, the manufacturer and retailer should share the cost of the consortium blockchain technology. It is beneficial to consumers when input costs and input level of consortium blockchain are controlled within a certain range. For the strategy that the input costs of the consortium blockchain are split by the manufacturer and the retailer, the smaller the proportion of the manufacturer's share is, the more favorable it is to the total profit of the supply chain.

Keywords: Dual Channel Supply Chain · Information Asymmetry · Investment in Consortium Blockchain Technology · Pricing Strategy

1 Introduction

An increasing number of people are choosing to shop online in the context of the Internet's rapid expansion and the widespread use of cell phones and other devices. Therefore, the majority of companies choose to sell their products through a dual-channel supply chain, which combines online and offline channels. For example, Hewlett-Packard, Lenovo, Gree, etc. Although the development of the supply chain's online and offline channels together improves the efficiency of product circulation between upstream and downstream, the information asymmetry that exists between upstream and downstream supply chain members causes numerous issues with the dual-channel retail model. Information asymmetry arises from the fact that supply chain participants have varying levels of information comprehension [1]. In this paper, we consider a dual-channel supply chain

© The Author(s), under exclusive license to Springer Nature Switzerland AG 2024
Y. P. Tu and M. Chi (Eds.): WHICEB 2024, LNBIP 515, pp. 86–97, 2024.
https://doi.org/10.1007/978-3-031-60264-1_8

pricing model under production cost information asymmetry, and we mainly discuss that the manufacturer conceals its true manufacturing cost, which allows the manufacturer to misrepresent its cost in order to seek more benefits [2].

This study suggests using consortium blockchain technology to mitigate the negative effects of information asymmetry on the coordinated development of the supply chain, given that cost information in the supply chain cannot be fully shared. Consortium blockchain belongs to one kind of blockchain technology. Since the consortium blockchain's processing speed is faster than that of the public chain, some commercial organizations and associations will choose to adopt it, such as the JD chain. The information on the consortium blockchain can only be read, written, and transmitted by the upstream and downstream of the supply chain, which is highly controllable [3]. At present, blockchain technology is being applied in a number of industries. When combined with Internet of Things (IoT) technology, blockchain technology can be used to solve a variety of issues in supply chains upstream and downstream, including those involving asymmetric, opaque information between record and storage [4].

Scholars both domestically and internationally concentrate on studying aspects of product quality, pricing, and services when explore the dual-channel supply chain. In this paper, we primarily examine two aspects: the consortium blockchain technology's input and the dual-channel supply chain with information asymmetry. Yan et al. [5] investigated the impact of manufacturers' misrepresentation of costs on the overall performance of the supply chain, and concluded that manufacturers' misrepresentation behaviors are beneficial to some participants in the supply chain, but detrimental to the entire supply chain. Yang H et al. [6] examined the impact of information asymmetry on revenue-sharing contracts and performance in a dual-channel supply chain, concluding that information asymmetry benefits the retailer but creates inefficiencies for the manufacturer and the entire supply chain. Allenbrand C [7] proposes that federated blockchains improve the problem of upstream and downstream information distortion, thus facilitating an optimal coordination equilibrium between manufacturers and retailers. Zhang et al. [8] explored the impact of introducing blockchain on risk-averse members in a dual-channel supply chain, and found that unit blockchain operating costs, direct selling costs, and demand fluctuations are the key points affecting members' decision-making. Zhu et al. [9] constructed two models to analyze the impact of blockchain on solving the problem of fake and shoddy products' damage to brand owners, and found that adopting blockchain is always favorable for retailers.

Currently, there are relatively few studies on the consortium blockchain. Some previous research on blockchain has mostly focused on traditional offline channels, but this paper addresses the information asymmetry of upstream and downstream costs of dual-channel supply chains. By introducing consortium blockchain technology, it reduces the harm that information asymmetry causes to the supply chain's overall efficiency and investigates the effects of both the introduction of the consortium blockchain technology and its non-introduction on the supply chain's overall performance.

2 Problem Description and Parameterization

This paper studies a dual-channel supply chain consisting of a single manufacturer and a single retailer, as shown in the following Fig. 1. Depending on whether the consortium blockchain is adopted and who pays for the consortium blockchain technology input, it is divided into three categories: a dual-channel sales model without adopting the consortium blockchain, a dual-channel sales model in which the retailer bears the input cost of the consortium blockchain technology alone, and a dual-channel sales model in which the manufacturer-retailer shares the input cost of the consortium blockchain technology.

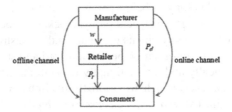

Fig. 1. The structure of dual-channel supply chain.

The retailer obtains the product from the manufacturer at the wholesale price w, and the consumer gains the product from the retailer at the retail price P_r, the manufacturer also owns the online channel and sells the product directly to the consumer at the direct price P_d through the online channel. The manufacturer will misrepresent its cost during the quotation process in an effort to increase profit. It is assumed that there exists a misrepresentation coefficient of λ, and the real cost of the manufacturer is c, so its misrepresented cost is λc [10]. The upstream and downstream of the supply chain introduced the consortium blockchain technology to improve this information asymmetry, assuming that the unit product input cost of the consortium blockchain is m, n represents the proportion of the consortium blockchain input cost that the manufacturer should bear for selling the unit product, $n \in (0, 1)$, θ represents the level of the consortium blockchain technology, $\theta \in (0, 1)$ [11]. The representation of the parameters involved in the model is shown in Table 1:

Table 1. Meaning of model parameters.

Symbol	Definition
D_r	Retailer offline channel demand
D_d	Manufacturer online channel demand
α	Consumer preference for retail channels
λ	Coefficient of misrepresentation

(*continued*)

Table 1. (*continued*)

Symbol	Definition
θ	Level of input in the consortium blockchain
Q	Potential market demand
a	Self-price elasticity coefficient of demand
b	Cross-price elasticity coefficient of demand
P_r	Retail price in offline channel
P_d	Direct price in the online channel
w	Wholesale price
c	Manufacturer's true cost
j	Sensitivity of supply chain members to information
m	Unit input cost of the consortium blockchain
n	Proportion of the input costs of the consortium blockchain to be borne by the manufacturer for each unit of product sold
$1-n$	Proportion of the input costs of the consortium blockchain to be borne by the retailer for each unit of product sold
$\prod_r$	Retailer's profit
$\prod_m$	Manufacturer's profit
π	Total supply chain profit

Establish the following demand function for retailers and manufacturers:

$$D_r = \alpha Q - aP_r + bP_d - \lambda j \tag{1}$$

$$D_d = (1 - \alpha)Q - aP_d + bP_r - \lambda j \tag{2}$$

Within the dual channel, the self-price elasticity of demand is more efficient than the cross-price elasticity, therefore, it is assumed here that $a > b > 0$ [12]. Three scenarios are taken into consideration in this paper to examine the role of consortium blockchain technology. In order to solve the above problems, this paper constructs a Stackelberg game model with the manufacturer as the leader and the retailer as the follower, and the decision sequence is that the manufacturer first decides the direct price P_d and wholesale price w in the online channel, and the retailer decides the offline retail price P_r [13].

3 Modeling and Solving

3.1 No Investment in Consortium Blockchain Technology

Model 1: In this scenario, the manufacturer's and retailer's profits are as follows:

$$\Pi_{m1} = (w_1 - \lambda c)(\alpha Q - aP_{r1} + bP_{d1} - \lambda j) + (P_{d1} - \lambda c)[(1 - \alpha)Q - aP_{d1} + bP_{d1} - \lambda j] \tag{3}$$

$$\Pi_{r1} = (P_{r1} - w_1)D_{r1} = (P_{r1} - w_1)(\alpha Q - aP_{r1} + bP_{d1} - \lambda j) \tag{4}$$

The optimal solutions for manufacturers and retailers are obtained using backward induction as follows [14].

$$P_{d1}^* = \frac{Q(a + b\alpha - a\alpha) - \lambda j(a + b) + c\lambda(a^2 - b^2)}{2(a^2 - b^2)}$$

$$w_1^* = \frac{Q(a\alpha + b - b\alpha) - \lambda j(a + b) + c\lambda(a^2 - b^2)}{2(a^2 - b^2)}$$

$$P_{r1}^* = \frac{Q(3a^2\alpha + 2ab - b^2\alpha - 2ab\alpha) + c\lambda(a^3 - b^3 - ab^2 + a^2b) - j\lambda(3a^2 - b^2 + 2ab)}{4a(a^2 - b^2)}$$

3.2 The Cost of Investing in Consortium Blockchain Technology is Borne Solely by the Retailer

Model 2: In this case, the retailer bears the cost of inputting the consortium blockchain alone. This paper assumes that only by bearing the cost of the consortium blockchain can they enjoy the information transparency brought by the introduction of the consortium blockchain technology, therefore, the demand profit functions of the manufacturer and the retailer are as follows.

$$D_{r2} = \alpha Q - aP_{r2} + bP_{d2} - (1 - \theta)\lambda j \tag{5}$$

$$D_{d2} = (1 - \alpha)Q - aP_{d2} + bP_{r2} - \lambda j \tag{6}$$

$$\Pi_{m2} = (w_2 - c)D_{r2} + (P_{d2} - c)D_{d2} = (w_2 - c)[\alpha Q - aP_{r2} + bP_{d2} - (1 - \theta)\lambda j] \\ + (P_{d2} - c)[(1 - \alpha)Q - aP_{d2} + bP_{r2} - \lambda j] \tag{7}$$

$$\Pi_{r2} = (P_{r2} - w_2 - m)D_{r2} = (P_{r2} - w_2 - m)[\alpha Q - aP_{r2} + bP_{d2} - (1 - \theta)\lambda j] \tag{8}$$

In this model, the optimal decisions of the supply chain members are as follows.

$$P_{d2}^* = \frac{Qa + (a^2 - b^2)c - Q\alpha(a - b) + (b\theta - b - a)\lambda j}{2(a^2 - b^2)}$$

$$w_2^* = \frac{Qb + (a^2 - b^2)(c - m) + Q\alpha(a - b) + (a\theta - a - b)\lambda j}{2(a^2 - b^2)}$$

$$P_{r2}^* = \frac{(a^3 - b^3)c + a^3m + Q\alpha(3a^2 - b^2) + ab(ac - bc - bm - 2Q\alpha + 2Q) - (3a^2 - b^2 - 3a^2\theta + b^2\theta + 2ab)\lambda j}{4a(a^2 - b^2)}$$

3.3 Costs of Investing in Consortium Blockchain Technology are Borne by Manufacturer and Retailer

Model 3: In this scenario, retailers and manufacturers share the cost of investing in the consortium blockchain. The demand profit functions of the manufacturer and the retailer are as follows.

$$D_{r3} = \alpha Q - aP_{r3} + bP_{d3} - (1 - \theta)\lambda j \tag{9}$$

$$D_{d3} = (1 - \alpha)Q - aP_{d3} + bP_{r3} - (1 - \theta)\lambda j \tag{10}$$

$$\Pi_{m3} = (w_3 - c - mn)[\alpha Q - aP_{r3} + bP_{d3} - (1 - \theta)\lambda j] + (P_{d3} - c - mn)[(1 - \alpha)Q - aP_{d3} + bP_{r3} - (1 - \theta)\lambda j] \tag{11}$$

$$\Pi_{r3} = [P_{r3} - w_3 - (1 - n)m]D_{r3} = [P_{r3} - w_3 - (1 - n)m][\alpha Q - aP_{r3} + bP_{d3} - (1 - \theta)\lambda j] \tag{12}$$

In this model, the optimal decisions of the supply chain members are as follows.

$$P_{d3}^* = \frac{Qa + ((a + b)(c + mn) - Q\alpha)(a - b) + (b + a)(\theta - 1)\lambda j}{2(a^2 - b^2)}$$

$$w_3^* = \frac{Qb + (a^2 - b^2)(c - m + 2mn) + Q\alpha(a - b) + (a + b)(\theta - 1)\lambda j}{2(a^2 - b^2)}$$

$$P_{r3}^* = \frac{a^3(c + m) - b^3(c + mn) + ab(2Q - bm + amn - 2Q\alpha) + Q\alpha(3a^2 - b^2) + (a^2 b - ab^2)c + (\theta - 1)(3a^2 - b^2 + 2ab)j}{4a(a^2 - b^2)}$$

Proposition 1. $\frac{\partial w_1^*}{\partial j} < 0$, $\frac{\partial P_{d1}^*}{\partial j} < 0$, $\frac{\partial P_{r1}^*}{\partial j} < 0$; $\frac{\partial P_{d2}^*}{\partial j} < 0$, $\frac{\partial w_2^*}{\partial j} < 0$, $\frac{\partial P_{r2}^*}{\partial j} < 0$; $\frac{\partial P_{d3}^*}{\partial j} < 0$, $\frac{\partial w_3^*}{\partial j} < 0$, $\frac{\partial P_{r3}^*}{\partial j} < 0$.

From Proposition 1, the optimal pricing of supply chain members decreases with increasing sensitivity to information both before and after the introduction of the consortium blockchain. Before the introduction of consortium blockchain technology, there is information asymmetry in the upstream and downstream of the supply chain, and they choose to set lower prices to attract consumers to buy products. After the introduction of consortium blockchain technology, supply chain members need to invest a certain amount of consortium blockchain costs, but the demand of the upstream and downstream of the supply chain will also increase, so the increase in the unit cost of the product will make the supply chain members make up for the loss of profit by lowering the price and thus increasing the sales volume.

4 Comparative Analysis of Three Models

4.1 Price Comparison of Three Models

Proposition 2. When $\theta < \frac{c(a^2 - b^2)(\lambda - 1)}{b\lambda j}$, $P_{d2}^* < P_{d1}^*$; when $\theta < \frac{(a^2 - b^2)(c\lambda - c + m)}{a\lambda j}$, $w_2^* < w_1^*$; when $\theta < \frac{c(a^3 - b^3 - ab^2 + a^2 b)(\lambda - 1) + (ab^2 - a^3)m}{(3a^2 - b^2)\lambda j}$, $P_{r2}^* < P_{r1}^*$; when $\theta > \frac{(b^2 - a^2)mn}{a\lambda j}$, $P_{d3}^* > P_{d2}^*$; when $\theta > \frac{2(b^2 - a^2)mn}{b\lambda j}$, $w_3^* > w_2^*$; when $\theta > \frac{(b^3 - a^2 b)mn}{2ab\lambda j}$, $P_{r3}^* > P_{r2}^*$.

From Proposition 2, when the degree of input of the consortium blockchain technology is controlled within a certain range, the pricing of supply chain members after the introduction of the consortium blockchain technology is lower than that when it is not introduced, this is because the introduction of the consortium blockchain technology improves the problem of the asymmetry of the cost information, and the supply chain upstream and downstream are more transparent. Therefore, supply chain members lower prices to attract more price-sensitive consumers. With the adoption of consortium blockchain, as the degree of consortium blockchain input rises, supply chain members' pricing is higher when the input cost of the consortium blockchain is shared by the manufacturer and the retailer than when the input cost of the consortium blockchain is borne by the retailer alone, this is because the inputs of the technology makes the manufacturers and retailers to sell unit product profit is reduced, so supply chain members will choose to increase the wholesale price, retail price way to increase the profit per unit product.

4.2 Comparison of Three Model Profits

Proposition 3. When $\frac{A_1+B_1+C_1+D_1}{\lambda j(3a^2+b^2)} < \theta < 1$, and $m < -\frac{A_1+B_1+C_1}{3a^3-3ab^2}$, $\pi_2^* > \pi_1^*$. Which $A_1 = (3a^3 - 3ab^2 + a^2b - b^3)c$, $C_1 = (3a^2 + b^2 + 4ab)\lambda j$, $D_1 = (3a^3 - 3ab^2)m$, $B_1 = Q(4ab\alpha - 4ab - 3a^2\alpha - b^2\alpha)$; when $0 < \theta < \frac{A_2+C_2+D_2}{B_2}$, $\pi_2^* > \pi_3^*$, conversely, when $\frac{A_2+C_2+D_2}{B_2} < \theta < 1$, $\pi_2^* < \pi_3^*$, which $C_2 = -4ab^2mn - b^3mn + 4a^3mn + 4a^2\lambda j - 4ab^2c$,

$A_2 = sqrt[16Q^2a^4(\alpha - 1)^2 - 16Q^2a^2b\alpha(2a\alpha - 2a - b\alpha) + 32Qa^4c(a\alpha - a - b\alpha) - 8Qa^4bmn(10\alpha - 7)$

$+(32Qa^4\lambda j - 32Qa^3b^2c)(\alpha - 1) + 8Qab^2mn(a^2\alpha + 10ab\alpha - b^2\alpha - 7ab) - 32Qa^2b(a\lambda j - b^2c\alpha - b\lambda\alpha j)$

$-8a^5bmn(4c + 3mn - 3m) + 16a^5c(2\lambda j + ac) - 8a^4b^2c(4c - 3mn) - a^4b^2m^2n(11n - 48) + b^6m^2n^2$

$+16a^4\lambda j(2bc - 2bmn + \lambda j) + 8a^3b^3mn(5c + 3mn - 3m) + 8ab^2\lambda jmn(4ab + b^2) - 8b^5mnac$

$-8a^3b\lambda j(4bc + bmn - 4\lambda j) + 16a^2b^2(b^2c^2 - 2bc\lambda j + \lambda^2j^2) - 2a^2b^4mn(12c - 5mn - 24m)]$

$B_2 = 4a\lambda j(a + 2b)$, $D_2 = 4Qa^2\alpha + 4ab\lambda j - 4Qab\partial + 4a^3c - 4Qa^2 + a^2bmn$.

Proposition 3 shows that when the degree of consortium blockchain input and input costs are within a certain range, the total profit of the supply chain is larger when the consortium blockchain technology is input than when it is not, which is because the input of the consortium blockchain technology makes the market demand rise, at the same time, the upstream and downstream information of the supply chain is more transparent, therefore, the profit of the supply chain members rises, which offsets market losses due to cost information asymmetry. After the input of consortium blockchain technology, it can be seen that there is a threshold value for the input degree of consortium blockchain, when θ is smaller than the threshold value, the total profit of the supply chain is the highest when the cost of choosing to input the consortium blockchain is borne by the retailer alone; when θ is larger than the threshold value, a strategy in which the input cost of the consortium blockchain is shared between the manufacturer and the retailer should be chosen. Therefore, for the supply chain as a whole, the introduction of consortium blockchain technology is favorable.

4.3 Impact of Cost Sharing Ratio on Total Supply Chain Profitability

Proposition 4. When $n < \frac{A_3 - B_3 - C_3 - D_3}{(4a^4 - 6a^2b^2 + 2b^4)m^2 + bm(a^2 - b^2)}$, $\frac{\partial \pi_3^*}{\partial n} < 0$; conversely, $\frac{\partial \pi_3^*}{\partial n} > 0$. Which $A_3 = (2Qb\alpha m + 2abcm + 2abm^2)(a^2 - b^2)$; $B_3 = (4Qa^3 m - 4Qab^2 m)(\alpha - 1)$; $C_3 = (4ab^2 + 2b^3 - 4a^3 - 2a^2 b)\lambda jm(\theta - 1)$; $D_3 = 2cm(2a^4 - 3a^2b^2 + b^4)$.

Proposition 5 shows that for model 3, there exists a threshold value for the proportion n, when the proportion n is smaller than this threshold value, the total profit of the supply chain decreases with the increase of the proportion of the costs shared, and when the proportion of the costs shared is larger than this threshold value, the total profit of the supply chain increases with the larger proportion n of the costs shared. Therefore, it can be concluded from the proposition that to make the total profit of the supply chain higher, the manufacturer should be made to bear as small a proportion of the consortium blockchain cost as possible. This is because the manufacturer has both online and offline demand channels, while the retailer has only offline channels. If the manufacturer shares less of the costs, its profit per unit of product will be higher.

5 Numerical Analysis

To confirm the validity of the analysis presented above, this section uses Matlab to do a case study analysis. The parameter settings are given here as follows: $Q = 100$, $c = 2.5$, $a = 10$, $b = 7$, $\lambda = 2$, $\alpha = 0.4$, $m = 5$, $n = 0.5$. The parameters are substituted into the three models to test the pricing strategies of the supply chain members before and after adopting the consortium blockchain chain technology as shown below:

As illustrated in Fig. 2, the pricing of supply chain members is negatively related to their level of sensitivity to information, both with and without the input of consortium blockchain technology, consistent with the inference of Propositions 1. Comparing the relationship between profit and the degree of input to the consortium blockchain in the three models, taking $j = 5$, $n = 0.5$, $\theta \in (0, 1)$, the results are shown in the following figure:

Figure 3 reveals that the total profit of the supply chain is higher when the consortium blockchain technology is input than when it is not. After the introduction of the consortium blockchain technology, there exists a threshold value for the degree of input of the consortium blockchain, supply chain members can choose the appropriate consortium blockchain introduction strategy based on this threshold value. Meanwhile, Fig. 3 demonstrates that the total profit of the supply chain all increases with the increase of the degree of input of the consortium blockchain, so the input of the consortium blockchain technology is favorable for the supply chain as a whole. After adopting the consortium blockchain technology, the results of comparing the changes in pricing of the three model supply chain members with the level of inputs of the consortium blockchain technology are shown in the figure below:

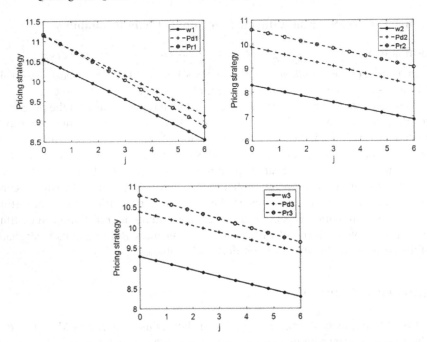

Fig. 2. Relationship between supply chain members' pricing and sensitivity to information j.

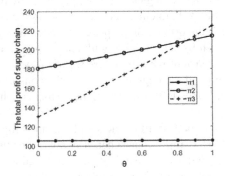

Fig. 3. Relationship between total supply chain profit and consortium blockchain input level.

From Fig. 4, it can be seen that the pricing of supply chain members is higher when the input costs of the consortium blockchain are shared by the manufacturer and the retailer than when the input costs of the consortium blockchain are borne by the retailer alone, $\theta \in (0, 1)$, which is consistent with the conclusion of Proposition 3. For Model 3, explore an appropriate sharing ratio that maximizes the total profit of the supply chain. Taking $\theta = 0.5$, $n \in (0, 1)$, and substituting the above parameters into the model, the results obtained are shown below:

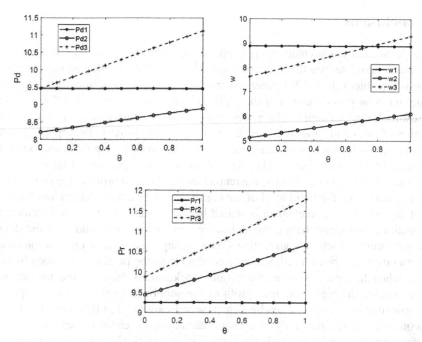

Fig. 4. Relationship between supply chain member pricing and consortium blockchain input level.

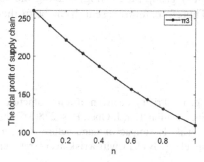

Fig. 5. Impact of consortium blockchain cost sharing ratio on total profit of supply chain members.

Figure 5 proves that the total profit of the supply chain will be higher when the proportion of input costs per unit of product consortium blockchain borne by the manufacturer is lower. Thus for Model 3, it is advantageous to explore an appropriate sharing ratio for the total profit of the supply chain members.

6 Conclusions

This paper studies a dual-channel supply chain that suffers from cost information asymmetry and investigates whether the problem can be solved by introducing the technology of consortium blockchain. This paper constructs three models and investigates the pricing and the total profit changes of the supply chain members under the three models. The results show that supply chain members usually set lower prices to mitigate the reduction of sales and benefits caused by information asymmetry; the input of consortium blockchain technology is beneficial to the total profit of supply chain; when the input level of the consortium blockchain is small and the input cost of the consortium blockchain is chosen to be borne by the retailer alone, the total profit of the supply chain is the highest; when the input level of the consortium blockchain is high and the input cost of the consortium blockchain is shared by the manufacturer and the retailer, the total profit of the supply chain is the highest; When the input cost and the input degree of the consortium blockchain are within a certain range, the optimal price of the supply chain members can be reduced, which is conducive to the purchase of goods by consumers; when the input cost of the consortium blockchain is shared by the manufacturer and the retailer, the higher the total profit of the supply chain is when the proportion of the manufacturer's share is smaller. The research presented in this paper has certain shortcomings. Firstly, the study of a dual-channel supply chain model with a single manufacturer and retailer is a little too simplistic, in reality, there are many competing manufacturers and retailers; additionally, some retailers have opened up online channels due to the rise of community group purchasing, making the study of a multi-channel model more meaningful. Therefore, future research can be further extended around these two aspects.

References

1. Zhou, J., Zhao, R., Wang, W.: Pricing decision of a manufacturer in a dual-channel supply chain with asymmetric information. Eur. J. Oper. Res. **278**(3), 809–820 (2019)
2. Chen, P., Li, B., Jiang, Y., et al.: The impact of manufacturer's direct sales and cost information asymmetry in a dual-channel supply chain with a risk-averse retailer. Int. J. Electron. Commer. **21**(1), 43–66 (2017)
3. Dib, O., Brousmiche, K.L., Durand, A., et al.: Consortium blockchains: overview, applications and challenges. Int. J. Adv. Telecommun **11**(1), 51–64 (2018)
4. Song, J.M., Sung, J., Park, T.: Applications of blockchain to improve supply chain traceability. Procedia Comput. Sci. **162**, 119–122 (2019)
5. Yan, B., Wang, T., Liu, Y., et al.: Decision analysis of retailer-dominated dual-channel supply chain considering cost misreporting. Int. J. Prod. Econ. **178**, 34–41 (2016)
6. Yang, H., Cao, E., Lu, K.J., et al.: Optimal contract design for dual-channel supply chains under information asymmetry. J. Bus. Ind. Mark. **32**(8), 1087–1097 (2017)
7. Allenbrand, C.: Smart contract-enabled consortium blockchains for the control of supply chain information distortion. Blockchain Res. Appl. **4**(3), 100134 (2023)
8. Zhang, T., Dong, P., Chen, X., et al.: The impacts of blockchain adoption on a dual-channel supply chain with risk-averse members. Omega **114**, 102747 (2023)
9. Zhu, S., Li, J., Wang, S., et al.: The role of blockchain technology in the dual-channel supply chain dominated by a brand owner. Int. J. Prod. Econ. **258**, 108791 (2023)

10. Huang, S., Wang, Y., Zhang, X.: Contracting with countervailing incentives under asymmetric cost information in a dual-channel supply chain. Transport. Res. Part E: Logist. Transport. Rev. **171**, 103038 (2023)
11. Zhong, Y., Yang, T., Yu, H., et al.: Impacts of blockchain technology with government subsidies on a dual-channel supply chain for tracing product information. Transport. Res. Part E: Logist. Transport. Rev. **171**, 103032 (2023)
12. Pi, Z., Fang, W., Perera, S.C., et al.: Enhancing the online buyer perception of consumer experience products in a dual-channel supply chain: a new role of free-riding. Int. J. Prod. Econ. **253**, 108600 (2022)
13. Zhang, K.: Manufacturer warranty service outsourcing strategies in a dual-channel supply chain. Protein Pept. Lett. **27**(6), 2899–2926 (2020)
14. Liu, C., Lee, C.K.M., Zhang, L.L.: Pricing strategy in a dual-channel supply chain with overconfident consumers. Comput. Ind. Eng. **172**, 108515 (2022)

The Effects of Anthropomorphism of Government Q&A Robot on Users' Perceived Government Trust

Min Zhang[1(✉)], Hui Li[2], and Wen Lin[2]

[1] Center for Studies of Information Resources, Wuhan University, Wuhan 430072, China
zhangmin@whu.edu.cn
[2] School of Information Management, Wuhan University, Wuhan 430072, China

Abstract. Government services have the characteristics of seriousness and authority that distinguish them from commercial services, and the application of anthropomorphism may strengthen the public's stereotypical impression of the government, cause negative attitudes towards the government, and reduce the credibility of the government if the application of anthropomorphism is completely copied from the experience in the commercial field, so it is necessary to explore the application of anthropomorphism of the government Q&A robot and its relationship with the government trust. With the level of anthropomorphism as the core, we select four influencing variables, namely, government affinity perception, service result valence, authoritarianism obeys personality, and government trust, formulate research hypotheses and construct an empirical research model, and conduct one pre-experiment and three formal experiments using the method of contextual manipulation experiments. The experimental results show that the anthropomorphism degree of the government Q&A robot positively affects government trust; government affinity perception plays a mediating role in the above process; service result valence moderates the relationship between the anthropomorphism degree of the government Q&A robot and government trust; and authoritarianism obeys personality moderates the relationship between the anthropomorphism degree of the government Q&A robot and government cognitive trust, but does not moderate the relationship between the anthropomorphism degree and government emotional trust.

Keywords: Anthropomorphism · Government Q&A robot · Digital Government · Government trust · Authoritarianism obeys personality

1 Introduction

Government Q&A robots are often defined as computer programs in the field of government affairs based on artificial intelligence technology that respond to user inquiries by recognizing, processing, and analyzing natural language [1]. With the launch of AI chatbot models ChatGPT and GPT-4 by US-based OpenAI triggering a new wave of technology worldwide, government Q&A robots have received an unprecedentedly

Y. P. Tu and M. Chi (Eds.): WHICEB 2024, LNBIP 515, pp. 98–109, 2024.
https://doi.org/10.1007/978-3-031-60264-1_9

high level of attention, both in academia and in industrial practice. Anthropomorphism of robots is a research priority in the field of human-robot interaction. It has been widely practiced in the field of business marketing for developers to elicit positive impressions and responses from users by making robots designed to be more human-like. Anthropomorphic design tools have also been introduced in the field of digital government services to create intelligent Q&A robots. However, government services are different from commercial services in terms of seriousness and authority, so the application of anthropomorphism may not be able to completely copy the experience of the commercial sector, otherwise the phenomenon of "not suited to the local environment" may occur.

Public trust in government is at the center of the government-public relationship. Some studies have found that the exposure and use of digital government services can help improve the public's perception of the government's efficiency, transparency and responsiveness, improve the public's evaluation of government performance, and improve the public's internal trust in the government [2]. Therefore, government Q&A robots play an important role in shaping government image, perceiving government performance, and forming government trust to a certain extent. However, there is limited research on the government's adoption of intelligent Q&A robots and their impacts, especially on how the anthropomorphism strategy of government Q&A robots affects the formation of government trust. Therefore, this study proposes core scientific questions: (1) Can the application of anthropomorphism in government Q&A robots influence the formation of government trust? (2) How does the application of anthropomorphism in government Q&A robots affect the mechanism of trust formation in government? (3) Does the impact of anthropomorphism in government Q&A robots vary in different contexts?

2 Literature Review

Throughout the domestic and international research literature, studies on the anthropomorphism of robots are mostly focused on the commercial field, but rarely involve the political field. Existing studies mainly include three categories: (1) Studies on the anthropomorphic design of robots, such as external image anthropomorphism, behavioral anthropomorphism, verbal communication anthropomorphism, etc., focusing on how to design intelligent robots in business scenarios so that anthropomorphism can really work [3]; (2) Studies on ethical issues of anthropomorphism applied in robots, discussing whether anthropomorphic attributes can create an issue of ethical risk [4]; (3) Studies on the impact of anthropomorphism on users. This study focuses on the third category, the study of the impact of anthropomorphism on users. Many empirical studies have verified the positive results of anthropomorphism [5], such as enhancing users' satisfaction and consumption willingness; some scholars have also investigated the negative effects of anthropomorphism, e.g., based on the theory of the Valley of Horror, Zhang Yi et al. [6] found that when the anthropomorphism of a service robot exceeds a certain threshold, consumers will feel disgusted instead. Very few scholars have studied the effect of anthropomorphism on the communication effect of political microblogging in the field of government affairs.

Many researchers have paid attention to the impact of new models of government services based on digital government in government trust [7]. How to enhance public trust in government with the application of digital government is one of the primary goals of digital government development. For the path of the role of data government contact on government trust, existing studies divide it into two categories: (1) Participatory government path, emphasizing that digital government can enhance the level of public trust in government by promoting public political participation; (2) Enterprise government path, emphasizing that the government can create a service-oriented digital public service system with the help of information technology, and enhance the public's trust in the government by improving the public's perception of the performance of public services. Studies have been conducted to explore the influencing factors of government trust under the perspective of digital government engagement based on the two aforementioned paths of government trust formation, and this paper categorizes the perspectives of these studies into those based on the perspective of public political participation and those based on the perspective of service performance perception.

According to the literature combing, this paper believes that there are three research gaps worth exploring: Firstly, the extension of anthropomorphism-related theories in the governmental domain is worth exploring; secondly, more research perspectives such as human-computer interaction are called for in the study of the impact of digital government contact on government trust; finally, there is a lack of mature theoretical guidance on the influence mechanisms and boundary conditions of anthropomorphism in digital government. Our study aims to fill these three research gaps. To address research gap 1, this study explores the impact of anthropomorphism on government Q&A robots by demonstrating the applicability of anthropomorphism's spillover effect in the government domain. This part of the study answers RQ 1. Addressing research gap 2, this study explores the impact of the anthropomorphism of government Q&A robots on government trust from the perspective of human-computer interaction, combining social response theory and institutional performance theory. This part of the study also answers RQ 2. To address research gap 3, this study integrates interdisciplinary theories of human-computer interaction and political psychology, constructs and validates a research model, and explores how the mediating variable (government affinity perception), and moderating variables (service result valence, and authoritarianism obeys personality) affect the influence of the anthropomorphism degree of government Q&A robot on government trust. This part of the study answers RQ 2 and RQ 3.

3 Hypothesis Formulation and Model Construction

3.1 Theoretical Foundation

Social Response Theory and Institutional Performance theory are two of the most significant theoretical foundation applied in our research. Social Response Theory is a classic theory in the field of human-computer interaction. The theory states that human-computer interaction is inherently social: individuals automatically or unconsciously perceive computers as social actors, even if they know that the machine has no feelings or intentions [8]. In this context, when computers have cues related to human behavior, people unconsciously or autonomously apply human social rules to their interactions with computers, such as norms of politeness and personality responses [9]. It has been shown that users develop a sense of social presence when interacting with anthropomorphic virtual machine agents. Even a few anthropomorphic cues can trigger an individual's sense of social presence and social norms, which in turn prompts the user to display behaviors and reactions similar to those in human-to-human interactions.

Government trust is the focus of this study. In the field of government trust research, Institutional Performance Theory and Social Capital Theory are the two dominant explanatory theories. The difference between these two theories is that Institutional Performance Theory focused on the performance of the government, while the social capital theory emphasizes the importance of socio-cultural context and public participation. According to the context of our research, we prefer to adopt Institutional Performance Theory. Institutional performance theory argues that government trust stems from the public's perception and rational assessment of government governance performance or institutional performance [10]. The level of government trust depends not only on objective institutional performance such as economic growth and government transparency, but also on subjective perceptions such as public satisfaction with public services and a sense of political efficacy. However, whether emphasizing objective institutional performance or the impact of subjective feelings of performance on government trust, institutional performance theory stresses the endogenous nature of government trust, emphasizing that government trust comes from the results of the government system's own operation, and that the public's choice of trusting or distrusting the government is based on rational calculations.

3.2 The Effect of Anthropomorphism of Government Q&A Robot on Government Trust

According to Social Response Theory, when interacting with robots, people automatically or unconsciously perceive the computer as a social actor, even if they know that the machine has no feelings or intentions. It has been noted that if people perceive intelligent robots to be more similar to people, they will have more positive attitudes towards them and develop positive emotions, which in turn increase user trust and satisfaction. Further research has found that the anthropomorphic characteristics of robots can generate spillover effects, which can help increase users' attitudes and emotional connection towards the websites or brands represented by the robots. For users in the governmental domain, highly anthropomorphic Q&A robots may also be associated with the level of digitization and intelligence of government services. Therefore, this study hypothesizes that highly anthropomorphic government Q&A robots in the governmental domain also help increase users' trust in the governmental agencies represented by the robots. Drawing on Du Fan and Wu Xuanna's [11] categorization, this study refines government trust into cognitive trust and emotional trust in government.

H1 The degree of anthropomorphism of government Q&A robots positively affects users' trust in government.

H1a The degree of anthropomorphism of government Q&A robots positively affects users' cognitive trust in government.

H1b The degree of anthropomorphism of government Q&A robots positively affects users' emotional trust in government.

3.3   The Mediating Role of Government Affinity Perception

Highly anthropomorphic service robots can give users a stronger desire to engage with them and bring them closer to the psychological distance between them and the robot [12]. This study hypothesizes that this effect can also apply to the relationship between the user and the government that provides the government Q&A robots, e.g., increasing the sense of closeness with the government. Drawing on existing research, this paper introduces the concept of government affinity perception. Government affinity perception refers to the degree to which a user perceives that the government exhibits characteristics such as enthusiasm and efficiency in government services and develops an affinity with the government on a psychological level. We infer that anthropomorphic government Q&A robots can evoke users' perception of government affinity and thus enhance trust in the government. Therefore, based on the above analyses, this study proposes the following hypotheses:

H2 Government affinity perception mediates the relationship between anthropomorphism level and government trust.
H2a Government affinity perception mediates the relationship between anthropomorphism level and government cognitive trust.
H2b Government affinity perception mediates the relationship between the degree of anthropomorphism and government emotional trust.

3.4   The Moderating Role of Service Result Valence

According to institutional performance theory, public trust in government depends on the perceived performance of public services. When users interact with government Q&A robots, they often want to obtain information or get help, so whether the robots can solve problems is what users focus on, which will largely affect their performance perception of government services. In interviews with consumers, Deng Shichang et al. [13] found that the inability of AI robots to practically solve the user's problems can lead to a poor experience. In the existing anthropomorphism literature, many scholars have examined the impact of anthropomorphism based on the context of robot service success, and some scholars have also focused on the role of anthropomorphism in the context of service failure [14], but the existing studies tend to focus on only one of the scenarios of success or failure, and very few studies have examined both the success and failure scenarios of the service from an integrated perspective. For these two different service result contexts, users' information processing and perception may differ, thus affecting the identification, perception, and subsequent role of anthropomorphic cues. Therefore, this study introduces service result valence as a moderating variable to examine the differences in anthropomorphic influence on positive and negative outcomes. Synthesizing the above analyses, this study proposes the following hypotheses:

H3 Service result valence moderates the effect of anthropomorphism degree on government trust.
H3a Service result valence moderates the effect of anthropomorphism degree on government cognitive trust; in the positive outcome, anthropomorphism degree of government Q&A robots does not have a significant effect on government cognitive trust; in the

negative outcome, high anthropomorphism degree of government Q&A robots is more likely to enhance users' government cognitive trust.

H3b Service result valence moderates the effect of anthropomorphism degree on government emotional trust; under positive outcome, anthropomorphism degree of government Q&A robots has no significant effect on government emotional trust; under negative outcome, high anthropomorphism degree of government Q&A robots is more able to enhance users' emotional trust in government.

3.5   The Moderating Role of Authoritarianism Obeys Personality

When studying the cognitive formation of users, it is important not to ignore the differences between individual traits. It has been pointed out that intrinsic personality and extrinsic environmental variables affect their political awareness tendencies and political attitudes. The anthropomorphism of the government Q&A robot belongs to the extrinsic environmental variables, so the intrinsic personality is also an indispensable variable in the study of the formation of government trust. It has been pointed out that authoritarianism obeys personality is one of the important variables in the study of the relationship between public and government trust. Individuals with an authoritarianism obeys personality usually exhibit authority over law, adhere to traditional values and concepts, and are not allowed to express dissatisfaction with authority [15]. Therefore, the stronger the authoritarianism obeys personality, the more subconsciously one identifies with the current authoritative government, i.e., the higher the level of trust in the government, and the less sensitive this trust is to changes in the external environment. Based on this, the present study hypothesizes that the effect of anthropomorphism level on trust in government is likely to be moderated by the moderating effect of authoritarianism obeys personality. This study proposes the following hypothesis:

H4 Authoritarianism obeys personality moderates the effect of the degree of anthropomorphism on government trust.

H4a Authoritarianism obeys personality moderates the effect of anthropomorphism degree on government cognitive trust; for high authoritarianism obeys personality, anthropomorphism degree of government Q&A robots has no significant effect on government cognitive trust; for low authoritarianism obeys personality, high anthropomorphism degree of government Q&A robots is more likely to enhance users' government cognitive trust.

H4b Authoritarianism obeys personality moderates the effect of anthropomorphism degree on government emotional trust; for high authoritarianism obeys personality, the anthropomorphism degree of government Q&A robots has no significant effect on government emotional trust; for low authoritarianism obeys personality, government Q&A robots with high anthropomorphism degree are more able to enhance users' emotional trust in the government.

Based on the above assumptions, the research model of this paper is constructed as shown in Fig. 1.

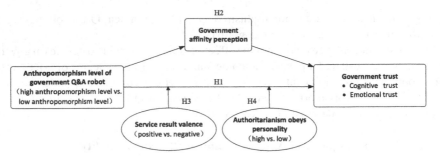

Fig. 1. A research model to study the effect of anthropomorphism level of government Q&A robot on government trust.

4 Research Design and Experimental Validation

4.1 Pre-experiment: Anthropomorphic Manipulation Design and Effect

This study chooses to manipulate it in a "picture"-based way, focusing on "ID card processing process consulting" as a common government affairs consulting topic, and designing different levels of anthropomorphic dialogue interfaces between the government Q&A robot and the user. This study recruits 80 subjects to participate in an online contextual experiment through the "Credamo" platform. First, the subjects are randomly divided into two groups, with one group browsing high-form anthropomorphic manipulation materials and the other browsing low-form anthropomorphic manipulation materials. Next, the subjects are asked to fill out an experimental questionnaire, which consists of four anthropomorphism measurement questions of the government Q&A robot and personal information.

A total of 78 valid samples are obtained in the pre-experiment. The internal consistency coefficient of the anthropomorphism measurement scale is greater than 0.7, indicating a high degree of inter-question agreement. An independent-samples t-test is used in this study, which shows that the anthropomorphic manipulation approach in the pre-experiment is valid and that it can be used in subsequent formal experiments.

4.2 Experiment 1: Main Effect of Degree of Anthropomorphism and the Mediating Effect of Government Affinity Perception

In Experiment 1, a one-way (high vs. low anthropomorphism) between-groups design is used to recruit 80 subjects from the "Credamo" platform. The first part of the formal experiment consists of randomly dividing the subjects into two groups and then subjecting them to the same anthropomorphic manipulation as in the pre-experiment. In the second part, the subjects are asked to imagine that they are a college student who has just come to the city A for employment and needs to apply for a new ID card in A after moving their household registration to A. They then ask the intelligent Q&A robot on the government service platform of A about the current process of applying for an ID card; then, the subjects will see a screenshot of their dialogue with the Q&A robot. The third part is to fill in the experimental questionnaire, which includes four anthropomorphism measures, two government affinity perception measures, three government cognitive trust measures, three government emotional trust measures and personal information.

A total of 69 valid samples are eventually obtained for Experiment 1. The internal consistency coefficients for all measurement scales are greater than 0.7. Firstly, Experiment 1 still tests the validity of the anthropomorphism manipulation. Secondly, an independent-samples t-test is used to verify the effect of anthropomorphism level on trust in government, which shows that compared to the low anthropomorphism group, users in the high anthropomorphism group have higher cognitive trust in government ($M_{high\ anthropomorphism}$ = 6.11, SD = 0.62; $M_{low\ anthropomorphism}$ = 5.23, SD = 0.95; t = 4.546, p < 0.001), and their emotional trust is also higher ($M_{high\ anthropomorphism\ level}$ = 5.91, SD = 0.81; $M_{low\ anthropomorphism\ level}$ = 5.28, SD = 1.03; t = 2.781, p = 0.007 < 0.01); the effect of anthropomorphism level on the perceived affinity for the government is also validated, with users in the high anthropomorphism group generating higher perceptions of affinity for the government than those in the low anthropomorphism group ($M_{high\ anthropomorphism}$ = 5.75, SD = 1.01; $M_{low\ anthropomorphism}$ = 4.40, SD = 1.34; t = 4.702, p < 0.001). Next, in order to verify the mediating effect of government affinity perception, the Bootstrap method is chosen for this study. The results show that the indirect effect of anthropomorphism degree on government cognitive trust through government affinity perception is significant (β = 0.137, [0.019,0.267]), and the direct effect is significant (β = 0.187, [0.013,0.361]), which indicates that government affinity perception produces a partial mediating effect; and that the degree of anthropomorphism has a significant indirect effect on the emotional trust of the government through the perception of government affinity (β = 0.236, [0.109,0.389]), and the direct effect is not significant (β = 0.089, [−0.091,0.269]), indicating that the perception of government affinity produces a complete mediating effect.

4.3 Experiment 2: Moderating Effects of Service Result Valence

In Experiment 2, a 2 (anthropomorphism level: high vs. low) x 2 (service result valence: positive vs. negative) two-factor between-groups experimental design is used, and 160 subjects are recruited from the "Credamo" platform. In the first part of the main experiment, all subjects are randomly assigned to two groups, and the same anthropomorphic manipulation as in the pre-experiment is performed on the subjects; next, the two groups are subdivided into two groups, and the subjects are set up with the scenarios of successful and unsuccessful service outcomes. The second part of the main experiment is for the subjects to imagine that they are a college student who has just come to the city A for employment, recently intends to apply for a passport in order to facilitate overseas travel, so asks the intelligent Q&A robot of the city A's government service platform about the current process of applying for a passport; the subject is then shown a screenshot of the complete dialogue between himself/herself and the Q&A robot. The third part of the main experiment is to fill out the questionnaire, which contains the same anthropomorphism, government affinity perception, government cognitive trust, and affective trust measurements of the government intelligent Q&A robot as in the previous experiments, one service outcome validity measurement, one situational imagery difficulty measurement, and personal information.

Experiment 2 ends up with a total of 136 valid samples. The internal consistency coefficients for all measurement scales are greater than 0.7. First, Experiment 2 tests the validity of the manipulation. Second, Experiment 2 again verifies the main effect of anthropomorphism level on government trust and the mediating effect of government affinity perception. Finally, the moderating effect of service result valence on the relationship between the degree of anthropomorphism and government trust is tested. A two-way ANOVA is used to test the interaction between service result valence and anthropomorphic degree on government trust, and the results show that the main effects of anthropomorphic degree and service result valence on cognitive trust and emotional trust of the government are both significant; and the interaction effect of anthropomorphic degree*service result valence is significant on cognitive trust of the government ($F = 8.90, p = 0.003 < 0.01$), and the interaction effect on emotional trust of the government is equally significant ($F = 9.34, p = 0.003 < 0.01$).

Further simple effects analyses show that under the positive outcome, the government cognitive trust for users in the high and low anthropomorphism group is 5.93 and 5.68 respectively, and the simple effect of anthropomorphism on cognitive trust is not significant ($F = 0.86, p = 0.355 > 0.05$); the government emotional trust for users in the high and low anthropomorphism group is 5.99 and 5.74 respectively, and the simple effect of anthropomorphism on emotional trust is not significant ($F = 0.73, p = 0.395 > 0.05$). Under the negative outcome, users in the high anthropomorphism group have significantly higher cognitive trust ($M_{high\ anthropomorphism} = 4.59$) than those in the low anthropomorphism group ($M_{low\ anthropomorphism} = 3.21$), and the simple effect of anthropomorphism on cognitive trust is significant; users in the high anthropomorphism group have significantly higher government emotional trust ($M_{high\ anthropomorphism} = 4.73$) than those in the low anthropomorphism group ($M_{low\ anthropomorphism} = 3.21$), and the simple effect of anthropomorphism on emotional trust is significant.

4.4 Experiment 3: Moderating Effects of Authoritarianism Obeys Personality

Experiment 3 is a one-way (anthropomorphism: high vs. low) between-groups design, in which a measure of the psychological value of authoritarianism obeys personality is included in the experiment. A total of 160 subjects are recruited from the "Credamo" platform. The first part of the main experiment consists of randomly dividing all subjects into two experimental groups and then subjecting them to the same anthropomorphic manipulation as in the pre-experiment. The second part of the main experiment is for the subjects to imagine that they have moved their household registration to the new city M because of their work, and they need to apply for a new ID card in M. They then ask the intelligent Q&A robot of the M city's government service platform for advice on the process of applying for an ID card now; next, the subjects will be presented with a screenshot of the dialogue between themselves and the Q&A robot. The third part of the main experiment is for the subjects to fill out a questionnaire, which includes the same anthropomorphism level of the Q&A robot, government affinity perception, cognitive trust, government affective trust, and situational imagery difficulty measurement questions as in the previous experiments, the four authoritarianism obeys personality measurement items, and personal information.

Experiment 3 ends up with a total of 117 valid samples. The internal consistency coefficients for all measurement scales are greater than 0.7. First, Experiment 3 tests the validity of the anthropomorphism manipulation again. Second, Experiment 3 continues to validate the effect of anthropomorphism level on government trust and the mediating effect of government affinity perception. Again, the moderating effect of authoritarianism obeys personality is tested. The average of the four measures of authoritarianism obeys personality is taken as the score of authoritarianism obeys personality, and the samples with scores above the median are classified as the high authoritarianism obeys personality group, and those below the median are regarded as the low authoritarianism obeys personality group. Finally, a two-way ANOVA is also used to test the interaction of authoritarianism obeys personality and anthropomorphism level on government trust. The results show that the main effect of degree of anthropomorphism and authoritarianism obeys personality on government cognitive trust is significant ($F_{degree\ of\ anthropomorphism} = 17.16, p < 0.001; F_{authoritarianism\ obeys\ personality} = 26.07, p < 0.001$) respectively and the interaction effect of degree of anthropomorphism* authoritarianism obeys personality on government cognitive trust is significant ($F = 4.498, p = 0.036 < 0.05$); the main effects of degree of anthropomorphism and authoritarianism obeys personality are significant on emotional trust ($F_{degree\ of\ anthropomorphism} = 22.50, p < 0.001; F_{authoritarianism\ obeys\ personality} = 32.48, p < 0.001$) respectively, but the interaction term of degree of anthropomorphism * authoritarianism obeys personality is not significant for government emotional trust ($F = 2.047, p = 0.155 > 0.05$).

Simple effect analyses of anthropomorphism and authoritarianism obeys personality on government cognitive trust show that for high authoritarianism obeys personality, the simple effect of anthropomorphism on government cognitive trust is not significant ($M_{high\ anthropomorphism} = 6.01, SE = 0.18; M_{low\ anthropomorphism} = 5.70, SE = 0.18; F = 2.02, p = 0.158 > 0.05$); for low authoritarianism obeys personality, the simple effect of anthropomorphism on government cognitive trust is significant ($M_{high\ anthropomorphism} = 5.53, SE = 0.18; M_{low\ anthropomorphism} = 4.40, SE = 0.18; F = 19.79, p < 0.001$). Thus, the moderating effect of authoritarianism obeys personality on the relationship between anthropomorphism and government cognitive trust is validated. In addition, there is no moderating effect of authoritarianism obeys personality between anthropomorphism and emotional trust, as the interaction effect between anthropomorphism and authoritarianism obeys personality on government emotional trust is not significant.

5   Discussion of the Results

The results of Experiment 1 validate H1 and H2. First, the results demonstrate that a high degree of anthropomorphism enhances users' cognitive trust and emotional trust. Second, the mediation test reveals the mechanism by which the degree of anthropomorphism affects government trust. Government affinity perception partially mediates the effect of anthropomorphism degree on cognitive trust and fully mediates the effect of anthropomorphism degree on emotional trust. Therefore, compared with the cognitive trust, government affinity perception occupies a stronger dominant role in the process of anthropomorphism promoting the formation of emotional trust.

The results of Experiment 2 verifies H3, and also again verifies H1 and H2. When the service outcome is positive, there is no significant difference between the effects of high and low anthropomorphism on cognitive trust and emotional trust in the government; and when the service outcome is negative, high anthropomorphism enhances the cognitive trust and emotional trust of the users more than low anthropomorphism.

The results of Experiment 3 partially support H4, i.e., H4a is valid, but H4b is not. Experiment 3 also again tests H1 and H2. The results of Experiment 3 indicate that authoritarianism obeys personality plays a moderating role in the relationship between anthropomorphism degree and cognitive trust, but not significantly in the relationship between anthropomorphism degree and emotional trust in government. Specifically, for high authoritarianism obeys personality, there is no significant difference between the effects of high and low anthropomorphism degree on government cognitive trust; for low authoritarianism obeys personality, high anthropomorphism degree is more effective than low anthropomorphism degree in enhancing users' government cognitive trust. For both high and low authoritarianism obeys personalities, a high anthropomorphism level can significantly enhance users' emotional trust in the government.

6 Conclusion

This study focuses on the impact of anthropomorphism degree of government Q&A robots on government trust, firstly, based on literature combing and analysis, summarizing the results and shortcomings of existing research and determining the research idea of this paper; secondly, combining theory and existing research to put forward relevant research hypotheses and constructing an empirical research model; lastly, one pre-experiment and three formal experiments are carried out using context manipulation experiments to verify the research hypotheses. This study shows that the anthropomorphism degree of government Q&A robot positively affects government trust, and that the government affinity perception plays a mediating role in this process; that the service result valence moderates the relationship between the anthropomorphism degree of government Q&A robot and government trust; and that the authoritarianism obeys personality moderates the relationship between the anthropomorphism level of government Q&A robot and cognitive trust in government, but doesn't moderate the relationship between anthropomorphism level and emotional trust in government. Our findings not only make a meaningful contribution to the theoretical development of anthropomorphism and government trust research, but also provide valuable suggestions for the product design of government Q&A robots, effective ways of guiding the public by government administrations, as well as policy formulation.

Although this paper has done a lot of work to ensure the accuracy and scientificity of the study, due to the researcher's own ability and the limited reality of the conditions, there are still some shortcomings in this paper. In terms of research objects, this paper mainly explores the virtual, text-based, intelligent Q&A robots, but there are still some other types of intelligent Q&A robots, which can be further explored in the future. In addition, in terms of data acquisition, although this study uses contextual descriptions plus dialogue pictures to simulate as much as possible the usage scenarios of governmental intelligent Q&A bots, it still doesn't quite match the real-life usage scenarios. Therefore, future research can optimize the design of the experimental scene and use technical means to build a more simulated experimental environment.

References

1. Dahiya, M.: A tool of conversation: chatbot. Int. J. Comput. Sci. Eng. **5**(5), 158–161 (2017)
2. Ni, K., Liu, X., Liang, W.: Digital access and local government trust: is contact an effective way to improve trust? J. Econ. **9**(04), 216–242 (2022). (in Chinese)
3. David, D., Hayotte, M., Thérouanne, P., d'Arripe-Longueville, F., Milhabet, I.: Development and validation of a social robot anthropomorphism scale (SRA) in a french sample. Int. J. Hum Comput Stud. **162**, 102802 (2022)
4. Murtarelli, G., Gregory, A., Romenti, S.: A conversation-based perspective for shaping ethical human–machine interactions: the particular challenge of chatbots. J. Bus. Res. **129**, 927–935 (2021)
5. Seo, S.: When female (male) robot is talking to me: effect of service robots' gender and anthropomorphism on customer satisfaction. Int. J. Hosp. Manag. **102**, 103166 (2022)
6. Zhang, Y., Wang, Y.: A research on the influence mechanism of anthropomorphic service robots on consumer usage intention: the moderating effect of social class. Foreign Econ. Manag. **44**(03), 3–18 (2022). (in Chinese)
7. Morgeson, F.V., III., VanAmburg, D., Mithas, S.: Misplaced trust? exploring the structure of the e-government-citizen trust relationship. J. Public Adm. Res. Theory **21**(2), 257–283 (2011)
8. Nass, C., Moon, Y.: Machines and mindlessness: social responses to computers. J. Soc. Issues **56**(1), 81–103 (2000)
9. Epley, N., Waytz, A., Cacioppo, J.: On seeing human: a three-factor theory of anthropomorphism. Psychol. Rev. **114**(4), 864–886 (2007)
10. Mishler, W., Rose, R.: What are the origins of political trust? testing institutional and cultural theories in post-communist societies. Comp. Pol. Stud. **34**(1), 30–62 (2001)
11. Du, F., Wu, X.: The influence of procedural justice and uncertainty on acceptance of public policy: the mediating effect of affective trust and cognitive trust. Psychol. Sci. **40**(02), 448–454 (2017). (in Chinese)
12. Li, X., Sung, Y.: Anthropomorphism brings us closer: the mediating role of psychological distance in User–AI assistant interactions. Comput. Hum. Behav. **118**, 106680 (2021)
13. Deng, S., Tian, Q., Lin, X.: The emotional competency model and measurement index for artificial intelligence in customer service. J. Shanghai Univ. Int. Bus. Econ. **27**(04), 100–110 (2020). (in Chinese)
14. Wang, H., Xie, T., Zhan, C.: When service failed: the detrimental effect of anthropomorphism on intelligent customer service agent avatar - Disgust as mediation. Nankai Manag. Rev. **24**(04), 194–206 (2021). (in Chinese)
15. Altemeyer, B.: The authoritarians. Winnipeg (2007)

Research on the Evolutionary Analysis of Online Public Opinion Reversal Events Based on Social Combustion Theory

Ke Dong[1], Feiyang Yuan[2], and Jiachun Wu[1(✉)]

[1] Research Institute for Data Management and Innovation, Nanjing University, Suzhou 215163, China
hdu_wjc@163.com

[2] School of Information Management, Wuhan University, Wuhan 430072, China

Abstract. [Purpose] By constructing an improved model of online public opinion reversal events, we explore the evolutionary pattern with reversal attributes in multiple dimensions, and provide practical support for relevant public opinion governance. [Methodology] This research is based on the social combustion theory, which will map to the sentiment, opinion leader and theme of the opinion reversal event from three perspectives of combustion materials, combustion agents and ignition temperature, to further select the Hu Xinyu incident for empirical research. [Results] The results show that the interaction of opinion leaders' influence, theme changes and netizens' emotional confrontation leads to the continuous "combustion" of public opinion reversal events, and jointly advances the evolution of public opinion. Opinion leaders play the role of "accelerant" in the incident, and good media can promote the positive development of netizens' emotions. [Conclusions] Facing the reversal of public opinion, the mainstream media should take up the main responsibility in the process of public opinion management and promote the maximization of the impact of effective information; netizens should make rational judgement and voices on public opinion, trust the government, and maintain a positive mindset.

Keywords: Online Public Opinion · Opinion Reversal · Incident Evolution · Social Combustion Theory

1 Introduction

Reversal events, as a special type of online events, are characterized by the fact that netizens' discussions will culminate and change direction repeatedly through event's progress. Public sentiment is susceptible to redundant information in various media, especially undesirable media, which creates ambiguous perceptions [1]. During changes in reversal events, public sentiment is prone to more intense emotional confrontation and cyber violence, because news facts fail to make a timely appearance resulting in a proliferation of false information and a gradual loss of control of public opinion [2]. Hence, it is of great practical significance for public governance to explore the evolutionary characteristics and laws of public opinion reversal events.

© The Author(s), under exclusive license to Springer Nature Switzerland AG 2024
Y. P. Tu and M. Chi (Eds.): WHICEB 2024, LNBIP 515, pp. 110–119, 2024.
https://doi.org/10.1007/978-3-031-60264-1_10

Few studies have taken into account the influence of opinion leaders on netizen sentiment, despite the fact that previous research has examined the evolution of public opinion based on the social combustion theory and has introduced the themes of netizen sentiment and events. This paper puts the emotions, events, and themes of public opinion reversal events to the three elements of "combustion substance," "accelerant," and "ignition temperature" in social combustion theory, and then introduces the multi-dimensional evolution model based on inter-sequence when opinion leaders are constructed, before selecting the Hu Xinyu event for empirical analysis and making targeted recommendations.

2 Literature Review

In instances of public opinion reversal, the distorted reporting of undesirable media not only impedes the search for the truth of the incident, but also further aggravates the public's emotions, which can easily lead to the direction of public opinion deviating from the right track [3]. In the post-truth era, the study of public opinion reversal events has received extensive attention from scholars. Scholars chose the theme of the public opinion reversal event, the dynamics of official releases and public psychology as the features of the evolution mechanism of public opinion reversal, and simulated and modelled them [4, 5]. Scholars mainly use the infectious disease model [5, 6] and social combustion theory [7] to simulate the evolutionary path of public opinion reversal events. In research on the governance of public opinion reversal events, scholars have proposed that public opinion governance should continuously strengthen platform regulation, encourage the media to adhere to the industry's responsibility, and strengthen public awareness [8, 9].

To sum up, the content aspects of current research on opinion reversal events ignore the function of opinion leaders in influencing the direction of public opinion and arousing the public' emotions, and instead concentrate on the public level. Current research on reversal events lacks a sentiment corpus suitable for analyzing public opinion, and existing techniques primarily use quantitative word frequency features and do not recognize variables at the semantic level.

3 Research Design

Public opinion reversal event is the intervention of a reversal event in the process of public opinion evolution, resulting in the views and emotions of different netizens tending to develop in the opposite direction [10]. This research classifies the stages of public opinion reversal events according to their reversal points, and further studies the mechanism of public opinion generation and the synergistic evolution from the three elements of social combustion theory. Owing to the contradictions and conflicting views of netizens can be visualized as emotional confrontation over the same event, this study analogizes the " sentiment" as the "combustion materials"; and further introduces the intentional guidance of public opinion by the media, especially the opinion leaders, as " combustion agent"; as the theme of the public opinion reflects the event's connotation, this study regards " event theme" as " ignition temperature". Based on the improved model (see Fig. 1), this article intends to select typical reversal events and analyze the multi-attribute characteristics and evolution trends of opinion leaders, event themes and emotional confrontation at each stage, revealing the synergistic evolution law of public opinion reversal events.

Fig. 1. Evolutionary Analysis Model of Public Opinion Reversal Events Based on Social Combustion Theory

3.1 Research Methods

Analysis of Opinion Leaders. Online opinion leaders, as the intermediate link between media information and influence, can guide the formation of users' opinions [11]. Opinion leader analysis helps to improve the accuracy of opinion research and judgement. This paper achieves multi-stage opinion leader influence assessment by applying an improved opinion leader evaluation system [12], which assigns weights to parameters such as the number of fans, retweets, comments and likes.

Analysis of Theme. Public opinion events' themes react to the focus of netizens' attention. As LDA can achieve good topic feature extraction for texts with high similarity and poor differentiation under the same event, this paper applies the topic model to identify multiple topics for the development of public opinion events, and further uses the perplexity to determine the optimal number of topics. The perplexity calculation formula is as follows:

$$perplexity(D) = \exp\left(-\frac{\sum \log p(w)}{\sum_{d=1}^{M} N_d}\right)$$

$$p(w) = p(w/t) * p(t/d)$$

where d denotes a document, the denominator is the total length of all unit words of the document, p(w) denotes the probability that a feature word occurs, p(w/t) denotes the probability that a feature word occurs in a topic, and p(t/d) denotes the probability that a topic occurs in a document.

Analysis of Emotional. Sentiment analysis helps to explore the mindset of public groups on specific topics [13]. The Snow-NLP tool has defects such as poor generalization ability and failure to consider semantic features, therefore, this paper proposes to combine Word2vec and Bi-LSTM for sentiment analysis. The Word2vec is able o achieve more accurate semantic similarity expression. The Bi-LSTM model is able to improve the gradient disappearance problem triggered by the increase of the number of layers in the network. It can be seen that the complementary characteristics of the two models fit the processing requirements of our dataset very well.

3.2 Data Collection and Processing

The "Hu Xinyu" incident attracted widespread attention from the news media in late 2022. It started with the strange disappearance of Hu Xinyu at school, and netizens' failure to make progress on the case for a long time led to heated discussions on social media, mainly attacking the school's concealment behavior and the police's lack of competence, and even pushed public opinion to the brink of loss of control at one point. The public opinion was later calmed down when the truth was clarified at a press conference. In the "Hu Xinyu" incident, netizens' emotions are intense, the sensitivity of the subject is high, the investigation cycle is long, and the public opinion of the incident is reversed in the process. Hence, this paper chooses this public event as the research object, collects the contents and comments of the related microblogs, and obtains 29,210 microblogs after cleaning. The fields of this research dataset including user's ID, microblog text, time, retweet number, comment's number and text.

3.3 Public Opinion Life Cycle

This research integrates the Baidu index of the "Hu Xinyu" incident, combines manual interpretation, and initially obtains the two-stage reversal characteristics of public opinion of the incident, and further fits the "bimodal" propagation model of network information [14], dividing the incident cycle into: beginning stage (November 21, 2022-January 28, 2023), outbreak stage (January 29, 2023), first decline stage (January 30, 2023-February 2, 2023), second outbreak stage (February 2, 2023), second decline stage (February 3, 2023-February 6, 2023), and calming stage (February 7, 2023-February 12, 2023). As shown in Fig. 2, we find that the causes of the two peaks are "Hu Xinyu's body was found" and "Hu Xinyu's press conference". As the revelation of the truth of the incident made the public opinion space rational return, point E as the public opinion reversal point of the incident, after the reversal of the public opinion heat gradually calmed down.

4 Results Analysis

4.1 Analysis of Opinion Leaders

This paper, based on existing experience, assigns values to the number of retweets, comments, likes, and blogger followers of microblogs: in 0.25, 0.25, 0.125, and 0.375 [12], calculates the influence of opinion leaders at each stage, and takes the top ten to be analyzed.

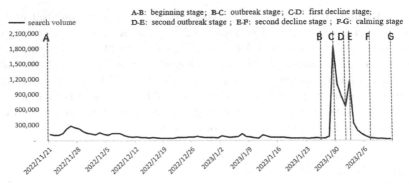

Fig. 2. The Life Cycle Stages of Internet Public Opinion on the "Hu Xinyu Incident"

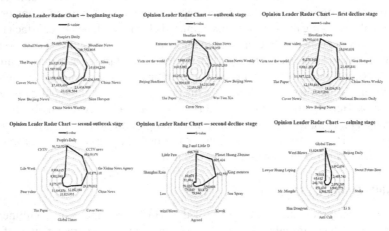

Fig. 3. Radar Chart of Opinion Leaders' Influence at Various Stages of Public Opinion Reversal Events

As depicted in Fig. 3, it could be seen that there are large differences in the opinion leaders corresponding to each stage. Overall, mainstream media occupy the foci of influence, they have professional reporting power, are trusted by the public and have wide influence. Furthermore, there are many relatively less influential self-media outlets among the opinion leaders. It is evident that public opinion is influenced by both mainstream media and self-published media, and its governance should rightly be shared by both.

4.2 Evolution Analysis of Theme

Under the influence of significant public opinion events, the content of the topics discussed at each stage of public opinion has been continuously fluctuating and changing. With instinctive concern for the life of a teenager, netizens have continued to pay attention to and follow up on the disappearance of Hu Xinyu. By determining the optimal number of themes for each stage, this paper further lists the high-frequency words under each theme (see Table 1).

Table 1. Distribution of thematic feature words at each stage of public opinion reversal events

Developmental stage	Topics	Feature words
Beginning stage	TopicI-1	Hope, Find, Child, Concern
	TopicI-2	Tape recorders, Organs, Playgrounds
	TopicI-3	Video, Search, Rescue, Police
	TopicI-4	Surveillance, School, Disappearance
Outbreak stage	TopicII-1	Death, Found, Results
	TopicII-2	Blessings, Children, Hope, Students
	TopicII-3	Search, School, Corpse
	TopicII-4	Truth, Forensics, Blessings, Tape recorders
First decline stage	TopicIII-1	Truth, Hope, Expectation, Concern
	TopicIII-2	Warehouses, Discoveries, Woods, Granaries
	TopicIII-3	Media, Press, Families
Second outbreak stage	TopicIV-1	Children, Parents, Mental Health, Teenagers
	TopicIV-2	Corpse, Work, Search
	TopicIV-3	Deceased, RIP, Surveillance, Granary
	TopicIV-4	Conspiracy, Disinformation, Media, Truth
Second decline stage	TopicV-1	Police, Suicide, Truth, chool
	TopicV-2	Children, Psychology, Parents, Teachers
	TopicV-3	Parents, Teachers, Depression, Blessings
Calming stage	TopicVI-1	Media, Disinformation, Punishment
	TopicVI-2	Truth, Officials Launch
	TopicVI-3	News, Account, Disposition

Table 1 shows that: in the beginning stage, the themes included rumors and police actions, with netizens not knowing the truth and having diverse opinions. In the outbreak stage, the themes include the discovery of the body, the police's ineffective handling of the case, intense discussions among netizens, and an increase in rumors. In the first recession stage, themes include suspicions about the case, existing findings. In the second outbreak stage, themes included the release of the truth and clarification of doubts, netizens' focus shifted from the incident itself to the mental health of the youth, and the discussion of psychological issues brought the heat of the incident to its peak once again. In the second recession stage, the theme focused on the psychological education of teenagers, and netizens gradually returned to rationality. In the calming phase, the theme included rumor accounts and media, and netizens condemned the behavior of some bad media for eating "human blood buns". Moreover, this paper finds that a portion of the themes run through multiple stages, which indicates their continuous concern. Relevant management departments can summarize the key points of netizens' concerns accordingly and take reasonable diversionary measures.

4.3 Evolution Analysis of Emotional

This paper statistics on the proportion of the public' sentiment tendency in each stage (see Fig. 4). Netizens' sentiments were stable before the second outbreak. Netizens' negative emotions accounted for about 1/3 of the total, due to the long investigation and the misleading of the bad media which made the negative emotions rise in the public opinion space, and the negative text's viewpoints were focused on the dissatisfaction with the police work, with remarks such as "it feels like a show", on the other hand, there were fewer positive emotions, about 20%, which were mainly the prayers for the family members of the person concerned. Netizens' neutral sentiments were often characterized by doubts and discussions about the case, such as "why no case was filed". With the convening of the press conference and the clarification of the truth, the "Hu Xinyu" incident has ushered in a second outburst of public opinion. Netizens' positive sentiments rose 2.41 times, and related microblogs began to express trust in officials and gradually focused on the youth mental health issues. In the second decline stage when the content of Hu Xinyu's recordings was disclosed, netizens' positive sentiment peaked as opinion leaders called for the care of young people's mental health. In the calming stage, netizens were extremely dissatisfied with the disposition and punishment of the rumour-mongering media announced by the Internet Information Office, and demanded that the punishment be increased, causing the proportion of negative sentiment expressed in the relevant microblogs to rise to 48.1%. However, as the case came to an end, the public gradually withdrew from the centre of public opinion on the incident, and the whole public opinion reversal incident came to an end.

Developmental stage	Proportion of negative emotions	Proportion of Neutral Emotions	Proportion of Positive Emotions
Beginning stage	29.37%	56.23%	14.40%
Outbreak stage	30.63%	55.13%	14.24%
first decline stage	31.24%	56.41%	12.35%
second outbreak stage	30.75%	40.11%	29.14%
second decline stage	29.49%	41.32%	29.19%
calming stage	48.13%	43.48%	8.39%

Fig. 4. Distribution of Public Sentiment at Various Stages of Public Opinion Reversal Events

4.4 Co-evolution Analysis

This research, combined with the social combustion theory, finds that the spread and reversal of the "Hu Xinyu" incident is influenced by the interaction of opinion leaders, event themes, and netizens' emotions, so this paper analyses the synergistic evolution of opinion leaders, event themes, and netizens' emotions, and obtains Fig. 5 and Fig. 6. The opinion leaders, such as Headline News and China News, provided timely reports after the outbreak of the incident (in Fig. 5), promoting effective information to play a positive role, and prompting netizens' positive emotions to rebound and outweigh the negative emotions. While Sina, Global Times, and Beijing Daily failed to fulfil their responsibilities in order to bring up the tempo, which triggered the rise of negative sentiments among netizens. We find that opinion leaders contribute to the polarization of netizens' sentiments and exacerbate the potential danger of "burning" when public opinion is constantly erupting.

Developmental Stage	Opinion leaders	Negative emotional ratio	Neutral emotion ratio	Positive emotion ratio
beginning stage	People's Daily	30%	58%	12%
	Headline News	28%	53%	19%
outbreak stage	Headline News	16%	61%	23%
	China News	16%	51%	33%
first decline stage	Headline News	24%	38%	38%
	Sina	36%	52%	12%
second outbreak stage	People's Daily	21%	37%	42%
	CCTV news	35%	36%	29%
second decline stage	Big J and Little D	8%	31%	61%
	Planet Huang Zhixian	8%	34%	58%
calming stage	Global Times	52%	44%	4%
	Beijing Daily	56%	36%	8%

Fig. 5. Public Sentiment Distribution of Opinion Leaders at Various Stages of Opinion Reversal Events

In Fig. 6, this study finds that social events stimulate conflicts in cyberspace and trigger emotional confrontation among netizens. In the beginning stage, the proportion of positive emotions within the topics of the "Hu Xinyu" incident, such as the police's ineffective handling of the case (Topic I-3), "Disappearance" (Topic I-4), and "Organ trading" (Topic I-2), was less than 10%. In the first outbreak stage, topics such as "human remains discovery" (Topic II-1) pushed the proportion of positive sentiment to 35%. In the first decline stage, the distribution of sentiment varies greatly among different topics, with "pursuing the truth" tending to be positive, "searching" tending to be neutral,

Developmental stage	Topic	Proportion of negative emotions	Proportion of Neutral Emotions	Proportion of Positive Emotions
Beginning stage	TopicI-1	21%	28%	51%
	TopicI-2	33%	59%	8%
	TopicI-3	37%	58%	5%
	TopicI-4	28%	66%	6%
Outbreak stage	TopicII-1	28%	59%	13%
	TopicII-2	31%	52%	17%
	TopicII-3	29%	61%	10%
	TopicII-4	35%	44%	21%
first decline stage	TopicIII-1	28%	37%	35%
	TopicIII-2	21%	75%	4%
	TopicIII-3	43%	45%	12%
second outbreak stage	TopicIV-1	19%	24%	56%
	TopicIV-2	32%	53%	15%
	TopicIV-3	29%	54%	17%
	TopicIV-4	40%	40%	20%
second decline stage	TopicV-1	22%	43%	35%
	TopicV-2	31%	42%	26%
	TopicV-3	35%	35%	30%
calming stage	TopicVI-1	51%	39%	10%
	TopicVI-2	49%	43%	8%
	TopicVI-3	45%	46%	9%

Fig. 6. Theme-Sentiment Distribution at Various Stages of Opinion Reversal Events

and "families seeking help through the media" tending to be negative. With the truth released, netizens expressed regret while gradually observing the social issues about caring for the mental health of youth (Topic IV-1), and the proportion of positive sentiment came to 56%. In the calming stage, public announcement of the punishment of some rumour-mongering media (Topic VI-1) inspired netizens denounce, and the proportion of negative sentiment rose.

5 Conclusion

This article analogizes the opinion leaders, themes and netizens' emotions of opinion reversal events to the three elements of the social combustion theory, and conducts an empirical study through the "Hu Xinyu" incident. The interaction of opinion leaders' influence, theme change and netizens' emotional confrontation leads to the continuous "combustion" of public opinion reversal events, and jointly advances the evolution of public opinion. This research finds that opinion leaders play the role of "accelerant" in the diffusion of public opinion, especially in the early stage of the incident, and that good media can promote the positive development of netizens' sentiment. Hence, mainstream media should take the main responsibility in the process of public opinion management to maximize the effect of effective information and prevent the public from being misled by "invalid and junk information". Netizens, as an important group of participants in public opinion events, should strive to get rid of the emotional errors caused by social stereotypes, make rational judgements and voice out information in the online public opinion space, trust the government, and face the public opinion reversal events with a positive attitude. Nevertheless, this research has certain research limitations. For example, our dataset is limited to text data from microblogs, multimodal data, such as images and videos, is not taken into account. In future research, deep learning and other similar models can be used to accomplish recognition and classification of multimodal data.

Acknowledgement. This research was supported by the National Social Science Foundation of China under Grant 21CTQ017.

References

1. Yin, F., et al.: Hot-topics cross-propagation and opinion-transfer dynamics in the Chinese Sina-microblog social media: a modeling study. J. Theor. Biol. **566**, 111480 (2023)
2. Wang, J., et al.: Spatiotemporal pattern evolution and influencing factors of online public opinion——evidence from the early-stage of COVID-19 in China. Heliyon. **9**(9), e20080 (2023)
3. Zhu, H., Hu, B.: Impact of information on public opinion reversal—an agent based model. Physica A **512**, 578–587 (2018)
4. Chen, T., Wang, Y., Yang, J., Cong, G.: Modeling public opinion reversal process with the considerations of external intervention information and individual internal characteristics. Healthcare **8**, 160 (2020)
5. Jiang, G., Li, S., Li, M.: Dynamic rumor spreading of public opinion reversal on Weibo based on a two-stage SPNR model. Physica A **558**, 125005 (2020)

6. Cong, J., et al.: Research on the governance path of the public opinion reversal of emergency: based on information interaction perspective. J. China Soc. Sci. Tech. Inf. **41**(06), 594–608 (2022). (in Chinese)

7. Peng, G., Cheng, X.: The generation mechanism of reversal news public opinion based on social burning theory. Inf. Sci. **41**(01), 80–85+109 (2023) (in Chinese)

8. Gao, Y.: Analysis of the reasons and countermeasures for the reverse of public opinion in the post truth era. Press Outpost. (05), 32–34 (2021) (in Chinese)

9. Li, Y., Chen, Q.: Analysis of the reversal phenomenon of public opinion due to audience misinterpretation under stereotypical thinking – taking the case of "Xi'an Domestic Violence" as an example. Press Outpost. **15**, 27–28 (2022). (in Chinese)

10. Proietti, C.: The dynamics of group polarization. In: Baltag, A., Seligman, J., Yamada, T. (eds.) LORI 2017. LNCS, vol. 10455, pp. 195–208. Springer, Heidelberg (2017). https://doi.org/10.1007/978-3-662-55665-8_14

11. Chen, J., et al.: The guidance of opinion leader on followers' opinions–based on opinion similarity and closeness perspective. Procedia Comput. Sci. **221**, 49–56 (2023)

12. Li, Y., et al.: Evaluation model of micro-blog opinion leader. Inf. Secur. Commun. Priv. **02**, 79–81 (2013). (in Chinese)

13. Zhou, Z., et al.: Evolution of online public opinions on major accidents: Implications for post-accident response based on social media network. Expert Syst. Appl. **235**, 121307 (2024)

14. Jia, Y., An, L., Li, G.: On the Online information dissemination pattern of city emergencies. J. Intell. **34**(04), 91–96+90 (2015). (in Chinese)

The Impact of Enterprise Digital Transformation on Customer Service Innovation Performance

Minghan Su, Qi Feng, and Jianming Zhou[✉]

Guangdong University of Finance and Economics, School of Business Administration, Guangzhou 510320, Guangdong, China
jmzhou@gdufe.edu.cn

Abstract. In the context of the digital economy, the emerging digital technologies have made the digital transformation of enterprises an unavoidable trend to help improving customer service. This paper conducted a sample survey of 139 Chinese companies and used multiple regression equation analysis to try to explore the mechanism between enterprise digital transformation and customer service innovation performance. The research results showed that: (1) Enterprise digital transformation had a significant direct positive impact on customer service innovation performance; (2) Enterprise cross-border activities played a partial mediating role in the process of enterprise digital transformation affecting customer service innovation performance; (3) Both proactive market orientation and reactive market orientation positively moderated the positive relationship between enterprise digital transformation and enterprise cross-border activities. That is, the higher the enterprise's proactive market orientation and reactive market orientation, the stronger the impact of enterprise digital transformation on enterprise cross-border activities. The above research results have important theoretical and practical significance for understanding the complex relationship between enterprise digital transformation and customer service innovation, and for improving the enterprise's ability to serve customers.

Keywords: Enterprise Digital Transformation · Cross-border Activities · Market Orientation · Customer Service Innovation Performance

1 Introduction

The new round of technological revolution and industrial transformation is promoting the rapid development of digital industrial technologies such as artificial intelligence, cloud computing, and big data, which in turn promotes the continuous and deep integration of digital technology and the real economy, and accelerates the digital transformation of enterprises. Entering the era of digital knowledge economy, customer service innovation has become an important driving force for companies to quickly respond to customer needs and improve corporate service quality. However, in the past, enterprises' emphasis on innovation was often limited to the technical level, and insufficient attention was paid

© The Author(s), under exclusive license to Springer Nature Switzerland AG 2024
Y. P. Tu and M. Chi (Eds.): WHICEB 2024, LNBIP 515, pp. 120–130, 2024.
https://doi.org/10.1007/978-3-031-60264-1_11

to service innovation in the service department (Zhang et al., 2010) [1]. In fact, enterprise service innovation is the process of breaking through previous technical limitations and utilizing the services provided by new technologies (Qi and Wang, 2022) [2]. Service innovation not only involves the improvement of service technology, but also includes the integration of optimizing customer service, service delivery systems and technology selection (Johne and Storey, 1998) [3]. For enterprises, customer service innovation is a key factor in improving their core competitiveness. Therefore, it is of great significance to study the impact of enterprises digital transformation on customer service innovation performance.

Based on the development of new technologies, enterprises can cross their own organizational boundaries and seek external resources and knowledge to make up for their own insufficient endowments and shortcomings in their capability structures. This cross-border search for knowledge is called cross-border activities (Wu et al., 2015) [4]. Existing research on cross-border activities pays more attention to the impact of cross-border activities driven by new technologies on cooperation between enterprises and other organizations and the efficiency of resource acquisition. This study includes the cross-border activities of enterprises as mediating variables to explore their role on enterprise digital transformation affecting customer service innovation performance.

In addition, the choice of different market orientations by enterprises will affect cross-border knowledge search, thereby affecting corporate innovation (Qu, 2021) [5]. This study incorporates market orientation as a boundary condition into the model to explore the impact of different market orientations on enterprise digital transformation affecting cross-border activities.

Based on this, this study attempts to conduct an empirical study to find out whether and how enterprise digital transformation affects customer service innovation performance, by focusing on the meditating role of enterprise cross-border activities and moderating role of market orientation under the background of digitalization, so as to help companies strengthen their service capabilities and service efficiency.

2 Literatures Review and Research Hypotheses

Enterprise digital transformation is the process of using a variety of digital technologies to promote the reconstruction and optimization of all levels of the enterprise, enabling enterprises to reduce production costs, improve production and service efficiency, control business risks, and thereby enhance their core competitiveness (Pei et al., 2023) [6]. Based on the research on enterprise digital transformation by many scholars, the impact of enterprise digital transformation behavior on enterprises is multi-level, diversified, and throughout the entire process, while the impact on customer service is rarely touched upon.

In the context of digitalization, a large number of studies have proven that the rapid development of technology has a significant positive effect on enterprise service innovation performance (Jian et al., 2014) [7], at the same time, the enterprise's own ability to absorb new technologies will also affect the enterprise's service innovation performance (Xiao, 2013) [8]. It can be seen from a large number of studies that there is a strong correlation between an enterprise's customer service innovation performance and its use of new technologies. Based on this, this study puts forward the following hypothesis:

H1: Enterprise digital transformation has a significant positive impact on customer service innovation performance.

Rosenkopf and Nerkar (2001) [9] proposed the concept of cross-border search, which refers to the activities that enterprises will carry out to search for external knowledge across organizational boundaries and knowledge bases in a dynamic environment. Cross-border activities enable enterprises to contact the outside and obtain innovation knowledge. Enterprise cross-border activities are an important way to help enterprises innovate, and they will also affect the innovation performance of enterprises (Wang and Wei, 2017) [10], that is, the enterprise's cross-border activities have a good positive impact on corporate innovation. To sum up, the cross-border activities of enterprises have a direct and positive relationship with customer service innovation performance. Accordingly, this study proposes the following hypotheses:

H2: Enterprise cross-border activities have a significant positive impact on customer service innovation performance.

The digital transformation of enterprises can help enterprises cross the "digital divide" and promote customer service innovation (Zhu, 2023) [11]. Cross-border activities can help companies break through their own boundaries to obtain external technology and information (Wu et al., 2015; Fu, 2023) [4][12]. The technical resources acquired by enterprises through cross-border activities will help enterprises apply it to customer service innovation in the process of digital transformation. Based on this, combined with the previous hypothesis analysis, this study proposes the following hypotheses:

H3: Enterprise cross-border activities mediate the relationship between enterprise digital transformation and customer service innovation performance.

Market orientation is a series of behaviors or activities that collect, disseminate and respond to market intelligence (Wu et al., 2021) [13]. Narver et al. (2004) [14] and others divided market orientation into proactive market orientation and reactive market orientation based on customers' explicit and implicit needs. Proactive market orientation is to proactively focus on the potential needs of customers, not limited to the needs and knowledge currently expressed by customers, and always maintain sensitivity to new markets, new technologies and new ideas (Xu, 2019) [15]. The reactive market orientation focuses on the explicit needs of customers and also pays attention to the information of the existing market. The proactive market orientation and the reactive market orientation use exploratory knowledge resources and exploitative knowledge resources respectively to guide enterprises to carry out exploratory knowledge resources and exploitative activities (Jian et al., 2018) [7]. The higher level of market orientation, the more it can promote cross-border activities under the impact of enterprise digital transformation. Accordingly, this study proposes the following hypotheses:

H4a: Proactive market orientation mediates the relationship between enterprise digital transformation and cross-border activities. That is, the higher level of proactive market orientation, the stronger positive impact of enterprise digital transformation on cross-border activities.

H4b: Reactive market orientation mediates the relationship between enterprise digital transformation and cross-border activities. That is, the higher level of reactive market orientation, the stronger positive impact of enterprise digital transformation on cross-border activities.

3 Research Design

3.1 Research Framework

According to the previous literature review, this paper's research framework and hypotheses are presented as Fig. 1.

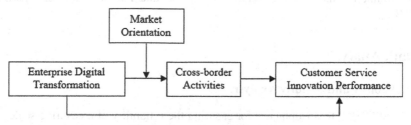

Fig.1. The research framework

3.2 Measurement

In measuring variables, this study mainly used tested high-cited measurement scales to ensure the validity and reliability of the research tools. All measurement scales are Likert-5 rating scales.

Among them, the enterprise digital transformation scale comes from the research of (Chi, 2020) [16] to design the questionnaire, with a total of 3 items. The cross-border activity scale mainly refers to the research of (Wang et al., 2023) [17] to design the questionnaire, including two dimensions: cross-border search for technical knowledge (5 items) and cross-border search for market knowledge (4 items), with a total of 9 items Question composition. The proactive market orientation scale mainly refers to the research of (Zhu et al., 2016) [18] to design the questionnaire, with a total of 5 items. The reactive market orientation scale mainly refers to the research of (Zhu et al., 2016) [18] to design the questionnaire, with a total of 5 items. The customer innovation service performance scale mainly refers to the research of (Avlonitis et al., 2001) [19] to design the questionnaire, which includes two dimensions: customer service financial performance (6 items) and customer service non-financial performance (5 items), with a total of 11 items.

3.3 Sampling

The data for this study were collected from the middle and senior leaders responsible for enterprise digital management in 139 enterprises in a provincial association in China. A total of 150 questionnaires were distributed and lasted for one week. A total of 150 questionnaires were recovered, of which 142 were completed with complete answers. After excluding 3 questionnaires with complete logical questions, a total of 139 valid questionnaires were obtained, with an effective recovery rate of 94.7%. Among the 139 manager samples, the majority are male managers, with 114 people accounting for 82%;

In terms of age, they are mainly young and middle-aged managers, with an average age of 34.9 years (standard deviation = 5.8 years); In terms of educational background, employees with high education account for a large proportion. There are 45 people with master's and doctoral degrees, accounting for 32.4%, 79 people with bachelor's degrees, accounting for 56.8%, and 15 people with junior college or below, accounting for 10.8%; At the management level, there are 122 senior managers, accounting for 87.8%, 16 middle managers, accounting for 11.5%, and 1 junior manager, accounting for 0.7%.

4 Data Analysis

4.1 Reliability and Validity Analysis

We used SPSS19.0 to do alpha test for ensuring the reliability of measuring scales, and the tested results indicated that all Cronbach's α value were greater than the standard value of 0.7 which presented in Table 1, showing that the measuring scales of Enterprise Digital Transformation, Cross-border Activities, Market Orientation, and Customer Service Innovation Performance have good reliability.

Table 1. Cronbach's α value of measuring scales.

Variables	α value
Enterprise digital transformation	0.75
Cross-border activities	0.77
Proactive market orientation	0.84
Reactive market orientation	0.83
Customer service innovation performance	0.85

And the validity test of Enterprise digital transformation, Cross-border activities, Market Orientation, and Customer Service Innovation Performance was used CFA method. The results presented in Table 2 indicated that all AVE (average variance extracted) and CR (composite reliability) values are higher than the standard of 0.45 and 0.7, suggesting that all measuring scales of Enterprise digital transformation, Cross-border activities, Market Orientation, and Customer Service Innovation Performance have good validity.

Table 2. AVE and CR values of measuring scales.

Variables	AVE value	CR value
Enterprise digital transformation	0.45	0.75
Cross-border activities	0.46	0.89
Proactive market orientation	0.51	0.84
Reactive market orientation	0.49	0.82
Customer service innovation performance	0.49	0.91

4.2 Descriptive Statistical Analysis

Table 3 performs descriptive statistical analysis on the variables and control variables of this study, and summarizes the mean, variance and correlation coefficient of the study variables of Enterprise digital transformation (EDT), Cross-border activities (CBA), Proactive Market Orientation (PMO), Reactive Market Orientation (RMO) and Customer Service Innovation Performance (CSIP) and control variables of Gender (GEN), Age, Education (EDU), Position Level (PL). Correlation analysis results show that enterprise digital transformation has a significant positive correlation with cross-border activities ($r = 0.76$, $p < 0.01$), proactive market orientation ($r = 0.22$, $p < 0.01$), reactive market orientation ($r = 0.20$, $p < 0.05$) and customer service innovation performance ($r = 0.76$, $p < 0.01$). Cross-border activities have a significant positive correlation with customer service innovation performance ($r = 0.86$, $p < 0.01$). Positive correlation results provide good guarantee for the verification of the research hypothesis of this study.

Table 3. Means, standard deviations, and correlations

Variables	1	2	3	4	5	6	7	8	9
1. GEN	1.00								
2. AGE	−0.02	1.00							
3. EDU	−0.13	−0.04	1.00						
4. PL	0.07	−0.25**	0.02	1.00					
5. EDT	−0.07	−0.59**	0.08	0.37**	1.00				
6. CBA	−0.05	−0.45**	0.08	0.25**	0.76**	1.00			
7. PMO	0.00	−0.15	−0.03	−0.02	0.22**	0.33**	1.00		
8. RMO	0.00	−0.16	−0.13	−0.05	0.20*	0.31**	0.83**	1.00	
9. CSIP	−0.05	−0.48**	0.03	0.24**	0.76**	0.86**	0.23**	0.27**	1.00
Mean	0.18	34.92	2.21	2.87	3.34	3.36	3.37	3.37	3.30
SD	0.39	5.78	0.62	0.36	0.88	0.78	0.84	0.79	0.77

Notes: $N = 139$. ** $p < 0.01$, * $p < 0.05$

4.3 Hypotheses Test

Hierarchical multiple regression analysis with SPSS 19.0 was used to test hypotheses by entering in control variables (i.e., age, gender, education and position level), independent variable (i.e., Enterprise digital transformation), mediator variable (i.e., Cross–border activities), and moderator variable (i.e., Proactive market orientation, Reactive market orientation) on separate steps. Table 4 presents the results.

Table 4. Hierarchical regression hypothesis test results

	CSIP			CBA				
	Model1	Model2	Model3	Model4	Model5	Model6	Model7	Model8
Control variables								
GEN	−0.07	0.00	−0.02	−0.01	−0.21	−0.30	−0.18	0.02
AGE	−0.45**	−0.06	−0.12*	−0.05	−0.03	0.01	0.00	−0.01
EDU	0.00	−0.03	−0.04	−0.04	0.18	0.19	0.14	0.03
PL	0.14*	−0.05	0.01	−0.03	−0.03	−0.01	−0.02	−0.03
Independent variable								
EDT		0.75**		0.24**	0.21 *	0.76**	0.73**	0.73**
Mediator								
CBA			0.80**	0.66**				
Moderator								
PMO							0.17**	
RMO								0.20**
Interaction								
EDT × PMO							0.21**	
EDT × RMO								0.15**
R^2	0.26	0.58	0.75	0.77	0.23	0.57	0.63	0.62
ΔR^2	0.26	0.33	0.49	0.19	0.23	0.34	0.05	0.05
F	11.48**	37.23**	81.21**	74.61**	10.07*	35.53**	31.26**	30.81**
ΔF	11.48**	104.72**	268.48**	109.56**	10.07*	105.90**	9.38**	8.71**

Notes: $N = 139$. ** $p < 0.01$, * $p < 0.05$

According to the results of model M2 in Table 4, it is found that enterprise digital transformation has a significant positive impact on customer service innovation performance (M2, $\beta = 0.75$, $p < 0.01$), and H1 is established.

According to the results of model M3, it can be found that cross-border activities also have a significant positive impact on customer service innovation performance (M3, $\beta = 0.80$, $p < 0.01$), and H2 is established.

It can be known from model M4 that when the mediating variable cross-border activities is added to the regression equation of model M4, the impact coefficient of enterprise digital transformation on customer service innovation performance (M2, β = 0.75, p < 0.01) is significantly weakened by 72% (M4, β = 0.24, p < 0.01). In addition, the results of model M6 also show that enterprise digital transformation has a significant positive impact on enterprise cross-border activities (M6, β = 0.76, p < 0.01). Therefore, based on the above empirical results, this paper can draw the following conclusion that cross-border activities play a partial mediating role between enterprise digital transformation and knowledge-based customer service innovation performance. Thus, H3 is supported by the data.

This study draws on Hayes (2013) [20], Zhou and Zhou (2021) [21] and others recommended the Bootstrapping method to further test the significance of the mediating effect of cross-border activities. The results show that the mediating effect of cross-border activities on enterprise digital transformation and customer service innovation performance is 0.440, and its 95% confidence interval is [0.275, 0.658]. The confidence interval of the mediating effect of cross-border activities does not include zero. Therefore, the mediating effect of cross-border activities is significant, and H3 is further supported by the data, that is, the significance of part of the mediating effect of cross-border activities has been verified.

4.4 Analysis of the Regulatory Effect of Market Orientation

By comparing models M6 and M7, it can be found that after the interaction variable "enterprise digital transformation $\times$ proactive market orientation" is introduced in model M7, the variance explanatory power (R^2) of model M7 not only significantly increases by 10.5%, but also the interaction variable also has a significant impact on Cross-border activities (M7, $\beta = 0.21$, p < 0.01), indicating that proactive market orientation moderates the relationship between enterprise digital transformation and cross-border activities significantly. That is, the higher the proactive market orientation, the stronger the positive impact of enterprise digital transformation on corporate cross-border activities. H4a is supported. Figure 2 shows the influence pattern of this interaction.

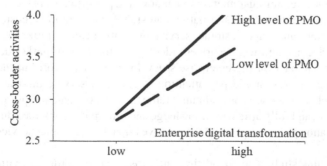

Fig.2. Differences of proactive market orientation on enterprise digital transformation impacting enterprise cross-border activities

By comparing models M6 and M8, it can be found that after the interaction variable "enterprise digital transformation × reactive market orientation" is introduced in model M8, the variance explanatory power (R^2) of model M8 not only significantly increases by 8.8%, but also the interaction variable has a significant positive impact (M8, $\beta = 0.15$, p < 0.01), indicating that reactive market orientation has a significant positive moderating effect in the process of enterprise digital transformation positively affecting enterprise cross-border activities. That is, the higher the reactive market orientation, the stronger the positive impact of enterprise digital transformation on enterprise cross-border activities. H4b is supported. Figure 3 shows the influence pattern of this interaction.

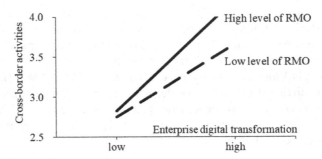

Fig.3. Differences of reactive market orientation on enterprise digital transformation impacting enterprise cross-border activities

5   Conclusions and Discussion

This study conducted a sample survey of 139 Chinese companies and used multiple regression equation analysis to try to explore the mechanism between enterprise digital transformation and customer service innovation performance. The results have theoretical and practical significance.

Firstly, this study confirmed that enterprise digital transformation was a powerful positive variable affecting customer service innovation performance in the context of digitization. Enterprise digital transformation can significantly improve customer service innovation performance, and customer service innovation can optimize the enterprise's customer service capabilities, accurately identify customer and market demands, and have a positive impact on the enterprise's development. Therefore, in the context of digitization, enterprises should pay attention to customer service innovation, actively utilize new technologies such as artificial intelligence and big data to optimize customer service systems, and fully utilize the knowledge and information obtained during the digital transformation process to expand the positive impact on customer service innovation performance.

Secondly, this study also found that enterprise's cross-border activities mediated the positive relationship between enterprise digital transformation and customer service innovation performance. Clarifying how enterprise digital transformation contributes to customer service innovation is of significant importance for people to gain a deeper understanding of how enterprise digital transformation enhances customer service innovation performance. It is evident that in the process from enterprise digital transformation to cross-border activities to the impact on customer service innovation performance, if an enterprise wants to innovate in customer service during the digital transformation, it needs to use new digital technologies. This process of seeking knowledge requires enterprises to break through their organizational boundaries to obtain external resources and information, including innovatively reforming the enterprise's strategic goals, collaborating with technology companies in different industries, establishing new technology research and development departments, and hiring technical experts to enable the enterprise to more efficiently obtain and utilize external new knowledge and technology. This allows the enterprise to effectively explore market changes and consumer demands, innovate in serving customers, optimize customer service processes, and ultimately enhance customer service innovation performance.

Thirdly, the empirical results of this study indicated that different market orientations chosen by enterprises will affect the degree of participation in cross-border activities during enterprise digital transformation, thereby influencing the enterprise's customer service innovation performance. By introducing market orientation as an important extension of the impact of enterprise digital transformation on customer service innovation performance, this study explored the boundary of the moderated role of proactive market orientation and reactive market orientation on enterprise digital transformation affecting customer service innovation performance. Therefore, in the process of enterprise digital transformation, the selected market orientation should match the formulated enterprise strategy, and analyzing the enterprise's own market orientation will enable the enterprise to more efficiently and effectively search for and use external knowledge and technology, reducing exploration costs and improving the efficiency of knowledge search and transformation.

Finally, this paper explored the relationship between enterprise digital transformation and customer service innovation performance, as well as focusing on the mediating and moderating effects of cross-border activities and market orientation, and makes certain theoretical and managerial contributions. However, there are still some limitations: (1) This study is too broad in its conceptual research on enterprise digital transformation, and in the future, it can conduct more in-depth research on digital transformation to refine the independent variables; (2) This paper primarily focuses on studying the effects of cross-border activities and market orientation on customer innovation performance. Future research can delve further into additional mediating and moderating variables to better optimize the enterprise's digital transformation customer innovation service performance model.

Acknowledgments. This work was supported by Guangdong Provincial Philosophy and Social Science Project (GD23YGL10).

References

1. Zhang, R.Y., Liu, X.M., Wang, H.Z., Nie, K.: The impact of customer-enterprise interaction on service innovation: based on the perspective of organizational learning. Chin. J. Manag. (2), 218–224 (2010)

2. Qi, L., Wang, X.: Research on external resource acquisition, collaborative capabilities and service innovation performance of advanced manufacturing enterprises. Learn. Explor. (10), 113–120 (2022)
3. Johne, A., Storey, C.: New service development: a review of the literature and annotated bibliography. Eur. J. Mark. **32**(3/4), 184–251 (1998)
4. Wu, Z.Y., Chen, Y.R., Wu, B.: Review and prospects of research on the connotation, boundaries and models of cross-border search. Sci. Technol. Prog. Countermeas. **32**(19), 153–160 (2015)
5. Qu, X.Y.: The impact of market orientation, knowledge search and failure learning matching on naive innovation. Sci. Technol. Prog. Countermeas. **38**(13), 29–36 (2021)
6. Pei, X., Liu, Y., Wang, W. H.: Enterprise digital transformation: driving factors, economic effects and strategic choices. Reform (5), 124–137(2023)
7. Jian, Z.Q., Chen, J.H., Zheng, X.Y.: Research on the impact of network capabilities and relationship learning on service innovation performance. J. Manag. Eng. **28**(3), 91–99 (2014)
8. Xiao, Z.X.: Empirical study on the impact of knowledge absorptive capacity on service innovation performance - empirical evidence from service outsourcing companies. J. Zhejiang Gongshang Univ. (6), 73–80 (2013)
9. Rosenkopf, L., Nerkar, A.: Beyond local search: boundary-spanning, exploration, and impact in the optical disk industry. Strateg. Manag. J. **22**(4), 287–306 (2001)
10. Wang, L., Wei, J.: Research on the relationship between knowledge-intensive service embedding, cross-border search and service innovation of manufacturing enterprises. Sci. Technol. Prog. Countermeas. **34**(16), 48–55 (2017)
11. Zhu, X. F.: The impact path of digital transformation on the performance of new retail enterprises - the intermediary effect based on consumption upgrade. Bus. Econ. Res. (16), 151–154 (2023)
12. Fu, X.Y., Ding, M.X.: The impact of cross-border search and dual innovation on the growth of new retail enterprises under the background of digital economy. Bus. Econ. Res. (12), 165–168 (2023)
13. Wu, W.Q., Huang, X., Wu, C.H.: Technological boundary-spanning search, crowdfunding interaction and crowdfunding innovation performance: a mediated moderation model of knowledge sharing. Enterp. Inf. Syst. **15**(3), 352–372 (2021)
14. Narver, J.C., Slater, S.F., Maclachlan, D.L.: Responsive and proactive market orientation and new-product success. J. Prod. Innov. Manag. **21**(5), 334–347 (2004)
15. Xu, J.Z., Li, F.S., Pan, W., Fu, J.W.: The impact of dual knowledge search on corporate innovation performance: the moderating role of market orientation. China Sci. Technol. Forum (7), 119–127 (2019)
16. Chi, M.M., Ye, D.L., Wang, J.J., Zhai, S.S.: How my country's small and medium-sized manufacturing enterprises improve new product development performance-from the perspective of digital empowerment. Nankai Manag. Rev. **23**(3), 63–75 (2020)
17. Wang, L.J., Wang, W.W., Tian, H.N.: Research on the impact of cross-border search and knowledge integration on the servicization performance of manufacturing enterprises. China Soft Sci. (6), 155–166 (2023)
18. Zhu, Y.X., Zhou, F., Sha, Z.Q.: The relationship between cross-border search and business model innovation—from the perspective of absorptive capacity. Econ. Manag. **42**(11), 92–104 (2016)
19. Avlonitis, G.J., Papastathopoulou, P.G., Gounaris, S.P.: An empirically-based typology of product innovativeness for new financial services: success and failure scenarios. J. Prod. Innov. Manag.Manag. **18**(5), 324–342 (2001)
20. Hayes, A.F.: An Introduction to Mediation, Moderation and Conditional Process Analysis: A Regression-Based Approach. Guilford Press, New York (2013)
21. Zhou, J., Zhou, Y.: Knowledge inertia and knowledge creation behavior: the role of organizational memory and innovation atmosphere. Sci. Res. **39**(6), 1103–1110+1119 (2021)

Effect of Consumers' Perceived Financial Constraint on Online New Product Purchase Intention

Qi Feng, Minghan Su, and Jianming Zhou(✉)

School of Business Administration, Guangdong University of Finance and Economics,
Guangzhou 510320, GD, China
jmzhou@gdufe.edu.cn

Abstract. The study reported here examined the relationship between online consumers' perceived financial constraint and online new product purchase intention by focusing on the mediating effect of online consumers' risk-taking tendency and moderating effect of online consumers' online shopping impulsivity. Data from a survey of 209 students in three undergraduate classes and one professional master student class was used to conduct empirical study. Results found that the perceived financial constraint was negatively related to consumers' online new product purchase intention while risk-taking tendency mediated this relationship significantly. In additional, consumers' online shopping impulsivity was negatively moderating the relationship between online consumers' perceived financial constraint and risk-taking tendency. Moreover, consumers' online shopping impulsivity had a significant negative impact on perceived financial constraint. Finally, implications of the findings were discussed for preventing or reducing the perceived financial constraint from the perspective of online merchants and online consumers.

Keywords: Perceived Financial Constraint · Risk-taking Tendency · Online Shopping Impulsivity · Online New Product Purchase Intention

1 Introduction

As production and manufacturing capabilities continue to progress, a multitude of new products are being generated daily, while the evolution of network technology has led to a considerable number of these new products being offered for sale online. Nevertheless, it is prudent to consider whether these fresh online offerings are able to elicit purchase intentions from online consumers. The acceptance of new products by consumers is a multifaceted process, encompassing five key stages: awareness, interest, evaluation, trial, and adoption (Rogers et al., 2014) [1]. Consequently, it is essential to address how to enhance online consumers' inclination to buy new products online, the factors influencing this online purchase process, and the elucidation of the motives and mechanisms guiding online consumers' purchasing decisions.

The impact of an individual's financial status is not solely derived from their objective wealth, but also extends to their subjective perception. A growing number of consumers

© The Author(s), under exclusive license to Springer Nature Switzerland AG 2024
Y. P. Tu and M. Chi (Eds.): WHICEB 2024, LNBIP 515, pp. 131–141, 2024.
https://doi.org/10.1007/978-3-031-60264-1_12

believe that their economic circumstance no longer satisfies their consumption requirements, leading to a perceived financial constraint which, in turn, influences their intention to purchase new products online. In previous research on factors influencing the online new product purchase intention, the characteristics of the online product itself will affect the online new product purchase intention (Huang and Sengupta, 2020) [2]. In addition, consumption context is also one of the factors that influence the online new product purchase intention (Jiang, 2021) [3]. However, there is currently a scarcity of specific and systematic analyses on the influence of online consumers' perceived financial constraints on their intention to purchase new products online. Thus, further research in this area is imperative.

In organizational behavior, scholars refer to risk-taking tendency by the concept that individuals tend to evaluate their own likelihood of success when faced with risky behavior. The level of an individual's risk-taking tendency affects their risk preferences, and subsequently the decisions and behaviors they will take (Llewellyn and Sanchez, 2008) [4]. Therefore, this study includes risk-taking tendency as a mediating variable to explore its mediating role between the perceived financial constraint and the intention to purchase new products online.

Considering the rise of the online shopping model, Jiang et al. (2014) [5] believed that online consumers' impulse purchases in online shopping were not utilitarian purchases, but experiential purchases that pursue hedonism. The online shopping impulsivity makes online consumers not think too much about internal and external negative impacts, as well as the consequences of their purchasing behavior, but instead make them more adventurous in purchasing online products. Therefore, this study intends to further analyze the role of online shopping impulsivity on online consumers' perceived financial constraint, and its moderating role between the perceived financial constraint and online consumers' risk-taking tendencies.

Therefore, this study aims to study the relationship between online consumers' perceived financial constraint and online new product purchase intention by focusing on the mediating effect of online consumers' risk-taking tendency and moderating effect of online consumers' online shopping impulsivity, so as to find out the way to help new products sale online.

2   Literatures Review and Research Hypotheses

The perceived financial constraint refers to a subjective psychological feeling that individuals believe that their financial situation limits their consumption desires, emphasizing the limitations and constraints of existing financial conditions on expected consumption (Tully et al., 2015) [6]. Hamilton et al. (2019) [7] pointed out that when consumers feel a sense of financial constraints, they will adopt a three-stage response model. The first stage is that consumers' thinking and decision-making are disturbed, and they will react. The second stage is that consumers begin to change their thinking and actions in response to financial resource constraints. In the third stage, if the perceived financial constraint persists for a long time, consumers will gradually adapt to this constraint and take its impact into future decisions and behaviors.

The purchase intention of new product refers to the subjective willingness of consumers in the process of purchasing products or services, and is a subjective probability

(Fishbein et al., 1975) [8]. There are two factors that affect the online new product purchase intention. Internal factors include individual differences among consumers, consumer perceived value, and consumer satisfaction. External factors include corporate image, socioeconomic factors, situational factors, and the influence of others. Based on this, this paper argues that the perceived financial constraint will cause online consumers to limit and restrict their expected consumption and reduce their desire to purchase new products online. Therefore, we propose the following assumption:

H1: Online consumers' perceived financial constraint has a significant negative impact on online new product purchase intention.

Risk-taking tendency refers to the behavioral pattern of an individual in a certain risk situation, which reflects the degree to which an individual judge various factors in the risk situation, thereby predicting future events and making risky decisions (Brochhaus, 1980) [9]. Individuals with high risk-taking tendencies will adopt a positive attitude towards risk and like to get involved in new areas, and they will pay more attention to the benefits brought by risky activities. This attitude will subtly affect the subsequent behavioral tendencies (Ronay and Kim, 2006) [10]. Based on this, this paper argues that high risk-taking tendency may have a positive impact on online new product purchase intention. Therefore, we propose the following assumption:

H2: Online consumers' risk-taking tendency has a significant positive impact on online new product purchase intention.

The reason why the perceived financial constraint will have a negative impact on online consumers' online new product purchase intention is mainly because a strong perceived financial constraint will make online consumers less aggressive in consumption and afraid of trying online products with a high risk, thereby reducing the online new product purchase intention. Based on this, this paper argues that the negative impact of the perceived financial constraint on online new product purchase intention is likely to be through reducing the risk-taking tendency of online consumers. Hence, we propose the following hypothesis:

H3: Risk-taking tendency plays a mediating role between perceived financial constraint and online new product purchase intention.

Impulse buying is a complex purchasing behavior that is characterized by suddenness, convincingness, and hedonic, and the rapid purchase decisions made by consumers prevent them from considering various information and alternatives carefully. Therefore, impulsive buying can be regarded as an irrational behavior of consumers (Chung et al., 2017) [11]. To determine whether a purchase decision is impulsive, we can consider it with the following three criteria. The first criterion is that the purchase decision is spontaneous and unplanned. The second criterion is that consumers rarely consider the consequences of their purchasing decisions. The third criterion is that this purchase decision is triggered by some irresistible factors or uncontrollable personality, situation and other temptation factors. These temptations will prompt consumers to gain immediate satisfaction and develop a strong emotional attachment to the product, thus causing consumers to have a strong, sudden and irresistible urge to buy immediately (Spiteri, 2020) [12].

Online shopping impulsivity is defined as an individual's strong desire to purchase after being stimulated by some external environment, and under the control of this desire to purchase, the emotional response is much higher than the individual's rational judgment of online shopping behavior. Yang and Lu (2013) [13] pointed out that the reason for the high incidence of impulse buying behavior on the Internet is that there are various stimulating factors in the online shopping environment (such as product characteristics, consumer characteristics, advertising promotions, website characteristics). Based on this, this paper argues that consumers with high online shopping impulsivity will become more aggressive and more courageous to purchase new online products that exceed their financial affordability. They will not carefully consider the possible adverse consequences of their purchase. Therefore, we propose the following hypotheses:

H4: Online shopping impulsivity has a significant negative impact on online consumers' perceived financial constraint.

H5: Online shopping impulsivity plays a moderating role in the relationship between online consumers' perceived financial constraint and risk-taking tendency.

3   Method and Design

3.1   Research Framework

According to the previous literature review, this paper's research framework and hypotheses are presented in Fig. 1.

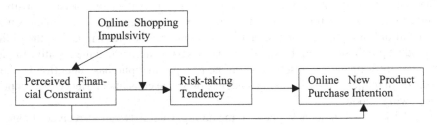

Fig. 1. The research framework

3.2   Research Samples

The research data in this paper was collected from students in three undergraduate classes and one professional master student class in colleges. Relevant data collection received strong support and cooperation from the leaders and students of the colleges. In the survey, we collected the data of student background information (i.e. age, sex, education, expenses, frequency), financial situation, online shopping impulsivity level, risk-taking tendency level and the willingness to purchase new products online. It took us one month to send out a total of 250 coded questionnaires and returned 223 with 209 were completed and valid, which represents a response rate of 83.6%.

By matching the survey data, questionnaires with obvious logical errors were eliminated, and a total of 209 student questionnaires were used for hypothesis verification. Of these 209 students, 88 people were males (accounting for 42%), and 121 people were females (accounting for 58%); the average age was 20.59 years old (standard deviation = 1.01); in terms of education background, 150 people were undergraduates (accounting for 71.8%), 59 people were master students (accounting for 28.2%); in terms of monthly expenses, 43 people had a monthly expenses of less than 1,000 Yuan, 126 people had a monthly expenses of 1,001–2,000 Yuan, 27 people had a monthly expenses of 2001–3000 Yuan, and 13 people had a monthly expenses of more than 3000 Yuan; in terms of the frequency of purchasing new online products every month, 60 people purchased new online products once or less (accounting for 28.7%), 124 people purchased new online products 2–5 times (accounting for 59.3%), 17 People purchased new online products 5–9 times (accounting for 8.1%), and 8 people purchased new online products 10 times or more (accounting for 3.8%). The characteristics of the samples were basically in line with the characteristics of online consumers.

3.3 Measurements

In order to ensure the validity and reliability of the measuring scales of the perceived financial constraint, online shopping impulsivity, risk-taking tendency, and online new product purchase intention, this research used five-point Likert scales that frequently cited in academic literature and revised partially according to the research purpose and the suggestions of business people and experts in related fields. SPSS 26.0 was used for testing the reliability with Cronbach's α and AMOS 22.0 was used for testing the convergent validity with Average Variance Extracted (AVE) and Composite Reliability (CR).

Perceived Financial Constraint. The measuring scale of perceived financial constraint was development by Paley (2019) [14] which comprised 4 items. Cronbach's α was 0.85 (higher than 0.70), while AVE was 0.59 (higher than 0.50) and CR was 0.85 (higher than 0.70) for perceived financial constraint, indicating that the construct of perceived financial constraint has good reliability and convergent validity.

Online Shopping Impulsivity. The measuring scale of online shopping impulsivity was development by Li and Guo (2015) [15] which comprised 5 items. Cronbach's α was 0.88 (higher than 0.70), while AVE was 0.59 (higher than 0.50) and CR was 0.88 (higher than 0.70) for online shopping impulsivity, indicating that the construct of online shopping impulsivity has good reliability and convergent validity.

Risk-Taking Tendency. The risk-taking tendency scale was mainly measured using the International Personality Inventory Library (IPIP) developed by Goldberg (1998) [16]. The IPIP contained a 10-item scale. This paper selected 6 positive items among them. Cronbach's α was 0.89 (higher than 0.70), while AVE was 0.57 (higher than 0.50) and CR was 0.89 (higher than 0.70) for risk-taking tendency, indicating that the construct of risk-taking tendency has good reliability and convergent validity.

Online New Product Purchase Intention. The measuring scale of online new product purchase intention was development by Pavlou (2003) [17] which comprised 4 items. Cronbach's α was 0.87 (higher than 0.70), while AVE was 0.63 (higher than 0.50) and CR was 0.87 (higher than 0.70) for online new product purchase intention, indicating that

that the construct of online new product purchase intention has good reliability and convergent validity.

4   Results

4.1   Confirmatory Factor Analysis (CFAs)

Confirmatory factor analysis (CFAs) with AMOS 22.0 was used to examine the discriminant validity of Perceived financial constraint (PFC), Online shopping impulsivity (OSI), Risk-taking tendency (RT) and Online new product purchase intention (ONPPI) with χ^2/df, RMSEA, RFI, and GFI. The results in Table 1 showed that by the comparison between the four-factor model, the three-factor model and the single-factor model, the four-factor model had the best fit indexes (χ^2/df = 133.457/146 = 0.914; RMSEA = 0.001 was less than 0.08, TLI = 1.007 was greater than 0.9, CFI = 1.000 was greater than 0.9), indicating that the measuring scales used in this study has good discriminant validity.

Table 1. Results of CFAs for the measures of the variables

Model	Factors	χ^2/df	RMSEA	RFI	GFI
Four-factor	PFC, OSI, RT, ONPPI	0.914	0.001	0.933	0.937
Three-factor -1	PFC+OSI, RT, ONPPI	2.585	0.087	0.811	0.802
Three-factor -2	PFC+RT, OSI, ONPPI	2.655	0.089	0.806	0.793
Three-factor -3	PFC+ONPPI, OSI, RT	2.509	0.085	0.816	0.800
Three-factor -4	PFC, OSI+RT, ONPPI	1.482	0.048	0.892	0.881
Three-factor -5	PFC, OSI+ONPPI, RT	1.821	0.063	0.867	0.851
Three-factor -6	PFC, OSI, RT+ONPPI	2.519	0.085	0.816	0.784
One-factor	PFC+OSI+RT+ONPPI	4.586	0.131	0.664	0.684

Notes: RMSEA is the root-mean-square error of approximation; RFI is the robust fitting index; and GFI is the goodness-of-fit index

4.2   Descriptive Statistics

Table 2 presents the means, standard deviations, and zero-order Pearson correlations of all main variables and controlled variables. Results in Table 2 showed that the perceived financial constraint was negatively correlated with the risk-taking tendency (r = − 0.42, p < 0.01) and the online new product purchase intention (r = −0.44, p < 0.01), and the perceived financial constraint was also negatively correlated with the online shopping impulsivity (r = − 0.41, p < 0.01). Risk-taking tendency was positively correlated with the online new product purchase intention (r = 0.51, p < 0.01) and online shopping impulsivity (r = 0.75, p < 0.01). In addition, the online new product purchase intention had no significant correlations with age (r = − 0.04, p > 0.05), sex (r = 0.10, p > 0.05), education (r = − 0.01, p > 0.05), monthly expenses (r = −0.01, p > 0.05) and online shopping frequency (r = − 0.11, p > 0.05). These results provide initial support for the further hypotheses test in this study.

Table 2. Mean, variance and correlation coefficient of main variables

Variables	1	2	3	4	5	6	7	8	9
1. Age	1.00								
2. Sex	0.00	1.00							
3. Education	0.94**	-0.00	1.00						
4. Expenses	0.03	0.09	0.00	1.00					
5. Frequency	0.00	0.06	0.02	0.57**	1.00				
6. PFC	−0.07	0.04	−0.04	0.02	0.05	1.00			
7. OSI	−0.02	0.08	−0.03	0.07	−0.05	−0.41**	1.00		
8. RT	−0.00	0.10	0.02	0.04	−0.03	−0.42**	0.75**	1.00	
9. ONPPI	−0.04	0.10	−0.01	−0.01	−0.11	−0.44**	0.67**	0.51**	1.00
Mean	20.59	0.58	2.28	2.05	1.87	3.29	3.40	3.37	3.34
SD	1.01	0.49	0.45	0.76	0.71	0.98	0.90	0.88	0.89

Notes: N = 209, * Significant at P < 0.05; ** Significant at P < 0.01. Sex is coded "0" = male, "1" = female. Education is coded "0" = holding no degree, "1" = holding Bachelor's degree, "2" = holding Master's degree

4.3 Hypothesis Test

Hierarchical multiple regression analysis with SPSS 26.0 was used to test hypotheses by entering in control variables (i.e., students' age, sex, education, monthly expenses and online shopping frequency), independent variable (i.e., perceived financial constraint), mediator variable (i.e., risk-taking tendency), and moderator variable (i.e., online shopping impulsivity, perceived financial constraint × online shopping impulsivity) on separate steps. Table 3 presents the results.

H1 proposed that perceived financial constraint had a significant negative impact on online new product purchase intention. As shown in Table 3, perceived financial constraint was negatively associated with online new product purchase intention (M2, β = − 0.46, p < 0.01). Thus, H1 was supported.

H2 proposed that risk-taking tendency had a significant positive impact on online new product purchase intention. As shown in Table 3, risk-taking tendency was positively associated with online new product purchase intention (M3, β = 0.50, p < 0.01). Thus, H2 was supported.

H3 proposed that risk-taking tendency mediated the relationship between perceived financial constraint and online new product purchase intention. As shown in Table 3, the results indicated that perceived financial constraint had a significant negative impact on risk-taking tendency (M6, $\beta = -0.14$, $p < 0.01$), and the influence coefficient of the perceived financial constraint on online new product purchase intention (M2, $\beta = -0.46$, $p < 0.01$) is significantly weakened (M4, $\beta = -0.30$, $p < 0.01$) after entering risk-taking to M2. Thus, H3 was supported.

Table 3. Hierarchical regression hypothesis test results

	PFC	ONPPI			RT		
	M1	M2	M3	M4	M5	M6	M7
Control Variables							
Sex	0.07	0.12*	0.06	0.08	0.12	0.05	0.06
Age	−0.36	−0.45*	−0.20	−0.33	−0.34	−0.20	−0.13
Education	0.29	0.40*	0.18	0.29	0.32	0.21	0.15
Expense	0.06	0.09	0.04	0.05	0.09	−0.00	−0.01
Frequency	−0.02	−0.16*	−0.13	−0.13	−0.08	0.00	0.02
Independent Variable							
PFC		−0.46**		−0.30**	−0.43**	−0.14**	−0.23**
Mediating Variable							
RT			0.50**	0.37**			
Moderator							
OSIP	−0.42**					0.69**	0.57**
Interaction							
PFC × OSIP							0.20**
R^2	0.19**	0.25**	0.28**	0.35**	0.20**	0.58**	0.61**
ΔR^2	0.19	0.06	0.09	0.10	−0.05	0.38	0.03
F	7.92**	10.91**	13.06**	15.61**	8.56**	40.35**	39.05**
ΔF	43.36**	55.44**	67.85**	33.32**	46.12**	184.48**	13.03**

Notes: N = 209, * Significant at $P < 0.05$; ** Significant at $P < 0.01$

Since the mediating effect analysis recommended by Baron and Kenny (1986) [18] has the disadvantage that the significance of the mediating effect cannot be tested, bootstrap method recommended by Hayes (2013) [19] was also used for the mediating effect test. Results of bootstrapping test with 5000 times repeated sampling showed that there was a significant mediating effect of risk-taking tendency on the relationship between perceived financial constraint and online new product purchase intention (mediating effect value = 0.10, 95% confidence interval was [0.04, 0.18] included no zero). Hence, H3 got further supported.

H4 proposed that online shopping impulsivity had a significant negative impact on perceived financial constraint. As shown in Table 3, online shopping impulsivity was negatively associated with perceived financial constraint (M1, $\beta = -0.42$, p < 0.01). Thus, H4 was supported.

H5 proposed that online shopping impulsivity moderated the relationship between perceived financial constraint and risk-taking tendency. Results in Table 3 showed that the interaction of perceived financial constraint × online shopping impulsivity was positively related to risk-taking tendency (M7, $\beta = 0.20$, p < 0.01), and the interaction effect accounted for 61% of the explained variance in risk-taking tendency ($\Delta R^2 = 0.03$, $\Delta F = 13.03$, P < 0.01). Moreover, to determine the nature of the moderating effect, we plotted the interaction using Aiken and West's (1991) [20] procedure of computing slopes one standard deviation above and below the mean of online shopping impulsivity. Figure 2 illustrated the pattern of this interaction. Hence, H5 was supported.

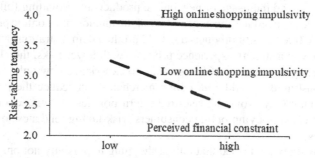

Fig. 2. The moderating effect of online shopping impulsivity on the relationship between perceived financial constraint and risk-taking tendency

5 Discussion and Conclusion

Taking 209 students from three undergraduate classes and one professional master student class in colleges as study samples, this study empirically explored the effect and impacting mechanism of online consumers' perceived financial constraint on online new product purchase intention. Through the hierarchical multiple regression analysis of the data collected by the questionnaire, it was found that: (1) Perceived financial constraint was negatively related to online new product purchase intention. (2) Risk-taking tendency was positively related to online new product purchase intention, and mediated the relationship between perceived financial constraint and online new product purchase intention significantly. (3) Online shopping impulsivity moderated the relationship between perceived financial constraint and risk-taking tendency. Moreover, online shopping impulsivity had a significant negative impact on perceived financial constraint. The results have theoretical and practical significance.

Firstly, this study confirmed that the perceived financial constraint was a negative predictive variable that affected the online new product purchase intention. It can significantly reduce consumers' online new product purchase intention. Therefore, online merchants should conduct sufficient market research to identify the reasons for the decline in online consumers' purchase intention, and then make adjustments to their online products, including improving product functions, enhancing product quality, and increasing product value to meet the actual needs of consumers. In addition, online merchants should also reconsider pricing strategies and increase promotion efforts and advertising investment for online products to stimulate the online consumers' online new product purchase intention, thereby effectively weakening the negative impact of the perceived financial constraint.

Secondly, this study confirmed that risk-taking tendency played a significant mediating role between perceived financial constraint and online new product purchase intention. This research result uncovered the "black box" between perceived financial constraint and online new product purchase intention, suggesting that the perceived financial constraint can reduce consumers' online new product purchase intention by inhibiting online consumers' risk-taking tendency. Therefore, online merchants can help online consumers understand the usage of new online products by providing fully transparent product information to reduce consumers' fear of the unknowns of online products. They can also provide free trials of products and hold product demonstrations and experience activities to allow consumers experience products with lower risks, thereby effectively weakening the negative impact of being afraid to experience new online products due to financial constraints. In addition, online merchants can reduce the perceived risks of online consumers by providing risk-free return policies or satisfaction guarantees, thereby effectively improving online consumers' risk-taking tendency to purchase the online products.

Finally, this study confirmed that online shopping impulsivity not only directly had a significant negative impact on online consumers' perceived financial constraint, but also moderated the relationship between perceived financial constraint and risk-taking tendency. This conclusion is an important extension of the research on the impact of online consumers' perceived financial constraint on online new product purchase intention. It is the first time to explore the moderating influence of individual online shopping impulsivity on the process of financial constraints from the perspective of individual traits, and helps to reveal the transmission mechanism and boundary conditions between the perceived financial constraint and online new product purchase intention. Therefore, various measures should be taken to enhance customers' shopping impulsivity, thereby decrease the negative impact of perceived financial constraint on online consumers' risk-taking tendency.

Acknowledgments. This work was supported by Guangdong Provincial Philosophy and Social Science Project (GD23YGL10).

References

1. Rogers, E.M., Singhal, A., Quinlan, M.M: Diffusion of innovations. In: An Integrated Approach to Communication Theory and Research, pp. 432–448. Routledge, Abingdon (2014)

2. Huang, Y., Sengupta, J.: The influence of disease cues on preference for typical versus atypical products. J. Consum. Res. **47**(3), 393–411 (2020)
3. Jiang, Y.: The impact of new product brand names on consumer purchasing decisions – the mediating effect of brand association. Enterp. Econ. **40**(2), 72–81 (2021)
4. Llewellyn, D.J., Sanchez, X.: Individual differences and risk taking in rock climbing. Psychol. Sport Exerc. **9**(4), 413–426 (2008)
5. Jiang, S., Zhao, H.X., Meng, L.: Research on B2C online shopping online interaction and consumer impulse buying behavior. Inquiry into Econ. **5**, 64–73 (2014)
6. Tully, S.M., Hershfield, H.E., Meyvis, T.: Seeking lasting enjoyment with limited money: Financial constraints increase preference for material goods over experiences. J. Consum. Res. **42**(1), 59–75 (2015)
7. Hamilton, R.W., Mittal, C., Shah, A., Thompson, D.V., Griskevicius, V.: How financial constraints influence consumer behavior: An integrative framework. J. Consum. Psychol. **29**(2), 285–305 (2019)
8. Fishbein, M., Ajzen, I.: Belief, attitude, intention and behavior: an introduction to theory and research. Philos. Rhetoric **41**(4), 842–844 (1975)
9. Brockhaus, R.H., Sr.: Risk taking propensity of entrepreneurs. Acad. Manag. J. **23**(3), 509–520 (1980)
10. Ronay, R., Kim, D.Y.: Gender differences in explicit and implicit risk attitudes: a socially facilitated phenomenon. Br. J. Soc. Psychol. **45**(2), 397–419 (2006)
11. Chung, N., Song, H.G., Lee, H.: Consumers' impulsive buying behavior of restaurant products in social commerce. Int. J. Contemp. Hospitality Manag. **29**(2), 709–731 (2017)
12. Spiteri Cornish, L.: Why did I buy this? Consumers' post-impulse-consumption experience and its impact on the propensity for future impulse buying behavior. J. Consum. Behav. **19**(1), 36–46 (2020)
13. Yang, K., Lu, W.W.: Analysis of consumer impulse buying behavior on the Internet environment. Mod. Manag. Sci. **8**, 102–104 (2013)
14. Paley, A., Tully, S.M.: Sharma, E: Too constrained to converse: The effect of financial constraints on word of mouth. J. Consum. Res. **45**(5), 889–905 (2019)
15. Li, H., Guo, D.: Research on the relationship between online shopping experience sharing and impulsive buying behavior - based on the perspective of knowledge sharing. J. Hebei Univ. Econ. Bus. Compr. Ed. **15**(3), 77–80 (2015)
16. Goldberg, L.R.: A scientific collaboratory for the development of advanced measures of personality and other individual differences. International Personality Item Pool (1998)
17. Pavlou, P.: A: consumer acceptance of electronic commerce: integrating trust and risk with the technology acceptance model. Int. J. Electron. Commer. **7**(3), 101–134 (2003)
18. Baron, R.M., Kenny, D.: A: The moderator–mediator variable distinction in social psychological research: conceptual, strategic, and statistical considerations. J. Pers. Soc. Psychol. **51**(6), 1173–1182 (1986)
19. Hayes, A.F.: An Introduction to Mediation, Moderation and Conditional Process Analysis, A Regression-Based Approach. Guilford Press, New York (2013)
20. Aiken, L.S.: Multiple Regression: Testing and Interpreting Interactions. Sage Publications, Oaks (1991)

Timing Strategies in Introducing Digital Sensory Technologies for Online Retailers

Zhenglong Zhou[1], Fengying Hu[2(✉)], and Xiaonan Chen[1]

[1] School of Information Management, Central China Normal University, Wuhan 430079, China
[2] Business School, Hubei University, Wuhan 430062, China
fengyinghu@hubu.edu.cn

Abstract. This paper builds a dynamic multi-stage technology supply chain model including a technology provider and two competitive retailers, explores the timing strategies in introducing digital sensory technologies (the DSTs) for online retailers and analyses the impact of technology provider's response polices on retailers' decision-making. The results show that, when a retailer firstly introduces the DSTs and another retailer is taking a wait-and-see attitude towards introducing the DSTs (i.e., under the WAS strategy), a long period of monopoly period can stimulate retailers to introduce the DSTs, and the lower technology service fee will encourage the latter (retailer) to enter the market ahead of time, so that the latter retailer has an incentive to shift strategy choices and introduce the DSTs together with the competitor or sooner. Instead, the retailers will choose the AAS strategy, i.e., they vie to be the first to introduce the DSTs. Under certain conditions, the technology provider can satisfy the strategic needs of both the former and the latter through different (uniform /reinforcing /weakening) response policies, and strengthen or weaken the relationship between two competitive retailers through the standardized technology service fee, which plays a "Management Leverage" role.

Keywords: Online Retailers · Digital Sensory Technologies · Timing Strategies · Response Policies

1 Introduction

1.1 Motivations and Questions

When browsing online retailers' websites, consumers not only want to know how their clothes look, but also how they feel on their skin. This has to be done with digital sensory technologies (i.e., the DSTs), those that can generate sensory inputs and can enhance the consumer's shopping experience and prompt consumers to make purchasing decisions (Petit et al. 2019). DSTs include virtual reality (Pfeiffer et al. 2020), augmented reality (Pamuru et al. 2021, Wuttke et al. 2022), and other multi-sensory-enabling technologies. According to the researches of Pfeiffer et al. (2020), Pamuru et al. (2021) and Wuttke et al. (2022), virtual reality (VR) and augmented reality (AR) technologies have been used to improve psychological and emotional states that consumers interact with products in an online environment. Crucially, the seemingly more pleasurable experiences adopted by these VR and AR technologies were found to have a positive impact on consumers' willingness to pay and purchasing intentions (Petit et al. 2022, Barta et al. 2023, Branca et al. 2023).

From the embodied cognition theory, enjoyable shopping experiences are built on specific processing systems of physical states and sensory morphology in the brain (Ruusunen et al. 2023). Thus, all consumer experiences are based on the integration of sensory inputs that influence the latter's judgments and behaviors (Krishna 2012). In other words, the DSTs can more effectively influence consumers' sensory experience of a product, which in turn drives their buying decisions as quickly as possible (Krishna 2012, Shahid et al. 2022). Therefore, the DSTs provides a new online environment and presents a multi-sensory experience similar to that observed in the real world. For instance, the DSTs of realsee.com allows consumers to manipulate any product that they are interested in online store, and to rotate it through a 3D interactive view; and further, consumers can click on the dot to display the item of product and get the relevant information[1].

Therefore, online retailers have an incentive to introduce the DSTs to attract consumers to find the interested product (by rotating or zooming in the product image), which helps improve sensory consistency in product search (Fürst et al. 2021). Pfaff and Spann (2023) showed unfavorable AR contexts negatively affect consumers' product-related purchase intention. Von Der et al. (2023) emphasized the plausibility of AR content, e.g., a rational and deliberate assessment of AR content will impact utilitarian benefits. Thus, introducing the DSTs to build a good virtual environment cannot always provide consumers with a more comprehensive experience.

With that in mind, this paper wants to solve the following question.

Q1: When considering the DSTs can build a good virtual environment, whether introducing the DSTs is profitable for retailers or not?

In fact, not all online retailers are willing to introduce the DSTs in a context where emerging technologies are transforming the retail industry. On the one hand, some customers are averse (i.e., technology-biased) about emerging technologies (Allen and Choudhury 2022), so that retailers have no incentive to introduce technology, or they are willing to wait a while before considering introducing the DSTs. On the other hand, retailers have to consider cost and positive ROI; for instance, according to Zipline's 2022 retail technology report, retailers are making technology purchase decisions based upon the technology cost[2]. From the perspective of transaction cost economics, if the transaction costs of introducing the DSTs exceed the benefits of the DSTs, then online retailers have no incentive to introduce the DSTs (i.e., the DSTs don't generate effective market spillovers). As a result, some retailers are taking a wait-and-see attitude towards introducing new technologies and choosing a *wait-and-see strategy (i.e., WAS strategy)* based on the trade-off between benefits and costs. However, even though some retailers face great uncertainty and market risk, they vie to be the first to introduce the DSTs. This may be because traditional retailers are participating in the transformation and

---

[1] Source: https://www.realsee.com/website/solution/business.
[2] Source: https://getzipline.com/resources/retail-technology-report/.

technology upgrading under the new retail environment, so that they choose an *act-at-once (soon) strategy (i.e., AAS strategy)*. With this in mind, we attempt to address the following question.

Q2: Which (wait-and-see v.s act-at-once) strategy is better for competitive retailers under considering the introduction timing in the DSTs Introduction?

1.2 Contribution Statements

To properly answer these research questions, we consider a technology supply chain model between a technology provider and a retailer (or two competitive retailers) under different technology introduction strategies. Our studies has two main contributions. First, there is currently a scarcity of literature on the timing of technology introduction by retailers, both domestically and internationally. Thus, this paper has a certain degree of innovation and novelty. Additionally, this research will provide management insights and suggestions for the formulation of technology solutions by technology providers. Second, this paper considers the strategy choices of retailers regarding the timing of technology introduction and factors such as the level of technological output, adopting insights into strategy choices for technology transactions in the dynamic multi-agent supply chain system of the new retail market. This has significant practical value.

2   Main Model

2.1   Model Assumption

This paper constructs a dynamic multi-stage technology supply chain model involving a technology provider S and two competitive retailers R_i and R_j $(i, j = (1, 2), j \neq i)$. To address the timing of the DSTs introduction by retailers, this model sets a continuous time variable τ for the DSTs introduction, and τ is a continuous variable ranging from $[0, T]$ (Tan et al. 2022). At $\tau = \tau_1$, any retailer begins to decide the time of introducing the DSTs and signs a technology service contract with the provider, specifying the start date for technology application. When the technology provider and retailer(s) sign the contract, the technology service fee for per unit product can be set as w, the technological functionality or technology output level is θ, and to achieve a technology output, the technology R&D cost is a convex increasing function $F(\theta)$ in which $F\prime(\theta) > 0$ and $F''(\theta) > 0$. Following the extant literature (e.g., Biswas et al. 2023), to facilitate result development and derive more closed-form results, we consider the case when $F(\theta)$ is quadratic, i.e., $F(\theta) = \gamma\theta^2/2$, where γ $(\gamma > 0)$ represents the technology cost coefficient.

The strategies of introducing the DSTs can be divided into (a) WAS strategy and (b) AAS strategy:

(a) **WAS strategy:** When the first retailer R_1 decides to introduce the DSTs at time τ_1, the second retailer R_2 takes a wait-and-see attitude towards introducing the DSTs (e.g., observes and waits for a period). This results in the retailers introducing the DSTs through a sequential manner. Consequently, retailer R_1 operates as a monopolist and profits during the entire period $[\tau_1, \tau_2)$, known as *Period I—the Monopoly Period*.

In Period I, the technology provider initially decides the technology output level $\theta_{=1\backslash*\text{ROMAN}}$ for retailer R_1. Subsequently, retailer R_1 sets the price $p_{1,=1\backslash*\text{ROMAN}}$ for its product. It is not until time τ_2 that the second retailer R_2 decides to introduce the DSTs. Since retailer R_1 does not exit the market, both R_1 and R_2 will coexist in the period $[\tau_2, T)$ which is set as *Period II—the Competition Period*. The technology provider decides the technology output level θ_{II} for this period, and both retailers independently set the prices for their products, $p_{1,\text{II}}$ and $p_{2,\text{II}}$ during the competitive period $(\tau_2, 1]$. Let $t_I = \tau_2 - \tau_1$ and $t_{II} = T - \tau_2$ represent the lengths of Periods I and II respectively.

(b) **AAS strategy:** If both retailers (denoted as R_f and R_l) choose to introduce the DSTs simultaneously, i.e., at $\tau_f = \tau_l(\tau_f, \tau_l \in (0, T])$, they enter Period II—the Competition Period together and the lengths of Period II is $t_{II} = T - \tau_{f(l)}$. In this strategy, the market comprises two competitive retailers, R_f and R_l. For simplicity, we assume $T = 1$ and the technology provider adopts homogeneous technological functionality with the technology output level θ. Subsequently, both retailers simultaneously decide their respective prices $p_{f,\text{II}}$ and $p_{l,\text{II}}$.

To facilitate result development and derive more closed-form results, we assume that the technology provider adopts the following three polices to meet the varying needs of two retailers, where ρ is a discount factor and $0 < \rho < 1$:

(1) **Uniform policy:** The technology provider adopts the same technological functionality to both R_1 and R_2 in both Periods I and II, satisfying the technology output level $\theta_{1,\text{I}} = \theta_{1,\text{II}} = \theta_{2,\text{II}} = \theta$.

(2) **Reinforcing policy:** When only one retailer enters in the market of DSTs (Period I), the technology provider adopts a higher level of technological functionality to the former (retailer R_1), i.e., strengthens technological support for the first retailer and attracts them to early sign a technology contract. In Period II, the latter (i.e., retailer R_2) joins the market and obtains the lower technology output. Considering the competition in Period II, the technology output of retailer R_1 is the same to that of R_2, satisfying $\theta_{1,\text{I}} = \theta$, $\theta_{1,\text{II}} = \theta_{2,\text{II}} = \rho\theta$.

(3) **Weakening policy:** Contrary to the reinforcing policy, the technology provider will focus on increasing the technology output level in the competitive period (Period II) to meet the competitive demands of R_1 and R_2, thereby diminishing the technology output level provided solely to the monopolist R_1 in Period I. Hence, $\theta_{1,\text{I}} = \rho\theta$, $\theta_{1,\text{II}} = \theta_{2,\text{II}} = \theta$.

2.2 Decision Analysis

We assume that the demand rate λ of retailers (market demand for per unit time) is sensitive to the market price p set by retailers and the technology output level θ provided by the technology provider. Following the extant literature (e.g., Biswas et al. 2023), we set $\lambda = u - p + \beta\theta$, where $u(u > 0)$ represents the potential market demand, and $\beta(\beta > 0)$ is the enhancement effect of the technology output level on demand (e.g., products' sensory congruency through the DSTs). Furthermore, in a competitive market environment (in Period II), the demand rate of two competitive retailers (R_i and $R_{j,j\neq i}$) is $\lambda_{i,\text{II}} = u - p_i + \beta\theta + \eta(p_{j,\text{II}} - p_{i,\text{II}})$, $j \neq i$, where $\eta(\eta > 0)$ represents the competitive intensity between two retailers.

Thus, the demand rates for retailers under the WAS strategy in each period can be expressed as follows (note that during Period I, retailer R_2 does not introduce the DSTs, and only R_1 is present in the market, thus $\lambda_{2,I} = 0$):

$$\text{Period I-Monopoly}: \lambda_{1,I} = u - p_{1,II} + \beta\theta_{II}, \lambda_{2,I} = 0 \tag{1}$$

$$\text{Period II-Competition}: \lambda_{i,II} = u - p_{i,II} + \beta\theta_{II} + \eta(p_{j,II} - p_{i,II}) \tag{2}$$

Correspondingly, $j \neq i, i, j \in \{1, 2\}$. Under the AAS strategy, the market only exists in Period II, so that the demand rate for each retailer can be expressed as (2), and $i, j \in \{f, l\}$.

Following the model proposed by Tang et al. (2022), the demand of retailer $i \in \{1, 2, f, l\}$ in period $n \in \{I, II\}$ is the product of the corresponding demand rate and the period lengths, i.e., $D_{i,n} = \lambda_{i,n}t_n$. Therefore, the corresponding profit function can be expressed as $\Pi_i = D_{i,I} \times (p_{i,I} - w) + D_{i,II} \times (p_{i,II} - w)$. Based on the model assumption of Figs. 1(a), the total profit function of retailer R_1 under the WAS strategy equals the sum of the profits in the two periods. Retailer R_2, with zero demand rate in Period I, derives the total profit solely from Period II, which are respectively shown in Formula (3) and (4). Table 1 lists the profit functions of two retailers under different scenarios.

$$\begin{aligned}
\Pi_1(p_{1,II}, p_{2,II}, \theta_I, \theta_{II}) &= D_{1,I} \times (p_{1,I} - w) + D_{1,II} \times (p_{1,II} - w) \\
&= \lambda_{1,I}t_I \times (p_{1,I} - w) + \lambda_{1,II}t_{II} \times (p_{1,II} - w) \\
&= (u - p_{1,I} + \beta\theta_I)t_I \times (p_{1,I} - w) + [u - p_{1,II} + \beta\theta_{II} + \eta(p_{2,II} - p_{1,II})]t_{II}(p_{1,II} - w)
\end{aligned} \tag{3}$$

$$\begin{aligned}
\Pi_2(p_{1,II}, p_{2,II}, \theta_I, \theta_{II}) &= D_{2,I} \times (p_{2,I} - w) + D_{2,II} \times (p_{2,II} - w) \\
&= \lambda_{2,I}t_I \times (p_{2,I} - w) + \lambda_{2,II}t_{II} \times (p_{2,II} - w) \\
&= 0 + [u - p_{2,II} + \beta\theta_{II} + \eta(p_{1,II} - p_{2,II})]t_{II} \times (p_{2,II} - w) \\
&= [u - p_{2,II} + \beta\theta_{II} + \eta(p_{1,II} - p_{2,II})]t_{II} \times (p_{2,II} - w)
\end{aligned} \tag{4}$$

Further, we obtain the profit function of the technology provider under different strategies, the result under the WAS strategy is as following:

$$\Pi_S = w \times (D_{1,I} + D_{1,II} + D_{2,II}) - max\left\{\frac{1}{2}\gamma\theta_I{}^2, \frac{1}{2}\gamma\theta_{II}{}^2\right\} \tag{5}$$

The result under the AAS strategy is as following:

$$\Pi_S{}^{AAS} = w \times (D_{f,II} + D_{l,II}) - \frac{1}{2}\gamma\theta^2 \tag{6}$$

Note that, the technology service fee for per unit product is multiplied by the total demand under introducing the DSTs, and then minus the total R&D cost. Under the WAS strategy, to avoid double-counting R&D cost in both periods, we use the larger R&D cost in Period I and Period II to represent $F(\theta)$.

Table 1. Profit Function of Retailers

	Uniform policy (U)	$\Pi_1^U = (u - p_{1,I} + \beta\theta)t_I \times (p_{1,I} - w) + [u - p_{1,II} + \beta\theta + \eta(p_{2,II} - p_{1,II})]t_{II} \times (p_{1,II} - w)$ $\Pi_2^U = [u - p_{2,II} + \beta\theta + \eta(p_{1,II} - p_{2,II})]t_{II} \times (p_{2,II} - w)$
WAS strategy	Reinforcing policy (R)	$\Pi_1^R = (u - p_{1,I} + \beta\theta)t_I \times (p_{1,I} - w) + [u - p_{1,II} + \rho\beta\theta + \eta(p_{2,II} - p_{1,II})]t_{II} \times (p_{1,II} - w)$ $\Pi_2^R = [u - p_{2,II} + \rho\beta\theta + \eta(p_{1,II} - p_{2,II})]t_{II} \times (p_{2,II} - w)$
	Weakening policy (W)	$\Pi_1^W = (u - p_{1,I} + \rho\beta\theta)t_I \times (p_{1,I} - w) + [u - p_{1,II} + \beta\theta + \eta(p_{2,II} - p_{1,II})]t_{II} \times (p_{1,II} - w)$ $\Pi_2^W = [u - p_{2,II} + \beta\theta + \eta(p_{1,II} - p_{2,II})]t_{II} \times (p_{2,II} - w)$
AAS strategy		$\Pi_f(p_{f,II}, p_{l,II}, \theta) = [u - p_{f,II} + \beta\theta + \eta(p_{l,II} - p_{f,II})]t_{II} \times (p_{f,II} - w)$ $\Pi_l(p_{f,II}, p_{l,II}, \theta) = [u - p_{l,II} + \beta\theta + \eta(p_{f,II} - p_{l,II})]t_{II} \times (p_{l,II} - w)$

3 Retailers' Strategy Analysis

3.1 Equilibrium of Retailers' Strategies

For obtaining the equilibrium results of retailers under different strategies, we externalize the technology provider's variables θ and w to simplify the solving process. After taking the WAS strategy as an example and using backward induction, we obtain the solving model sequence as following:

$$\begin{cases} \max_{p_{1,II}} \Pi_1(p_{1,II}, p_{2,II}, \theta) \\ \max_{p_{2,II}} \Pi_2(p_{1,II}, p_{2,II}, \theta) \end{cases} \rightarrow \max_{p_{1,II}} \Pi_1(p_{1,I}, \theta) \qquad (7)$$

Under the condition where the technology provider adopts the uniform policy to retailers, we get the equilibrium prices and profits for retailers R_1 and R_2 under the WAS and AAS strategies, as shown in Lemma 1 (the proof is is omitted).

Lemma 1: Equilibrium results under different strategies exhibit significant similarities, but primarily differ in the discount factor ρ of the technology output level, as shown in the following (Table 2).

Table 2. Equilibrium results under different strategies

(a) Equilibrium Solution under the WAS strategy		
Uniform policy (U)	Reinforcing policy (R)	Weakening policy (W)
$p_{1,\mathrm{II}}{}^{U} = p_{2,\mathrm{II}}{}^{U} = \dfrac{\beta\theta+u+w+\eta w}{\eta+2}$	$p_{1,\mathrm{II}}{}^{R} = p_{2,\mathrm{II}}{}^{R} = \dfrac{\beta\theta+u+w+\eta w}{\eta+2}$	$p_{1,\mathrm{II}}{}^{W} = p_{2,\mathrm{II}}{}^{W} = \dfrac{\beta\theta+u+w+\eta w}{\eta+2}$
$p_{1,\mathrm{I}}{}^{U} = \dfrac{\beta\theta+u+w}{2}$	$p_{1,\mathrm{I}}{}^{R} = \dfrac{\beta\theta+u+w}{2}$	$p_{1,\mathrm{I}}{}^{W} = \dfrac{\rho\beta\theta+u+w}{2}$
$\Pi_{1}{}^{U} = \dfrac{(\beta\theta+u-w)^{2}}{4}\left[t_{\mathrm{I}} + \dfrac{4(\eta+1)t_{\mathrm{II}}}{(\eta+2)^{2}}\right]$	$\Pi_{1}{}^{R} = \dfrac{(\beta\theta+u-w)^{2}t_{\mathrm{I}}}{4} + \dfrac{(\eta+1)(\rho\beta\theta+u-w)^{2}t_{\mathrm{II}}}{(\eta+2)^{2}}$	$\Pi_{1}{}^{W} = \dfrac{(\rho\beta\theta+u-w)^{2}t_{\mathrm{I}}}{4} + \dfrac{(\eta+1)(\beta\theta+u-w)^{2}t_{\mathrm{II}}}{(\eta+2)^{2}}$
$\Pi_{2}{}^{U} = \dfrac{(\eta+1)(\beta\theta+u-w)^{2}t_{\mathrm{II}}}{(\eta+2)^{2}}$	$\Pi_{2}{}^{R} = \dfrac{(\eta+1)(\rho\beta\theta+u-w)^{2}t_{\mathrm{II}}}{(\eta+2)^{2}}$	$\Pi_{2}{}^{W} = \dfrac{(\eta+1)(\beta\theta+u-w)^{2}t_{\mathrm{II}}}{(\eta+2)^{2}}$

(b) Equilibrium solution under the AAS strategy
$p_{f,\mathrm{II}} = p_{l,\mathrm{II}} = \dfrac{\beta\theta+u+w+\eta w}{\eta+2}, \ \Pi_{f} = \Pi_{l} = \dfrac{(\eta+1)(\beta\theta+u-w)^{2}t_{\mathrm{II}}}{(\eta+2)^{2}}$

3.2　Different Strategy Choices of Retailers

Combining the equilibrium results under different strategies, we obtain Proposition 1 and Proposition 2 for the sake of demonstrating the strategic trade-off between the WAS strategy and the AAS strategy.

Proposition 1: Setting a longer monopoly period can inspire retailers to take the initiative in introducing the DSTs. In this way, the retailer's strategy choice will be unaffected by the technology provider's differentiated response polices.

(1) Under the condition that $t_{\mathrm{I}} > t^{*}$, the WAS strategy is comprehensively advantageous;
(2) Under the condition that $t_{\mathrm{I}} \leq t^{*}$, the WAS strategy is partially advantageous, wherein,

$$t^{*} = \frac{4\left[(\beta\theta+u-w)^{2}-(\rho\beta\theta+u-w)^{2}\right](\eta+1)t_{\mathrm{II}}}{(\beta\theta+u-w)^{2}(\eta+2)^{2}}.$$

Proposition 1 shows that, as long as the monopoly period length for retailer R_{1} is sufficiently long, regardless of the response polices adopted by the technology provider, retailer R_{1} will choose the WAS strategy. That is, only when the monopoly period length is short, the profits gained by introducing the DSTs simultaneously with competing retailers might be higher. Additionally, we find the maximum profits for the technology provider adopting a uniform policy or a weakening policy are greater than those under the AAS strategy.

A longer monopoly period ensures that the former who introduces the DSTs firstly have stronger bargaining power, helping to secure more favorable technology service fees and terms from the technology provider, thereby reducing investing costs. In practice, retailers taking the initiative to sign technology service contracts with technology providers can also create a win-win situation. For example, in China's new retail industry, according to the 2020 semi-annual report of Sun Art Retail, Alibaba, as the technology provider, contributed to a 16.8% increase in net profit year-over-year and brought nearly 50 million users to Sun Art Retail, with nearly 13 million active users; Alibaba's financial report for the first quarter of the fiscal year 2021 also showed that up to the first half of 2020, the revenue contributed to Sun Art Retail by Alibaba's empowerment accounted for about 15% of the total revenue.

Proposition 2: Lowering of the technology service fee will motivate the latter (e.g., retailer R_2) to enter the market earlier, giving them the incentive to change their strategy and choose to introduce the DSTs simultaneously with competitors.

(1) Under the condition that $w > \frac{\beta\theta(1+\rho)}{2} + u$, it follows that $\Pi_2{}^R > \Pi_l$ (or $\Pi_2{}^U$ or $\Pi_2{}^W$), i.e., the WAS strategy is more advantageous;

(2) Under the condition that $w \leq \frac{\beta\theta(1+\rho)}{2} + u$, it follows that $\Pi_2{}^R \leq \Pi_l$ (or $\Pi_2{}^U$ or $\Pi_2{}^W$), i.e., the AAS strategy is more advantageous.

Proposition 2 shows that for retailer R_2, it is advisable to avoid introducing the DSTs at the same time as competitors when the service fee is high, and R_2 will choose a waiting and convince the technology provider to choose a reinforcing policy, i.e., providing a higher technology output level to competitor R_1 during the monopoly period. On one hand, a higher technology service fee can increase the financial burden on the business, affecting the profits of the latter. For example, retailer R_2 can control the total cost of the enterprise by convincing the technology provider to lower the technology output level; on the other hand, the latter hope to "free ride", not only share the demand driven by the former's technology marketing, but also obtain best practices and expert opinions which are of reference value and guiding significance, helping the latter to understand the technology environment and market competition more quickly. For example, the technology provider may release reports on technology trends and industry development after collaborating with retailer R_1, so that retailer R_2 can hitch a ride to optimize the strategy choice.

Proposition 3: Under the WAS strategy, lowering of the technology service fee will encourage two retailers to form an alliance and jointly persuade the technology provider to choose a uniform policy; whereas increasing the technology service fee will prevent the alliance of two retailers.

Proposition 3 shows that if the technology service fee is lower, two retailers (R_1 and R_2) are willing to introduce the DSTs under the WAS strategy, and prefer the technology provider to adopt a uniform policy to maximize their profits; when the technology service fee is higher and the monopoly period length is shorter, two retailers (R_1 and R_2) are willing to prefer the technology provider to adopt a reinforcing policy; when the technology service fee is higher and the monopoly period length is longer, retailer R_2 wants the strategy to remain unchanged, i.e., prefer the technology provider to adopt a reinforcing policy, while retailer R_1 prefers the technology provider to adopt a weakening policy.

In summary, under the condition of $w \leq \frac{\beta\theta(1+\rho)}{2} + u$, the WAS strategy can achieve a win-win result for both retailers, and they should form an alliance to jointly persuade the technology provider to choose a uniform policy; subsequently, increasing the technology service fee will prevent the alliance of the two retailers. For example, in Period I (with $t_1 \geq \frac{4(\eta+1)t_{II}}{(\eta+2)^2}$) under the higher technology service fee, retailer R_1 prefers a weakening policy, and retailer R_2 prefers a reinforcing policy; under $t_1 \leq t^* < \frac{4(\eta+1)t_{II}}{(\eta+2)^2}$), retailer R_1 prefers a AAS strategy (as shown in Proposition 1(2)), and retailer R_2 prefers a reinforcing policy. Therefore, we argue that the technology provider can adopt a homogenized technology service fee which simultaneously satisfies the strategic needs of the former and the latter, and the homogenized technology service fee also effectively strengthens or weakens the alliance between two retailers, i.e., plays a "Management Leverage" role.

4 Extension and Discussion

In Sect. 3.2, we find setting a longer monopoly period (i.e., $t_1 > t^*$) can inspire retailers to take the initiative in introducing the DSTs. This result is valuable for retailers, and can guide retailers to make rational choices. However, which Measures should retailers take to effectively introduce new technology? Previous studies lack analysis. Thus, this section analyses the impact of the product competition intensity (η) and the discount factor (ρ) on t^*, so that take specific measures for retailers.

To facilitate result development and derive more closed-form results, we set $\tau_1 = 0$, $\tau_2 = t$, and thus $t_1 = t$ and $t_{II} = 1 - t$. According to Proposition 1, we show that t^* changes as t^{**}, i.e.,

$$t^{**} = \frac{4(\eta + 1)[(\beta\theta + u - w)^2 - [(\rho\beta\theta + u - w)^2]}{(\beta\theta + u - w)^2(\eta + 2)^2 + 4(\eta + 1)[(\beta\theta + u - w)^2 - [(\rho\beta\theta + u - w)^2]},$$

thereby giving Proposition 5, and the proof is shown in the Appendix.

Proposition 4: Retailers should reduce the competition intensity and response the differentiated policies.

(1) Time length t^{**} in period I decreases with the increase of the competition intensity (η), i.e., $\partial t^{**}/\partial\eta < 0$;

(2) When $w > \rho\beta\theta + u$, it follows that $\partial t^{**}/\partial\rho > 0$, when $w < \rho\beta\theta + u$, it follows that $\partial t^{**}/\partial\rho < 0$, and when $\rho = 1$, it follows that $t^{**} = 0$.

To verify the conclusion of Proposition 4, this paper uses the following figure to characterize it numerically.

Proposition 4 show that, retailers should reduce the intensity of their product competition, which can lessen the impact of technology providers' differentiated response policies on the DSTs introduction strategies. For example, each retailer just need to introduce the DSTs for the new or exclusive products. In general, new products or exclusive products are less competitive, so that retailers who firstly introduce the DSTs can obtain the longer time of period I, as shown in Fig. 1(a). Moreover, if the technology provider provide the lower technology service fee, the former retailers should require the technology providers to enhance their differentiated response policies, such as offering larger discounts. Thus, technology providers strengthen the technological support for the first retailer and attracts them to early sign a technology contract. On the contrary, if the technology provider provide the higher technology service fee, retailers should require the technology providers to reduce the difference between response policies, as shown in Fig. 1(b).

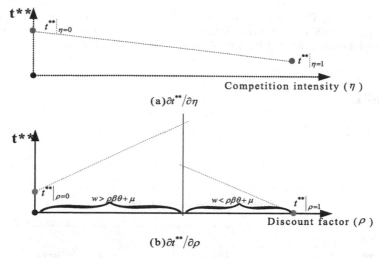

Fig. 1. The impact of η and ρ on the time length in period I

5 Conclusions

This paper builds a dynamic multi-stage technology supply chain model involving a technology provider and two competitive retailers. To address the strategic timing choice of two retailers for introducing the DSTs, the model employs a continuous time variable; further, considering the real-world context where the technology provider adopts differentiated technology response policies to retailers: an uniform policy, a reinforcing policy, and a weakening policy. And the results show that, when a retailer firstly introduces the DSTs and another retailer is taking a wait-and-see attitude towards introducing the DSTs (i.e., under the WAS strategy), a long period of monopoly period can stimulate retailers to introduce the DSTs, and the lower technology service fee will encourage the latter (retailer) to enter the market ahead of time, so that the latter retailer has an incentive to shift strategy choices and introduce the DSTs together with the competitor or sooner. Instead, the retailers will choose the AAS strategy, i.e., they vie to be the first to introduce the DSTs. Under certain conditions, the technology provider can satisfy the strategic needs of both the former and the latter through different (uniform /reinforcing /weakening) response policies, and strengthen or weaken the relationship between two competitive retailers, which plays a"Management Leverage" role.

However, there are still limitations in this study. First, future research could relax assumptions such as the linear impact of factors like technology output level on demand, and strengthen the conclusions of this paper by comparing equilibrium results under linear and nonlinear models. Second, for the customer who are anxious or averse about emerging technologies (Kundu and Ramdas 2022), they will not use DSTs and cannot enjoy the value brought by DSTs functionality; for the customer who are willingly using the emerging technology functionality to gain additional value (Sun and Ji 2022). Thus, future research can consider the above consumer segmentation, i.e., relax assumptions that not all online retailers are willing to introduce DSTs, thereby strengthening our research conclusions.

Acknowledgement. This research was supported by the National Social Science Foundation of China (23FGLB083), the National Natural Science Foundation of China (72302080), the Fundamental Research Funds for the Central Universities (CCNU24ZZ134).

Appendix

Appendix 1

See Table 3.

Table 3. The notations of H and A

WAS strategy		
$H^U = \frac{1+\eta}{2+\eta}$,	$H^R = \frac{2+\eta+\rho\eta}{2+\eta}$,	$H^W = \frac{2\rho+\eta+\rho\eta}{2+\eta}$,
$A^U = 4t_{II}H^U + t_{II}$	$A^R = 2t_{II}H^R + t_I$	$A^W = 2t_{II}H^W + \rho t_I$

AAS strategy
$H^{AAS} = \frac{1+\eta}{2+\eta}$, $A^{AAS} = 2t_{II}H^{AAS}$

Proofs of Proposition 1 and Proposition 2.

(1) The inequality $\Pi_1{}^U - \Pi_f = \frac{(\beta\theta+u-w)^2 t_I}{4} > 0$ always holds, and $\Pi_1{}^U > \Pi_f$. In addition, it is easy to see that $\Pi_2{}^U = \Pi_l$.

(2) Let $\Pi_1{}^R - \Pi_f = \frac{4(\eta+1)t_I[(\rho\beta\theta+u-w)^2-(\beta\theta+u-w)^2]+(\beta\theta+u-w)^2(\eta+2)^2t_I}{4(\eta+2)^2} = 0$, then

we find: $When = \frac{4[(\beta\theta+u-w)^2-(\rho\beta\theta+u-w)^2](\eta+1)t_{II}}{(\beta\theta+u-w)^2(\eta+2)^2}$, we have $\Pi_1{}^R = \Pi_f$;

when $t_I > \frac{4[(\beta\theta+u-w)^2-(\rho\beta\theta+u-w)^2](\eta+1)t_{II}}{(\beta\theta+u-w)^2(\eta+2)^2}$, we have $\Pi_1{}^R > \Pi_f$; when $t_I < \frac{4[(\beta\theta+u-w)^2-(\rho\beta\theta+u-w)^2](\eta+1)t_{II}}{(\beta\theta+u-w)^2(\eta+2)^2}$, we have $\Pi_1{}^R < \Pi_f$.

Let $\Pi_2{}^R - \Pi_l = \frac{(\eta+1)t_{II}[(\rho\beta\theta+u-w)^2-(\beta\theta+u-w)^2]}{(\eta+2)^2} = 0$, then we find:

$When w = \frac{\beta\theta(1+\rho)}{2} + u$, we have $\Pi_2{}^R = \Pi_l$; when $w > \frac{\beta\theta(1+\rho)}{2} + u$, we have $\Pi_2{}^R > \Pi_l$; when $w < \frac{\beta\theta(1+\rho)}{2} + u$, we have $\Pi_2{}^R < \Pi_l$.

(3) The inequality $\Pi_1{}^W - \Pi_f = \frac{(\rho\beta\theta+u-w)^2 t_I}{4} > 0$ always holds, so $\Pi_1{}^W > \Pi_f$. In addition, it is easy to see that $\Pi_2{}^W = \Pi_l$. Proposition 1 is proved.

Similarly, when $w > \frac{\beta\theta(1+\rho)}{2}+u$, $\Pi_2{}^R > \Pi_l$; when $w \leq \frac{\beta\theta(1+\rho)}{2}+u$, $\Pi_2{}^R \leq \Pi_l$, and $\Pi_2{}^U = \Pi_2{}^W = \Pi_l$. That is, Proposition 2 is proved. Q.E.D.

Proof of Proposition 3.

The proof of Proposition 3 is similar to the proofs of Proposition 1 and Proposition 2, can be omitted.

Proof of Proposition 4.

The proofs of Proposition 4 is similar to the proofs of Proposition 1 and Proposition 2, can be omitted.

References

Allen, R., Choudhury, P.: Algorithm-augmented work and domain experience: the countervailing forces of ability and aversion. Organ. Sci. **33**(1), 149–169 (2022)

Barta, S., Gurrea, R., Flavián, C.: Using augmented reality to reduce cognitive dissonance and increase purchase intention. Comput. Hum. Behav. **140**, 107564 (2023). https://doi.org/10.1016/j.chb.2022.107564

Branca, G., Resciniti, R., Loureiro, S.M.C.: Virtual is so real! Consumers' evaluation of product packaging in virtual reality. Psychol. Mark. **40**(3), 596–609 (2023)

Fürst, A., Pečornik, N., Binder, C.: All or nothing in sensory marketing: must all or only some sensory attributes be congruent with a product's primary function? J. Retail. **97**(3), 439–458 (2021)

Krishna, A.: An integrative review of sensory marketing: engaging the senses to affect perception, judgment and behavior. J. Consum. Psychol. **22**(3), 332–351 (2012)

Kundu, A., Ramdas, K.: Timely after-sales service and technology adoption: evidence from the off-grid solar market in Uganda. Manuf. Serv. Oper. Manag. **24**(3), 1329–1348 (2022)

Pamuru, V., Khern-am-nuai, W., Kannan, K.: The impact of an augmented-reality game on local businesses: a study of Pokémon go on restaurants. Inf. Syst. Res. **32**(3), 950–966 (2021)

Petit, O., Javornik, A., Velasco, C.: We eat first with our (digital) eyes: enhancing mental simulation of eating experiences via visual-enabling technologies. J. Retail. **98**(2), 277–293 (2022)

Petit, O., Velasco, C., Spence, C.: Digital sensory marketing: integrating new technologies into multisensory online experience. J. Interact. Mark. **45**(1), 42–61 (2019)

Pfaff, A., Spann, M.: When reality backfires: product evaluation context and the effectiveness of augmented reality in e-commerce. Psychol. Mark. **40**, 2413–2427 (2023)

Pfeiffer, J., Pfeiffer, T., Meißner, M., Weiß, E.: Eye-tracking-based classification of information search behavior using machine learning: evidence from experiments in physical shops and virtual reality shopping environments. Inf. Syst. Res. **31**(3), 675–691 (2020)

Ruusunen, N., Hallikainen, H., Laukkanen, T.: Does imagination compensate for the need for touch in 360-virtual shopping? Int. J. Inf. Manag. **70**, 102622 (2023). https://doi.org/10.1016/j.ijinfomgt.2023.102622

Shahid, S., Paul, J., Gilal, F.G., Ansari, S.: The role of sensory marketing and brand experience in building emotional attachment and brand loyalty in luxury retail stores. Psychol. Mark. **39**(7), 1398–1412 (2022)

Sun, C., Ji, Y.: For better or for worse: impacts of IoT technology in e-commerce channel. Prod. Oper. Manag. **31**(3), 1353–1371 (2022)

Tan, Y.C., Chandukala, S.R., Reddy, S.K.: Augmented reality in retail and its impact on sales. J. Mark. **86**(1), 48–66 (2022)

Tang, W., Wang, T., Xu, W.: Sooner or later? The role of adoption timing in new technology introduction. Prod. Oper. Manag. **31**(4), 1663–1678 (2022)

Von Der Au, S., Rauschnabel, P.A., Felix, R., Hinsch, C.: Context in augmented reality marketing: does the place of use matter? Psychol. Mark. **40**, 2447–2463 (2023)

Wuttke, D., Upadhyay, A., Siemsen, E., Wuttke-Linnemann, A.: Seeing the bigger picture? Ramping up production with the use of augmented reality. Manuf. Serv. Oper. Manag. **24**(4), 2349–2366 (2022)

Bibliometric Analysis of Open Innovation Communities Based on Citespace

Jiangping Wan[1](✉), Siting Lin[1](✉), and Xuanqi Liu[2]

[1] School of Business Administration, South China University of Technology,
Guangzhou 510640, China
csjpwan@scut.edu.cn, 202220131906@mail.scut.edu.cn
[2] School of Engineering and Technology, Yangen University, Quanzhou 362011, China

Abstract. [Purpose/Significance] With the continuous development of Internet technology, open innovation communities (OICs) have become a crucial force driving scientific and technological progress as well as industrial development. In-depth research and analysis of OICS are of significant importance in understanding their developmental trends, influencing factors, and future tendencies. [Method/Process] A total of 129 Chinese core literature articles were selected from the China National Knowledge Infrastructure (CNKI) database within a specific time range. English literature data were collected from the SCI and SSCI of the Web of Science Core Collection, totaling 128 articles. CiteSpace, a visualization knowledge mapping tool, was utilized for bibliometric analysis, examining the growth trends, current status, and research hotspots in the OIC field. Based on this analysis, potential areas for future research emphasis were identified. [Results/Conclusion] Building upon the definitions provided by domestic and international scholars concerning open innovation communities, this paper summarized five major characteristics of these communities: virtuality, goal orientation, interactivity, network structure, and voluntariness. The results of literature growth trends indicate a general increase in the number of publications within the OIC field, garnering widespread attention in academia. By comparing keyword clustering maps of Chinese and English literature, it was observed that common focal points revolve around community user creative management, user behavior analysis, and corporate performance research. However, differences exist as domestic literature emphasizes leading user identification while foreign literature pays more attention to research on open-source software communities within OICs. Future research should concentrate on leading user identification and demand analysis.

Keywords: Open Innovation Communities · Knowledge Mapping · CiteSpace

1 Introduction

The surge of globalization and rapid advancement in information technology have significantly impacted corporate innovation. Relying solely on internal resources for closed innovation is no longer sufficient to adapt to the complex and ever-changing competitive environment. Many enterprises are establishing Open Innovation Communities (OICs) in response, inviting external users to participate in innovative activities such as internal product development and service design through online platforms. As an emerging content generation platform, OICs have garnered widespread attention and high regard in both industry and academia. In the industry, OICs have flourished, with prominent communities like Salesforce, Starbucks' MyStarbucksIdea, Dell IdeaStorm, Xiaomi's MIUI Community, Huawei's Pollen Club, Honor's Club, Haier's HOPE Community, among others. User-contributed content within OICs significantly enhances a company's innovation performance. Statistics show that one-third of modification suggestions for Xiaomi's MIUI operating system are provided by community users [4], and MyStarbucksIdea amassed 150,000 ideas within just five years. In academia, the emergence and rapid development of OICs have sparked extensive scholarly research and practical discussions. Increasingly, both domestic and international scholars have regarded OICs as an important research topic in innovation management. Research on open innovation communities abroad has reached a relatively mature stage, accumulating a vast amount of literature and case studies. However, domestic research in this field is still in an exploratory and nascent stage, necessitating further in-depth research and practical experience to refine the theoretical framework and methodologies within this domain.

Over the past few decades, significant progress has been made in the research field of OICs both domestically and internationally, covering numerous related topics such as community member participation behavior, knowledge sharing mechanisms, construction and management of innovation ecosystems, and value co-creation. However, due to the broad scope of research content and the extensive volume of related literature covering various research themes, an effective method is required to synthesize and analyze these works, enabling a better understanding of research hotspots and trends. Given the vast number of publications, the visualization analysis tool CiteSpace can conduct bibliometric research within specific academic disciplines, revealing research hotspots, frontiers, and developmental trends within a discipline during a certain period, providing a clear overview of a particular academic domain. Hence, this paper will utilize CiteSpace for bibliometric analysis systematically to explore the research progress and trends within the OICs field. Through the implementation of this research, we aim to offer new methods and perspectives for the study and practice of open innovation communities, providing valuable references for future research endeavors.

2   Understanding and Characteristics of Open Innovation Communities

2.1   Essence of Open Innovation Communities

OICs originated from the concept of open innovation proposed by Professor Chesbrough in 2003 [1]. The concept emphasizes the permeability of organizational boundaries and the significance of external resources [2]. Enterprises can purposefully import and export innovative resources, maximizing the value of these resources, effectively enhancing innovation capabilities, and assisting in achieving and sustaining innovation. OICs serves as a pivotal platform for enterprises to achieve open innovation [3]. It is a user-centric virtual community established by enterprises or third-party platforms [4], fundamentally operating as an internet-based user-generated content platform.

The rise and application of OICs have garnered widespread attention, leading researchers from various academic fields to propose different definitions and interpretations. Gangi et al. consider OICs as communities composed of individuals distributed across different locations, focusing on solving general issues or developing new solutions through computer-mediated communication [10]. This definition emphasizes the distributed nature of OICs and their use of computer communication to support collaboration and innovation. The primary goal of open innovation communities is to address problems and develop new solutions, thereby increasing their influence on enterprise innovation. West et al. propose that OICs are voluntary, non-coercive associations, typically lacking prior organizational affiliations among community members, who unite to achieve a shared goal of creation or advancement of innovation [11]. Schröder et al. interpret OICs as virtual communities comprising numerous voluntarily participating individuals aiming to seek new, creative solutions, encompassing both product-related issues and personal needs [13]. Zhang Keyong views OICs as open collaborative environments developed based on internet technology, serving as crucial platforms for enterprises to coordinate internal and external innovation resources to achieve technological, product, or service innovation [14]. Zhang Ning and colleagues define OICs as vital channels for value co-creation between enterprises and consumers, primarily using the internet as a communication medium, with consumers and enterprise R&D personnel as main members, aiming to address product issues or gather innovative product suggestions [15].

Among these scholars' perspectives, the definitions of OICs generally encompass four aspects: entity, technology, scope, and purpose. This paper considers OICs as online virtual communities established by enterprises using internet technology, centered around users. Their purpose is to encourage users to collaboratively develop new innovative ideas through social interaction, integrating these ideas into enterprise product development and service design processes to support the realization of specific innovations.

2.2 Characteristics of Open Innovation Communities

Based on the analysis of domestic and international scholars' definitions of OICs, this paper summarizes five major characteristics of OICs: virtuality [4, 10, 13, 14], goal orientation [11, 12, 15], interactivity [13], network structure [10, 11, 16], and voluntariness [11, 13].

Virtuality: This characteristic is reflected in its dependence on the internet and digital technology, enabling members to communicate and collaborate without being restricted by time or space, anytime and anywhere.

Goal Orientation: The establishment of OICs is aimed at attracting more external users to participate in internal innovation and driving the achievement of innovative goals. OICs aim to foster the generation of new and creative ideas and solutions, introducing them into the market to meet user needs or address specific problems.

Interactivity: This is manifested in multiple interactions between community members, platform interfaces, among community members, and between community members and community managers. Firstly, community members contributing knowledge can understand the innovation needs of the enterprise and the creative content of other members through the platform, thereby engaging in knowledge creation. Secondly, community members can share innovative ideas and provide feedback through various means such as likes, comments, and bookmarks, fostering interactions not limited to one-on-one communication. Community members can interact simultaneously with multiple others, collectively propelling innovation. Furthermore, community managers gain insights and ideas from members, providing resources, support, feedback, and rewards to promote innovation prosperity.

Network Structure: Within OICs, community members engage in social interactions through internet platforms, such as liking, commenting, or bookmarking each other's ideas and creativity, collectively addressing problems or developing innovations. These interactions establish social relationships, interconnecting community members, forming a social network. This social network significantly influences information dissemination, knowledge sharing, and collaboration within OICs.

Voluntariness: Participation by community members is based on personal willingness and interest rather than mandatory requirements or specific organizational affiliations. Member involvement is voluntary, where they autonomously choose to join the community, share innovative ideas, interact with other members, and collectively achieve innovation goals.

3   Current Research Status of Open Innovation Communities

Chinese literature data were obtained from the China National Knowledge Infrastructure (CNKI) database using the search term 'Open Innovation Community' with no specified time range. Irrelevant or minimally related documents such as handbooks or book reviews were excluded, and duplicate literature was removed, resulting in a final dataset of 129 articles. English literature data were sourced from the Science Citation Index (SCI) and Social Sciences Citation Index (SSCI) within the Web of Science Core Collection. The search query used was 'TS=("Open Innovation Communit*") OR TS=(" Innovation Communities *")'. After excluding irrelevant literature, a total of 128 articles were obtained.

CiteSpace software was employed for bibliometric analysis, utilizing visualization methods to delve into the scientific knowledge structure, regularities, and distribution of literature in the field of OICs. The analysis primarily focuses on the following dimensions: (1) Analysis of literature growth trends; (2) Keyword clustering maps: Analysis of research hotspots.

3.1   Analysis of Literature Growth Trends

Growth Trends in Chinese Literature. Using the built-in bibliometric function in CNKI to analyze the publication volume changes in the field of OICs (as shown in Fig. 1): Literature research in this field commenced in 2013, marking a nascent phase from 2013 to 2016 with slow development. In 2017, there was an explosive growth in the number of publications, reaching 18 articles. From 2018 onwards, the field entered a fluctuating development stage, with the annual publication count maintaining a relatively high level. Overall, over the past decade, Chinese literature has shown a general upward trend, indicating a gradual increase in attention within the domestic academic community toward this field.

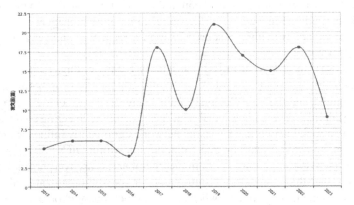

Fig. 1. Growth Trend of Chinese Literature in the OIC Field

The research on domestic OICs began in 2013. Xia Shanjun et al. analyzed and integrated three subsystems of knowledge transfer and flow, human capital flow, and innovation income growth, proposing a systemic dynamic model of the OICs network operation [17]. The model highlights the important state variables connecting these three subsystems: the number of network members, R&D investment, patent quantity, and innovation income. Starting from these three key variables, the study suggests that effective management of OICs by enterprises is crucial, emphasizing the integration of human capital, funds, and intellectual capital; diversification of innovation income growth; and cultivation of an open innovation culture. This research reveals the operation mechanism of OICs, indicating three key factors to enhance enterprise open innovation performance, holding significant practical and theoretical value. The most frequently cited paper is 'Research on Online User Contribution Behavior of Enterprise Open Innovation Community Based on CAS Theory: Taking a Well-Known Domestic Enterprise Community as an Example' [18] by Qin Min et al., which divides community users' contribution behavior into active contribution and reactive contribution. Drawing on complex adaptive system theory, it explains user contribution behavior, categorizing the influencing factors of user contribution behavior into individual factors, interaction factors, and user-community environmental impact factors, conducting empirical research using a questionnaire survey. This study defines and quantitatively develops two behavior scales—online user active contribution and reactive contribution—uncovering differences in the influencing mechanisms of these two types of contribution behaviors, laying a foundation for in-depth exploration of enterprise OIC user behavior.

Growth Trends in English Literature. Growth trends in English literature (Fig. 2): The bar chart represents publication volume, and the line chart depicts citation count. The publication volume shows a fluctuating upward trend, reaching its peak in 2022; citation count displays a noticeable growth trend, indicating that this field is gradually becoming a current research hotspot.

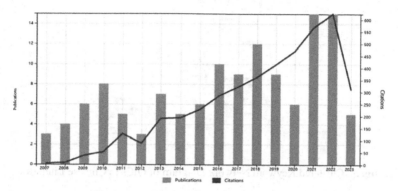

Fig. 2. Growth Trends of English Literature in the OICs Field

Research on OICs abroad started earlier. The earliest publication with the highest citations is 'Open innovation and strategy' [19]. Scholars such as Chesbrough used the global collaborative development of the Linux operating system as an example to deeply analyze the open-source business model in the software industry. They pointed out two major challenges posed by the open innovation model to traditional business models: the first being the questioned principle of needing ownership of resources that create value, and the second principle of excluding others' ability to replicate the product. The paper also emphasizes crucial considerations for companies implementing open strategies: firstly, how to attract a broad range of contributors to actively participate and maintain their engagement over time. Secondly, given the scarcity of contributors who can significantly drive the community, how can companies stand out in a competitive contributor market? Additionally, as each OIC comprises internal and external participants, how can companies effectively balance their collaborative relationships? Finally, how can companies find profitable avenues from open innovation initiatives and ensure sustained involvement in these initiatives? The posing of these questions marks the beginning of research in the OICs field, offering essential research directions for further exploration of the impact and applications of the open innovation model.

3.2 Analysis of Research Hotspots

Keywords serve as highly refined and summarized representations of the literature content. Keyword analysis was conducted using CiteSpace software, which involved merging semantically similar nodes and removing nodes with minimal relevance to the research topic, resulting in a clustered keyword network diagram.

Research Hotspots in Chinese Literature. The clustered keyword network diagram for Chinese literature is illustrated in Fig. 3, summarizing the primary keyword distributions within the top four major categories (Table 1).

Fig. 3. Clustered Keyword Network Diagram of OICs in Chinese Literature

Table 1. List of Hotspot Keywords in OICs

Cluster	Hotspot Keywords
Leading Users	Source Credibility, Clustering Algorithms, Identification, Text Mining, Innovation Capability, Social Network Connections, Needs Analysis
Online Communities	Innovation Communities, User Creativity, Knowledge Creation, Innovation Sources, Absorptive Capacity
Influencing Factors	Innovation Models, Corporate Performance, Knowledge Contribution, Game Theory
Community Networks	Knowledge Evolution, Knowledge Collaborative Innovation, Operation Mechanisms, Innovation Resources, Trust Mechanisms

The hotspot keywords represent the research focus and trends in this field. By observing and analyzing the table data along with relevant literature, the current research hotspots in OICs have been summarized as identification of leading users, management of user creativity in communities, the impact factors on corporate performance and user knowledge sharing behavior, and research on community networks.

Research Hotspots in English Literature. From the results of the analysis of hotspot keywords in English literature, the current research hotspots include technological innovation in open-source software communities, user creative adoption in OICs communities, OICs case studies (focusing on corporate innovation performance), social media technologies, and user behavior analysis (Fig. 4).

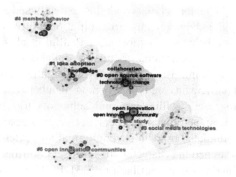

Fig. 4. Clustered Keyword Network Diagram of OICs in English Literature

From the results of the analysis of hotspot keywords in English literature, the current research hotspots include technological innovation in open-source software communities, user creative adoption in OICs communities, OICs case studies (focusing on corporate innovation performance), social media technologies, and user behavior analysis.

3.3 Comparative Analysis of Domestic and Foreign Literature

Comparing the research hotspots in domestic and foreign studies, both share common focuses on managing user creativity in communities, user behavior analysis, and corporate performance research. The difference lies in domestic literature placing more emphasis on identifying leading users, while foreign literature shows more interest in researching open-source software communities within OICs.

The related studies on creative management emphasize the full utilization of knowledge resources to optimize the process of screening and evaluating creativity. Scholars primarily explore how to accurately identify high-quality ideas when facing the challenge of a vast pool of ideas. For instance, Gangi et al. identified factors influencing creative adoption using mixed case studies based on survey data and objective data from the Dell community. Their results indicate that the complexity, observability, and trialability of ideas are equally important in determining the adoption of user-generated ideas [10]. Hossain and Islam analyzed 320 adopted ideas in the Starbucks community, categorizing ideas into three types: product, experience, and involvement, establishing empirical models for each. Their research indicates that the implementation of ideas depends significantly on factors such as the number of votes and points obtained by the idea, the time of posting, and the contributor's points [20]. Zhang et al. approached value co-creation, using signal transmission theory to study factors influencing idea adoption, such as idea information entropy, emotional intensity, idea length, views, and comments, from the perspective of co-creating value [15]. Zhang Lanlan, based on Aristotle's persuasion theory, summarized factors influencing idea adoption from dimensions like personality appeal, logical appeal, and emotional qualities [3].

In the study of user behavior, scholars both domestically and abroad focus mainly on methods for identifying leading users, user participation motivations, and factors influencing user contribution behavior. For instance, Paulini et al. found through surveys that most participants in OICs are contributors or collaborators, primarily motivated by fun and challenge, with intrinsic motivation outweighing extrinsic motivation, and passionately engaged participants are typically new members [21]. Fang et al. explored motivations influencing users' willingness and behaviors for continued participation from psychological, social, and functional perspectives, suggesting that user participation motivations are stimulated by both psychological and external factors [22]. Mahr et al. qualitatively researched the characteristics of user contribution behavior in OICs, dividing it into active and reactive contributions [23]. Building upon this, Qin et al. borrowed from the theory of complex adaptive systems to explain user contribution behavior, categorizing the influencing factors into three dimensions: individual user factors, user interaction factors, and user-community environmental influence factors [18]. Zhang Lanlan, based on social exchange theory, analyzed users' motivations for participating in innovation from an input-output perspective [3].

Regarding corporate innovation performance, several scholars' research demonstrates that engaging in open innovation has a positive impact on enhancing corporate innovation performance. Cheng et al., through a survey of 223 Asian service companies, found a significant positive correlation between companies conducting open innovation activities and four dimensions of innovation performance: innovativeness of new products/services, success rate of new products/new services, customer performance, and financial performance. The impact was relatively stronger on the innovativeness of new services and financial performance [24]. Dong et al. drew from the dynamic capabilities framework and the innovation value chain perspective, conducting empirical research using panel data collected from Dell and Starbucks communities. They proposed two dimensions of dynamic capabilities - enterprise ideation capability and enterprise ideation implementation capability - and discussed their impact on corporate performance from the perspective of corporate value [25]. Xia et al. constructed a three-party game model involving enterprises, competitive enterprises, and customers, examining the influence of closed, semi-open, and open innovation models on corporate innovation performance. They advocated for companies to establish OICs communities to enhance innovation capabilities [26]. Various scholars use different performance measurement indicators for corporate innovation performance. Some use company metrics, including financial performance indicators [24], sales growth indicators [26], market share indicators [27], while others use innovation metrics such as R&D intensity, the number of new products developed and commercialized, speed of new product development, and the number of patents [28].

The identification of leading users is a primary area of focus in domestic research, and in foreign studies related to user behavior, identifying leading users is also a key area. The concept of leading users was initially proposed by Hippel, and with the application of the leading user theory, more characteristics of leading users have been discovered. Synthesizing scholars' viewpoints, leading users possess the following characteristics: they have needs ahead of ordinary users [7, 8, 32], anticipate benefiting from innovation [7, 29], have a strong motivation for innovation [7, 31–33], possess strong innovation capabilities [30, 32, 33], have extensive expertise (product usage experience and product knowledge) [8, 23, 32, 33], adopt new products faster than ordinary users [8, 33], have potential as opinion leaders [8, 32, 33], and higher intermediary centrality [9] (Table 2). The methods for identifying leading users mainly include: group screening, pyramid method, crowdsourcing, network volunteerism, and identification algorithms based on data mining technology (Table 3).

Table 2. Characteristics of Leading Users

Characteristics	Source
Needs ahead of ordinary users	Hippel[7]; Lüthje[8]; Belzl[32]
Anticipation of benefiting from innovation	Hippel[7]; Morrison[29]
Strong motivation for innovation	Hippel[7]; Bogers[31];Belzl[32];Pajo[33]
Strong innovation capabilities	Belzl[32];Pajo[33];GuozhengHe[30]
Rich expertise (product usage experience and product knowledge)	Lüthje[8]; Mahr[23]; Belzl[32]; Pajo[33]
Faster adoption of new products than ordinary users	Lüthje[8]; Pajo[33]
Potential as opinion leaders	Lüthje[8]; Belzl[32];Pajo[33]
Higher intermediary centrality	Özaygen[9]

Table 3. Comparison of Leading User Identification Methods

Method	Characteristics
Group Screening Method	Advantages: Easy to implement and operate without requiring professional training for researchers Disadvantages: Tedious process of questionnaire distribution, collection, and data analysis; high human and physical costs resulting in low efficiency; lack of objectivity in the obtained results
Pyramid Method	Advantages: Less workload and higher efficiency compared to group screening methods Disadvantages: May overlook some highly innovative but less socially influential leading users; lack of objectivity in the results

(continued)

Table 3. (*continued*)

Method	Characteristics
Crowdsourcing Method	Essentially a method for recruiting and aggregating users for innovative tasks, doesn't fully utilize the automatic data mining and processing capabilities of user innovation communities
Network Log Method	Advantages: Qualitative research method, collects more objective data Disadvantages: Requires researchers to have rich experience and keen observation skills, otherwise, potential leading users might be overlooked
Identification Methods Based on Data Mining	Advantages: Saves manpower and resources, increases efficiency; more objective results Disadvantages: The effectiveness is highly reliant on the constructed indicator system

4 Conclusion and Implications

Based on the definition of open innovation communities by scholars both domestically and internationally, this study outlined five major characteristics of open innovation communities: virtuality, goal orientation, interactivity, networked structure, and voluntariness. Using CiteSpace for bibliometric analysis of 129 Chinese and 128 English papers, the trend in literature growth indicated an overall increasing trend in the field of Open Innovation Communities (OICs). This suggests a growing academic interest in this area. Comparing the keyword clustering maps of Chinese and English literature, it was found that both domestic and foreign studies share common focuses on community user creativity management, user behavior analysis, and enterprise performance research. However, there are differences, with domestic literature focusing more on identifying leading users while foreign literature emphasizes research on open-source software communities within OICs. Notably, in foreign literature, the study of leading users stands out in user behavior-related research. The objective results of bibliometrics affirm that identifying leading users is a current hot topic in academia and holds substantial research value. This study suggests that future research could focus on the following aspects:

Identification of Leading Users Issue. Füller et al. highlighted that the stability, persistence, and effectiveness of OICs communities rely on mobilizing and managing user heterogeneity [5]. Leading users are the main drivers of innovation within OICs, being the most active and innovative group, often characterized by forward-looking needs. Their insights and demands significantly influence product and service innovation. However, these users are both active and scarce within OICs [6]. With a large user base and few leading users, accurately identifying them is crucial for enterprises to enhance innovation performance.

Issue 1: How to construct an effective system of identification metrics based on leading user theory and rapidly identify leading users? How can the effectiveness of this process be validated?

Leading User Needs Analysis Issue. OICs communities, as emerging platforms for user-generated content, play a crucial role in fostering innovation. Leading user theory emphasizes the forward-looking nature of these users' needs. Their insights and demand predictions significantly impact product and service innovation. The text data within posts or replies by leading users contain implicit real opinions about products or services. By mining this textual data from leading users, enterprises can obtain valuable market insights, guide product development and innovation strategies, anticipate user needs, enhance competitiveness, and foster sustainable community growth. Understanding and meeting the needs of leading users are pivotal factors in driving innovation and the success of the community in the context of OICs.

Issue 2: How to extract and classify user needs from the textual data of leading users? How to quantify the importance and level of improvement of different types of needs?

Issue 2: For various types of needs, how to extract valuable insights and provide effective recommendations for enterprises?

References

1. Chesbrough, H.W.: Open Innovation. The New Imperative for Creating and Profiting from Technology. Cambridge: Harvard Business School Press, USA (2003)
2. Zhang, Z., Chen, J.: The Composition, Characteristics and Management of Enterprises' Innovation Resource Based on Open Innovation Pattern. Science of Science and Management of S.&.T. 2008(11), 61–65(2018). (in Chinese)
3. Zhang, L.: Research on user behavior mechanisms in open innovation communities. Shanghai: Shanghai University of Finance and Economics (2021). (in Chinese)
4. Bai, Y., Guo, L., Yin, H.: Research on the growth mechanism of proprietary intellectual property rights, brand-driven entrepreneurship, and the case study of Xiaomi technology Co. Ltd. Sci. Technol. Progr. Policy 32(12), 79–85 (2015). (in Chinese)
5. Füller, J., Hutter, K., Hautz, J., et al.: User roles and contributions in innovation-contest communities. J. Manag. Inf. Syst. 31(1), 273–308 (2014)
6. Hippel, E.V., Ogawa, S., Jong, J.P.: The age of the consumer-innovator. MIT Sloan Manag. Rev. 53(1), 27–35 (2011)
7. Von Hippel, E.: Lead users: a source of novel product concepts. Manag. Sci. 32(7), 791–805 (1986)
8. Lüthje, C., Herstatt, C.: The lead user method: an outline of empirical findings and issues for future research. R&D Manag. 34(5), 553–568 (2004)
9. Özaygen, A., Balagué, C.: Idea evaluation in innovation contest platforms: a network perspective. Decis. Support. Syst. 2018(112), 15–22 (2018)
10. Di Gangi, P.M., Wasko, M.: Steal my idea! Organizational adoption of user innovations from a user innovation community: a case study of Dell IdeaStorm. Decis. Support. Syst. 48(1), 303–312 (2009)
11. West, J., Lakhani, K.R.: Getting clear about communities in open innovation. Ind. Innov. 15(2), 223–231 (2008)
12. Fichter, K.: Innovation communities: the role of networks of promotors in open innovation. R&D Manag. 39(4), 357–371 (2009)

13. Schröder, A., Hölzle, K.: Virtual communities for innovation: influence factors and impact on company innovation. Creativity Innov. Manag. **19**(3), 257–268 (2010)
14. Keyong, Z.: Research on Knowledge Sharing in Open Innovation Communities. Jilin University, Changchun (2018). (in Chinese)
15. Ning, Z., Wenfei, Z., Zhiliang, P., et al.: Research on the influencing factors of user idea adoption in enterprise's open innovation community: based on the value co-creation perspective. Sci. Technol. Prog. Policy **38**(16), 91–100 (2021). (in Chinese)
16. Qi Guijie, Li Yiying.: Research on the Contribution Degrees of Online Users in the Open Innovation Communities for Enterprises. Science & Technology Progress And Policy 33(14),81–87(2016). (in Chinese)
17. Xia, E., Zhang, M., Zhu, H.: System dynamics of open innovation community network. Sci. Technol. Prog. Policy **30**(08), 14–19 (2013). (in Chinese)
18. Qin, M., Qiao, H., Chen. L.: Online user contribution behavior in enterprise-hosted open innovation communities based on complex adaptive system: an example of Chinese famous enterprise-hosted community. Manag. Rev. **27**(01), 126–137 (2015). (in Chinese)
19. Chesbrough, H.W., Appleyard, M.M.: Open innovation and strategy. Calif. Manage. Rev. **50**(1), 57–76 (2007)
20. Hossain, M., Islam, K.M.Z.: Generating ideas on online platforms: a case study of "My Starbucks Idea." Arab Econ. Bus. J. **10**(2), 102–111 (2015)
21. Paulini, M., Maher, M.L., Murty, P.: Motivating participation in online innovation communities. Int. J. Web Based Communities **10**(1), 94–114 (2014)
22. Fang, C., Zhang, J.: Users' continued participation behavior in social Q&A communities: a motivation perspective. Comput. Hum. Behav. **2019**(92), 87–109 (2019)
23. Mahr, D., Lievens, A.: Virtual lead user communities: drivers of knowledge creation for innovation. Res. Policy **41**(1), 167–177 (2012)
24. Cheng, C.C.J., Huizingh, E.K.R.E.: Wen is open innovation beneficial? The role of strategic orientation. J. Prod. Innov. Manag. **31**(6), 1235–1253 (2014)
25. Dong, J.Q., Wu, W.: Business value of social media technologies: evidence from online user innovation communities. J. Strateg. Inf. Syst. **24**(2), 113–127 (2015)
26. Enjun, X., Ming, Z., Sujuan, W., et al.: Study on innovation performance of community network of open innovation——based on mathematical analysis and empirical test. Chin. J. Manag. Sci. **21**(S2), 549–556 (2013). (in Chinese)
27. Koçoğlu, İ, İmamoğlu, S.Z., İnce, H., et al.: The effect of supply chain integration on information sharing: enhancing the supply chain performance. Procedia Soc. Behav. Sci. **2011**(24), 1630–1649 (2011)
28. Qin, W., Shanxing, G.: Study on dynamic games model of open source software innovation based on open knowledge disclosure. J. Ind. Eng. Eng. Manag. **24**(04), 104–109 (2010). (in Chinese)
29. Morrison, P.D., Roberts, J.H., Midgley, D.F.: The nature of lead users and measurement of leading edge status. Res. Policy **33**(2), 351–362 (2004)
30. He, G., Chen, R.: Research on leading user identification methods in the consumer goods industry. Stat. Decis. **2009**(4), 15–17 (2009). (in Chinese)
31. Bogers, M., Afuah, A., Bastian, B.: Users as innovators: a review, critique, and future research directions. J. Manag. **36**(4), 857–875 (2010)
32. Belz, F.M., Baumbach, W.: Netnography as a method of lead user identification. Creativity Innov. Manag. **19**(3), 304–313 (2010)
33. Pajo, S., Verhaegen, P.A., Vandevenne, D., et al.: Analysis of automatic online lead user identification. In: Smart Product Engineering: Proceedings of the 23rd CIRP Design Conference, pp. 505–514. Germany: Springer Berlin Heidelberg, Berlin(2013). https://doi.org/10.1007/978-3-642-30817-8_49

Why College Students Prefer to Study on Online Video-Sharing Platforms: The Case of Bilibili Platform

Jing Yang[1], Tingyu Zhang[1(✉)], Jiaxin Gao[2], Zheshi Bao[1], Hongyan Liang[1], and Hangming Zhang[3]

[1] College of Business Administration,
Nanjing University of Finance and Economics, Nanjing, China
1589101448@qq.com
[2] Hongshan College, Nanjing University of Finance and Economics, Nanjing, China
[3] School of Management Science and Engineering, Nanjing University of Finance and Economics, Nanjing, China

Abstract. Acknowledging the growing preference of university students for studying on the Bilibili platform, this study explores their motivations using the theory of transactional distance and social identity theory. The research investigates the relationship between perceived interactivity and students' continuance intention to study on Bilibili, with self-identity and social identity as mediating variables. The study also integrates emotional needs, based on social identity theory, as a moderating variable. Data from 371 valid survey responses out of 384 potential participants, predominantly senior students regularly using Bilibili for study, were analyzed. The findings reveal that perceived interactivity positively influences students' self-identity and social identity, which significantly enhances their intention to continue using Bilibili for educational purposes. The research demonstrates that perceived interactivity indirectly affects continuance intention, mediated by self-identity and social identity, while emotional needs positively moderate this mediating process.

Keywords: Online video-sharing platform · Bilibili platform · Perceived Interactivity · Self-identity · Social identity

1 Introduction

In recent years, a new mode of learning has emerged among the younger generation. With the onset of the COVID-19 pandemic in early 2020, which severely impacted everyday activities including education, China had to shift entirely to online education. Leveraging internet platforms and digital learning resources, the scale of online education platforms grew massively, with over 100 million users in online learning spaces.

Some studies have identified that online video-sharing has become a popular social and educational practice. Platforms like Bilibili, originally intended for general video sharing, are increasingly recognized for their educational potential. These platforms enable individuals to publish topics, searches and watch videos of interest, interact through comments and bullet chats, and find like-minded individuals. CCTV's report describes Bilibili as a new type of social learning platform favored by Generation Z. While existing research has primarily concentrated on MOOCs and similar online teaching platforms, it was observed that students' autonomy, motivation, and learning capabilities influence their continued learning engagement significantly. Therefore, this study centers around why an increasing number of university students prefer using online video-sharing platforms for learning, with a focus on Bilibili.

The research employs a quantitative approach, integrating the Theory of Transactional Distance and Social Identity Theory into an empirical model, validated using statistical methods. The study's contributions include revealing the critical role of interactivity on Bilibili in attracting students for learning, enhancing understanding of online learning phenomena, and exploring the impact of identity theory on students' online learning willingness. It also finds that individuals with higher emotional needs are more influenced by this process, underscoring the role of entertainment and social interaction in online learning and helping to understand the popularity of video-sharing platforms in remote learning.

2 Literature Review

2.1 Online Learning

Online learning, first coined in 1995 with WebCT's development, has expanded beyond its initial scope of utilizing LMS for uploading texts and PDFs. This growth now encompasses e-learning, blended learning, and various online courses, significantly diversifying digital educational activities [1].

Research exploring the characteristics of teaching content in online learning highlights its unique ability to enhance learning and interactivity, both in synchronous environments with live lectures and real-time interactions, and asynchronous settings where learning content is accessed independently, impacting student motivation and outcomes [2]. Further studies have discussed the distinct technological aspects of online learning, which facilitate a shift from traditional didactic methods to more learner-managed modes. This transition is characterized by enhanced dialogue, involvement, and support for individual learning styles, thus promoting learner autonomy [3]. Additionally, research has uncovered the community and social attributes inherent in e-learning, where communities of practice within these platforms foster shared interests and collaborative learning. However, these communities are often confined to structured discussions within LMS and are limited to specific groups like university classes [4]. Lastly, a comprehensive review by Hoi et al. [5] categorizes online learning methods into supervised, with limited feedback, and unsupervised types, while Vonderwell et al. [4] identify technology, course interface, group behavior, and student personas as significant factors influencing learner participation and outcomes in online courses.

2.2 Continuous Intention of Online Video-Sharing Platform

In our study, "continuous intention" refers to the learner's ongoing behavioral tendency and attitude towards engaging with online course platforms. Such behavioral intention, as identified by Chen et al. [6], is a dynamic belief influencing behavior execution.

The usage of various media types on social platforms varies according to the application. The emergence of new platforms introduces novel media exchange methods, with video becoming a widely utilized medium for knowledge sharing across social media and MOOC platforms. Key variables influencing users' continuous intentions on video-sharing platforms are explored by researchers. Some study found that the ease of access to knowledge in comment section will help viewers understand a big picture of knowledge introduced in the video. Research of Wu et.al. [7] has showed that collaboration is crucial for increasing users' engagement in knowledge sharing. Users on a collaborative video platform are more willing to share their opinions and knowledge than in a traditional forum platform. A study proposes a model based on the technology acceptance model (TAM) and social influences theory by conducting a survey of 206 male and 135 female video sharers of YouTube to test model. The results indicate that perceived ease of use is an important determinant of the intention to use YouTube to share video [8].

3 Theoretical Framework and Hypotheses

3.1 Perceived Interactivity

The Theory of Transactional Distance, originally proposed by Moore, plays a pivotal role in this study's exploration of distance education. It integrates four core concepts: structure, dialogue, transactional distance, and learner autonomy. Among these, Transactional distance refers to the psychological and communicational space created by physical distance in online education, depending on the platform's structure and dialogue capabilities.

Interactivity, as defined by Kiousis [9], signifies the simulated interpersonal communication experience in an information technology-driven environment. This aspect of online platforms, as noted by Fernandes and Neves [10], significantly enhances user experience. For instance, YouTube is known for video sharing, Instagram for photos and videos, and Twitter for text messages. In platforms like Bilibili, features such as bullet chats and comment sections foster a dynamic learning environment. Zhang and Cassany [11] highlight the unique interactive nature of bullet chats on Bilibili, offering a real-time, anonymous space for viewers to freely express opinions and engage in dialogues.

This study posits a key reason that university students are drawn to online video-sharing platforms like Bilibili for learning is the enhanced perception of interactivity these platforms offer. Grounded in the Theory of Transactional Distance, it is suggested that the perceived interactivity positively influences online learning. Education fundamentally involves social interactions like student-teacher and student-student dialogues. Elements such as course structure and interactive features are crucial in shaping the online learning experience. Bilibili, with its interactive design, effectively reduces the transactional distance (TDST and TDSS), thereby fostering a more engaging learning environment. Features like bullet chats and comment sections on Bilibili enhance this interactivity. Bullet chats, appearing in real-time alongside videos, offer an anonymous and spontaneous way for users to express themselves and engage in cross-temporal dialogues [11]. While the anonymity of bullet chats might limit direct replies, comment sections allow for more structured interactions, including questions and responses from other users or video creators. This unique blend of interactive elements contributes to Bilibili's distinctive learning atmosphere.

H1: Perceived interactivity on online video-sharing platforms significantly and positively influences the continuous learning intention of university students on these platforms.

3.2 Self-identity and Social Identity as Mediators

Identity is a sense of belonging to a group that is expressed in terms of personal attributes, group membership, and social roles. It is an extremely important aspect of self-concept [12]. Human identity has two levels: self-identity and social identity [1].

Self-identity is the awareness of one's uniqueness, and thus, self-identity establishes the individual as the same person in time and space rather than others [13]. Social identity is the recognition that one belongs to a particular social group, and also the recognition of the emotional and value significance that being a group member brings [14].

Social identity theory argues that everyone makes an assessment of their own image and puts their subjective image into a social context to seek self-positioning, thus obtaining a sense of identity [14]. One's social group membership and group category are an important part of one's self-concept, and it advocates that people strive to obtain and maintain positive social identity, thereby enhancing self-esteem. This positive identity is largely derived from the comparison of in-groups and relevant out-groups. Existing research has discussed the influencing factors of identity from multiple aspects, such as demographic characteristics, gender and age [13], and social factors such as religious beliefs and culture [15].

This paper argues that when college students generate a sense of interactivity on online video sharing platforms, it will produce a sense of self and social identity. The interactivity of college students using Bilibili to learn mainly manifests itself in the process of sending barrage or leaving messages in the video comment area, through interaction and communication with bloggers or other users. When college students learn on Bilibili and receive interactive feedback, they will have two feelings. First, social identity perception, in the context of watching videos on Bilibili, college students can perceive that there are other users who have also watched the same video and left their footprints through the scrolling barrage, and the real-time number of online viewers allows users to perceive that there are other users learning together at any time. This cross-temporal companionship learning also allows users to realize that they are not alone in the process of watching videos, and there are classmates in the same situation as them learning on the other end of the Internet. This will stimulate a sense of group unity, that is, social identity perception. Second, self-identity perception, when college students express their personal opinions or questions through barrage or comment area, and receive responses and likes from video bloggers or other users, they will think that their understanding and cognition are unique and valuable, and they have gained the respect of others. Their sense of accomplishment is enhanced, thus realizing the identity of individual identity. Therefore, we propose hypotheses 2 and 3:

H2: The interactivity perception of college students learning on Bilibili will significantly positively affect individual identity.

H3: The interactivity perception of college students learning on Bilibili will significantly positively affect social identity.

Identity perception affects the behavior of individuals on information platforms, which has been found in many studies. Jiang et al. [16] investigated Weibo and, based on the theory of planned behavior, studied the impact of identity on Weibo usage intention. They found that Weibo platforms promote continuous usage intention through group social identity and individual personal identity. There are also studies that use identity theory to understand the teaching process. Hwang [13] found that individual social identity and self-identity play a decisive role in developing emotional commitment and the innate motivation to share knowledge through email in the study of the role of identity in modern auxiliary teaching media learning. This paper argues that identity will affect college students' sustained learning intention on Bilibili.

Based on the above discussion, the interactivity perception generated by college students' learning on Bilibili will affect social identity and self-identity. At the same time, this social identity and self-identity will have a separate impact on the sustained learning intention of the platform. Therefore, we believe that social identity and self-identity play a mediating role between interactivity perception and platform learning intention. Therefore, we propose hypotheses 4 and 5:

H4: Interactivity perception will significantly positively affect college students' sustained learning intention on online video sharing platforms through personal identity.

H5: Interactivity perception will significantly positively affect college students' sustained learning intention on online video sharing platforms through social identity.

3.3 The Regulating Role of Emotional Needs

This study examines the role of emotional needs in the context of online learning, conceptualizing them as pleasurable emotions experienced during interactions and relationships within the digital platform. Emotional needs, as defined by Katz et al. [17], pertain to the desires for aesthetic, pleasurable, and emotional experiences during platform engagement.

Emotions play a significant role in online learning processes. While they can distract, emotions, when managed, may enhance thinking, decision-making, and engagement. Research on emotional presence within an online community of inquiry demonstrates the salience of emotion in online learning. Given this reality, emotion must be considered, if not a central factor, at least as a ubiquitous, influential part of learning—online and otherwise. The Colmode model by Garrison et al. [18] suggests that emotional presence is evident in social, cognitive, and teaching aspects of online learning communities. Emotions in online learning environments are not just peripheral but are influential and pervasive aspects of the learning experience, both online and in traditional settings.

This research hypothesizes that the emotional needs of university students learning on Bilibili influence the process from perceived interactivity to identity recognition and, ultimately, to the willingness to learn online. Identity Theory emphasizes the emotional and value significance of belonging to a social group [14]. There's a strong correlation between emotional needs and social identity recognition. Higher emotional needs often lead to a more profound sense of belonging and self-awareness, stimulated by inter-actions. Observations of students on Bilibili affirm this: those with higher emotional needs actively seek self-identity construction, engaging more with the community. This engagement, in turn, boosts their identity recognition and motivates continued learn-ing on the platform. Conversely, students with lower social needs show less desire for such interactions and identity recognition, resulting in lower motivation for continuous learning on Bilibili.

H6:Emotional needs modulate the relationship between perceived interactivity and social identity recognition. Higher emotional needs strengthen the positive relationship between perceived interactivity and social identity recognition.

H7:Similarly, emotional needs also modulate the relationship between perceived interactivity and personal identity recognition. When emotional needs are higher, the positive correlation between perceived interactivity and personal identity recognition becomes stronger.

Furthermore, emotional needs are believed to not only moderate the relationship between interactivity and self-identity recognition but also affect the mediating role of social identity recognition. Students with high emotional needs feel less isolated through interactions on Bilibili, fostering temporary companionship, group solidarity, and enhanced social identity, thus motivating continuous learning. In contrast, stu-dents with lower social needs engage less with others, leading to lower social identity recognition and motivation to continue learning on the platform (Fig. 1).

H8: Emotional needs moderate the mediating effect of social identity recognition in the relationship between the perceived interactivity on Bilibili and the continuous learning intention on the platform.

H9 Emotional needs moderate the mediating effect of self-identity recognition in the relationship between the perceived interactivity on Bilibili and the continuous learning intention on the platform.

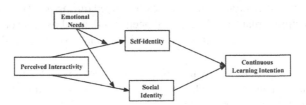

Fig. 1. Research Model

4   Data Analysis and Results

4.1   Data Collection

This study focuses on college students and utilizes a questionnaire survey to collect the necessary data via an online platform. Ultimately, there were 400 online surveys administered, out of which 371 were deemed valid after eliminating any invalid submissions. The criteria for identifying invalid questionnaires include selecting the same option across all scales, indicating no prior knowledge or usage of Bilibili, or completing the questionnaire in less than 100 s.

The demographic and descriptive statistics includes information on gender, grade, usage time and useful frequency. Amongst the 371 college students surveyed, the gender breakdown of the group is 32.6% male and 67.4% female. The majority of participants were seniors in terms of their academic year. The usage time of Bilibili is broken down into several categories, including less than 1 year (10.2%), 1 to 3 years (26.7%), 3 to 5 years (30.5%), 5 to 10 years (28.6%), and more than 10 years (4.0%). The useful frequency of Bilibili for learning, within a week's time frame, is also broken down into several categories, including 0 times (13.5%), 1 to 3 times (40.4%), 3 to 5 times (17.3%), and more than 5 times (28.8%).

4.2   Measurement Tools

In this research, perceived interactivity was developed and revised based on Ridings et al. [19], was measured by 3 items. Continuous intention was modified from Lin and Wang [20], were measured with 6 items. Self-identity and social identity were developed and revised based on Cheek et al. [1]. Self-identity was measured by 5 items, and social identity was also measured by 5 items. The emotional needs refer to Park et al.'s [21] study included a total of 5 items. All questionnaire items were based on a 7-point Likert scale (5 = strongly agree and 1 = strongly disagree). In order to mitigate the influence of confounding factors, this study controls for other variables that may impact the findings. Specifically, four control variables are selected: gender, grade, usage time and useful frequency.

4.3   Results

Reliability and Validity. In this study, SPSS 26.0 was tested for the reliability of the questionnaire scale. Each item demonstrated a factor loading above 0.7, the CR values of each variable were more than 0.7, and the Cronbach's alpha coefficients of all items in the questionnaire were over 0.8, indicating excellent reliability of the constructed scale. To further validate the model, confirmatory factor analysis was performed using AMOS 26.0 software in this study. The overall results of the fitting evaluation are as follows: $\chi 2/DF = 2.830 < 3$, CFI $= 0.953 > 0.9$, NFI $= 0.929 > 0.9$, RMSEA $= 0.070 < 0.1$. These results indicate an ideal data fitting effect. Furthermore, the square root of each variable's average variance extracted (AVE) is greater than its correlation coefficient absolute value, suggesting good discriminant validity. Given that we used and modified existing mature scales for this study's purposes, it ensures good content validity.

Common Method Biases. To eliminate common method bias, the unrotated exploratory factor analysis in this study was conducted using SPSS 26.0. The results revealed a total of five factors with eigenvalues greater than 1, and the largest factor was 19.532%, less than 20%. Moreover, the variance inflation factor (VIF) for all variables is less than 3. In conclusion, it indicates that there was no serious multicollinearity problems.

Test of Hypotheses. The standardized path coefficients and hypothesis testing results of the model are shown in * MERGEFORMAT Table 1. Results of path coefficient. For Hypothesis 1, perceived interactivity on online video-sharing platforms was found to be positively correlated with the continuous learning intention of university students ($\beta = 0.417$, $p < 0.001$), and thus hypothesis 1 is supported. In the same way, Hypothesis 2 ($\beta = 0.259$ $p < 0.001$), Hypothesis 3 ($\beta = 0.309$, $p < 0.001$) are all supported, perceived interactivity was found to be positively correlated with self-identity and social identity.

Table 1. Results of path coefficient

Hypothesis	Path	β	T-value	Result
H1	Perceived Interactivity → Continuous learning intention	0.417	9.850***	Supported
H2	Perceived Interactivity → Self-identity	0.259	5.063***	Supported
H3	Perceived Interactivity → Social identity	0.309	6.059***	Supported
H6	Perceived Interactivity*Emotional needs → Social identity	0.131	2.598*	Supported
H7	Perceived Interactivity*Emotional needs → Self-identity	0.156	3.112**	Supported

Note:* P < 0.05, ** P < 0.01, *** P < 0.001

To test the mediation effect, 371 samples were tested by Bootstrap method. The bootstrapping program was used to construct a 95% confidence interval for the bias correction of the indirect effect, the results are shown in Table 2. Mediation effect test. Hypothesis 4 and Hypothesis 5 are supported. Perceived Interactivity can significantly positively affect college students' willingness to continue learning on online video sharing platforms through self-identity and social identity. To test the moderating effect, as shown in Table 1, Hypothesis 6 ($\beta = 0.131$ $p < 0.05$) and Hypothesis 7 ($\beta = 0.231$ $p < 0.01$) are supported too. Emotional needs modulate the relationship between perceived interactivity and social identity and the relationship between perceived interactivity and self-identity. And moderating effect diagrams are shown in Fig. 2 and Fig. 3.

For Hypothesis 8 and Hypothesis 9, the results are shown in Table 2. Hypothesis 8 and Hypothesis 9 are supported. Emotional needs moderate the mediation effect of social identity and self-identity in the relationship between the perceived interactivity and the continuous learning intention on Bilibili.

Table 2. Mediation effect test

Hypothesis	Path	Effect	SE	LLCI	ULCI	Result
H4	Perceived Interactivity →Self-identity →Continuous learning intention	0.0288	0.014	0.0059	0.0603	Supported
H5	Perceived Interactivity →Social identity →Continuous learning intention	0.0301	0.0163	0.0039	0.0679	Supported
H8	Perceived Interactivity*Emotional needs →Social identity →Continuous learning intention	0.018	0.0104	0.0006	0.0404	Supported
H9	Perceived Interactivity*Emotional needs →Self-identity →Continuous learning intention	0.0172	0.0094	0.0004	0.0366	Supported

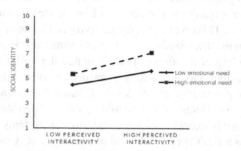

Fig. 2. The moderating effect diagram of emotional needs on social identity

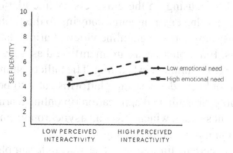

Fig. 3. The moderating effect diagram of emotional needs on self-identity

5 Conclusions

This study, based on research involving 371 university students, arrives at several conclusions. Firstly, perceived interactivity in online video-sharing platforms enhances the willingness to continue learning. This inclination arises from a sense of identity recognition induced by interactive experiences. Moreover, social presence is not merely about perceiving group belonging but also involves realizing one's self-worth. Our study goes a step further by suggesting that such interaction fosters not only a sense of belonging to a community but also an individual's self-awareness. Secondly, the perception of interactivity influences continuous learning intention through personal and social identity recognition. Our study posits that the interactivity perceived by university students on online video-sharing platforms fosters both personal and social identity recognition. This process of identity recognition, stimulated by perceived interactivity, fuels students' willingness to continue using the platform for learning purposes. Thirdly, the emotional needs of university students intensify the process wherein interactivity perception influences continuous learning intention through identity recognition. These emotions, which are complex and multifaceted, encompassing emotions arising from social interactions and entertainment experiences. Emotions experienced during online learning can stimulate identity recognition, ultimately affecting the willingness to use the platform.

Our study has some theoretical contributions. First, further clarify the concept of "online video sharing platform". The study may provide some enlightening significance for clarifying its concept and promoting its standardization. Secondly, from the perspective of interactivity, we explore the impact on college students' willingness to continue learning on the platform. This reveals that interactivity on online video sharing platforms is an important reason to attract students to use platforms for learning, and a more comprehensive understanding of the factors that influence the willingness of platforms to continue learning contributes to the existing literature on online learning. Thirdly, based on the new theoretical perspective of interactive distance theory and identity theory, the phenomenon of college students' tendency to use online video sharing platform is further interpreted. The study deepens the understanding of students' willingness to learn online learning and expands the research field of identity theory on the other hand.

Our study has some practical contributions. Firstly, the implications of this study emphasize the significance of interactivity and identity recognition in enhancing online learning experiences. By focusing on these aspects, online platforms can create more engaging and effective learning environments, catering to the evolving needs of modern learners. Moreover, this study found that online video-sharing platforms can satisfy students' emotional needs. Emotional needs are manifested as a desire for entertainment, aligning with the role of entertainment in learning. The bullet comment (danmu) and messaging mechanisms on online video-sharing platforms cater to both entertainment and social needs. This finding strengthened application on online learning platforms, particularly the bullet comment system, which offers an asynchronous interaction mechanism, fostering a sense of community and belonging.

This paper also has certain limitations. The research sample primarily consisted of university students, reflecting only a subset of Bilibili users, which might limit the study's generalizability. Future research could expand the sample size and diversify the subjects to deepen the study's insights. Moreover, bullet comments can also have negative impacts, such as inundating students with irrelevant information, which was initially designed to establish connections and a sense of belonging. This can distract students and affect their focus and concentration. Addressing these challenges and balancing the positive and negative aspects of such interactive features on online platforms is a crucial area for future exploration.

Acknowledgments. This research was supported by National Social Science Fund of. China (19CGL067), the Nanjing University of Finance and Economics Innovation Team Project (KYCTD202201), and Postgraduate Research & Practice Innovation Program of Jiangsu Province.

References

1. Cheek, J.M., Tropp, L.R., Chen, L.C., Underwood, M.K.: Identity orientations: Personal, social, and collective aspects of identity. In: Proceedings of the 102nd Annual Convention of the American Psychological Association, Los Angeles (1994)
2. Dhawan, S.: Online learning: a panacea in the time of COVID-19 crisis. J. Educ. Technol. Syst. **49**(1), 5–22 (2020)
3. Coomey, M., Stephenson, J.: Online learning: it is all about dialogue, involvement, support, and control — according to the research. In: Teaching & Learning Online, pp. 37–52. Routledge, Location (2018)
4. Vonderwell, S., Zachariah, S.: Factors that influence participation in online learning. J. Res. Technol. Educ. **38**(2), 213–230 (2005)
5. Hoi, S.C.H., Sahoo, D., Lu, J., Zhao, P.: Online learning: a comprehensive survey. Neurocomputing **459**, 249–289 (2021)
6. Chen, M., Wang, X., Wang, J., Zuo, C., Tian, J., Cui, Y.: Factors affecting college students' continuous intention to use online course platform. SN Comput. Sci. **2**, 1–11 (2021)
7. Wu, Q., Sang, Y., Zhang, S., Huang, Y.: Danmaku vs. forum comments: understanding user participation and knowledge sharing in online videos. In: Proceedings of the 2018 ACM International Conference on Supporting Group Work (2018)
8. Yang, C., Hsu, Y.-C., Tan, S.: Predicting the determinants of users' intentions for using YouTube to share video: moderating gender effects. Cyberpsychol. Behav. Soc. Netw. **13**(2), 141–152 (2010)
9. Kiousis, S.: Interactivity: a concept explication. New Media Soc. **4**(3), 355–383 (2002)
10. Fernandes, T., Neves, S.: The role of servicescape as a driver of customer value in experience-centric service organizations: the dragon football stadium case. J. Strateg. Mark. **22**(6), 548–560 (2014)
11. Zhang, L.-T., Cassany, D.: Making sense of danmu: coherence in massive anonymous chats on Bilibili.com. Discourse Stud. **22**(4), 483–502 (2020)
12. Deaux, K.: Reconstructing social identity. Pers. Soc. Psychol. Bull. **19**(1), 4–12 (1993)
13. Hwang, Y.: Investigating the role of identity and gender in technology-mediated learning. Behav. Inform. Technol. **29**(3), 305–319 (2010)
14. Tajfel, H., Turner, J.C.: The Social Identity Theory of Intergroup Behavior. In: Political Psychology, pp. 276–293. Psychology Press (2004)
15. Cunningham, G.B.: The influence of religious personal identity on the relationships among religious dissimilarity, value dissimilarity, and job satisfaction. Soc. Justice Res. **23**, 60–76 (2010)
16. Jiang, C., Zhao, W., Sun, X., Zhang, K., Zheng, R., Qu, W.: The effects of the self and social identity on the intention to microblog: an extension of the theory of planned behavior. Comput. Hum. Behav. **64**, 754–759 (2016)
17. Katz, E., Haas, H., Gurevitch, M.: On the use of the mass media for important things. Am. Sociol. Rev. **38**(2), 164–181 (1973)
18. Garrison, D.R., Anderson, T., Archer, W.: Critical inquiry in a text-based environment: Computer conferencing in higher education. Internet High. Educ. **2**(2–3), 87–105 (1999)
19. Ridings, C.M., Gefen, D., Arinze, B.: Some antecedents and effects of trust in virtual communities. J. Strateg. Inf. Syst. **11**(3–4), 271–295 (2002)

20. Lin, W.S., Wang, C.H.: Antecedences to continued intentions of adopting e-learning system in blended learning instruction: a contingency framework based on models of information system success and task-technology fit. Comput. Educ. **58**(1), 88–99 (2012)
21. Park, N., Kee, K.F., Valenzuela, S.: Being immersed in social networking environment: Facebook groups, uses and gratifications, and social outcomes. Cyberpsychol. Behav.Behav. **12**(6), 729–733 (2009)

The Impact of Digital Leadership
on the Dynamic Capabilities in Micro-startups:
A Case Study in China

Yuan Gao[1]([✉]), Xiao Wang[2], and Jinijn Lu[1]

[1] Department of Educational Studies, Xi'an Jiaotong-Liverpool University,
Suzhou 215123, China
Yuan.gao1703@student.xjtlu.edu.cn
[2] International Business School
Suzhou, Xi'an Jiaotong-Liverpool University, Suzhou 215123, China

Abstract. Dynamic capabilities are essential for micro-startups to identify and exploit opportunities in the era of digitalization. Entrepreneurs must exercise their digital leadership to enhance organizational dynamic capabilities, particularly in fragile micro-startups with weak structures and unclear work routines. The case study adopted a constructivist grounded theory to explore how entrepreneurs adopt their digital leadership to influence the micro-startups' dynamic capabilities in China. Semi-structured interviews were conducted with 15 entrepreneurs managing micro-ventures in the digital sectors in East China. Five themes were identified to interpret the impact: 1) opportunities beneath the uncertainty, 2) constraints evoke breakthroughs, 3) ambition balance furthers entrepreneurship, 4) maintaining entrepreneurship in flux, and 5) shared vision engines the entrepreneurship team. The study broadens the theoretical understanding of digital leadership and dynamic capabilities. It also provides digital practitioners with insights to improve their leadership, benefiting the survival and development of micro-startups within the digital context.

Keywords: Digital leadership · Dynamic capabilities · Digitalization · Micro-Startups

1 Introduction

Due to the rapid development of technology and innovation in the digital era, most enterprises have difficulty maintaining advantages in the process of digitalization. Confronted with varying challenges in digitalization, micro-startups face more severe survival and management issues due to their liabilities of newness and immature organizational structure [1]. Research pointed out that in the digital context of rapid technological and market changes, the dynamic capability of an organization is a crucial ability for enterprises to create, acquire, and rearrange resources to adapt to the ever-changing business environment [2]. Teece's [3] research suggests that dynamic capability consists of three

Y. P. Tu and M. Chi (Eds.): WHICEB 2024, LNBIP 515, pp. 179–190, 2024.
https://doi.org/10.1007/978-3-031-60264-1_16

dimensions: 1) sensing opportunities and threats, 2) seizing opportunities, and 3) reconfiguring resources. Numerous studies have indicated that micro-startups must establish solid dynamic capabilities to efficiently identify and develop opportunities [4]. Consequently, they can survive and further develop within the emerging and complex digital economy.

Although dynamic capabilities provide a strategic solution for micro-startups, the construction and utilization of dynamic capabilities still heavily depend on the leadership of entrepreneurs, especially digital leadership in this era [4]. Digital leadership is an evolved form of leadership under the global digitization; it refers to leaders incorporating digital technology into their mindset and behaviors to improve efficiency and create value for the company [6–8]. The emergence and discussion on digital leadership stem from the diverse challenges and difficulties in the current digital process, such as complex information processing and digital business patterns. These challenges require entrepreneurs in the digital sectors to transfer their traditional leadership (e.g., transactional leadership) to embrace the new digital leadership, which enables them to achieve digital strategic goals through evolutive and dynamic leading styles.

While a growing body of literature recognizes the importance of digital leadership in enterprise development in the digital era, the extant studies primarily concentrate on its process and implications [2]. There is a lack of interpretation regarding how digital leadership influences diverse aspects of startups, such as organizational dynamic capabilities. Besides, some studies have examined the association between digital leadership and enterprise dynamic capabilities [1, 8], there is a gap in the literature regarding a thorough exploration and comprehensive understanding of the impact between these two constructs. This gap is particularly evident in the absence of insights from the experiences of digital leaders in various cases. To better understand how entrepreneurs in micro startups adopt their digital leadership to influence organizations' dynamic capabilities, we proposed the following research question:

How do entrepreneurs influence organizational dynamic capabilities through their digital leadership?

To address this research question, we collected different cases of Chinese micro-startups in digital sectors. Through in-depth interviews among these leaders, several themes emerged in thematic analysis to illustrate how entrepreneurs exercise their digital leadership to influence micro-startups' dynamic capabilities. This study contributes to the literature by linking digital leadership and dynamic capabilities, thereby expanding the theoretical understanding of both. It also underscores the practical importance of this relationship, emphasizing the need for entrepreneurs to embrace digital leadership in addressing challenges posed by global digitalization and ensuring the survival and development of micro-startups in the digital economy.

2 Theoretical Background

2.1 Dynamic Capabilities in Micro-startups

The dynamic capability was initially conceptualized as a company's ability to integrate, develop, and reconfigure internal and external capabilities to help the company adapt to ever-changing environments [2, 3]. It concerns the creation and development of an organization's sustainable competitive advantages, encompassing three aspects: 1) sensing opportunities and threats, 2) seizing opportunities, and 3) maintaining competitiveness through the reconfiguration of resources [3]. In a turbulent and unstable market environment, numerous studies have investigated and recognized the indispensable role of dynamic capabilities in organizational management and strategic development [2]. For instance, research highlights the mediating role of dynamic capabilities between strategic growth and business models, ensuring companies' strategic updates.

However, enterprises encounter various challenges and opportunities within the digital economy context during digital transformation. This has increased research focus on updating dynamic capabilities in the digital landscape [1]. For instance, Guo's [5] study explored the development of digital startups from a dynamic capabilities' perspective, emphasizing the need for strategic updates through the integration of technological innovation and value proposition innovation [6]. Similarly, for micro-startups with lower risk resistance, continual development of dynamic capabilities is essential to coordinate limited resources and develop integrated business models suitable for their unique business and digital context [3]. Thereby, they can gain a competitive edge and ensure a sustainable source of advantage. However, given the absence of a well-established management team and organizational structure in micro startups, the development of dynamic capabilities heavily relies on the leadership of entrepreneurs.

2.2 Digital Leadership of Entrepreneurs

Digital leadership refers to leaders integrating digital technology into their leadership style, identifying and exploiting opportunities through innovative and efficient digital technology to create value for the company [7]. The current research investigating the characteristics and roles of digital leadership is in a preliminary and emerging stage. For instance, Zhu's [14] study categorized five characteristics of digital leadership: thoughtful, creative, global visionary, inquisitive, and profound. Additionally, research has emphasized the pivotal role of digital leadership in the digital transformation of startups. These digital leaders possess combined skills in digital, market, business, strategic, etc. In the digital era, they lead entrepreneurial teams with a visionary approach, achieving sustainable advantages in the ever-changing market environment [13]. Similar roles of digital leadership are further supported by some notable business cases, such as the digital transformation in Schneider Electric and DBS Bank [8].

Although leaders and scholars have gradually recognized the role of digital leadership in enterprise innovation and management, related research is still in its early stages. Most research in the context of digitalization does not distinguish between digital leadership and general leadership, thus overlooking some of the digital literacy of leaders [6]. Further research is needed to investigate the role of digital leadership in organizational management, including its impact on organizations' dynamic capabilities.

2.3 Study Context

Global digitalization is a distinctive context in our study. Due to its transformative nature, digitalization brings varying challenges to startups in reshaping the traditional business models, communication channels, and operational processes, etc. To stay survival and competitive in the digital era, research indicated that dynamic capabilities are a critical factor for micro-startups [1, 4]. Therefore, entrepreneurs need to enhance their digital leadership to build solid dynamic capabilities of micro startups, thereby confronting the challenges and opportunities brought by digitalization. However, the current research on digital leadership is still underexplored, and the impact of digital leadership on dynamic abilities, especially in micro startups has not been fully investigated [7, 8, 13]. We thereby conducted this study to explore the impact of entrepreneurs' digital leadership on dynamic capabilities among micro-startups. This research enhances our theoretical understanding of digital leadership, and it also inspires future digital leaders to utilize their leadership more efficiently in practical management scenarios, improving the dynamic capability of startups.

3 Methods

The qualitative research employed the constructivist grounded theory to explore the impacts of entrepreneurs' digital leadership on dynamic capabilities among varying micro-startups [9]. The constructive grounded theory is appropriate for the case study [15]. First, the research issue of the influence of digital leadership on micro startups' dynamic capabilities is lacking clarity, requiring further exploration. Grounded theory is suitable for the exploratory topic, and it can employ systematic research procedures to analyze collected data, extract theory, and address current research gaps [15]. Second, unlike building a conceptual framework based on prior knowledge, grounded theory advocates that theories and themes would emerge from the raw data through inductive analysis [15]. This meets our research needs by inductively constructing a theoretical framework on the narratives and experiences of participants, to reveal the influencing process of digital leadership on startups' dynamic capabilities. Third, grounded theory is suitable for conducting research within a unique context [15]. Digitalization is a special context for leaders and startups due to its transformative nature in many aspects, such as business models and human resource management. Grounded theory effectively aids researchers in iteratively comparing and analyzing the participants' responses to identify the patterns and themes, showing how digital leadership influences the dynamic capabilities of micro-startups.

3.1 Participants

Utilizing the theoretical sampling technique and data saturation criteria [9], our study enlisted 22 individuals at first, and 15 participants met the recruitment standards. These 15 participants are active entrepreneurs managing their micro-ventures from digital sectors across diverse Chinese cities. The study specifically selected entrepreneurs from Jiangsu, Zhejiang, and Shanghai, as these places exhibited similar economic levels, industrial structures, and a comparable cultural context that embraced entrepreneurship. Additionally, these southern coastal areas are famous for incubating digital micro-startups, owing to their advantageous locations and supportive local government policies. As Table 1 illustrates, the study also considered the demographic factors of participants. The gender ratio was relatively balanced among all participants, encompassing nine males and six females. Those entrepreneurs are all involved in digital sectors, including E-commerce, machine learning, cloud computing, cybersecurity, etc. The average duration of their business was two years and a half. The entrepreneurial team size was between two and five people, which belongs to a typical micro-startup in China.

Table 1. Demographics of participants

Participants	Gender	Age	Education (Degree)	Business	Years of Business	Location (City)	Team Members
1	Male	26	Bachelor	Software	2	Suzhou	2
2	Male	32	Master	E-commerce	3	Suzhou	3
3	Female	29	Bachelor	Telecommunication	1.5	Suzhou	5
4	Male	44	High school	E-commerce	2	Hangzhou	3
5	Female	34	Master	Artificial Intelligence	3.5	Shanghai	4
6	Female	32	Bachelor	Software	2	Suzhou	3
7	Male	21	Bachelor	Social Media	1	Shanghai	2
8	Female	32	Master	Cybersecurity	2.5	Suzhou	3
9	Male	22	Bachelor	Digital Games	1	Suzhou	4
10	Male	35	High school	Software	3.5	Hangzhou	4
11	Female	29	Bachelor	Software	1	Hangzhou	5
12	Female	28	Bachelor	Social Media	2	Hangzhou	3
13	Male	33	Master	E-commerce	3	Hangzhou	3
14	Male	27	Bachelor	E-commerce	1.5	Wenzhou	5
15	Male	29	High school	Digital Games	2	Wenzhou	4

3.2 Interview Procedure

Semi-structured interviews were conducted individually, lasting approximately 90 min each. After obtaining the ethics approval, researchers conducted the face-to-face interviews, with eight predetermined questions guiding the discussion [9]. First, the participants would be guided to talk about their venture's basic situation, entrepreneurial progress, and market contexts, followed by the main interview question, "Please briefly introduce the entrepreneurial process of your enterprise, and corresponding digital context within the market." Second, we introduced the participants to the concepts of dynamic capabilities and digital leadership. Afterward, those participants would be required to narrate their roles of digital leadership in running a business, such as allocating resources, sensing opportunities and threats, and handling challenges. An example question could be, "What specific digital leadership practices do you employ to create and acquire resources that your startup needs?".

In addition, the entrepreneurs' communication mode, behavioral style, and daily routine as a digital leader would also be discussed. They aim to identify their managerial roles in their team. For example, "Please tell me about your digital leadership in different management scenarios, such as how to get along and communicate with your team members. How does this affect the development of the startups?" These responses could comprehensively demonstrate the roles and responsibilities of a digital leader, and how they exercise leadership to impact the micro-startups' dynamic capabilities.

3.3 Analysis

Our study utilized the three-step coding method to process the interview data via NVivo 12 [9, 15]. The initial step involves open coding. By reading the transcribed texts repeatedly, the researcher deconstructed the data into smaller, manageable units with descriptive codes, which capture the essence of the information. In the second step, focused coding is adopted to refine and consolidate codes identified in open coding, leading to the emergence of central themes or core categories that explain the primary phenomenon. The third step is theoretical coding. Through considering the interactions and causality among categories, researchers extract and interconnect sub-themes to unveil a comprehensive theoretical explanation within the research.

During the coding process, we followed the procedures of comparative analytical standards in grounded theory to compare data, codes, and categories [15]. In addition, the other co-authors conducted a review of the interview data and coding results, contributing to the data exploration and reinforcing its credibility. Figure 1 illustrates the data collection and analysis process.

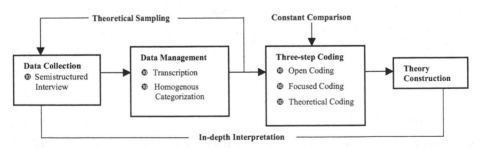

Fig. 1. Data collection and analysis process

4 Findings

The research yielded five main themes: 1) opportunities beneath the uncertainty, 2) constraints evoke breakthroughs, 3) ambition balance furthers entrepreneurship, 4) maintaining entrepreneurship in flux, and 5) shared vision engines the entrepreneurship team. These five themes offer valuable insights into how entrepreneurial leaders influence organizational dynamic capabilities through their digital leadership.

4.1 Opportunities Beneath the Uncertainty

The first theme refers to the fact that some participants with digital leadership could better handle the uncertainty in digital transformation, thereby identifying value opportunities in turbulence. Specifically, those digital leaders tended to look at unknown entrepreneurship from a rational perspective, employing digital technologies to foresee some pitfalls, and identify opportunities. Although the innate fearful dispositions toward uncertainty sometimes upset the whole team, those digital leaders liked to take responsibility for the ambiguity and steer the business development. For instance, participant 11 remarked, "I like to use data analytics to achieve valuable insights on the chaotic internet... They[insights] inspired my buddies [employees]."

In this theme, the respondents demonstrated a high level of digital literacy in their leadership style, effectively addressing the uncertainties of entrepreneurship. Unlike conventional leaders, these digital leaders exhibit a firm grasp and analytical ability concerning digital information, thereby better perceiving opportunities and threats. This further aligns with the dimension of dynamic capabilities. A representative quote from participant 7 was listed to support this finding:

"It's so important that I will spend three hours per day reading news from all digital media, regarding the latest market conditions, customer comments, and policy iteration... I gradually get used to the uncertain market...I can extract unique opportunities from it, and those opportunities provide directions for my business transformation."

4.2 Constraints Evoke Breakthroughs

This theme pertains to certain digital leaders who are limited in resources, but they can flexibly reconfigure scarce resources through digital systems, creating opportunities to promote entrepreneurial progress. Such a process boosts the development of micro-startups' dynamic capabilities. Specifically, micro startups often encounter unexpected events, and constrained resources may hinder business development, and even disrupt team collaboration. Our participants emphasized that digital leadership could integrate digital technologies to provide a more efficient workflow through the redistribution and combination of resources. Participant 5 noted that "this can enable startups to achieve unexpected breakthroughs in restrictions."

Furthermore, this theme also indicates that entrepreneurs with digital leadership have an untrammeled attitude towards business running. Some participants expressed that stereotypes in consumption patterns are an intangible limitation, and they tend to challenge so-called trends. Digital thinking allows them to "jump out of the box", and ultimately provide disruptive products or services in the sectors. Participant 3 made the comments:

"The desperate situation in entrepreneurship made me realize what [resources] I currently have, which furthered me to think about how to reallocate them to cater to the market... I start to understand the formula '1+1>2', which means maximizing profits with the least number of people and things... For example, using DingTalk [a digital management platform] to improve workflow efficiency."

4.3 Ambition Balance Furthers Entrepreneurship

Under this theme, digital leadership entails leaders setting ambitious goals for enterprise development, while maintaining a clear awareness of the organization's actual resources and production capacity. Challenges reflecting leaders' ambition can stimulate business development, as some participants noted that setting higher standards and goals than expected would pose challenges to the team. Overcoming these setbacks in challenges enhanced the overall ability of the entrepreneurial team, aiding micro-startups in effectively integrating resources, boosting dynamic capabilities, and driving venture progress.

However, these digital leaders must balance their ambitions, as challenges beyond the team's capabilities can jeopardize the entire business. Our cases illustrated that excessive ambition in leaders can bring overwhelming challenges, causing uncontrollable damage to the organization's inherent goals, shared vision, and team cohesion. Participant 4 stated, "radically taking orders is actually a result of my inadequate resource allocation as a leader." Therefore, leaders need to acquire organized skills from digital culture, better balancing their ambition for organizational development with precise control over resources. Participant 8 made the remarks:

"As the principal within my company, I benefited from the digital technology to have a clear understanding, lets' say big picture, of the resources and team of the entire company... Sometimes I have an over passion and ambitious plan for my business, but I realized that this is not based on reasonable resource allocation."

4.4 Maintaining Entrepreneurship in Flux

This theme indicates that entrepreneurial leaders need to upgrade the company's digital layout, lead their organizations to align with the digital market, and maintain stable and efficient communications with other units in the digital context. Specifically, the development of digital technologies has brought earth-shattering changes to all aspects of a typical enterprise, including its production pattern, supply chain management, marketing strategies, customer experience, and so on. The dilemma in digital transformation poses great challenges for most startups, especially those in traditional industries. Some participants who have successfully navigated digital transformation have expressed that they would strive to enhance their digital knowledge and skills, leverage the advantages of digital technology, negotiate with internal and external stakeholders, and seek benefits while eliminating obstacles for their business.

Hence, the "flux" in this theme implies that organizations, under the management of digital leaders, need to establish dynamic links with the digital era to achieve management upgrades, effective communication, and resource reconfiguration. The role of digital leadership in this process clearly aligns with the characteristics of dynamic capabilities in startups. Participant 6 expressed the following opinions:

"I used to scoff at those fancy digital technologies... But I realized that traditional operations and management patterns are gradually being phased out by the digital age... The old set makes it almost impossible for my company to 'communicate' with the trendy enterprises and customers... This [upgrade through digitalization] effect is very positive, and the most obvious one is that we are able to keep up with the pace of digital changes, which helps us expand our more innovative business."

4.5 Shared Vision Engines the Entrepreneurship Team

Under this theme, digital leaders use the strength of digital technologies to establish a shared vision and make full use of the human resources within entrepreneurial teams, thereby enhancing organizational dynamic capabilities. Specifically, entrepreneurial leaders are required to refine their strategies for team management in the digital context. Participants highlighted that by utilizing digital technologies, such as online collaborative work platforms, task and project management applications, and cloud-based file sharing, leaders could effectively construct a digital culture within the team, thereby improving the workflow of micro-startups to further the business venturing.

Furthermore, participants revealed that as entrepreneurs, they liked to exercise their digital leadership to empower team members by providing a shared vision. Building on improved digital workflows, leaders fostered team cohesion through thoughtful communication and concrete actions such as team-building activities. Consequently, participants have observed that team members in a highly committed alliance are motivated to exert more significant efforts in assisting businesses with resource allocation and development in digitalization, ultimately realizing a shared vision. Despite potential unintentional friction among subordinates, Participants 12 and 4 stated that they would play the role of a "lubricant" to mediate employee relationships and stimulate a spirit of teamwork. A representative quote from participant 10 was listed:

"A very important but easily overlooked issue is that I [as the leader] have transformed, or upgraded my digital thinking, but I have not timely trained, or led my team to adapt to the situation digital transformation... It's not just about putting a digital system on the company... But I believe it's more important to integrate digital culture into the company, establish a strategic goal and blueprint that fits the current market, in order to continuously motivate our partners."

5 Discussion

This study explored how micro-startup leaders use their digital leadership to enhance organizational dynamic capabilities. Through in-depth interviews with 15 entrepreneurial leaders in the digital sectors, we have identified five main themes from the analysis to illustrate the impact of digital leadership on organizational dynamic capabilities, which are: 1) opportunities beneath the uncertainty, 2) constraints evoke breakthroughs, 3) ambition balance furthers entrepreneurship, 4) maintaining entrepreneurship in flux, and 5) shared vision engines the entrepreneurship team. This qualitative research has significantly contributed to both theoretical understanding and practical applications.

Firstly, our research found that leaders employ digital leadership to sense opportunities and threats within the market uncertainty, thereby enhancing the organization's dynamic capabilities. This aligns with the previous that the judgments made by leaders under uncertainty are key factors affecting startups' development, and the judgment is a comprehensive analysis of varying factors in strategic management [13]. This trait corresponds with the existing literature's portrayal of digital leadership, wherein entrepreneurial leaders make full use of advanced technologies and data-driven insights to anticipate potential trends or challenges in uncertain markets [7, 8]. This proactive approach aligns with the perceived dimensions of dynamic capabilities, enabling the identification and exploitation of opportunities for startups in their digital transformation [3]. Secondly, micro startups may encounter numerous obstacles and constraints in the context of digitalization, such as funding shortages, lack of interpersonal capital, and weak structures [1, 4]. We observed that some entrepreneurs employ digital leadership to explore potential resources and, more importantly, restructure resources to drive the development of the enterprises. This finding is consistent with the literature's depiction of digital leadership, suggesting that the evolution of digital technology equips leaders with diverse analytical and decision-making tools that they must integrate into their daily management to enhance operational efficiency and capitalize on opportunities for businesses [6–8]. In addition, the process also aligns with the understanding of dynamic capabilities in research, which involves enterprises providing suitable and sustainable resources through integration and reconfiguration [1, 2]. The execution of this process necessitates the involvement of digital leadership.

Regarding the impact of digital leadership that balanced ambition could enhance the organization's dynamic capabilities, the finding is expected in literature but also represents an innovation in digital leadership. Previous research echoes the finding from the perspective of entrepreneurial leadership, emphasizing that entrepreneurs need to possess the trait of "framing the challenge" to navigate the organization through corresponding challenges [11, p. 247]. Related studies further supported the notion that overly confident and optimistic ambitious leaders may find it hard to accurately assess the organization and market situation, thereby presenting greater obstacles to opportunity development [7, 14]. Although this impact is seldom discussed in digital leadership research, we believe it should be considered to enrich the understanding on digital leadership. As digital development introduces more opportunities and challenges to startups, digital leadership should underscore that leaders shall achieve a delicate balance between their aggressiveness and the actual ability of their organizations., thus promoting entrepreneurial development in a rational manner.

Our research also revealed that digital leaders enhance dynamic capabilities by maintaining the internal and external interactions between the organizations and the environment, thereby effectively facilitating the organization to gain more opportunities and resources. Prior research supported this finding that in the digital era, entrepreneurs need to employ digital leadership to enable continuous interaction between organizations and markets to fully exploit opportunities, aligning with the dynamic and collaborative perspective in dynamic capabilities [3, 7]. This impact of digital leadership appears to be particularly emphasized among Chinese entrepreneurial leaders, potentially linked to the importance placed on relationships in commercial intercourse in Chinese society [12]. Future research can further investigate the phenomenon.

Furthermore, our research uncovered that digital leaders are adept at employing a shared vision to cultivate a highly committed team, thereby enhancing the organizations' dynamic capabilities. This aligns with the literature's emphasis on the crucial role of digital leadership in fostering team collaboration, instilling enthusiasm, and fostering a high commitment to common goals among team members to propel the company forward [7, 8]. Additionally, this finding aligns with research on dynamic capabilities, suggesting that a positive team spirit, including loyalty to entrepreneurial values, a harmonious team atmosphere, and a trusting environment, can effectively enhance an organization's dynamic capabilities [3, 10].

5.1 Implications

Our research holds substantial significance for scholars and practitioners in the era of digitalization. Firstly, our research innovatively explores how digital leadership can impact micro startups. Despite extensive research on the connections between general leadership and organizational dynamic capabilities, entrepreneurs still need to upgrade their general leadership into digital leadership to enhance organizational dynamic capabilities, thereby coping with digital challenges and opportunities in this era. Based on this, our research conducted in-depth interviews with 15 digital leaders and identified five central themes that show how entrepreneurs exercise their digital leadership to impact the dynamic capabilities of micro startups. This addresses a research gap by bridging and exploring the connections between digital leadership and dynamic capabilities across different levels of construction (individual and organizational). Findings of the research also enrich the theoretical understanding of digital leadership and dynamic capabilities within the current literature. Moreover, the study contributes a unique perspective of micro startups in the Chinese context. Micro startups have distinctive structures and features, but lack substantial research on them. Meanwhile, prior studies on digitalization often focused on digital transformations and corporate development in Western contexts, our case analysis in the Chinese setting provides valuable and authentic insights for scholars seeking to understand digital leadership styles among Chinese entrepreneurs.

This study also holds practical importance, inspiring entrepreneurial practitioners by highlighting the impact of digital leadership on organizational dynamic capabilities. In micro startups, leaders' influence is magnified, urging emerging entrepreneurs and business consultants to recognize the expectations for leaders to undergo capacity audits. This intentional effort to enhance digital literacy fortifies the overall dynamic capabilities of the enterprise, offering potential shortcuts for startup development in the digital landscape [6]. Additionally, education and training practitioners can leverage these insights to develop targeted digital courses.

5.2 Limitations and Future Research

Some limitations are present in this study, offering avenues for future research. Firstly, entrepreneurship is a dynamic process shaped by various sociocultural factors, including entrepreneurial legitimacy, policies, and regulations. Future research should consider these factors to extend the scope of the study. Secondly, our qualitative study involved a limited number of participants and was conducted in the Yangtze River region in China. Subsequent research could benefit from a more diverse participant pool across various locations.

Additionally, incorporating quantitative methods, such as constructing structural equation models, can validate the impact of digital leadership on dynamic capabilities. Thirdly, the relationship between digital leadership and dynamic capabilities is not one-sided. Investigating the reverse effects, specifically how dynamic capabilities influence digital leadership, and understanding the mechanisms between these two constructs, could offer valuable insights.

References

1. Karimi, J., Walter, Z.: The role of dynamic capabilities in responding to digital disruption: a factor-based study of the newspaper industry. J. Manag. Inf. Syst. **32**(1), 39–81 (2015)
2. Warner, K.S.R., Wäger, M.: Building dynamic capabilities for digital transformation: an ongoing process of strategic renewal. Long Range Plan. **52**(3), 326–349 (2019)
3. Teece, D.J.: Explicating dynamic capabilities: the nature and microfoundations of (sustainable) enterprise performance. Strateg. Manag. J. **28**(13), 1319–1350 (2007)
4. Feng, L., Qin, G., Wang, J., Zhang, K.: Disruptive innovation path of start-ups in the digital context: the perspective of dynamic capabilities. Sustainability **14**(19), 12839 (2022)
5. Guo, H., Yang, J., Han, J.: The fit between value proposition innovation and technological innovation in the digital environment: implications for the performance of startups. IEEE Trans. Eng. Manage. **68**(3), 797–809 (2021)
6. Kane, G.C., Phillips, A.N., Copulsky, J., Andrus, G.: How digital leadership is (n't) different. MIT Sloan Manag. Rev. **60**(3), 34–39 (2019)
7. Sheninger, E. C.: Digital leadership: Changing Paradigms for Changing Times. Corwin, Thousand Oaks (2019)
8. Benitez, J., Arenas, A., Castillo, A., Esteves, J.: Impact of digital leadership capability on innovation performance: The role of platform digitization capability. Inf. Manag. **59**(2), 103590 (2022)
9. Creswell, J.W.: Research Design: Qualitative, Quantitative, and Mixed Methods Approaches (4th ed.). Sage Publications Ltd, Thousand Oaks (2014)
10. Fainshmidt, S., Frazier, M.L.: What facilitates dynamic capabilities? The role of organizational climate for trust. Long Range Plan. **50**(5), 550–566 (2017)
11. Gupta, V., MacMillan, I.C., Surie, G.: Entrepreneurial leadership: developing and measuring a cross-cultural construct. J. Bus. Ventur. **19**(2), 241–260 (2004)
12. Liu, J., Nandhakumar, J., Zachariadis, M.: When Guanxi meets structural holes: exploring the Guanxi networks of Chinese entrepreneurs on digital platforms. J. Strateg. Inf. Syst. **27**(4), 311–334 (2018)
13. Tigre, F.B., Curado, C., Henriques, P.L.: Digital leadership: a bibliometric analysis. J. Leadersh. Organ. Stud. **30**(1), 40–70 (2023)
14. Zhu, P.: Digital Master: Debunk the Myths of Enterprise Digital Maturity. Lulu Publishing Services, Morrisville (2014)
15. Corbin, J., Strauss, A.: Basics of Qualitative Research: Techniques and Procedures for Developing Grounded Theory (4th ed.). Sage, Thousand Oaks (2015)

Understanding Consumers' Negative Word-of-Mouth Intention in the Aftermath of AI-Based Service Failure Through Attribution Theory

Ruibin Tan, Yixiao Li[✉], Shuiqing Yang, Surong Yan, and Kang Lin

School of Information Management and Artificial Intelligence,
Zhejiang University of Finance and Economics, Hangzhou 310018, China
yxli@zufe.edu.cn

Abstract. This article explores the consequences of AI-based service failures on consumers' negative word-of-mouth (NWOM) communication. Utilizing attribution theory, the study investigates how consumers' attributions of failure, including locus, stability, and controllability, influence their NWOM intentions, taking into account their trust in AI-based services. Through eight scenario experiments and questionnaires, the research unveils that internal attributions or attributions to high stability and controllability increase NWOM intention, with controllability having a stronger negative impact. Interactive effects between locus and stability/controllability are observed, mediated by trust in AI-based services. This study contributes to understanding consumer behavior in AI-based service environments, providing theoretical and practical insights for service providers to navigate the impact of AI-based service failures.

Keywords: Service Failure · Attribution Theory · NWOM · Trust

1 Introduction

Over the past decade, there has been a rapid advancement in artificial intelligence (AI) technology. Recognizing this transformative trend, either leading enterprises or SMEs have actively embraced the integration of AI into their operational to enhance performance efficiency [1]. This adoption is widespread across sectors, notably in hospitality, catering, and tourism, driven by AI's efficiency, accuracy, and convenience, indicating a keen interest in leveraging AI to improve service delivery [2].

While AI-based services offer unparalleled efficiencies, their deployment can lead to failures in complex scenarios, such as biased algorithms, creation of filter bubbles by recommendation systems, and inaccurate forecasts. These incidents not only tarnish the reputation of service providers but also diminish public trust in AI, fostering negative behaviors. Despite the prevalence of service failures related to AI, academic research in this area remains in its early stages. As Huang have discovered, in contrast to traditional human services, consumers appear to be less inclined to share their negative experiences following adverse outcomes from AI services [3]. This article seeks to explore this discrepancy by examining how consumers respond to AI service failures. Specifically, we focus on understanding consumers' willingness to engage in negative word-of-mouth (NWOM) after encountering such service failures, given its importance in the service industry [3]. Additionally, considering the fundamental role of trust in shaping customer reactions in traditional service interactions [4], this article also investigates the mediating effect of user trust on the relationship between failure attributions and NWOM sharing in context of AI-based services.

Our research contributes in several aspects. Firstly, by examining AI-based service failures through the lens of attribution theory, we extend the literature on service failures beyond traditional incidents caused by companies and staff, injecting novelty into the theory. Secondly, we find that failures deemed highly stable or controllable significantly increase negative behavioural intentions among consumers, with controllability having a stronger impact than stability. Additionally, an interaction effect exists between locus and these variables. Thirdly, our research reveals that consumer trust mediates the relationship between failure attributions and the likelihood of sharing NWOM, shedding light on how different attributions affect consumer responses to AI service failures. Finally, building on these theoretical insights, we present several practical managerial recommendations for service providers.

2   Literature Review

2.1   AI-Based Service Failure and Negative Word-of-Mouth

In recent years, amidst the ongoing progress in artificial intelligence, various sectors have seamlessly incorporated AI services. Nonetheless, within service environments, service failures remain inevitable due to the intricacies of direct user interactions and customer demands—a reality extending to AI-based services. It is essential to note that AI services exhibit unique characteristics in comparison to human employees. Therefore, obtaining a comprehensive understanding of customer responses to failures of this innovative technology is crucial.

Consumers exhibit various negative behaviors following service failures, with the expression of negative word-of-mouth (NWOM) standing out as a significant manifestation. NWOM refers to a commonplace behavior wherein individuals share negative experiences, either in casual conversations with friends or on social media platforms [3]. Extensive research has identified three primary motivations that consumers engage in NWOM [3]. Firstly, consumers warn potential customers to be cautious about service providers to prevent similar negative experiences. Secondly, NWOM's influential impact on service providers may lead consumers to share negative experiences as retaliation. Thirdly, sharing NWOM provides an outlet for consumers who feel unfairly treated to express grievances. Therefore, understanding the willingness of consumers to engage in NWOM following AI-based service failures is of paramount importance.

However, limited research has appraised the negative impact of AI-induced service failures on consumers' NWOM behavior. Building upon Huang and Philp [3] revelation of fundamental distinctions between AI-based and traditional service failures, our study opts to investigate the backdrop of service failures in AI-based recommendation systems and their influence on consumers' inclination to share NWOM.

2.2 Attribution Theory

Attribution theory provides a comprehensive framework for elucidating the mechanisms through which individuals assign causes to their experiences, especially in the context of failures or negative outcomes. This analytical lens is particularly vital for dissecting AI-based service failures, offering a clear understanding of the reasons of consumers' adverse reactions to such failures and, in turn, furnishing service providers with strategic insights for mitigating these responses. Central to this theory is the premise that consumers' negative behaviors stem from their attributions regarding the nature of service failures. Specifically, attribution theory posits that consumers assess the causality of failures along three critical dimensions: locus, stability, and controllability.[5]. Existing literature underscores that the manner in which consumers attribute responsibility for a failure significantly impacts their emotional states and subsequent behaviors [6], thereby rendering this framework valuable for studying service failures in the context of new technology [7].

Locus of causality scrutinizes the origin of issues, discerning whether they arise from internal factors (i.e., consumers themselves) or external factors (e.g., service providers) [5]. Recent studies, exemplified by research on patients in smart healthcare, have disclosed that distinct attributions of self-responsibility yield varying levels of trust in AI-provided medical services [8]. Acknowledging consumers' tendency not to attribute failures to themselves, our study makes a clear distinction between internal attribution (assigning blame to the service provider) and external attribution (attributing blame to environmental factors) in the investigation of the locus of causality. This distinction lays the foundation for our hypothesis:

H1: When users make internal attributions (i.e., assigning responsibility to the service provider), it leads to a higher intention to share NWOM.

Stability refers to the persistence or transience of factors contributing to service failures and the likelihood of similar outcomes occurring in the future [5]. The higher the stability, the more resistant the causes of service failure are to change and the more likely they are to persist. Therefore, when consumers perceive failures as highly stable, they question the provider's competence, leading to negative behaviors as an outlet for their dissatisfaction. Drawing on attribution theory, Researchers [9] corroborated this, revealing that those attributing failure to high stability are expected to diminish confidence in the provider's competence, reduce satisfaction, and instigate negative behaviors, including NWOM. Given the significant implications of highly stable failures, it is essential to better comprehend how locus influences outcomes based on the differentiation of stability levels. Building upon previous research on stability attribution, we assume that varying stability levels in AI-based failures will elicit distinct effects on user behavior. Thus, we hypothesize:

H2a: High stability attribution for service failures will lead to a higher level of willingness among users to share NWOM.

H2b: Under conditions of high stability failure, the internal attribution (versus external attribution) will significantly enhance users' propensity to share NWOM.

H2c: Under conditions of low stability failure, locus of causality do not exert a significant impact on users' willingness to engage in NWOM.

Controllability, as defined by Weiner [5], refers to the extent to which the service provider can alter the causes of failure, while the outcome "could have been otherwise." Akin to stability, perceiving that the service provider had the capacity to avert failure but failed to do so heightens the probability of negative emotions and behaviors [10]. Scholars have similarly observed a negative association between stability, controllability, and user trust and loyalty in service failure scenarios [4]. Thus, we hypothesize that users will demonstrate varying degrees of negative behavior when encountering AI-based service failures of varying controllability, presenting the following hypotheses:

H3a: High controllability attribution for service failures will result in a greater willingness on the part of users to share NWOM.

H3b: The internal attribution has a more significant positive impact on users' willingness to share NWOM in situations of high controllability failure.

H3c: Locus of causality do not significantly affect users' willingness to share NWOM in situations of low controllability failure.

User trust is pivotal in shaping users' negative behaviors post-service failures. Previous research indicates that attributions of stability and controllability in failures profoundly affect user trust [4]. While user trust is fundamental in traditional services for maintaining lasting relationships [11], its role in AI-based services, especially concerning NWOM, remains underexplored. This gap highlights the need for integrating trust with attribution theory in the context of AI service failures. We propose that the diverse locus typically indicate varying degrees of relevance between the cause and the service provider, resulting in different levels of user trust, which ultimately influences their negative behaviors. Thus, we formulate the following hypothesis:

H4a: When stability of the failure is certain, user trust negatively mediates the impact of the locus of causality on NWOM intent.

H4b: When controllability of the failure is certain, user trust negatively mediates the impact of the locus of causality on NWOM intent.

The conceptual model of our study is illustrated in Fig. 1.

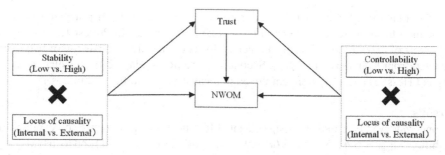

Fig. 1. Conceptual model

3 Overview of Studies

We conducted eight between-subjects scenario experiments across two studies to test these hypotheses. In each study, we explored how AI-based service failures influenced users' inclination to share NWOM by manipulating distinct attributions based on attribution theory. Specifically, Study 1 investigated the impact of AI-based service failures with varying stability levels on users' willingness to engage in NWOM. Similarly, in Study 2, we examined the effects of different degrees of controllability in AI-based service failures on their intention to share NWOM. Both studies also provided mediation evidence related to user trust, elucidating the underlying mechanisms.

4 Study 1

4.1 Pretest 1

Experimental Design

To validate our scenarios, we conducted pretest 1 with 204 participants recruited through a professional survey platform's paid sample service. The pretest involved manipulating stability and locus of causality, resulting in four distinct scenarios. Participants were randomly assigned to one of the groups and asked to rate their perceptions of stability and locus related to the service failure using a 7-point Likert scale.

The scenario described participants planning a 10-day trip with the aid of an AI system named "Travel Master", whose recommendations turned out to be disastrous. Specifically, in the high stability group, internally attributed participants were informed that they received recommendations from "Travel Master" that closely resembled their historical preferences, while they currently lacked interest in those attractions. Externally attributed participants faced service failures caused by overcrowding at various tourist destinations during the National Day holiday, despite "Travel Master's" efforts to implement backup plans.

In the low stability group, internally attributed participants encountered a service failure attributed to an AI system upgrade, resulting in inaccuracies in historical data reading and the generation of inappropriate recommendations. Conversely, participants with external attributions experienced a service failure caused by an unexpected thunderstorm, disrupting the AI's data-reading capabilities and rendering the system incapable of providing personalized recommendations.

The majority of constructs in our research were adapted from prior studies, with some modifications for alignment with the study's objectives. In Pretest 1, we assessed the levels of two variables. Firstly, perceived locus of causality, consisting of two items adapted from Kaltcheva et al. [12]. Secondly, three items adapted from Belanche et al. [7] and Hess Jr et al. [13] were employed to measure the stability of failures.

Results

A one-way ANOVA indicated significant differences in participants' perceptions of stability ($M_{high} = 5.41$, $M_{low} = 3.68$, $F(1,204) = 140.239$, $p < 0.001$) and locus ($M_{internal} = 2.88$, $M_{external} = 4.96$, $F(1,204) = 113.960$, $p < 0.001$). These results suggested that our manipulation of the scenario was successful.

4.2 Formal Experiments

Measurement

In order to test the interaction effect between stability and locus, a 2 (stability: low vs. high) × 2 (locus: internal vs. external) between-subjects design was employed. We enlisted 320 participants (56.25% female, $M_{age} = 31$) through a survey platform for the experiment, maintaining consistency with the pretest procedures. 249 responses were deemed valid, resulting in a 77.8% validity rate with 55.0% female participants.

In the formal experiment, we broadened our scope of measurements, Firstly, drawing inspiration from Xie and Peng [14], we utilized three items to gauge user trust. Secondly, three items adapted from Kaltcheva et al. [12] were employed to assess the willingness to share NWOM. To account for potential interference, we included one item adapted from Roggeveen et al. [15] to assess the severity of the presented service failure and another item adapted from Fu et al. [10] to evaluate authenticity of scenarios.

We ensured demographic balance across all scenarios, finding no significant differences in gender ($F(1,249) = 0.285$, $p = 0.837$), age ($F(1,249) = 1.681$, $p = 0.172$), education ($F(1,249) = 0.610$, $p = 0.609$), or income levels ($F(1,249) = 1.033$, $p = 0.379$). The analysis confirmed the robustness of our scales, with Cronbach's α exceeding 0.75 and confirmatory factor analysis supporting structural validity through AVE and CR values above 0.5 and 0.7, respectively. A Harman's single-factor test further validated our measures by showing no single factor accounted for more than 40% of the variance, underscoring the reliability and validity of our approach.

Manipulation Check

Prior to analysis, a normality test using the Shapiro-Wilk test confirmed that the measured data followed a normal distribution, allowing for subsequent parametric tests. A one-way ANOVA revealed significant differences in stability ($M_{high} = 5.53$, $M_{low} = 3.54$, $F(1,249) = 206.877$, $p < 0.001$) and locus ($M_{internal} = 2.54$, $M_{external} = 5.17$, $F(1,249) = 279.389$, $p < 0.001$) among different groups, indicating successful manipulation.

To validate scenario authenticity, we employed a one-sample t-test on mean scores across the four scenarios (ranging from 5.35 to 5.63). Results exhibited a significant elevation of mean values above the neutral scale value of 4 ($t = 26.591$, $p < 0.001$). Hence, these scenarios were perceived by the participants as realistic. Moreover, a one-way ANOVA scrutinized the failure severity across the four scenarios, indicating no significant differences in severity (F(1,249) = 1.341, p = 0.262), effectively avoiding the interference of severity.

Hypothesis Test

Independent samples t-tests revealed a significant difference in NWOM intentions based on locus of causality, with higher intentions observed for participants with internal attributions compared to those with external attributions ($M_{internal}$ = 4.22, $M_{external}$ = 3.73, p = 0.004). Furthermore, participants in the high stability failure group exhibited significantly higher NWOM intentions compared to the low stability group (M_{high} = 4.27, M_{low} = 3.70, p = 0.001), providing support for H1 and H2a.

A two-way ANOVA indicated significant main effects of both stability and locus (p < 0.01), and their interaction was significant at the 0.05 level (p = 0.011). The interaction effect is illustrated in Fig. 2. Specifically, in instances of high-stability failures, consumers who made internal attributions were found to be more actively engaged in NWOM ($M_{internal}$ = 4.70, $M_{external}$ = 3.80, p < 0.001). However, in cases of low-stability failures, the locus of causality no longer played a significant differentiating role ($M_{internal}$ = 3.74, $M_{external}$ = 3.67, p = 0.759). Therefore, H2b and H2c are supported.

The mediating effect of user trust was tested using Model 4 in the PROCESS plugin. A 95% bias-corrected bootstrap (based on 5000 samples) revealed the significant mediating effect of user trust in both high-stability (indirect effect: CI [-0.2480, -0.0738]) and low-stability (indirect effect: CI [-0.1921, -0.0498]) service failures. However, user trust exhibited distinct mediation effects depending on the level of stability. Specifically, in highly stable scenarios, trust demonstrated a partial mediating effect (direct effect: CI [-0.3758, -0.1318]), whereas in low-stability scenarios, it exerted a complete mediating effect (direct effect: CI [-0.0912, 0.1595]). Therefore, H4a is supported.

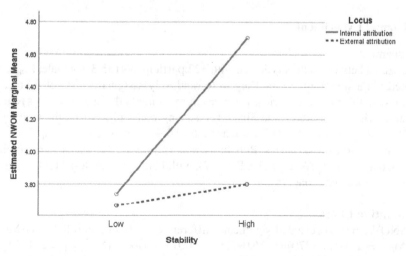

Fig. 2. The interaction between stability and locus of causality on NWOM

5 Study 2

5.1 Pretest 2

Experimental Design
In a setup similar to pretest 1, we engaged 202 participants via the same platform, assigning them randomly to one of four scenarios. In the high controllability group with internal attribution, participants faced a service failure where recommended attractions had excessive fees and were misaligned with their interests, indicating a clear lack of suitable alternatives. For external attribution, the failure was attributed to poor management and rude staff at the suggested location.

Conversely, in the low controllability group, participants with internal attribution used keywords not reflecting their interests, leading "Travel Master" to rely solely on these keywords and past data, failing to offer appropriate destinations due to limited processing capabilities. In the external attribution scenario, a sudden heavy rain led to the closure of many attractions.

In pretest 2, we measured participants' evaluations of the controllability and locus of causality of failures experienced in the given scenario. The measurement for locus remained consistent with pretest 1. Additionally, three items were adapted from Chang et al. [16] to measure controllability.

Results
A one-way ANOVA indicated significant differences in participants' perceptions of controllability (M_{high} = 5.06, M_{low} = 2.88, $F(1,202)$ = 212.258, $p < 0.001$) and locus ($M_{internal}$ = 2.71, $M_{external}$ = 5.45, $F(1,202)$ = 301.153, $p < 0.001$), confirming successful manipulation.

5.2 Formal Experiment

Measurement
We utilized a between-subjects design with 322 participants (55.3% female, M_{age} = 32) recruited via a survey platform. They were randomly assigned to one of four groups, aligning with the pretest scenarios. The measurement methods for all variables remained consistent with the pretest 2 and Study 1, ensuring continuity across the study, yielding 270 valid responses (83.85% response rate, 55.9% female). Demographic analysis showed no significant variances. Reliability and validity of the scales were confirmed (Cronbach's $\alpha > 0.75$, AVE > 0.5, CR > 0.7), with Harman's single-factor test negating common method bias concerns.

Manipulation Check
The ANOVA results revealed significant differences in both controllability (M_{high} = 5.06, M_{low} = 2.93, $F(1,270)$ = 256.092, $p < 0.001$) and locus ($M_{internal}$ = 2.66, $M_{external}$ = 5.26, $F(1,270)$ = 327.573, $p < 0.001$) between the two groups. These results validate the successful manipulation. Consistent with Study 1, participants considered the four scenarios highly realistic and relevant to real-life situations, with mean scores ranging from 5.28 to 5.49 ($t = 23.152$, $p < 0.001$). Additionally, there were no significant

differences in the severity of the failures among the four groups (F(1,270) = 0.603, p = 0.613).

Hypothesis Test
Similar to the findings in Study 1, a one-way ANOVA indicated that users with internal attribution ($M_{internal}$ = 4.17, $M_{external}$ = 3.82, p = 0.031) and high controllability (M_{high} = 4.35, M_{low} = 3.66, p < 0.001) were significantly more inclined to share NWOM, thus supporting H1 and H3a.

A two-way ANOVA revealed a significant main effect of controllability (p < 0.001) and an interaction with locus (p < 0.05) on NWOM sharing. Internal attribution users were more inclined to share NWOM in low controllability cases ($M_{internal}$ = 4.016, $M_{external}$ = 3.347, p = 0.003). However, no significant difference in sharing intention emerged between internal and external attributions in high controllability cases ($M_{internal}$ = 4.306, $M_{external}$ = 4.414, p = 0.636), contradicting expectations and invalidating H3b and H3c. The interaction effect is depicted in Fig. 3.

The PROCESS Model 4 mediation analysis revealed that user trust fully mediated the effect of locus on NWOM sharing in both low controllability (indirect effect: CI [-0.3156, -0.1129]; direct effect: CI [-0.2341, 0.0064]) and high controllability failures (indirect effect: CI [-0.3089, -0.1095]; direct effect: CI [-0.0112, 0.2687]). Therefore, this finding supports H4b.

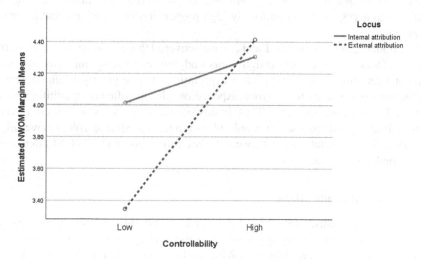

Fig. 3. The interaction between controllability and locus of causality on NWOM

6 Conclusion and Discussion

6.1 Discussion

This article aims to explore consumers' willingness to share NWOM following failures in AI-based services and the underlying mechanisms, drawing on attribution theory.

Studies 1 and 2 demonstrate a clear link between the perceived stability or controllability of AI-based services and consumers' propensity to engage in NWOM. Specifically, when users perceive AI-based services as stable or controllable, it can increase tendency to believe that the service provider failed in fulfilling their obligations, leading to a sense of mistrust and prompt NWOM. Conversely, attributing service failures to uncontrollable or accidental factors tends to soften consumer reactions, reducing the likelihood of NWOM dissemination. Furthermore, the research explores the impact of responsibility attribution and establishes a link between the locus and the propagation of NWOM. Consumers attributing negative experiences internally are more prone to share them, regardless of stability or controllability attributions.

Our findings indicate a nuanced interaction effect between attributions perceptions and NWOM sharing. When failures are perceived as stable and internally attributed, there's a marked increase in NWOM sharing, a trend that lessens with instability. Interestingly, controllability perceptions lead to varied responses. In low controllability situations, consumers holding internal attributions are more inclined to share NWOM, possibly due to viewing the service provider as somewhat responsible despite limited control. Contrastingly, high controllability failures prompt high degree NWOM intentions across both internal and external attribution groups. This phenomenon can be elucidated by the heightened negative emotions experienced by consumers in the presence of controllability attributions [6], which drive more widespread negative behaviors. Therefore, in instances where negative emotions dominate, the precise cause of failure becomes less significant to users, driving a uniformly high propensity for negative behavior among consumers.

Additionally, in both Studies 1 and 2, we discovered that user trust plays an intermediary role. Drawing on previous insights, this study places a strong emphasis on stability as a pivotal determinant in shaping future expectations. Consequently, when stable negative outcomes occur, users tend to form expectations that are often disappointing and can easily lead to negative behaviors. Thus, in this situation, as users can observe a service that will disappoint them, user trust only plays a partial mediating role. Conversely, in other scenarios, the relationship between failure attribution and NWOM intentions is entirely mediated by user trust.

6.2 Theoretical Implications

Three theoretical contributions have been made in this through our study. Firstly, it contributes to the literature by applying attribution theory to comprehend consumers' responses to AI-based service failures. While existing research has shown the impact of consumer attributions on emotions, there is a dearth of exploration in the context of AI-based service failures. Addressing this gap, we investigated how consumers' perceptions of stability and controllability influence their intentions to share NWOM. Utilizing a two-way ANOVA, we analyze interactions between the locus of causality and these factors, shedding light on the internal mechanisms of consumer attributions in AI-based service failures.

Secondly, our research explores the impact of consumers' attributions on NWOM intentions in the context of AI-based service failures. Social media have permeated into practically every single pore and cell of human society. Understanding the driving forces behind consumers' NWOM intentions in such situations is crucial due to the amplifying effect of social media on service failure-related events, potentially leading to crises. By exploring interactions between different levels of stability, controllability, and locus, our study identifies situations where NWOM is significantly propelled. Although rooted in AI-based service failures, this finding contributes to understanding key factors influencing consumers' NWOM in the era of social media.

Finally, we investigated the role of consumer trust in shaping NWOM intentions following AI-based service failures. Previous research has lacked studies considering user trust as an intermediary variable in the influence of attributions on negative behaviors, particularly in the context of artificial intelligence services. The study revealed that user trust serves as a negative mediator in the formation of NWOM intentions, regardless of stability and controllability levels, when consumers face AI-based service failures. This enriches our understanding of how user trust impacts behavioral intentions in situations involving failures in technology-driven services.

6.3 Managerial Implications

This paper provides some implications for managerial strategies in addressing the challenges posed by NWOM, especially in the social media era. AI service providers should be particularly alert to stable and controllable failures. Even if negative feedback isn't promptly shared, it's essential to acknowledge potential user dissatisfaction in controllable situations. Proactively enhancing AI's personalized recommendations through better user data management can effectively reduce controllable mistakes, emphasizing the importance of continuous improvement in AI systems.

Secondly, providers should devise resolution strategies tailored to the locus of causality, considering the substantial impact of users' causal attributions on NWOM intentions. Strengthening internal controls can proactively prevent issues attributed to internal errors, and communicating contingency plans with consumers will clarify compensation procedures in the event of service failures.

Finally, Elevating trust levels is identified as an effective means to reduce NWOM occurrences. Given the confirmed mediating role of user trust, maintaining transparency in the AI's operational mode and recommendation process may fosters user trust. Implementing measures to provide insights into AI operational mode demonstrates the company's commitment to excellence and sincerity, reinforcing trust in the realm of AI-based services.

6.4 Limitations and Future Research

The study has limitations. Firstly, using scenario-based experiments may constrain external validity. Future research should prioritize field studies for a more precise understanding of user responses to AI service failures. Secondly, the focus on AI systems for travel destination recommendations may limit generalizability. Exploring diverse scenarios in future studies would enhance applicability.

Acknowledgement. This research was partially supported by the NSFC (61972337).

References

1. Vlačić, B., Corbo, L., e Silva, S.C., Dabić, M.: The evolving role of artificial intelligence in marketing: a review and research agenda. J. Bus. Res. **128**, 187–203 (2021). https://doi.org/10.1016/j.jbusres.2021.01.055
2. Li, M., Yin, D., Qiu, H., Bai, B.: A systematic review of AI technology-based service encounters: implications for hospitality and tourism operations. Int. J. Hosp. Manage. **95**, 102930 (2021)
3. Huang, B., Philp, M.: When AI-based services fail: examining the effect of the self-AI connection on willingness to share negative word-of-mouth after service failures. Serv. Ind. J. **41**, 877–899 (2021)
4. Nikbin, D., Hyun, S.S., Iranmanesh, M., Maghsoudi, A., Jeong, C.: Airline travelers' causal attribution of service failure and its impact on trust and loyalty formation: the moderating role of corporate social responsibility. Asia Pac. J. Tourism Res. **21**, 355–374 (2016)
5. Weiner, B.: Attributional thoughts about consumer behavior. J. Consum. Res. **27**, 382–387 (2000)
6. Van Vaerenbergh, Y., Orsingher, C., Vermeir, I., Larivière, B.: A meta-analysis of relationships linking service failure attributions to customer outcomes. J. Serv. Res. **17**, 381–398 (2014)
7. Belanche, D., Casaló, L.V., Flavián, C., Schepers, J.: Robots or frontline employees? Exploring customers' attributions of responsibility and stability after service failure or success. J. Serv. Manag. **31**, 267–289 (2020)
8. Huo, W., Zheng, G., Yan, J., Sun, L., Han, L.: Interacting with medical artificial intelligence: Integrating self-responsibility attribution, human–computer trust, and personality. Comput. Hum. Behav. **132**, 107253 (2022)
9. Weitzl, W., Hutzinger, C., Einwiller, S.: An empirical study on how webcare mitigates complainants' failure attributions and negative word-of-mouth. Comput. Hum. Behav. **89**, 316–327 (2018)
10. Fu, X., Liu, X., Hua, C., Li, Z., Du, Q.: Understanding tour guides' service failure: Integrating a two-tier triadic business model with attribution theory. J. Hosp. Tour. Manag. **47**, 506–516 (2021)
11. Morgan, R.M., Hunt, S.D.: The commitment-trust theory of relationship marketing. J. Mark. **58**, 20–38 (1994)
12. Kaltcheva, V.D., Winsor, R.D., Parasuraman, A.: Do customer relationships mitigate or amplify failure responses? J. Bus. Res. **66**, 525–532 (2013)
13. Hess, R.L., Jr., Ganesan, S., Klein, N.M.: Service failure and recovery: the impact of relationship factors on customer satisfaction. J. Acad. Mark. Sci. **31**, 127–145 (2003)
14. Xie, Y., Peng, S.: How to repair customer trust after negative publicity: the roles of competence, integrity, benevolence, and forgiveness. Psychol. Mark. **26**, 572–589 (2009)
15. Roggeveen, A.L., Tsiros, M., Grewal, D.: Understanding the co-creation effect: when does collaborating with customers provide a lift to service recovery? J. Acad. Mark. Sci. **40**, 771–790 (2012)
16. Chang, H.H., Tsai, Y.-C., Wong, K.H., Wang, J.W., Cho, F.J.: The effects of response strategies and severity of failure on consumer attribution with regard to negative word-of-mouth. Decis. Support. Syst. **71**, 48–61 (2015)

Pricing Strategies of Dual-Channel Green Supply Chain Considering Government Subsidies and Blockchain Technology

Qing Fang and Luyao Wang[✉]

School of Management, Wuhan University of Science and Technology, Wuhan 430065, China
W13461685055@163.com

Abstract. As consumers pay more attention to green products, the issue of trust in green products has become increasingly prominent. In recent years, enterprises have invested in blockchain technology to provide consumers with product traceability information. This paper introduces three variables of green product trust, blockchain technology and government subsidies in a dual-channel green supply chain to study the optimal pricing strategies of three models without blockchain, with blockchain without government subsidies and with blockchain with government subsidies. The research indicates that as consumers' trust in green products increases, manufacturers are more inclined to invest in blockchain technology; investment in blockchain technology raises the price of green products, while government subsidies for blockchain can both lower and raise the price of green products; investment in blockchain technology and government subsidies can benefit manufacturers and retailers only when consumer green preference is high.

Keywords: Green Supply Chain · Blockchain Technology · Government Subsidies

1 Introduction

In January 2023, the State Council Information Office of China released the White Paper "Green Development in China in the New Era," emphasizing the need to steadfastly pursue the path of green development, continuously promote the optimization and upgrading of green industry structure, and facilitate the green transformation of social development [1]. As the government pays more attention to green and low-carbon development, consumers are gradually realizing the impact of personal behaviors on society and enterprises. Consumers' purchasing preferences for green products influence the level of green inputs by enterprises. In order to expand market share and increase revenue, many enterprises have established online direct sales channels to sell their products in addition to traditional retail channels. Due to information asymmetry, consumers find it challenging to access information related to the origin and processing of products, leading to their frequent skepticism about the greenness of such products. Blockchain, as a product of the development of new-generation information technology, is characterized by decentralization, traceability of information and difficulty in tampering with

Y. P. Tu and M. Chi (Eds.): WHICEB 2024, LNBIP 515, pp. 203–213, 2024.
https://doi.org/10.1007/978-3-031-60264-1_18

data, and is considered to be one of the most promising technologies for improving the traceability of product information [2]. Enterprises can utilize blockchain to record information such as raw materials, places of origin and quality inspection reports of green products, and consumers can trace this information by scanning the QR codes on product packaging, thereby increasing their trust and willingness to purchase green products [3].

Due to the limited widespread adoption of blockchain technology, enterprises still face high costs when using blockchain, which not only dampens enthusiasm but also increases the selling price of green products. The government plays an important role in formulating and enforcing various regulations and subsidy policies, which guide the operational decisions of enterprises. In order to encourage enterprises to adopt blockchain technology, improve the market competitiveness of traceable green products, and alleviate the problem of high application costs of blockchain, the government can formulate relevant policies for subsidies. Therefore, it is of great significance to study the dual-channel green supply chain considering government subsidies and blockchain technology, based on consumer green preferences and product trust.

The rest of the paper is organized as follows: Sect. 2 provides a brief summary of the relevant literature. Section 3 introduces the model description and relevant assumptions. Model construction and solution are presented in Sect. 4. In Sect. 5, a case study analysis of the optimal decisions from the aforementioned models was conducted. Finally, Sect. 6 summarizes the relevant conclusions and proposes future research directions.

2 Literature Review

This paper is closely related to two research directions. The first is the dual-channel green supply chain, and the second is the application of blockchain technology and government subsidies in the supply chain. In terms of dual-channel green supply chain, Yu et al. [4] consider the impact of product greenness and free-rider effect on dual-channel green supply chain and design a cooperative contract to coordinate channel conflicts. Pal et al. [5] established a two-level game model to explore the optimal pricing, green innovation, and promotion effort levels of each subject under centralized decision-making, manufacturer leadership, and Nash strategy. Zhao et al. [6] found that increasing the product assortment in a retailer's dual-channel supply chain improves total profitability when there are multiple suppliers. Using a two-stage optimization approach and Stackelberg game, Peng et al. [7] found that customer satisfaction has a significant impact on green marketing inputs in supply chains. Meng et al. [8] compared the impact of government subsidies on the pricing of green products while considering consumer channel preferences.

In the application of blockchain and government subsidies, Liu et al. [9] proposed cost-sharing and revenue-sharing contracts to achieve Pareto improvement in investment decisions for green agricultural products under the information services of big data and blockchain. Lin et al. [10] studied the product pricing decision problem of manufacturers investing in blockchain technology under the cost-sharing and revenue-sharing contracts provided by retailers. Wu et al. [11] found in the livestreaming supply chain of agricultural products that government subsidies to suppliers can improve the freshness of agricultural products, while subsidies to anchors can enhance marketing effectiveness. By constructing a three-way evolutionary game model, Guo et al. [12] found that government subsidies have a positive impact on the behavioral strategies of manufacturers and consumers. Xu and Duan [3] examined blockchain adoption strategies when the government subsidizes manufacturers, retailers, and consumers, respectively. Zhong et al. [13] studied the additional benefits brought to the supply chain by manu-facturers adopting blockchain technology in a dual-channel supply chain. They found a win-win-win situation when the government provides subsidies.

However, in the aforementioned research on dual-channel green supply chains, few scholars have focused on the issue of consumer trust in green products and the application of blockchain technology. Studies on the application of blockchain are mostly concen-trated in single-channel supply chains, with limited research on dual-channel supply chains. Additionally, in the aspect of government subsidies, the focus has primarily been on exploring subsidies for products and various subjects in the supply chain, with a lack of research on subsidies for blockchain. Therefore, based on the consideration of con-sumer green preferences and product trust, this paper constructs a dual-channel supply chain model without blockchain, with blockchain without government subsidies, and with blockchain with government subsidies. The study explores and compares the vari-ations in product greenness, pricing strategies for online and offline channels, as well as profit outcomes among different models.

3 Model Description and Assumptions

This paper focuses on a dual-channel green supply chain consisting of a manufacturer and a retailer, where the manufacturer sell green products through both traditional retail and online direct sales channels. Due to asymmetric market information, consumers question the greenness of the products. To improve consumer trust, the manufacturer can use blockchain technology for product traceability, but investing in blockchain will also increase the cost pressure of the manufacturer, so the government can provide subsidies to manufacturer. The decision sequence in this paper is as follows: First, the manufacturer decides whether to adopt blockchain technology, and if so, the government decides whether to subsidize it; Second, the manufacturer decides the greenness, wholesale price and online price of the product; Finally, the retailer decides the retail price of the product. The symbols involved in the model are shown in Table 1.

In order to make the model description more detailed, the following assumptions are made in this paper:

1. The manufacturer and the retailer are assumed to maintain risk neutrality and aim to maximize their own profits.
2. To simplify the model, the manufacturer's unit cost of producing green products is not considered.
3. The value range of the cross-price sensitivity coefficient is $0 < \beta < 1$.
4. According to Hsieh and Lathifah [14], the manufacturer adopting blockchain needs to bear unit usage cost c, where $c < w$.
5. The manufacturer bears the responsibility for green product research and develop-ment. The green research and development cost function is represented as $c(e) = \frac{ke^2}{2}$, where k is the green product research and development cost coefficient.

Table 1. Model symbols and meanings

Symbol	Definition
a	Potential market demand
β	Cross-price sensitivity coefficient
w	Wholesale price
θ	Consumer trust in green products
e	Product greenness
λ	Consumer green preferences
k	Green product research and development cost coefficient
c	The unit application cost of blockchain
γ	Proportion of government subsidies for blockchain unit application costs
p_r	Offline retail price
p_d	Online direct sales price
D_r	Retail channel market demand
D_d	Direct sales channel market demand
π_r	Retailer's profit
π_m	Manufacturer's profit
$N/B/T$	Represent without blockchain/with blockchain without government subsidies/with blockchain with government subsidies

6. Referring to Zhang et al. [15], when the manufacturer does not adopt blockchain technology, consumers have doubts about the greenness of the product, in this case $0 < \theta < 1$. When using blockchain for product information traceability, consumer concerns can be completely eliminated, in this case $\theta = 1$.

According to the above assumptions, the demand function without blockchain adoption can be expressed as:

$$D_r^N = a - p_r + \beta p_d + \theta \lambda e \tag{1}$$

$$D_d^N = a - p_d + \beta p_r + \theta \lambda e \tag{2}$$

The demand function for adopting blockchain without government subsidies and adopting blockchain with government subsidies can be expressed as follows:

$$D_r^{B/T} = a - p_r + \beta p_d + \lambda e \tag{3}$$

$$D_d^{B/T} = a - p_d + \beta p_r + \lambda e \tag{4}$$

4 Model Construction and Solution

4.1 Model Without Blockchain

When not adopting blockchain technology, the manufacturer only needs to bear the green product research and development cost. The profit function is:

$$\pi_m^N = wD_r^N + p_d D_d^N - \frac{1}{2}ke^2 \tag{5}$$

The profit function for the retailer is:

$$\pi_r^N = (p_r - w)D_r^N \tag{6}$$

In the model where the manufacturer does not adopt blockchain, using the method of backward induction for solution, when $0 < \lambda < \sqrt{\frac{4k(1-\beta)}{\theta^2(3+\beta)}}$, the optimal decision is as follows:

$$p_d^{N*} = \frac{2ak}{4k(1-\beta) - \lambda^2\theta^2(3+\beta)}$$

$$p_r^{N*} = \frac{ak(3-\beta)}{4k(1-\beta) - \lambda^2\theta^2(3+\beta)}$$

$$w^{N*} = \frac{2ak}{4k(1-\beta) - \lambda^2\theta^2(3+\beta)}$$

$$e^{N*} = \frac{a\lambda\theta(3+\beta)}{4k(1-\beta) - \lambda^2\theta^2(3+\beta)}$$

$$\pi_r^{N*} = \frac{a^2k^2(\beta-1)^2}{[4k(1-\beta) - \lambda^2\theta^2(3+\beta)]^2}$$

$$\pi_m^{N*} = \frac{a^2k(3+\beta)}{2[4k(1-\beta) - \lambda^2\theta^2(3+\beta)]}$$

Proposition 1 The relationship between consumer trust in green products and the various equilibrium solutions is as follows:

$$\frac{\partial e^{N*}}{\partial\theta} > 0, \frac{\partial w^{N*}}{\partial\theta} > 0, \frac{\partial p_r^{N*}}{\partial\theta} > 0, \frac{\partial p_d^{N*}}{\partial\theta} > 0, \frac{\partial D_r^{N*}}{\partial\theta} > 0, \frac{\partial D_d^{N*}}{\partial\theta} > 0, \frac{\partial \pi_r^{N*}}{\partial\theta} > 0, \frac{\partial \pi_m^{N*}}{\partial\theta} > 0$$

From Proposition 1, it can be inferred that an increase in consumer trust in green products will enhance both online and offline market demand, thereby encouraging the manufacturer to invest more funds to improve the greenness of their products. With the increase in costs, the manufacturer chooses to raise the wholesale and direct selling prices of green products to enhance profits, and the retailer also increases the retail price to shift the added costs to consumers.

4.2 Model with Blockchain Without Government Subsidies

When the manufacturer adopts blockchain technology, consumers can trace the origin of green products, and at this point $\theta = 1$. In addition to the research and development costs of green products, the manufacturer also needs to bear the unit application costs of blockchain. The profit function for the manufacturer at this point is:

$$\pi_m^B = (w - c)D_r^B + (p_d - c)D_d^B - \frac{1}{2}ke^2 \tag{7}$$

The profit function for the retailer is:

$$\pi_r^B = (p_r - w)D_r^B \tag{8}$$

In the model where the manufacturer adopts blockchain without government subsidies, using the method of backward induction for solution, when $0 < \lambda < \sqrt{\frac{4k(1-\beta)}{(3+\beta)}}$, the optimal decision is as follows:

$$p_d^{B*} = \frac{2k(a + c - \beta c) - \lambda^2 c(3 + \beta)}{4k(1 - \beta) - \lambda^2(3 + \beta)}$$

$$p_r^{B*} = \frac{ak(3 - \beta) + ck(1 - \beta^2) - \lambda^2 c(3 + \beta)}{4k(1 - \beta) - \lambda^2(3 + \beta)}$$

$$w^{B*} = \frac{2k(a + c - \beta c) - \lambda^2 c(3 + \beta)}{4k(1 - \beta) - \lambda^2(3 + \beta)}$$

$$e^{B*} = \frac{\lambda(3 + \beta)(a - c + \beta c)}{4k(1 - \beta) - \lambda^2(3 + \beta)}$$

$$\pi_r^{B*} = \frac{k^2(\beta - 1)^2(a - c + \beta c)^2}{[4k(1 - \beta) - \lambda^2(3 + \beta)]^2}$$

$$\pi_m^{B*} = \frac{k(\beta + 3)(a - c + \beta c)^2}{2[4k(1 - \beta) - \lambda^2(3 + \beta)]}$$

Proposition 2 The relationship between the unit application cost of blockchain and various equilibrium solutions is as follows:

1. $\frac{\partial e^{B*}}{\partial c} > 0$, $\frac{\partial D_d^{B*}}{\partial c} > 0$, $\frac{\partial D_r^{B*}}{\partial c} > 0$.
2. When $0 < \lambda < \sqrt{\frac{2k(1-\beta)}{3+\beta}}$, $\frac{\partial w^{B*}}{\partial c} > 0$, $\frac{\partial p_d^{B*}}{\partial c} > 0$; otherwise, $\frac{\partial w^{B*}}{\partial c} < 0$, $\frac{\partial p_d^{B*}}{\partial c} < 0$. When $0 < \lambda < \sqrt{\frac{k(1-\beta^2)}{3+\beta}}$, $\frac{\partial p_r^{B*}}{\partial c} > 0$; otherwise, $\frac{\partial p_r^{B*}}{\partial c} < 0$.
3. When $0 < c < \frac{a}{1-\beta}$, $\frac{\partial \pi_r^{B*}}{\partial c} < 0$, $\frac{\partial \pi_m^{B*}}{\partial c} < 0$; otherwise, $\frac{\partial \pi_r^{B*}}{\partial c} > 0$, $\frac{\partial \pi_m^{B*}}{\partial c} > 0$.

According to Proposition 2, with the increase of the unit application cost of blockchain, the manufacturer will choose to reduce the greenness of the product in order to avoid a significant increase in the cost of green products. Obviously, if the greenness of the product is reduced, consumers with a preference for green products will be unwilling to purchase products with low greenness at the same price. Therefore, the market demand for online and offline channels will also decrease. For the manufacturer and the retailer, if consumer green preferences are low and the unit application cost of blockchain is below a certain threshold, then with the increase in blockchain application costs, channel members will choose to increase the wholesale and online and offline price of green products to minimize losses due to reduced demand. However, at this time, the increase in the price of green products cannot compensate for the losses suffered by channel members due to increased costs and reduced demand, therefore the profit of the channel members will be reduced.

4.3 Model with Blockchain with Government Subsidies

In order to encourage the manufacturer to adopt blockchain technology, the government can provide subsidies for the unit application cost of blockchain. Let γ be the proportion of government subsidies for the unit application cost of blockchain, where $0 < \gamma < 1$. Thus, the profit function for the manufacturer is:

$$\pi_m^T = (w - c(1 - \gamma))D_r^T + (p_d - c(1 - \gamma))D_d^T - \frac{1}{2}ke^2 \tag{9}$$

The profit function for the retailer is:

$$\pi_r^T = (p_r - w)D_r^T \tag{10}$$

In the model where the manufacturer adopts blockchain with government subsidies, using the method of backward induction for solution, when $0 < \lambda < \sqrt{\frac{4k(1-\beta)}{(3+\beta)}}$, the optimal decision is as follows:

$$p_d^{T*} = \frac{2ak + c(1 - \gamma)(2k - 3\lambda^2 - 2\beta k - \beta\lambda^2)}{4k(1 - \beta) - \lambda^2(3 + \beta)}$$

$$p_r^{T*} = \frac{ak(3 - \beta) + c(1 - \gamma)(k - 3\lambda^2 - \beta\lambda^2 - \beta^2 k)}{4k(1 - \beta) - \lambda^2(3 + \beta)}$$

$$w^{T*} = \frac{2ak + c(1 - \gamma)(2k - 3\lambda^2 - 2\beta k - \beta\lambda^2)}{4k(1 - \beta) - \lambda^2(3 + \beta)}$$

$$e^{T*} = \frac{\lambda(3 + \beta)[a + c(\gamma - 1)(1 - \beta)]}{4k(1 - \beta) - \lambda^2(3 + \beta)}$$

$$\pi_r^{T*} = \frac{k^2(\beta - 1)^2[a + c(\gamma - 1)(1 - \beta)]^2}{[4k(1 - \beta) - \lambda^2(3 + \beta)]^2}$$

$$\pi_m^{T*} = \frac{k(3 + \beta)[a + c(\gamma - 1)(1 - \beta)]^2}{2[4k(1 - \beta) - \lambda^2(3 + \beta)]}$$

Proposition 3 The relationship between the government subsidy proportion for the unit application cost of blockchain and the various equilibrium solutions is as follows:

1. $\frac{\partial e^{T*}}{\partial \gamma} > 0$, $\frac{\partial D_d^{T*}}{\partial \gamma} > 0$, $\frac{\partial D_r^{T*}}{\partial \gamma} > 0$.

2. When $0 < \lambda < \sqrt{\frac{2k(1-\beta)}{3+\beta}}$, $\frac{\partial w^{T*}}{\partial \gamma} < 0$, $\frac{\partial p_d^{T*}}{\partial \gamma} < 0$; otherwise, $\frac{\partial p_d^{T*}}{\partial \gamma} > 0$, $\frac{\partial p_d^{T*}}{\partial \gamma} > 0$.

   When $0 < \lambda < \sqrt{\frac{k(1-\beta^2)}{3+\beta}}$, $\frac{\partial p_r^{T*}}{\partial \gamma} < 0$; otherwise, $\frac{\partial p_r^{T*}}{\partial \gamma} > 0$.

3. When $0 < c < \frac{a}{(1-\gamma)(1-\beta)}$, $\frac{\partial \pi_r^{T*}}{\partial \gamma} > 0$, $\frac{\partial \pi_m^{T*}}{\partial \gamma} > 0$; otherwise, $\frac{\partial \pi_r^{T*}}{\partial \gamma} < 0$, $\frac{\partial \pi_m^{T*}}{\partial \gamma} < 0$.

According to Proposition 3, since government subsidies directly benefit the manufacturer, as the proportion of government subsidies increases, the manufacturer will be more motivated to increase the greenness of their products, thereby increasing consumer purchasing intentions and driving an increase in market demand for online and offline channels. For consumers with low green preference, who are not sensitive to changes in product greenness. The manufacturer and retailer, in order to further expand market demand, will lower the price of green products for consumers. Moreover, the higher the government subsidy proportion, the greater the reduction in the price of green products. It is found that channel members' profits do not always show a monotonically increasing (decreasing) trend with the increase in the proportion of government subsidies. When the unit application cost of blockchain is below a threshold, increasing government subsidies reduces the actual costs for the manufacturer. This enables the manufacturer to offer more competitive green products to expand their market presence, and the retailer can also benefit from the government subsidy due to the free-rider effect.

Proposition 4 When the manufacturer adopts blockchain, comparing with and without government subsidies, the following equilibrium results can be obtained:

1. $e^{T*} > e^{B*}, D_d^{T*} > D_d^{B*}, D_r^{T*} > D_r^{B*}$.

2 When $0 < \lambda < \sqrt{\frac{2k(1-\beta)}{3+\beta}}$, $w^{T*} < w^{B*}, p_d^{T*} < p_d^{B*}$; otherwise, $w^{T*} > w^{B*}, p_d^{T*} > p_d^{B*}$. When $0 < \lambda < \sqrt{\frac{k(1-\beta^2)}{3+\beta}}$, $p_r^{T*} < p_r^{B*}$; otherwise, $p_r^{T*} > p_r^{B*}$.

3 When $0 < c < \frac{2a}{(1-\beta)(2-\gamma)}$, $\pi_r^{T*} > \pi_r^{B*}, \pi_m^{T*} > \pi_m^{B*}$; otherwise, $\pi_r^{T*} < \pi_r^{B*}, \pi_m^{T*} < \pi_m^{B*}$

From Proposition 4, it is clear that the greenness of products and the market demand in online/offline channels are always higher in the case of the manufacturer adopting blockchain and with government subsidies than in the case of no government subsidies. Only when consumers have a low preference for green products, the wholesale and online/offline prices of green products under the scenario with government subsidies are lower than those without government subsidies. In addition, the profits of the manufacturer and the retailer are influenced by the unit application cost of blockchain, and when the unit application cost of blockchain is below a certain threshold, both the manufacturer and the retailer can benefit from government subsidies.

5   Numerical Analysis

In order to analyze the variations in the wholesale price of green products, online and offline prices, as well as the profits of the manufacturers and the retailer in the three models mentioned above, numerical analysis is conducted in this section using Matlab. The parameter values in the models are set as follows: $a = 50$, $\beta = 0.4$, $k = 5$, $\theta = 0.5$, $\gamma = 0.3$, $c = 10$, $0 < \lambda < 1.5$.

5.1   The Impact of Consumer Green Preferences on Prices

It can be observed from Figs. 1 and 2 that as consumer green preference increases, the wholesale and online/offline price of green products also increase. Furthermore, regardless of whether the government provides subsidies, the wholesale and online/offline

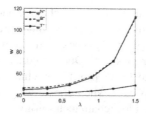

Fig. 1. The relationship between consumer green preference and wholesale price

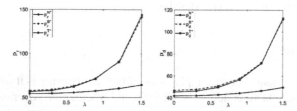

Fig. 2. The relationship between consumer green preferences and selling price

price of green products are higher when the manufacturer adopts blockchain compared to the scenario where blockchain is not adopted. Since government subsidies directly benefit the manufacturer, when consumer green preference is relatively low, the manufacturer may moderately reduce the wholesale and direct selling prices of green products to attract consumers. In order to maintain their own profits, the retailer also choose to lower the retail price. In this scenario, the wholesale and online /offline price of green products with government subsidies are lower than those without government subsidies. With the increase in consumer green preference, the wholesale and online/offline price of green products with government subsidies will eventually be higher than those without government subsidies.

5.2 The Impact of Consumer Green Preferences on Profits

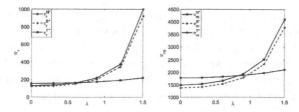

Fig. 3. The relationship between consumer green preferences and profit

It can be observed from Fig. 3 that the higher the consumer's green preference, the higher the profits for the manufacturer and the retailer. Regardless of whether the government subsidizes or not, the sensitivity of channel members' profits to changes in consumer green preferences under the blockchain model is significantly higher than that of the without blockchain model. When consumer green preferences are relatively low, the investment of manufacturers in blockchain technology has limited impact on expanding the market for green products. Due to increased production costs, adopting blockchain technology leads to lower profits for channel members compared to the without blockchain model. However, when consumer green preferences are relatively high, the manufacturer utilizing blockchain technology for product traceability not only cater to consumer demands but also contribute to market expansion. In this scenario, channel members can increase prices to gain more profits, and the profits reach the highest in the case of government subsidies.

6 Conclusions

Based on the dual-channel green supply chain, this paper constructs three models based on whether the manufacturer adopts blockchain and whether the government subsidizes blockchain, and analyzes the changes in pricing and profits of supply chain members in different models.

The main research conclusions are as follows: First, in the model where manufacturers does not adopt blockchain, the increase in consumer trust in green products can benefit the entire supply chain, so manufacturers have an incentive to invest in blockchain to increase consumer trust in the product. Second, although the adoption of blockchain by manufacturers is unfavorable for the greenness of the product, when the government subsidizes the unit application cost of blockchain, it can increase the greenness of the product. In this case, the greenness of the product is always higher than that without government subsidies. Third, the changes in the wholesale price and online/offline prices of green products are influenced by consumer green preferences. In the model with blockchain technology, the prices set by manufacturers and retailers are higher than in the model without adopting blockchain. In this case, government subsidies for blockchain can either increase or decrease wholesale and selling prices. Finally, for manufacturers and retailers, the investment in blockchain technology is a double-edged sword, only when consumer green preferences are relatively high, the investment in blockchain technology and government subsidies can enable manufacturers and retailers to obtain more profits.

This paper investigates the optimal pricing strategy for a dual-channel green supply chain considering blockchain and government subsidies with a manufacturer as the leader. In reality, many large retailers such as Walmart, Amazon have a large audience, significant purchasing power, and strong bargaining capabilities. Therefore, future research can delve into the impact of blockchain technology and government subsidies on green supply chain decisions under different power structures.

References

1. The State Council Information Office of the People's Republic of China. http://www.scio.gov.cn/zfbps/zfbps_2279/202303/t20230320_707649.html. Accessed 9 Mar 2024

2. Lin, Q., Liu, M.W., Wang, X.W.: Research on green supply chain decision-making embedded with information transfer function of blockchain. Comput. Integr. Manuf. Syst. **30**(01), 355–368 (2024). (in Chinese)
3. Xu, J., Duan, Y.: Pricing and greenness investment for green products with government subsidies: when to apply blockchain technology? Electron. Commer. Res. Appl. **51**, 101108 (2022)
4. Yu, N.N., Wang, P.C., Zhao, C.: Study on coordination of dual-channel supply chain considering product green degree. Oper. Res. Manage. Sci. **31**(04), 75–81 (2022). (in Chinese)
5. Pal, B., Sarkar, A., Sarkar, B.: Optimal decisions in a dual-channel competitive green supply chain management under promotional effort. Expert Syst. Appl. **211**, 118315 (2023)
6. Zhao, Y.P., Huang, W.J., et al.: Pricing and green promotion decisions in a retailer-owned dual-channel supply chain with multiple manufacturers. Cleaner Logistics Supply Chain. **6**, 100092 (2023)
7. Peng, Y.G., Wang, W., et al.: Competition and cooperation in the dual-channel green supply chain with customer satisfaction. Econ. Anal. Policy. **76**, 95–113 (2022)
8. Meng, Q., Li, M., et al.: C preferences. Sustain. Prod. Consumption. **26**, 1021–1030 (2021)
9. Liu, P., Long, Y., et al.: Investment decision and coordination of green agri-food supply chain considering information service based on blockchain and big data. J. Clean. Prod. **277**, 123646 (2020)
10. Lin, Q., Liu, M.W., Zou, Z.C.: Carbon emission reduction and pricing decisions of supply chain embedded in blockchain under different incentive contracts. Comput. Integrated Manuf. Syst. **12**(5), 1–20 (2024). (in Chinese). https://doi.org/10.3390/math12050704
11. Wu, G.K., Yang, W.S., et al.:Agri-food supply chain under live streaming and government subsidies: strategy selection of subsidy recipients and sales agreements. Comput. Ind. Eng. **185**, 109647 (2023)
12. Guo, L.B., Zhang, Q.Q., et al.: An evolutionary game model of manufacturers and consumers' behavior strategies for green technology and government subsidy in supply chain platform. Comput. Ind. Eng. **189**, 109918 (2024)
13. Zhong, Y., Yang, T., et al.: Impacts of blockchain technology with government subsidies on a dual-channel supply chain for tracing product information. Transp. Res. Part E: Logistics Transp. Rev. **171**, 103032 (2023)
14. Hsieh, C.C., Lathifah, A.: Exploring the spillover effect and supply chain coordination in dual-channel green supply chains with blockchain-based sales platform. Comput. Ind. Eng. **187**, 109801 (2024)
15. Zhang, L.R., Peng, B., Cheng, C.Q.: Research on government subsidy strategy of low-carbon supply chain based on block-chain technology. Chin. J. Manage. Sci. **31**(10), 49–60 (2023). (in Chinese)

Brain Functional Connectivity Mechanisms of FNIRS-Based Security Warnings Affecting Phishing Recognition

Zhiying Wang[(✉)] and Yuting Zhang

School of Economics and Management, Jiangsu University of Science and Technology,
Zhenjiang 212100, Jiangsu, China
wangzy_20066@163.com

Abstract. In the face of the severe threat posed by phishing to information security, the role of security warnings has received a lot of attention. Existing studies on the effects of security warnings on users' ability to identify phishing have yet to reached a unified conclusion, while the cognitive neural changes behind the phenomenon need to be further explored. In this study, we utilized functional near-infrared technology to investigate the effects of security warnings on users' functional brain connectivity for identifying phishing. It was found that the security warning did not significantly affect users' functional connectivity in the prefrontal lobe but significantly reduced the functional connectivity of the right temporoparietal lobe and between the right middle temporal gyrus and the left superior frontal gyrus in women. The possible explanation is that although the security warning reduced users' trust in phishing emails, it is difficult to affect users' cognitive abilities because trust and cognition do not constantly interact, resulting in a lack of improvement in users' ability to recognize phishing. Expanding the research on the functional brain connectivity mechanisms by which security warnings affect users' recognition of phishing from the cognitive neuroscience perspective can help improve phishing security intervention strategies.

Keywords: Phishing · Security Warning · Functional Brain Connectivity · fNIRS

1 Introduction

Phishing is a criminal behavior that uses social engineering and technology to steal consumers' personal identification data and financial account credentials [1]. Phishing, as a form of online fraud, has become one of the severe threats in today's digital age. According to the "Phishing Activity Trend Report for the Second Quarter of 2023" released by the International Anti-Phishing Group [2], a total of 1,286,208 phishing attacks occurred in the second quarter of 2023, which is the third highest quarterly total ever recorded by APWG. As traditional information security emphasizes security protection technology, phishing defense technology has also received much attention. Although cybersecurity technology tools attempt to flag or delete suspicious emails,

Y. P. Tu and M. Chi (Eds.): WHICEB 2024, LNBIP 515, pp. 214–225, 2024.
https://doi.org/10.1007/978-3-031-60264-1_19

phishing attacks still inevitably infiltrate a user's inbox, making users' identification of phishing the last line of defense [3]. However, many users fail to adopt effective defense strategies when facing phishing, causing them to become victims of phishing attacks and may even suffer them multiple times. Therefore, user identification of phishing is the core defense against phishing attacks.

Existing research has conducted many studies on users' identification of phishing and designed a series of user-centered security warning intervention strategies. Security warnings deter users from complying with information security behaviors by passively or actively reminding them of potential phishing risks [4]. However, current research has yet to reach a unified conclusion on the effectiveness of security warnings on users' identification of phishing. Such studies usually use questionnaires and other methods to obtain users' subjective data, only to explore the impact of security warnings on users' identification of phishing; the cognitive neural mechanism behind this impact still needs to be clarified. Therefore, this study utilizes fNIRS to investigate the effects of security warnings on the functional brain connectivity of users' phishing recognition from the perspective of neuroscience, and the results of this study can help to reveal the cognitive neural mechanisms of security warnings on phishing recognition and guide more effective phishing recognition practices.

2 Literature Review

2.1 Intervention in Phishing Identification

In order to deal with the threat of phishing and effectively reduce the risk of users becoming victims of phishing attacks, researchers are committed to developing and improving various security interventions. Among them, existing interventions for phishing identification are mainly security warnings. However, the conclusions of existing studies on the effectiveness of security warning interventions on phishing recognition are not uniform.

Some studies have concluded that users' compliance with security warnings can effectively reduce phishing risks. Akhawe and Felt [5] showed that security warnings proved to be an effective means of deterring users from visiting phishing websites and that the user experience of the warnings may significantly impact user behavior. Petelka et al. [6] found that link-centric phishing warnings improved users' phishing recognition capabilities compared with email banner warnings, where forced-attention warnings are the most effective. Desolda et al. [7] created a warning dialog box that not only warns users of possible attacks but also explains why the website is suspicious, helping users deny access to malicious websites.

However, other studies have found that users do not always comply with security warnings. Xiong et al. [8] used an eye tracker in a laboratory environment and found that passive warnings cannot effectively help users identify phishing. Jenkins et al. [9] found that warning prompts did not have the expected effect but made users more likely to ignore warnings. Vance et al. [10] conducted experiments to explore users' understanding of warnings from the perspectives of warning comprehension, semantics, syntax, and pragmatics and found that users had difficulty understanding warning content and did not comply with warnings.

2.2 Methods of Phishing Identification

In order to investigate the factors that affect users' recognition of phishing, most existing studies use questionnaires or contextual experimental designs to obtain subjective data. For example, Sarno et al. [3] used a questionnaire to obtain users' individual differences and phishing identification data to explore the effect of individual differences on phishing identification. Xu and Rajivan [11] used a situational experiment to collect user decision-making data when facing phishing to explore the effect of deception-related mental language factors in phishing email texts on identifying phishing. Jensen et al. [12] used a questionnaire and situational experiment to collect users' level of phishing recognition and their attitudes towards the effectiveness of training to explore the effectiveness of mindfulness-based training on users' identification of phishing.

Some scholars have also used cognitive neuroscience methods to obtain objective data on users' responses to phishing. Cognitive neuroscience can mine physiological signals, behavior, and other data to help researchers better understand human decision-making behaviors and cognitive processes in information security [13]. Neupane et al. [14] used fMRI to explore the underlying neural activity of users when distinguishing between legitimate and phishing websites and heeding security warnings of malware. Vance et al. [15] used fMRI and ET to longitudinally explore how habituation to security warnings affects security warning compliance and whether the polymorphic design of warnings could reduce habituation. Valecha et al. [16] used EEG to explore the role of cognitive and related brain responses in phishing contexts.

Based on the above analysis, existing studies have explored the impact of security warnings on users' recognition of phishing. Still, the conclusions obtained are not uniform. Meanwhile, most existing studies obtain subjective data on users' responses to phishing through questionnaires or situational experiments. Although some scholars also use eye trackers and other measures to measure users' identification of phishing, further exploration is still needed to reveal the functional connectivity of the brain in identifying phishing. fNIRS has higher spatial resolution and better robustness, and it is less sensitive to interfering signals with head and eye movements. Therefore, this study utilizes fNIRS to explore the brain's functional connectivity mechanism of security warnings for users to identify phishing and help optimize the design and formulation of security intervention strategies.

3   Research Design

3.1   Subjects

Referring to the number of near-infrared experiment subjects in existing studies, this study recruited volunteers online by posting a registration link, and a total of 24 undergraduates and postgraduates were enrolled as subjects, including 12 males and 12 females. Age ranged from 18 to 31 years old (22.15 ± 2.86). All subjects were right-handed, had normal or corrected-to-normal vision, had no color blindness or color weakness, and had no history of mental illness. The subjects signed the consent form before the experiment and were given course credits or cash rewards afterward.

3.2 Experimental Procedure

This experiment was carried out in the human factors engineering laboratory of the college. The phishing emails used in this study are mainly adapted and designed based on the common types of phishing emails on Millersmiles, with a 50% occurrence rate of phishing emails. A large number of studies have shown that the prefrontal lobe of the brain is closely related to high-level cognition [17], and the right temporoparietal junction area plays a vital role in guessing the intentions of others [18]. Therefore, this experiment placed sensors in a 3 × 3 arrangement in the brain's prefrontal lobe and right temporoparietal junction area. According to the existing anatomy calibration system, the region of interest (ROI) was divided into six regions. The experiment was presented by E-prime and divided into pretest, intervention, and post-test stages.

(1) Pretest stage: The subjects were required to identify the email's legitimacy. All the experimental materials were presented randomly. After the email was presented, the subjects pressed the T (True) or F (False) key according to their judgment of its legitimacy. T indicated that the email was considered legitimate, and F indicated that the email was considered a phishing email. The pretest phase of the experiment was completed when the participants judged the validity of the 24 emails.
(2) Safety intervention stage: The subject relaxed for 120 s, and then a safety warning intervention was conducted. Security warning interventions are implemented by presenting relevant images that emphasize the serious negative consequences of clicking on emails with specific features. All intervention materials were presented for the 180s.
(3) Post-test phase: After a 120-s rest, the subjects were asked to judge the 24 emails again. The specific steps were the same as those in the pretest stage.

4 Data Analysis

4.1 Behavioral Data Analysis

To quantify and evaluate the behavioral performance of users in identifying phishing, this study uses the Matthews Correlation Coefficient (MCC) as the evaluation metric. Since MCC considers both false positive and false negative errors, it is usually regarded as a balanced evaluation metric. In this study, we treat users as classifiers and use the Matthews correlation coefficients to evaluate users' behavioral performance in identifying phishing before and after security warning intervention, calculated as shown in (1).

$$MCC = \frac{TP * TN - FP * FN}{\sqrt{(TP + FP)(TP + FN)(TN + FP)(TN + FN)}} \tag{1}$$

Using MCC as an evaluation metric for users to identify phishing behaviors, the MCC value of each subject was calculated based on the behavioral data of subjects' phishing identification, and the MCC value of user recognition of phishing before and after the security warning stimulus is shown in Fig. 1.

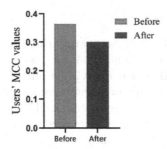

Fig. 1. Users' MCC values before and after security warning intervention

To test the effect of security warning on the brain functional connectivity of users to identify phishing, repeated measures ANOVA was conducted on the MCC values of subjects under the stimulation of security warning intervention, and the results are shown in Table 1, which shows that before and after the security warning intervention, there is no statistically significant difference between the percentage of the users' correctness to recognize phishing.

Table 1. Repeated measures ANOVA of MCC values

	Type III Sum of Squares	df	Mean Square	*F*	Sig
Time	0.050	1	0.050	1.672	0.209
Error	0.687	23	0.030		

The role of gender factor was further considered to explore whether gender affects the effect of security warnings on users' recognition of phishing. The results are shown in Table 2, which shows that the main effects of time and gender, as well as the interactions of time and gender, did not have a statistically significant difference ($p > 0.05$). Therefore, gender does not significantly affect the role of security warnings on users' recognition of phishing.

Table 2. Repeated measures ANOVA of MCC values by gender

	Type III Sum of Squares	df	Mean Square	*F*	Sig
Intercept	5.304	1	5.304	38.438	0.000
Time	0.050	1	0.050	1.774	0.196
Gender	0.045	1	0.045	0.326	0.574
Time × Gender	0.068	1	0.068	2.416	0.134
Error	0.619	222	0.028		

A paired-sample t-test was conducted on the MCC values of users identifying phishing before and after the security warning intervention of different genders. The results showed that under the stimulation of security warnings, the phishing identification for males did not significantly improve ($p = 0.904$), while the phishing identification for females was significantly reduced ($p = 0.006$). The MCC values for phishing identification by users of different genders before and after the security warning intervention stimulus are shown in Fig. 2.

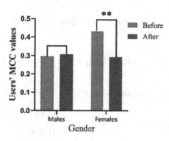

Fig. 2. MCC values of users of different genders before and after security warning intervention

4.2 Brain Functional Connectivity Analysis

Data Preprocessing
Experimentally measured data of HbO concentration changes were processed using NIRS_KIT software running on Matlab. First of all, due to the presence of noise, such as head movement and breathing, the data needs to be preprocessed. After that, each subject's Pearson correlation coefficient of each pair of time series of the ROI was calculated, and the correlation coefficients between the ROIs were taken as the functional connectivity strengths. The correlation coefficients were processed using the Fisher_Z transform to standardize them to a normal distribution.

Brain Functional Connectivity Analysis
Figure 3 shows the functional connectivity matrix between subjects' ROIs before and after the security warning stimulus, where the closer the color of the matrix is to yellow indicates stronger functional connectivity in the ROI, and the closer the color is to blue indicates weaker functional connectivity in the ROI.

Paired-sample t-tests were performed on the Z-values between the ROIs before and after the security warning intervention, in which the brain functional connectivity that underwent significant changes is shown in Table 3. Table 3 shows that security warnings caused a significant decrease in the functional connectivity of IPG_R - PCG_R and PCG_R - MTG_R, and the effect on the prefrontal lobe was insignificant.

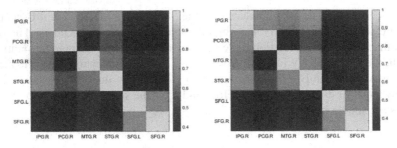

Fig. 3. Functional connectivity matrix before and after safety warning intervention

Table 3. Significantly changed functional connectivity

Connect the region	Pre-intervention r-value	Post-intervention r-value	Sig
IPG_R - PCG_R	0.973	0.850	0.007
PCG_R - MTG_R	0.503	0.399	0.008

Visualize the brain functional connectivity between ROIs before and after the security warning intervention stimulation, as shown in Fig. 4. The left side is the brain functional connectivity before the security warning intervention stimulation, and the right side is the brain functional connectivity after the intervention stimulation. The colors of the connecting lines between the brain regions indicate the strength of the functional concatenation, with the closer the color is to the red color indicating the stronger functional connectivity, and the closer the color is to the blue color indicating the weaker functional connectivity.

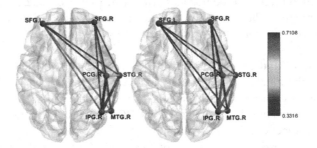

Fig. 4. Brain functional connectivity under safety warning intervention

The effect of security warnings on users' brain functional connectivity for recognizing phishing was further explored under different genders. The functional connectivity matrices between ROIs for users of different genders before and after the security warning intervention are shown in Figs. 5 and 6.

A paired-sample t-test was also performed on the Z-values between the ROIs, where the significantly changed connections are shown in Table 4. From Table 4, it can be found

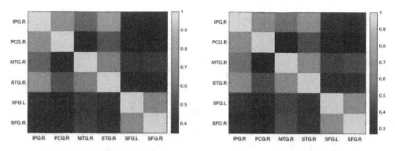

Fig. 5. Functional connectivity matrix of males before and after intervention

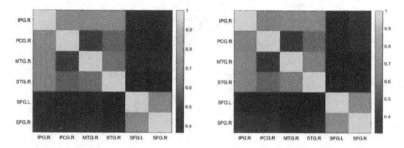

Fig. 6. Functional connectivity matrix of females before and after intervention

that for male subjects, the security warning significantly decreased the functional connectivity of PCG_R - MTG_R; for female subjects, the security warnings significantly decreased the functional connectivity of IPG_R - PCG_R and MTG_R - SFG_L.

Table 4. Significantly changed functional connectivity by gender

gender	ROI	Pre-intervention r-value	Post-intervention r-value	Sig
male	PCG_R - MTG_R	0.438	0.312	0.020
female	IPG_R - PCG_R	0.907	0.783	0.021
	MTG_R - SFG_L	0.477	0.347	0.007

Visualize the brain functional connectivity between ROIs for users of different genders before and after security warning intervention stimulation, as shown in Figs. 7 and 8.

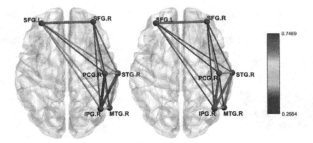

Fig. 7. Brain functional connectivity of males under intervention

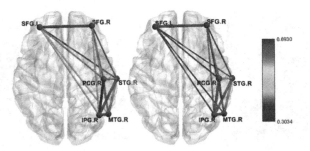

Fig. 8. Brain functional connectivity of females under intervention

5 Conclusion and Implications

5.1 Conclusion

This study explored the effects of a security warning intervention and gender on users' functional brain connectivity when recognizing phishing using the fNIRS technique. The main conclusions are as follows:

(1) By analyzing users' phishing recognition behavior before and after security warning intervention, our results show that security warning does not significantly affect users' phishing recognition behavior. Further exploring the effects of security warnings on brain functional connectivity, our results showed that functional connectivity in the user's right temporoparietal lobe was significantly decreased, and functional connectivity in the prefrontal lobe did not change significantly after security warning stimulation.

(2) Further explore whether gender factors will affect the effect of security warnings. Our research results show that under the intervention of security warnings, there was not much difference in the accuracy of male users' phishing recognition while phishing recognition was significantly reduced among females under the security warning intervention. Further exploring the effects of security warnings on brain functional connectivity of users of different genders, it was found that security warnings not only reduced the functional connectivity of the right temporoparietal lobe in both males and females but also between the right middle temporal gyrus and the left superior frontal gyrus in female users.

5.2   Implications

Theoretical Implications

This research has important theoretical significance, as follows:

(1) From the cognitive neuroscience perspective, this study explores the effect of security warnings on users' brain functional connectivity in identifying phishing and enriches phishing recognition research from the perspective of brain functional connectivity. Current research has yet to reach a unified conclusion on the effectiveness of security warnings on users' identification of phishing, and most of them are obtained from subjective data. So, it remains to be proved through what mechanism security warnings affect users' phishing identification. Therefore, from the cognitive neuroscience perspective, this paper explores the brain functional connectivity mechanism of security warnings. Studies have shown that the right temporoparietal lobe plays a vital role in inferring the intentions of others [18]; however, once a person's intentions are predictable or expected, the activity of the right temporoparietal lobe diminishes [19]. With the security warning, the user may become alert and suspicious of the email in advance. Thus, the functional connectivity of the right temporoparietal lobe decreases. However, the security warnings did not significantly affect the functional connectivity of the prefrontal lobe, indicating that the security warnings did not significantly change users' cognitive levels by enhancing the functional connectivity of the prefrontal lobe. Therefore, a possible explanation is that although security warnings decreased users' trust in email since trust and cognition do not constantly interact, the security warning did not significantly affect users' cognitive abilities and their ability to process email messages, which led to a lack of significant enhancement of users' phishing recognition abilities.

(2) Gender plays a crucial role in the anatomy and function of the human brain as well as in human behavior, and also has an impact on connectivity between regions [20], so we explored whether gender factors could affect the role of security warnings, further revealing the factors that influence the effectiveness of security warnings. Our research shows that while security warnings reduce male users' trust in phishing, they did not change their perceptions, making the security warnings ineffective. However, for female users, while security warnings reduced users' distrust of email, this distrust affected users' ability to process email messages, resulting in a greater tendency for female users to judge distrusted emails as phishing emails.

Practical Implication

In terms of practice, this study is vital for formulating strategies to improve phishing identification capabilities. Current automated phishing detection techniques are ineffective in preventing and protecting users in real-time, and relevant training for users and understanding how users recognize and distinguish whether a phishing email or website is phishing is an effective way to prevent users from being phished. By exploring the brain functional connectivity related to phishing recognition and monitoring the real-time neural activity of users identifying phishing emails under the intervention of security warnings, the effect of security warnings on users' recognition of phishing is explored, which will help the relevant departments to formulate more effective anti-phishing training and help to improve the users' phishing recognition ability.

5.3 Limitation

This paper also has certain limitations that deserve to be explored in depth in future research. The sample of the experiment was college students and graduate students, and the sample size was only 24. Although the sample represents active Internet users, it may not represent a broader population, so subsequent research can expand the sample to make the conclusions more stable.

Acknowledgement. This research was supported by National Natural Science Foundation of China under Grant 72074101.

References

1. Alsharnouby, M., Alaca, F., Chiasson, S.: Why phishing still works: user strategies for combating phishing attacks. Int. J. Hum.-Comput. Stud. **82**, 69–82 (2015)
2. Anti-Phishing Working Group. Phishing Activity Trends Report. 2st Quarter 2023. https://apwg.org/ (2023)
3. Sarno, D.M., Harris, M.W., Black, J.: Which phish is captured in the net? Understanding phishing susceptibility and individual differences. Appl. Cogn. Psychol. **37**(4), 789–803 (2023)
4. Chen, J., Mishler, S., Hu, B., Li, N.H. Proctor, R.W.: The description-experience gap in the effect of warning reliability on user trust and performance in a phishing-detection context. Int. J. Hum.-Comput. Stud. **119**, 35–47 (2018)
5. Akhawe, D., Felt, A.P.: Alice in warningland: a large-scale field study of browser security warning effectiveness. In: 22nd USENIX Security Symposium (USENIX Security 13), pp. 257–272 (2013)
6. Petelka, J., Zou, Y., Schaub, F., Assoc Comp, M.: Put your warning where your link is: improving and evaluating email phishing warnings. In: CHI Conference on Human Factors in Computing Systems (CHI), pp.1–15 (2019)
7. Desolda, G., Aneke, J., Ardito, C., Lanzilotti, R., Costabile, M.F.: Explanations in warning dialogs to help users defend against phishing attacks. Int. J. Hum.-Comput. Stud. **176**, 1–20 (2023)
8. Xiong, A., Proctor, R.W., Yang, W., Li, N.: Is domain highlighting actually helpful in identifying phishing web pages? Hum. Factors. **59**(4), 640–660 (2017)
9. Jenkins, J.L., Anderson, B.B., Vance, A., Kirwan, C.B., Eargle, D.: More harm than good? How messages that interrupt can make us vulnerable. Inf. Syst. Res. **27**(4), 880–896 (2016)
10. Vance, A., Jenkins, J.L., Anderson, B.B., Kirwan, C.B., Bjornn, D.: Improving security behavior through better security message comprehension: fMRI and eye-tracking insights. In: NeuroIS Retreat Conference (NeuroIS Retreat), pp.11–17 (2018)
11. Xu, T., Rajivan, P.: Determining psycholinguistic features of deception in phishing messages. Inf. Comput. Secur. **31**(2), 199–220 (2023)
12. Jensen, M.L., Dinger, M., Wright, R.T., Thatcher, J.B.: Training to mitigate phishing attacks using mindfulness techniques. J. Manag. Inf. Syst. **34**(2), 597–626 (2017)
13. Wang, Z., Deng, H., Wang, N., Ge, S.: A review on cognitive neuroscience in information security behavior. In: 18th Annual Wuhan International Conference on E-Business (WHICEB), pp.471–478 (2019)
14. Neupane, A., Saxena, N., Maximo, J.O., Kana, R.: Neural markers of cybersecurity: an fMRI study of phishing and malware warnings. IEEE Trans. Inf. Forensics Secur. **11**(9), 1970–1983 (2016)

15. Vance, A., Jenkins, J.L., Anderson, B.B., Bjornn, D.K., Kirwan, C.B.: Tuning out security warnings: a longitudinal examination of habituation through fMRI, eye tracking, and field experiments. MIS Q. **42**(2), 355–385 (2018)

16. Valecha, R., Gonzalez, A., Mock, J., Golob, E.J., Rao, H.R.: Investigating phishing susceptibility-an analysis of neural measures. In: Information Systems and Neuroscience (NeuroIS) Retreat Workshop, pp.111–119 (2019)

17. Carter, R.M., Bowling, D.L., Reeck, C., Huettel, S.A.: A distinct role of the temporal-parietal junction in predicting socially guided decisions. Science **337**(6090), 109–111 (2012)

18. Hirshfield, L., Bobko, P., Barelka, A., Sommer, N., Velipasalar, S.: Toward interfaces that help users identify misinformation online: using fNIRS to measure suspicion. Augmented Hum. Res. **4**(1), 1–13 (2019)

19. Koster-Hale, J., Saxe, R.: Theory of mind: a neural prediction problem. Neuron **79**(5), 836–848 (2013)

20. Gong, G., He, Y., Evans, A.C.: Brain connectivity: gender makes a difference. Neuroscientist **17**(5), 575–591 (2011)

Research on the Influence of Knowledge Marketing Characteristics on Consumer Stickiness in E-commerce Live Broadcasting: The Mediating Role of Flow Experience

Lei Han and Ying Xiong[✉]

China University of Geosciences, Wuhan 430074, China
thamansa@126.com

Abstract. This study builds the relationship model of knowledge marketing characteristics, flow experience, and consumer stickiness based on SOR theory and communication persuasion theory. The results of a survey and analysis using structural equation modeling indicate that anchor professionalism, knowledge relevance, knowledge interest, living atmosphere, empathetic atmosphere, and interactive atmosphere have a positive influence on the level of consumers' stickiness in live streaming. Flow experience serves as an intermediary element in the connection between anchor professionalism, knowledge relevance, knowledge interest, empathic atmosphere, interactive atmosphere, and customer stickiness. Product involvement enhances the effect of knowledge relevance on consumers' flow experience but diminishes the effect of knowledge interest on consumers' flow experience.

Keywords: E-commerce live broadcast · Knowledge marketing · Flow experience · Product involvement · Consumer stickiness

1 Introduction

commerce live streaming facilitates the connection of customers and merchandise in a real-time virtual space using one or more communication technologies [1]. Nevertheless, the issues of poor industry standardization and declining client stickiness to e-commerce live streaming rooms are brought about by the growth of e-commerce live streaming. The emergence of a knowledge marketing live carriers format based on emotional recognition and containing various features, such as information transfer, was signaled in 2022 when Dong Yuhui distinguished himself among the many carriers with his emotionally charged knowledge narrative talent. From the standpoint of the user, after continuous consumption of entertainment-related content, users require deep value content in addition to shallow emotional content. Knowledge marketing has regained prominence.

Since knowledge marketing is fundamentally the distribution of information, which variables will influence consumer behavior during the knowledge marketing dissemination process? In what ways can e-commerce brands increase user retention through the use of knowledge marketing? To sum up, this study employs the flow experience as an intermediary variable, introduces the product involvement degree as a moderating variable, develops a research model that examines the impact of knowledge marketing characteristics on consumer stickiness, conducts an empirical analysis of the entire influencing process. Providing a reference basis for enterprise live management.

2 Theoretical Background

2.1 Communication Persuasion Theory

The theory of communication persuasion includes three external stimuli of persuasion subject, persuasion information, persuasion situation, and one internal factor of persuasion object. Together, internal and external stimuli have an impact on the persuasion object's attitude [2]. In this study, the anchor, the knowledge the anchor conveys to the audience, and the live streaming scenario act as external stimuli that induce attitude change in consumers when using persuasion theory in the e-commerce live streaming scenario. The customer is the target of persuasion, and the alteration in the consumer's behavioral intention and attitude is predominantly manifested in the consumer's desire to act. This study constructs a research framework by employing the relevant content of persuasion theory.

2.2 Knowledge Marketing

Knowledge marketing is mainly carried out through knowledge means. Based on the media environment, knowledge marketing is an innovative marketing approach where companies use internet technology to provide consumers with valuable content related to their products. This content is delivered through effective channels of knowledge dissemination to help consumers solve complex problems and enhance the brand's value [3]. The knowledge marketing in this paper refers to the live streaming brand in the marketing process with knowledge as the core, the high-value content related to the brand and products through effective communication methods to the target audience, help them to more deeply understand the knowledge and cultural connotations related to the product, and then influence their consumption behavior of the marketing method.

Online transactions are the mainstay of knowledge marketing. In e-commerce live broadcasting, the anchor plays a crucial role as the driving force for companies to generate and acquire value through knowledge. Knowledge content with far-reaching impact is the core of knowledge marketing, which provides users with the knowledge to realize the double value premium of the brand. According to Tomita, knowledge is reliant on context, and different experience contexts created by enterprises in marketing will produce different effects. Consequently, this paper intends to consider the impact on consumer stickiness from the perspectives of marketing subject, knowledge content, and marketing context in knowledge marketing.

3 Study Hypothesis and Study Model

3.1 The Role of Persuasive Subject

The example of network opinion leaders, according to Quester [4], can increase audience consumption. Anchors are the most influential on consumer opinion in live broadcasting. Anchors' professionalism entails their mastery of the knowledge and skills pertaining to the the products they recommend. Anchors must possess extensive knowledge bases in linked domains due to the specificity of "knowledge" transmission in knowledge marketing. Cultural literacy and knowledge are directly proportional to an anchor's level of expertise in the field of knowledge, the greater the anchor's level of expertise, the more effectively they can deliver an immersive and pleasurable process experience to users.

According to Ruther, customer stickiness is the tendency of customers to visit more frequently and stay longer [5], and it is a feature of customers who make recurrent purchases of a good or service [6]. In this paper, consumer stickiness is defined as the duration of a user's engagement with a live broadcast and their propensity to visit repeatedly. Professional anchors can establish a distinct anchor image through their advantages, provide the audience with an unprecedented live broadcast experience, and thus encourage consumers to remain in the live room. Therefore, this study proposes the following hypothesis:

H1a Anchor Professionalism has a positive impact on flow experience.
H1b Anchor Professionalism has a positive impact on consumer stickiness.

3.2 The Role of Persuasive Information

The quality of information impacts consumers' capacity to receive it [7]. Relevance is a dimension of the quality of information, and the correlation between information and individual tasks has an impact on consumer decision-making [8]. Within the realm of live broadcasting, when anchors impart knowledge that is directly related to the information about products, it can effectively fulfill the practical needs of consumers watching e-commerce live broadcasts. Then, bringing a positive emotional impact to consumers, enhancing their pleasure and increasing their willingness to visit the live broadcasting room repeatedly. A significant incentive for users to watch live broadcasting is the opportunity to gain entertainment [9]. Hedonic experience can make consumers enter a state of immersion [10]. In the process of knowledge dissemination, anchors take into account the interestingness of knowledge, which is conducive to attracting consumers to stay, establishing emotional connections with users, and enhancing consumer stickiness. In e-commerce live broadcasting, whether the information acquired by the subject has actual value to itself affects consumers' judgment of the quality of the information. Knowledge belongs to a kind of information, useful knowledge can make users realize the relevance of the knowledge taught by the anchor and their requirements, to resonate with the anchor and generate a flow experience. Moreover, practical knowledge can enhance the interaction between consumers and anchors, thereby fostering consumer interest and purchasing behavior towards related products, ultimately enhancing consumer stickiness. Therefore, this study proposes the following hypothesis:

H2a Knowledge relevance has a positive impact on flow experience.
H2b Knowledge relevance has a positive impact on consumer stickiness.
H3a Knowledge interest has a positive impact on flow experience.
H3b Knowledge interest has a positive impact on consumer stickiness.
H4a Knowledge practicality has a positive impact on flow experience.
H4b Knowledge practicality has a positive impact on consumer stickiness.

3.3 The Role of Persuasive Situation

Live broadcast situations including two components: real situations and virtual situations. According to the distraction theory in the persuasion context, consumers' vigilance towards the disseminated information can be diminished via distraction, while in the virtual context, the atmosphere plays an important role, which can affect people's emotions and potentially enhance their propensity to make a purchase [11]. The persuasion situation studied in this paper mainly refers to the atmosphere created in the broadcast room.

When the anchor imparts knowledge to consumers during an e-commerce live broadcast, specialized terminology will inevitably surface, if it is too rigid, it is easy to make consumers resent the atmosphere of the live broadcast. The main way of establishing a living atmosphere is the anchor language's proximity to reality. Anchor will be esoteric knowledge popularization to the audience, to real friendly spoken reduce the physical distance with the audience, enhance the sense of familiarity with the consumer, and then make it produce a sense of pleasure, to enhance its desire to remain in the live room. Empathy is the ability of individuals to comprehend and produce comparable emotions and subsequent actions. In the marketing process, the brand creates a situation that inspires consumer empathy, thereby potentially mitigating consumer estrangement. Fostering an empathetic atmosphere in live e-commerce broadcasting enables anchors to genuinely connect with consumers, which is conducive to shaping a virtual community with a sense of belonging, empowering users with a sense of identity and worth, and increasing consumer stickiness. Interaction in e-commerce live broadcasting refers to the reciprocal exchange of information between the anchor and the audience, as well as between members of the audience [12]. In the process of knowledge marketing, knowledge dissemination is a reciprocal flow process that invites the audience to actively engage, express their wishes, and co-construct the cultural connotation. The anchor, as the frontline of the live broadcast, can create a good interactive atmosphere for customers to participate in the behavior. In the product display, employing targeted engagement with the audience who asked questions can eliminate consumer concerns and form emotional resonance. Therefore, this study proposes the following hypothesis:

H5a Living atmosphere has a positive impact on flow experience.
H5b Living atmosphere has a positive impact on consumer stickiness.
H6a Empathic atmosphere has a positive impact on flow experience.
H6b Empathic atmosphere has a positive impact on consumer stickiness.
H7a Interactive atmosphere has a positive impact on flow experience.
H7b Interactive atmosphere has a positive impact on consumer stickiness.

3.4 The Role of Flow Experience

According to the SOR theoretical model, when someone encounters an external stimulus, it will generate mental or emotional cognitions that will lead the individual to react with appropriate attitudes or behaviors. User stickiness is manifested by the increase in usage time and frequency, and the characteristics of flow experience are the key to triggering this performance [13]. The flow experience in an online context is a psychological feeling [14], which is intuitively manifested as a weakened sense of time. Watching live e-commerce can stimulate the flow experience of consumers and make them more focused on the live broadcast room, thus increasing the time consumers stay in the live e-commerce broadcast and increasing the possibility of repeated visits to the live broadcast room. Whether it be anchor professionalism, knowledge relevance, knowledge interest, knowledge practicality, living atmosphere, empathic atmosphere, or interactive atmosphere, live broadcasting in e-commerce can enhance consumers' flow experiences, which in turn increases consumer stickiness by prolonging their stay in the broadcast room. Consequently, it is speculated that flow experience plays an intermediary role between the characteristics of knowledge marketing and consumer stickiness. Therefore, this paper proposes the following hypothesis:

H8 Flow experience has a positive impact on consumer stickiness.

H9a Flow experience mediates the relationship between anchor professionalism and consumer stickiness.

H9b Flow experience mediates the relationship between knowledge relevance and consumer stickiness.

H9c Flow experience mediates the relationship between knowledge interest and consumer stickiness.

H9d Flow experience mediates the relationship between knowledge practicality and consumer stickiness.

H9e Flow experience mediates the relationship between living atmosphere and consumer stickiness.

H9f Flow experience mediates the relationship between empathic atmosphere and consumer stickiness.

H9g Flow experience mediates the relationship between interactive atmosphere and consumer stickiness.

3.5 The Moderating Role of Product Involvement

Product involvement refers to the degree to which consumers determine the product and their interests through the cognition of their needs, that is, the degree of effort paid for the purchase[15]. Diverse products can potentially elicit varying mental states and behaviors among individuals. Consumers with a high degree of product involvement are more focused when choosing products and will have a stronger sense of pleasure[16]. A high level of engagement in live shopping encourages customers to invest more time in acquiring knowledge about products, attentively listen to information delivered by anchors and user interaction, focus on and actively participate in live activities, and are stimulated to generate a more intense flow experience. Therefore, this paper proposes the following hypothesis:

H10a Product involvement positively affect the relationship between anchor profession-alism and flow experience.

H10b Product involvement positively affect the relationship between knowledge relevance and flow experience.

H10c Product involvement positively affect the relationship between knowledge interest and flow experience.

H10d Product involvement positively affect the relationship between knowledge practicality and flow experience.

H10e Product involvement positively affect the relationship between living atmosphere and flow experience.

H10f Product involvement positively affect the relationship between empathic atmo-sphere and flow experience.

H10g Product involvement positively affect the relationship between interactive atmo-sphere and flow experience.

Based on the above hypothesis, we can construct the study model as shown in Fig. 1.

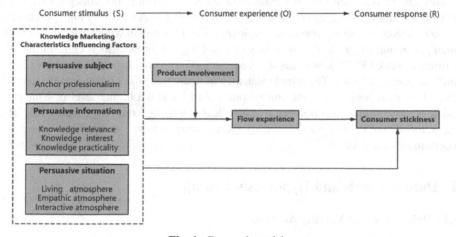

Fig. 1. Research model

4 Research Design

4.1 Questionnaire Design and Measurement

The questionnaire was designed according to the framework of this paper. To ensure the reliability and validity of the questionnaire, this study adopted the more mature scales and modified the scales with the content of the study, anchor professionalism is derived from the study by Fang et al., knowledge relevance is assessed using Yang's study scale, knowledge interest referred to Lin's research, knowledge practicality is determined using Cheung's study, living atmosphere referred to Liu's research, empathic atmosphere originates from Chen's measuring scale, interactive atmosphere is based on

Meng's scale, flow experience is adapted from Zhang's scale, product involvement is developed from Zaichkowsky's study, customer stickiness is obtained from Lu's scale. A seven-point Likert scale was used to rate attitudes from "strongly disagree" to "strongly agree". To improve the accuracy of the scale, 70 consumers who had watched the live broadcast of the knowledge marketing strategy were selected to conduct a pre-survey, summarize the suggestions made by the respondents and test the reliability and validity of the collected data to form a formal survey scale.

4.2 Survey Design and Data Organization

This study used the platform to generate electronic questionnaires and released them in a snowball fashion through major social platforms, which was conducive to collecting information from various types of samples. The research object was online users who had watched the live broadcast of knowledge-based marketing e-commerce, and a total of 418 questionnaires were collected, of which 389 were valid, with an effective rate of 93%. Among the respondents, women accounted for 62.2%. The age group was mainly 26–35 years old (57.8%). Education concentrated in junior college, bachelor's degree, and master's degree or above accounted for 70.2%. A relatively high percentage (57.6%) was comprised of corporate employees. The majority of whom earned over 5000 yuan per month (67.9%). The frequency of watching live broadcasts is concentrated 2–3 times a week (34.7%), whereas the frequency of live broadcast purchasing exceeds once per week (69.4%). The sample statistics indicate that women between the ages of 26 and 35 who possess specific consumption abilities and a higher level of education pay more attention to e-commerce live broadcasting using knowledge marketing. The characteristics of the sample align with the webcasting audience group, which possesses a certain reference value.

5 Data Analysis and Hypothesis Testing

5.1 Reliability and Validity Analysis

Cronbach'sαcoefficient was employed to test the questionnaire's reliability. The overall reliability of the questionnaire was 0.932, and the Cronbach's α coefficient of each sub-scale was greater than 0.7, indicating high reliability of the scale. AMOS24.0 software was used to conduct confirmatory factor analysis. The results showed that the standardized factor load for thirty-six items exceeded 0.7, the CR value for ten variables exceeded 0.8, and the AVE value for each variable exceeded 0.6. These results indicated that the research data possessed a satisfactory combination of reliability and convergence validity. Table 1 displays the differential validity test of the overall data. The results indicate that the correlation coefficients among latent variables are all below the square root of AVE, indicating good differential validity. To sum up, the whole data scale has good credibility and validity.

Table 1. Correlation coefficient matrix

	1	2	3	4	5	6	7	8	9	10
1.Professionalism	0.746									
2.Relevance	-0.030	0.739								
3.Interest	-0.228***	0.542***	0.727							
4.Practicality	0.389***	0.474***	0.109	0.779						
5.Living	0.050	0.455***	-0.078	0.436***	0.775					
6.Empathic	0.048	0.429***	0.245***	0.442***	0.372***	0.684				
7.Interactive	0.071	0.636***	0.397***	0.448***	0.456***	0.597***	0.692			
8.Flow experience	0.288***	0.630***	0.556***	0.491***	0.260***	0.555***	0.647***	0.604		
9.Involvement	-0.145*	0.441***	0.781***	0.064	0.038	0.272***	0.477***	0.582***	0.619	
10.Stickiness	0.131*	0.662***	0.541***	0.375***	0.307***	0.450***	0.485***	0.692***	0.476***	0.662
Square root	0.864	0.860	0.853	0.883	0.880	0.827	0.832	0.777	0.787	0.814

Note: * represents $P < 0.05$, ** represents $P < 0.01$, *** represents $P < 0.001$

5.2 Model Fit Analysis and Path Checking

Structural equation modeling was constructed through AMOS to verify the causal relationship between the variables. The output results are shown in Table 2, where the relevant indicators of model fitness are in line with the research criteria, indicating that the overall fitness of the model is good.

Table 2. Model fit index

x^2/df	GFI	AGFI	RMSEA	CFI	NFI	IFI	TLI	RFI
1.781	0.896	0.872	0.045	0.963	0.923	0.964	0.958	0.911

After the model fit analysis, the hypothesis path was examined using AMOS. The results are shown in Table 3. Except knowledge practicality and living atmosphere have no significant impact on flow experience and knowledge practicality has no significant impact on consumer stickiness, the remaining paths all pass the significance test. The hypothesis H1a, H1b, H2a, H2b, H3a, H3b, H5b, H6a, H6b, H7a, H7b, H8 is verified. The hypothesis of H4a, H4b, and H5a were not passed. The reason may be that live streaming emphasizes immediacy, while knowledge practicality focuses more on long-term information accumulation and application. Knowledge practicality makes it difficult to create consumer stickiness in the short term. Moreover, due to the diverse backgrounds of users who watch live e-commerce broadcasts, it is difficult for anchors to provide practical knowledge that caters to all customers. Although the living atmosphere can create a cordial and natural situation for the broadcast room, it may struggle to strike an emotional chord with consumers, and thus fail to significantly affect the establishment of the flow experience.

Table 3. Model parameter estimation results

trails	Non-standardized coefficient	Standardized coefficient	S.E.	C.R.	P	Conclusion
Anchor professionalism → Flow experience	0.208	0.345	0.031	6.619	***	Found
Knowledge relevance → Flow experience	0.093	0.187	0.037	2.533	**	Found
Knowledge interest → Flow experience	0.170	0.398	0.029	5.934	***	Found
Knowledge practicality → Flow experience	0.024	0.037	0.037	0.657	0.511	False
Living atmosphere → Flow experience	0.001	0.001	0.038	0.014	0.989	False
Empathic atmosphere → Flow experience	0.093	0.230	0.023	4.112	***	Found
Interactive atmosphere → Flow experience	0.117	0.190	0.041	2.834	**	Found
Anchor professionalism → Consumer stickiness	0.098	0.132	0.046	2.137	*	Found
Knowledge relevance → Consumer stickiness	0.207	0.337	0.048	4.310	***	Found
Knowledgel interest → Consumer stickiness	0.138	0.260	0.041	3.338	***	Found
Knowledge practicality → Consumer stickiness	0.057	0.071	0.047	1.228	0.220	False
Living atmosphere → Consumer stickiness	0.115	0.139	0.049	2.359	**	Found
Empathic atmosphere → Consumer stickiness	0.065	0.131	0.030	2.166	*	Found
Interactive atmosphere → Consumer stickiness	0.125	0.164	0.053	2.336	**	Found
Flow experience → Consumer stickiness	0.405	0.328	0.123	3.306	***	Found

Note: * represents $P < 0.05$, ** represents $P < 0.01$, *** represents $P < 0.001$

5.3 Mediating Effect Analysis

The mediation effect of flow experience was tested through Bootstrap. Since hypotheses H4a and H5a are not valid after testing and do not meet the premise of mediating effect, flow experience does not constitute a mediating effect in the influence of knowledge practicality and living atmosphere on consumer stickiness, the hypotheses H9d and H9e do not pass. The sampling is now repeated 5000 times using the bias-corrected test method, and a 95% confidence interval is calculated to test the mediating effect of other hypotheses. If the indirect effect does not contain 0 in the 95% confidence interval, the mediating effect is significant. The test results are shown in Table 4. Flow experience has a significant mediating effect on the influence of anchor professionalism, knowledge relevance, knowledge interest, empathic atmosphere, and interactive atmosphere on consumer stickiness. Hypotheses H9a, H9b, H9c, H9f and H9g have been confirmed.

Table 4. The mediating effect test results of flow experience

Impact pathways	Type of effect	efficiency value	SE	Bias-corrected 95%CI		
				Lower	Upper	P
Anchor professionalism → Flow experience → Consumer stickiness	indirect effect	0.084	0.073	0.004	0.291	0.040
	direct effect	0.098	0.078	-0.075	0.211	0.156
	aggregate effect	0.182	0.037	0.115	0.264	0.001
Knowledge relevance → Flow experience → Consumer stickiness	indirect effect	0.038	0.040	0.002	0.169	0.035
	direct effect	0.207	0.065	0.086	0.329	0.006
	aggregate effect	0.245	0.057	0.141	0.366	0.001
Knowledge interest → Flow experience → Consumer stickiness	indirect effect	0.069	0.063	0.005	0.257	0.037
	direct effect	0.138	0.075	-0.049	0.243	0.096
	aggregate effect	0.207	0.038	0.137	0.285	0.001
Empathic atmosphere → Flow experience → Consumer stickiness	indirect effect	0.038	0.032	0.001	0.121	0.025
	direct effect	0.065	0.044	-0.028	0.142	0.126
	aggregate effect	0.103	0.031	0.041	0.165	0.004
Interactive atmosphere → Flow experience → Consumer stickiness	indirect effect	0.047	0.050	0.003	0.205	0.032
	direct effect	0.125	0.069	-0.031	0.251	0.053
	aggregate effect	0.172	0.050	0.165	0.038	0.018

5.4 Moderating Effect Analysis

Hierarchical regression was used to test the moderating effect of product involvement. The lack of significant influence on flow experience from knowledge practicality and living atmosphere in the path test failed to satisfy the prerequisite for the moderating effect test, therefore, hypotheses H10d and H10e were deemed invalid. The test results of the adjustment effects of other hypotheses are shown in Table 5. The interaction coefficients of knowledge relevance and knowledge interest were significant with product involvement. The interaction coefficients of anchor professionalism, empathic atmosphere and interactive atmosphere were not significant with product involvement. Product involvement positively moderates the influence of knowledge relevance on flow experience and negatively moderates the influence of knowledge interest on flow experience. Assume that H10b is verified, H10c is reversely verified, and H10a, H10f, and H10g are not verified. The reason may be that whether it is the high professionalism of the anchor, the resonance atmosphere that produces emotional resonance with consumers, or the interaction that can prompt the anchor to communicate with the audience instantly, all of them can trigger a strong sense of pleasure, have a greater impact on the flow experience, transcend the limitations imposed by product involvement, forming a pleasing shopping experience.

To more clearly present the regulatory mechanism of product involvement, the regulatory effect diagram shown in Fig. 2 is drawn. The diagram illustrates that as product involvement increases, the impact of knowledge relevance on flow experience becomes stronger, whereas the influence of knowledge interest on flow experience diminishes. This suggests that product involvement strengthens the relationship between knowledge relevance and flow experience, and weakens the relationship between knowledge interest and flow experience.

Table 5. Results of moderating effect analysis

Variable		implicit variable:Flow experience		
		Model 1	Model 2	Model 3
independent variable	Anchor professionalism	0.283^{***}	0.281^{***}	0.252^{***}
	Knowledge relevance	0.186^{***}	0.193^{***}	0.176^{***}
	Knowledge interest	0.333^{***}	0.211^{***}	0.189^{***}
	Empathic atmosphere	0.199^{***}	0.190^{***}	0.126^{**}
	Interactive atmosphere	0.189^{***}	0.142^{**}	0.108^{*}
moderator variable	Product involvement		0.202^{***}	0.112^{*}

(*continued*)

Table 5. (*continued*)

Variable		implicit variable:Flow experience		
		Model 1	Model 2	Model 3
interaction term	Anchor professionalism*Product involvement			0.088
	Knowledge relevance*Product involvement			0.028^*
	Knowledge interest*Product involvement			-0.173^{**}
	Empathic atmosphere*Product involvement			0.013
	Interactive atmosphere*Product involvement			0.027
model parameter	R^2	0.564	0.584	0.621
	ΔR^2	0.556	0.575	0.606
	ΔF	70.290^{***}	66.678^{***}	40.821^{***}

Note: * represents $P < 0.05$, ** represents $P < 0.01$, *** represents $P < 0.001$

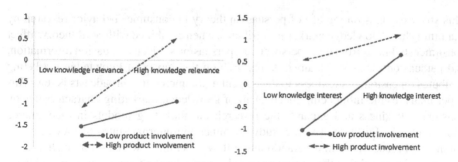

Fig. 2. Moderating effect of Product involvement

6 Conclusions and Future Research

6.1 Research Findings and Management Insights

This paper explores the impact of knowledge marketing characteristics on customer stickiness in e-commerce live streaming, drawing upon SOR and communication persuasion theory. It considers the mediating effect of flow experience and the moderating effect of product involvement. The results of an empirical analysis of the questionnaire data using SPSS and Amos indicate that consumer stickiness is positively influenced by anchor professionalism, knowledge relevance, knowledge interest, living atmosphere, empathic atmosphere, and interactive atmosphere. The practicality of knowledge has no significant effect on consumer stickiness. Flow experience mediates the relationship between anchor professionalism, knowledge relevance, knowledge interest, empathic atmosphere, interactive atmosphere, and consumer stickiness, but the mediating effect between knowledge practicality, living atmosphere, and consumer stickiness is not significant. Product involvement positively moderates the effect of knowledge relevance on flow experience and negatively moderates the effect of knowledge interest on flow experience.

According to the research findings, the following management insights are obtained: first, enterprises should select appropriate anchors and focus on training them. Anchors should possess a comprehensive understanding of the products displayed in the live broadcast and effectively integrate explanation and knowledge dissemination. Second, construct e-commerce live broadcasting with higher quality content, combining knowledge relevance and knowledge interest. To attract consumers' attention, the live broadcast's content should be closely related to the core of the product and can demonstrate the advantages of introducing products from a new dimension of knowledge. Third, enterprises should create a good atmosphere in the live broadcast room and innovate the live broadcast format. Enterprises can use situational description, enhance the sense of the picture, close to consumer life. Furthermore, it strengthens the interaction with consumers, enhances the audience's sense of participation, and improves consumer stickiness.

6.2 Theoretical Contributions

This study expands on the use of persuasion theory in consumer behavior research by examining how knowledge marketing attributes, when combined with SOR theory, affect consumer stickiness from three perspectives: persuasion subject, persuasion information, and persuasion scenario. Meanwhile, research on the impact of knowledge marketing attributes on customer stickiness in the current e-commerce live broadcasts is few. This paper analyzes the influencing mechanism of knowledge marketing characteristics on consumer stickiness and expands the research on marketing models in e-commerce live broadcasts. Furthermore, this study examines the internal states of viewers of e-commerce broadcasts from the standpoint of flow experience, which offer an alternative viewpoint for examining the impact of knowledge marketing traits on viewer stickiness in e-commerce live broadcasts.

6.3 Limitations and Future Research Directions

The participants completed the questionnaire by recalling their previous experience of watching live video, rather than immediately after the viewing, which may deviate from the choices made in real scenarios. In future studies, the questionnaire can be conducted using the scenario experiment method to enhance the accuracy of predicting customers' feelings and behaviors while viewing live streams. Besides, the impact of knowledge marketing characteristics on consumer stickiness is a complex process. Aside from flow experience and product engagement, more elements affect the relationship between them, which can be the focus of future investigation.

References

1. Chen, C.C., Lin, Y.C.: What drives live-stream usage intention? The perspectives of flow, entertainment, social interaction, and endorsement. Telematics Inform. **35**(1), 293–303 (2018)
2. Hovland, C.I.: Reconciling conflicting results derived from experimental and survey studies of attitude change. Am. Psychol. **14**(1), 8 (1959)
3. Salojaervi, H., Sainio, L.M., Tarkiainen, A.: Organizational factors enhancingcustomer knowledge utilization in the management of key accountrelationships. Ind. Mark. Manage. **39**(8), 1395–1402 (2010)
4. Quester, P., Lin, L.A.: Product involvement/brand loyalty: is there a link? Journal of product & brand management **12**(1), 22–38 (2003)
5. Ruther.: An exploration of flow during internet use. Internet Research: Electronic Networking Application and Policy 11(2), 103–113 (2001)
6. McCloskey, D.: Evaluating electronic commerce acceptance with the technology acceptance model. Journal of Computer Information Systems **44**(2), 49–57 (2004)
7. Wang, R.Y., Strong, D.M.: Beyond accuracy: What data quality means to data consumers. J. Manag. Inf. Syst.Manag. Inf. Syst. **12**(4), 5–33 (1996)
8. Ganesan, M.Z., Richard, Y.: Managing Data Qualityin Dynamic Decision Environment:An Information Product Approach. Journal of Database Management **14**(4), 14–32 (2003)
9. Hilvert-Bruce, Z., Neill, J.T., Sjöblom, M., et al.: Social motivations of live-streaming viewer engagement on Twitch. Comput. Hum. Behav.. Hum. Behav. **84**, 58–67 (2008)
10. Thai, T.D.H., Wang, T.: Investigating the effect of social endorsement on customer brand relationships by using statistical analysis and fuzzy set qualitative comparative analysis (fsQCA). Comput. Hum. Behav.. Hum. Behav. **113**, 106499 (2020)
11. KOTLER P.: Atmospherics as a marketing tool. Journal of retailing (4), 48–64 (1973)
12. Tong, J.: A study on the effect of web live broadcast on consumers' willingness to purchase. Open Journal of Business and Management **5**(02), 280 (2017)
13. Rettie, Ruth.: An exploration of flow during Internet use. Internet Research 11(2), 218–250 (2001)
14. Hoffman, D.L., Novak, T.P.: Marketing in hypermedia computer-mediated environments: conceptual foundations. J. Mark. **3**, 50–68 (1996)
15. Zaichkowsky, J.L.: Measuring the Involvement Construct. Journal of Consumer Research **12**(3), 341–352 (1985)
16. Koufaris, Marios.: Applying the technology acceptance model and flow theory to online consumer behavior. Information Systems Research 13(2), 205–223 (2002)

Bibliometrics-Based Visualization and Analysis of E-commerce Poverty Alleviation Research

Xiuyuan Gong and Pengkai Sun[✉]

Nanjing Normal University, 1 Wenyuan Road, Nanjing 210023, China
Sunpk2001@163.com

Abstract. E-commerce poverty alleviation is an effective way to achieve accurate poverty alleviation and has become a research hotspot in recent years. To comprehensively understand the e-commerce poverty alleviation research topics and frontier evolution trends, this paper applied Citespace to visualize and analyze relevant core journal articles in the Web of Science (WOS) and China Knowledge Network (CNKI). Based on the existing research results, this paper constructed an integrated analytical framework to analyze the specific content of the research topics on e-commerce poverty alleviation from research on the effects of e-commerce poverty alleviation policies, research on e-commerce poverty alleviation modes and influencing factors, and research on the effects of e-commerce poverty alleviation. Finally, this paper proposed that future research can be further explored and analyzed in research on the integration of live streaming and e-commerce poverty alleviation, research on corporate social responsibility in e-commerce poverty alleviation, and research on e-commerce poverty alleviation model optimization.

Keywords: E-commerce poverty alleviation · Citespace · Bibliometric analysis · Frontier trends · Rural revitalization

1 Introduction

Poverty is one of the world's most difficult problems constraining human development, and poverty eradication is one of the top priorities among the 17 sustainable development goals of the United Nations 2030 Agenda for Sustainable Development [1]. China successfully realized the task of poverty eradication in 2020, and tens of millions of rural poor people have been lifted out of absolute poverty, and poverty alleviation efforts have further shifted to alleviating relative poverty [1, 2]. With the development of the information revolution based on information and communication technology (ICT), e-commerce poverty alleviation represented by information poverty alleviation is considered an innovative solution to the poverty problem [3]. In 2014, China incorporated e-commerce poverty alleviation into the "Ten Projects for Precise Poverty Alleviation". More and more e-commerce platforms are entering the poverty alleviation market, not only increasing the proportion of poverty-alleviation products sold but also gradually forming a boom in e-commerce poverty alleviation.

The traditional poverty alleviation approach aims to introduce external resources that are not accessible to poor areas, and these solutions are often only temporary and of limited help to sustainable poverty alleviation [4]. E-commerce poverty alleviation incorporates e-commerce into the poverty alleviation and development system. It is an innovative way of poverty alleviation supported by information technology and based on market activities [4, 5]. Its precise poverty alleviation function is mainly reflected in the following aspects: first, e-commerce poverty alleviation can effectively alleviate the information asymmetry between urban and rural areas and overcome the barriers of time and space [6]. Secondly, e-commerce poverty alleviation plays an important role in accelerating the construction of rural infrastructure, improving the marketization level of agricultural products, and accelerating the process of agricultural industrialization. Finally, e-commerce poverty alleviation can effectively help poor farmers expand the sales channels of agricultural products, reduce transaction costs and risks, and increase income [7]. Therefore, e-commerce poverty alleviation has significant effectiveness and sustainability compared with traditional poverty alleviation methods, and its research now needs to be further sorted out to better serve rural revitalization.

Due to the different starting points of scholars, the existing studies are scattered and lack a common knowledge base, failing to analyze and explore the entire research field from a systemic and holistic perspective. Therefore, with the help of Citespace, this paper visualized and analyzed the research on e-commerce poverty alleviation in Web of Science (WOS) and China Knowledge Network (CNKI), analyzed the evolution and trend of e-commerce poverty alleviation research from the perspective of the system as a whole, and grasped the hotspots and research frontiers of research.

2 Methodology

2.1 Research Data

In this paper, Citespace version 6.2 R6 was used as the main tool for literature analysis in this study. The Chinese literature of this study was obtained from the core journals of the CNKI. The English literature was obtained from the core collection of WOS. The subject terms of Chinese literature were e-commerce poverty alleviation, rural e-commerce, live streaming e-commerce poverty alleviation, and e-commerce poverty alleviation live streaming. Each subject term was logically connected by "OR", and the type of literature was limited to journal literature, and the source of the journal was CSSCI, with a total of 402 articles retrieved, and the period was from January 2015 to October 2023. After manually eliminating some severely missing articles, the remaining 395 documents were exported in Reworks format and converted to format using Citespace, resulting in 395 pieces of data in WOS format. The search terms for the English literature were: live streaming poverty alleviation, e-commerce poverty alleviation, and rural e-commerce, each term was logically connected by "OR". The type of literature was limited to "Article", and the source of journals was SSCI, SCI, and SCIE of WOS Core Collection, and a total of 269 articles were retrieved, spanning the period from 2003 to October 2023.

2.2 Data Handling

Data were imported using Citespace 6.2. R6 and the period was set to January 2015-October 2023 for CNKI data and January 2003-October 2023 for WOS data. The time slices were all set to 1 year. Subject to the maximum number of limitations of software nodes, the network analysis criterion for CNKI data was g-index with a K-value set to 25, and for WOS data was g-index with a K-value set to 24.

3 Basic Characteristics Analysis

3.1 Analysis of the Number of Publications

Research in the field of e-commerce poverty alleviation has entered a period of vigorous development. From the data in Fig. 1, the earliest publication in this field was in 2005, but the number of publications in the decade 2003–2015 has been at a low level. Since the release of "The Decision of the CPC Central Committee and State Council on Winning the Battle against Poverty" in 2015, domestic scholars have actively flocked to the field of e-commerce poverty alleviation, and the number of publications has been explosive growth. It shows that the relevant research in the field of e-commerce poverty alleviation has entered a stage of rapid development. As the 2023 data is not yet fully included, but it also exceeded the data for the whole year of 2018 and approached the data for the whole year of 2019, it is expected that the number of postings in 2023 will reach another record high.

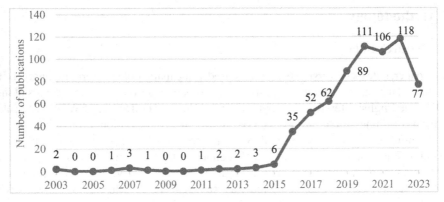

Fig. 1. Number of publications on e-commerce poverty alleviation research

3.2 Global Distribution of Research Countries

There are differences in research progress and research focus in the field of e-commerce poverty alleviation between China and the international countries, with China in the lead. The country with the highest number of publications is China with 195 articles, accounting for 52.85%. It is followed by 37 articles from the United States, accounting for 10.02%. Intermediary centrality mainly indicates the importance of the node in the network, and the top three countries in terms of intermediary centrality are China (0.98), the United States (0.52), and the United Kingdom (0.23).

3.3 Distribution of Source Journals

Research in e-commerce poverty alleviation has a low number of publications but high quality. Table 1 demonstrates the source journals with a high volume of publications included in WOS and CNKI. It can be found that the impact factors of the source journals are relatively high, indicating that the original literature set of this study is of high quality and has a certain academic influence. Further digging reveals that the topics of journals with high publication volume are related to sustainable development, and agricultural and rural issues, which also initially indicates the hot area of e-commerce poverty alleviation.

Table 1. Main journals for e-commerce poverty alleviation literature

Journal (WOS)	Num	IF	Journal (CNKI)	Num	IF
Sustainability	34	3.9	Issues in Agricultural Economy	10	6.1
Journal of Rural Studies	15	5.1	Journal of China Agricultural Resources and Regional Planning	10	2.2
Journal of Theoretical and Applied Electronic Commerce Research	8	5.6	Chinese Rural Economy	7	10.3

4 Keyword Analysis

4.1 Keyword Frequency Analysis

In the field of e-commerce poverty alleviation, there are differences in research hotspots between China and other countries. The high-frequency keywords appearing in the literature of this field represent the research hotspot for a certain period. Keywords appearing more frequently in WOS and CNKI are shown in Table 2. Through the preliminary analysis of keyword frequency, it is found that "rural e-commerce" is a common hot issue globally, and the frequency of CNIK is 65, ranking first, while the frequency of WOS is 26, ranking fourth. The keyword "e-commerce" is the most frequent keyword in WOS. The keyword "e-commerce poverty alleviation" is the second most frequent word in the CNKI, with 23 frequencies. The difference is that Chinese scholars are more concerned with research on poverty alleviation approaches at the macro level, identifying specific poverty alleviation paths and paradigms, such as precision poverty alleviation and e-commerce poverty alleviation. International scholars pay more attention to micro-level research, especially poverty alleviation research related to information technology, such as "information", "technology", and "internet". This also shows that international research has paid attention to information poverty alleviation and is committed to eliminating the digital divide and getting rid of relative poverty.

Table 2. E-commerce poverty main keywords

CNKI	Centrality	Num	WOS	Centrality	Num
rural e-commerce	0.6	65	e-commerce	0.25	52
e-commerce poverty alleviation	0.16	23	impact	0.07	39
rural revitalization	0.08	20	information	0.2	32
targeted poverty alleviation	0.09	16	rural e-commerce	0.04	26
poverty alleviation	0.09	9	adoption	0.3	26

Figures 2 and 3 are keyword co-occurrence maps, which is an undirected network. Each node represents a keyword, the color represents the time range in which the keyword appears, and the thickness of the color circle represents the number of occurrences in that time range. The node size represents the frequency of keyword occurrence and the centrality, if the centrality of the node is greater than 0.1, a purple border will appear, indicating that the node has a higher degree of importance. The thickness of the line between the nodes represents the strength of the relationship between the keywords, the thicker the line, the greater the co-occurrence strength between the keywords. We can find that (1) after China achieved comprehensive poverty alleviation in 2020, the heat

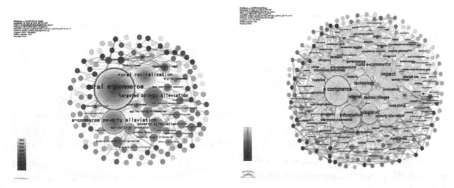

Fig. 2. CNKI keywords co-occurrence map   **Fig. 3.** WOS keywords co-occurrence map

of attention to the studies on poverty alleviation and targeted poverty alleviation gradually decreased. Instead, research on information technology-based rural e-commerce and digital economy soon gradually become a new hotspot. (2) Although international research on e-commerce poverty alleviation started earlier, it became a research hotspot only in recent years, especially after 2020, when the frequency of each keyword has risen sharply.

4.2 Analysis of Keyword Importance

Keyword bursts primarily reflect surges in keyword attention. The red line in the graph represents the duration of the keyword's heat, the longer the red line represents the longer the duration of the keyword's heat. Strength represents the strength of the keyword's heat, the higher the value the higher the strength of the keyword's heat. According to Figs. 4, and 5, it can be found that there are 11 burst keywords in CNKI and WOS. The keywords with the greatest intensity of international bursts as seen in the graph are digital divide (2.44) and model (2.22) come in second place. The ones that are still hot for research in 2023 are "model" and "inequality". China's top three keywords in terms of burst strength are poverty alleviation (2.73), target poverty alleviation (1.85), and precision poverty alleviation (1.69).

By comparing the keyword emergence chart, it can be found that international research focused more on information technology-based research early. However, the research heat has gradually shifted to poverty alleviation models and inequality in recent years. In China, the research focuses more on poverty alleviation models. Meanwhile, combined with the keyword co-occurrence maps, it can be found that international research is mostly based on the case of China and focuses on information technology-based fields, such as e-commerce, the Internet, and the digital divide. There is also a trend for Chinese research to move into the area of information technology, which suggests that information poverty alleviation will become a new hotspot in the field of e-commerce poverty alleviation.

Top 11 Keywords with the Strongest Citation Bursts

Keywords	Year	Strength	Begin	End	2015 - 2023
taobao village	2016	1.1	2016	2018	
cultural precise poverty alleviation	2016	0.83	2016	2018	
targeted poverty alleviation	2017	1.85	2017	2020	
poor areas	2017	1.02	2017	2019	
competency model	2017	0.99	2017	2018	
precision poverty alleviation	2018	1.69	2018	2019	
efficiency of poverty alleviation	2018	0.84	2018	2019	
big data	2019	1.08	2019	2020	
poverty alleviation	2017	2.73	2020	2021	
farmers income increase	2020	0.75	2020	2021	
ethnic minority areas	2020	0.75	2020	2021	

Fig. 4. CNKI keywords based on burst strength

Top 11 Keywords with the Strongest Citation Bursts

Keywords	Year	Strength	Begin	End	2013 - 2023
digital divide	2013	2.44	2013	2017	
internet	2013	1.99	2013	2016	
culture	2013	1.43	2013	2019	
determinants	2014	1.49	2014	2019	
case study	2016	1.39	2016	2020	
developing country	2017	1.74	2017	2019	
ict	2019	2.19	2019	2020	
taobao villages	2019	1.4	2019	2020	
agriculture	2019	1.36	2019	2021	
model	2021	2.22	2021	2023	
inequality	2021	1.54	2021	2023	

Fig. 5. WOS keywords based on burst strength

The centrality of a keyword reacts to the importance of the keyword in the network, and high centrality can distinguish clusters in the network, indicating that the node has a higher degree of importance in the network structure. Combined with Fig. 2 and Fig. 3, the node with the purple outer box in the graph represents that the keyword has high centrality (no less than 0.1), and has a higher degree of importance in the whole network structure. Keywords with higher centrality in China are rural e-commerce and e-commerce poverty alleviation. Keywords with higher centrality in international are e-commerce, information, adoption, internet, and technology.

Timeline mapping analysis incorporates the time dimension into the clustering relationship, which can show the clustering relationship and evolution trend of each direction in e-commerce poverty alleviation. The darker color of the connecting lines and cluster labels in the graph indicates an earlier start time for a given cluster, and the length of the timeline indicates the period of a given cluster. There are differences in research themes and evolutionary trends in e-commerce poverty alleviation between China and other countries. CNKI studies can be categorized into 9 clusters, as shown in Fig. 6. The Q-value of clustering is 0.7435 and S-value is 0.9601, which indicates that the clustering result is highly reliable. The most important clustering 0 rural e-commerce has evolved gradually from early content analysis of rural e-commerce and policy instrument content analysis to digital financial influence, social grooming behavior, and so on. The clustering 1 e-commerce poverty alleviation has evolved gradually from early content analysis of farmers endowment and e-commerce poverty reduction to research focusing on structural equation models and mediating effect model.

Fig. 6. The CNKI timeline of keyword clusters   **Fig. 7.** The WOS timeline of keyword clusters

The studies in the WOS database are categorized into 10 clusters, as shown in Fig. 7. The Q-value of clustering is 0.5963 and S-value is 0.8084, which indicates that the clustering result is highly reliable. The most important cluster, 0 technical efficiency, evolved gradually from agricultural exploitations and information technology to e-commerce applications, technical efficiency, and governance rethinking. The clustering 1 technology has evolved gradually from early content analysis of information, benefits, and geography to the economy-emotion-place framework and brand trust.

5   Hot Spots and Frontier Trends Analysis

By analyzing the importance of keywords in the field of e-commerce poverty alleviation, this paper reveals the important research topics and research directions in the field of e-commerce poverty alleviation at the macro level. The specific research contents under these important research topics still need to be further excavated and analyzed based on a research framework. As shown in Fig. 8.

China's achievements in the field of e-commerce poverty alleviation cannot be separated from the guiding and regulating role of government policy, which is an important driving force for the development of e-commerce poverty alleviation. But how its actual effect is and how it should be improved in the future to adapt to the development of the new era has become an issue of wide concern in the academic community. To effectively play the role of e-commerce in poverty alleviation, it is not only necessary to correctly guide the government policy, but also to accurately identify the influencing factors of the e-commerce poverty alleviation development model, and develop an efficient e-commerce poverty alleviation model according to local conditions. The implementation of the e-commerce model for poverty alleviation does not mean that poverty eradication efforts are successful. As a long-term and arduous task, it is necessary to analyze and evaluate the actual effects of poverty alleviation through e-commerce promptly. On this basis, the effectiveness of the work should be summarized, and the policy guidelines and development model should be optimized promptly, to provide new development advice for the subsequent practical work. Based on this, this paper constructed an integrated analytical framework (as shown in Fig. 8.) from the research on the effect of e-commerce poverty alleviation policies, the research on e-commerce poverty alleviation models and influencing factors, and the research on the effect of e-commerce poverty alleviation and analyzes the specific research content in the field of e-commerce poverty alleviation.

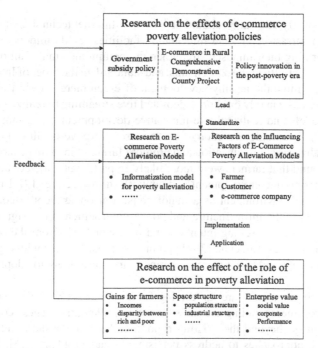

Fig. 8. Research framework for e-commerce poverty alleviation

5.1 Research on the Effect of E-commerce Poverty Alleviation Policies

Enhancing policy guidance for poverty alleviation in e-commerce and harnessing the endogenous power of policy guidance are crucial policy directions for advancing e-commerce and fostering the development of rural areas. The positive significance of the government's supportive policies to promote rural e-commerce has been proven. From the perspective of subsidy methods, the two methods of subsidizing by purchase volume and subsidizing by purchase price will have impacts on the tripartite decision-making of the government, e-commerce companies, and farmers [8]. In terms of subsidy targets, government subsidies to farmers and shopping platforms can effectively promote the economic incomes of both, and under either centralized or decentralized decision-making, subsidies to farmers or shopping platforms are better than subsidies to consumers [9]. From the perspective of government macro policies, macro policies have strong guidance and often produce significant positive effects. Qin et al. (2023) focus on macro government policies and use the "Comprehensive Demonstration of E-commerce in Rural Areas" policy as a quasi-natural experiment to prove that government support policies effectively promote the economic development of rural areas [10].

5.2 Research on E-commerce Poverty Alleviation Models and Influencing Factors

E-commerce poverty alleviation should be based on Internet technology to improve the construction of infrastructure and information facilities, guide impoverished individuals in transforming their mindset, strengthen the communication of all organizations, enhance the interactivity of the participants, and standardize the order of Internet poverty alleviation to promote the healthy development of e-commerce poverty alleviation. In addition, rural areas can rely on short videos and live streaming to realize the innovation of business models and realize the re-innovative development of e-commerce poverty alleviation [11]. The implementation of e-commerce for poverty alleviation provides a new way to realize rural revitalization and promote farmers' income generation. Leroux et al. (2001) found that farmers were more likely to participate in e-commerce sales in areas with better computer equipment and network infrastructure [12]. Li et al. (2021) identified the rural environment as a major constraint on farmers' e-commerce selling behavior, where the infrastructure and policy environment has a significant impact on farmers' e-commerce selling intention and behavior [13]. From the perspective of farmers' characteristics, Lin et al. (2021) pointed out that farmers with higher levels of resource endowment and e-commerce awareness are more likely to adopt e-commerce sales [14].

E-commerce enterprises are the driving force of market activities and the bridge connecting e-commerce trading activities for poverty alleviation. These company social innovations can go beyond the existing rigid social service system and use creative and sustainable approaches to address persistent social problems [15]. Private firms can leverage market knowledge and access to a wide range of resources to develop innovative business models that provide viable and effective solutions to social problems [16]. Recently, how to attract consumers and enhance their satisfaction has become an important influence on the long-term development and sustainable success of the e-commerce poverty alleviation model. Improving the quality and safety of agricultural products in poverty-stricken areas is an important means of attracting more consumers. Utilizing online review texts as well, Yin et al. (2022) found that logistics services, merchant services, product quality, and sales platforms all positively affect consumer satisfaction [17].

5.3 Research on the Effect of E-commerce Poverty Alleviation

In terms of farm household income, precision poverty alleviation can effectively narrow the income gap between urban and rural areas [1]. In terms of increasing the income of rural households, Liu et al. (2021) found that even though the operation of e-commerce entails considerable costs for farmers, farmers continue to participate because of the consistently increasing benefits, and the closer they are to the township, the more they benefit from e-commerce [18]. In terms of spatial structure, the change of spatial structure by e-commerce poverty alleviation has led to an increase in farmers' willingness to shop online [3], and farmers' voluntary participation in market activities, increasing their opportunities to communicate with the outside world. This not only increases farmers' incomes but also helps in the continuous upgrading of farmers' skills and promotes investment in their children's education [15]. In terms of spatial aggregation effects, rural e-commerce has fundamentally altered urbanism, changing the social and spatial reorganization of cities. Taobao Village, as a typical rural e-commerce, is the embodiment of the industrial aggregation of e-commerce for poverty alleviation. Rural e-commerce industrial agglomeration represented by Taobao villages reshapes traditional urban-rural relations and promotes the level of rural urbanization [19]. However, the aggregation effect of rural e-commerce cannot be generalized, the development of Taobao villages will not only increase the difficulty of rural governance but also undermine the operation of the original leading enterprises, thus inhibiting the growth of farmers' income [20]. In terms of corporate value, participation in poverty alleviation activities is a way for e-commerce companies to fulfill their corporate social responsibility and create significant corporate social value. When private firms engage in activities involving charitable poverty alleviation it leads to a more positive market response, which significantly increases the overall market value of the firm [21]. In particular, participation in government-sponsored CSR activities can better enhance corporate value compared to a firm's own CSR activities [22]. In recent years, e-commerce poverty alleviation still has certain drawbacks in the process of its development. For example, issues such as environmental pollution, financial risks brought about by debt leverage amplification, and public information security are often overlooked. The problems of low service quality, unmet individualized consumer needs, low marketability, and lack of product competitiveness in market activities have also not been addressed [5].

6 Prospects for Future Research

Through the literature analysis and review, this study concludes that future research can be further developed in the following areas.

First, research on the integration of live streaming and e-commerce poverty alleviation. More and more scholars recognize that e-commerce live streaming is gradually becoming a new mode of e-commerce poverty alleviation, which has significant economic effects and social benefits in helping farmers increase their income and the mainstay out of poverty. However, how effective live e-commerce is in alleviating poverty has yet to be studied relatively few studies on the policy, development model, and effects of livestreaming e-commerce poverty alleviation. Second, there is still a significant lack of research on the social responsibility of e-commerce poverty alleviation enterprises. For most enterprises, how to create social value while taking into account the economic returns of the enterprise has become a real problem that needs to be solved urgently. Third, research on e-commerce poverty alleviation model optimization. The analysis of the existing literature on the disadvantages of e-commerce poverty alleviation is not yet perfect, such as the lack of services for e-commerce poverty alleviation, the difficulty of solving the "one-kilometer problem" and the instability of poverty alleviation benefit linkage, which still needs further research and exploration.

7 Conclusion

First, Chinese and international research on poverty alleviation through e-commerce has a different focus. Research on e-commerce poverty alleviation is now in a booming phase and IT-based research on poverty alleviation through e-commerce is a research priority now. Second, the clustering results for the field of e-commerce poverty alleviation are different in China and internationally. Chinese research can be subdivided into 9 categories and international research can be subdivided into 10 categories. Thirdly, this paper analyzed the frontier research on e-commerce poverty alleviation based on the analytical framework and proposed the main research directions for the future.

Acknowledgement. This research was supported by the National Natural Science Foundation of China under Grant: 72001114.

References

1. Tang, J., Gong, J., Ma, W.: Narrowing urban–rural income gap in China: the role of the targeted poverty alleviation program. Econ. Anal. Policy **75**, 74–90 (2022)
2. Chao, P., Biao, M.A., Zhang, C.: Poverty alleviation through e-commerce: village involvement and demonstration policies in rural China. J. Integr. Agric.Integr. Agric. **20**, 998–1011 (2021)
3. Han, F., Li, B.: Exploring the effect of an enhanced e-commerce institutional mechanism on online shopping intention in the context of e-commerce poverty alleviation. Inf. Technol. People **34**, 93–122 (2020)
4. Li, L., Du, K., Zhang, W., Mao, J.-Y.: Poverty alleviation through government-led e-commerce development in rural China: an activity theory perspective. Inf. Syst. J. **29**, 914–952 (2019)
5. Wu, J., Zhang, J., Zhao, N.: How to boost e-commerce for poverty alleviation? A perspective on competitiveness analysis using online reviews. Electronic Commerce Research (2023)
6. Liu, Y., Zhou, M.: Can rural e-commerce narrow the urban–rural income gap? evidence from coverage of Taobao villages in China. China Agricultural Economic Review (2023)

7. Xu, N., Xu, C., Jin, Y., Yu, Z.: Research on the operating mechanism of E-Commerce poverty alleviation in agricultural cooperatives: an actor network theory perspective. Front. Psychol. **13** (2022)
8. Pu, X., Lai, D., Jin, D.: Subsidy based on purchase volume or purchase price? —the government subsidy policy for poverty alleviation through E-commerce. Chinese J. Manage. Sci. **31**, 32–40 (2023). (in Chinese)
9. Zhong, Y., Lai, I.K.W., Guo, F., Tang, H.: Research on government subsidy strategies for the development of agricultural products E-commerce. Agriculture **11**, 1152 (2021)
10. Qin, Q., Guo, H., Shi, X., Chen, K.: Rural E-commerce and county economic development in China. Chin. World. Econ. **31**, 26–60 (2023)
11. Xia, H., Weng, J., Zhang, J.Z., Gao, Y.: Rural E-commerce model with attention mechanism: role of Li ziqi's short videos from the perspective of heterogeneous knowledge management. J. Glob. Inf. Technol. Manag.Manag. **25**, 118–136 (2022)
12. Leroux, N., Wortman, M.S., Jr., Mathias, E.D.: Dominant factors impacting the development of business-to-business (B2B) e-commerce in agriculture. Int. Food Agribusiness Manage. Rev. **4**, 205–218 (2001)
13. Li, X., Sarkar, A., Xia, X., Memon, W.H.: Village environment, capital endowment, and farmers' participation in e-commerce sales behavior: a demand observable bivariate probit model approach. Agriculture **11**, 868 (2021)
14. Lin, H., Li, R., Hou, S., Li, W.: Influencing factors and empowering mechanism of participation in e-commerce: an empirical analysis on poor households from Inner Mongolia. China. Alexandria Eng. J. **60**, 95–105 (2021)
15. Huang, C., et al.: The effects of an innovative e-commerce poverty alleviation platform on Chinese rural laborer skills development and family well-being. undefined. 116 (2020)
16. Fang, L., Huang, C.-C.: Targeted poverty alleviation in China: evidence from Jingdong e-commerce poverty alleviation. Poverty Public Policy **12**, 386–396 (2020)
17. Yin, T., Yu, L., Bao, W.: Study on consumer satisfaction and influence factors of poverty alleviation products through E-commerce. J. Appl. Stat. Manage. **41**, 599–609 (2022). (in Chinese)
18. Liu, M., Min, S., Ma, W., Liu, T.: The adoption and impact of E-commerce in rural China: application of an endogenous switching regression model. J. Rural. Stud. **83**, 106–116 (2021)
19. Lin, J., Lin, M., You, X., Wu, S.: The effects of Taobao villages' spatiotemporal agglomeration on urbanization: a case study of Quanzhou. Fujian. J. Geograph. Sci. **33**, 1442–1460 (2023)
20. Tang, W., Zhu, J.: Informality and rural industry: Rethinking the impacts of E-Commerce on rural development in China. J. Rural. Stud. **75**, 20–29 (2020)
21. Huang, H., Shang, R., Wang, L., Gong, Y.: Corporate social responsibility and firm value: evidence from Chinese targeted poverty alleviation. Manag. Decis.. Decis. **60**, 3255–3274 (2022)
22. Jing, J., Wang, J., Hu, Z.: Has corporate involvement in government-initiated corporate social responsibility activities increased corporate value?—evidence from China's targeted poverty alleviation. Humanities Soc. Sci. Commun. **10**, 1–16 (2023)

Consumers' Intention to Purchase Through the O2O Catering Platform: A Study Based on a Stimulus-Organism-Response (SOR) Model

Yun Liu[✉], Tian Liao, Jiawen Chen, and Changlin Ye

School of Economics and Management, Xiamen University of Technology, Xiamen 361024, China
liuyun@xmut.edu.cn

Abstract. With the rapid development of information technology, it is now fast and convenient for consumers to get food service through the O2O catering platform. Based on stimulus-organism-response (SOR) theory, this study examines how external stimulus variables (the platform's recommendation mechanism and preferential policies, online evaluation, platform stores' monthly sales volumes, the platform's supervision mechanism, and contactless delivery) all affect consumers' intention to purchase through the O2O catering platform under the inner organism intermediary variables (perceived value and perceived risk). In this study, 424 sample questionnaires were collected and the data were analyzed by structural equation model. The results show that the platform's recommendation mechanism and preferential policies, the platform stores' monthly sales volumes, and the platform's supervision mechanism all positively affect consumers' perceived value, which in turn positively affects consumers' purchase intentions. Conversely, online evaluation, the platform stores' monthly sales volumes, the platform's supervision mechanism, and contactless delivery all negatively affect consumers' perceived risk. In addition, perceived risk negatively affects consumers' purchase intention. The findings have implications for the O2O catering platform to develop a suitable marketing strategy.

Keywords: SOR Model · O2O Catering Platform · Purchase Intention · Perceived Value · Perceived Risk

1 Introduction

With the rapid development of mobile Internet, urbanization, and the catering industry, China's O2O (online to offline) catering platform has experienced remarkable growth. According to the latest data released by CNNIC, the number of catering takeout users in China reached 535 million as of June 2023, an increase of 2.6% over the end of last year [1]. However, with the booming development of the catering takeout industry, some problems have emerged, particularly in terms of poor customer experience [2]. Therefore, it is necessary to identify the factors that affect consumers' intention to purchase through the O2O catering platform to optimize marketing strategy and improve customer experience for better development of the O2O catering platform.

© The Author(s), under exclusive license to Springer Nature Switzerland AG 2024
Y. P. Tu and M. Chi (Eds.): WHICEB 2024, LNBIP 515, pp. 252–264, 2024.
https://doi.org/10.1007/978-3-031-60264-1_22

Compared with traditional catering, there are few empirical studies analyzing consumers' intention to purchase through the O2O catering platform [3]. In existing studies, Elaboration Likelihood Model and Technology Acceptance Model were applied most in online catering and scholars mainly focused on perceived usefulness and ease of use of platforms in terms of consumers' intention to purchase catering takeout [4]. In this paper, we adopt the stimulus-organism-response (SOR) model and closely combine the unique characteristics of online catering ordering to further study the influencing factors that promote consumers' intention to purchase intention through the O2O catering platform from the perspective of psychological perceived value and risk. The main contributions of this paper are as follows: (1) This study focuses on the catering takeout industry and makes a systematic empirical study of the consumers' intention to purchase through the O2O catering platform, which further expands the research scope of traditional catering. (2) Considering the sudden public crises, this paper integrates the risks brought about by uncertain factors such as consumers' perceptions of external self-stimulation, as well as consumers' perceptions of value in consumption, which helps to provide management suggestions for better development of O2O catering platform.

2 Literature Review

2.1 Consumers' Purchase Intentions and O2O Catering Platform

The term O2O catering platform means that customers place food orders through an online catering takeout platform; delivery persons then deliver the food provided by offline catering enterprises [4]. According to previous studies, there are several factors that influence consumers' O2O catering purchase intentions, including food quality, distribution service quality, post-purchase service quality and price promotion strategies [2-5]. With the threat of sudden public crises (such as the COVID-19 epidemic), some scholars paid more attention to the food safety issues of O2O catering platform, which leads to suggestions on supervision mechanism. Yang et al. (2021) analyzed the content of customer reviews on Chinese O2O catering platform and found that taste, freshness and brand credibility significantly affect consumers' purchase intentions [3].

In summary, previous researchers have mostly focused on the impact of food characteristics on consumers' purchase intentions but few combine the characteristics of the platform. Therefore, it is necessary to conduct further empirical research on consumers' intention to purchase through the O2O catering platform.

2.2 Customer Perceived Value and Perceived Risk

The theory of customer perceived value proposed by Zeithaml holds that enterprises should start from customer orientation and prioritize the customer's perception of value when designing, creating and providing value for customers [6]. That is, they should conduct an overall evaluation of the utility of products or services after weighing the benefits perceived by customers and the costs of obtaining those products or services.

The theory of perceived risk was introduced into the category of marketing in 1960, and has become one of the most important concepts of the combination of psychology and marketing [7]. When consumers generate purchase intentions due to various stimuli from both the outside and themselves, they often face a number of uncertain factors before making the final purchase decisions. Therefore, they feel a sense of risk and a need to analyze the possibility of potential losses. This judgment process is called perceived risk. Some empirical studies have found that a strong correlation exists between consumers' perceived risk and their purchase intentions [8]. In fact, the consumption decision-making process is affected by the psychological comparison and judgment of benefits, costs and other uncertain factors. Catering takeout is affected by many special characteristics and factors, such as the personalized experience of the food itself and the timeliness of food safety in the process of express delivery. It is therefore necessary to further analyze the effects of the psychological feelings and decision-making factors of catering consumers before purchasing on the platform.

2.3 Stimulus-Organism-Response (SOR) Model

The "stimulus-organism-response" (SOR) is a model of cognitive psychology, originally proposed by Mehrabian et al. (1974) [9]. The SOR model is mainly used to explain the impact of environmental external stimuli on consumers' psychology and behavior, which has been widely used in the research of online platform consumer behavior. Previous studies have applied the SOR model to investigate the effects of trust, discounts, social presence, perceived value and immersion experience on purchase intentions. However, there is a lack of empirical analysis on personality factors in the catering takeaway industry. Consumers search and browse information on the O2O catering platform, make catering food choices, and engage in ordering behavior, which is stimulated by external platform functions, forming psychological changes and consumption cognition, ultimately affecting purchase intentions. This paper attempts to use the SOR model as the theoretical framework to explain the factors influencing consumers' catering consumption intentions on the O2O catering platform.

3 Conceptual Model and Research Hypotheses

3.1 Model Framework

Based on the above literature research results, the research model is shown in Fig. 1

3.2 Research Hypotheses

Platform's Recommendation Mechanism. The platform's recommendation mechanism usually includes the establishment of a business ranking list, specific business and commodity recommendations, and so on. It stimulates consumers' perceptions of the products and services by selectively presenting some specific aspects of the businesses or catering products. Sun et al. (2016) found that personalized recommendations of the platform are conducive to improving consumers' shopping experience [10]. Therefore, the following assumptions are proposed:

H1: A platform's recommendation mechanism has a positive impact on consumers' perceived value of the O2O catering platform.

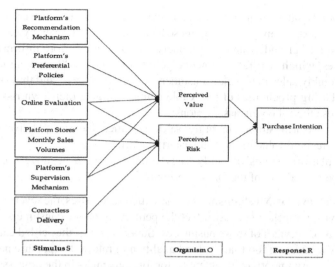

Fig. 1. Theoretical research model

Platform's Preferential Policies. The platform's 'preferential policies' refer to the activities launched by the online takeout platform, whose purpose is to stimulate consumers' purchase intention through various means of changing prices. Pan and Ha (2022) found that the price discounts on the platform are positively accepted, thus affecting consumers' purchase behavior [5]. Many kinds of catering products are available on the O2O catering platform. When consumers face many choices, promotion strategies (such as low prices and gifts) will play a positive role in consumers' choices of catering products, thus forming both a shopping impulse and a decision-making process. Based on the above, the following assumption is proposed:

H2: The platform's preferential policies have a positive impact on consumers' perceived value of the O2O catering platform.

Online Evaluation. 'Online evaluation' refers to the evaluation of consumers' scores for businesses in the platform, as well as services and goods. Consumers often take evaluations as the judgment standard in the process of making purchasing decisions [11]. By corroborating the interaction between negative online reviews and consumers' perceived risk, some scholars have found that consumers tend to be more inclined to use negative reviews as a reference [12]. Effective and accurate online evaluations help consumers to obtain useful information, which can be used as the judgment basis for decision-making. Therefore, this study makes the following assumptions:

H3: Online evaluations have a positive impact on consumers' perceived value of the O2O catering platform.

H4: Online evaluations have a negative impact on consumers' perceived risk of the O2O catering platform.

Platform Stores' Monthly Sales Volumes. The monthly sales volumes of catering stores on the O2O platform reflect the intensity of consumers' willingness to buy goods in stores. Zhu et al. (2020) researched the enterprise Meituan and found that businesses with high monthly sales often have more comments, precisely because consumers have a strong willingness to buy goods from these businesses [13]. Driven by curiosity, consumers like to further understand the products, and they want more information about their purchases, which will further encourage them to buy by "following the crowd". Also, high monthly sales may make consumers feel more at ease, and they may believe that the purchasing proclivities of a sizeable cohort mitigate their own risk. Based on this, we propose the following assumptions:

H5: The platform stores' monthly sales volumes have a positive impact on consumers' perceived value of the O2O catering platform.

H6: The platform stores' monthly sales volumes have a negative impact on the consumers' perceived risk of the O2O catering platform.

Platform's Supervision Mechanism. For the settled businesses, the severity of the platform's supervision mechanism may affect the perceived risk of consumers with regard to the products or services of those businesses. Supervision of the settled catering businesses mainly focuses on food safety, food quality and relevant expo-sure mechanisms. Food safety is a very important judgment factor for consumers in the process of risk perception. Since the outbreak of sudden public crises, consumers are increasingly paying attention to potential eating and drinking risks. The platform's supervision mechanism ensures that the quality and safety of food on the platform, which increases consumers' trust and perceived value in the platform. Wang and Cui (2018) believed that the supervision of food safety on the online takeout platform has a very significant impact on consumers' online takeout behavior [10]. Based on this, the following assumptions are put forward:

H7: The platform's supervision mechanism has a positive impact on consumers' perceived value of the O2O catering platform.

H8: The platform's supervision mechanism has a negative impact on consumers' perceived risk of the O2O catering platform.

Contactless Delivery. 'Contactless delivery' in the O2O catering platform means that, after consumers order food and confirm the order with the takeout courier, the courier places the goods at the location designated by consumers. This delivery method can effectively reduce the probability of the spread of the virus, to some extent, under the background of sudden public crises. In the post-COVID-19 era, contactless delivery will be able to improve the "last mile" distribution mechanism, that is, avoid direct face-to-face contact with customers at the end of the whole logistics link [14]. This alleviates consumers' anxiety, reduces consumers' perceived risk, and ultimately promotes consumers' purchase intentions. Based on this, the following assumption is proposed:

H9: Contactless delivery has a negative impact on consumers' perceived risk of the O2O catering platform.

Perceived Value. In this study, 'perceived value' mainly includes five value forms: functional value, emotional value, social value, cognitive value and situational value. When consumers use the O2O catering platform for information browsing and comparison purposes, perceived value will usually affect their purchase intention at the purchase level, product level and brand level. Consumers can get a perception of the value of the taste, price and other gains and losses of the catering food consumption experience, as well as a psychological perception, via the content of pictures, comments and recommendation platforms. Liu et al. (2020) found that perceived value is one of the factors that influence consumers' purchase intentions from the perspective of cognitive psychology [15]. Based on this, the following assumption is proposed:

H10: Perceived value has a positive impact on consumers' intention to purchase through the O2O catering platform.

Perceived Risk. When consumers use the O2O catering platform, the risks they perceive are food safety risk as well as contactless delivery. Since all early consumer decision-making behaviors are completed online, (including ordering), all elements that have been directly evaluated by offline stores are completely hidden. They cannot know the situation of food before they get it, which will bring anxiety and ultimately affect consumers' purchase intentions [8]. Based on this, the following assumption is proposed:

H11: Perceived risk has a significant negative impact on consumers' intention to purchase through the O2O catering platform.

4 Questionnaire Design and Data Collection

4.1 Questionnaire Design

The variables and the measurement indicators involved in this research were mainly derived from existing literature. In order to verify the assumptions with regard to consumers' intention to purchase through the O2O catering platform, the questionnaire mainly includes two parts. The first part includes the survey participants' sample demographic characteristics and the second part includes variables and the scale, including the platform's recommendation mechanism (REC) [16], preferential policy of the platform (SYS) [5], online evaluation (COM) [11], platform stores' monthly sales volumes (QUAN) [13], platform's supervision mechanism (SUP) [10], contactless delivery (DIS) [14], perceived value (PV) [15], perceived risk (PR) [8], and purchase intention (PU) [17]. The questionnaire was compiled with a 5-level Likert scale, ranging from (1) completely disagree to (5) completely agree.

4.2 Questionnaire Distribution and Data Collection

In order to further ensure the quality of the questionnaire items, a preliminary survey of the questionnaire was carried out, and a total of 87 valid questionnaires were collected. The Cronbach's α coefficients are greater than 0.7, and greater than Cronbach's α after deleting the item. The KMO values of the nine latent variables are above 0.6. The sphere test meets the significance level requirements, and the cumulative explanatory variance of factor analysis is more than 50%. Therefore, the questionnaire has good reliability and can be used for formal research. The questionnaire study was distributed through the Questionnaire Star platform, over a period of 2 months; a total of 470 questionnaires were collected. After excluding invalid questionnaires, 424 valid questionnaires were confirmed, for an effective response rate of 90.21% [18].

4.3 Sample Description

The first part of the questionnaire fully reflects the sample division of 424 valid questionnaires. The detailed demographic information is shown in Table 1.

Table 1. Demographic description

Characteristics	Category	Frequency	%	Characteristics	Category	Frequency	%
Gender	Male	172	40.6	Occupation	Students	224	52.8
	Female	252	59.4		Individual businesses	32	7.5
Age	Less than 18 years	10	2.4		Staff	122	28.8
	18–25 years	261	61.6		Freelance	13	3.1
	26–30 years	79	18.6		Institution personnel	27	6.4
	31–35 years	58	13.7		Others	6	1.4
	35 + years	16	3.7	O2O Catering Platforms Used	Meituan takeout	282	66.5
Highest Education Level Attained	High school and below	25	5.9		Ele.me	269	63.4
	Junior college	134	31.6		Star.Ele	120	28.3
	Undergraduate	253	59.7		Koubei	126	29.7
	Master's	10	2.4		Dazhongdianping	137	32.3
	Doctorate and above	2	0.4		Others	13	3.1

5 Research Results

5.1 Reliability and Validity Test

A reliability test was used to judge the internal stability of the questionnaire data and the reliability of the measurement results [19]. As shown in Table 2, the Cronbach's α coefficients of all latent variables are between 0.845 and 0.900, higher than 0.7. The Cronbach's α values and CITC values are consistent with their reference standard values. Therefore, the questionnaire has good reliability for the measurement of variables.

As shown in Table 2, the factor load of the standardized coefficient reflects the importance of the variable on the common factor. Also, the factor load of all variables is greater than 0.6, ranging from 0.758 to 0.882, with all exceeding the threshold value of 0.5. The combined reliability (CR) is greater than 0.7. The AVE value of each variable is distributed between 0.646 and 0.751; all values are more than 0.5. Therefore, the convergence validity of the sample data can be judged to meet the required standard.

The discriminant validity results are shown in Table 3. The AVE arithmetic square root values of the diagonal lines are much higher than the values of the relevant factors in the same column. This finding indicates that each potential variable can be distinguished from each of the others by high discriminant validity.

Table 2. Analysis of reliability and convergence validity

Latent Variables	Item	CITC	Cronbach's α after Deleting the Item	Cronbach's α Coefficient	Factor Load	CR	AVE
REC	REC1	0.757	0.812	0.870	0.825	0.870	0.691
	REC2	0.756	0.814		0.836		
	REC3	0.742	0.826		0.832		
SYS	SYS1	0.756	0.742	0.845	0.829	0.845	0.646
	SYS2	0.694	0.801		0.824		
	SYS3	0.687	0.809		0.758		
COM	COM1	0.788	0.829	0.886	0.857	0.886	0.722
	COM2	0.761	0.854		0.834		
	COM3	0.785	0.832		0.859		
QUAN	QUAN1	0.746	0.810	0.866	0.826	0.866	0.683
	QUAN2	0.756	0.801		0.826		
	QUAN3	0.733	0.822		0.827		
SUP	SUP1	0.706	0.819	0.856	0.788	0.856	0.665
	SUP2	0.728	0.798		0.837		
	SUP3	0.751	0.776		0.820		
DIS	DIS1	0.750	0.801	0.863	0.814	0.864	0.680
	DIS2	0.739	0.809		0.827		
	DIS3	0.735	0.815		0.831		
PV	PV1	0.763	0.812	0.872	0.834	0.872	0.695
	PV2	0.758	0.817		0.847		
	PV3	0.744	0.830		0.819		
PR	PR1	0.746	0.768	0.851	0.841	0.852	0.657
	PR2	0.712	0.801		0.788		
	PR3	0.705	0.807		0.803		
PU	PU1	0.792	0.866	0.900	0.858	0.900	0.751
	PU2	0.796	0.862		0.860		
	PU3	0.818	0.844		0.882		

Table 3. Discrimination validity

	REC	SYS	COM	QUAN	SUP	DIS	PV	PR	PU
REC	**0.831**								
SYS	0.717	**0.804**							
COM	0.468	0.449	**0.850**						
QUAN	0.698	0.685	0.497	**0.827**					
SUP	0.605	0.605	0.377	0.594	**0.815**				
DIS	0.758	0.714	0.473	0.684	0.593	**0.824**			
PV	0.748	0.721	0.462	0.714	0.721	0.725	**0.834**		
PR	−0.726	−0.685	−0.481	−0.675	−0.624	−0.686	−0.707	**0.811**	
PU	0.758	0.742	0.471	0.734	0.683	0.738	0.802	−0.781	**0.866**

5.2 Hypothesis Test

Amos23.0 was used to construct the structural equation for model fitting and the effect was good: $\chi 2/df = 1.262$. The AGFI, NFI, IFI, and CFI values were 0.924, 0.960, 0.991, and 0.991, respectively. The RMESA value was 0.025. These results met the recommended standard of model fitting, and were suitable for further path analysis [20] (Fig. 2).

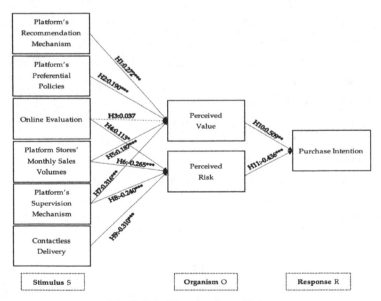

Fig. 2. Model and path coefficient

Table 4. Hypothesis test results

Hypothesis	Path	Std	UStd	S.E	C.R	P	Results
H1	REC → PV	0.272	0.267	0.041	6.542	***	Supported
H2	SYS → PV	0.190	0.192	0.041	4.634	***	Supported
H3	COM → PV	0.037	0.035	0.028	1.227	0.220	Not supported
H4	COM → PR	−0.113	−0.106	0.034	−3.087	*	Supported
H5	QUAN → PV	0.187	0.194	0.042	4.617	***	Supported
H6	QUAN → PR	−0.265	−0.278	0.048	−5.744	***	Supported
H7	SUP → PV	0.316	0.336	0.037	9.067	***	Supported
H8	SUP → PR	−0.240	−0.259	0.044	−5.921	***	Supported
H9	DIS → PR	−0.310	−0.320	0.047	−6.817	***	Supported
H10	PV → PU	0.509	0.522	0.033	15.626	***	Supported
H11	PR → PU	−0.436	−0.442	0.033	−13.396	***	Supported

Notes: "Std." means "Normalized Path Coefficient"; "UStd." means "Nonstandardized Path Coefficients"; "S.E." means "Standard Error"; "C.R." means "Critical Ratio"; *** $p < 0.001$; * $p < 0.05$; $p > 0.05$ (not significant)

The hypothesis test results of the theoretical model are shown in Table 4. It shows that the p-values of all relationships are significant, except for the online evaluation assumption of perceived value. To test the mediating effects of perceived value and perceived risk, this study used the bootstrapping method, as described in Table 5 (the number of samples is 5000, with a confidence level of 95%). As can be seen, except for the route "COM → PV → PU", 95% confidence interval of other impact paths does not cover 0. It indicates that online evaluation does not have a significant indirect impact on purchase intention through perceived value and perceived risk. Thus, the platform's recommendation mechanism and preferential policy, the platform stores' monthly sales volumes, and the platform's supervision mechanism all have a significant indirect impact on purchase intention through perceived value. The platform stores' monthly sales volumes, online evaluation, the platform's supervision mechanism, and contactless delivery all have a significant indirect impact on purchase intention through perceived risk.

Table 5. The mediating effect analysis

Mediation Paths	Indirect Effects	Lower Bound	Upper Bound	p
REC → PV → PU	0.055	0.020	0.092	0.003
SYS → PV → PU	0.041	0.011	0.074	0.012
QUAN → PV → PU	0.044	0.015	0.077	0.006
QUAN → PR → PU	0.041	0.012	0.074	0.009
COM → PV → PU	0.007	−0.008	0.022	0.396
COM → PR → PU	0.021	0.005	0.044	0.030
SUP → PV → PU	0.084	0.034	0.126	0.000
SUP → PR → PU	0.048	0.019	0.074	0.001
DIS → PR → PU	0.035	0.001	0.067	0.040

6   Conclusions and Suggestions

According to the test results in Table 5, the conclusions can be interpreted as follows: (1) The platform's recommendation mechanism has a significant positive impact on the consumers' perceived value of the O2O catering platform ($\gamma = 0.272$, p < 0.001). Therefore, H1 is supported, which verifies the research conclusions of Sun [16]. Also, the platform's preferential policies have a significant positive impact on consumers' perceived value of the platform ($\gamma = 0.190$, p < 0.001). Thus, H2 is supported, which is consistent with the research conclusions of Pan [5]. (2) The effect of an online evaluation of consumers' perceived value fails to reach a significant level ($\gamma = 0.037$, p = 0.220). Thus, H3 is untenable, which is inconsistent with the research results of Chiang and Guo [11] because quick purchase decisions may discourage consumers from reviewing lengthy comments. Online evaluation has a significant negative impact on consumers' perceived risk of the platform ($\gamma = -0.113$, p < 0.05). Thus, H4 is supported. (3) The platform stores' monthly sales volumes have a significant impact on consumers' perceived value ($\gamma = 0.187$, p < 0.001) and perceived risk ($\gamma = -0.265$, p < 0.001). Thus, H5 and H6 are supported. (4) The platform's supervision mechanism has a significant positive effect on consumers' perceived value ($\gamma = 0.316$, p < 0.001), but has a significant negative effect on consumers' perceived risk ($\gamma = -0.240$, p < 0.001). Therefore, H7 and H8 are supported. This shows that, the smaller the degree of the platform's supervision of food is, the greater the perceived risk of consumers to food safety will be, which also verifies the research results of Wang [10]. Similarly, contactless delivery has a significant negative impact on the perceived risk of takeout platform consumers ($\gamma = -0.310$, p < 0.001). Therefore, H9 is supported, which is consistent with those of Huang [14]. (5) Perceived value has a significant positive impact on consumers' purchase intention ($\gamma = 0.509$, p < 0.001). Thus, H10 is supported. This confirms that the research results of Liu et al. [15] are also applicable to the platform. Perceived risk has a significant negative impact on consumers' purchase intention ($\gamma = -0.436$, p < 0.001). Therefore, H11 is supported.

Based on the conclusions above, the realistic suggestions are proposed for O2O catering platform enterprises and catering merchants. Firstly, the platform should improve the recommendation mechanism to push consumers' favorite catering foods more accurately. Secondly, it is suggested that O2O catering platform managers should formulate a reasonable price system and promote strategies, according to their consumption ability level, in order to improve their perceived value. Thirdly, the platform should apply social marketing promotion strategies and properly integrate visual social marketing elements such as short videos and live broadcasts to attract store visitors. Finally, the O2O catering platform should establish a perfect supervision and punishment system, further standardizing the standardized operation of businesses. Also, the platform should strengthen the service quality, which ensures the safety, hygiene and timely delivery of takeout food by setting up intelligent access cabinets, providing heat preservation, storage, sterilization, non-contact distribution and other services.

Based on the theory of consumer perceived value and perceived risk, this study enriches the research variables, constructs a SOR model of consumers' intention to purchase through the O2O catering platform, and studies the factors that affect consumers' purchase intention on the platform. However, the paper still has some limitations. Firstly, this study does not analyze the differences in age, gender and education level of different groups. Secondly, this study has not examined the reasons of consumers who are unwilling to order on the platform. Therefore, future research can consider subdividing the attributes of consumers, conducting detailed research on the factors that influence purchase intentions on the platform by categories. Such studies could further investigate and analyze the consumers who are unwilling to order meals online, so as to develop more suitable e-business strategies for the O2O catering platform.

References

1. The 52th Statistical Report on Internet Development in China. https://cnnic.cn/n4/2023/0828/c199-10830.html. Accessed 28 Aug 2023. (in Chinese)
2. Shi, C.Y., Pei, Y.L., Li, D.D., Wu, T.: Influencing factors of catering O2O customer experience: an approach integrating big data analytics with grounded theory. Tehnički vjesnik **28**(3), 862–872 (2021)
3. Yang, F.X., Li, X.P., Lau, V.M., Zhu, V.Z.: To survive or to thrive? China's luxury hotel restaurants entering O2O food delivery platforms amid the COVID-19 crisis. Int. J. Hosp. Manag.Manag. **94**, 102855 (2021)
4. Shankar, A., Jebarajakirthy, C., Nayal, P., Maseeh, I.H., Kumar, A., Sivapalan, A.: Online food delivery: a systematic synthesis of literature and a framework development. Int. J. Hosp. Manag.Manag. **104**, 103240 (2022)
5. Pan, H., Ha, H.Y.: The moderating role of mobile promotion during current and subsequent purchasing occasions: the case of restaurant delivery services. Int. J. Contemp. Hosp. Manag.Manag. **34**(2), 601–622 (2022)
6. Zeithaml, V.A.: Consumer perceptions of price, quality, and value: a means-end model and synthesis of evidence. J. Mark. **52**, 2–22 (1988)
7. Bauer, R.A.: Consumer Behavior as Risk Taking. American Marketing Association, Chicago, IL, USA (1960)
8. Liu, H., Zhao, H.: Research on purchase intention of mobile terminal based on takeout apps. Manage. Rev. **33**(2), 207–216 (2021). (in Chinese)

9. Mehrabian, A., Russell, J.A.: An Approach to Environmental Psychology. The MIT Press, Cambridge (1974)
10. Wang, T., Cui, B., Wu, Q.S., Lu, R.J., Qin, X., Pan, X.F.: Research on the influencing factors of consumers' online takeout consumption behavior – Based on the survey data of Jiangsu Province. J. Researches Dietetic Sci. Culture **35**, 15–21 (2018). (in Chinese)
11. Chiang, C.F., Guo, H.W.: Consumer perceptions of the Michelin Guide and attitudes toward Michelin-starred restaurants. Int. J. Hosp. Manag.Manag. **93**, 102793 (2021)
12. Zhang, Y.M., Su, Y.Y., Zhang, Y.Y.: Research on the impact of negative online comments on consumers' perceived risks. J. Hebei Univ. Econ. Business **41**(1), 100–108 (2020). (in Chinese)
13. Zhu, L.J., Zou, Y.L., Zheng, Y.Q.: Study on influencing factors of monthly sales volume of merchants settled in Meituan takeout platform. Market Modernization **22**, 1–3 (2020). (in Chinese)
14. Huang, H.L.: Challenges for contactless online food delivery services during the COVID-19 pandemic in Taiwan: Moderating effects of perceived government response. Eval. Program Plann.Plann. **97**, 102249 (2023)
15. Liu, J.Y., Liu, W.X., Li, J.F., Zhang, Q.L.: Research on the influence of online opinion leaders on consumers' purchase intention based on SOR model. J. Chongqing Univ. Technol. (Soc. Sci.) **34**, 70–79 (2020). (in Chinese)
16. Sun, L.P., Zhang, L.J., Wang, P.: Review and Prospect of online personalized recommendation research. Foreign Econ. Manage. **38**(6), 82–99 (2016). (in Chinese)
17. Cai, R.F.: Research on Influencing Factors of consumer behavior based on SOR model – YSL "Star" marketing stimulation. Ind. Sci. Tribune **16**, 90–92 (2017). (in Chinese)
18. Hare, J., Black, W, Babin, B.: Multivariate data analysis: a global perspective.7th edn. Pearson Education Ltd., London (2010)
19. Fornell, C., Larcker, D.F.: Evaluating structural equation models with unobservable variables and measurement error. J. Mark. Res. **18**, 39–50 (1981)
20. Guo, Z.Y., Yao, Y., Chang, Y.C.: Research on customer behavioral intention of hot spring resorts based on SOR model: the multiple mediation effects of service climate and employee engagement. Sustainability **14**(14), 8869 (2022)

The Effect of Anthropomorphic Features of Virtual Streamers on Consumers' Purchase Intention-The Mediating Role of Sense of Trust

Yang Tong, Yajing Diao[✉], and Bingxue Liu

Jiangsu University of Science and Technology, Zhenjiang 212000, Jiangsu, China
dyj1979829@163.com

Abstract. Live streaming e-commerce has become increasingly popular due to its instant, interactive, and entertaining features. This is especially true in light of the 2020 epidemic and related policies, which have led to explosive growth in live streaming with goods. Additionally, the rapid development of digital technologies such as artificial intelligence, virtual reality, and three-dimensional images has led to the gradual emergence of virtual streamers in the field of live streaming. The article presents a mediation model of virtual streamer's anthropomorphic features influencing consumer purchase behavior through trust, based on SOR theory. Empirical research is conducted to support the model. The study findings indicate that virtual streamers' affinity has a positive impact on consumers' purchase intention. Additionally, the sense of competence and intimacy also positively affect consumers' purchase intention. However, the mimicry and responsiveness of virtual streamers do not significantly influence consumers' purchase intention. Furthermore, the sense of competence and trust partially mediate the relationship between anthropomorphic features of virtual streamers and consumers' purchase intention. The article's results expand on relevant research regarding virtual streamers in live streaming and provide insights for enterprises and practitioners to better utilize virtual streamers for live streaming with goods.

Keywords: virtual streamers · anthropomorphic features · trust · consumers' purchase intention

1 Introduction

Compared to traditional e-commerce shopping, livestream e-commerce market products through the streamer's presentation and real-time interaction with consumers. The choice of streamer is a key factor in live streaming and can affect product sales. Recently, virtual streamers have been introduced to live streaming through digital technologies such as artificial intelligence, virtual reality, and 3D imagery. A report by Avery Consulting since 2020 shows that the number of virtual streamers participating in Shake and Taobao live business platforms has reached 948 new registered businesses [1]. The virtual streamer industry is driven by economic, social, and technological factors. Respondents noted that they are easily attracted to virtual streamers by their business skills, voice appearance, and characterisation.

Y. P. Tu and M. Chi (Eds.): WHICEB 2024, LNBIP 515, pp. 265–276, 2024.
https://doi.org/10.1007/978-3-031-60264-1_23

Research on virtual streamers has shown that consumers tend to interact with them by liking and commenting [2]. Virtual streamers have advantages such as low cost, uninterrupted live streaming, and accurate information provision using idle time traffic. However, some studies have found that people may show aversion to AI virtual digital people. For instance, it was discovered that individuals tend to favor books and films recommended by other people rather than those suggested by robots [3].

Research found that consumers have a low intention to adopt AI due to the technology's failure to meet user expectations [4]. Trust is frequently mentioned as a crucial factor in the adoption of new technologies. However, research on how to foster consumer trust in virtual streamers is still limited, despite the emergence of virtual streamers. As a result, there is a lack of research on building trust in virtual streamers in the context of e-commerce and the relationship between anthropomorphic traits and trust in virtual streamers.

Based on this, we focus our study on virtual streamers in live streaming rooms to explore in depth how the anthropomorphic features of virtual streamers inspire consumers to generate trust and influence purchase intention. We collected 323 questionnaire responses about virtual streamer anthropomorphic features and their impact on consumers' purchase intention, which were analyzed using structural equation modeling. The analysis shows that virtual streamers' affinity can increase consumers' purchase intention. However, anthropomorphism and responsiveness do not have a direct effect on purchase intention. Instead, they mediate through the sense of competence and intimacy, which in turn increases consumers' purchase intention. This study sheds light on the role of trust in the research field of virtual streamers. Additionally, this text provides practical implications for live merchants.

2   Review of Relevant Theories and Research

2.1   Virtual Streamers

The field of virtual streamers has gained attention and research due to the advancements in artificial intelligence, graphics, and animation technology. Virtual streamers are digital entities created and utilized through computer means such as computer graphics, graphic rendering, motion capture, deep learning, and speech synthesis [5]. Virtual streamers are interactions between people and technology. Some scholars explore the interactivity characteristics of virtual streamers from the perspective of embodied communication. However, in certain contexts, the appeal of virtual streamers may not significantly impact consumers' purchasing desires [6].

2.2   Anthropomorphism

Anthropomorphism was first defined as the tendency to view humans in non-human forms and events [7]. Later, it was redefined as the tendency to attribute human traits, motives, intentions, or emotions to non-human subjects, whether real or imagined [8]. Existing research is primarily divided into three dimensions: appearance anthropomorphism, language anthropomorphism, and action anthropomorphism, concerning anthropomorphism in artificial intelligence.

Appearance anthropomorphism is the first anthropomorphic manifestation to receive attention. Anthropomorphic appearance helps to increase consumers' willingness to purchase hedonic products when compared to non-anthropomorphic appearance. Sinha et al. [9] also measured the anthropomorphism of robot arms.

Linguistic anthropomorphism refers to attributing human-like qualities to non-human entities, such as thinking, feeling, awareness, behavior, action, communication, and interaction. According to Crolic et al. [10], the use of anthropomorphic language can have a negative impact on customer satisfaction, particularly when customers are angry and engaging in chat. The results showed that anthropomorphic language had both positive and negative effects on different types of errors.

Action anthropomorphism is the process of giving non-human things (e.g. products, services, brands, etc.) human characteristics to form a living image. The effects of chatbot anthropomorphism on consumers from the perspective of trust and relationship norms and found that anthropomorphism strengthens consumer trust [11]. Brand anthropomorphism moderates consumers' perceived warmth.

2.3 Virtual Streamer Anthropomorphism

Virtual streamers' use of sensory-like language leads to lower purchase intention. Appearance anthropomorphism plays a significant role in human-computer interaction. Virtual streamer anthropomorphism's three components - perceived warmth, perceived physical resemblance to humans, and perceived competence - affect customers' perceptions of the service's value, such as emotional and utilitarian value. This paper classifies the anthropomorphic characteristics of virtual streamers as affinity, mimicry, and responsiveness based on these studies.

Affinity forms the basis of social relationships and is a feeling left behind by the degree to which someone is perceived as friendly, kind and pleasant [12]. It has been found that affinity during viewing enhances consumers' willingness to share. Mimicry is a significant concept in cognitive psychology. It refers to the influence of internal models on people's perception, judgement, and performance of their surroundings and things [13]. Virtual streamers are designed to mimic the appearance, voice, and other characteristics of real human beings through computer technology. Responsiveness refers to the ability to quickly respond to consumer requests [14]. In the context of live e-commerce streaming, responsiveness can be defined as the virtual streamer's ability to instantly respond to consumer questions. The virtual streamer's responsiveness is critical to the success of live streaming due to its interactive nature.

2.4 The Mediating Role of Trust

Trust is the willingness of an individual to accept the effects of another party's behavior. Currently, research on trust in AI has primarily been conducted from a two-dimensional perspective, focusing on rational assessment processes and emotional reflections arising from interactions. The definition of trust has been interpreted mainly in terms of cognitive and affective dimensions [15]. The two dimensions are trust in the virtual streamer's competence and emotional trust, competence and intimacy.

Competence refers to the objective perception of one's or another's ability to perform a task effectively[16]. Trust in competence is established by the virtual streamer's ability to demonstrate competence, for example, by providing accurate and thorough answers or reliable solutions.

In social psychology, intimacy refers to the sharing of behavioral, physical, cognitive, and emotional experiences between two people. The anthropomorphism of an AI can cause consumers to feel intimate with it [17]. The trust of the user in the emotional connection and emotional resonance generated by the virtual streamer is what defines intimacy. In this paper, intimacy is defined as consumers developing emotional attachment, identification, and trust in virtual streamers.

This study aims to examine the anthropomorphic characteristics of virtual streamers, including appearance, language, and action anthropomorphism. Additionally, it seeks to investigate the impact of these characteristics on consumers' purchase intention, with consumers' sense of trust serving as a mediator.

3 Research Hypotheses and Models

The S-O-R theoretical model explains how external stimuli influence behavioral responses through an individual's organismic state. This paper explores how the anthropomorphic features of virtual streamers (i.e. affinity, mimicry, and responsiveness) influence consumers' purchase intention through the mediating role of trust, using the SOR framework. Figure 1 shows the specific theoretical framework diagram.

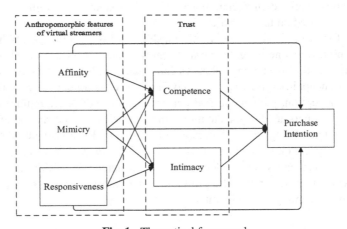

Fig. 1. Theoretical framework

3.1 Anthropomorphic Features of Virtual Streamers

Virtual streamers create the first impression of affinity. When interacting with a friendly virtual streamer, consumers perceive the streamer as approachable. The main factors influencing consumers' willingness to purchase are the streamer's affinity and expertise.

A positive evaluation of the streamer can enhance the consumer's shopping experience [18]. Additionally, affinity helps to build trust and emotional connection between the consumer and the machine [19]. In conclusion, the higher the affinity of the virtual streamer, the more it helps to increase consumers' willingness to buy as well as increase their trust. Therefore, this paper proposes the hypothesis.

H1. Affinity positively affects sense of competence(a), intimacy(b), consumers' purchase intention (c).

Anthropomorphism is the perception that virtual streamers are alive [13]. The appearance, voice, and gestures of AI-based virtual streamers are all anthropomorphic features. The human-like appearance and voice help to create a perception of the robot's humanity and make consumers feel that the virtual streamer is real [20]. When consumers perceive a high degree of anthropomorphism in a virtual streamer, it can help build trust and create an emotional connection that promotes purchase intention. This emotional connection can also enhance consumers' curiosity and interest in the virtual streamer, which in turn increases their attention to the recommended product and purchase intention [21]. Therefore, we propose the following hypotheses.

H2. Mimicry positively affects competence(a), intimacy(b), consumers' purchase intention (c)

Live streaming's biggest appeal lies in the interactivity between the consumer and the streamer. The streamer's responsiveness plays a crucial role in the success of the stream [22]. A quick response from the streamer creates trust in the consumer and gives them a sense of the streamer's competence. This, in turn, influences the consumer's willingness to make a purchase [23]. Streamers have a significant impact on consumers' purchase intention by interacting with them through various channels. When consumers receive a satisfactory response, their trust in streamers increases. Therefore, we propose the following hypotheses.

H3. Responsiveness positively affects competence(a), intimacy(b), consumers' purchase intention (c).

3.2 Trust and Purchase Intention

Competence has a positive influence on consumer psychology and behavior [16]. When individuals perceive themselves, others, or other subjects as highly competent, it enhances their behavior. In the context of virtual streamers, the demonstration of competence by virtual streamers increases consumers' trust, which in turn leads to purchase intentions. This, in turn, leads to consumers' willingness to purchase the goods recommended by virtual streamers [24]. Therefore, we propose hypotheses based on the idea that consumers' increased sense of competence towards virtual streamers generates positive emotions and enhances their positive evaluations of virtual streamers' affinity, mimicry, and responsiveness.

H4. Competence positively influences consumers' purchase intention.

H5. Competence positively mediates the effect of affinity(a), mimicry(b), responsiveness(c) on consumers' purchase intention.

This intimacy can be highly influential in building and solidifying trust, leading to consumer brand loyalty, satisfaction, word-of-mouth recommendations [25]. Virtual streamers build emotional resonance with consumers through their approachability, mimicry, and responsiveness. When consumers emotionally identify with and connect to virtual streamers, they are likely to develop interest in and trust in the products recommended by the virtual streamers [26]. The paper proposes a hypothesis that intimacy positively impacts consumer-virtual streamer interactions [27]. We therefore propose the following hypotheses.

H6. Intimacy positively mediates the effect of consumer's purchase intentions.

H7. Intimacy positively mediates the effect of affinity(a), mimicry(b), responsiveness (c) on consumers' purchase intention.

4   Research Design

4.1   Scale Design and Sample Collection

All of measurement items were adapted from previous research and modified to suit the context of live streaming commerce. All of items were measured on a 7-point Likert scale to gauge respondents' views on the impact of anthropomorphic traits of virtual streamers on consumer purchase intentions, ranging from 1 (strongly disagree) to 7 (strongly agree).

To test the research hypothesis, this paper collected data using a questionnaire distributed through the 'Questionnaire Star' platform. The questionnaire includes a question to verify if the participant has watched the live broadcast of the virtual streamer. To ensure the validity of the data, a link to the virtual streamer video was provided only to those who have watched the broadcast, preventing those who have not from filling out the questionnaire.

The online questionnaire survey comprises three main sections. The first section introduces the purpose of the study and assures respondents that their information will be kept safe and anonymous. The second section measures demographic variables of the questionnaire respondents and investigates whether they have watched virtual streamers and their knowledge of live streaming. The third section measures the anthropomorphic features of virtual streamers, as well as consumers' trust and willingness to buy. A total of 333 data points were collected, and after excluding invalid questionnaires, 323 valid questionnaires remained. Descriptive statistics were performed on these 323 samples to understand the distribution, as shown in Table 1.

Table 1. Table of demographic variables

Variant	Sample characteristics	Number	Percentage
Gender	Male	171	52.90%
	Female	152	47.10%

(*continued*)

Table 1. (*continued*)

Variant	Sample characteristics	Number	Percentage
Age	Under 18	14	4.30%
	18–25	88	27.20%
	26–30	104	32.20%
	31–40	51	15.80%
	41–50	17	5.30%
	51–60	49	15.20%
Education	Below junior high school	7	2.20%
	High school	39	12.10%
	Undergraduate	235	72.8%
	Postgraduate and above	42	13.00%
Watched	Yes	221	68.40%
	No	102	31.60%
Platform	Taobao	173	53.56%
	Dou yin	154	47.68%
	Jing dong	82	25.39%
	Kuai shou	60	18.58%
	Little Red Book	78	24.15%
	Bilibili	95	29.41%
	The rest	3	0.93%
Purchases	0	33	10.22%
	1–3	50	15.48%
	4–9	149	46.13%
	9 or more	91	28.17%

5 Data Analysis and Results

5.1 Model Fit

We use SPSS and Amos to conduct the data analysis. The models were evaluated for reliability and validity. Table 2 shows that the Cronbach's alpha coefficient and KMO values for all constructs were greater than the desired value of 0.7, indicating good reliability of the questionnaire.

The questionnaire items have a high ability to explain the corresponding variables, as evidenced by their standard loading coefficients being greater than 0.6. Additionally, the component reliabilities of affinity, mimicry, responsiveness, competence, intimacy, and willingness to buy are all greater than 0.7, indicating good convergent validity with AVE values greater than 0.5, The recommended threshold of 0.5 is therefore exceeded.

Discriminant validity was then assessed by comparing the structural correlations to the AVE square root for each structure. The results in Table 3 show that all values of the AVE square root are greater than any correlation coefficient, indicating good discriminant validity.

Table 2. Validated factor analysis of variables and reliability and validity analysis

Variable	Item	Standard Load	AVE	CR	Cronbach α	KMO
Affinity	qhl1	0.862	0.7161	0.9008	0.909	0.847
	qhl2	0.813				
	qhl3	0.853				
	qhl4	0.856				
Mimicry	nth1	0.831	0.6902	0.899	0.899	0.848
	nth2	0.832				
	nth3	0.859				
	nth4	0.8				
Responsiveness	xyx1	0.807	0.6772	0.8934	0.893	0.848
	xyx2	0.868				
	xyx3	0.816				
	xyx4	0.799				
Competence	srg1	0.831	0.7004	0.8751	0.875	0.739
	srg2	0.862				
	srg3	0.817				
Intimacy	qmg1	0.867	0.7127	0.8815	0.881	0.746
	qmg2	0.842				
	qmg3	0.823				
Purchase intention	gmyy1	0.823	0.6935	0.8716	0.871	0.740
	gmyy2	0.824				
	gmyy3	0.851				

Table 3. Table of differentiated validity

	Affinity	Mimicry	Responsiveness	Competence	Intimacy	Purchase intention
Affinity	**0.846**					
Mimicry	.507**	**0.831**				
Responsiveness	.659**	.562**	**0.823**			
Competence	.608**	.653**	.617**	**0.837**		
Intimacy	.611**	.485**	.590**	.611**	**0.844**	
Purchase Intention	.618**	.500**	.516**	.614**	.591**	**0.833**

**. Significantly correlated at the .01 level (bilaterally)

5.2 Hypothesis Testing

The path coefficients of mimicry and responsiveness on consumers' purchase intention are not significant, with p-values of 0.502 and 0.191, respectively. Therefore, hypotheses H2c and H3c are not valid. The study found that the virtual streamers' mimicry and responsiveness did not have a significant impact on consumers' purchase intention. The

Table 4. Mediation effects test table

Mediation path	Estimate	95% confidence		
		Lower	Upper	P
H5a.Affinity → competence → purchase intention	0.093	0.025	0.212	0.006**
H5b.Affinity → intimacy → purchase intention	0.106	0.036	0.218	0.005**
H5c.Responsiveness → competence → purchase intention	0.076	0.011	0.205	0.017*
H7a.Mimicry → competence → purchase intention	0.152	0.039	0.32	0.008**
H7b.Mimicry → intimacy → purchase intention	0.043	0.007	0.118	0.014*
H7c.Responsiveness → intimacy → purchase intention	0.072	0.02	0.18	0.008**

Note:***: $P < 0.001$, **: $P < 0.01$, *: $P < 0.05$

hypotheses H1a, H1b, H1c, H2a, H4, and H6 were significant at the 0.001 level, while H3a and H3b were significant at the 0.01 level. H2b was significant at the 0.05 level. Figure 2 shows the specific path coefficients.

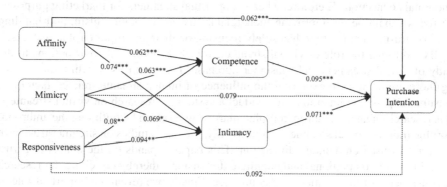

Fig. 2. Path factor diagram

5.3 Mediation Effect Test

We use the Bootstrap interval estimation test to verify the mediation effect of anthropomorphic features (affinity, mimicry, responsiveness) of virtual streamers on the sense of trust (competence, intimacy) and consumer purchase intention. The bias-corrected nonparametric percentile method was chosen as the sampling method, with a sample size of 2000 and a confidence level of 95% for the confidence interval. The mediating effect was considered significant when the confidence interval did not contain 0. Table 4 shows that the mediation effect of competence and intimacy is significant, and none of the confidence intervals contain 0. This indicates that competence and intimacy have a mediating effect on the consumer's willingness to buy. Therefore, H5a, H5b, H5c, H7a, H7b, and H7c are valid.

6 Results and Conclusions

We construct virtual streamer anthropomorphic features based on SOR theory, and use trust as a mediator to study consumers' purchase intention, and finally draw the following conclusions: (1) The affinity of virtual streamers has a positive effect on consumers' purchase intention. (2) Anthropomorphism and responsiveness of virtual streamers do not significantly impact consumers' purchase intention. (3) Competence and intimacy have a positive effect on consumers' purchase intention. (4) Competence and trust partially mediate the relationship between anthropomorphic characteristics of virtual streamers and consumers' purchase intention. We found that the anthropomorphism and responsiveness of virtual streamers do not have a direct and positive impact on consumers' purchase intentions. The lack of real emotions and human touch in virtual streamers, despite their ability to simulate realistic appearance and interaction through technical means, is believed to be the reason for this. It is important to avoid anthropomorphizing virtual streamers and instead focus on creating a clear and objective user experience. Consumers typically prefer to establish an emotional connection with real people or brands when making purchasing decisions. Virtual streamers cannot completely replace this emotional connection. Therefore, when using virtual streamers for marketing purposes, the focus should be on improving their relatability, anthropomorphism, and building viewers' trust in them, rather than solely focusing on their anthropomorphic features.

By exploring the role of virtual streamer, we offer theoretical contributions to the study of virtual streamers and consumer purchase intention. Firstly, while most existing literature focuses on exploring the influence of human streamer-related factors on consumers' purchase intention, we conduct a systematic research on virtual streamers. This research enhances anthropomorphic marketing research by outlining the anthropomorphic traits of virtual streamers. Additionally, previous studies on streamer trust have primarily focused on a single dimension. This paper expands on the concept of trust by dividing it into emotional and cognitive dimensions, thereby enriching the research on consumer trust in streamers in e-commerce. Finally, we reveal the important role of virtual streamers in live business. Avatars, as an advanced technology, have been studied by scholars in the fields of education and marketing. However, their impact in live e-commerce is little known. The study of virtual streamers' anthropomorphic features provides new insights through the study of non-virtualised people.

It has a guiding significance for the marketing of virtual streamers in business practice. With the continuous improvement of artificial intelligence technology, virtual streamers are becoming increasingly sophisticated. We offer the following recommendations for merchants, platforms, and virtual streamer designers: Firstly, when selecting virtual streamers, merchants should opt for those with a high degree of anthropomorphism to promote consumer trust. To enhance brand awareness and sales, it is recommended to establish a long-term relationship with virtual streamers that have a high degree of anthropomorphism. The platform should provide stable technical support to ensure that the anthropomorphic features of virtual streamers are sufficiently obvious. Additionally, data analysis and machine learning algorithms can be used to provide anthropomorphic services for the audience. For virtual streamer designers, it is necessary to create virtual streamers with a high degree of anthropomorphism to attract consumers and increase their trust in the virtual streamers. This, in turn, promotes consumers' purchase intention.

However, there are some shortcomings in this paper. We focused solely on virtual streamers. Future research could explore the comparison between different types of virtual streamers to gain a deeper understanding of their behavior and performance. Secondly, future studies could explore the interaction between task types and virtual streamer types to gain a more comprehensive understanding of their performance in different contexts. Additionally, the impact of virtual streamer anthropomorphic features on purchase intention is a complex process that may be influenced by various factors. Future research can explore other factors that may affect the relationship between anthropomorphic features and purchase intention. This will deepen our understanding of the influence of virtual streamers on purchase intention.

Acknowledgement. This research was supported by the National Social Science Foundation of China under Grant 23BGL305.

References

1. iiMedia Research: China's Live Broadcast E-commerce Industry Operation Big Data Analysis and Trend Research (2023). https://report.iimedia.cn/repo13-0/43334.html. Accessed 30 Mar 2023. (in Chinese)
2. Arsenyan, J., Mirowska, A.: Almost human? a comparative case study on the social media presence of virtual influencers. Int. J. Hum. Comput. Stud.Comput. Stud. 155, 102694 (2021)
3. Yeomans, M., Shah, A., Mullainathan, S., Kleinberg, J.: Making sense of recommendations. J. Behav. Decis. Mak.Behav. Decis. Mak. 32(4), 403–414 (2019)
4. Ashfaq, M., Yun, J., Yu, S., Loureiro, S.M.C.: I, Chatbot: Modeling the determinants of users' satisfaction and continuance intention of AI-powered service agents. Telematics Inform. 54, 101473 (2020)
5. Gao, W., Jiang, N., Guo, Q.: How do virtual streamers affect purchase intention in the live streaming context? a presence perspective. J. Retail. Consum. Serv.Consum. Serv. 73, 103356 (2023)
6. Kim, H., Park, M.: Virtual influencers' attractiveness effect on purchase intention: A moderated mediation model of the Product–Endorser fit with the brand. Comput. Hum. Behav. 143 (2023)
7. Bourdillon, M.F.C., de Mahieu, W., Sahay, K.N., Teran-Dutari, J., Guthrie, S.: On a cognitive theory of religion. Curr. Anthropol.. Anthropol. 21(4), 535–538 (1980)
8. Epley, N., Waytz, A., Cacioppo, J.T.: On seeing human: a three-factor theory of anthropomorphism. Psychol. Rev. 114(4), 864–886 (2007)
9. Sinha, A.K., Thalmann, N.M., Cai, Y.: Measuring anthropomorphism of a new humanoid hand-arm system. Int. J. Soc. Robot. (2023)
10. Crolic, C., Thomaz, F., Hadi, R., Stephen, A.T.: Blame the bot: anthropomorphism and anger in customer-chatbot interactions. J. Mark. 86(1), 132–148 (2021)
11. Cheng, X., Zhang, X., Cohen, J., Mou, J.: Human vs. AI: understanding the impact of anthropomorphism on consumer response to chatbots from the perspective of trust and relationship norms. Inform. Process. Manage. 59(3) (2022)

12. Ellegaard, C.: Interpersonal attraction in buyer–supplier relationships: a cyclical model rooted in social psychology. Ind. Mark. Manage. **41**(8), 1219–1227 (2012)
13. Lakoff, G.: Explaining embodied cognition results. Top. Cogn. Sci.Cogn. Sci. **4**(4), 773–785 (2012)
14. Wongkitrungrueng, A., Assarut, N.: The role of live streaming in building consumer trust and engagement with social commerce sellers. J. Bus. Res. **117**, 543–556 (2020)
15. Velasco, F., Yang, Z., Janakiraman, N.: A meta-analytic investigation of consumer response to anthropomorphic appeals: the roles of product type and uncertainty avoidance. J. Bus. Res. **131**, 735–746 (2021)
16. Weiner, B.: Intrapersonal and interpersonal theories of motivation from an attributional perspective. Educ. Psychol. Rev. **12**(1), 1–14 (2000)
17. Komiak, S.Y.X.: The impact of internalization and familiarity on trust and adoption of recommendation agents (2003)
18. Chen, H., Zhang, S., Shao, B., Gao, W., Xu, Y.: How do interpersonal interaction factors affect buyers' purchase intention in live stream shopping? the mediating effects of swift guanxi. Internet Res. **32**(1), 335–361 (2022)
19. Nagel, D.M., Giunipero, L., Jung, H., Salas, J., Hochstein, B.: Purchaser perceptions of early phase supplier relationships: the role of similarity and likeability. J. Bus. Res. **128**, 174–186 (2021)
20. Borau, S., Otterbring, T., Laporte, S., Fosso Wamba, S.: The most human bot: Female gendering increases humanness perceptions of bots and acceptance of AI. Psychol. Mark. **38**(7), 1052–1068 (2021)
21. Balakrishnan, J., Dwivedi, Y.K.: Conversational commerce: entering the next stage of AI-powered digital assistants. Annals of Operations Research (2021)
22. Mutum, D., Ghazali, E.: Perceived Online Interactivity of Blogs (2010)
23. Xue, J., Liang, X., Xie, T., Wang, H.: See now, act now: How to interact with customers to enhance social commerce engagement? Inf. Manage. **57**(6), 103324 (2020)
24. Balasubramanian, S., Konana, P., Menon, N.M.: Customer satisfaction in virtual environments: a study of online investing. Manage. Sci. **49**(7), 871–889 (2003)
25. Park, J., Yoo, J.W., Cho, Y., Park, H.: Examining the impact of service robot communication styles on customer intimacy following service failure. J. Retail. Consum. Serv.Consum. Serv. **75**, 103511 (2023)
26. Mou, Y., Zhang, L., Wu, Y., Pan, S., Ye, X.: Does self-disclosing to a robot induce liking for the robot? testing the disclosure and liking hypotheses in human–robot interaction. Int. J. Hum.–Comput. Interac., 1–12 (2022)
27. Jodén, H., Strandell, J.: Building viewer engagement through interaction rituals on Twitch.tv. Inf. Commun. Soc. **25**(13), 1969–1986 (2022)

Influencer-Focused Barrages in Product Demo Videos: An Exploratory Study

Juntao Wu[1], Yanli Pei[1(✉)], Shan Wang[2], and Fang Wang[3]

[1] International Business School, Beijing Foreign Studies University, Beijing, China
peiyanli@bfsu.edu.cn
[2] Edwards School of Business, University of Saskatchewan, Saskatoon, SK S7N 5A7, Canada
[3] Lazaridis School of Business & Economics, Wilfrid Laurier University, Waterloo, ON N2L 3C5, Canada

Abstract. Barrages, or live comments from viewers, are a popular and important element in videos on social media platforms, facilitating active viewer interaction and content co-creation. Prior studies have examined the impacts of barrage volume on video effectiveness, overlooking its content types. Drawing from uses and gratification theory, this study investigates a specific type of barrage—those on influencers—and its impact on the effectiveness of product demo videos. An empirical study on 186,842 barrages in 151 influencer-led product demo videos on social media confirms the positive effect of barrage volume on video effectiveness measured by "likes" and "collects" counts. Intriguingly, influencer-focused barrages, although small in volume (7%), exert additional positive impacts. Moreover, while video effectiveness diminishes with longer duration, the effect of influencer-focused barrages increases with video duration, being more prominent in longer videos than shorter ones. This study underscores the necessity of delving into and comprehending barrage content, shedding light on its heterogeneous intrinsic values.

Keywords: Barrage · Video Influencer · Social Media

1 Introduction

As social media platforms continue to rapidly evolve, multimedia communication, particularly in the form of videos, has garnered immense popularity. Barrage, also known as live comments, danmu comments, or bullet screens, are real-time comments that video viewers directly contribute onto the video screen. Originating from Niconico videos in Japan during the 2010s, barrages are now widely implemented by social media video platforms such as Acfun, Bilibili, and Tencent Video [1]. These real-time comments empower viewers to express opinions [2], adding valuable content to social media videos and fostering social presence and an interactive, co-viewing atmosphere [3]. Consequently, barrages can engage viewers and enhance video effectiveness [4].

An emerging line of research has studied the impact of barrages, focusing on barrage volume and its temporal features. These studies have predominantly highlighted the

Y. P. Tu and M. Chi (Eds.): WHICEB 2024, LNBIP 515, pp. 277–286, 2024.
https://doi.org/10.1007/978-3-031-60264-1_24

positive effect of barrages on audience engagement and video effectiveness, as evidenced by post-viewing responses such as "likes" and "collects" counts. Moreover, prior studies have identified nuanced patterns of such effects. For example, Zhang et al. [1] find that the intensity of barrages at the end of videos, but not at the beginning, increases audience engagement.

Nevertheless, the existing literature has seldomly delved into barrage content to comprehend its heterogeneous values. Barrages manifest in various content types, such as topic-related barrages (i.e., those pertaining to the central topics of a video), influencer-focused barrages (i.e., comments about the video influencer(s)) [5], and self-expression barrages (i.e., those unrelated to the video topics or influencers). These distinct barrage content types could potentially wield differing impacts on viewers, consequently influencing video effectiveness in heterogeneous ways. However, their specific effects remain largely unexplored.

To further understand barrage effects, this research zones in on influencer-focused barrages in product demo videos. Product demo videos, a major category of influencer content on social media, feature influencers showcasing products, explaining their features, and commenting on their functions and values. In such videos, the majority of barrages naturally revolve around product-related discussions. However, viewers also post comments on the influencer to express their opinions and engage in one-sided conversation. Barrages on the influencers in product demo videos are off-topic but reflect individual audiences' interest in influencers, thereby raising questions about their values and contribution to the effectiveness of the product demo videos.

Drawing on uses and gratification theory, we posit the positive effect of influencer-focused barrages and its variation along with video durations. An empirical study on a sample of 186,842 barrages within 151 influencer-led product demo videos on Bilibili confirms a positive association between barrage volumes and video effectiveness. Specifically, influencer-focused barrages exert an additional positive impact on video effectiveness. Furthermore, the effects of barrages are heterogeneous based on video duration, being more prominent in longer videos than in shorter ones.

2 Literature Review

Barrages are mostly short comments closely aligned with the video content's timeline, creating a pseudo-synchronous effect that enriches video content, promotes viewer engagement, and enhances video effectiveness [5]. Existing research has examined the value of barrages in videos, indicating their positive effect on viewer responses.

Particularly, prior studies have examined the effect of barrages through various metrics, including the presence of barrage functionality, its frequency, fluctuation, temporal features, length, and sentiment. Fang et al. [3], in a survey study, suggest that the use of barrages (compared to no barrage) can increase the perceived social presence of a video website and thus increase viewers' intention to revisit the website and promote positive word-of-mouth. Analyzing live streaming videos, Zhou et al. [2] report a positive association between viewers' gift-giving to live streamers and barrage features such as the number of words in barrages, the level of debate in barrages, word similarity of barrages, and the number of excitement-related words in barrages within the same period. Wei

[6] shows that the number and the density of barrage peaks influence subsequent barrage and comment inputs. Zhang et al. [1] examine the temporal sequence of barrages, revealing that barrage intensity at the end of, but not the beginning, of a video is positively associated with user engagement measured by the number of likes, comments, and shares. Zhang et al. [4] report that moment-to-moment synchronicity between temporal variations in barrage volume and those in movie content predicts viewer appreciation of movies. Wei et al. [7] report the interaction of barrage sentiment and influencers' perceived competence in affecting likes, views, collects, and shares a video receives.

Several theories have been used to explain the effects of barrages, including signaling theory, social impact theory [6], the stimulus-organism-response framework [3], and the emotions as social information model [7]. Empirical studies have predominantly utilized secondary data, with viewer responses such as the counts of "likes" and "collects" being employed to measure video effectiveness [1, 7], which were also used in our studies.

3 Research Hypothesis

This research examines the effects of barrages, particularly influencer-focused barrages, on the effectiveness of product demo videos on social media. Figure 1 provides the research framework. We examine video effectiveness using "likes" and "collects" counts. "Likes" provides a venue for viewers to express their immediate positive assessment of a video, whereas "collects" allows viewers to bookmark or save a video for future use or reference. They measure distinct aspects of the value of social media videos to viewers. Because of their differences, we posit and test their relationships with barrage features separately.

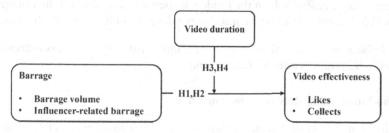

Fig. 1. Research model

3.1 Barrages and Video Effectiveness

Barrages can enhance video effectiveness in multiple ways. First, they can provide interpretations and new meaning-making to video content, serving as a content co-creation venue for audiences. Barrages can supply complementary information and add useful insights to a video, aiding viewers in comprehending video content. Moreover, they can introduce different perspectives for understanding a scenario or the characterization of individuals/entities portrayed in the video. In addition, barrages foster social interaction in the viewer community. It signifies the social presence of community members [3] and facilitates emotional exchange and information sharing [2]. Chen et al. [8] observe that a lonely audience pays more attention to emotionally appealing barrages, with longer gaze time and more fixation.

Uses and gratification theory, a popular communication theory, posits that audiences seek out media to satisfy their social and psychological needs such as information seeking and social relationships [9, 10]. Applied to the context of video barrages, the theory implies that barrages can fulfill various gratifications such as information sharing, entertainment, and social interactions for viewers. A barrage-strengthened video can become more engaging and effective for viewers than the original content alone. This positive effect of barrage numbers on video effectiveness has been evident in previous studies [6, 11]. Thus, we hypothesize:

H1: Barrages in a product demo video positively affect video effectiveness reflected in "likes" (H1a) and "collects" (H1b) counts.

Moreover, we posit that influencer-focused barrages may have an additional value in promoting product demo videos. Influencer-focused barrages are not directly related to the topics under discussion in content-sharing videos (i.e., product demos in our context of study) but pertain to the information presenters in the videos. These barrages can make the influencers more salient to the audience and direct audience attention to the influencers [12]. As the creator of and the main character in the video content, influencers' credibility, expertise, and likeability are crucial factors that affect audiences' overall assessment of the video and its content [13]. Additionally, influencer-focused barrages can be captive to the audience socially. Social media is characterized by social connections and a strong focus on people-oriented social communication. Given that influencers play a central role in their video, audiences may naturally find interest and enjoyment in learning about peer opinions regarding the influencers. We hypothesize:

H2: Influencer-focused barrages positively affect video effectiveness reflected in "likes" (H2a) and "collects" (H2b) counts.

3.2 The Moderating Role of Video Duration

Video duration may moderate the barrage effects. Video duration is an important factor affecting video effectiveness. Munaro et al. [14] suggest that longer videos can provide sufficient information and connect with the audience emotionally, and report in their empirical study that longer videos receive more comments than shorter videos on YouTube. However, research across multiple domains also indicates that audiences have limited attention spans [15]. Consequently, it is hard to keep audiences interested and engaged with longer videos. Particularly, social media users can be easily distracted and prefer immediate gratification. They may lose focus for longer videos [16].

Barrages can add useful and interesting viewer-created content to videos. The value of barrages may be more prominent in longer video duration because they help engage audiences and keep their attention on the video. We hypothesize:

H3: The impact of barrage volume on video effectiveness, reflected in "likes" (H3a) and "collects" (H3b) counts, is contingent upon video duration, with its effect being more pronounced in longer videos compared to shorter ones.

H4: The impact of influencer-focused barrages on video effectiveness, reflected in "likes" (H4a) and "collects" (H4b) counts, is contingent upon video duration, with its effect being more pronounced in longer videos compared to shorter ones.

4 Methodology

4.1 Data Collection

We chose Bilibili, a popular video platform in China, as our data resource for it is one of earliest video platforms to use barrages technology and in good operation. A total of 151 videos were randomly collected from the popular video list in the technology section of Bilibili between September 2022 and November 2023. These videos were from 37 video influencers, who are of a wide range of popularity with fan numbers ranging from thousands to millions.

The collected data included video serial number, duration, upload date, total views received, counts of "likes" and "collects", the name of the video influencer, their fan/follower counts, and whether the influencer chooses to highlight a particular audience comment at the top of the video comment section. Barrage data for each video were obtained via Bilibili's APIs.

4.2 Measures

Table 1 summarizes the dependent, independent, and control variables in this study. Consistent with prior studies [1] and aligning with our theoretical development above, the dependent variables measuring video effectiveness are the counts of "likes" and "collects" that a video accumulates.

The independent variables under study include the total number of barrages (Barrage) and the total number of influencer-focused barrages in a video (BarrageInf). To obtain the latter variable, two researchers independently reviewed and assessed barrage content to code whether a barrage comment is related to the influencer in a video. In cases of coding discrepancies, the researchers collaboratively reviewed the barrage content to reach a consensus. Examples of influencer-focused barrages include comments like "You look very nice today!", "The influencer has a high EQ," or "You are very fast in producing and uploading this product video."

Table 2 presents descriptive statistics of the variables in our study. Given that most variables are log-transformed, we provide a brief of their raw data statistics here. In our sample, the average counts of "likes" and "collects" per video are 13,186 and 1,679, respectively. The total number of barrages in our sample is 186,842, with an average of 1,237 per video. The average number of influencer-focused barrages is 86 per video, constituting about 7% of the total barrage volume. The majority of barrages in these product demo videos pertain to product comments. The average duration of the video is 616 s (i.e., 10 min 16 s), ranging from 133 to 2,499 s (i.e., just over 2 min to over 41 min).

Table 1. Variable Operationalizations.

Variables	Measures
Dependent variable	
VEffect	Video effectiveness, measured by the number of "likes" and the number of "collects" a video receives. The measurements are log-transformed
Independent variables under study	
Barrage	Barrage volume in a video, measured by the number of barrages. The measurement is log-transformed
BarrageInf	Influencer-focused barrage volume in a video, measured by the number of influencer-focused barrages. The measurement is log-transformed
Control variables	
VDuration	Length of a video, measured by the number of seconds of a video. The measurement is log-transformed
Followers	Number of followers of a video influencer. The measurement is log-transformed
Followees	Number of followees of a video influencer. The measurement is log-transformed
Views	Number of views a video receives. The measurement is log-transformed
HComment	A dummy variable indicating whether a video has a highlight comment or not (1 = Yes, 0 = No). Highlight comments are comments that a video influencer chooses to display at the top of the video's comment section
Ad	A dummy variable indicating whether a video contains advertisement or not (1 = Yes, 0 = No)
PostTime	Video posted time, measured by the number of days between a video's upload date and the data collection date

Table 2. Descriptive statistics of the variables

	Mean	SD	Minimum	Maximum
VEffect$_{Like}$	3.867	0.510	2.243	5.079
VEffect$_{Collect}$	2.898	0.522	1.322	4.380
Barrage	2.848	0.485	1.580	3.949
BarrageInf	1.683	0.509	0.000	2.740
VDuration	2.728	0.225	2.124	3.400
Followers	5.528	0.681	3.568	6.613
Followees	2.161	0.631	0	3.090
Views	5.349	0.485	3.597	6.568
HComment	0.390	0.490	0	1
Ad	0.140	0.347	0	1
PostTime	8.200	11.677	0	100

5   Results

An OLS linear regression model was used to test the hypotheses, and data analysis was conducted employing SPSS. Table 3 reports the regression results for three models.

Model 1 includes the variable Barrage along with all control variables, testing H1. Model 2 adds BarrageInf, testing H2. Model 3 further incorporates the interaction terms between barrage volume variables and video duration, testing H3. The models achieve good fits. All VIFs are below the threshold of 10; multicollinearity is not a major concern in the analysis.

Table 3. Regression results

	Model 1		Model 2		Model 3	
	VEffect$_{Like}$	VEffect$_{Collect}$	VEffect$_{Like}$	VEffect$_{Collect}$	VEffect$_{Like}$	VEffect$_{Collect}$
Barrage	0.538***	0.443***	0.457***	0.290*	0.450***	0.279*
	(0.068)	(0.117)	(0.070)	(0.121)	(0.067)	(0.115)
BarrageInf			0.112**	0.212**	0.135***	0.250***
			(0.035)	(0.060)	(0.034)	(0.058)
Barrage × VDuration					−0.373	−0.584
					(0.198)	(0.340)
BarrageInf × VDuration					0.625**	1.027**
					(0.182)	(0.312)
VDuration	−0.450***	0.297*	−0.438***	0.318*	−0.408***	0.363**
	(0.077)	(0.132)	(0.074)	(0.127)	(0.075)	(0.128)
Followers	0.060*	−0.035	0.066*	−0.024*	0.065*	−0.027
	(0.028)	(0.048)	(0.027)	(0.046)	(0.026)	(0.044)
Followees	0.005	0.092**	0.006	0.094**	0.011	0.102*
	(0.020)	(0.035)	(0.020)	(0.034)	(0.019)	(0.032)
Views	0.532***	0.497***	0.520***	0.474***	0.514***	0.464***
	(0.056)	(0.097)	(0.055)	(0.094)	(0.052)	(0.090)
HComment	−0.008	0.033	−0.005	0.038	−0.007	0.035
	(0.027)	(0.047)	(0.026)	(0.045)	(0.025)	(0.043)
Ad	0.057	0.041	0.032	−0.006	0.010	−0.042
	(0.037)	(0.064)	(0.037)	(0.063)	(0.035)	(0.061)
PostTime	0.001	0.001	0.002	0.002	0.002	0.003
	(0.001)	(0.002)	(0.001)	(0.002)	(0.001)	(0.002)
N	151	151	151	151	151	151
R^2	0.912	0.750	0.917	0.769	0.925	0.791

Robust standard errors are reported in parentheses; ***$p < 0.001$, **$p < 0.01$, *$p < 0.05$.

As shown in Table 3, the estimates for Barrage in Model 1 and all other models are significantly positive, being 0.538 ($p < 0.001$) in the regression of the dependent variable VEffectLike and 0.443 ($p < 0.001$) in the regression of VEffectCollect in Model

1. The total barrage volume is positively associated with video effectiveness, H1a and H1b are supported. Moreover, the estimates for VDuration in models of VEffectLike are all significantly negative, suggesting a general preference among audiences for shorter videos. Interestingly, the estimates for VDuration in models of VEffectCollect are all significantly positive, suggesting that longer videos may provide higher collection value to audiences for further reference.

In addition, the estimates for BarrageInf in Model 2 are all significantly positive, being 0.112 (p < 0.01) in the regressions of VEffectLike and 0.212 (p < 0.01) in the regression of VEffectCollect. This suggests that, on top of the positive effect of barrages, influencer-focused barrages offer additional content value to viewers. H2a and H2b are supported.

Furthermore, the estimates for the interaction term Barrage × VDuration in Model 3 are negative but insignificant. H3a and H3b, which posit positive interaction effects, are not supported. The results suggest no significant difference in the effect of barrages based on video durations.

Intriguingly, the estimates for the interaction term BarrageInf × VDuration are significantly positive, being 0.625 (p < 0.01) in the regression of VEffectLike and 1.027 (p < 0.01) in the regression of VEffectCollect. H4a and H4b are supported. While the effect of overall barrages on video effectiveness remains consistent across different video durations, the impact of influencer-focused barrages is contingent on video durations. The positive effect becomes more pronounced in longer videos compared to shorter ones.

6 Discussions

This study builds on and extends prior research on barrage volume [1, 3] and investigates the effects of influencer-focused barrages on the effectiveness of product demo videos. Although constituting a relatively small proportion (about 7%) of the total barrages in product demo videos, influencer-focused barrages can contain valuable information that captures audiences' attention. An empirical study of influencer-led product demo videos on social media verifies that the overall barrage volume within a video increases video effectiveness, as measured by "likes" and "collects" counts. This result aligns with those from previous studies [5]. Moreover, influencer-focused barrages exhibit additional positive impacts on video effectiveness. Furthermore, this positive effect of influencer-focused barrages is moderated by video durations, being more pronounced in longer videos than in shorter ones. This means influencer-focused barrages play a crucial role in capturing viewer attention and enhancing engagement, particularly in extended video content where audiences have more time to learn about the influencer's characters. Results also reveal that audiences generally like shorter videos but tend to collect longer videos for further reference and rewatching. These are in line with previous studies suggesting that longer videos provide more information [14] and shorter ones can better catch user attention.

This research contributes to the literature on barrage in social media videos. Firstly, it diverges from the current focus on the total barrage volume and its temporal features by highlighting the importance of delving into various barrage types [6, 11]. To our knowledge, this study is among the first to examine the effect of influencer-focused barrages, a sporadic but ever-presenting barrage component in product demo videos. Secondly, it unveils novel, interesting insights into the value of barrages in social media videos. The increasing impact of influencer-focused barrages, compared with the consistent effect of the overall barrage volume, based on video duration underscores the significant interest of viewers in peer opinions on the influencer. For the practical implications, this research can provide product demo video influencers with some suggestions to change the focus of their video content to achieve their desired video effectiveness.

As an exploratory study, this research is limited in its scope, which can be further developed. Theoretically, we focus on one type of barrage—those on influencers. Additional types of barrages can be coded and analyzed. Moreover, further exploration of content variables, such as sentiment regarding influencers, could provide additional insights into influencer-focused barrage content and its effects. Methodologically, efforts to enlarge the sample size are ongoing to enhance the reliability of findings and enable robustness tests, such as multigroup analysis.

References

1. Zhang, X., Zhao, Z., Wang, K.: The effects of live comments and advertisements on social media engagement: application to short-form online video. Journal of Research in Interactive Marketing ahead-of-print (2023)
2. Zhou, J., Zhou, J., Ding, Y., Wang, H.: The magic of danmaku: a social interaction perspective of gift sending on live streaming platforms. Electron. Commer. Res. Appl. **34**, 100815 (2019)
3. Fang, J., Chen, L., Wen, C., Prybutok, V.R.: Co-viewing experience in video websites: the effect of social presence on e-loyalty. Int. J. Electron. Commer. **22**, 446–476 (2018)
4. Zhang, Q., Wang, W., Chen, Y.: In-consumption social listening with moment-to-moment unstructured data: the case of movie appreciation and live comments. Mark. Sci. **39**, 285–295 (2020)
5. Kineta Hung, Tse, D.K., Chan, T.H.: E-commerce influencers in China: Dual-route model on likes, shares, and sales. J. Advertising 51(4), 486–501 (2022)
6. Wei, K.: The impact of barrage system fluctuation on user interaction in digital video platforms: a perspective from signaling theory and social impact theory. J. Res. Interact. Mark. **17**, 602–619 (2023)
7. Wei, Z., Zhang, M., Qiao, T.: Effect of personal branding stereotypes on user engagement on short-video platforms. J. Retail. Consum. Serv. **69**, 103121 (2022)
8. Chen, G., Zhou, S., Zhi, T.: Viewing mechanism of lonely audience: evidence from an eye movement experiment on barrage video. Comput. Hum. Behav. **101**, 327–333 (2019)
9. Blumler, J.G., Katz, E.: The Uses of Mass Communications: Current Perspectives on Gratifications Research. Sage Publications, Beverly Hills (1974)
10. Farivar, S., Wang, F., Yuan, Y.: Opinion leadership vs. para-social relationship: Key factors in influencer marketing. J. Retailing Consumer Serv. **59**, 102371 (2021)
11. Wang, F., Fu, X., Sun, Z.: A comparative analysis of the impact of barrage and comments on video popularity. IEEE Access **9**, 164659–164667 (2021)
12. Farivar, S., Wang, F.: Effective influencer marketing: a social identity perspective. J. Retail. Consum. Serv. **67**, 103026 (2022)
13. Karimi, S., Wang, F.: Online review helpfulness: Impact of reviewer profile image. Decis. Support. Syst. **96**, 39–48 (2017)
14. Munaro, A.C., Hübner Barcelos, R., Francisco Maffezzolli, E.C., Santos Rodrigues, J.P., Cabrera Paraiso, E.: To engage or not engage? the features of video content on YouTube affecting digital consumer engagement. J. Consumer Behav. **20**, 1336–1352 (2021)

15. Bediou, B., Adams, D.M., Mayer, R.E., Tipton, E., Green, C.S., Bavelie, D.: Meta-analysis of action video game impact on perceptual, attentional, and cognitive skills. Psychol. Bull. **144**, 77–110 (2018)
16. Richtel, M.: Growing Up Digital, Wired for Distraction. The New York Times **21**, 1–11 (2010)

Analyzing Consumer Switching Intentions in Short Video E-commerce: A Comprehensive Examination Through the Lens of Push, Pull, and Mooring Factors

Yijia Ma[1], Yi Cui[1], Jie Li[2(✉)], and Yonghui Li[1,1]

[1] Communication University of China, Beijing 100024, China
[2] Hangzhou Dianzi University Information Engineering College, Hangzhou 311305, Zhejiang, China
lij@hziee.edu.cn

Abstract. The rapid dissemination of short video platforms has prompted enterprises to explore their potential applications in the e-commerce domain, leading to the emergence of a novel paradigm termed short video e-commerce. As an increasing number of consumers turn to short video e-commerce for their shopping endeavors, both academia and industry have shown a growing interest in this phenomenon. However, current research primarily focuses on qualitative investigations and analyses of user adoption behavior, with limited quantitative exploration into the factors influencing consumer switching behavior. To address this research gap, the present study, rooted in the Push-Pull-Mooring (PPM) model, examines the impact of platform attributes and consumer comparative perception on consumer conversion intention. Subsequently, it employs structural equation modeling to elucidate the causal mechanisms underlying these influencing factors. By uncovering consumers' shopping needs on short video platforms, this paper contributes to the theoretical advancement of e-commerce research. Furthermore, it assists industry professionals in formulating appropriate strategies to retain existing consumers and attract new ones.

Keywords: Switching Intention · Short Video E-commerce · Push-Pull-Mooring Framework · Social Commerce

1 Introduction

With the development of internet technology and the increasing pace of daily life, short videos have become an essential component of people's everyday routines. In the United States, over 70% of surveyed individuals watch short videos on their smartphones, while in China, short video users make up a staggering 94.8% of the total online population. In recent years, short videos have expanded beyond their initial roles in information dissemination and social entertainment [1], progressively being explored for their e-commerce potential by various businesses. In 2022, platforms like Douyin and Kuaishou saw a

161% year-on-year increase in the total value of goods transactions generated by content consumption, with Kuaishou's e-commerce goods transactions reaching 222.4 billion yuan (30.54 billion USD) in the third quarter alone. This highlights the significant development potential of short video e-commerce, which is expected to continue influencing consumer behavior both presently and in the future. Understanding consumer switching behavior is paramount for businesses [2]. However, the predominant focus of current research remains on qualitative analysis [1], with the majority of studies concentrating on exploring users' continued usage behavior rather than their migration behavior [3]. This study addresses this research gap by investigating the factors influencing consumers' transition from traditional e-commerce to short video e-commerce, posing the following two questions:

RQ1: What factors affect consumer switching intention from traditional e-commerce to short video e-commerce?
RQ2: What is the mechanism by which these factors shape consumer switching intention?

Given the initial dearth of theoretical grounding in the realm of short video platforms, this study delves into the examination of user transfer intentions using the PPM theory.

This study contributes to both theory and practice of short video e-commerce. It quantitatively unveils the factors and mechanisms influencing consumer switching intention from traditional e-commerce to short video e-commerce. Secondly, this research shows that the pull factors exert a stronger influence on comparative perceived enjoyment than the push factors. This suggests that consumers' positive shopping experiences in terms of enjoyment primarily stem from the alignment between short video e-commerce and contemporary consumer shopping habits, rather than deficiencies in traditional e-commerce functionality. Thirdly, the study finds that social presence has a more substantial impact on comparative perceived trust and comparative perceived enjoyment than information quality. This underscores the greater importance of emotional appeals over rational appeals in short video e-commerce. As a result, the findings of this study offer pertinent recommendations for short video platforms, traditional e-commerce platforms, and merchants.

2 Literature Review and Theoretical Background

2.1 Short Video E-commerce

"Short videos" denote videos with a duration of fewer than 5 min that fulfill users' needs for both knowledge acquisition and entertainment. Users can create concise and fragmented videos by incorporating elements such as music, editing, and other components [1].

The main differences between short videos and traditional or online media can be classified into personalized attributes, entertainment features, and social characteristics [4]. Practitioners have validated the potential of short videos in e-commerce and conducted relevant research on consumer behavior [5, 6]. The analysis of literature on short videos reveals that short video e-commerce exhibits both entertainment features and e-commerce potential, leading to consumer channel migration behavior, which merits further investigation.

2.2 Switching Behavior

In comparison to research on short videos, the study of switching behavior constitutes a relatively mature research field. Switching behavior refers to the action of users migrating from one service provider to another. It is often triggered by user dissatisfaction with existing products and services and the perception of relative advantages of alternative products and services [7]. This paper investigates consumer transfer behavior from traditional e-commerce to short video e-commerce.

Research on switching behavior between e-commerce platforms encompasses three distinct types of switching behavior, including cross-media channel switching between PC-based e-commerce and mobile e-commerce [8], homogeneous service switching in mobile e-commerce [9], and non-homogeneous service switching between traditional e-commerce and social e-commerce [10]. For traditional e-commerce, short video e-commerce not only demonstrates excellence in matching algorithms and video presentation but also showcases innovation in social, entertainment, and media functions. Research into switching behavior from traditional e-commerce to short video e-commerce constitutes a more intricate study, combining cross-media channel switching with non-homogeneous service switching. Therefore, this paper examines consumer switching behavior by using the differences between these two e-commerce models as influencing factors.

2.3 Push-Pull-Mooring

The PPM theory is widely employed in the study of consumer switching behavior, particularly in the field of marketing. This theory is a general theoretical framework that does not specify particular variables such as push, pull, and mooring factors within a specific research context. This theoretical framework is particularly suitable for exploratory research in new scenarios where the foundational theoretical basis may be relatively scarce. Therefore, synthesizing the push, pull, and mooring factors from existing research in different scenarios will aid in delineating the scope of these factors in this study [8, 10].

Through the above summary of the literature related to the PPM theory, it is evident that there has been no research on short video media, whether within the context of e-commerce or social media. This underscores the fact that specific propulsive and attractive factors in the context of short video media have not yet received attention or recognition. Hence, the application of the PPM theory to investigate channel transition behaviors between traditional e-commerce and short video e-commerce holds certain academic and practical significance.

3 Hypothesis Development and Research Model

The motivation behind consumers' intention to switch from traditional e-commerce to short-video e-commerce is jointly determined by two pivotal factors: platform attributes and comparative perceptions. Regarding platform attributes, this study employs the PPM framework to delve into the exploration, positing hypotheses H1–H5. Concerning comparative perceptions, grounded on the fusion of short-video content and entertainment features, this research advances hypotheses H7 and H8. Based on this, the model is formulated as depicted in Fig. 1.

According to research from Shiu et al., consumer confusion is characterized by a consumer's inability to form accurate explanations for various aspects of a product or service during the decision-making process [11]. Consumer confusion is regarded as a crucial factor impacting consumer satisfaction. For example, study on the transition from traditional e-commerce to live-streaming e-commerce, consumer confusion is identified as a motivating factor leading to dissatisfaction with traditional e-commerce [12]. In traditional e-commerce settings, sellers primarily use images and text to showcase product characteristics, prices, and usage to consumers. Therefore, when multiple stores offer similar products, consumers must sift through numerous web pages, expending substantial time on filtering and comparison. This process can lead to consumer confusion when making product purchases. The worse the consumer's experience with traditional e-commerce, the stronger the relative perceived enjoyment towards short video e-commerce. Thus, we posit the following hypothesis:

H1: The consumer confusion of traditional e-commerce is positively related to comparative perceived enjoyment.

Information quality pertains to the degree of relevance, accuracy, comprehensibility, and utility of the information generated by an e-commerce website about consumer needs. Extant research indicates that the quality of information furnished by websites can foster consumer trust, and consequently bolster consumer purchase intent [8, 9]. Divergent from conventional e-commerce's reliance on static imagery and text, short video e-commerce employs dynamic video presentations, augmenting the intelligibility of information and broadening content coverage. Short video creators adopt a buyer-centric approach in product introductions, thereby significantly heightening the perceived reliability of information by consumers. Accompanied by fitting musical accompaniments and witty dialogue, this also amplifies the readability of information. The stronger a consumer's sense of immersion and trust in the short video platform, the more pronounced their relative perceived enjoyment and trust. Thus, we posit the following hypotheses:

H2: The information quality of short video e-commerce is positively related to comparative perceived enjoyment.
H3: The information quality of short video e-commerce is positively related to comparative perceived trust.

Social presence is defined as the extent to which consumers are perceived as "real individuals" in mediated communication, and is frequently employed in media research [13]. Short video platforms not only offer convenient short video creation tools but also promote high-quality short video content, encouraging user-generated short videos [2]. In this way, short video e-commerce facilitates interaction between consumers and short video creators. Consumers experience a higher level of social presence when using short video platforms. Social interactions can be pivotal in enhancing consumer understanding, fostering trust [5], and influencing cognitive adjustments, expectation setting, and coordination improvements [9]. Thus, we posit the following hypotheses:

H4: The social presence of short video e-commerce is positively related to comparative perceived enjoyment.

H5: The social presence of short video e-commerce is positively related to comparative perceived trust.

Social influence refers to how individuals or groups can affect the thoughts, feelings, and behaviors of others. Social influence encompasses informational normative social influence, which respectively impact consumer trust and hedonic experiences. It often reflects an individual's attempt to comply with others' expectations to gain rewards, recognition, and enhance their self-image through connections with others [9, 10]. Given the widespread global usage and increasing trend of short video platforms among users, there is a considerable level of social influence. Thus, we proposed the following hypotheses:

H6: Social influence is positively related to consumer switching intention.

Perceived enjoyment has its origins in the concept of flow theory, which denotes the feeling of dedicating one's mental energies completely to a particular activity. Simultaneously, the experience of flow is accompanied by a heightened sense of excitement and a feeling of fulfillment, leading to positive emotions [14]. In an online environment, consumers' perceived enjoyment can induce impulsive purchases [15] and bolster consumer satisfaction as well as platform reputation [4, 5]. Short video platforms are often regarded as platforms with social and entertainment functions. Watching short videos can bring joy to consumers and evoke positive emotions, thereby enhancing consumers' relative perceived enjoyment. Therefore, we posit the following hypothesis:

H7: Comparative perceived enjoyment is positively related to consumer switching intention.

Trust is defined as the willingness to engage in exchanges with reliable partners. In traditional commerce, trust is deemed indispensable and is typically established through interactions between consumers and sales representatives, as well as between consumers and suppliers. In the context of e-commerce, online perceived trust serves as the cornerstone of the willingness to make purchases [6, 8]. Research conducted by Nohria and Eccles pointed out a decrease in consumer trust in online environments, primarily attributed to the absence of auditory, visual, and tactile interactions between consumers [16]. Conversely, short videos offer heightened visual and auditory effects, along with enhanced social interaction, leading to an increased comparative perceived trust of consumers in short video platforms. Thus, we posit the following hypothesis:

H8: Comparative perceived trust is positively related to consumer switching intention.

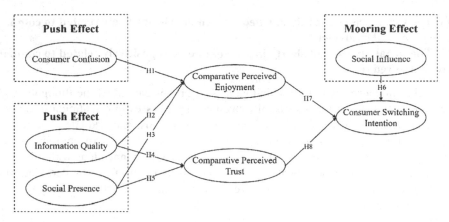

Fig. 1. Research model

4 Empirical Analysis

4.1 Measurement Development

To ensure the validity of our research, this study adapted existing literature and tailored a scale based on the characteristics of short video platforms. We adapted scales as outlined in Table 1. The questionnaire comprises two sections: one about the respondents' demographic information and the other focusing on measurement indicators for each variable. All items were assessed using a five-point Likert scale, ranging from 1 (strongly disagree) to 5 (strongly agree). The final survey instrument was developed through initial questionnaires, small-scale interviews, pre-testing, and subsequent revisions.

Table 1. Research scale

Constructs	Items	Sources
Consumer Confusion (CC)	4	Wang & Shukla (2013)
Social Presence (SP)	3	Animesh et al. (2011)
Information Quality (IQ)	3	DeLone & McLean (1992)
Social Influence (SI)	3	Holden & Karsh (2010)
Comparative Perceived Trust (CPT)	2	Lai et al. (2012)
Comparative Perceived Enjoyment (CPE)	3	Hsieh et al. (2012)
Consumer Switching Intention (CSI)	3	Hsieh et al. (2012)

4.2 Data Collection

Data collection was conducted through a specialized online survey website (www.wjx.cn). Respondents were motivated with randomly distributed red envelopes valued at

1–5 RMB. Over a two-week data collection period, we collected a total of 502 samples. Surveys with more than five missing data points and those showing identical responses were removed. Additionally, we conducted IP address verification to prevent multiple responses from a single participant. After the data cleaning process, we obtained 426 valid samples, resulting in an 84.9% effective response rate.

4.3 Data Analysis and Results

Following the two-step procedure recommended by Anderson and Gerbing, we initially examined the measurement model to validate the reliability and validity of the questionnaire. Subsequently, an assessment of the structural model was conducted. IBM SPSS 20.0 was employed for preliminary statistical analysis in this study, while IBM AMOS 24.0 was used for structural equation modeling analysis. Descriptive information regarding the dataset is presented in Table 2.

Table 2. Demographics of respondents

Demographic Factor	Category	Samples ($n = 426$)	Percentage (%)
Gender	Male	178	41.8
	Female	248	58.2
Age	Less than 25	325	76.3
	25–29	12	2.8
	30–39	24	5.6
	More than 39	65	15.3
Income in RMB (monthly)	Less than 2000	193	45.3
	2001–4000	119	27.9
	4001–6000	43	10.1
	6001–8000	18	4.2
	More than 8000	53	12.4

4.4 Common Method Bias

We conducted Harman's single-factor test by running an exploratory factor analysis of all the scale items. The result shows that all items are categorized into seven factors. All factors explain 78.25% of the variance in this study's constructs, with the first factor explaining 40.34% and the last explaining 3.41%. In addition, we compared correlations among constructs and found no constructs with correlations over 0.9. These results indicate that the common method bias is not a threat in the present study.

4.5 Measurement Model

To assess the reliability and validity of the sample data obtained from the survey questionnaire, we conducted tests for both reliability and validity. Detailed test results are presented in Table 3.

Table 3. Results of the confirmatory factor analysis.

Constructs	Items	Loading	Cronbach's Alpha	Composite Reliability	Average Variance Extracted
CC	CC1	0.834	0.872	0.873	0.634
	CC2	0.849			
	CC3	0.774			
	CC4	0.720			
SP	SP1	0.703	0.846	0.849	0.655
	SP2	0.871			
	SP3	0.843			
IQ	IQ1	0.744	0.832	0.833	0.625
	IQ2	0.819			
	IQ3	0.807			
SI	SI1	0.915	0.868	0.878	0.710
	SI2	0.908			
	SI3	0.684			
CPT	CPT1	0.831	0.838	0.838	0.722
	CPT2	0.868			
CPE	CPE1	0.838	0.897	0.897	0.744
	CPE2	0.866			
	CPE3	0.883			
CSI	CSI1	0.889	0.899	0.900	0.750
	CSI2	0.897			
	CSI3	0.809			

In addition, to assess discriminant validity, we followed the approach of Fornell and Larcker by comparing the square root of the AVE with the inter-variable correlations. As indicated in Table 4, the square root of AVE for each variable was consistently higher than the correlations among variables, confirming the strong discriminant validity of the model.

After examining the validity and reliability of the measurements, this study conducted a goodness-of-fit test using the maximum likelihood method, as shown in Table 5. All

Table 4. Correlations among constructs

Constructs	CC	SP	SI	IQ	CPT	CPE	CSI
CC	**0.796**						
SP	0.182	**0.809**					
SI	0.147	0.467	**0.843**				
IQ	0.191	0.700	0.606	**0.791**			
CPT	0.156	0.587	0.604	0.777	**0.850**		
CPE	0.291	0.575	0.460	0.730	0.650	**0.863**	
CSI	0.138	0.530	0.618	0.691	0.702	0.646	**0.866**

Note: Diagonal numbers in bold are the square root of the average variance extracted of each construct; Pearson correlations are shown below the diagonal

the indicators for model fit evaluation met the recommended criteria, thus confirming the adequacy of fit for both the measurement and structural models in this research.

Table 5. Summary of model fit

Model fit	Recommend	Measurement	Structural model
CMIN/DF	<3	2.063	2.193
RMR	<0.08	0.033	0.034
GFI	>0.9	0.904	0.920
AGFI	>0.8	0.874	0.890
NFI	>0.9	0.925	0.940
RFI	>0.9	0.908	0.925
IFI	>0.9	0.960	0.966
CFI	>0.9	0.959	0.966
RMSEA	<0.08	0.050	0.053

4.6 Structural Model and Hypothesis Testing

The results of structural model testing are presented in Table 6, and we depicted the results in Fig. 2.

Table 6. The results of SEM analysis

Path	Estimate	S.E.	C.R.	P-value	Result
H1:CC → CPE	0.148	0.050	3.518	***	Supported
H2:IQ → CPE	0.405	0.053	7.096	***	Supported
H3:IQ → CPT	0.423	0.047	8.067	***	Supported
H4:SP → CPE	0.535	0.052	10.22	***	Supported
H5:SP → CPT	0.558	0.054	9.886	***	Supported
H6:SI → CSI	0.260	0.044	5.209	***	Supported
H7:CPE → CSI	0.312	0.049	6.326	***	Supported
H8:CPT → CSI	0.362	0.055	6.776	***	Supported

Note: * p < 0.05, ** p < 0.01, *** p < 0.001

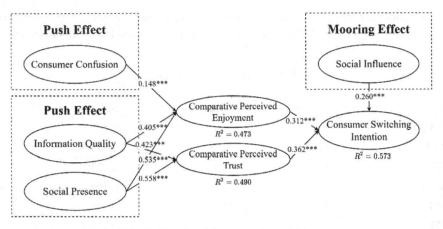

Fig. 2. Results of the research model tests

5 Conclusion and Implications

5.1 Theoretical Implication

This research contributes to the existing literature in several ways. Firstly, it enhances the study of transition behavior by investigating the factors and mechanisms influencing consumer switching intention from traditional e-commerce to short video e-commerce.

Secondly, in this study, both social presence and information quality significantly contribute to comparative perceived trust and enjoyment of short video e-commerce, with social presence exerting a more pronounced influence. This finding not only enriches the theoretical landscape of e-commerce but also underscores the greater prominence of media characteristics compared to informational characteristics in the context of short video e-commerce. Social presence emerges as a critical driver of consumer adoption of short video e-commerce, indirectly emphasizing the greater significance of emotional elements over rational ones.

Lastly, the results of this research show that platform attributes have a substantial impact on comparative perceptions, subsequently influencing consumer switching intention. It becomes apparent that comparative perceptions play a pivotal role in mediating the relationship between platform attributes and consumer switching intention, serving as a crucial conduit.

5.2 Practical Implication

Based on the PPM theory, this research investigates the key drivers of consumer switching intention from traditional e-commerce to short video e-commerce, offering substantial practical significance. Firstly, short video e-commerce retailers must address consumer confusion. For example, before crafting short videos, retailers should clearly define product positioning and target consumer demographics. Short video platforms should also enhance product search and ranking mechanisms, recommending highly rated and promising items to potential consumers.

Secondly, merchants in short video e-commerce need to enhance information quality and social immediacy. Specifically, merchants should provide more concise and precise product presentations and introductions. Moreover, high-quality filming and editing techniques should be employed when recording videos.

Thirdly, utilizing social influence can stimulate consumers' propensity to switch. For instance, short video platforms leverage viral marketing to publicize their e-commerce capabilities, thus converting more typical short video users into short video e-commerce consumers.

Lastly, in short video e-commerce, consumers' emotional appeal holds more weight than rational arguments. Short video e-commerce merchants can sacrifice some information quality to enhance the sense of social presence. For example, merchants can judiciously utilize special effects and filters in short videos, creating a series of short videos and collaborating with internet celebrities. However, even when sacrificing information quality, a requisite level of accuracy and detail must be upheld to fulfill consumers' fundamental requirements.

5.3 Conclusion

Short videos applications have become an indispensable and integral part of people's lives, demonstrating significant advantages in information dissemination and social entertainment. Numerous businesses highly value these advantages. The application value of short videos in the field of e-commerce has been deeply explored, giving rise to a new e-commerce model known as "short video e-commerce." Consequently, consumers are switching from traditional e-commerce to short video e-commerce. To expand the knowledge base in the existing field of short video e-commerce, and to provide practitioners with development strategies for short video e-commerce, this study adopts the PPM theory framework to thoroughly investigate the key factors influencing consumers' transition from traditional e-commerce platforms to short video e-commerce platforms and analyze their underlying impact mechanisms.

The study reveals that push factors encompass consumer confusion caused by traditional e-commerce platforms, while pull factors include information quality and social presence on short video e-commerce. These factors influence consumer switching intention from traditional e-commerce to short video e-commerce through comparative perceived trust and comparative perceived enjoyment. Furthermore, social influence, as a mooring factor, also plays a certain role in consumer switching intention.

Acknowledgement. This research was supported by the National Natural Science Foundation of China under Grant 72202219.

References

1. Sheng, M.Y., Basha, N.K.: A conceptual framework to study effective short-video platform advertising on Chinese generation y consumer online purchase intention. WSEAS Trans. Environ. Dev. **18**, 1055–1072 (2022)
2. Zhang, K.Z.K., Cheung, C.M.K., Lee, M.K.O.: Online service switching behavior: the case of blog service providers. J. Electron. Commer. Res. **13**(3), 184–197 (2012)
3. Boe, T., Gulbrandsen, B., Sorebo, O.: How to stimulate the continued use of ICT in higher education: integrating information systems continuance theory and agency theory. Comput. Hum. Behav. **50**(9), 375–384 (2015)
4. Gan, C., Li, H.: Understanding the effects of gratifications on the continuance intention to use WeChat in China: a perspective on uses and gratifications. Comput. Hum. Behav. **78**, 306–315 (2018)
5. Xie, X.J., Tsai, N.C., Xu, S.Q., Zhang, B.Y.: Does customer co-creation value lead to electronic word-of-mouth? An empirical study on the short-video platform industry. Soc. Sci. J. **56**(3), 401–416 (2019)
6. Wang, Y.: Humor and camera view on mobile short-form video apps influence user experience and technology-adoption intent, an example of TikTok (DouYin). Comput. Hum. Behav. **110**, 106373 (2020)
7. Hsieh, J.K., Hsieh, Y.C., Chiu, H.C., Feng, Y.C.: Post-adoption switching behavior for online service substitutes: a perspective of the push-pull-mooring framework. Comput. Hum. Behav. **28**(5), 1912–1920 (2012)
8. Lai, J.Y., Debbarma, S., Ulhas, K.R.: An empirical study of consumer switching behaviour towards mobile shopping: a push-pull-mooring model. Int. J. Mob. Commun. **10**(4), 386–404 (2012)
9. Zhou, T.: Examining user switch between mobile stores: a push-pull-mooring perspective. Inf. Resour. Manag. J. **29**(2), 1–13 (2016)
10. Li, C., Ku, Y.: The power of a thumbs-up: will e-commerce switch to social commerce? Inf. Manag. **55**(3), 340–357 (2017)
11. Shiu, J.Y.L.: Risk-reduction strategies in competitive convenience retail: how brand confusion can impact choice among existing similar alternatives. J. Retail. Consum. Serv. 61, 102547 (2021)
12. Zhao, Q., Chen, C., Zhou, Z., Mao, R.: Factors influencing consumers' intentions to switch to live commerce from push-pull-mooring perspective. J. Glob. Inf. Manag. **31**(1), 1–30 (2023)
13. Park, H., Cameron, G.T.: Keeping it real: exploring the roles of conversational human voice and source credibility in crisis communication via Blogs. Journal. Mass Commun. Q. **91**(3), 487–507 (2014)
14. Mikalef, P., Giannakos, M., Pateli, A.: Shopping and word-of-mouth intentions on social media. J. Theor. Appl. Electron. Commer. Res. **8**(1), 17–34 (2013)

15. Cui, Y., Zhu, J.R., Liu, Y.P.: Exploring the social and systemic influencing factors of mobile short video applications on the consumer urge to buy impulsively. J. Glob. Inf. Manag. **30**(1), 1–23 (2022)
16. Nohria, N., Eccles, R.C.: Face-to-Face: Making Network Organizations Work. Harvard Business School Press, Boston (1992)

Team Faultlines in Online Visual Programming Learning Platform: Considering the Effect of Team Leaders' Characteristics

Xiaobin Zhang, Zujun Shi, Shouxiang Qiu$^{(\boxtimes)}$, and Ling Zhao

Huazhong University of Science and Technology, Wuhan 430074, China
shouxiang_qiu@hust.edu.cn

Abstract. This study investigates the impact of faultlines, created by differences in multiple attribute characteristics among team members, on the learning performance of online programming teams, utilizing data from all studios on the Codemao platform. Contrasting with traditional offline work teams or online crowdsourcing competition teams, online learning teams exhibit lower competitiveness and a more flexible internal structure. Our findings reveal that team faultlines impede team interaction, thereby negatively affecting overall team performance, and the leader ability controversially exacerbate the adverse effects of team faultlines on interaction and performance. We also discovered that task-oriented rather than relationship-oriented team management is more conducive for early-stage teams, serving as a complementary factor to mitigate the negative impacts of faultlines. Lastly, the study discusses the theoretical and practical implications of these findings, proposes future research directions, and acknowledges the limitations of the current research.

Keywords: team faultlines · virtual learning team · team performance · team leader's characteristics · team interaction

1 Introduction

Online visual programming learning (VPL) platform is an emerging and special type among those various online learning platforms, which serve as crucial avenues for specialized knowledge and skill acquisition [1]. By furnishing learners with visualized and modular programming environments, various VPL platforms, such as Scratch and Codemao, offer an alternative to traditional code-based programming learning. It is demonstrated that VPL could lower the entry barriers for novices and enhance the interest and engagement of learners [1].

To promote learners' participation and learning performance, VPL platforms facilitate intensive interaction among learners through team-based or group-based strategies [1]. Taking Codemao, the largest VPL platform in China, as an example. Codemao has launched a unique 'studio' feature, which is a team-based strategy that encourage learners to form teams on the platforms. One or several leaders could launch a studio (e.g., team) and recruit team members. The leaders could also set goals and principles

Y. P. Tu and M. Chi (Eds.): WHICEB 2024, LNBIP 515, pp. 300–312, 2024.
https://doi.org/10.1007/978-3-031-60264-1_26

of the studio and manage the team. Both online and offline educational research have highlighted the effectiveness of team-based or group-based learning in enhancing Information flow and knowledge sharing [2]. However, challenges arise in such online VPL environments where learners are usually unfamiliar with each other, and simply forming teams online doesn't guarantee better team performance.

Though there are many factors that could influence a team's performance, this study focused on the team faultlines. Team faultlines, indicative of team diversity, are maginary boundaries that divide groups into relatively homogenous subgroups based on membership attributes [3] and regarded as a fundamental characteristic of team composition to exert significant influence on both the processes and performance of a team. Although plenty of studies have explored the impact of faultlines on offline work team performance, findings regarding its direction and magnitude remain inconclusive as both positive and negative impacts of team faultlines on team performance were found [4]. Researchers have explored the internal mechanisms of how faultlines influence team performance and potential boundary conditions [6]. This inquiry pivots towards understanding these dynamics within the virtual teams prevalent in online learning platforms. Unlike their counterparts in crowdsourcing tournaments, which Cao et al. (2022) examined [6], virtual teams dedicated to online learning environments are hypothesized to exhibit less competitive behavior and to possess a more loosely defined internal structure. This distinction raises pivotal questions about the nature and extent of faultlines' impact on team performance within these settings, as well as the identification of contingent factors that may modulate this relationship. The current study posits that the unique characteristics of virtual learning teams—marked by reduced competition and fluid organizational boundaries [5]—necessitate a reevaluation of established understandings derived from traditional, offline team settings.

On the VPL platform, due to the absence of external competitive pressure between teams, members within a team may lack a unified goal and the motivation to communicate and collaborate with members from different subgroups. This could lead to an increased negative impact of team faultlines on team performance. Concurrently, internal organization and management within the team may become more crucial, such as whether and how the team organizer (or leader) establishes consistent internal goals for the team. Therefore, we raise the following research questiones: How do team faultlines influence team performance within the online VPL platform? Additionally, what factors may enhance or mitigate this impact ?

To address the aforementioned questions, this study first collects the data of teams from a specific online programming platform as a case to examine the impact of team faultlines on team performance and the underlying mechanisms. We argue that, within virtual learning teams, team faultlines exert a detrimental influence on team performance, primarily by diminishing team interactions. Secondly, adopting the leadership lens, we introduce and analyze two mechanisms that could potentially mitigate this adverse effect: leader ability and team management orientation. Our research suggests that both mechanisms can alleviate the detrimental effects of team faultlines on performance, albeit through different pathways. Specifically, leader ability attenuates the negative effects of faultlines on team interactions, subsequently alleviating its adverse influence on performance. In contrast, leader orientation directly augments team interactions, thereby enhancing team performance.

This study significantly contributes to the literature by addressing the underexplored domain of team faultlines' effects on team performance in an online setting. We elucidate the adverse influence of faultlines on the performance of online learning teams, attributing much of this effect to the mediation of team interactions. Moreover, by embracing a leadership characteristic perspective, we unveil two pivotal mechanisms aimed at countering the detrimental ramifications of team faultlines. Notably, our insights hold paramount importance for shaping team-based learning strategies across online learning platforms, offering actionable recommendations to aid platforms in crafting optimal team architectures, thus circumventing the pitfalls associated with internal team divisions.

2 Literature Review

2.1 Team-Based Learning in Online Visual Programming Platform

Fig. 1. An example of studio in Codemao

Visual programming platforms facilitate entry for novices through visual and gamified elements like block-based coding and achievement badges. Prominent examples include Scratch, Blockpy, and Codemao. Team-based and group learning distinguish these visual programming platforms from traditional platforms, highlighting a unique approach to collaborative online education. For instance, Codemao, China's premier visual programming platform, allows learners to join studios that resonate with their creative style and skill level, fostering a collaborative learning environment. As depicted in Fig. 1, "江玖工作室" is the name of the studio. The head of this studio is "苏四象", and the deputy heads are "KevinSyXo", "你好吧 789", and "屑佬本尊". "江玖工作室" has 39 members, and "ImpostorBlack" is one of them. Studio members typically possess significant creative abilities and expertise, and their inclusion often brings dual support in terms of traffic and technical expertise, thereby enhancing both individual and team performance [3]. We note that studios operate as spontaneous team-based learning organizations, in which the internal structure is relatively loose, and most studios are still in the early stages. This becomes particularly problematic when multiple subgroups form within the team, potentially activating dormant faultlines and leading to potential conflicts and communication barriers. Therefore, investigating how boundary conditions and complementary mechanisms can mitigate the negative impacts of team fragmentation and guide the formation of effective internal structures and management strategies is of significant theoretical and practical importance for enhancing studio performance.

2.2 Team Faultline and Team Performance

Team faultlines, as conceptualized by Lau & Murnighan (2005), represent hypothetical divisions within a team based on one or more characteristics, such as race, gender, age, and education [3]. In terms of measuring faultlines, previous research primarily used social category attributes like gender and age, and informational characteristics like education and experience, employing the faultline algorithm developed by [4], which calculates the ratio of between-group variance to total variance. However, a notable difference in recent studies [6] is the focus on social dominance-based faultlines, not based on traditional demographic attributes but on social dominance traits granted by IT systems, such as rank and hierarchy. This approach is particularly insightful and applicable, as demographic attributes in online environments are often less observable, with more emphasis on attributes reassigned by online IT systems.

Empirical studies on how faultlines impact on team performance reveal a complex picture. Discrepancies exist in the direction and magnitude of faultlines' impact on team performance. Researchers adhering to social categorization perspective report a negative correlation, mediated by factors like team open communication [8], and subgroup formation and interaction quality [9]. In contrast, proponents of information-processing theory suggest a positive influence, mediated through intergroup learning [3], and team reflexivity [4]. Interaction and communication within teams are frequently considered as mediating variables in these studies [8, 9].

Additionally, Most research has concentrated on offline work environments [7], with limited focus on online settings. In online crowdsourcing environments, the direct impact of faultlines on team performance is less pronounced and is contingent on situational characteristics such as team ability and effort [6]. In contrast to teams in crowdsourcing competitions, teams on online programming platforms lack external competitive incentives like cash rewards, which can promote internal cooperation, potentially counteracting the negative effects of faultlines [9]. Therefore, the mechanisms through which team faultlines in online programming learning influence performance are multifaceted and deserve further exploration.

2.3 Team Leader Characteristics and Team Performance

Recent studies indicate the pivotal role of team leaders in influencing the creative process within various contextual backgrounds [10]. Social Information Processing (SIP) Theory posits team leaders are key agents reflecting the attributes of the work environment, especially online and serve as primary sources of information. Leaders who adopt a humble and task-centered management approach, despite their capabilities, send a strong signal of openness to constructive suggestions and appreciation of team contributions [11]. This management style can alleviate conflicts arising from social categorization and integrate diverse cognitive resources, thereby facilitating team interactions and enhancing performance.

This study focuses on leader abilities in terms of leader traits and management orientation in terms of leader behaviors. Leader ability refers to the ability of team leaders to use their creative experience to lead members towards greater achievements, thereby boosting overall studio performance [11]. Team management orientation, categorized into relational and task-oriented types, indicate leaders' approaches to managing the team's daily operations and outcomes. According to trait activation theory, traits manifest as behaviors only when activated, so leader traits generally do not directly impact team interaction and performance but are considered as boundary conditions [12]. Furthermore, from the perspective of managing online programming learning platforms, a leader's management behavior largely aims to facilitate information exchange and resource sharing among informal team members, thereby elevating overall team performance. Thus, this paper positions leaders' management orientation as direct antecedents to team interaction, exploring the complementary mechanisms through which team faultlines affect team performance.

3   Research Model and Hypotheses

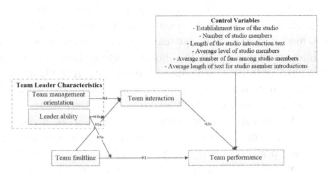

Fig. 2. Research model

Our research model, as depicted in Fig. 2, systematically investigates the interplay between team faultlines, leader characteristics, team interaction, and team performance within online visual programming platforms.

3.1   Effects of Team Faultline on Team Performance

Team faultlines, created based on varying member attributes, divide a team into subgroups. This division can lead to potential conflicts and communication barriers, amplifying differences between subgroups [3]. In teams with significant social category faultlines, an "us versus them" mentality can lead to fragmentation, adversely affecting team performance [13]. Therefore, we propose the following hypothesis:

H1: In the VPL platform, team faultline is negatively related to team performance.

3.2 Effects of Team Interaction

Team faultlines may also indirectly influence team performance by affecting interactions among team members. Team interaction, central to team building and management, involves cognitive, verbal, and action-oriented interactions among members. These interactions, bridging team inputs and outputs, significantly affect performance [13]. However, pronounced social category faultlines in teams may weaken task interdependence and cooperative efforts among members [4], thereby diminishing prosocial motivations and behaviors and inhibiting performance improvement. From the perspective of interactional efficacy, sub-group fissures impede the exchange of information and communication among team members, thereby exacerbating differences and a sense of boundary between sub-groups. The negative impacts of stereotyping, in-group favoritism, and out-group hostility further foster a pervasive atmosphere of antipathy. This may hinder effective problem-solving and reducing team performance [14]. Therefore, we propose the following hypothesis:

H2a: In the VPL platform, team faultline is negatively related to team interaction.
H2b: In the VPL platform, team interaction is positively related to team performance.

3.3 Effects of Team Leaders' Characteristics

Research indicates that autocratic and democratic leadership styles are crucial for effective leadership [11]. In the context of spontaneous learning teams on online programming platforms, democratic leadership, involving joint decision-making by leaders and team members, is more suitable in non-emergency and initial situations. However, high leadership abilities in a democratic setting may be counterproductive, increasing mistrust and disidentification among team members, thereby inhibiting communication, cooperation, and ultimately, team performance. According to SIP theory, stronger leadership abilities might foster a self-centered leadership style [12]. This can exacerbate conflicts arising from social categorization processes, and amplify differences and disagreements between subgroups [10], intensifying the negative impact of team faultlines on both team interaction and performance. Based on this logic, we propose the following hypotheses:

H3a: In the VPL platform, a higher level of leader's ability strengthens the negative relationship between team faultlines and team performance.
H3b: In the VPL platform, a higher level of leader's ability strengthens the negative relationship between team faultlines and the level of team interaction.

Task and relationship orientations form a continuum of leadership styles, which have been a focus of leadership research for years [15, 16]. Task-oriented leaders typically set detailed plans and high yet achievable goals [15]. In contrast, relationship-oriented leaders place greater emphasis on team culture and member relationships, encouraging trust and cooperation [16]. In newly formed teams, leaders tend to focus on subgroup relationships, hoping to bridge faultlines through social activities. However, this can exacerbate issues, as frequent relational contact in immature teams can lead to quick judgments and an emphasis on differences [17]. Conversely, a task orientation can centralize focus on common goals, effectively facilitating internal information and knowledge interaction, thereby enhancing team performance [10]. Therefore, we propose the following hypothesis:

H4: In the VPL platform, teams led by leaders with task-oriented rather than relationship-oriented will exhibit higher level of team interaction.

4 Research Method

4.1 Research Subject and Data Collection

This study collected data from Codemao (https://shequ.codemao.cn/) in August 2023, China's largest online programming platform for children. Since in October 2015, the platform has attracted over two million learners from 11 countries and regions. Codemao features a team-based learning function called "Studio", akin to offline study groups, facilitating collaborative and communicative learning around shared goals. See Fig. 3 for more details. After data cleansing, which involved removing officially banned studios and those with fewer than two members, the final sample comprised 4,844 studios and 49,627 learners.

Fig. 3. An example of the studio (left) and user profile (right) on Codemao

4.2 Measurement of Variables

(1) Team Performance (TeamPerformance). On the Codemao platform, members submit their previously published works to the studio, which other users can view and like. Quantity and quality of submissions are crucial reference indicators for earning studio points and determining studio rank. Therefore, we measure TeamPerformance using the logarithm of the weighted average of the quantity and quality scores of all submissions to the studio. The rationale for calculating the quality score on the basis that one "like" is equivalent to two "view" is rooted in Codemao's standard scoring system for submissions, which assigns equal weight to one "like" and two "view".

(2) Team Faultlines (TeamFaultline). This study adopts an algorithm proposed by Thatcher et al. (2012) and calculates the TeamFaultline using formula (1) [4]. This algorithm has been widely applied in information systems research. We use user levels and the number of submissions as attribute indicators for calculating team faultlines since these attributes effectively reflect the creative abilities and activity levels of users on the platform. Considering the different scales of user levels and the number of submissions, we first logarithmically transform the submissions indicator and then normalize it, while the user levels indicator is directly normalized.

$$Fau = \frac{\sum_{k=i}^{2}\sum_{j=1}^{p} n_k^{(g)} (\bar{x}_{jk} - \bar{x}_{j.})^2}{\sum_{k=i}^{2}\sum_{j=1}^{p}\sum_{i=1}^{n_k^{(g)}} (x_{ijk} - \bar{x}_{j.})^2}, g = 1, 2 \ldots S$$

$$Fau = max(Fau_g) \tag{1}$$

In the aforementioned formula, x_{ijk} represents the value of feature j for member i in subteam k. The term $\bar{x}_{j.}$ denotes the average value of feature j across all team members, while $\bar{x}_{jk}$ signifies the average value of feature j within the members of subteam k. The variable $n_k^{(g)}$ corresponds to the number of members in subteam k in the g-th dichotomy. The maximum value of Fau_g computed for a team represents the strength of team faultline. This value typically ranges between 0 and 1, with values closer to 1 indicating a stronger faultline in the team.

(3) Level of Team Interaction (AveInteraction). A higher number of discussions and comments within a studio generally indicates a greater level of interaction. Hence, this study employs the logarithm of the per capita total number of discussions and comments made by studio members as a measure of team interaction.

(4) Leader Ability and Management Orientation (LeaderAbility & ManagementOrientation). The head and deputy head, who initially established the studio, are responsible for comprehensive management tasks. The LeaderAbility is quantified using the number of contributions made by the head and deputy head. Regarding the ManagementOrientation, this is categorized into task-oriented and relationship-oriented types [10]. A task-oriented management orientation (marked as 1) is inferred when the studio's description includes specific task requirements for members; otherwise, it is considered relationship-oriented (marked as 0).

(5) Control Variables. This study aims to encompass a comprehensive range of variables, including the studio's establishment time (EstablishTime), the number of studio members (StudioSize), the length of the studio's introduction text (DescriptionLength), the average level of studio members (AveMemLevel), the average number of fans per studio member (AvefansTotal), and the average length of the members' introduction texts (AveMemDescriptionLength). Furthermore, to minimize heteroscedasticity, a logarithmic transformation was applied to all continuous variables.

4.3 Empirical Model

We employ causal stepwise regression to test the proposed hypotheses, constructing three distinct linear regression models.

Model 1 examines the impact of team faultlines on team performance and the moderating effect of leadership ability. All control variables are included.

$$TeamPerformance = \beta_0 + \beta_1 TeamFaultline + \beta_2 LeaderAbility$$
$$+ \beta_3 LeaderAbility \times TeamFaultline + Controls + \varepsilon \qquad (2)$$

Model 2 investigates the effect of team faultlines on the extent of team interaction, along with the moderating role of leadership ability. This model also incorporates leaders' team management orientation and all control variables.

$$AveInteraction = \beta_0 + \beta_1 TeamFaultline + \beta_2 ManagementOrientation$$
$$+ \beta_3 LeaderAbility + \beta_4 LeaderAbility \times TeamFaultline + Controls + \varepsilon \qquad (3)$$

Model 3 explores the combined influence of team faultlines, leadership ability and the level of team interaction on team performance. All control variables are included in the analysis.

$$TeamPerformance = \beta_0 + \beta_1 TeamFaultline + \beta_2 AveInteraction$$
$$+ \beta_3 LeaderAbility + \beta_4 LeaderAbility \times TeamFaultline + Controls + \varepsilon \qquad (4)$$

A comprehensive analysis integrating Models 1, 2, and 3 is conducted to assess the mediating effect of team interaction.

5 Results

5.1 Data Analysis and Results

Table 1 present the results of the descriptive statistics. We performed a VIF test, indicating no serious multicollinearity. Table 2 presents the results of Model 1, 2 and 3. As shown in Model 1, Team faultlines significantly negatively affect team performance ($\beta = -0.296$, $p < 0.05$), supporting H1. The interaction between leadership ability and team faultlines is significantly negative ($\beta = -0.457$, $p < 0.01$), supporting H3a. In Model 2, Team faultlines significantly negatively influence the level of team interaction ($\beta = -0.299$, $p < 0.01$), supporting H2a. Moreover, the interaction of leadership ability with team faultlines is significantly negative ($\beta = -0.106$, $p < 0.05$), supporting H3b. Leadership team management orientation significantly positively affect team interaction ($\beta = 0.121$, $p < 0.01$), supporting H4. In Model 3, Team interaction significantly positively influences team performance ($\beta = 0.282$, $p < 0.01$), supporting H2b. Combining the results of Models 1, 2 and 3, the level of team interaction partially mediates the impact of team faultlines on team performance.

Table 1. Descriptive Statistics of Variables

Variable	N	Mean	SD	Min	Max
TeamPerformance	4844	4.129	2.072	0	13.112
TeamFaultline	4844	0.788	0.240	0	1
ManagementOrientation	4844	0.113	0.317	0	1
LeaderAbility	4844	1.822	1.067	0	5.784
AveInteraction	4844	1.235	0.853	0	6.656
StudioSize	4844	1.710	0.535	1.099	3.135
DescriptionLength	4844	3.333	1.067	0.693	5.198
AveMemLevel	4844	0.678	0.234	0	1.705
AveFansTotal	4844	2.218	1.311	0	9.216
AveMemDescriptionLength	4844	1.696	0.955	0	3.932
EstablishTime	4844	2.619	0.851	0	3.970

Table 2. Results of regression analysis

DV	Model 1	Model 2	Model 3
	TeamPerformance	AveInteraction	TeamPerformance
TeamFaultline	−0.296***	−0.299***	−0.210**
	(0.105)	(0.0557)	(0.104)
LeaderAbility	0.951***	0.155***	0.908***
	(0.0243)	(0.0110)	(0.0253)
LeaderAbility × TeamFaultline	−0.457***	−0.106**	−0.426***
	(0.0888)	(0.0423)	(0.0878)
ManagementOrientation		0.121***	
		(0.0388)	
AveInteraction			0.282***
			(0.0327)
Controls	included	included	included
LR chi2	−8430.3	−5140.8	−8380.1
N	4844	4844	4844

* $p < 0.1$, ** $p < 0.05$, *** $p < 0.01$

5.2 Robustness Test

This study employed two methods for robustness test: data truncation and variable substitution. To mitigate the impact of outliers, a 1% bilateral truncation was applied to the continuous variables. In order to more accurately measure studio leadership ability, we use "head" to replace "head" and "deputy head". The results remained consistent under both methods, demonstrating the robustness of the our conclusions.

6 Discussion and Implication

6.1 Discussion of Findings

This study unveils several intriguing findings. Initially, by defining faultlines based on user level and the number of submissions on an online programming learning platform, the study delineates team faultlines aligned with these platform-specific attributes. Consistent with prior research [8, 9], our findings indicate a negative impact of team faultlines on team performance, mediated by team interactions.Secondly, considering the pivotal role of leaders in enhancing team identification in both offline corporate and online self-organized teams, we introduce two classic variables in leadership research: leadership ability and team management orientation [11, 16]. Interestingly, it was found that stronger leadership ability can worsen the negative effects of team faultlines on interaction and performance. This may be due to the fact that strong leadership can create perceptions of autocracy and distrust among team members, resulting in reduced cooperation and communication, ultimately diminishing team performance.Lastly, following conventional leadership research [11], we distinguish between task-oriented and relationship-oriented leadership styles. The empirical result validates the complementary mechanism of team management orientation: directly fostering team interaction and thereby enhancing overall team performance, while mitigating the negative impact of team faultlines in another logical chain.

6.2 Implications

The research offers several theoretical insights. Firstly, our study enriches the relatively scarce research on how faultlines affect the performance of virtual teams by focusing on the unique and emerging context of VPL platforms, and reveals the diversity in how faultlines influence team performance across different types of virtual teams. Secondly, by exploring the mediating role of team interaction – where faultlines indirectly affect team performance, this study contributes to the research on faultline impact mechanisms. Thirdly, this paper introduces the variables of leadership ability and team management orientation to investigate their roles in moderating and complementing the impact of faultlines on virtual team performance. Our findings reveal that leader characteristics and behaviors significantly, yet differently, influence the strengthening or weakening of faultlines' negative effects in virtual teams.

This research also holds significant practical value. For leaders aiming to enhance studio development and overall team performance, it is advisable to adopt measures to mitigate the negative effects of faultlines. During the initial stages of studio development, leaders should avoid overly demonstrating their capabilities, instead adopting a humble approach to signal appreciation for team members' constructive feedback or substantial contributions. This can reduce the obstructive impact of existing faultlines on team interaction. Encouraging members from different subgroups to break barriers, learn from each other, and collectively accumulate experience and improve skills can lead to a qualitative leap in overall team performance.

6.3 Limitations and Future Research

This study is not without limitations. Firstly, the data was exclusively collected from Codemao. This may limit the applicability of our findings to programming platforms active in different cultural contexts. Additionally, this study broadly defines team fault-lines as differences in subgroup alignment within studios based on user level and number of contributions. Future research could endeavor to obtain more comprehensive demographic data (such as gender) through surveys or interviews.

Acknowledgement. This work is partially supported by a grant from the Humanities and Social Sciences Foundation of the Ministry of Education (23YJA630142), a grant from the Social Science Foundation of China (22VRC153), and also supported by a Hubei Universities Provincial Teaching and Research Project (2022059).

References

1. Zhang, X., et al.: Learning performance in block-based programming education for children: predictors and moderator. In: PACIS 2022 Proceedings, pp. 1–16 (2022)
2. Wang, C., et al.: Learning performance and behavioral patterns of online collaborative learning: impact of cognitive load and affordances of different multimedia. Comput. Educ. **143**(2020), 1–14 (2020)
3. Lau, D., Murnighan, J.: Interactions within groups and subgroups: the effects of demographic faultlines. Acad. Manag. J. **48**(4), 645–659 (2005)
4. Thatcher, S.M.B., Patel, P.C.: Group faultlines: a review, integration, and guide to future research. J Manag. **38**(4), 969–1009 (2012)
5. Dulebohn, J.H., Hoch, J.E.: Virtual teams in organizations. Hum. Resour. Manag. R. **27**(4), 569–574 (2017)
6. Cao, F., et al.: Do social dominance-based faultlines help or hurt team performance in crowdsourcing tournaments? J. Manag. Inform. Syst. **39**(1), 247–275 (2022)
7. Bezrukova, K., et al.: Do workgroup faultlines help or hurt? A moderated model of faultlines, team identification, and group performance. Organ. Sci. **20**(1), 35–50 (2009)
8. Yao, J., Liu, X.: The effect of activated resource-based faultlines on team creativity: mediating role of open communication and moderating role of humble leadership. Curr. Psychol. **42**(16), 13411–13423 (2023)
9. Zhang, Y., Chen, H.: How surface-level and deep-level faultlines influence team performance through subgroup formation and team interaction quality: a meta-analytic review. Manag. Organ. Rev. **19**(5), 876–909 (2023)
10. Tabernero, C., et al.: The role of task-oriented versus relationship-oriented leadership on normative contract and group performance. Soc. Behav. Personal. **37**(10), 1391–1404 (2009)
11. Connelly, M.S., et al.: Exploring the relationship of leadership skills and knowledge to leader performance. Leadersh. Q. **11**(1), 65–86 (2000)
12. Ye, S., et al.: Feeling trusted or feeling used? The relationship between perceived leader trust, reciprocation wariness, and proactive behavior. Psychol. Res. Behav. Manag. **14**(2021), 1461–1472 (2021)

13. Hambrick, D.C., et al.: Structural interdependence within top management teams: a key moderator of upper echelons predictions. Strateg. Manag. J. **36**(3), 449–461 (2015)
14. Zhang, H., et al.: A study on the impact of team interdependence on cooperative performance in public-private partnership projects: the moderating effect of government equity participation. Sustainability (Switzerland). **15**(17), 1–22 (2023)
15. Montano, D., et al.: A meta-analysis of the relative contribution of leadership styles to followers' mental health. J. Leadersh. Organ. Stud. **30**(1), 90–107 (2023)
16. Chang, S.-M., Lin, S.S.J.: Team knowledge with motivation in a successful MMORPG game team: a case study. Comput. Educ. **73**(2014), 129–140 (2014)
17. Pregernig, U.: Chapter 16: Breaking bad? The effect of faultline strength and distance on relationship conflict, and performance in teams. A conditional process model. Progr. Int. Bus. Res. **12**(2017), 379–402 (2017)

AI-Enabled Blended Collaborative Education

Xiaoxia Wang[✉]

School of Traffic and Transportation, Beijing Jiaotong University, Beijing 100044, People's
Republic of China
xxwang@bjtu.edu.cn

Abstract. The COVID-19 epidemic has accelerated the worldwide popularization of online education. The birth of generative artificial intelligence has greatly
promoted the widespread application of AI, which also brings great opportunities
and challenges to education. To keep up with the innovative age and address society's needs, this paper explores the digital transformation of education 4.0 based
on a literature review. The findings are as follows: (1) For lifelong learning and
self-improvement education 4.0, the evolution path of technology-based education is illustrated; the elements and composition of AI-based digital education 4.0
is shown, which shaping interactive digital learning environment; (2) Enabling
students to better adjust to the ever-changing social environment, co-creation and
collaborative blended learning is the trend. From the perspective of educational
practice, this paper presents two sets of case studies to demonstrate AI improving
collaborative education and building a collaborative project society. The results
contribute to the education reform in China.

Keywords: Digital Transformation · Collaborative Blended Learning ·
AI-enabled

1 Introduction

The Covid-19 pandemic has accelerated the development and adaptation of online education with IT infrastructure and equipment updates. Schooling takes place at home or
outside school, for regional and international borders disappear. After the emergency, in
November 2022, the ChatGPT model added chat content based on Instruct GPT technology was officially released and opened a test version to the public. A more intelligent
and personalized chat experience of ChatGPT brings challenges and opportunities to the
advancing digital transformation in post-epidemic online education.

School is the condensation and rehearsal of social life (*Xigui Li*). The research
objectives of this paper are as follows. Explore the practical path of digital technology in
expanding school teaching time and space, sharing high-quality resources, optimizing
course content and teaching processes, optimizing student learning methods, and accurately conducting teaching evaluations. Construct a new teaching and learning model
under the digital background, improve school teaching efficiency and quality, reasonably
carry out self-directed learning, and improve the quality of preparatory teaching.

© The Author(s), under exclusive license to Springer Nature Switzerland AG 2024
Y. P. Tu and M. Chi (Eds.): WHICEB 2024, LNBIP 515, pp. 313–324, 2024.
https://doi.org/10.1007/978-3-031-60264-1_27

The research question is with the ChatGPT innovation the digitalization in education has developed to what degree and where to go in the post-COVID-19 environment.

The remainder of this paper is arranged as follows. Section 2 introduces the research method and conducts a literature review; Sect. 3 discusses review results on the digital transformation of personalized education 4.0 to construct co-creation and collaborative blended learning. Section 4 demonstrates case studies in two ways. One is that AI applications are introduced by educational management institutions; the other is driven by teachers and students for a project society. The last section summarized the conclusions.

This study seeks to fill the following gaps in the literature: (1) How AI applications comprehensively improve collaborative education involving institutions, teachers, and students; (2) Empirical case observation for the trend of collaborative project society.

The result will contribute to the practice of education reform in China, such as the *Notice of the General Office of the Ministry of Education on Recommending Experimental Zones and Schools for Compulsory Education Teaching Reform (Education Foundation Office Letter [2023] No. 30).*

2   Research Method and Literature Review

To focus on the impact of the COVID-19 pandemic, the literature is acquired with search expression ("digital transformation" and "digital learning" and ("AI-enabled" or "AI" or "bot" or "customization") within 2020-) in the ScienceDirect database. The preliminary review approach is reading the literature one by one, assisting with ChatFile of Baidu's *YiYan* (ChatGPT bot) and Baidu AI Translation. As a result, the above literature can be divided into the following three categories.

2.1   Review Articles

Mukul and Büyüközkan (2023) [1] contribute a structured overview of Education 4.0 with the digital transformation in education; Ng and Ching et al. (2023) [2] focus on online learning in management education employing a bibliometric and content analysis. Five sub-themes are identified for receiving the most scholarly attention, such as pedagogy, technology, assessment methods, learning outcomes or skills, and challenges. Based on sentiment analysis and a multi-country review of university students' and educators' perceptions of the use of digital and social media platforms, results by Al-Hail and Zguir et al. (2023) indicate that various barriers to effectively fulfilling online learning still exist. Findings also revealed the lack of, and therefore need for, proper teaching and learning material and strategies suitable for digital education [3]. Sarker and Ullah (2023) [4] identified the criteria for quality assessment in e-learning can be centered around five major themes: technological infrastructure, ICT competency, and adaptability, pedagogy for online education, collaboration, partnership, and motivation, as well as a blended learning environment.

2.2 Empirical Studies Following Two Paths

One stream investigates different regions' educational practices, e.g. changes in Indonesian private universities [5]; digital transformation (strategy for)/of higher education in Australia [6], and conflict-affected Syria [7]; the other examines different majors, such as a commentary of business education [8]; a case study of the digital-enabled redesign of entrepreneurship education [9]; AI-enabled talent training for the cross-cultural news communication talent [10].

2.3 AI-Based Perspective

Al Darayseh (2023) [11] employs the technology acceptance model to explore the acceptance of AI in teaching science and finds that the factors of self-efficacy, expected benefits, ease of use, and attitudes toward AI applications have the greatest influence on teachers' behavioral intention towards AI applications. Lakshmi and Kumar et al. (2023) [12] focused on collaborative technical education and addressed how AI can make e-learning more interesting, efficient, and tailored to each learner; and how AI can be used to promote diversity and equity. The future research is to create mixed-reality artifacts and to support collaborative educational environments. In addition, there are some specific cases. For example, Capatina and Patel et al. (2023) [13] explore immersive learning experiences in a safe metaverse to elevate students' lives; Vidanaralage and Dharmaratne et al. (2022) [14] assess the impact of gamified video-based learning through schema and emotion analysis.

3 Review Results and Discussion on Digital Transformation of Education 4.0

Based on the above literature review and focused on the trend of post-pandemic, this part analyzed basic related concepts, clarified the evolutionary path, constructed a framework based on the relationship of elements, and studied the improvement path of AI-based blended collaborative learning for co-creation.

3.1 Personalized Education 4.0

Under the 4th industrial revolution, education 4.0 [1] is a new experience-based education system for lifelong learning and self-improvement, which brings technology, individuality, and exploratory learning into our lives.

Evolution of Technology-based Education Terms. To keep up with the innovative age and address society's needs, the process of education is associated with the evolving technology as Fig. 1, working in Industry 4.0 environments. And transdisciplinary systems approach contributes to the realization of digital transformation [15].

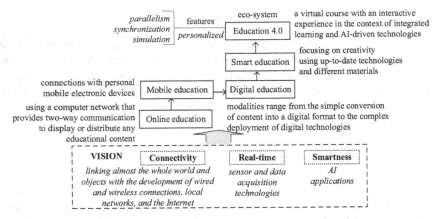

Fig. 1. Definitions and evolution of technology-based education terms.

Interactive Digital Learning Environment. Digital transformation is not just a technical issue, but a comprehensive change involving education models, teaching methods, and the roles of teachers and students as Fig. 2. Teachers have transformed from knowledge transmitters to instructors and facilitators, and even become guides for students' morality, emotion, etc. [11].

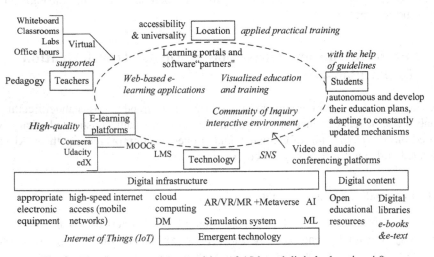

Fig. 2. The elements and composition of AI-based digital education 4.0.

To support learning and development, educational institutions provide not only stable and reliable digital infrastructure with constant upgrading but also easily available sufficient and diversified digital content. E-learning platforms combined with rich interactive tools facilitate knowledge, resources, and expertise exchanging, sharing, and integrating, as a result, promoting collaborative research, interactive communication [16], and cooperation, expanding coverage and influence, increasing the accessibility and universality of education.

3.2 Co-creation and Collaborative Blended Learning

Creatively Education Plans for Innovation. In addition to traditional academic achievements when complying with national or regional curriculum standards, students are encouraged to motivate non-traditional thinking explore independently, and pay more attention to developing their comprehensive quality and ability as Fig. 3 [1], which helps them succeed in their future studies and careers.

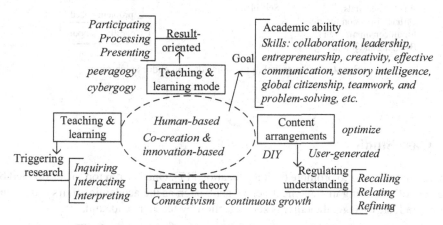

Fig. 3. Co-creation and innovation-based educational system.

Teaching methods and strategies aimed at cultivating students' core competencies, which comply with outcome-based education. Table 1 illustrates analytical skills that produce corresponding thinking.

Table 1. Analytical skills and corresponding thinking.

Analytical skills	Produce thinking
to feel and define world problems correctly	critical
innovative ideas for their solution	creative
to use the right methods and techniques for such solutions	scientific and analytical

Collaborative Blended Learning. For enriched and agile personalized learning, teachers carry out deep redesign courses based on technological pedagogical content knowledge [2] with innovation and efficiency. As Fig. 4, blended learning, which expands equal opportunities in education, combines synchronous and asynchronous learning elements, and encodes based on different learning strategies, bringing synergistic effects [3, 7, 12, 16].

Educators should actively explore interactive, heuristic, exploratory, and experiential teaching methods based on context and problem orientation.

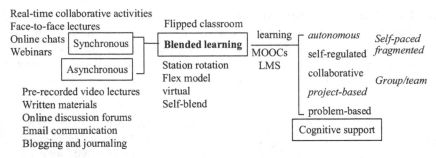

Fig. 4. Instructional approaches design endorse learning.

4   Case Studies

There are two paths to promote digital education [17]. One is from top to bottom, led by the school's teaching management department, such as the academic affairs office, and undergraduate college; the other is self-selection by teachers and students.

4.1   AI Applications Comprehensively Improve Collaborative Education

Undergraduate review and professional certification are two objective criteria to evaluate the quality of teaching in universities. For instance, Fig. 5 presents the architecture diagram of education and teaching products offered by *BEIJING JINGYEDA TECHNOLOGY CO., LTD.* (abbr. *JYD*).

Implement the teaching and examination evaluation of core accomplishments concepts, educational institutions focus on comprehensive, process-oriented, practical, and developmental evaluation, and play the guiding, diagnostic, feedback, and motivating role of evaluation to promote the comprehensive development of students.

For each course or subject, Fig. 6 illustrates digital empowerment and AI-based personalized adaptive learning systems [14], to promote personalized teaching, customized learning, and process evaluation. This provides students with more guidance and support so that they can adapt to self-regulated learning enabling students to better adjust to the ever-changing social environment.

The organic connection between teaching-learning-evaluation follows these steps. (1) Using AI/ML to adapt to different learners and autonomously arrange the learning process, based on self-discipline and time management skills, customize their learning plans (schedules and tasks), and provide flexibility. (2) Assess learning effectiveness

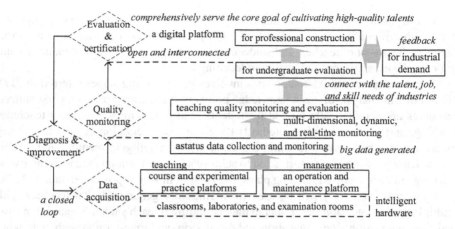

Fig. 5. Architecture diagram of education and teaching products.

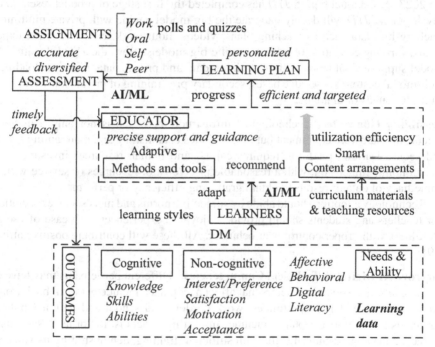

Fig. 6. AI-based adaptive learning customized educational experience

and quality with optimized evaluation methods, explore the implementation of evidence-based evaluation, value-added evaluation, negotiated evaluation, and performance evaluation, and cultivate self-reflection and critical thinking skills. (3) After objectively evaluating and analyzing learning outcomes, guide students to make reasonable use of evaluation results to improve learning strategies and methods. (4) Continuous improvement with self-confidence and self-efficacy. Only with the active participation and continuous adjustment of teachers and students can we better cope with this challenge and improve the effectiveness and quality of teaching [18].

The development of AI components involves the following stages referred to *JYD*. (1) Intelligent analysis of weak knowledge points in the learning process, personalized resources are automatically pushed to students, and a system of intelligent teaching, learning, and practice is constructed; (2) Based on the integration of multimodal big model engines and private teaching big data, virtual intelligent mentors and intelligent teaching assistants are constructed to achieve adaptive learning diagnosis, analysis, warning, and personalized learning plans; (3) A large model + privatized data + AIGC ("AI-generated content") will be used to intelligently generate digital teachers with multiple professional abilities, in-depth understanding of each student's learning needs, real-time interaction, communication and discussion, and long-term growth, achieving personalized education for thousands of people and faces on a large scale. Referring to the 2023 semi-annual report, *JYD* has completed the first stage of product research and development. *JYD* will deeply integrate the big model engine with private multimodal teaching big data such as teaching plans, videos, homework tests, and exam experiments, forming education or school-specific big models. Now, the *JYD* Education Big Model supports dual loading of pre-training data and private data, real-time loading of multimodal custom knowledge bases, secondary pre-training of private knowledge, and multiple rounds of dialogue.

Feasibility Guarantee. Technological infrastructure, which is not only a matter of purchasing hardware equipment but also includes establishing and maintaining a stable and secure learning platform, requires capital and human resources investment. For the economic dimension, with a reasonable price/cost of resources or service with the immediacy of data or results to obtain gratifying efficiency or performance.

Technology adoption should abide by subjective norms and meet social expectations. For teachers and students should provide enjoyable experiences with ease of use and usefulness with proper control over behavior. All these will contribute positive attitude [19].

Improve AI Digital & Technical Competencies. Different participants may have different levels of acceptance. Factors that affect acceptance include personal background, experience, understanding, attitudes, work burden, and school and regional policies. Strategies to increase acceptance include supporting to acquisition of necessary digital literacy, enhancing technical skills with sufficient training, demonstrating its value and potential, building trust and confidence (safety, privacy protection), providing practical opportunities, establishing cooperation and community, considering individual needs, and providing continuous support and feedback.

4.2 Collaborative Project Society

For a learning society and ubiquitous learning, Fig. 7 illustrates the basic general learning framework and methods for collaborative learning.

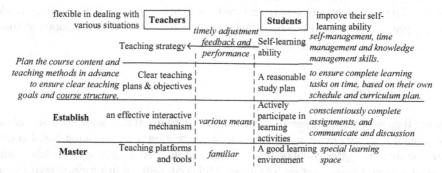

Fig. 7. The general learning framework and methods for collaborative learning.

Here presents learning community tools to demonstrate the continuous innovation and development progress of some learning organizational structures, processes, culture, and achieve.

Swarma Club (pattern). The Swarma Science Community is the most influential scientific community in China with a focus on complex systems, building a research institute without walls.

Xiao'e Tong, a Good Helper for Enterprise Digital Management. Private domain operation is gradually becoming an important means of digital management, and promoting the upgrading of enterprises' business and organizational construction. As a one-stop tool for private domain operations, *Xiao'e Tong* focuses on knowledge products and user services, solving pain points such as product and service delivery, marketing customer acquisition, user operation, organizational role management, and brand value output, and forming a closed loop.

Youshu Academy is Provided by Netease Shufan. *Youshu Academy* is the official learning, training, and communication platform of *NetEase Youshu*. Here, learners can efficiently learn the knowledge and skills of various big data products, and acquire ability endorsements, and career development. At the same time, learners can also use what they have learned to answer questions and clarify, communicate and share with others, and gain happiness.

Luojilab.com for the New Business App. Obtaining the *New Business App*, serving entrepreneurs from small and medium-sized enterprises across the country, providing courses related to business operations, including audio, video, and live classes. The APP will also provide a community for entrepreneurs to discuss and exchange ideas, share experiences, and provide guidance on their entrepreneurial experiences, helping them solve business problems.

Feishu from ByteDance. With a people-oriented user experience and a customer perspective product architecture, *Feishu* is an advanced enterprise collaboration and management platform that integrates functions such as instant communication, calendar, audio and video conferencing, cloud documents, cloud storage, and workbenches, achieving greater efficiency and enjoyment for both organizations and individuals. The genes of internet companies provide it with a lightweight and flat operating mode, greatly promoting enterprise office efficiency and creating infinite development space for efficient and easy collaborative work [20].

5 Conclusions

Facing the challenges of ChatGPT, personalized digitalized education with an interactive digital learning environment should face co-creation and innovation-based educational system and offer collaborative blended learning. And there are two-level loops of teaching-learning-evaluation. The upper level is educational institutions paying more attention to undergraduate review and professional certification; the lower level is teachers and students who care about AI-based adaptive learning customized educational experience. For a ubiquitous learning society, project-based collaborative learning is a trend. For instance, the operation structure of *Swarma Club*, digital features of *Xiao's Tong*, *Youshu Academy* integrated with industry, the *New Business App* offered by Luojilab.com serving entrepreneurs, and *Feishu* from *ByteDance* creating infinite space for efficient and easy collaborative work.

When we focus on innovation and reform, and great importance should be attached to network security and privacy protection to ensure that personal information is not leaked or abused. It is necessary to provide sufficient flexibility and adaptability to cope with emergencies and changes.

It is important to create a cultural atmosphere that supports and encourages digital transformation, be aware of its importance in improving the quality of education, and actively participate in and support the transformation. Strengthen the application training of the national smart education platform, and encourage daily use. The institutions need to engage in more exchanges and cooperation with international partners to obtain more technical support and resource sharing.

The 4th Plenary Session of the 19th Central Committee of the Communist Party of China in 2019 proposed that "data can participate in distribution as a factor of production according to its contribution", clarifying the important concept of the data factor market. The Ministry of Finance issued the *Provisional Regulations on Accounting Treatment of Enterprise Data Resources* on August 21, 2023, which will come into effect on January 1, 2024. The inclusion of data elements in the table refers to the conversion of future costs of an enterprise into assets, so that the value of normally invisible data can be seen, quantified, and recognized. The proposal of data element inclusion in the table aims to standardize the accounting treatment of enterprise data resources and strengthen the disclosure of relevant accounting information. This inclusion is beneficial for visualizing the value of data resources, revitalizing the value of data assets, and promoting digital transformation. In January 2024, the National Data Administration and 17 other departments jointly issued the *"Data Elements ×" The Three Year Action Plan (2024–2026)* aims to promote the high-level application of data elements, promote collaborative optimization, reuse and, efficiency enhancement, and integration innovation of data elements. The market-oriented construction of data elements has progressed from conceptual formation to practical exploration. As a result, new requirements have been proposed for the development direction of education 4.0.

Acknowledgement. This research was supported by the undergraduate education reform project of "Logistics Distribution under the Internet Environment" (textbook) and the postgraduate education reform project of "Managerial Economics" (core course), School of Traffic and Transportation, Beijing Jiaotong University.

References

1. Mukul, E., Büyüközkan, G.: Digital transformation in education: a systematic review of education 4.0. Technol. Forecast. Soc. Change **194**, 122664 (2023)
2. Ng, D.T.K., Ching, A.C.H., Law, S.W.: Online learning in management education amid the pandemic: a bibliometric and content analysis. Int. J. Manag. Educ. **21**(2), 100796 (2023)
3. Al-Hail, M., Zguir, M.F., Koç, M.: University students' and educators' perceptions on the use of digital and social media platforms: a sentiment analysis and a multi-country review. iScience **26**(8), 107322 (2023)
4. Sarker, M.F., Ullah, M.S.: A review of quality assessment criteria in secondary education with the impact of the COVID-19 pandemic. Soc. Sci. Human. Open **8**(1), 100740 (2023)
5. Anggadwita, G., Indarti, N., Ratten, V.: Changes in Indonesian private universities educational practices in the post COVID-19 environment. Int. J. Manag. Educ. **22**(1), 100905 (2024)
6. D'Ambra, J., Akter, S., Mariani, M.: Digital transformation of higher education in Australia: understanding affordance dynamics in E-Textbook engagement and use. J. Bus. Res. **149**, 283–295 (2022)
7. Habib, M.: Digital transformation strategy for developing higher education in conflict-affected societies. Soc. Sci. Human. Open **8**(1), 100627 (2023)
8. Krishnamurthy, S.: The future of business education: a commentary in the shadow of the Covid-19 pandemic. J. Bus. Res. **117**, 1–5 (2020)
9. Secundo, G., Mele, G., Vecchio, P., et al.: Threat or opportunity? A case study of digital-enabled redesign of entrepreneurship education in the COVID-19 emergency. Technol. Forecast. Soc. Chang. **166**, 120565 (2021)
10. Shen, G.: AI-enabled talent training for the cross-cultural news communication talent. Technol. Forecast. Soc. Chang. **185**, 122031 (2022)
11. Al Darayseh, A.: Acceptance of artificial intelligence in teaching science: Science teachers' perspective. Comput. Educ. Artif. Intell. **4**, 100132 (2023)
12. Lakshmi, A.J., Kumar, A., Kumar, M., et al.: Artificial intelligence in steering the digital transformation of collaborative technical education. J. High Technol. Manag. Res. **34**(2), 100467 (2023)
13. Capatina, A., Patel, N., Mitrov, K., et al.: Elevating students' lives through immersive learning experiences in a safe metaverse. Int. J. Inf. Manag. 102723 (2023)
14. Vidanaralage, A.J., Dharmaratne, A.T., Haque, S.: AI-based multidisciplinary framework to assess the impact of gamified video-based learning through schema and emotion analysis. Comput. Educ. Artif. Intell. **3**, 100109 (2022)
15. Hashmi, M.A., Mo, J.P.T., Beckett, R.C.: Transdisciplinary systems approach to realization of digital transformation. Adv. Eng. Inform. **49**, 101316 (2021)

16. De Notaris, D., Canazza, S., Mariconda, C., et al.: How to play a MOOC: practices and simulation. Entertain. Comput. **37**, 100395 (2021)
17. Konstantinou, E., Nachbagauer, A., Wehnes, H.: Editorial: digital learning and education in a project society. Project Leadersh. Soc. **4**, 100083 (2023)
18. Hofer, S.I., Nistor, N., Scheibenzuber, C.: Online teaching and learning in higher education: lessons learned in crisis situations. Comput. Hum. Behav. **121**, 106789 (2021)
19. Yazdani, M., Pamucar, D., Erdmann, A., et al.: Resilient sustainable investment in digital education technology: a stakeholder-centric decision support model under uncertainty. Technol. Forecast. Soc. Chang. **188**, 122282 (2023)
20. Wang, X.: A case study of collaborative learning within a digitalization learning environment. In: Tu, Y., Chi, M. (eds.) WHICEB 2023. LNBIP, vol. 480, pp. 84–94. Springer, Cham (2023). https://doi.org/10.1007/978-3-031-32299-0_8

Can Gamification Motivate Doctors' Online Contributions? Empirical Evidence from an Online Healthcare Platform in China

Zhiying Cheng, Zilong Wang, and Hualong Yang[✉]

Guangdong University of Technology, 161 Yinglong Road, Guangzhou 510520, China
hualongyang_gut@sina.com

Abstract. Online healthcare has enormous potential in optimizing the allocation of medical resources and alleviating the shortage of medical resources in China. As providers of medical services and knowledge on online healthcare platforms, doctors' active contributions are key to the long-term development of these platforms. To incentivize doctors to contribute online, an increasing number of online healthcare platforms are introducing gamification mechanisms. However, it is currently unclear whether and how gamification impacts doctors' online contributions. To investigate this research question, this study built an empirical model based on self-determination theory and social exchange theory. Data from doctors in China's largest online medical platform were collected to validate the impact of gamified achievements on their online contributions. Our findings reveal that doctors' gamified achievements on the platform have a significant positive impact on their online contributions; external rewards received by doctors on the platform (economic and reputation rewards) mediate the relationship between doctors' gamified achievements and their online contributions. Furthermore, this study confirms that doctors' professional status can moderate the relationship between external rewards received by doctors and their online contributions. The results of this study can help us better understand the functions of gamification, provide insights for optimizing the operations of online healthcare platforms, enhancing doctors' understanding of platform mechanisms, and assisting patients in making better decisions when selecting doctors.

Keywords: Online healthcare · gamification · doctor's contribution behavior

1 Introduction

Maintaining and motivating user contribution behavior is a critical challenge faced by online platforms and communities. Negative user engagement may have adverse effects on the sustained operation of the platform [1]. In online healthcare platforms, doctors are the providers of medical services and knowledge, making them a key resource within the platform. Therefore, incentivizing doctors to contribute online is an important way to ensure the sustainable development of online healthcare platforms. In recent years, gamification has garnered widespread attention as a new paradigm for incentivizing user

Y. P. Tu and M. Chi (Eds.): WHICEB 2024, LNBIP 515, pp. 325–336, 2024.
https://doi.org/10.1007/978-3-031-60264-1_28

contribution behavior in online healthcare platforms. Gamification refers to the use of game design elements in non-gaming environments, with the aim of creating experiences similar to those found in gaming environments [2]. By introducing elements such as points, badges, leaderboards, and other gamification features, platforms can enhance user incentives [3], attracting continued usage and promoting sustained user contribution [4]. Currently, gamification mechanisms have been widely applied across various online communities, including online healthcare platforms.

Self-determination theory posits that individual behavior motivation is primarily driven by three basic psychological needs, including autonomy, competence, and relatedness [5]. Autonomy refers to an individual's control and choice over their own behavior; competence needs entail the individual's desire for continuous development and improvement of skills, knowledge, and abilities; and relatedness needs refer to the individual's desire to establish positive, supportive, and meaningful relationships with others. Self-determination theory primarily focuses on innate needs for self-regulation in humans [6] and has been widely applied in online community research to explain the relationship between motivational factors and user contribution [7]. Gamification is considered to be able to fulfill individuals' basic psychological needs. Specifically, the voluntary participation in games can satisfy individuals' need for autonomy; the goals and feedback systems in games can meet individuals' need for competence; and the social connections embedded in game systems can effectively fulfill individuals' need for relatedness. According to self-determination theory, gamification may influence users' online contribution behavior. Research by Von et al. also found that gamification in online Q&A communities can promote user online contributions, with user contributions peaking on the day they receive badges [8]. However, there is relatively limited research on whether gamification can impact user contribution behavior in professional communities such as online healthcare platforms. In online healthcare platforms, gamification is specifically manifested as gamified achievements for doctors, including gamification points, badges, and rankings obtained by doctors. While some studies have confirmed that introducing gamification mechanisms in online healthcare platforms can increase the overall contribution of a department of doctors [9], there is a lack of research at the individual doctor level to explore whether gamified achievements of doctors can incentivize their online contributions. There are limitations in the research perspectives of previous studies.

The motivating factors for promoting user engagement and contribution can generally be categorized into two types: intrinsic motivation and extrinsic motivation. Intrinsic motivation involves individuals performing certain behaviors for the sake of happiness and satisfaction, such as a sense of self-worth and enjoyment in helping others [6]. Extrinsic motivation, on the other hand, involves external rewards such as reputation and monetary incentives [10]. For the group of doctors, providing only intrinsic motivation is not sufficient to sustain their contributions on online medical platforms. Social exchange theory is commonly used to explain social interactions and behaviors in interpersonal relationships, suggesting that all individual actions are exchanges driven by self-interest and rewards [11]. Previous research on doctors' participation in online medical platforms, based on social exchange theory, suggests that their involvement is not purely an economic exchange but a social exchange [12]. This article confirms that a doctor's professional capital can determine the social and economic rewards they receive on the platform. Here, professional capital refers to a special, scarce, durable, and valuable capital possessed by social professionals (such as doctors, lawyers, teachers), which can represent the qualifications and abilities of professionals. In this context, gamified achievements of doctors align with the characteristics of professional capital and can partly reflect the quality of service and attitude of doctors on online medical platforms. However, it remains unclear whether gamified achievements can bring social and economic rewards to doctors.

Furthermore, there is limited research on the moderating effects of physician characteristics on the relationship between motivating factors and physician behavior. The professional status of physicians is often associated with their economic situation and social influence, making it one of the key characteristics influencing physicians' online behavior [12]. Physicians with higher professional status typically have better personal financial situations and higher social standing, whereas those with lower professional status are the opposite. According to goal-setting theory, different goals have different effects on individual performance [13]. This study speculates that doctors with different professional statuses may have different goals when participating in online healthcare platforms, leading to heterogeneity in the impact of incentive factors on doctors with different professional statuses.

Based on the above analysis, this article proposes the following research questions: (1) Can physicians' gamified achievements influence their online contributions? (2) What is the mechanism through which physicians' gamified achievements affect their online contributions? (3) Does physicians' professional status moderate the relationship between motivating factors and online contributions? To address the research questions posed, this study collected data from 55,479 physicians on China's largest online medical platform, "Haodf," over a period of three months to test our hypotheses and run our research model. The results of the study indicate: (1) Physicians' gamified achievements can promote their online contributions on the online medical platform; (2) Gamified achievements can bring economic and reputational rewards to physicians, with economic and reputational rewards partially mediating the effect of physicians' gamified achievements on their online contributions; (3) Physicians' professional status plays a moderating role in the rewards gained by physicians and their online contributions, with lower-status physicians placing more importance on economic and reputational rewards compared to higher-status physicians.

This study makes several contributions. Firstly, it validates at the individual physician level that gamified achievements can enhance physicians' online contributions, further exploring the functionality of gamification and supplementing research perspectives on gamification and user-generated content. Secondly, by employing social exchange theory, this article reveals the mechanism through which physicians' gamified achievements influence their online contributions, identifying the motivating role of physicians' external needs on their contributions and expanding the application scope of social exchange theory. Lastly, by integrating goal-setting theory, this study explores the moderating effect of physicians' professional status on the relationship between motivating factors and online contributions. It provides practical insights for the management personnel of online healthcare platforms to optimize system design.

2   Theory and Hypothesis

2.1   Gamification Achievements and Doctor's Contribution Behavior

In online medical platforms, physicians' contribution behaviors mainly involve providing medical services to patients and sharing medical knowledge and information. Since knowledge and information are considered personal to physicians [10], physicians' online contributions need to be motivated by relevant factors. According to self-determination theory, individuals' behavioral motivation is primarily driven by psychological needs for autonomy, competence, and relatedness. In online healthcare platforms, the gamified achievements obtained by physicians through gamification design can provide intrinsic motivation for physicians' online contributions. Specifically, firstly, the ways in which physicians achieve gamified achievements on the platform are not unique, indicating a high level of autonomy for physicians. Secondly, the gamification mechanisms in online healthcare platforms provide clear goals for physicians, and physicians' online contributions can be displayed through gamified achievements such as points, badges, or leaderboards, providing timely feedback to satisfy their need for competence. Lastly, achieving physicians' gamified achievements requires utilizing the social attributes of online healthcare platforms to engage in good communication with patients, meeting the interpersonal relationship needs of the physician. In summary, physicians' gamified achievements can effectively satisfy physicians' psychological needs, generating intrinsic motivation to promote physicians' online contributions. Based on this, this article proposes the following research hypothesis:

Hypothesis 1: Gamification achievements of doctors on online healthcare platforms positively influence their contribution behavior.

2.2   Analysis of the Mechanisms Through Which Gamification Achievements Impact Doctor's Online Contribution

Compared to traditional offline medical channels, online healthcare platforms can more efficiently provide recognition and rewards to physicians. Previous research has shown that physicians in online healthcare platform receive two significant types of rewards: social rewards and economic rewards [12]. Social rewards mainly include a physician's visibility and reputation within the community, including the number of virtual gifts, thank-you notes, and likes received. Social rewards are crucial for physicians in online healthcare platforms because they not only represent recognition of their abilities and work, motivating physicians, but also help attract more patients. In addition to social rewards, online healthcare platforms can also provide economic rewards to physicians, primarily including fees earned from consulting patients and electronic gifts given by patients. Economic rewards are a direct form of compensation that can offset the costs of contributions made by physicians in the platform while also meeting their financial needs.

The doctor-patient communication in online healthcare platforms is a form of social exchange behavior, not just economic exchange. There exists a significant information asymmetry between doctors and patients, with patients facing higher risks. Therefore, in addition to economic exchanges, the healthcare system needs to establish interactive relationships to foster gratitude and trust. According to social exchange theory, the process of doctors' online contributions can be seen as a social exchange process, where doctors provide medical services to patients, and patients, in return, have the obligation to bring rewards such as money and reputation to doctors. Previous research has used the concept of professional capital to explain the prerequisites for doctors to receive economic and social rewards on online medical platforms. Professional capital can be divided into two aspects: status capital and decision capital. Status capital represents individual and social advantages, while decision capital refers to the ability to make correct judgments and commit to social professions. The research findings indicate that doctors' status capital and decision capital have a significant positive impact on their social and economic rewards [12]. Doctors' gamified achievements align with the characteristics of professional capital, reflecting not only their status in the community but also the level of time and effort invested and their professional abilities, which can bring economic and social rewards to doctors.

Money is a tangible form of reward that individuals use to improve their financial situation [13], and it is also a crucial factor in promoting doctors' contributions online. In online healthcare platforms, doctors primarily receive economic rewards through online consultations or phone consultations, and after the consultation is completed, patients can also purchase electronic gifts to provide financial feedback to the doctors. According to social exchange theory, individual behavior is aimed at maximizing benefits, and when the economic rewards obtained from doctors' online contributions can meet their own needs and cover the costs they incur, doctors have the motivation to continue contributing. Additionally, based on research by Ryan and Deci, although economic rewards may not directly satisfy doctors' intrinsic needs, these external motivational factors can indirectly translate into intrinsic motivators, thereby promoting doctors' online contributions.

Reputation is an external motivational factor that enhances personal image [14]. In online healthcare platforms, doctors' reputation rewards mainly come from patients' ratings, reviews, electronic gifts, thank-you letters, and more. Positive feedback from patients helps doctors establish online credibility, build a good reputation, and attract more online patients. Conversely, negative feedback can significantly impact doctors in healthcare platforms built on trust. Research by Liu et al. found a positive correlation between doctors' appointment numbers and their offline and online reputations, indicating that online reputation directly influences doctors' professional influence and holds significant importance for them. Therefore, this study proposes the following hypothesis:

Hypothesis 2: Economic rewards mediate the relationship between gamified achievements and doctors' contribution behavior.

Hypothesis 3: Reputation rewards mediate the relationship between gamified achievements and doctors' contribution behavior.

2.3 Analysis of the Moderating Role of Doctor's Professional Status

In online healthcare platforms, professional status refers to a doctor's professional title, ranking, and position in the hospital. In China, doctors' professional titles range from low to high, including resident physician, attending physician, associate chief physician, and chief physician. A doctor's professional status reflects their professional knowledge and achievements in the healthcare field, serving as an important signal for patients when choosing a doctor [15]. Generally, doctors with higher professional status have better offline financial conditions [12] and can also gain more reputation and gamified achievements on online medical platforms. Therefore, for doctors with different professional status, there are significant differences in the impact of different motivational factors on doctors' online contributions.

Goal-setting theory suggests that different goals have different effects on individual performance, and individuals can also set and manage their performance through self-regulation. Existing research has shown that when easier goals are set, individuals' performance will be lower compared to when more difficult goals are set. Doctors with higher professional status often need to deal with more offline patients, leaving limited energy for online patients. When doctors have limited energy, the difficulty level of the goals is often set lower [16], leading to lower willingness and intensity of online contributions compared to doctors with lower professional status. Additionally, due to inconsistent intrinsic needs, doctors with different professional statuses have different goal settings when entering the health community. Doctors with higher professional status already have sufficient economic and reputational rewards, and their contributions to the community are more motivated by intrinsic factors. Their demand for external incentives such as economic and reputational rewards is relatively lower compared to doctors with lower professional status, and the goals they expect to achieve in the community are relatively easier. Therefore, the following hypothesis is proposed:

Hypothesis 4: Economic rewards have a stronger positive effect on doctors with lower professional status than on doctors with higher professional status.

Hypothesis 5: Reputational rewards have a stronger positive effect on doctors with lower professional status than on doctors with higher professional status.

Figure 1 shows the research model in this paper.

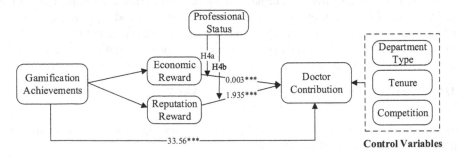

Fig. 1. Research model

3 Empirical Research

3.1 Data Analysis

The data in this study comes from the most famous online healthcare platform "Haodafu" website in China (www.haodf.com). This website is very popular among doctors, so it can provide rich data for the research in this article. To ensure that our sample is unbiased, this study collected data from doctors in all departments. After deleting invalid data, such as incomplete doctor information or doctors no longer using online consultation services on the website, this article collected data from 55479 doctors from December 2022 to February 2023 to test our hypothesis and run our research model.

3.2 Research Model

Main Effect Model

Our research establishes an empirical model to examine the impact and mechanism of gamification achievements on doctors' online contribution in online healthcare platforms. Our empirical model adopts fixed effects. The empirical model is as follows:

$$DocContribution_{i,t} = a_i + \beta_0 + \beta_1 Achievement_{i,t} + \beta_2 \log(Tenure)_{i,t}$$

$$+\beta_3 Competition_{i,t} + \beta_4 DepartmentType_{i,t} + v_i + u_t + \varepsilon_{i,t} \tag{1}$$

where $i = 1, 2, \ldots$, represents the sample doctor, t represents the month, log (Tenure), Competition, DepartmentType represents the control variable, u_i represents the fixed effect of time, and v_i represents the fixed effect of an individual, ε is a random perturbation term, β is the parameter to be estimated. This study uses a fixed effects model to conduct regression tests on formula (1).

Moderation Effect Model

Using the mediation effect model to test Hypothesis 2 and 3, the testing process is divided into three steps: first, to test the impact of the gamification achievement on doctors' online contribution; Secondly, to examine the impact of the mediating variable on doctors' online contribution. If it is not significant, stop testing; Finally, to examine the impact of mediating variables and gamification achievement on doctors' online contribution. Therefore, the following mediation effect model is constructed:

$$y_{i,t} = a_0 + a_1 x_{i,t} + a_j Controls + year_t + cp_i + \varepsilon_{i,t} \tag{2}$$

$$m_{i,t} = b_0 + b_1 x_{i,t} + b_j Controls + year_t + cp_i + \varepsilon_{i,t} \tag{3}$$

$$y_{i,t} = c_0 + c_1 x_{i,t} + c_2 m_{i,t} + c_j Controls + year_t + cp_i + \varepsilon_{i,t} \tag{4}$$

3.3 Empirical Results

Results of Main Effect

Our empirical model was examined using Stata 16. The results of our empirical model are presented in Table 1. First, H1 suggests that gamification achievements are positively associated with doctors' online contribution. The empirical results support H1 ($\beta = 33.56$, $p < 0.01$), which implies that an increase in doctor's gamification achievement leads to an increase in their consultations with patients. In terms of controlling variables, the length of doctors' usage time in online healthcare platforms has a significant impact on their contribution; The effort level of department colleagues has a significant impact on the contribution of doctors. The type of department where a doctor is located has a significant impact on their contribution.

Results of Mediation Effect

Our research also examines the mediation effect. Hypotheses H2 and H3 suggest that economic reward and reputation reward mediate the relationship between gamification achievements and doctors' contribution behavior. These hypotheses are supported by empirical results. Firstly, the empirical results mentioned earlier demonstrate a significant influence of gamification achievements on doctors' contribution behavior. Secondly, using Eq. (3), we tested the impact of gamification achievements on economic reward and reputation reward, and the regression results are presented in Table 1. Specifically, an increase in doctors' gamification achievements significantly increases economic reward ($b_1 = 3357.6$, $p < 0.01$), and it also has a significant positive effect on reputation reward ($b_1 = 1.488$, $p < 0.01$). Thirdly, following the testing requirements mentioned earlier, we used Eq. (4) to examine the mediating effect by incorporating the significantly influenced variables as the mediator variables. From Table 1, it can be observed that even after including the mediator variable of economic reward in the baseline regression, the coefficient of doctors' contribution behavior remains significant ($\beta = 22.87$, $p < 0.01$), and the coefficient of economic reward is also significant ($c_2 = 0.00318$, $p < 0.01$), indicating that higher economic reward leads to greater doctors' online contribution. Thus, economic reward partially mediates the relationship. Similarly, after including the mediator variable of reputation reward in the baseline regression, the coefficient of doctors' contribution behavior remains significant ($\beta = 30.68$, $p < 0.01$), and the coefficient of reputation reward is also significant ($c_2 = 1.935$, $p < 0.01$), suggesting that higher reputation reward leads to greater doctors' online contribution. Therefore, reputation reward partially mediates the relationship. Consequently, it can be concluded that increasing economic and reputation rewards for doctors serves as an important mediating pathway through which gamification achievements promote doctors' contribution behavior.

Results of Moderating Effect

In order to further investigate whether the external motivation of doctors with different professional status has heterogeneity to their online contribution, this study categorized the sample doctors into two groups: low-professional status and high-professional status, and conducted grouped regression analysis. Regression shows that for doctors with high-professional status and low-professional status, economic reward can promote their online contribution. In addition, the results of grouped regression also showed that the

Table 1. Empirical results

Variables	DocContribution	EconomicReward	DocContribution	ReputationReward	DocContribution
Achievement	33.56*** (32.81)	3357.6*** (11.17)	22.87*** (15.59)	1.488*** (18.27)	30.68*** (25.41)
Economic Reward			0.003*** (5.71)		
Reputation Reward					1.935*** (3.54)
LnTenure	−0.594* (−1.91)	211.0*** (4.84)	−2.187*** (−5.36)	−0.0177 (−0.84)	−0.559 (−1.87)
Competition	0.065*** (5.21)	8.234** (2.98)	−1.265*** (−4.67)	0.00174* (1.99)	0.062*** (5.20)
Department Type	−2.503*** (−5.36)	−99.47 (−1.12)	0.039*** (3.40)	−0.0846* (−2.07)	1.935*** (3.54)
Constant	−105.5*** (−26.08)	−12891.8*** (−10.44)	−64.49*** (−11.66)	−4.820*** (−14.02)	−96.21*** (−21.37)
Individual	Yes	Yes	Yes	Yes	Yes
Period	Yes	Yes	Yes	Yes	Yes
N	166095	166100	166095	166100	166095
R2	0.1977	0.1909	0.5826	0.1933	0.2705

coefficient of doctors with low-professional status ($\beta = 0.014$, $p < 0.01$) was higher than that of doctors with high-professional status ($\beta = 0.003$, $p < 0.01$). In order to verify whether the coefficient difference between the two groups is significant, this paper makes a seemingly unrelated estimation (suest) of the grouped regression results, and the empirical P value of the difference is 0.00, indicating that there is heterogeneity in the incentive effect of economic return on doctors with different professional status. The incentive effect of economic reward on the online contribution of doctors with low-professional status is stronger than that of doctors with high-professional status. Doctors with low-professional status may prefer to get more economic reward from the online healthcare platforms to make up for the lack of offline economic reward.

This study also analyzed the heterogeneity of reputation reward on doctors' online contributions with different characteristics. The grouped regression results show that for doctors with high and low professional status, reputation rewards can promote their online contributions. The results of group regression also showed that the coefficient of doctors with low professional status ($\beta = 4.151$, $p < 0.01$) was higher than that of doctors with high professional status ($\beta = 1.889$, $p < 0.01$). Furthermore, a seemingly unrelated estimation was conducted on the grouped regression results, and the empirical P-value of the coefficient difference was 0.0789, which is significant at the 10% level, indicating heterogeneity in the motivational effect of reputation reward on doctors of different professional status. The incentive effect of reputation rewards on doctors' online contributions with low-professional status is stronger than that of doctors with high-professional status. Compared to doctors with higher professional status, doctors with lower professional status may prefer to gain a comparative advantage in reputation from online healthcare platforms (Table 2).

Table 2. Moderating effect of doctor's professional status

Variables	Low-professional status	High-professional status	Low-professional status	High-professional status
Economic Reward	0.014*** (5.27)	0.003*** (5.27)		
Reputation Reward			4.151*** (5.55)	1.889** (3.29)
LnTenure	−0.426 (−0.90)	0.176 (0.42)	1.105 (1.67)	1.514** (3.13)
Competition	0.033 (1.84)	0.051** (3.28)	0.078** (3.29)	0.087*** (5.48)
Department Type	0.072 (0.09)	−1.949** (−3.25)	−0.442 (−0.44)	−1.769** (−2.60)
Constant	4.858 (1.51)	4.826 (1.48)	−4.698 (−0.96)	−4.550 (−1.20)
Individual	Yes	Yes	Yes	Yes
Period	Yes	Yes	Yes	Yes
N	42879	123216	42879	123216
R2	0.4266	0.5883	0.1256	0.1445
Suest	0.00		0.0798	

4   Discussion and Implications

4.1   Discussion

This study explored the impact of gamification achievement on doctors' contribution behavior in online healthcare platforms and its mechanism. Table 3 shows the hypothesis testing results in this paper.

Table 3. Hypothesis testing results

Hypotheses		Support
H1	Gamification Achievements → Doctor Contribution	Yes
H2	Economic Reward → Doctor Contribution	Yes
H3	Reputation Reward → Doctor Contribution	Yes
H4a	Professional Status → Economic Reward and Doctor Contribution	Yes
H4b	Professional Status → Reputation Reward and Doctor Contribution	Yes

First, gamification achievements can promote doctors to contribute in online healthcare platforms. Gamification can satisfy doctors' intrinsic needs, including autonomy, competence, and relatedness, thereby motivating them to make contributions online. Second, the economic and reputational rewards that doctors receive are important mediating factors in the process of gamified achievements promoting their online contributions. Gamified achievements can bring economic and reputational rewards to doctors, thereby promoting their online contributions. The gamification achievements of doctors can be seen as a professional capital for doctors, which can reduce the decision-making risks of patients in the case of information asymmetry between doctors and patients, thereby attracting more online patients for doctors. On the other hand, achieving the achievements of doctors requires a significant amount of cost. Only when patients who are attracted to the doctor can bring external benefits that cover the cost, can the doctor's contribution behavior continue and complete the closed loop of social exchange. Third, this study also found that there is heterogeneity in the promotion effect of external incentive factors on doctors' online contribution with different professional status. Doctors with lower professional status place more emphasis on economic and reputation rewards than those with higher professional status. There are significant differences in the external needs and goals that doctors with different professional status hope to achieve in the community. Doctors with lower professional status have a higher demand and intensity for economic and reputation rewards than those with higher professional status. From the perspective of goal setting, the difficulty of achieving goals for doctors with low-professional status is generally higher than that of doctors with high-professional status, so there are also differences in their contributions.

4.2　Implications

This study has made several theoretical contributions. Firstly, while there have been numerous studies exploring factors influencing user participation and contribution in online communities, research on doctors' online contributions is relatively scarce. This study utilized individual-level data of doctors to confirm the positive impact of gamified achievements on their online contributions in medical platforms, providing a new perspective on the study of doctors' contribution behaviors. Secondly, this research incorporated social exchange theory to consider how gamified achievements provide external incentives to doctors, treating doctors' online contributions as a dynamic social exchange process, revealing the mechanism through which gamified achievements influence doctors' online contributions. Lastly, based on goal-setting theory, this study confirmed significant differences in the effects of external incentives such as economic rewards and reputation on the online contributions of doctors with different professional statuses, showing that doctors with different goals contribute to online medical platforms to varying degrees. This finding enhances our understanding of the impact of various motivations on different doctors and contributes to the literature on online medical platforms.

This study also offers practical implications. Firstly, for operators of online medical platforms, gamification mechanisms can indeed motivate doctors to make online contributions, so platforms should prioritize and improve relevant mechanisms. Additionally, for doctors with relatively low gamified achievements, platforms can consider providing them with some degree of resource tilt to promote their continued contributions, thereby increasing the overall activity of the medical community. Furthermore, the conclusions of this study suggest that platforms should implement different incentive measures for doctors with different professional statuses to maximize their contributions on the platform. Secondly, for the group of doctors, the conclusions of this study can encourage them to focus on their gamified achievements and adjust their platform operation strategies in a timely manner. Thirdly, for patients, given the asymmetry of knowledge and information between doctors and patients, this study suggests that patients can evaluate doctors' abilities and qualifications through their gamified achievements, assisting patients in choosing doctors to obtain higher quality online medical services.

Acknowledgement. This study was partially funded by the National Natural Science Foundation of China Grant (72001049; 71901073).

References

1. Ren, Y., Kraut, R., Kiesler, S.: Applying common identity and bond theory to design of online communities. Organ. Stud. **28**(3), 377–408 (2007)
2. Deterding, S., Dixon, D., Khaled, R., et al.: From game design elements to gamefulness: defining "gamification". Paper presented at the Proceedings of the 15th International Academic MindTrek Conference: Envisioning Future Media Environments (2011)
3. Hamari, J., Koivisto, J., Sarsa, H.: Does gamification work? – A literature review of empirical studies on gamification. Paper presented at the 2014 47th Hawaii International Conference on System Sciences (2014)
4. Harwood, T., Garry, T.: An investigation into gamification as a customer engagement experience environment. J. Serv. Mark. **29**(6/7), 533–546 (2015)
5. Ryan, R.M., Deci, E.L.: Self-determination theory and the facilitation of intrinsic motivation, social development, and well-being. Am. Psychol. **55**(1), 68 (2000)
6. Xi, N., Hamari, J.: Does gamification satisfy needs? A study on the relationship between gamification features and intrinsic need satisfaction. Int. J. Inf. Manag. **46**, 210–221 (2019)
7. Dholakia, U.M., Bagozzi, R.P., Pearo, L.K.: A social influence model of consumer participation in network-and small-group-based virtual communities. Int. J. Res. Mark. **21**(3), 241–263 (2004)
8. von Rechenberg, T., Gutt, D., Kundisch, D.: Goals as reference points: empirical evidence from a virtual reward system. Decis. Anal. **13**(2), 153–171 (2016)
9. Liu, J., Zhang, X., Meng, F., et al.: Deploying gamification to engage physicians in an online health community: an operational paradox. Int. J. Prod. Econ. **228**, 107847 (2020)
10. Sun, Y., Fang, Y., Lim, K.H.: Understanding sustained participation in transactional virtual communities. Decis. Support Syst. **53**(1), 12–22 (2012)
11. Homans, G.C.: Social behavior as exchange. Am. J. Sociol. **63**(6), 597–606 (1958)
12. Guo, S., Guo, X., Fang, Y., et al.: How doctors gain social and economic returns in online health-care communities: a professional capital perspective. J. Manag. Inf. Syst. **34**(2), 487–519 (2017)
13. Latham, G.P., Locke, E.A.: Self-regulation through goal setting. Organ. Behav. Hum. Decis. Process. **50**(2), 212–247 (1991)
14. Li, D., Hu, L.: Exploring the effects of reward and competition intensity on participation in crowdsourcing contests. Electron. Mark. **27**, 199–210 (2017)
15. Lin, H.F.: The role of online and offline features in sustaining virtual communities: an empirical study. Internet Res. **17**(2), 119–138 (2007)
16. Dang, Y., Guo, S., Song, H., et al.: Setting goal difficulty in monetary incentives to physicians: evidence from an online health knowledge-sharing platform. Inf. Technol. People (ahead-of-print) (2023)

Research on the Combination Model Based on DPMM and IForest

Jiangping Wan[⊠], Siting Lin, and Yinsuo Zhang

School of Business Administration, South China University of Technology, Guangzhou 510640, China
csjpwan@scut.edu.cn

Abstract. This paper proposes a combined model based on DPMM (Dirichlet Process Mixture Model) and IForest (Isolation Forest), providing an effective solution to address the challenges of cold start and customer drift in credit risk management. Focusing on the scenario of a large amount of unlabeled data in credit risk management, the approach initially employs DPMM to cluster a small number of labeled normal and default samples. By calculating the Euclidean distance between unlabeled samples and each cluster, the model obtains a default similarity score for the unlabeled samples. Subsequently, considering the imbalance in sample distribution, the IForest algorithm constructs multiple random isolation trees to identify anomalies in the dataset, calculating the anomaly score as a measure of default abnormality. Finally, a weighted combination of the default similarity and anomaly scores from the two models is used for classification of unlabeled samples. Simulation experiments on the German credit risk dataset, with IForest model and self-training model as two control groups, demonstrate that the combined model exhibits superior predictive performance, particularly in scenarios with a low proportion of default samples, effectively mitigating the challenges associated with the cold start problem.

Keywords: Cold start problem · Dirichlet Process Mixture Model (DPMM) · Isolation Forest · Mixture model

1 Introduction

Credit business holds a significant share in the field of Internet finance [1]. Commercial banks and financial institutions can provide credit services to individual customers through online platforms, aiming to meet the financial needs of individuals or small and micro-enterprises. The current online credit business faces two major challenges: the cold start problem and customer drift. Emerging online lending platforms often encounter challenges in acquiring a sufficient number of investors and borrowers at the initial stage. The platform's lack of sufficient participants can lead to liquidity shortages, impacting its operation and development. Accompanying the cold start problem is the issue of customer drift. In the initial stage of platform development, its efficient and convenient features make it easier to attract high-net-worth and creditworthy borrowers. However, with intense market competition and changes in regulatory policies, platforms, to further expand profit margins, choose to increase efforts in customer diversification. With the expansion of the customer base, the platform comes into contact with a more diverse group of borrowers with varying credit conditions, including those with higher credit risks that are difficult to assess. This increases the platform's credit risk, making it susceptible to possibilities of overdue payments and bad debts.

This article introduces machine learning techniques into credit risk models, proposing an approach that combines Dirichlet Process Mixture Models (DPMM) and Isolation Forest (IForest) to address the cold start problem and enhance the accuracy of user default predictions. The credit risk model is essentially a supervised binary classification model aimed at predicting whether users applying for loans pose a default risk. Firstly, for a small amount of labeled data, DPMM is employed to model the data, clustering labeled normal and default samples separately. This method does not require specifying the number of clusters, automatically determining the cluster quantity, thus avoiding the impact of manually specifying cluster numbers. Considering the limited number of labeled samples, Gibbs sampling is used to solve the DPMM model. After clustering labeled samples, the default similarity of unlabeled samples is computed based on the distance between unlabeled samples and each cluster center. Secondly, for a large amount of unlabeled data, considering the issue of imbalanced sample distribution where the number of normal users far exceeds default users, and the behavior of default users is unpredictable, unsupervised anomaly detection algorithm IForest is employed to calculate the default anomaly degree of unlabeled samples. Finally, combining default similarity and default anomaly degree, the classification and iteration of unlabeled samples are completed for prediction. The technical roadmap of the study is illustrated in Fig. 1.

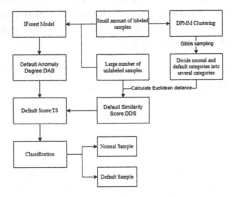

Fig. 1. Technology Roadmap

2 Current Research Status at Home and Abroad

In 1936, Fisher [1] introduced credit discriminant analysis based on grouping problems, laying a crucial foundation for subsequent research. Altman [2] proposed the classic Z-score model, fitting data using multivariate regression to measure the credit risk level of the borrowing party. Empirical studies by Campbell et al. [3] and Charitou et al. [4]

employed the Logit model, revealing factors such as unemployment rate, interest rate, loan-to-value ratio, among others, influencing loan risk levels. Bill Fair and others developed the FICO (Fair Isaac Corporation) scoring system, assigning different weights to five dimensions (customer's credit repayment history, number of credit accounts, length of credit usage, types of credit in use, and newly opened credit accounts), ultimately calculating the user's credit score for decision-making [1]. Traditional credit assessment models primarily rely on reviewing individual credit histories and the FICO scoring system. This model, in some cases, tends to exclude specific groups lacking traditional credit histories, such as young people or new immigrants. The rise of big data, blockchain, cloud computing, and other digital technologies has brought revolutionary changes to credit assessment models. By collecting and analyzing large-scale data, including but not limited to consumer behavior and social media activity data, financial institutions can customize credit assessment schemes, effectively improving assessment accuracy and specificity. For example, Tsang et al. [5] combined deep learning models with a genetic algorithm to construct a hybrid model, validated on the German credit dataset, demonstrating excellent predictive performance. Rishehchi et al. [6], through social network analysis, derived network metrics for cooperating participants in the surveyed SCF. They integrated these metrics with six classification algorithms (including Naive Bayes, Logistic Regression, Multilayer Perceptron, Random Forest, Logistic Model Trees, REP Tree, Sequential Minimal Optimizations) to develop an enhanced predictive model. Caruso et al. [7] considered quantitative and qualitative customer features, proposing a clustering method based on mixed data. Experimental results confirmed the clustering method's untapped potential in estimating credit risk.

Compared to foreign countries, domestic research in this field started relatively late, primarily focusing on the factors, measurement, and management of credit risk, yielding substantial results. For instance, Luo Jinhui et al. [8] conducted research on P2P platforms, indicating that the problem of asymmetric information between the supply and demand sides of funds leads to an increase in bank credit risk. Hu Lingling [9] pointed out in her study that the proficiency of financial institution staff and whether business units meet quality standards are significant factors affecting statistical indices in credit risk management. Concerning the measurement of credit risk, Yu Muqing et al. [10] demonstrated the adaptability of the KMV model in quantitatively assessing bank credit risk. Zeng Lingling [11] combined the KMV model with BP neural networks for measurement. Gao Yijie [12] constructed six basic models of machine learning, optimizing each basic model's parameters and integrating them using methods like Voting and Adaboost. Experimental results showed that Adaboost significantly improved the effectiveness of basic models.

In practical applications, especially in the initial stages of credit product development or when dealing with emerging markets, there is often a situation of extremely limited labeled data or a large amount of unlabeled data. Due to the insufficient amount of labeled data, the predictive accuracy of traditional models is severely affected, highlighting the importance of improving model robustness in cold start scenarios. The advantage of integrated models lies in their combination of the strengths of different technologies and methods, overcoming the limitations of a single model. DPMM, as a non-parametric Bayesian method, possesses high flexibility and adaptability, effectively handling a small amount of labeled data or even unlabeled data, thereby addressing data scarcity or cold start issues. In contrast, IForest, as an anomaly detection method, efficiently identifies abnormal samples in large-scale unlabeled data, providing robust support for discovering potential risk signals. Considering these factors, this paper proposes a combined model based on DPMM and an enhanced version of IForest to tackle the cold start problem in credit risk management. By leveraging the strengths of both models, this approach more accurately assesses credit risk in the absence of labeled data, offering financial institutions a more reliable risk management tool when facing emerging markets or introducing new products.

3 Construction of the Credit Risk Control Model

The sample space is defined as $X = R^d$. The sample label set is denoted as $Y = \{-1, 0, +1\}$. The Y value of $+1$ indicates that the user has defaulted on repayment, making it a default sample. When $Y = 0$, the sample is considered normal. For $Y = -1$, the sample is unlabeled. The dataset can be represented as $D = \{(x_1, y_1), \ldots, (x_l, y_l) \ldots (x_n, y_n)\}$, where n is the total number of samples. It is assumed that the first l samples in the dataset constitute the labeled sample set D^l, and the remaining n-l samples form the unlabeled sample set D^u. The unlabeled samples include both normal and default samples, with the normal sample set denoted as D_0^l and the default sample set as D_{+1}^l.

3.1 Calculation of Default Similarity Based on DPMM Model

Overview of DPMM Model The DP (Dirichlet distribution) is commonly used to describe the prior distribution of parameters in a multinomial distribution. The DP characterizes the probability distribution parameters defined in a discrete space. The DP is an extension of the Dirichlet distribution to continuous spaces. The definition is as follows: suppose there exists a random probability distribution G_0 defined on a measure space Ω, α is a concentration parameter, and $A_1 \ldots A_r$ are arbitrary finite partitions of the measure space θ, $\Omega = A_1 \cup A_2 \cup \ldots A_r$. A probability distribution G on the space θ satisfies:

$$(G(A_1), \ldots, G(A_r)) \sim \text{Dirichlet}(\alpha G_0(A_1), \ldots, \alpha G_0(A_r)) \tag{1}$$

It is considered that G follows a DP with parameters G_0 and α, denoted as $G \sim DP(G_0, \alpha)$. Here, G_0 represents some base distribution, and as the value of α increases, the distribution of G_0 and G becomes closer.

The construction methods of the DP mainly include three approaches: stick-breaking, Chinese Restaurant Process (CRP), and Polya urn scheme [1]. Among these, the CRP, compared to the other two construction methods, exhibits excellent clustering characteristics and stronger interpretability, making it widely applicable. This study adopts the CRP for construction. The construction process is as follows: assuming there is an infinite number of tables available for customers in a restaurant, and each table can accommodate any number of customers. The first customer who arrives sits at the first table. For the nth new customer, the following two rules are followed: first, if choosing to sit at a table with people, the probability is proportional to the number of customers already at the table, given by $\frac{n_k}{\alpha_0+n-1}$ (where n_k represents the current number of customers at table k); second, if choosing to sit at an empty table, the corresponding probability is $\frac{\alpha_0}{\alpha_0+n-1}$. When employing CRP for clustering, each table can be considered as a class, and there is no need to specify the number of categories; the model will adaptively choose the number of categories during the training process.

The DP exhibits favorable clustering properties, allowing samples with the same values to be grouped together. However, when data groups are not entirely identical, the DP struggles to effectively cluster them, regardless of their similarities. To overcome this limitation, researchers introduced the DPMM. DPMM is a Bayesian non-parametric model built upon the DP, treating it as a prior distribution. Assuming a set of samples x_i follows a distribution $F(\theta_i)$, with the prior distribution for the distribution parameters θ_i being a DP G, and utilizing the construction method of the DP for inference of posterior and prior distributions of parameters, the model is referred to as DPMM. Specifically, it satisfies the following formula: $x_i|\theta_i \sim F(\theta_i)$, $\theta_i|G \sim G$, $G \sim DP(\alpha, G_0)$. Here, x independently follows a distribution F with parameters θ, and the posterior distribution of θ regarding G follows a DP with parameters α and G_0.

Solution of the DPMM Model The current methods for deriving parameters in DPMM models can be mainly classified into two categories: variational methods and Markov Chain Monte Carlo methods (MCMC). Among these, Gibbs sampling is a widely used and straightforward MCMC method. In comparison to variational methods, Gibbs sampling is highly feasible, often requiring no approximation, and it is easy to find global optimal solutions.

For a dataset $D = \{x_1, \ldots x_n\}$, assuming each data point has a corresponding latent variable Z_i, representing its cluster label, the label set is $Z = \{z_1, \ldots z_n\}$. There are a total of K clusters, and the parameter set is $\phi = \{\phi_1, \ldots, \phi_K\}$, where each element in the set corresponds to the expectation of each class. In the experiment, the data consists of multidimensional continuous variables, assuming the data follows a multidimensional Gaussian distribution, expressed as $p(x_i|\phi, z) \sim N(\mu_{z_i}, \sum)$. According to Bayes' theorem, we have $p(\phi, z|D) \propto p_0(\phi)p_0(z)p(D|\phi, z)$. For the prior distribution $p_0(\phi)$, a conjugate prior can be obtained using the conjugate prior $p_0(\phi_k) \sim N(0, \sigma^2 I)$. In the study, the construction of the Dirichlet process is done using CRP, and the prior probability $p_0(z_k)$ for each cluster is given by:

$$\begin{cases} p(z_i = k|z_{-i}) = \frac{n_k}{n-1+\alpha} \\ p(z_i = k+1|z_{-i}) = \frac{\alpha}{n-1+\alpha} \end{cases} \tag{2}$$

The process of solving the DPMM model using Gibbs sampling involves randomly initializing z and ϕ at the beginning of the model. For each z_i, the following sampling method is employed:

$$p(z_i = k|D, \phi, z_{-i}) \propto p(z_i = k|z_{-i})p(x_i|z, \phi) = \frac{n_k}{n+1+\alpha}\frac{1}{2\pi^{\frac{d}{2}}|\Sigma|^{\frac{1}{2}}}\exp\{-\frac{1}{2}(x_i -$$

$$\mu_k)^T\Sigma^{-1}(x_i - \mu_k)\} \tag{3}$$

$$p(z_i = k|D, \phi, z_{-i}) \propto p(z_i = k|z_{-i})p(x_i|z, \phi) = \frac{n_k}{n+1+\alpha} \frac{1}{2\pi^{\frac{d}{2}}|\Sigma|^{\frac{1}{2}}} \exp\{-\frac{1}{2}(x_i -$$

$$\mu_k)^T \Sigma^{-1}(x_i - \mu_k)\} \qquad (4)$$

where $\sum' = (\frac{1}{\sigma^2}I + \sum^{-1})^{-1}$. After assigning categories to the new samples, the parameters ϕ are updated as follows: $p(\phi_k|D, z) \propto p_0(\phi_k) \prod_{i=1}^{n} p(x_i|z, \phi)$.

After classifying the labeled samples, compute the Euclidean distance between each unlabeled sample and each cluster center, given by $dist(x, \mu) = \sqrt{(x - \mu)^T (x - \mu)}$. Taking into account the minimum distance of each unlabeled sample to the cluster centers of the normal class, denoted as distnormal, and the minimum distance to the cluster centers of the default class, denoted as $distdefault(x) = min_{i=1}^{t} dist(x, \mu_i)$, define default similarity to assess the likelihood of a sample being in default:

$$DDS = \frac{distnormal(x)}{distdefault(x) + distnormal(x)} \qquad (5)$$

From the above formulas, it can be observed that as the DDS value approaches 1, the sample is more likely to be a default sample; as DDS approaches 0, the sample may be a normal sample. When DDS is close to 0.5, it implies that the sample exhibits some characteristics similar to default samples and some characteristics similar to normal samples, making it difficult to definitively determine its default risk.

3.2 Calculation of Default Anomaly Based on Improved IForest Model

The IForest algorithm is an anomaly detection algorithm based on tree models and randomization. This algorithm efficiently calculates default anomaly scores, is unaffected by data distribution and sample imbalances, and exhibits good classification performance. The algorithm performs non-replacement sampling on the training data and uses these samples to construct multiple random isolation trees, forming an isolation forest. Each isolation tree is a random binary tree constructed as follows: randomly select an attribute q from the attribute set Q; randomly select a value p for that attribute; classify each sample based on the p value, assigning samples with q values $<$ p to the left child node and others to the right child node; then recursively construct the left and right child nodes until the tree is complete or reaches the maximum height. After constructing the isolation forest, calculate the average path length $E(h(x))$ and obtain the anomaly score $S(x)$ for each sample as $S(x) = 2^{-E(h(x))}$. Considering that, when constructing the isolation forest, if there are many data points, the resulting tree height may be high, and it may require multiple splits to separate the anomaly points. To address this, normalize parameter $C(n) = 2H(n) - 2(1 - 1/n)$ is used to improve the model, and the improved anomaly score $IS(x) = 2^{-E(h(x))/C(n)}$. The harmonic parameter $H(n)$ in the formula can be estimated using $\ln(n) + 0.5772156649$ (Euler's constant). The sample's anomaly score IS is considered as the default anomaly degree (DAS). When the value of $E(h(x))$ tends to 0, the DAS value tends to 1, indicating the sample is classified as a default sample; when the value of $E(h(x))$ tends to n-1, the DAS tends to 0, indicating a normal sample.

3.3 Credit Risk Control Cold Start Problem Based on DPMM and IForest Models

DPMM can handle situations with few labeled data or a large amount of unlabeled data, exhibiting good adaptability to the cold start problem. The IForest algorithm is not influenced by data distribution and sample imbalances. Considering the strengths and weaknesses of both models, the study plans to adopt a fusion model for prediction. In order to identify potential default samples and reliable normal samples from the unlabeled data set, a weighted combination of DAS and DDS is considered: $TS(x) = \theta DDS(x) + (1 - \theta)DAS(x)$. A higher TS value indicates a higher probability of the sample being a default sample, while a lower TS value suggests a higher probability of the sample being normal. To further determine the threshold for distinguishing default and normal samples, the mean of TS for normal samples in the labeled data is taken as α, and the mean of TS for default samples is β. The calculation formulas for α and β are as follows:

$$\alpha = \frac{1}{|D_0^l|} \sum_{i=1}^{|D_0^l|} TS(x_i), \beta = \frac{1}{|D_{+1}^l|} \sum_{i=1}^{|D_{+1}^l|} TS(x_i) \tag{6}$$

If the TS value of an unlabeled sample, $TS(x)$, is greater than or equal to α, it is classified as a normal sample. If the TS value is less than or equal to β, the sample is classified as a default sample. Unlabeled samples with TS values between α and β are not predicted at this stage. Subsequently, the predicted samples are incorporated into the training set, and the model is retrained. For the samples to be predicted, the newly trained model is used. This process is repeated iteratively until all samples have completed training.

4 Simulation Experiments

4.1 Experimental Dataset and Experimental Environment

The data for this study is sourced from the German Credit Risk dataset in the UCI repository, a classic dataset used for credit risk assessment. This dataset provides personal and financial information of German bank customers, including 24 feature indicators (such as gender, age, housing situation, etc.) and 1 categorical label. There are a total of 1000 valid data entries, with 300 instances of default, resulting in a default rate of 30%. The key fields of the dataset are explained in Table 1.

The experiments were conducted by writing Python code, running on the Jupyter Notebook compiler in the Anaconda integrated development environment. In the experiments, a grid search method was employed to find the optimal hyperparameter combinations for each classifier, and five-fold cross-validation was utilized to assess the performance of each classifier.

Table 1. Explanation of datasets

Data field name	Explanation	Data field name	Explanation
status_account	Status of existing checking account	property	Property currently owned
duration	Duration in month	age	Age
credit_history	Credit history	inst_plans	Other installment plans
purpose	Purposses of credit	housing	Housing
amount	Credit amount	num_credits	Number of existing credits at this bank
saving_account	Savings account/bonds	job	Job
present_emp	Present employment since	dependents	Number of people being liable to provide maintenance for
income_rate	Installment rate in percentage of disposable income	telephone	Telephone (registered under the customers name)
personal_status	Personal status and sex	foreign_worker	foreign worker
other_debtors	Other debtors / guarantors	target	Class(1 = Good, 2 = Bad)
residence_info	Present residence since		

4.2 Algorithm Performance Evaluation Indicators

The Confusion Matrix is a commonly used table for evaluating model performance in classification problems (Table 2). In binary classification, samples are categorized as positive or negative. In this experiment, positive instances represent customers with credit defaults, while negative instances represent customers who repay on time. True Positive (TP) is when the model correctly predicts positive instances, True Negative (TN) indicates the model correctly predicts negative instances, False Positive (FP) is when the model incorrectly predicts negative instances as positive, and False Negative (FN) occurs when the model incorrectly predicts positive instances as negative. Generally, accuracy and recall, defined based on the confusion matrix, are suitable for balanced data samples [13]. In imbalanced datasets, where the number of positive instances is much larger or much smaller than the number of negative instances, accuracy may fail to distinguish between the correct classifications in different classes, potentially losing its significance as an evaluation metric.

Therefore, this study utilizes the Area Under the Curve (AUC) value of the ROC (Receiver Operating Characteristic) curve to assess algorithm performance. The ROC curve plots the true positive rate (TP_rate) against the false positive rate (FP_rate) by drawing the relationship curve between the true positive rate and false positive rate at different thresholds. In the ROC curve, the horizontal axis represents the probability of false positives, while the vertical axis represents the probability of false negatives. The curve closer to the top-left corner indicates better model performance. AUC is obtained

Table 2. Confusion Matrix

Heading level	Actual Positive	Actual Negative
Predicted Positive	True Positive	False Positive
Predicted Negative	False Negative	True Negative

by calculating the area under the ROC curve, with values ranging generally between 0.5 and 1. A value of 0.5 suggests model performance equivalent to random guessing, while 1 indicates perfect prediction. A higher AUC value implies better model performance.

$$TP_{rate} = \frac{TP}{TP + FN} \tag{7}$$

$$FP_{rate} = \frac{FP}{FP + FN} \tag{8}$$

4.3 Analysis of Experimental Results

In addition, two control experiments were set up in this study. One experiment solely employed the Isolation Forest (IForest) algorithm, while the other experiment utilized a self-training approach to train the model. Self-training is a semi-supervised learning method that involves training an initial model using labeled data and then using this model to predict unlabeled data. Samples with high confidence in the predictions are added to the training set, and this process is iterated, gradually expanding the training set to enhance model performance. The models used in this study and the self-training method both require setting a classifier, with the Support Vector Machine (SVM) method chosen for experimentation. Initially, to simulate a scenario with a large amount of unlabeled data, the experiment randomly split the dataset into a training set and a test set in an 8:2 ratio. The results of the three models are presented in Table 3.

Table 3. AUC values for different algorithms

Model	Auc
DPMM-IForest-SVM	0.6344605475040258
IForest	0.504830917874396
Self-Training-SVM	0.594654918490681

From the experimental results, it can be observed that the algorithm proposed in this paper, based on DPMM and IForest, outperforms the other two algorithms, demonstrating the best classification performance. This suggests that the fused algorithm effectively balances the true positive rate and false positive rate in credit risk assessment, alleviating certain cold-start issues. The IForest model exhibits the poorest classification performance, with an AUC value around 0.5, indicating that the model's performance is close to random classification. This underscores the significant limitations of the IForest model in addressing cold-start issues and indirectly supports the rationale behind the proposed fused model in this study. The Self-Training-SVM algorithm shows classification performance slightly below our model, possibly due to the repeated iteration of early misclassifications into later data training, posing some challenges to the algorithm's robustness and generalization performance.

To assess the robustness of the algorithm model, considering the impact of the proportion of default samples on the classification performance, the following experimental results were obtained by adjusting the number of default samples in the training set (Fig. 2). Generally, the number of default samples is smaller than normal samples, so only the variation range of the proportion of default samples in the training set between 0.1 and 0.5 is considered.

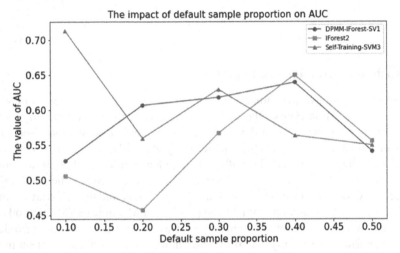

Fig. 2. The impact of default sample proportion on AUC

By observing the results in Fig. 2, it is found that the self-training model performs best when the proportion of default samples is low in the training set. However, with an increase in the number of default samples, the model's accuracy shows significant fluctuations, indicating its high sensitivity to input data. In comparison, contrasting with the DPMM-IForest-SVM model and the IForest model, it is evident that, in scenarios with a low proportion of default samples, the predictive performance of the DPMM-IForest-SVM algorithm surpasses that of the IForest model. It is noteworthy that when the proportion of default samples exceeds 0.4, the IForest model performs best among the three models; however, achieving such a high value for the proportion of default samples is challenging in real-world situations. In conclusion, the DPMM-IForest-SVM model proposed in this study demonstrates robustness in addressing the cold start problem, being less susceptible to the influence of the proportion of default samples and exhibiting good classification performance.

5 Conclusion

With the development of financial technology, credit risk management faces challenges not only from traditional finance but also unique issues in the field of internet finance, with the cold start problem and customer sinking problem being particularly prominent. To address these challenges, this paper proposes a composite model based on DPMM and IForest. Handling a large amount of unlabeled data in the credit domain, the DPMM is first employed to cluster a limited number of labeled normal and default samples. By calculating the Euclidean distance between unlabeled samples and each class of samples, the model obtains the default similarity scores for unlabeled samples. To tackle imbalanced sample distribution, the IForest algorithm is then utilized to construct multiple random isolation trees, identifying anomalous data and calculating anomaly scores as default anomaly indicators. Finally, a weighted combination of the similarity scores and anomaly scores from both models enables successful classification of unlabeled samples. In simulated experiments on the German credit risk dataset, the composite model demonstrates significant achievements. Compared to control groups using only the IForest model or self-training model, the experiment results, as indicated by the AUC values, show superior predictive performance of the composite model, particularly in scenarios with a low proportion of default samples. This success effectively mitigates the cold start problem, providing strong evidence for the rationality of the proposed composite model in this study.

The research in this paper still faces some challenges and limitations. Firstly, the experimental results of the study are limited in validating the model's generalization ability and stability due to constraints in the dataset. Future research could enhance validation by using more extensive and diverse real credit datasets, testing the model's applicability in a broader range of scenarios. Secondly, apart from the cold start and customer sinking issues, the credit risk domain currently encounters challenges from emerging fraud attacks in the black and gray industries [14]. With continuous technological developments, innovations in fraud attacks by black and gray industries are becoming more complex, and traditional credit risk models may struggle to cope with unknown attack methods. Future research can delve into advanced and intelligent credit risk models, such as incorporating AI big model technologies, to improve detection capabilities against unknown fraudulent activities, building upon an in-depth understanding of novel fraud attacks in the black and gray industries.

References

1. Liu, Z.: Research on credit risk control on machine learning. Nanjing: Nanjing University of Posts and Telecommunications (2020). (in Chinese)
2. Altman, E.I.: Bankrupt firms equity securities as an investment alternative. Financ. Anal. J. **25**(4), 129–133 (1969)
3. Campbell, T.S., Dietrich, J.K.: The determinants of default on insured conventional residential mortgage loans. J. Financ. **38**(5), 1569–1581 (1983)
4. Charitou, A., Lambertides, N., Trigeorgis, L.: Managerial discretion in distressed firms. Br. Account. Rev. **39**(4), 323–346 (2007)

5. Tsang, S., Koh, Y.S., Dobbie, G., et al.: Detecting online auction shilling frauds using supervised learning. Expert Syst. Appl. **41**(6), 3027–3040 (2014)
6. Rishehchi Fayyaz, M., Rasouli, M.R., Amiri, B.: A data-driven and network-aware approach for credit risk prediction in supply chain finance. Ind. Manag. Data Syst. **121**(4), 785–808 (2021)
7. Caruso, G., Gattone, S.A., Fortuna, F., Di Battista, T.: Cluster analysis for mixed data: an application to credit risk evaluation. Socio-Econ. Plann. Sci. **73**, 100850 (2021). https://doi.org/10.1016/j.seps.2020.100850
8. Luo, J., Chen, H., Xu, W.: Do borrowing histories of the borrowers on the P2P lending platform send a signal to the lenders? Evidence from China's"Renren Loan"Lending Platform. Contemp. Acc. Rev. **10**(01), 1–22 (2017). (in Chinese)
9. Hu, L.: Exploration of credit risk management in banks under the new situation. China Circ. Econ. **12**, 149–151 (2020). (in Chinese)
10. Yu, M., Han, Z.: Research on credit risk measurement of listed banks in china based on KMV model. Manage. Adm. **07**, 81–85 (2019). (in Chinese)
11. Zeng, L., Pan, Xiao., Ye, M.: Credit risk measurement of non listed companies based on BP-KMV model. Finance Account. Mon. **18**, 47–55 (2017). (in Chinese)
12. Gao, Y.: Study on credit default prediction based on optimal base model ensemble algorithm. Intell. Comput. Appl. **13**(07), 64–70+75 (2023). (in Chinese)
13. Li, Z.: Research on imbalance data classification based on hybrid model. Nanjing: Nanjing University of Posts and Telecommunications (2018). (in Chinese)
14. Chen, Z.: Credit risk control enters the "big model era".21st Century Business Herald (2023). (in Chinese)

Research on Consumer Repurchase Intention of Mystery Boxes—Based on Structural Equation Model

Wanqing Feng, Zilu Yang, and Lu Huang[✉]

Sichuan University, No. 29 Wangjiang Road, Chengdu, People's Republic of China
huanglu@scu.edu.cn

Abstract. In recent years, the phenomenon of mystery boxes has emerged as a notable consumption trend, demonstrating substantial market potential and cultivating a base of highly engaged enthusiasts. However, the repurchase rate of mystery boxes is declining year by year, making it important to identify factors that influence customers repurchase intention. Based on survey data from 230 questionnaires, this paper conducts an empirical study using a structural equation model to explore the impact of the four dimensions of customer experience: aesthetic experience, symbolic experience, emotional experience and social experience as well as the promotion focus in customer personality through the mediating role of customer perceived value and customer satisfaction on repurchase intention. The results show that the symbolic experience, emotional experience, social experience and promotion focus all have significant positive impact on consumer repurchase intention through the mediation of perceived value and customer satisfaction, while the aesthetic experience does not have a significant impact on repurchase intention. The conclusion of the study is of great theoretical and practical significance for mystery boxes enterprises to carry out accurate marketing strategies according to the characteristics of young consumers and improve the repurchase rate of loyal consumers.

Keywords: Mystery boxes · Customer experience · Promotion focus · Customer perceived value · Customer satisfaction · Repurchase intention

1 Introduction

Mystery boxes, also known as blind boxes, are characterized by their uniform packaging while containing varied styles of film, animation, and independently designed doll images. Their allure lies in the element of surprise, as consumers do not know which specific style they will receive until the box is opened. Since 2015, China's mystery box industry has seen remarkable growth, with companies like POPMART and IP STATION emerging as key players, significantly impacting the market and demonstrating substantial economic value. According to the Mob Research Institute, the market size of mystery boxes industry in China is expected to reach 30 billion yuan in 2024. This burgeoning interest has led to a "mystery box fever," particularly among younger consumers.

© The Author(s), under exclusive license to Springer Nature Switzerland AG 2024
Y. P. Tu and M. Chi (Eds.): WHICEB 2024, LNBIP 515, pp. 349–362, 2024.
https://doi.org/10.1007/978-3-031-60264-1_30

The inherent addiction mechanism and emotional appeal of mystery boxes result in a divided consumer base, with a significant portion of sales attributable to loyal fans who frequently repurchase. Official statistics from POPMART indicate that members constituted 92.20% of its sales in 2021, underscoring the importance of repeat customers. Nonetheless, according to POPMART's IPO disclosures, the member repurchase rate declined from 58.00% in 2020 to 44.50% in 2023. Consequently, mystery box companies and the industry at large face the pressing challenge of maintaining and expanding their base of loyal enthusiasts while encouraging repeat purchases, a critical issue necessitating immediate and effective solutions.

Mystery boxes, as a distinctive market segment, are defined by their probabilistic nature and focus on experiential consumption, which crucially shapes consumer repurchase intentions. Differing from standard goods, these boxes offer the chance to acquire an item from a set at random, with consumer preferences influenced by factors such as perceived risk and the valuation of products (Fay & Xie, 2008). The allure of mystery boxes transcends the physical product, embracing the excitement and satisfaction from the selection, purchase, and unveiling process. This study examines how the characteristics of the product and consumer personality affect purchase intentions and delves into the experiential consumption of mystery boxes to understand the drivers behind repurchase intentions.

The theoretical contributions of this research are multifaceted: Firstly, it addresses a gap in the analysis of repurchase intentions for mystery boxes by integrating an examination of both product characteristics and individual psychological factors, offering a more holistic view than prior studies which tended to focus on one aspect in isolation. Secondly, the study leverages the concept of customer experience to delve into the decision-making psychology of mystery box consumers, highlighting the experiential nature of mystery box consumption as a critical differentiator from more traditional forms of consumption. This approach addresses the shortcomings in previous research concerning the experiential aspects of mystery boxes. Thirdly, by applying regulatory focus theory to distinguish between individual differences among mystery box consumers, this study expands the scope of research into mystery box consumption and enriches the theoretical landscape related to probabilistic goods. These findings can assist managers in designing targeted and accurate marketing strategy that can benefit the sustainable development of mystery boxes enterprises and even the whole industry.

2 Conceptual Background and Research Hypothesis

2.1 The Impact of Customer Experience on Perceived Value and Customer Satisfaction

We explain the deeper mechanisms of mystery boxes consumption based on customer experiential theory, which describe customer experience as the subjective response of customers to the products and service, including perception, emotion, feeling, behavior and interaction (Schmitt, 1999). Based on the previous classification of customer experience dimensions (Schmitt, 1999; Lemon & Verhoef, 2016), combined with the characteristics of mystery boxes consumption, the mystery boxes customer experience is divided into aesthetic experience, symbolic experience, emotional experience and social experience.

Aesthetic Experience. Aesthetic experience emerges from the interplay of cognition, imagination, and emotion during the consumption of aesthetically appealing products. This experience is shaped by the product's aesthetic allure and the consumer's personality traits, influencing their cognitive, emotional, and behavioral responses (Wanzer et al., 2020). Research indicates that visually attractive products elicit a stronger purchase intent and behavior (Lin & Ryu, 2023). Aesthetic experiences provide hedonic pleasure from product aesthetics, enhancing perceived value. This emotional stimulation can lead to enjoyment and heightened arousal, underpinning customer satisfaction. Based on these insights, the following hypotheses are proposed:

H1a: Aesthetic experience positively affect perceived value.
H2a: Aesthetic experience positively affect customer satisfaction.

Symbolic Experience. With the increasing escalation and complexity of consumption, the symbolic value of some products is gradually greater than its functional value (Granulo et al., 2021). Consumers display their personality, values, lifestyle, social status and so on by buying some special products of symbolic value, which results in symbolic consumption (Grant, 1986). Consumers also buy mystery boxes because of their motivation to win social prestige, social identity and internal self-expression. Under the influence of Veblen effect, that is, showing off and comparing, consumers hope to improve their social reputation by owning hidden and popular style of mystery boxes. Under the influence of "Bandwagon effect", that is, conformity, consumers can integrate into a specific community by buying mystery boxes to obtain the identity and the sense of belonging. This process of self-presentation and self-identification results in benefits, so that the consumers perceived value increased, at the same time, the sense of achievement, group belonging and other positive feelings will make consumers have a satisfactory overall evaluation. The following hypotheses were developed:

H1b: Symbolic experience positively affect perceived value.
H2b: Symbolic experience positively affect customer satisfaction.

Emotional Experience. Emotional experience refers to individual consciousness and perception of their current emotional state, which is composed of physical arousal of external stimulation and self-feeling of internal psychology (Ballard, 2020). Consumers are gradually not satisfied with material consumption, but are more willing to pay for spiritual needs and the enjoy brought by emotional experience in consumption. The emotional experience brought about by uncertainty and seclusion is an important pursuit of mystery boxes consumers. The impulse, excitement and curiosity caused by uncertainty can promote consumers to repurchase; seclusion, that is, a sense of release from reality, also plays an important role in improving customer experience and loyalty. The emotional comfort and stimulation gained in mystery boxes consumption will bring positive value to consumers, which enhance customer perceived value and satisfaction. The following hypotheses were developed:

H1c: Emotional experience positively affect perceptual value.
H2c: Emotional experience positively affect customer satisfaction.

Social Experience. Social experience refers to the interactive behavior formed spontaneously by customers in the whole process of consumption, especially in the subsequent process (Arnold & Reynolds, 2003). Mystery boxes play the role of "social currency", connecting groups based on common interests through RED, Weibo, WeChat and other social platforms. The social experience of this collective carnival continues to attract consumers to join (Zollo et al., 2020). The close interaction and connection bring social benefits, while the excitement and pleasure improve satisfaction. The following hypotheses were developed:

H1d: Social experience positively affect perceived value.
H2d: Social experience positively affect customer satisfaction.

2.2 The Impact of Promotion Focus on Perceived Value and Customer Satisfaction

Regulatory focus theory considered that individuals have many kinds of self-regulating systems, including promotion focus and prevention focus, and thus form different internal guidance models (Higgins & Pinelli, 2020). People who promotion focus pay more attention to positive results and interests, and are less affected by negative results, while prevention focus people pay more attention to negative results and losses. The idea of promotion focus people is more open, more adventurous, and pays more attention to income rather than loss (Luqman et al., 2021), which is consistent with the characteristics of mystery boxes loyal consumers. Previous studies have shown that individuals who promotion focus are more likely to have impulsive buying behavior, and mystery boxes consumption is most of the time impulsive consumption, so mystery boxes purchase intention is closely related to promotion focus. Besides, promotion focus consumers will also have higher satisfaction after impulse purchase. Therefore, mystery boxes consumers who promotion focus will pay more attention to those experiences that meet their expectations in consumption and after consumption, which will produce higher perceived value and customer satisfaction. The following hypotheses were developed:

H3: Promotion focus positively affect perceived value.
H4: Promotion focus positively affect customer satisfaction.

2.3 The Impact of Perceived Value and Customer Satisfaction on Repurchase Intention

According to previous research, perceived value and customer satisfaction are two of the most important factors affecting customer repurchase intention (Sweeney & Soutar, 2001). Perceived value is the overall assessment of products or services after consumers measure gains and costs (El-Adly, 2019). After measuring the perceived acquisition and perceived pay of the products, consumers form the perceived value of the products, including practical value, emotional value, social value and so on. The higher the perceived value, the stronger the consumers' willingness to buy repeatedly.

Customer satisfaction is the consumers' evaluation of the products or services in order to judge whether they can achieve consumers' expected level, which is overall attitude to the consumption process (Giese & Cote, 2000; El-Adly, 2019). The satisfaction degree of consumers with this consumption will have a great impact on their subsequent repurchase behavior. If they are satisfied, their willingness to buy repeatedly will be stronger. The following hypotheses were developed:

H5: Perceived value positively affect repurchase intention.
H6: Customer satisfaction positively affect repurchase intention.

2.4 The Mediating Role of Perceived Value and Customer Satisfaction

According to the cognitive appraisal theory, consumer behavior follows the logical order of "cognition-emotion-attitude-behavior" (Lazarus, 1982). The complete consumption process consists of three stages: the formation of a general understanding of the product or service before the purchase, the formation of own attitude and evaluation of the product, service and brand in the purchase, and the guidance of the next behavior according to the cognitive and emotional status after the purchase. Meanwhile, the consumer repurchase intention is affected by the individual and the product both sides (Johnson et al., 2001). Therefore, in the process of mystery boxes consumption, customer experience and promotion focus in consumer personality jointly affect consumers' preliminary cognition of mystery boxes, forming the value evaluation and satisfaction evaluation of blind box, this kind of emotion or attitude to product affects whether consumers will buy again. And this relationship shows that the better the customer experience in mystery boxes consumption is, the more significant the promotion focus in consumer personality is, the higher the perceived value and customer satisfaction are, which leads to a higher willingness to repurchase. The following hypotheses were developed:

H7a: The effect of aesthetic experience on repurchase intention is mediated by perceived value.
H7b: The effect of symbolic experience on repurchase intention is mediated by perceived value.
H7c: The effect of emotional experience on repurchase intention is mediated by perceived value.
H7d: The effect of social experience on repurchase intention is mediated by perceived value.
H7e: The effect of promotion focus on repurchase intention is mediated by perceived value.
H8a: The effect of aesthetic experience on repurchase intention is mediated by customer satisfaction.
H8b: The effect of symbolic experience on repurchase intention is mediated by customer satisfaction.
H8c: The effect of emotional experience on repurchase intention is mediated by customer satisfaction.
H8d: The effect of social experience on repurchase intention is mediated by customer satisfaction.
H8e: The effect of promotion focus on repurchase intention is mediated by customer satisfaction (Fig. 1).

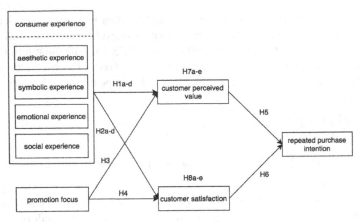

Fig. 1. The theoretical framework.

3 Methodology

3.1 Measurement Design

In the early stage of the survey, 30 mystery boxes loyal consumers were interviewed in depth, and the factors affecting their repurchase intention were summarized and extracted, according to which the questionnaire was designed in combination with the literature. The questionnaire is divided into two parts. The first part is the basic situation of the subjects, including age, sex, education, monthly disposable income, total expenditure on mystery boxes, etc. The second part is the specific problems of variable measurement, including "aesthetic experience", "symbolic experience", "social experience", "promotion focus", "customer perceived value", "customer satisfaction" and "repurchase intention". A total of 26 items (shown in Table 1) are measured by Likert five-point scale ranging from "(1) Strongly disagree" to "(5) Strongly agree".

3.2 Data Collection and Sample Characteristics

In our research, online questionnaires were used to collect research data. Since the study focused on the repurchase intention in mystery box consumption, we required all the participants to have experience in mystery box purchase. So, we randomly select 230 consumers have purchased blind boxes once or more using Credamo database. After excluding samples that did not pass the screening and were incomplete or mismatched, a total of 202 valid questionnaires were obtained, with an effective response rate of 87.830%. Among the interviewees, 61 were male (30.198%) and 141 were female (69.802%), which was in line with the basic proportion of mystery boxes customers. 167 (82.673%) interviewees aged from 18 to 30, which occupy the largest proportion, 16 (7.921%) were under 18 years old, and 19 (9.406%) were over 30 years old, which was basically consistent with the composition of loyal consumers of mystery boxes. The majority of interviewees received tertiary education, in total 191 (95.049%). 100 (49.505%) has monthly disposable income of 2000–4000 yuan, 60 (29.703%) have monthly disposable

Table 1. Questionnaire scale design and reliability

Variable	Items	Reference	Factor load	AVE	CR	α
Aesthetic experience (AE)	The design of mystery boxes is exquisite	Wanzer et al., (2020)	0.841	0.605	0.821	0.824
	The style of mystery boxes is very attractive to me		0.789			
	The appearance of mystery boxes is very conspicuous		0.697			
Symbolic experience (SE)	Mystery boxes expresses my personality and lifestyle	Granulo et al., (2021)	0.525	0.411	0.673	0.678
	Buying mystery boxes keeps me up with current trend		0.730			
	The IP image of mystery boxes is what I like and represent me		0.652			
Emotional experience (EE)	It makes me feel mysterious and curious that doesn't know the contents of mystery boxes before open it	Ballard (2020)	0.796	0.584	0.801	0.777
	The process of opening the mystery boxes made me excited		0.917			
	Mystery boxes make me feel relaxed and can temporarily forget the pressure and annoyance of reality		0.528			

(continued)

Table 1. (*continued*)

Variable	Items	Reference	Factor load	AVE	CR	α
Social experience (SOE)	Buying mystery boxes allows me to make like-minded friends	Arnold & Reynolds (2003)	0.902	0.768	0.909	0.905
	Mystery boxes is the bridge of communication with my colleagues		0.914			
	Talking to people about mystery boxes is my way of having fun		0.810			
Promotion focus (PF)	I often think about how I can succeed	Luqman et al. (2021)	0.772	0.492	0.793	0.756
	I often think about how I can realize my wishes and ideals		0.775			
	In contrast, I am more interested in gaining more benefits than in preventing losses		0.594			
	In general, I pay more attention to how to achieve more success than to avoid failure		0.646			
Customer perceived value (CPV)	The quality and feel of mystery boxes are good	El-Adly (2019)	0.699	0.411	0.731	0.796
	The price of mystery boxes is relatively reasonable		0.538			

(*continued*)

Table 1. (*continued*)

Variable	Items	Reference	Factor load	AVE	CR	α
	Buying mystery boxes makes me happy		0.767			
	Buying mystery boxes allows me to better maintain social relationships		0.526			
Customer satisfaction (CS)	On the whole, I am satisfied with the mystery boxes I bought	Giese & Cote (2000)	0.889	0.501	0.795	0.842
	Compared with my psychological expectations, I am satisfied with the mystery boxes I bought		0.722			
	Compared with other styles in the same series, I am satisfied with the mystery boxes I bought		0.646			
Repurchase intention (RPI)	I might buy mystery boxes again	El-Adly (2019)	0.869	0.551	0.825	0.851
	I will actively recommend the purchase of mystery boxes to my relatives and friends		0.867			
	I look forward to buying mystery boxes again		0.649			

income of 2000 yuan or less, and 25 (12.376%) have monthly disposable income of 6000 yuan or more. 87.129% of the interviewees spent no more than 800 yuan on mystery boxes, a total of 191.

4 Data Analysis

4.1 Factor and Reliability Analysis

KMO and Barlett's Spherical Test. Firstly, the KMO and Barlett's spherical tests of the model are carried out by SPSS26.0. The results are as follows: the KMO value is 0.911, which is greater than 0.600, the approximate chi-square value is 3416.046, the degree of freedom is 325, the significance level is 0.000, less than 0.010. The significant test with significant level of 1% shows that the scale is suitable for factor analysis.

Principal Component Extraction. The exploratory factor analysis is carried out, and the factor is extracted by principal component analysis. According to the variable situation, the number of factors is set to 8, the contribution rate of cumulative variance after rotation is 75.892%, greater than 70%, and the load coefficient of the corresponding factor after rotation is more than 0.500 (Table 1), which shows that the original data can be fully reflected.

Reliability Test. Cronbach's α coefficient was used to evaluate the reliability of the scale. Cronbach's α coefficient of each latent variable was between 0.678 and 0.905, which was higher than 0.6; the combined reliability CR ranged from 0.673 to 0.909, both higher than the baseline of 0.6; the AVE ranged from 0.411 to 0.768, both higher than the baseline of 0.4. This indicates the reliability of the measurement scale in this study, as shown in Table 1.

4.2 Structural Equation Model

Amos26.0 is used to test the structural equation model in our study. The $\chi 2/df = 2.964$, GFI = 0.915, NFI = 0.930, IFI = 0.904, CFI = 0.928, RMSEA = 0.078 in this model, indicating that the adaptability of the model is good.

The path analysis of the model shows that symbolic experience, emotional experience, social experience and promotion focus all have significant positive effects on perceived value and customer satisfaction, and both perceived value and customer satisfaction have significant positive effects on repurchase intention. It is assumed that H1b ~ d, H2b ~ d, H3, H4, H5, H6 are verified. However, aesthetic experience has no significant effect on perceived value and customer satisfaction, which is assumed that H1a and H2a are not valid (Table 2). Since the premise of mediating effect is that the independent variable has a significant influence on the mediating variable, H7a and H8a are also not valid. The standardized path coefficient results show the importance of the effects of each independent variables on dependent variables (Table 2).

Table 2. Structural equation model results

Hypothesized Paths	Estimate	Standardized Estimate	P	Hypothesis
H1a:AE → PV(+)	0.090	–	0.382	Not supported
H1b:SE → PV(+)	0.967	0.735	***	Supported
H1c:EE → PV(+)	0.283	0.256	*	Supported
H1d:SOE → PV(+)	0.301	0.338	***	Supported
H2a:AE → CS(+)	0.113	-	0.284	Not supported
H2b:SE → CS(+)	0.882	0.696	***	Supported
H2c:EE → CS(+)	0.434	0.374	**	Supported
H2d:SOE → CS(+)	0.110	0.108	*	Supported
H3:PF → PV(+)	0.244	0.223	*	Supported
H4:PF → CS(+)	0.472	0.368	*	Supported
H5:PV → RPI(+)	0.478	0.348	**	Supported
H6:CS → RPI(+)	0.635	0.442	**	Supported

4.3 Mediating Effect

Our research uses the PROCESS v3.4 in SPSS26.0 to test the mediating role of perceived value and customer satisfaction by Bootstrap method. Since aesthetic experience has no significant effect on perceived value and customer satisfaction, and does not meet the prerequisites of mediating role, we only test symbolic experience, emotional experience, social experience and promotion focus.

According to the Table 3, the effect value of symbolic experience-perceived value and customer satisfaction-repurchase intention is 0.438, and the Bias-corrected 95% confidence interval is (0.306, 0.580), which does not include 0, while the Bias-corrected 95% confidence interval of symbolic experience-repurchase intention is (0.021, 0.386), which also does not include 0. The results show that after the introduction of perceived value and customer satisfaction as mediator variables, the influence of perceived value and customer satisfaction on repurchase intention is still significant, but the influence of symbolic experience on repurchase intention is significantly weakened, so the mediating role of perceived value and customer satisfaction is established, and plays a partial mediating role, accounting for 68.76% of the mediating effect, which is the same for emotional experience, social experience and promotion focus. The mediating effect accounted for 68.257%, 57.778% and 76.508%, respectively. It was assumed that H7b-e and H8b-e were verified.

Table 3. Mediating effect

Paths	Effect value	S.E	Bias-corrected 95%CI		Relative effect value
			Lower	Upper	
SE → PV CS → RPI	0.438	0.071	0.306	0.580	68.760%
SE → RPI	0.198	0.095	0.021	0.386	31.083%
EE → PV CS → RPI	0.415	0.070	0.281	0.553	68.257%
EE → RPI	0.193	0.067	0.061	0.325	31.743%
SOE → PV CS → RPI	0.312	0.066	0.187	0.448	57.778%
SOE → RPI	0.227	0.071	0.087	0.368	42.037%
PF → PV CS → RPI	0.482	0.077	0.328	0.629	76.508%
PF → RPI	0.149	0.073	0.004	0.293	23.651%

5 General Discussion

5.1 Conclusion and Theoretical Contributions

First, symbolic, emotional, and social experiences associated with mystery box consumption positively impact both perceived value and customer satisfaction. Symbolic experience exerts the most significant influence on perceived value, followed by social and then emotional experiences. In terms of customer satisfaction, symbolic experience again has the most substantial effect, followed by emotional and then social experiences. This finding extends prior research by highlighting the importance of emotional and social dimensions and underscores the predominance of symbolic value in mystery box consumption (Lin & Ryu, 2023). These products serve as a medium through which young consumers express their identity, social status, and lifestyle aspirations.

Second, aesthetic experience does not significantly influence perceived value or satisfaction, suggesting pre-existing aesthetic expectations among consumers that do not substantially alter their overall assessment. This observation addresses a gap in earlier research focused on repurchase intentions.

Third, promotion-focused consumers tend to exhibit higher levels of perceived value and satisfaction, highlighting the importance of considering both personality traits and product attributes in understanding consumer behavior.

Fourth, customer perceived value and satisfaction directly influence repurchase intentions and act as significant mediators in the relationship between customer experience (symbolic, emotional, and social experiences), promotion focus, and repurchase intentions. This demonstrates that enhanced customer experiences and a pronounced promotion focus lead to greater perceived value and satisfaction, thereby increasing the likelihood of repurchase. This study not only reaffirms findings from previous research in the context of mystery box consumption (El-Adly, 2019) but also broadens the scope of inquiry into the effects of perceived value, customer satisfaction, and repurchase intentions.

5.2 Managerial Implications

Our study offers actionable insights for mystery box companies focused on building brand value, understanding emotional needs, fostering community engagement, and targeting promotion-focused consumers:

Enhance intellectual property (IP) for symbolic value: Strengthen IP development to imbue products with unique, precious, and irreplaceable qualities, akin to luxury goods and artworks. Elevating cultural and symbolic significance through storytelling, animations, and collaborations can distinguish products in a competitive market.

Address emotional needs: Cater to consumers' short-term excitement and long-term desires for nostalgia and companionship. Promote healthy consumption habits to build sustainable loyalty.

Foster community engagement: Enhance customer loyalty through active engagement in social media and community forums, encouraging interaction and a sense of belonging.

Target promotion-focused marketing: Design marketing strategies that emphasize the emotional and symbolic experiences, appealing to consumers' aspirations and sense of achievement.

5.3 Limitations and Future Research

Our study primarily focuses on the positive aspects of mystery box consumption, overlooking potential negative experiences such as disappointment from receiving undesired items or fear of uncertainty. Future research should explore how these negative experiences impact consumer psychology and purchasing decisions, incorporating factors like perceived risk.

Additionally, while our analysis distinguishes consumer personalities based on a long-term promotion focus, it's important to recognize that consumer focus can shift in the short term under specific circumstances. Subsequent studies could experiment with altering short-term consumer focus to assess its effect on purchasing intentions, considering variables like shopping environment and service quality.

Our research's scope is limited by using promotion focus as the sole variable to categorize consumer personality traits. Future studies should broaden this approach by incorporating additional personality variables such as self-conception and impulsivity. Meanwhile, consider their moderating effect within the model would be an expansion.

References

Fay, S., Xie, J.: Probabilistic goods: a creative way of selling products and services. Mark. Sci. **27**, 679–690 (2008)

Sheth, J.N., Newman, B.I., Gross, B.L.: Why we buy what we buy: a theory of consumption values. J. Bus. Res. **22**, 159–170 (1991)

Schmitt, B.: Experiential marketing. J. Market. Manag. **15**, 53–67 (1999)

Lemon, K.N., Verhoef, P.C.: Understanding customer experience throughout the customer journey. J. Mark. **80**(6), 69–96 (2016)

Wanzer, D.L., Finley, K.P., Zarian, S., Cortez, N.: Experiencing flow while viewing art: development of the aesthetic experience questionnaire. Psychol. Aesthet. Creat. Arts **14**(1), 113–124 (2020)

Lin, F., Ryu, K.: How product design affects repurchase intention, eWOM, and museum visit intention: museum mystery boxes in China. J. Travel Tour. Mark. **40**(5), 434–451 (2023)

Granulo, A., Fuchs, C., Puntoni, S.: Preference for human (vs. robotic) labor is stronger in symbolic consumption contexts. J. Consum. Psychol. **31**(1), 72–80 (2021)

Grant, M.C.: Culture and consumption: a theoretical account of the structure and movement of the cultural meaning of consumer goods. J. Consum. Res. **1986**, 71–84 (1986)

Ballard, B.S.: The epistemic significance of emotional experience. Emot. Rev. **13**, 175–209 (2020)

Arnold, M.J., Reynolds, K.E.: Hedonic shopping motivations. J. Retail. **79**, 77–95 (2003)

Zollo, L., Filieri, R., Rialti, R., Yoon, S.: Unpacking the relationship between social media marketing and brand equity: the mediating role of consumers' benefits and experience. J. Bus. Res. **117**, 256–267 (2020)

Higgins, E.T., Pinelli, F.: Regulatory focus and fit effects in organizations. Annu. Rev. Organ. Psych. Organ. Behav. **7**, 25–48 (2020)

Luqman, A., Talwar, S., Masood, A., Dhir, A.: Does enterprise social media use promote employee creativity and well-being? J. Bus. Res. **131**, 40–54 (2021)

El-Adly, M.I.: Modelling the relationship between hotel perceived value, customer satisfaction, and customer loyalty. J. Retail. Consum. Serv. **50**, 322–332 (2019)

Sweeney, C.J., Soutar, N.G.: Consumer perceived value: the development of a multiple item scale. J. Consum. Res. **77**, 120–131 (2001)

Giese, J.L., Cote, J.A.: Defining consumer satisfaction. Acad. Mark. Sci. Rev. **2000**, 1–24 (2000)

Lazarus, R.S.: Thoughts on the relations between emotion and cognition. Am. Psychol. **37**, 1019–1024 (1982)

Johnson, M.D., Gustafsson, A., Andreassen, T.W., et al.: The evolution and future of national customer satisfaction index models. J. Econ. Psychol. **22**, 217–245 (2001)

Research on the Method of Constructing Product Innovation Demands Graph Based on Competitive Product Reviews

Hongting Tang, Jie Gong, and Yanlin Zhang[✉]

Guangdong University of Technology, Guangzhou 510520, Guangdong, China
forest_zhang@163.com

Abstract. Nowadays, user review texts are the main source of product innovation demand for enterprises, but in the face of massive and unstructured user review texts, how to efficiently identify and visually express product innovation demand has become an urgent problem for enterprises. Although a series of studies have explored this issue, there is a lack of studies that cover the complete path of identifying, classifying, and visualising product innovation demand, and few studies have introduced reviews of competitive products for comparative analysis. Therefore, under the guidance of cognitive flexibility theory, this study firstly crawls the text data of user reviews of Huawei mate50 and Xiaomi 13, and then identifies the product innovation needs using BERT Fine-Tuning after data preprocessing; then the product innovation needs are clustered by themes using BERTopic, which classifies the themes into common and specific themes; finally, based on the theme clustering results, we use dependency parsing and association rules to construct a product innovation demand (comparison) graph under unique (shared) themes. The results of this research not only provide a new way of organising knowledge in the field of ill-structured knowledge, which is suitable for the development of cognitive flexibility theory in the era of big data, but also helps to guide enterprises to produce innovative products that really meet the needs of end-users, and promotes the transmutation of innovation from the production paradigm to the service paradigm in the era of knowledge economy.

Keywords: Online Comments · Opinion Mining · Visual Expression

1 Introduction

With the booming development of the e-commerce economy and the in-depth promotion of intelligent manufacturing, the user's demand for personalized, experiential, and intelligent products and services has become even stronger, and the speed of product iteration of enterprises has been accelerated. At the same time, the new generation of information technology for user empowerment, so that it has more right to speak and dominate, the user demand has gradually become the focus of enterprises to carry out product iteration and innovation. At present, many practitioners based on the application of open innovation platforms have discovered and proved the importance of innovation-oriented to user demand. For example, Xiaomi Technology has opened the MIUI community for its MIUI operating system and witnessed the achievement of listening to users' demand with the growing MIUI user base.

The remarkable performance of user demand in facilitating product innovation has attracted extensive attention from scholars in related fields such as knowledge management and data mining, e.g., user innovation mining [1], user demand mining [2], etc. However, there are still some gaps in the content and methodology of related research. First, in the discovery of product innovation demand, the existing literature focuses on the user data directly related to the product from the Internet platform and then carries out analyses, and few scholars have included the user reviews of competitive products in the process of discovering product innovation demand. User reviews of competitive products can help product manufacturers understand the strengths and weaknesses of the target product, and then more deeply understand user demand [3]. Secondly, there is a lack of research results covering the complete path of product innovation demand identification, classification, and visual representation. The cognitive flexibility theory, on the other hand, emphasizes the need for rich knowledge linkages in acquiring advanced knowledge in ill-structured domains [4], which implies the importance and necessity of developing intuitive and interconnected knowledge representations in the discovery process of product innovation demand. Focusing on the established results of opinion mining research, the task process from opinion identification [2], and opinion classification [5] to visual representation [6] fits this need.

Aiming at the above status quo, this paper will take user reviews in open innovation platforms as an example, and consider the method of constructing product innovation requirement graph for competitive product reviews under the guidance of cognitive flexibility theory. Specifically, this study crawls the user review data of Huawei mate50 and Xiaomi 13, identifies the product innovation demand using BERT Fine-Tuning model, then uses BERTopic to cluster the product innovation demand by themes, and finally constructs the (comparative) graph of the product innovation demand under the unique (shared) themes by using the dependency parsing and the association rules.

This study not only provides a new way of organizing knowledge in the ill-structured domain and adapts to the development needs of cognitive flexibility theory, but also incorporates competitive product reviews into the discovery study of product innovation demand, which improves the study of product innovation based on user intelligence.

2   Related Work

2.1   Knowledge Discovery Through Online Reviews

The emergence of Internet communities has greatly stimulated the enthusiasm of users to participate in product innovation, and users have published a large number of comments on various open platforms regarding their experiences of product use and product improvement demand. Based on this reality, many scholars have begun to explore how to extract user knowledge from online comments that is conducive to iterative product innovation, which is mainly classified into three aspects: (1) Product defect mining: Younas et al. detected product defects in mobile phones [7]; Zheng et al. identify and prioritise product defects [8]. (2) Creative innovation mining: Goldberg and Abrahams mined reviews related to the most useful innovation opportunities for the company [9]; while Zhang et al. identified innovative attributes of product reviews on Amazon [1]. (3) Product demand mining: Cong et al. proposed a small-sample data-driven approach to user requirements acquisition [10]; Zhang and Luo identified the types of consumer demand for product attributes based on online reviews [11]. Overall, product defects, product ideas, and product demand have been considered important materials that can assist product innovation in different studies, but product demand can be both product defects and direct ideas [1], which refer to various attributes of a potential product desired by users.

Focusing on the above corpus sources for product knowledge discovery studies, established studies rarely consider the inclusion of user reviews of competitive products in the discovery studies of product innovation needs. User reviews of competitive products can help manufacturers understand the strengths and weaknesses of target products while gaining a deeper understanding of user needs [3]. Therefore, incorporating competitive product reviews into the knowledge discovery process of the target product is conducive to the refinement of the knowledge discovery results.

2.2 Opinion Mining

Opinion mining is one of the tasks of knowledge discovery through online reviews. It denotes the extraction of people's attitudes or sentiments towards entities and their attributes from unstructured web texts [12]. This study summarises the task of opinion mining and its process by combining the existing results of opinion mining research. Specifically, the task process of opinion mining consists of five main parts: (1) Data acquisition, where the acquisition of the dataset is the first step in the process of opinion mining. (2) Opinion identification, where opinion-orientated texts are identified from the dataset. Ettrich et al. reconceptualised Needmining from a binary classification problem to a token classification problem to extract specific requirements from informative content [5]. (3) Aspect extraction, which identifies and extracts all aspects that are effective in improving classification results. Liu et al. proposed aspect-based pairwise opinion generation [13]. (4) Opinion classification, which uses different techniques to classify opinions. Ying Wang et al. classified the software demand embedded in APP user review data into five requirement categories [5]. (5) Visual representation to summarise and organize ideas and analyze them in the form of graphs.

The established literature focuses more on the research of aspect extraction and opinion classification, and relatively less on opinion identification and visual analysis, especially the lack of research results covering the complete path of opinion identification, opinion classification, and visual analysis. It is worth noting that the lack of advanced tasks tends to bring more noise or bias to the subsequent tasks, while the lack of subsequent tasks affects the effective utilization of opinion knowledge.

2.3 Visual Expression

Visual expression is the final expression and presentation of the opinion mining results. This link is very necessary for fine-grained opinion mining tasks, because fine-grained opinion mining results have more categorical attributes, and in the case of large datasets, there may even be a dimensionality explosion. Based on this, the established literature has made many attempts for the clear presentation and expression of opinion mining results. (1) semantic network visualization, e.g., based on keyword or entity extraction, the construction of knowledge network graph is completed by using semantic association relationships among entities [6, 14]. (2) Probabilistic relationship visualization, e.g., using the probabilistic results generated by association rule analysis to construct interconnected knowledge structure graph [15]. As far as the two different visualization graph methods are concerned, the semantic-based method is more in-depth in analysis and acquires a more systematic knowledge structure, but it requires a large amount of a priori knowledge and is inefficient in the case of big data; whereas the probabilistic-based method is fast, efficient, and does not require human intervention, with the disadvantage that the results are presented as floating on the surface and are poorly robust (easy to be interfered with by high-frequency words). These two methods have their own merits, but there is little literature combining the two for visualization studies. In addition, there is a lack of visual analytical frameworks for presenting contrasting views in established studies.

Therefore, in this study, we use dependent parsing to extract knowledge objects and their structural dependencies in the text, use association rule analysis to mine frequent knowledge sets and confidence relationships in the text, and then construct rules to generate a product innovation demand (comparison) graph in the form of a graph that takes into account semantic and probabilistic relationships under the specific (shared) themes.

3 Experiment

3.1 Data Description

The data for this study were selected from Xiaomi's MIUI community and Huawei's Pollen Club. In the investigation of this paper, we found that Huawei mate50 (the target product) and Xiaomi 13 (the competing product) have a competitive relationship, so we crawled the text of reviews about these two products in the community. Firstly, the acquired data is removed from duplicate posts and sentence breaks are applied to the content of all posts. Then, sentence cleaning work is performed, including removing English, numbers and emoticons, and traditional and simplified conversions, etc., in order to obtain valid sentences. Finally, sentences are manually labelled, if the sentence is a product innovation requirement, such as "Strongly suggest optimising the camera", it is labelled as 1, otherwise it is labelled as 0. A total of 10,000 sentences are labelled and the data details are shown in Table 1.

3.2 Identify Product Innovation Demand

To simplify the task of identifying product innovation demand and to ensure the accuracy of the task, this study adopts the BERT Fine-Tuning model to identify product innovation demand in review texts. BERT is a large-scale language model based on Transformer architecture. Unlike traditional unidirectional language models, BERT has the feature of

Table 1. Table of data details.

	Huawei mate50	Xiaomi 13
Total posts crawled	51301	57247
Valid posts (remove duplicates)	17186	28787
Total Sentences	23178	35275
Valid Sentences	18043	27993
Sentences with positive examples	1312	2316
Sentences with negative examples	2688	3684
Total tagged sentences	4000	6000

bidirectional modeling, which can take into account contextual information at the same time and better understand the meaning of words in different contexts. The training of BERT can be divided into two steps, namely pre-training and Fine-Tuning [16]. In this study, the BERT pre-training model will be invoked to classify text as the downstream task of Fine-Tuning, i.e., to identify whether a user review sentence is a product innovation demand.

Table 2. Table of relevant parameters defined.

Parameter	Set Values
Batchsize	16
Learning rate	2e-5
Optimizer	Adam
Loss function	BCELoss
Activation function	RELU Function, Sigmoid Function
Epoch	20
BertTokenizer	bert-base-chinese
BertModel	bert-base-chinese

In the identification part of product innovation demand, firstly, 10,000 sentences labeled in the data preprocessing are disordered and divided into a training set, validation set, and test set according to the ratio of 0.6:0.2:0.2. In the training process, relevant parameters need to be defined, see Table 2 for details. To determine the number of added linear layer layers, this paper conducts experiments by adding 1–10 linear layers. After every 20 epochs of training, the number of added linear layer layers is chosen to be 4 layers according to the accuracy, precision, recall, and F1 indexes of the test set. The final number of identified product innovation demand is 12,440, of which Huawei mate50 accounts for 5,149 and Xiaomi 13 accounts for 7,291. Some specific examples are shown in Table 3.

Table 3. Table of examples of partial results of product innovation demand identification.

Product	Product Innovation Demand
Huawei mate50	Strongly request to add back the super power-saving, too much power consumption!
Huawei mate50	Now the progress bar underneath is very slow to display and always fails to capture the desired image
Huawei mate50	When suggesting a camera, the focus interaction method provides the focal length button directly
Xiaomi 13	Suggested Optimised Shooting
Xiaomi 13	I wish there was a separate hibernation charging display for charging
Xiaomi 13	Add font size adjustment level

3.3 Theme Clustering

BERTopic is a BERT-based topic model. It combines the semantic representation capabilities of BERT with the statistical methods of traditional topic models to automatically cluster text in an unsupervised manner and assign a set of relevant keywords and representative documents to each generated topic. Compared to traditional topic models such as LDA, BERTopic has better semantic representation as well as easy interpretation of clustering results [17], so this paper chooses BERTopic for clustering product innovation demand topics. The specific settings are shown in Table 4.

Table 4. BERTopic related parameters table.

Parameter	Type of selection	Specified value
min_topic_size	–	20
language	–	"multilingual"
representation_model	Part Of Speech	"zh_core_web_trf"
embedding_model	SentenceTransformer	"paraphrase-multilingual-MiniLM-L12-v2"
vectorizer_model	CountVectorizer	jieba

Product innovation demand for Huawei mate50 and Xiaomi 13 are clustered thematically respectively, with 36 themes for Huawei mate50 and 62 themes for Xiaomi 13. In addition, BERTopic generates a topic label for each topic, i.e., the set of three keywords with the highest probability. According to the keyword collection of theme tags, through the Huawei mate50 and Xiaomi 13 theme tags two and two for the intersection, such as Huawei mate50 in the theme 6 theme tags for {"headphones", "sound quality", "Sound"}, the label of theme 0 in Xiaomi 13 is {"Headphones", "Sound", "Volume"}, the intersection of the two sets is {"headphones", "sound"} is more than one keyword, so it is judged to be a shared topic, and {"headphones", "sound"} is the tag of the shared topic. After the division of shared themes and unique themes, the final theme clustering results are shown in Table 5.

Table 5. Table of final thematic clustering results.

Shared themes	Theme tags	Number of sentences
0	Sound_Headphones	768
1	Map_Navigation	96
2	Heat_Game	142
…	…	…
12	Battery_Health	165
Huawei mate50 specific themes	Theme tags	Number of sentences
13	Stuttering_Continuity_Broken Stream	318
14	Swipe_Video_Sound	179
15	SMS_Message_Information	159
…	…	…
34	Background_Mode_Dark	24
Xiaomi 13 specific themes	Theme tags	Number of sentences
35	Video Recording_Video_Recording	249
36	Power_Saving_Power-Consumption	165
37	Housekeeping_Resilience_Capability	161
…	…	…
82	Color_Front_Red	20

3.4 Graph Construction

Dependency Parsing and Association Rules. Before constructing the product innovation demand graph, it is necessary to obtain the set of noun-verb nouns of target products and competitive products under each theme through dependency parsing. The purpose of dependency parsing is to automatically obtain the dependencies between words and their specific attributes in the product innovation requirements, and thus the syntactic information conveyed by the dependency structure, an example of which is shown in Fig. 1.

To obtain the probabilistic relationships in product innovation demand, this study uses association rule analysis to mine the noun-verb set obtained in the previous section. Before applying the association rule analysis, two association rule mining metrics will be used in this study: (1) Support indicates the frequency of keyword combinations in the

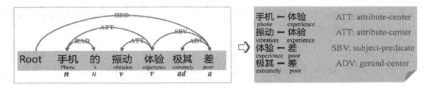

Fig. 1. Example of Dependency Parsing

dataset. (2) Confidence indicates the extent to which the rule is plausible. In this study, the FP-Growth algorithm is chosen for association rule analysis, which requires only two traversals of the target dataset, and does not need to iterate and enumerate all the data in each computation, which improves the efficiency significantly. The noun-verb set obtained by dependent parsing and the frequent items mined by the association rules are shown in Table 6, taking theme 0 as an example.

Table 6. Dependency Parsing and Association Rule Results Table for Theme 0.

Dependency Parsing		
Noun-Verb set	Dependency Relationship	Product
Virtual, Volume	ATT	Huawei mate50
Volume, Adjustment	SBV	Huawei mate50
Music, Control Interface	ATT	Huawei mate50
…	…	…
Sound, Open	VOB	Xiaomi 13
Volume, Down	SBV	Xiaomi 13
Bluetooth, Headset	ATT	Xiaomi 13
…	…	…
Association Rule		
Noun-Verb set	Confidence	Product
Variation, Sound Quality	1.0	Huawei mate50
Power, Headphones	1.0	Huawei mate50
Butler, Audio	1.0	Huawei mate50
…	…	…
Normalize, Sound	1.0	Xiaomi 13
Volume Button, Loose	1.0	Xiaomi 13
Charge, Sound	1.0	Xiaomi 13
…	…	…

Construction Methods. When creating the product innovation demand graph, the shared themes and unique themes were constructed in a slightly different way:

(1) The method of constructing product innovation demand graph under the unique theme: firstly, the frequent items mined under each unique theme, i.e. {A} → {B}, are obtained through association rules, and then the original sentences corresponding to the original sentences containing this frequent item are found sequentially. Through dependency parsing, we obtain the dominant and dominanted words of subject-predicate and verb-object relations in the sentence, i.e., the subject-predicate-object that represents the meaning of the main body of the sentence. After traversing all the frequent items, the subject-predicate and verb-object relation set pairs under the topic are finally obtained. Then, the subject labels are added to the graph first, and then the subject-predicate relation set pairs are added one by one, and finally, the verb-object relation set pairs are added sequentially.

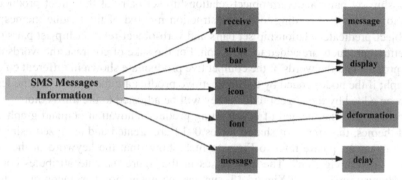

Fig. 2. Example of product innovation demand graph under the Huawei mate50 specific theme

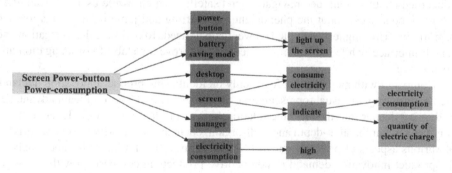

Fig. 3. Example of product innovation demand graph under the Xiaomi 13 specific theme

According to the method of constructing theme-specific product innovation demand graphs, the theme-specific product innovation demand graph of Huawei mate50 and Xiaomi 13 are constructed. As shown in Fig. 2, the theme of Huawei mate50 is "SMS Message Information", which reflects that users are concerned about the display of the status bar and icons when receiving messages, including the distortion of icons and fonts, and the delay of messages, etc.; as shown in Fig. 3, the theme of Xiaomi 13 is "Screen Power-button Power-consumption", which reflects that users are concerned about the problem of high power consumption. To improve these issues, Huawei could optimize the display of the status bar and icons, by improving software algorithms and increasing system performance. Xiaomi can provide a more detailed display of power consumption and optimize desktop and screen power consumption to help users better manage their power consumption.

(2) The method of constructing product innovation demand comparison graph under shared themes: firstly, the frequent items mined from the reviews of target products and competitive products under each shared theme are obtained through association rules, the theme labels of the shared themes are added firstly, and then the subject-predicate-relationship set pairs and verb-object-relationship set pairs of the target products are added to the graph according to the construction method of the unique themes; then the subject-predicate-relationship set pairs and verb-object-relationship set pairs of the competitive products are added to the graph. For the sake of contrast, the words of the target product and the words of the competitive product are shown in different colors in the graph; if the nodes added by the competitive product are the same as the nodes that have been added by the target product, they will be adjusted to the third color.

According to the method of constructing product innovation demand graph under shared themes, the graphs of shared topics 0–12 are created and analyzed using topic 1 as an example, please refer to Fig. 4, which shows that the keyword of the shared topic is "map navigation". The pink boxes in the figure indicate attributes common to the Huawei mate50 and Xiaomi 13, such as the navigation bar, incomplete display of lanes, and inaccurate map and compass directions. This suggests that users are more concerned about the precise positioning of navigation when using mobile phone products and that companies need to improve in this area. Comparison with the blue box (Huawei mate50) and the yellow box (Xiaomi 13) reveals that users of Huawei mate50 are more concerned about streamlined navigation and satellite search, while users of Xiaomi 13 are more concerned about the phenomenon of drifting and jumping in navigation and positioning. This suggests that the Huawei mate50 needs to optimize the navigation and search interface, while the Xiaomi 13 needs to improve the stability of navigation and positioning.

Compared with methods that focus only on identifying product innovation demand, theme clustering, or visual representation, the above method has significant advantages in digging deeper into the attribute relationships of product innovation demand. It can conduct a hierarchical in-depth and well-organized analysis to clarify the characteristics of various aspects of products under different themes. In addition, this paper analyses the product innovation demand of competitive products in comparison with the target product. This comparative analysis not only provides an understanding of the overall user demand for the product but also reveals the strengths of the target product over the competitive products. This provides key information for companies to improve their products to gain a favorable position in the market.

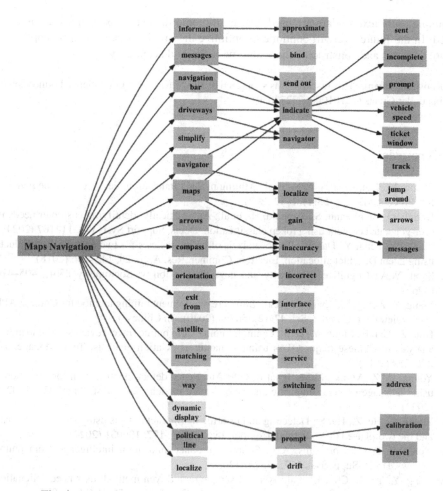

Fig. 4. Example of product innovation demand graph under a shared theme

4 Conclusion

This study effectively constructs a (comparative) graph of product innovation needs under the unique (shared) themes integrated into competitive products, clearly demonstrates users' product innovation needs, and realizes the study of the complete path of product innovation needs identification, classification, and visual expression. This study not only enriches and develops the methodological system of opinion mining, provides a new way of thinking for the application of machine learning methods to discover user opinions implied in the massive text, but also provides more ideas for product improvement, injects new inspiration for product innovation, guides enterprises to produce innovative products that truly satisfy the needs of end-users, and promotes the transmutation of innovation from the production paradigm to the service paradigm in the era of the knowledge economy. There are still some limitations in this study, for example, only textual data are used, and multimodal data such as pictures are not yet used. In the future, we will continue to optimize the graph so that it can be applied to more domains and constructed more automatically and accurately.

Acknowledgement. This research was supported by the National Natural Science Foundation of China under Grants (72101060, 72272039).

References

1. Zhang, M., Fan, B., Zhang, N., et al.: Mining product innovation ideas from online reviews. Inf. Process. Manage. **58**(1), 1–12 (2021)
2. Ettrich, O., Stahlmann, S., Leopold, H., et al.: Automatically identifying customer needs in user-generated content using token classification. Decis. Support Syst. **178**, 114107 (2024)
3. Wang, W., Feng, Y., Dai, W.: Topic analysis of online reviews for two competitive products using latent Dirichlet allocation. Electron. Commer. Res. Appl. **29**, 142–156 (2018)
4. Scott, W.A.: Cognitive complexity and cognitive flexibility. Sociometry **25**(4), 405–414 (1962)
5. Wang, Y., Zheng, L., Zhang, Y., et al.: Software requirement mining method for Chinese APP user review data. Comput. Sci. **47**(12), 56–64 (2020). (in Chinese)
6. Hou, Z., Cui, F., Meng, Y., et al.: Opinion mining from online travel reviews: a comparative analysis of Chinese major OTAs using semantic association analysis. Tour. Manage. **74**, 276–289 (2019)
7. Younas, M.Z., Malik, S.I.M., Ignatov, D.I.: Automated defect identification for cell phones using language context, linguistic and smoke-word models. Exp. Syst. Appl. **227**, 120236 (2023)
8. Zheng, L., He, Z., He, S.: Detecting and prioritizing product defects using social media data and the two-phased QFD method. Comput. Indust. Eng. **177**, 109031 (2023)
9. Goldberg, D.M., Abrahams, A.S.: Sourcing product innovation intelligence from online reviews. Decis. Supp. Syst. **157**, 113751 (2022)
10. Cong, Y., Yu, S., Chu, J., et al.: A small sample data-driven method: user needs elicitation from online reviews in new product iteration. Adv. Eng. Inform. **56**, 101953 (2023)
11. Zhang, Z., Luo, T.: Product demand analysis based on online review data mining and Kano model. Manage. Rev. **34**(11), 109–117 (2022). (in Chinese)
12. Hemmatian, F., Sohrabi, M.K.: A survey on classification techniques for opinion mining and sentiment analysis. Artif. Intell. Rev. **52**(3), 1495–1545 (2019)
13. Liu, Y., Li, F., Ji, D.: Aspect-based pair-wise opinion generation in Chinese automotive reviews: design of the task, dataset and model. Inf. Process. Manage. **58**(6), 102729 (2021)
14. Li, H., Gu, Y., Liu, J.: Research on data driven product demand recognition based on semantic similarity. Inf. Stud. Theory Appl. **45**(05), 99–106 (2022). (in Chinese)
15. Li, Z., Tang, H., Xu, X., et al.: Knowledge topic-structure exploration for online innovative knowledge acquisition. IEEE Trans. Eng. Manage. **68**(6), 1880–1894 (2021)
16. Devlin, J., Chang, M.W., Lee, K., et al.: BERT: pre-training of deep bidirectional transformers for language understanding. arXiv preprint arXiv:1810.04805 (2018)
17. Grootendorst, M.: BERTopic: neural topic modeling with a class-based TF-IDF procedure. arXiv preprint arXiv:2203.05794 (2022)

How Do Token Rewards Motivate User-Generated Content? Token Price Volatility and Peer Contribution Moderate the Effects of Token Rewards

Hongting Tang[ID], Jiachuan Yao[ID], and Yanlin Zhang[✉][ID]

School of Management, Guangdong University of Technology, Guangzhou 510520, Guangdong, China
forest_zhang@163.com

Abstract. This article elucidates the role of token rewards in influencing user contributions, proposing that token rewards can engender incentivizing effects on user contributions. Furthermore, it delves into the moderating effects of token price volatility and peer contribution on the relationship between token rewards and user contributions. Empirical research utilizing real data from Steemit is employed in this study. The results indicate that token rewards positively impact both the quantity and quality of user-generated content. Moreover, token price volatility positively/negatively moderates the positive effects of token rewards on the quantity/quality of user-generated content. Peer contribution negatively moderates the incentivizing effects of token rewards on user contributions. This article expands our understanding of blockchain-based online communities and provides management insights for such communities.

Keywords: User-generated content · Blockchain · Token rewards · Price volatility · Peer contribution

1 Introduction

User-generated content (UGC) is essential for the sustainable development of online communities [10]. However, due to its public nature as personal creations, UGC currently faces challenges related to insufficient supply and declining quality [13]. As a result, incentivizing user contributions has become a critical issue for online communities. In response, many communities have turned to using external incentives, especially monetary rewards, to motivate users. Despite this, monetary incentives have sometimes failed to produce the expected improvement in UGC quality [4]and have even led to reduced user contributions [14]. Consequently, more effective external incentives are urgently required.

Recently, a new generation of digital communities utilizing blockchain technology (blockchain-based online communities) has captured the attention of scholars and practitioners. Blockchain-based online communities influence user behavior by altering the incentive structure for content creation and curation [8]. Unlike traditional online communities, blockchain-based online communities use decentralized autonomy, while tokenizing usage, governance, ownership, and other rights within the online community, and employ token settlement transactions [6]. However, an important question remains regarding how such token impact user contributions in blockchain-based online communities.

The token incentive mechanism in blockchain-based online communities differs from monetary incentive mechanisms in three key aspects: value curation, value medium, and value distribution. Firstly, in terms of value curation, UGC in blockchain-based online communities undergoes value curation through community voting, rather than review by central entity or regulatory body [16]. Token rewards connect users' external and internal needs, suggesting that the psychological effects of receiving token rewards differ from those of monetary rewards. Secondly, concerning value medium, tokens are tradable assets on the blockchain, capable of being exchanged within the platform, converted into other cryptocurrencies or fiat currency outside the platform. Tokens require appropriate price volatility to ensure sufficient liquidity in the trading market. The token price volatility may affect the incentive effects of tokens. Lastly, in terms of value distribution, blockchain-based online communities allocate tokens based on the user contributions. These tokens stem from specific reward pools, and the tokens issued by the community within a certain period are finite. Do contributions from other users within the community serve as social norms or potential competition? Therefore, this paper will pose the following three questions:

Q1: How do token rewards for content creation influence user contributions?
Q2: Does and how does price volatility affect the effectiveness of token rewards?
Q3: Does and how does peer contribution affect the validity of token rewards?

This paper aims to investigate the effects of tokens and their inherent properties. Drawing on self-determination theory and social information processing theory to develop our hypotheses, we propose that token price volatility and peer contributions impact the quantity and quality of user contributions by moderating the direct effects of token rewards. The study utilizes Steemit as an empirical environment to test the hypotheses, enhancing our understanding of the relationship between the cryptocurrency market and blockchain-based online communities. Furthermore, it reveals that peer contributions can moderate the incentive effects brought about by external incentive mechanisms.

2 Related Work

2.1 Blockchain Technology and Blockchain-Based Online Communities

Blockchain-based online communities are decentralized online communities based on blockchain technology, which is one of the most promising application areas for the implementation of blockchain technology [9]. Existing studies have examined how tokens incentivize user behavior to achieve community autonomy within the blockchain context. Chen et al. (2023) investigated how token price volatility affects user contributions in tokenized digital platforms from the perspective of speculative nature of tokens

[5]. Delkhosh et al. (2023) analyzed the impact of bot participation on user contributions in the Steemit and the varying degree of token rewards on user contributions [8]. As tokens materialize ownership and governance rights within the community, Liu et al. (2022) suggested that tokens endow community members with a new identity—community owners and discussed the influence of this new identity on user contributions based on social capital theory and psychological ownership theory [16]. However, existing studies do not provide in-depth research on the properties of tokens, which have price volatility and are inherently scarce. How do price changes in the market and peer contribution within the community affect pass incentive effects? In other words, the relationship between token rewards and user contributions in the blockchain environment has not been thoroughly investigated.

2.2 Self-determination Theory and Social Information Processing Theory

To investigate the effects of token rewards on user participation, this paper adopts self-determination theory and social information processing theory as theoretical foundations. Self-determination theory is a macro theory concerning human motivation [7], which posits that individuals have three fundamental psychological needs—autonomy, competence, and relatedness. The fulfillment of these needs significantly enhances individuals' intrinsic motivation. Furthermore, existing research has overlooked the moderating role of token price and peer contributions when discussing the incentive effects of token rewards. Thus, focusing on the effectiveness of token rewards from the perspective of social information processing theory represents a meaningful extension of research on token rewards. According to social information processing theory, individual behavior is often influenced by complex environmental factors. Individuals interpret the information provided by the social environment and subsequently influence their attitudes and behaviors [17].

UGC contributions are voluntary prosocial behaviors and may be influenced by both external and internal environmental factors. As an external environmental factor, the market price of tokens can instantly reflect the actual benefits received by users, and existing research indicates that the value or variation of incentive elements can have an impact on individuals [5]. As an internal environmental factor, peers establish social connections with users, and numerous studies suggest that the number or performance of peers can influence individual behavior [15]. Existing research has focused more on the effects of different incentive mechanisms, the impacts of introducing incentive mechanisms on platforms, or the effects of accepting token rewards on individuals when exploring the efficacy of economic incentives, but these studies have overlooked the influence of environmental factors. Therefore, it is necessary to explore how and to what extent environmental factors, such as token prices and peers, affect the effectiveness of token rewards from the perspective of environmental information.

3 Research Model and Hypothesis Development

3.1 Direct Effect: Token Rewards

The present paper suggests that token rewards have a positive impact on user contributions, as evidenced by an increase in both the quantity and quality of UGC. According to self-determination theory, receiving performance related rewards enhances users' sense of competence. This implies that users who receive token rewards produce a greater quantity and higher quality of UGC. Similarly, Chen et al. (2019) demonstrated that monetary incentives effectively increase community content output and enhance content richness [4]. Another study also suggests that providing monetary incentives helps boost user engagement [2].

As high quality UGC often requires more time and effort, UGC quality represents the efforts exerted by the authors [14]. Previous research has indicated that UGC possesses public goods attributes [13], and the primary driver of UGC generation stems from users' intrinsic motivation. As tokens convey information about individuals' ability to produce high quality content, receiving token rewards associated with UGC quality may enhance users' intrinsic motivation [19]. Based on this, the present paper suggests that receiving token rewards will elevate users' level of effort, potentially leading to higher quality UGC, and puts forward the following hypotheses:

Hypothesis 1 (H1): Token rewards are positively associated with UGC quantity.
Hypothesis 2 (H2): Token rewards are positively associated with UGC quality.

3.2 Moderating Effect: Price Volatility

To maintain market stability, token prices exhibit a certain degree of volatility. On the one hand, appropriate token price volatility can attract more traders and investors, enhance token liquidity, and provide more trading opportunities [5]. On the other hand, token price volatility signifies uncertainty in the actual rewards received by users. The uncertainty in token prices is a significant factor that sets it apart from other reward elements. According to social information processing theory, users interpret social information and subsequently adjust their behavior [17]. Research indicates that the frequency of community information dissemination is significantly influenced by past market outcomes [18]. So, what changes occur in token rewards and user participation behavior when the cryptocurrency market fluctuates? From a theoretical perspective, prospect theory suggests that people are more inclined to avoid potential losses rather than pursue equivalent gains [12]. However, users' risk preferences and their performance when facing specific risks do not always align. Users often maintain an optimistic outlook in environments with uncertain rewards and enjoy the thrill of unveiling uncertainty [1]. Therefore, users may increase their level of effort to enhance their chances of gaining more tangible rewards. However, inevitably, users' autonomy may diminish as token price volatility intensifies. Based on this, the present paper anticipates that high volatility in token prices will incentivize user contributions and puts forward the following hypotheses:

Hypothesis 3a (H3a): Compared to low levels of token price volatility, high levels of token price volatility exert a positive impact of token rewards on the quantity of user contributions.

Hypothesis 3b (H3b): Compared to low levels of token price volatility, high levels of token price volatility result in a negative impact of token rewards on the quality of user contributions.

3.3 Moderating Effect: Peer Contribution

Upon establishing connections with the community, user behavior inevitably becomes subject to social factors. Social information processing theory emphasizes that people's behavior is significantly influenced by the surrounding social environment [17]. Other literature also indicates that social influence is a crucial factor affecting user behavior [20]. The tokens generated by the blockchain online community are limited each week. The community selects valuable UGC through community voting, and authors share the tokens in the reward pool based on the number of votes received. Furthermore, users' attention is deemed the most valuable and scarce resource on the internet. For users, receiving token rewards and social recognition serve as significant motivators for their contributions to the community. Research suggests that user contributions become more strategic in competitive environments, implying that they make fewer contributions when competition is intense. According to the competitive crowding out effect, when monetary incentives increase, some users may reduce or cease their contributions due to intensified competition [15]. Another study also indicates that as competition intensifies, user engagement levels significantly decline. Based on this, the present paper anticipates that peer contributions will inhibit user contributions and proposes the following hypotheses:

Hypothesis 4a (H4a): Compared to low levels of peer contributions, high levels of peer contributions exert a negative impact of token rewards on the quantity of user contributions.
Hypothesis 4b (H4b): Compared to low levels of peer contributions, high levels of peer contributions exert a negative impact of token rewards on the quality of user contributions.

Based on the above discussions, the research model is depicted in Fig. 1.

4 Research Method

4.1 Sample and Data Collection

The paper's research question delves into the influence of token rewards on user behavior in the blockchain environment. The study selects the renowned blockchain online community Steemit as the research subject. Initially, we chose the time window from December 27, 2018 to June 25, 2020. We obtained user information by accessing the Steem blockchain Application Programming Interface (API) at https://developers.ste em.io/. Subsequently, we acquired token prices from CoinMarketCap.com, a website that records trading information for most cryptocurrencies, to obtain historical STEEM prices.

Steemit distributes token rewards to users on a seven-day cycle. In this study, we statistically analyzed relevant variables on a weekly basis. To mitigate unobservable biases in UGC quality assessment, our research is confined to posts composed in English.

Moreover, to observe the process of changes in user participation behavior, we selected users who had posted and received tokens in at least 26 weekly periods as the subjects of our study. Ultimately, our dataset comprises 3,465 users and 254,555 data entries.

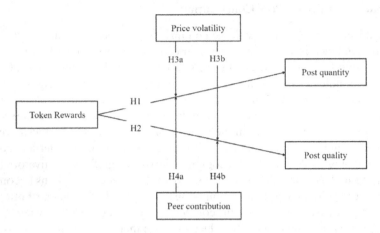

Fig. 1. Research framework

4.2 Measures

The study uses the number of token rewards to evaluate the rewards received by users. We define token price volatility as the standard deviation of the weekly STEEM opening prices. We define peer contributions as the number of posts by following users in a week. Additionally, we tabulate the number of posts each user publishes in a week to measure their level of participation. The images in Steemit community posts are crawled in the form of links, and this information is included in link count. Regarding measures of text quality, we consider text link count, text length, and fog index as three text variables to evaluate the quality of user posted articles through principal component analysis.

To ensure the accuracy of model estimation, and based on references from previous literature, this paper incorporates the following control variables: tenure, total number of posts, number of votes received, net votes received, number of comments, topic preferences, number of followers, and number of followings. To remove the long tail effect in data distribution, logarithmic transformations are applied to each variable.

4.3 Model Specification

We utilize ordinary least squares (OLS) to analyze our research model. The regression model is as follows:

$$Y_{i,t} = \alpha_i + \beta_1 Reward_{i,t-1} + \beta_2 Volatility_{t-1} + \beta_3 Reward_{i,t-1} * Volatility_{t-1}$$
$$+ \beta_4 Peercontribution_{i,t-1} + \beta_5 Reward_{i,t-1}$$
$$* Peercontribution_{i,t-1} + \tau Control_{i,t-1} + \lambda_i + \varepsilon_{i,t}$$

where α_i is the intercept, β_i are the primary parameter of interest in this paper. λ_i denotes the individual dummy variable. As the model includes macro variables, time dummy variables are not considered in the model to prevent multicollinearity issues. $\varepsilon_{i,t}$ is the error term. Furthermore, we conducted OLS regression analysis and robustness checks using Stata software version18.

5 Results

5.1 Estimation Results

Next, this section will report the interrelationships among the model variables. The Table 1 presents the regression results of the impact of token rewards on the quantity and quality of posts. According to the results of Model 1 and Model 4, token rewards are positively correlated with post quantity (coefficient $= 0.0335$, $p < 0.01$) and also positively associated with post quality (coefficient $= 0.0313$, $p < 0.01$). These findings strongly support H1 and H2, indicating that token rewards effectively promote user engagement and post quality.

In addition to the primary effects, this study also examines the moderating effects of token price volatility on peer contributions. Regarding the moderating effects of token price volatility, the interaction coefficient between token rewards and token price volatility is positive in Model 2 (coefficient $= 0.0111$, $p < 0.01$), indicating that at high levels of token price volatility, the incentive effects of token rewards is enhanced, leading to increased user engagement. This result supports H3a. According to the results of Model 5, the interaction between token rewards and token price volatility has a negative impact on post quality (coefficient $= -0.0028$, $p < 0.05$), suggesting that high token price volatility leads to a loss of quality, supporting our H3b. In terms of peer contributions, the impact of token rewards on post quantity is positively moderated, while the moderating variable simultaneously exerts a significant negative impact on post quantity/quality (coefficient $= -0.0099$, $p < 0.01$ and coefficient $= -0.0082$, $p < 0.01$). The results are support H4a and H4b.

5.2 Robustness Checks and Additional Analyses

5.2.1 Variable Substitution

To ensure the robustness of the results, this study replaces the original moderating variables with the volatility of STEEM closing prices and follower rewards, indicating a certain degree of robustness in the conclusions drawn in this paper. The results are shown in Table 2.

5.2.2 Double/Debiased Machine Learning

To address the setting bias of traditional linear regression models and the regularization bias of machine learning models, this paper further employs the double machine learning model proposed by Chernozhukov et al. (2018) for evaluation [3]. On one hand, this model can control the potential impact of high-dimensional disturbance parameters and

Table 1. Regression results on post quantity/quality.

DV	Quantity			Quality		
	Model 1	Model 2	Model 3	Model 4	Model 5	Model 6
Rewards	0.0335***	0.0287***	0.0390***	0.0313***	0.0326***	0.0358***
	(0.0071)	(0.0071)	(0.0076)	(0.0046)	(0.0047)	(0.0052)
Volatility		0.0150***			−0.0034*	
		(0.0023)			(0.0019)	
Reward × Volatility		0.0111***			−0.0028**	
		(0.0019)			(0.0014)	
Peer contribution			0.0840***			0.0724***
			(0.0084)			(0.0084)
Reward × Peer contribution			−0.0099***			−0.0082***
			(0.0034)			(0.0023)
Controls	Yes	Yes	Yes	Yes	Yes	Yes
User fixed effects	Yes	Yes	Yes	Yes	Yes	Yes
Number of observations	254555	254555	254555	254555	254555	254555
R^2	0.4733	0.4737	0.4757	0.2972	0.2973	0.3006

relax the linearity assumption. On the other hand, the model uses Neyman orthogonalization and cross-fitting to overcome the regularization bias and overfit issues in machine learning. Thus, this model can more accurately identify the causal effects between variables. Based on this, the paper utilizes double machine learning to estimate the impact of token rewards on UGC contributions.

This paper constructs the following partially linear model:

$$Y_{i,t} = \theta D_{i,t-1} + g(X_{i,t-1}) + U_{i,t-1}$$

$$E(U_{i,t-1} | D_{i,t-1}, X_{i,t-1}) = 0$$

i represents the individual, t denotes the week number. $Y_{i,t}$ represents the two dependent variables. $D_{i,t-1}$ denotes the treatment variable, representing the quantity of token rewards. θ is the core parameter of interest in this paper, measuring the marginal utility of token rewards. $X_{i,t-1}$ is a set of control variables, for which the specific functional form $g(X_{i,t-1})$ is estimated using machine learning methods. $U_{i,t-1}$ represents the error term. Following the recommendation of Chernozhukov et al. (2018), the model is split in a 1:4 ratio for cross-validation, and random forest is chosen as the machine learning method to fit the model, with the regression results shown in the table.

The models control for relevant variables. As seen from Model (1) and Model (4), the regression coefficients of token rewards on article quantity and quality are positive

Table 2. Robust Check(a).

DV	Quantity		Quality	
	Model 2	Model 3	Model 5	Model 6
Rewards	0.0306***	0.0406***	0.0326***	0.0394***
	(0.0071)	(0.0080)	(0.0047)	(0.0056)
Volatility	0.0103***		−0.0023	
	(0.0020)		(0.0016)	
Reward × Volatility	0.0079***		−0.0042***	
	(0.0017)		(0.0013)	
Peer contribution		0.0375***		0.0331***
		(0.0039)		(0.0035)
Reward × Peer contribution		−0.0092***		−0.0095***
		(0.0027)		(0.0019)
Controls	Yes	Yes	Yes	Yes
User fixed effects	Yes	Yes	Yes	Yes
Number of observations	254555	254555	254555	254555
R^2	0.4735	0.4753	0.2973	0.3007

and significant at the 1% level, indicating that token rewards can increase the quantity of articles users publish. Furthermore, to avoid the negative impact of specification bias of the double machine learning model on the conclusions, this paper modifies the parameter settings of the double machine learning model and the selection of neural networks. The sample splitting ratio for Model (2) and Model (5) is adjusted to 1:9, while random forest algorithm is replaced with neural networks for Model (3) and Model (6). The regression results obtained after resetting the double machine learning model are presented in the Table 3.

Table 3. Robust Check(b).

DV	Quantity			Quality		
	(1)	(2)	(3)	(4)	(5)	(6)
Rewards	0.0175***	0.01876***	0.0087***	0.0542***	0.0536***	0.0479***
	(0.0026)	(0.0027)	(0.0021)	(0.0023)	(0.0023)	(0.0020)
Controls	Yes	Yes	Yes	Yes	Yes	Yes
Number of observations	254555	254555	254555	254555	254555	254555

5.2.3 Instrumental Variable

To mitigate the issue of endogeneity in the regression analysis, this paper has endeavored to incorporate variables influencing user participation behaviors as comprehensively as possible and include the lagged explanatory variables in the model. However, it is inevitable that unobserved variables may still have a potential impact on the model. Therefore, this paper will use instrumental variable methods to further alleviate the endogeneity issue in the regression analysis. The paper employs the lagged token rewards as an instrumental variable to correct for biases caused by the core explanatory variables. Upon examination, this variable satisfies the exogeneity and relevance assumptions of instrumental variables. Leveraging instrumental variable two-stage least squares and constructing a partially linear instrumental variable model using double machine learning, the specific results are shown in the Table 4.

Table 4. Robust Check(c).

DV	IV		DMLIV	
	Quantity	Quality	Quantity	Quality
Rewards	0.3039^{***}	0.2123^{***}	0.0447^{***}	0.1046^{***}
	(0.0049)	(0.0041)	(0.0072)	(0.0071)
Controls	Yes	Yes	Yes	Yes
User fixed effects	Yes	Yes	No	No
Number of observations	251090	251090	251090	251090

6 Discussion and Conclusions

As a new generation of digital technology, blockchain and its derivative technologies provide a new perspective for effective incentivization. Within this framework, this article evaluates the level of contribution from users in the Steemit. It focuses on the dimensions of text quantity and text quality, with token rewards as the core explanatory variable, employing OLS to explore the impact and underlying mechanisms of token rewards on user contributions. Furthermore, it examines the moderating effects of token price volatility and peer contributions. Empirical results demonstrate that token rewards have a significantly positive influence on both the quantity and quality of user posts. The relationship between token rewards and user contributions is notably moderated by token price volatility and peer contributions, where token price volatility positively moderates the positive relationship between token rewards and the quantity of user posts, while negatively moderating the relationship between token rewards and post quality. Peer contributions negatively moderate the relationship between token rewards and both the quantity and quality of user posts.

This study focuses on the emerging blockchain online community to explore the incentivizing role of token rewards on user contribution behavior, holding important theoretical and practical significance. Firstly, it enriches the relevant research on token rewards in blockchain online communities. Secondly, it enhances the literature related to price volatility and peer contributions by considering the social environmental information within the blockchain context on the effectiveness of token rewards. Lastly, this article employs double machine learning to capture the complex causal relationships within the community, making the research conclusions more reliable. From a management perspective, Steemit should continue to practice token incentives and work to keep token prices under reasonable levels of volatility, while, at the same time, reducing the visibility of information related to peer contribution. However, this article has certain limitations. It solely focuses on the Steemit and does not further extend the research scope to validate the applicability of the research conclusions. Additionally, as online communities contain a large amount of textual and visual information, this article does not deeply explore image-related information, and the measurement of text quality requires further refinement.

Acknowledgement. We gratefully acknowledge the funding support from the National Natural Science Foundation of China (Grant 72101060, 72272039) and Guangzhou Basic and Applied Basic Research Foundation (Grant 202201010333).

References

1. Burke, J., et al.: Ambiguous sticks and carrots: the effect of contract framing and payoff ambiguity on employee effort. Account. Rev. **98**(1), 139–162 (2023)
2. Burtch, G., Hong, Y., Bapna, R., Griskevicius, V.: Stimulating online reviews by combining financial incentives and social norms. Manage. Sci. **64**(5), 2065–2082 (2017)
3. Chernozhukov, V., et al.: Double/debiased machine learning for treatment and structural parameters. Economet. J. **21**(1), c1–c68 (2018)
4. Chen, H., Hu, Y.J., Huang, S.: Monetary incentive and stock opinions on social media. J. Manag. Inf. Syst. **36**(2), 391–417 (2019)
5. Chen, K., Fan, Y., Liao, S.S.: Token incentives in a volatile crypto market: the effects of token price volatility on user contribution. J. Manag. Inf. Syst. **40**(2), 683–711 (2023)
6. Chod, J., Trichakis, N.S., Yang, A.: Platform tokenization: financing, governance, and Moral Hazard. Manage. Sci. **68**(9), 6411–6433 (2022)
7. Deci, E.L., Olafsen, A.H., Ryan, R.M.: Self-determination theory in work organizations: the state of a science. Annu. Rev. Organ. Psych. Organ. Behav. **4**(1), 19–43 (2017)
8. Delkhosh, F., et al.: Impact of bot involvement in an incentivized blockchain-based online social media platform. J. Manag. Inf. Syst. **40**(3), 778–806 (2023)
9. Gan, J. (Rowena), Tsoukalas, G., Netessine, S.: Decentralized Platforms: Governance, Tokenomics, and ICO Design, Management Science, pp. 6667–6683 (2023)
10. Huang, N., et al.: Motivating user-generated content with performance feedback: evidence from randomized field experiments. Manage. Sci. **65**(1), 327–345 (2019)
11. Huang, Y., Singh, P.V., Ghose, A.: A structural model of employee behavioral dynamics in enterprise social media. Manage. Sci. **61**(12), 2825–2844 (2015)
12. Kahneman, D., Tversky, A.: Prospect theory: an analysis of decision under risk. Econometrica: J. Econ. Soc. 263–291 (1979)
13. Ke, Z., Liu, D., Brass, D.J.: Do online friends bring out the best in us? The effect of friend contributions on online review provision. Inf. Syst. Res. **31**(4), 1322–1336 (2020)

14. Khern-am-nuai, W., Kannan, K., Ghasemkhani, H.: Extrinsic versus intrinsic rewards for contributing reviews in an online platform. Inf. Syst. Res. **29**(4), 871–892 (2018)
15. Liu, Y., Feng, J.: Does money talk? The impact of monetary incentives on user-generated content contributions. Inf. Syst. Res. **32**(2), 394–409 (2021)
16. Liu, Z., et al.: User incentive mechanism in blockchain-based online community: an empirical study of Steemit. Inf. Manag. **59**(7), 103596 (2022)
17. Saiancik, G.R., Pfeffer, J.: A social information processing approach to job attitudes and task design. Adm. Sci. Q. **23**(2), 224–253 (1978)
18. Xie, P.: The interplay between investor activity on virtual investment community and the trading dynamics: evidence from the bitcoin market. Inf. Syst. Front. **24**, 1287–1303 (2022)
19. Yu, Y., Khern-am-nuai, W., Pinsonneault, A.: When paying for reviews pays off: the case of performance-contingent monetary rewards. MIS Q. **46**(1), 609–625 (2022)
20. Zeng, Z., et al.: The impact of social nudges on user-generated content for social network platforms. Manag. Sci. **69**(9), 5189–5208 (2022)

A Human-Computer Automated Negotiation Model Based on Opponent's Emotion and Familiarity

Mukun Cao and Lei Xian[✉]

Xiamen University, Siming South Road 422, Xiamen 361005, China
xianlei@stu.xmu.edu.cn

Abstract. In e-commerce transactions, agent-based automated negotiation systems combine the advantages of artificial intelligence and bring great convenience to enterprises. However, few studies in agent-based model have considered the social characteristics of human interactions. In this paper, we propose a model with opponent's emotion and familiarity. Also use a capsule network to predict the type of an opponent based on bidding. We use opponent type, emotion, and familiarity as inputs to the improved TD3 to predict opponent' next round bidding. Through comparative experiments, our proposed model achieves better results in the transaction price, seller's utility, satisfaction, negotiation process and the negotiation rounds.

Keywords: Online Transaction · Emotion · Familiarity · Negotiation

1 Introduction

With the rapid development of the Internet and e-commerce, the number and scale of online transactions have increased rapidly. As an important part of business activities, negotiation is getting more and more attention. Automated negotiation, as a mode of business negotiation, replaces human beings in business negotiation through agent, which not only solves the spatial distance of offline negotiation but also saves time and cost and becomes the focus of scholars' attention (Cao et al., 2020).

Human-computer negotiation is when computers can accurately understand human language, capture human emotions, and use human language to start negotiation dialogues with them. Emotion is a critical factor influencing negotiation behavior results (Yip & Schweinsberg, 2017). Therefore, human-computer negotiation needs to empower the computer with semantic understanding and emotion recognition capability based on negotiation interaction, which improves agents' anthropomorphism.

Familiarity measures how well people are known during their interactions (Liu et al., 2016). In automated negotiation, familiarity can be used to measure the frequency of human-agent interactions and the strength of the relationship (Chen et al., 2023). When the agent and user are unfamiliar, it is difficult to communicate easily. Familiarity can reduce uncertainty in negotiation, promote trust between user and agent, and facilitate

Y. P. Tu and M. Chi (Eds.): WHICEB 2024, LNBIP 515, pp. 387–395, 2024.
https://doi.org/10.1007/978-3-031-60264-1_33

smooth communication. Therefore, familiarity can promote users' positive attitudes towards the agent and obtain better negotiation results (Chi et al., 2021).

In sum, this article designs a model for dynamic bidding with user emotion and familiarity to explore the impact on negotiation outcomes. We use a capsule net-work to predict the type of opponent, combined with the calculation of emotion and familiarity value as an input to improved TD3 and finally output the predicted opponent price.

2 Literature Review

2.1 Emotional Influence on Negotiation

Emotion, as an important way to get along with others, can effectively maintain inter-personal relationships and express action intentions. The social effects of emotions are embodied in that emotional expressions influence observer reactions, information processes and behaviors (Van Kleef & Cote, 2022).

Negotiation emotions include happiness, anger, fear, sadness, guilt, disapproval, etc. (Clempner, 2020). According to the complexity of emotions, there are single and mixed emotions. The influence of a single emotion can focus on observing the opponent's intention information in the context of specific social interactions (Keltner & Haidt, 1999). In negotiation process, the opponent's behavior changes and new information is transmitted, and the observer's emotion also changes dynamically (Scherer, 2009), so the study of mixed emotions may be more reality. Emotion is put forward as a social information model (EASI); emotions influence interaction processes, and negotiators generally use expression as a social information transmission (Van Kleef, 2009). Recognizing changes in the dynamics of the opponent's emotion during negotiation can help to adopt appropriate reply strategies and create a stronger sense of interaction for the user.

At present, there are abundant research results on negotiation influenced by emotions. It is mainly the influence of emotions on negotiation behavior (Wilson et al., 2016) and negotiation results (Yip & Schweinsberg, 2017). We designed an opponent bidding prediction model with psychometric indicators of emotion and familiarity to dynamically predict the user's next bidding with an appropriate emotional reply.

2.2 Agent-Based Automated Negotiation

Automated negotiation mainly uses game theoretic strategies, heuristic algorithms, argument-based strategies and machine learning strategies. Zhang (2010) proposed a solution to multi-person negotiation problems in bargaining situations and solved continuous negotiation problems. Keskin et al. (2023) presented a conflict-based opponent modeling technique and found that an automated negotiation agent could reach deals faster and accurately perceived users' behavioral preferences. Peng and Su (2020) used a new MAGDM approach to reduce group experts' workload and decrease the decision-making process's complexity. Kröhling et al. (2021) gave a model that used reinforcement learning to obtain contextual information to gain a competitive advantage, effectively facilitating higher benefits for the agent and social welfare.

The existing literature focuses on optimizing algorithms to improve the effectiveness of automated negotiation. Emotions and familiarity, as important factors in important social interactions, are modeled in conjunction with automated negotiation. The agent fully considers the human user's behavior and effectively improves intelligence.

3 Construction of a Human-Computer Negotiation System with Emotion and Familiarity

3.1 Opponent Bidding Prediction Negotiation Strategy

The opponent bidding prediction negotiation strategy is shown in Fig. 1. The agent obtains the opponent's price for three consecutive rounds as inputs to the module of the capsule network, and the opponent's type as the predicted output of the capsule network. At the same time, the values of emotion and familiarity are combined as inputs to the improved TD3 module, and the predicted offer of the opponent for the next round is output.

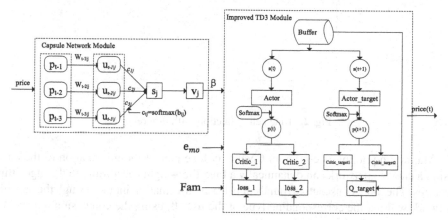

Fig. 1. The opponent' bidding prediction negotiation strategy framework

Time Belief Function

Time is the main constraint in the negotiation process, and we assume that users and agent have similar time beliefs. Time belief is the probability that the agent believes that the opponent accepts its offer (Chen et al., 2014).The agent will have a strict negotiation time, i.e., a maximum number of rounds of negotiation. Both parties want to reach a negotiation and have to keep compromising as time advances. According to Faratin et al. (1998), we consider the negotiating parties to be based on a time-dependent concession strategy function:

$$b(t) = e^{\left(1 - \frac{\min(t, t_{max})}{t_{max}}\right)^{\beta} \ln(K)},$$

$$(1)$$

where, t_{max} is the maximum negotiation time, and t is the current negotiation round; K is the negotiation coefficient; the value range of parameter β is between 0 and 50, which can determine the concavity and convexity of the curve. b(t) is a subtraction function related to time t, and b(t) $\in$ [0, 1]. Opponent's types are usually classified into three categories based on β: collaborative, neutral, and competitive. Agent thinks that collaborative opponent has a higher probability of accepting an offer, $\beta \in (1, 50]$, followed by neutral $\beta = 1$, and finally competitive $\beta \in (0, 1)$. Since the type of opponent may change dynamically, we use capsule networks to predict the type of opponent (Fig. 2).

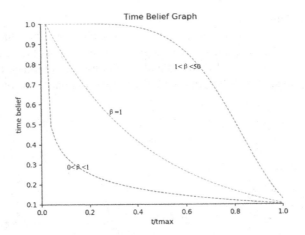

Fig. 2. Time belief function with different β

Maximum pooling operation in CNN may lose part of the information of the data, using a capsule network can dynamically adjust the weights according to the algorithm features. The three consecutive rounds of price as information input, through the capsule network will get the corresponding type of the user β, using the conversion matrix W_{tj} to map the price to the prediction vector u_{tj} :

$$u_{tj} = W_{tj}p_{tj}. \tag{2}$$

The prediction vector u_{tj} is weighted and summed with the coupling coefficients c_{tj} to obtain the output node s_j. At the same time, s_j is the input to the main capsule layer.

$$s_j = \sum_i c_{ij}u_{tj} \tag{3}$$

The main capsule layer s_j is compressed using the squash function:

$$v_j = \frac{\|s_j\|^2}{1 + \|s_j\|^2} \frac{s_j}{\|s_j\|}. \tag{4}$$

b_{ij} is updated by the correlation between the main capsule layer and subcapsule layer, and the coupling coefficient c_{ij} is larger when the similarity between u_{tj} and v_j is higher.

$$b_{ij} \leftarrow b_{ij} + u_{tj} \cdot v_j \tag{5}$$

The correlation between the main capsule layer and subcapsule layer is calculated by adjusting the weights through continuous iteration. Finally, the feature vector obtained from the main capsule layer is obtained.

Emotion

Emotions generally originate within the individual or are influenced by external events. Weber-Fechner Law describes the sensation of external physical stimuli on human mental stimuli (Wu et al., 2022). The calculation function is:

$$e_{mo} = k_m \log(1 + \Delta v), \tag{6}$$

where, e_{mo} is the emotion value, k_m is the normalized coefficient (usually $k_m = 1$), and Δv is the difference in stimulus. In negotiation, we use the change of the opponent's price as Δv.

$$\Delta v = \frac{p(t+1) - p(t)}{p^h} \tag{7}$$

Familiarity

As the number of negotiation rounds between the user and the agent increases, the familiarity between the two parties increases during the interaction. According to Qie et al. (2022), we construct the relationship between familiarity and experience value:

$$Fam = \frac{2}{1 + e^{-(t+E)}} - 1, \tag{8}$$

where t represents negotiation rounds, $t \in [0, t_{max}]$. E is the experience value between the user and the agent. For users with no experience in negotiating with the agent, their experience with the agent is 0. Familiarity is an increasing function for t and E. According to Zhang et al. (2007) in the context of negotiations, we construct experience formulas:

$$E = -\ln\left(\frac{2}{E_{initial} + t} - 1\right), \tag{9}$$

where $E_{initial}$ is the initial experience value of the user and agent, and the agent finds negotiation history from the database. If the agent and the user do not have historical negotiation records, the $E_{initial} = 0$.

Improved TD3 Module

TD3 is a deep learning algorithm that improves on the DDPG algorithm. At each round t, with a given state s, the agent selects actions a with reward r and the new environment $s(t + 1)$. The TD3 algorithm contains six networks: actor network: critic_1 network, critic_2 network, actor_target network, critic1_target network, critic2_ target network. The TD3 algorithm creates two independent critic networks by taking the smaller of the two when calculating the target value:

$$y_t = r_t + \gamma \min_{i=1,2} Q_{\theta_i^{t+1}}(s_{t+1}, \varphi(s_{t+1})), \tag{10}$$

where, r_t is the immediate reward at t, γ is the discount factor, y_t is the cumulative reward, and s_{t+1} is the state at $t + 1$.

To reduce the cumulative error, a delayed update strategy is adopted, where the first update of the critic network, followed by the update of the actor network:

$$\theta_i \leftarrow \min_{\theta_i} \frac{1}{N} \sum (y_t - Q_{\theta_i}(s, a))^2. \tag{11}$$

N is the critic network update period, and Q_{θ_i} is the critic network weight parameter, then the function is:

$$\nabla_\varphi J(\varphi) = \frac{1}{N} \sum \nabla_\varphi Q_{\theta_i}(s, a)|_{a=\pi_{\varphi(s)}}, \tag{12}$$

$$\theta_i^{t+1} \leftarrow r\theta_i + (1 - r)\theta_i^{t+1}|_{(i=1,2)}, \tag{13}$$

$$\varphi^{t+1} \leftarrow r\varphi + (1 - r)\varphi^{t+1}. \tag{14}$$

In the traditional TD3 algorithm, the data is sampled randomly during the training process, which leads to less efficient training. The Softmax changes actor network in accelerates the learning process in which the maximum network parameters are selected and recorded (Wu et al., 2023). The Softmax function maps the input values to a probability distribution representing the likelihood of a particular class. It is more sensitive to changes in input values and is suitable for neural network training.

$$\text{Softmax}(a_i) = \frac{e^{a_i}}{\sum_{i=1}^n e^{a_i}} \tag{15}$$

In summary, the predicted price p $(t + 1)$ of the agent is output by improved TD3 through the time belief b(t), the emotion value e_{mo} and familiarity Fam as environmental inputs.

The state is $s(t)$ at the time of the t^h quotation, and the quotation action is $p(t)$, and then it enters the next state $s(t + 1)$ after the quotation $p(t)$. Therefore, the Q function based on Q-learning learning can be defined as:

$$Q(s(t), p(t)) = r(s(t), p(t)) + \gamma \max_{p(t+1)} Q(\delta(s(t), p(t)), p(t + 1)) \tag{16}$$

If the negotiation is successful in the T quotation, the expected returns of the seller and the buyer:

$$Q = \int_{p_l}^{p_h} \left(p_h - p^T\right) b(t) e_{mo} Fam dp^T, \tag{17}$$

where p_l and p_h represent the user's initial bidding and reserve price.

The average expectation of the user's Q value is:

$$\overline{Q}(s(t), p(t)) = \frac{\sum_{i=t}^{T_b} \gamma^{i-t} b(i) e_{mo} Fam Q_e^b}{T_b - t + 1}. \tag{18}$$

The quotation strategy of the agent prediction is:

$$p(t + 1) = p^h - \overline{Q}(s(t), p(t)). \tag{19}$$

3.2 Reply Strategy

We divide the emotions in negotiation into five categories, namely, happy and satisfied, worried and anxious, disappointed and wronged, angry, and no emotion. There are three steps of the reply strategy: first, preprocess the user's text (word segmentation, stop words removal, etc.); second, realize the feature representation of the text through the text representation model; third, uses BERT to realize emotion classification based on the constructed classifier; fourth, responding to appropriate content according to different emotions.

4 Experiment Analysis

4.1 Experimental Results Measurement Method

Thompson and Leigh (1990) proposed that measuring negotiation results should include objective economic outcomes and subjective outcomes. The indicators for evaluating the objective consequences of negotiations generally include the transaction price, the negotiation rounds and the utility difference between negotiators. The subjective impact of negotiation from two aspects: satisfaction and negotiation process perception. Objective results are mainly obtained through human-computer experimental results. The results of subjective outcomes are collected according to the questionnaire after the human-computer experiment.

4.2 Human-Computer Negotiation Experiment

The participating members invited to this human-computer negotiation experiment are mainly students. After the personal recruitment, the experimenter ends the investigation through an online human-computer negotiation system. As for the questionnaire collection, the experiment group (EG) with proposed model of 113 samples, while the control group (CG) without proposed model of 106 samples.

The results show the descriptive statistical results of the two groups of experiments on various indicators and the ANOVA analysis results of the two groups of experiments. The transaction price ($M_{EG} = 68.62, M_{CG} = 61.13, p < 0.05$), seller's utility ($M_{EG} = 0.48, M_{CG} = 0.31, p < 0.05$), perceived satisfaction ($M_{EG} = 5.63, M_{CG} = 4.30, p < 0.05$) and perceived negotiation process ($M_{EG} = 5.36, M_{CG} = 4.12, p < 0.001$) perception of experiment group are significantly higher than the control group. While the negotiation rounds ($M_{EG} = 16, M_{CG} = 23, p < 0.001$) and buyer's utility ($M_{EG} = 0.25, M_{CG} = 0.40, p < 0.05$), of experiment group is lower than the control group. It shows that emotion recognition ability is conducive to improving negotiation efficiency.

5 Conclusion and Further Work

In this paper, we propose a model based on two social characteristics, opponent's emotion and familiarity, and also consider the type of opponent as an input to improved TD3 and respond according to the opponent's emotion. The experimental analysis shows that our model outperforms the model without emotion and familiarity regarding the transaction price, seller's utility, satisfaction, negotiation process and negotiation rounds. Although we achieved some research results, some things could still be improved in this paper.

Some aspects need to be supplemented and enhanced in the subsequent research. First, we mainly study the single-attribute negotiation between humans and computers about price. The negotiation issues should be further extended to multi-issue negotiation scenarios in future research. Second, we can consider more subjective emotion indicators for comparative experiments.

Acknowledgement. This work is supported by the National Natural Science Foundation of China (Grant # 72171199).

References

Cao, M.K., Hu, Q., Kiang, M.Y., Hong, H.: A portfolio strategy design for human-computer negotiations in e-retail. Int. J. Electron. Commer. 24(3), 305–337 (2020). https://doi.org/10.1080/10864415.2020.1767428

Chen, L., Dong, H., Zhou, Y.: A reinforcement learning optimized negotiation method based on mediator agent. Expert Syst. Appl. 41(16), 7630–7640 (2014)

Chen, X.Y., Chen, R.R., Wei, S.B., Davison, R.M.: Herd behavior in social commerce: understanding the interplay between self-awareness and environment-awareness. Internet Res. (2023). https://doi.org/10.1108/intr-05-2022-0359

Chi, O.H., Jia, S.Z., Li, Y.F., Gursoy, D.: Developing a formative scale to measure consumers' trust toward interaction with artificially intelligent (AI) social robots in service delivery. Comput. Hum. Behav. 118, 106700 (2021). https://doi.org/10.1016/j.chb.2021.106700

Clempner, J.B.: Shaping emotions in negotiation: a Nash bargaining solution. Cogn. Comput. 12(4), 720–735 (2020). https://doi.org/10.1007/s12559-020-09713-9

Faratin, P., Sierra, C., Jennings, N.R.: Negotiation decision functions for autonomous agents. Robot. Auton. Syst. 24(3–4), 159–182 (1998)

Keltner, D., Haidt, J.: Social functions of emotions at four levels of analysis. Cogn. Emot. 13(5), 505–521 (1999). https://doi.org/10.1080/026999399379168

Keskin, M.O., Buzcu, B., Aydogan, R.: Conflict-based negotiation strategy for human-agent negotiation. Appl. Intell. (2023). https://doi.org/10.1007/s10489-023-05001-9

Kröhling, D.E., Chiotti, O.J.A., Martinez, E.C.: A context-aware approach to automated negotiation using reinforcement learning. Adv. Eng. Inform. 47, 101229 (2021). https://doi.org/10.1016/j.aei.2020.101229

Liu, H.F., Chu, H.L., Huang, Q., Chen, X.Y.: Enhancing the flow experience of consumers in China through interpersonal interaction in social commerce. Comput. Hum. Behav. 58, 306–314 (2016). https://doi.org/10.1016/j.chb.2016.01.012

Peng, C., Su, C.: A multi-agent affective interactive MAGDM approach and its applications. Exp. Syst. 37(2), e12480 (2020). https://doi.org/10.1111/exsy.12480

Qie, X.T., Wu, J.H., Li, Y., Sun, Y.: A stage model for agent-based emotional persuasion with an adaptive target: from a social exchange perspective. Inf. Sci. 610, 90–113 (2022). https://doi.org/10.1016/j.ins.2022.07.147

Scherer, K.R.: The dynamic architecture of emotion: evidence for the component process model. Cognit. Emotion 23(7), 1307–1351 (2009). Article Pii 915419435. https://doi.org/10.1080/02699930902928969

Thompson, L.: Negotiation behavior and outcomes: empirical evidence and theoretical issues. Psychol. Bull. **108**(3), 515–532 (1990)

Van Kleef, G.A.: How emotions regulate social life: the emotions as social information (EASI) model. Curr. Dir. Psychol. Sci. **18**(3), 184–188 (2009). https://doi.org/10.1111/j.1467-8721. 2009.01633.x

Van Kleef, G.A., Cote, S.: The social effects of emotions. Annu. Rev. Psychol. **73**, 629–658 (2022). https://doi.org/10.1146/annurev-psych-020821-010855

Wilson, K.S., DeRue, D.S., Matta, F.K., Howe, M., Conlon, D.E.: Personality similarity in negotiations: testing the dyadic effects of similarity in interpersonal traits and the use of emotional displays on negotiation outcomes. J. Appl. Psychol. **101**(10), 1405–1421 (2016). https://doi. org/10.1037/apl0000132

Wu, C., Ruan, J., Cui, H., Zhang, B., Li, T., Zhang, K.: The application of machine learning based energy management strategy in multi-mode plug-in hybrid electric vehicle, part I: Twin Delayed Deep Deterministic Policy Gradient algorithm design for hybrid mode. Energy **262**, 125084 (2023). https://doi.org/10.1016/j.energy.2022.125084

Wu, J.H., Chen, H.Y., Li, Y., Liu, Y.H.: A behavioral assessment model for emotional persuasion driven by agent-based decision-making. Exp. Syst. Appl. **204**, 117556 (2022). https://doi.org/ 10.1016/j.eswa.2022.117556

Yip, J.A., Schweinsberg, M.: Infuriating impasses: angry expressions increase exiting behavior in negotiations. Soc. Psychol. Personal. Sci. **8**(6), 706–714 (2017). https://doi.org/10.1177/194 8550616683021

Zhang, D.M.: A logic-based axiomatic model of bargaining. Artif. Intell. **174**(16–17), 1307–1322 (2010). https://doi.org/10.1016/j.artint.2010.08.003

Zhang, J., Ghorbani, A.A., Cohen, R.: A familiarity-based trust model for effective selection of sellers in multiagent e-commerce systems. Int. J. Inf. Secur. **6**(5), 333–344 (2007). https://doi. org/10.1007/s10207-007-0025-y

Optimal Delivery Modes and the Impact of Fee Transparency Reform in Online Food Delivery Platforms

Xing Wan[✉] and Zhuoran Dong[✉]

School of Business Administration, Nanjing University of Finance and Economics, Nanjing 210023, China
1539802459@qq.com

Abstract. This study explores the optimal delivery modes and the impact of fee transparency reform on online food delivery platforms. By building models and conducting comparative analysis, we examine the effects of consumer demand for real-time delivery tracking, price thresholds, and platform fee transparency on merchants and platforms. The findings reveal that when consumers have low preference for real-time delivery tracking, merchants are more inclined to choose self-delivery to avoid high delivery costs and platform commissions. When the price threshold is low and there is moderate demand for real-time delivery tracking, merchants prioritize profits on each order and opt for platform delivery, while platforms tend to refrain from reform. However, in case of high consumer preference for real-time delivery tracking and a low price threshold, merchants choose platform delivery, and fee transparency reform further increases their profits. Finally, in case of high consumer preference for real-time delivery tracking and a high price threshold, the reform has no impact on merchant choices. This study provides decision support for online food delivery platforms and merchants, aiding them in selecting the optimal delivery modes and formulating fee strategies to improve efficiency and meet consumer demands.

Keywords: fee transparency reform · real-time delivery tracking · price thresholds · online food delivery platforms

1 Introduction

With the rapid development of the Internet and mobile technology, online food delivery platforms have risen worldwide. These platforms provide convenient food ordering and delivery services for consumers while offering new sales channels for merchants [1]. However, as the competition in the online food delivery industry intensifies, both platforms and merchants face a range of relevant decision-making issues.

One important issue is the selection of the optimal delivery mode. Numerous studies have addressed this topic. Ma distinguishes four logistics modes and indicates that merchants will choose the appropriate logistics service based on different management objectives [2]. Liu et al. analyzed the advantages and disadvantages of self-delivery [3], while Song analyzed the reasons for merchants choosing third-party delivery [4]. Du examined the impact of self-delivery-generated advertising effects and the consumer benefits from third-party platform promotion on merchant's food delivery strategies [5]. Li using Amazon as an example, found that providing fulfillment services is always beneficial for dominant retailers in the absence of competition. However, when competition exists, whether to offer fulfillment services depends on the extent of product valuation improvement and cost heterogeneity [6]. Tao discussed the pricing and delivery distance decisions for local merchants, and found that the app channel strategy is influenced by their own logistics capabilities and pricing power [7]. Du studied the impact of differential pricing on restaurant delivery modes [8]. Niu et al. explored the selection of online channel logistics delivery modes considering environmental sustainability [9]. Kimes identified delivery cost and capacity as key factors affecting O2O food delivery [10]. Liu et al. found that delivery service quality and speed are major influencing factors [11], while Arslan concluded that estimated delivery time is a primary measure of delivery capacity [12]. In summary, merchants and platforms need to weigh the pros and cons of different delivery modes from various perspectives in order to maximize profits and meet consumer demands.

In recent years, with the implementation of rate transparency reforms in the food delivery industry, the previous "fixed service fee" has been divided into "fulfillment service fee" and "technology service fee" [13], marking a significant progress in this structural reform. However, whether the reform that caters to the needs of merchants truly benefits them and whether structural reforms can genuinely meet the demands of merchants are still subject to further investigation.

Previous literature has combined merchants' delivery mode selection with platform development, pricing strategies, and other factors. This article, however, focuses on both merchants and platforms, taking into account the impact of real-time delivery on consumers and for the first time combines it with platform reform to identify the specific conditions for optimal merchant delivery, thus enriching existing research.

The purpose of this article is to explore the optimal strategy for merchants' delivery modes, focusing on the following research questions:

(1) How should merchants set product prices for each delivery mode?
(2) Are platform fee transparency reforms beneficial for merchants, and how do they influence merchants' choices of delivery modes?

2 Model

2.1 Symbol Specification

See Table 1 for symbol descriptions.

2.2 Model Framework and Assumptions

This model consists of a single merchant (selling only one type of product, and the price setter), a food delivery platform, and consumers, with consumers not participating in the decision-making process.

Assumption 1: This model focuses on the merchant's delivery mode selection before and after the fee reform. The basic model doesn't consider offline shopping scenarios and can be understood as the merchant solely engaged in online sales.

Assumption 2: To simplify the model, the basic model only considers the impact of product price on delivery fees. Factors such as delivery distance and time slots are not considered in the basic model.

Assumption 3: In reality, to prevent consumers from abandoning purchases due to delivery fees, merchants often bear the delivery fees and provide fee waivers to consumers [14]. For the sake of convenience, in this model, the delivery fees are entirely borne by the merchant.

Table 1. Notations.

Parameters	Variable	Descriptions
V	Consumer valuation of a product	Consumer valuations are the same regardless of the purchase route or delivery method
N/G	Platform reform or not	N: reform; G: non-reform
S/K	Delivery mode	S: self-delivery; K: third-party platform delivery
Pa_i	Online selling price	Discount coupons; $0 < Pa_i < 1$
d_i	Consumer demand	
u_i	Consumer utility	
F_i	Service fee before platform reform	
f_i	Commission after platform reform	$0 < f_i < 1$
c_{GK}	Delivery fee after platform reform	$0 < c_{GK} < 1$
c_R	Third-party platform delivery cost	$0 < c_R < 1$
c_S	Self-delivery cost	$0 < c_S < 1$
h_K	Real-time delivery tracking effect	$0 < h_K < 1$

We assume that the platform is the leader in this game and first decides whether to conduct a transparency reform in its strategic decision-making. Then, the merchant decides which delivery mode to choose, as shown in Fig. 1. For ease of representation, we use $\Omega = \alpha\beta$, where $\alpha \in \{N, G\}$ and $\beta \in \{K, S\}$, to denote the strategy combinations of the platform and the merchant. Specifically, the first letter $\alpha = N$ and S represent the platform's non-reform strategy and transparency reform strategy, respectively. $\beta = K$ and S represent the merchant's platform delivery mode and self-delivery mode, respectively [15]. It is worth noting that when the merchant chooses the self-delivery mode (S), the platform does not charge any delivery fees to the merchant. Therefore, in this model, under the assumption that the merchant chooses the self-delivery mode, the fees charged by the platform to the merchant remain the same before and after the reform, while other conditions remain unchanged. Thus, the basic model in this paper includes three strategy combinations: $\Omega = \{S, NK, GK\}$.

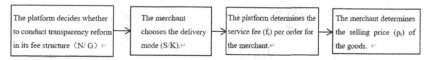

Fig. 1. The order of decisions for merchants and platforms in the model.

2.3 Demand Functions

Here, we will discuss the demand functions under different scenarios. We use "v" to represent the willingness of consumers to pay based on their value preferences for the product, which follows a uniform distribution over.

When $\Omega = S$, the consumer utility u_S is only influenced by the product price pa_S, and $u_S = v - pa_S$. The consumer will purchase the product only when $u_S > 0$; otherwise, the consumer will not make any purchases. Therefore, by integrating the utility function over $v \in [pa_S, 1]$, we obtain the demand function $d_S = 1 - pa_S$.

When $\Omega = NK$, consumers have real-time visibility of the distance between the delivery rider and the destination, providing improved user experience and delivery transparency. The consumer utility u_{NK} is influenced by the product price pa_{NK} and the real-time delivery tracking effect h_K, and the utility function is $u_{NK} = v - pa_{NK} + h_K$. The consumer will purchase the product only when $u_{NK} > 0$; otherwise, the consumer will not make any purchases. Therefore, the demand function is $d_{NK} = 1 - pa_{NK} + h_K$.

When $\Omega = GK$, the utility function is $u_{GK} = v - pa_{GK} + h_K$. The consumer will purchase the product only when $u_{GK} > 0$; otherwise, the consumer will not make any purchases. Therefore, the demand function is $d_{GK} = 1 - pa_{GK} + h_K$.

3 Analysis and Discussion

In this section, we first derive and discuss the equilibrium prices, demand, and profits under the three scenarios (S, NK, GK). Then, we conduct a comprehensive comparison to determine the equilibrium strategies for the platform and the merchant.

3.1 Equilibrium Solutions

Merchant Self-Delivery. In this scenario, the model in this paper assumes that the impact on the equilibrium profit of the merchant choosing self-delivery is minimal, whether before or after the transparency reform of the delivery fees. Therefore, in this model, the scenario of the merchant choosing self-delivery before the reform (NS) and the scenario of the merchant choosing self-delivery after the reform (GS) are combined into one scenario, referred to as "S" (Self-Delivery). In this case, after consumers place orders through the platform, the third-party platform charges the merchant a commission fee f_S per order. The merchant's delivery cost is represented as c_s. Therefore, under the self-delivery condition, the profit maximization models for the merchant and the platform are as follows:

$$\underset{d_S>0}{MAX}\ \Pi_b\ (pa_s) = (pa_s - f_S - c_S)d_S \tag{1}$$

$$\underset{d_S>0}{MAX}\ \Pi_P\ (f_S) = f_S d_S \tag{2}$$

As the leader, the platform first sets the commission fee f_S charged to the merchant per order. Then, the merchant determines her profit-maximizing selling price pa_S. Through backward induction, we obtain Lemma 1.

Lemma 1: Under the scenario of merchant self-delivery (S), the equilibrium solution is: $f_S = \frac{1-c_S}{2}$, $pa_S = \frac{3+c_S}{4}$, $d_S = \frac{1-c_S}{4}$, $\Pi_b = \frac{(1-c_S)^2}{16}$, $\Pi_p = \frac{(1-c_S)^2}{8}$, respectively.

Lemma 1 states that the optimal selling price for the merchant increases with the increase in the merchant's delivery cost, while the optimal commission fee charged by the platform decreases with the increase in the merchant's delivery cost. This is because in situations where the merchant's delivery cost is relatively high, the merchant will raise their price to ensure their profit, which inevitably leads to a decrease in consumer demand. In response, the platform may reduce its commission fee to attract and retain merchants. Furthermore, under the scenario of merchant self-delivery, the platform's profit is significantly higher than the merchant's profit. As the platform holds the advantage of being the leader, the equilibrium profit for the platform is twice that of the merchant's equilibrium profit.

Pre-reform Platform Delivery (NK): In this scenario, the platform does not undergo transparency reform in its fee structure, and the merchant uses the platform's delivery mode. Without the reform, the platform charges the merchant a service fee, denoted as F_{NK}, which does not differentiate between the technical service fee (commission) and the fulfillment service fee (delivery fee). Additionally, the platform sets a fixed amount c_R as the payment to the delivery rider per order. Therefore, under the condition of no transparency reform and the merchant choosing platform delivery, the profit maximization models for the merchant and the platform are as follows:

$$\underset{d_{NK}>0}{MAX}\ \Pi_b\ (pa_{NK}) = (pa_{NK} - F_{NK})d_{NK} \tag{3}$$

$$\underset{d_{NK}>0}{MAX}\ \Pi_P\ (F_{NK}) = (F_{NK} - c_R)d_{NK} \tag{4}$$

The platform first sets the service fee F_{NK} charged to the merchant. Then, the merchant determines her profit-maximizing selling price pa_{NK}. Through backward induction, we obtain Lemma 2.

Lemma 2: Under the scenario of no transparency reform in platform delivery fees and the merchant choosing platform delivery (NK), the equilibrium solution is: $F_{NK} = \frac{1+c_R+h_K}{2}$, $pa_{NK} = \frac{3+c_R+3h_K}{4}$, $d_{NK} = \frac{1-c_R+h_K}{4}$, $\Pi_b = \frac{(1-c_R+h_K)^2}{16}$ and $\Pi_p = \frac{(1-c_R+h_K)^2}{8}$, respectively.

Lemma 2 states: in the presence of platform delivery and without transparency reform in delivery fees, the equilibrium profit for the platform remains twice that of the merchant. When the merchant opts for platform delivery, the stronger real-time delivery tracking effect generated by the platform increases consumer willingness to purchase, leading the merchant to set higher prices for greater profits. Consequently, the platform may set higher service fees to maximize its own profit. Thus, in equilibrium, the optimal service fee for the platform and the optimal selling price for the merchant are higher, with the real-time delivery tracking effect having a more significant impact on product prices. Additionally, both the platform's optimal service fee and the merchant's optimal selling price increase with the payment to the delivery rider.

Post-reform Platform Delivery (GK): In this scenario, the platform undergoes transparency reform in its fee structure and charges the merchant in two parts: the technical service fee (commission) f_{GK} and the fulfillment service fee (delivery fee) c_{GK}. The fulfillment service fee c_{GK} is a function that varies with the merchant's selling price pa_{GK} in different stages. The specific forms of variation are as follows:

$$c_{GK} = \begin{cases} c_0, pa_{GK} \leq pa_0 \\ c_0 + t(pa_{GK} - pa_0), pa_{GK} \geq pa_0 \end{cases} \tag{5}$$

Here, $t < 1$ represents the additional delivery cost per unit price increase when the merchant's price pa_{GK} exceeds the threshold pa_0. c_0 represents the fixed delivery fee when the price does not exceed pa_0. Therefore, under the scenario of transparency reform in fees and the merchant choosing platform delivery, the profit maximization models for the merchant and the platform are as follows. When $pa_{GK} \leq pa_0$:

$$\underset{d_{GK}>0}{MAX} \, \Pi_b \, (pa_{GK}) = (pa_{GK} - f_{GK} - c_0)d_{GK} \tag{6}$$

$$\underset{d_{GK}>0}{MAX} \, \Pi_P \, (f_{GK}) = (f_{GK} + c_0 - c_R)d_{GK} \tag{7}$$

When $pa_{GK} \geq pa_0$, the profit maximization models are:

$$\underset{d_{GK}>0}{MAX} \, \Pi_b \, (pa_{GK}) = (pa_{GK} - f_{GK} - c_0 - t(pa_{GK} - pa_0))d_{GK} \tag{8}$$

$$\underset{d_{GK}>0}{MAX} \, \Pi_P \, (f_{GK}) = (f_{GK} + c_0 + t(pa_{GK} - pa_0) - c_R)d_{GK} \tag{9}$$

Similarly, the platform first sets the commission f_{GK} charged to the merchant. Then, the merchant decides profit-maximizing selling price pa_{GK}.

In the scenario where the merchant undergoes transparency reform in delivery fees and chooses platform delivery (GK), we can obtain the equilibrium solution when $pa_{GK} \leq pa_0$ as follows: $f_{GK} = \frac{1-2c_0+c_R+h_K}{2}$, $pa_{GK} = \frac{3+c_R+3h_K}{4}$, $d_{GK} = \frac{1-c_R+h_K}{4}$, $\Pi_b = \frac{(1-c_R+h_K)^2}{16}$, $\Pi_p = \frac{(1-c_R+h_K)^2}{8}$. If the equilibrium solution obtained at this point satisfies the predetermined range, $pa_{GK} \leq pa_0$, which implies $3 + c_R + 3h_K \leq 4pa_0$, then $pa_0 \geq \frac{3+c_R+3h_K}{4}$, the above solution is considered the equilibrium solution.

When $pa_{GK} > pa_0$, the equilibrium solution is as follows: $f_{GK} = \frac{(1-t)^2 - (2-t)c_0 + (1-t)c_R + (1-t)^2 h_K + t(2-t)pa_0}{2(1-t)}$, $pa_{GK} = \frac{c_R + (3-2t)(1+h_K)}{2(2-t)}$, $d_{GK} = \frac{1-c_R+h_K}{4-2t}$,

$\Pi_b = \frac{(1-t)(1-c_R+h_K)^2}{4(2-t)^2}$, $\Pi_P = \frac{(1-c_R+h_K)^2}{4(2-t)}$. Similarly, if the equilibrium solution obtained at this point satisfies the predetermined range, $pa_{GK} \geq pa_0$, which implies $3 + c_R + 3h_K \geq 4pa_0 + 2t(1 + h_K - pa_0)$, then $pa_0 \leq \frac{3+c_R+3h_K-2t(1+h_K)}{4-2t}$, the above solution is considered the equilibrium solution.

Combining the two scenarios, we can conclude the following: In the case where $pa_0 > \frac{3+c_R+3h_K}{4}$, the merchant strictly controls the product price below the threshold pa_0 by reducing the delivery costs, ensuring the maximization of their own profits. However, when $pa_0 < \frac{3+c_R+3h_K-2t(1+h_K)}{4-2t}$, indicating a lower threshold, the merchant strictly controls the selling price above the threshold to maximize their profits by increasing the product's selling price. And in the range where $\frac{3+c_R+3h_K}{4} \geq pa_0 \geq \frac{3+c_R+3h_K-2t(1+h_K)}{4-2t}$, the merchant allows the product price to fluctuate around the threshold pa_0, and the specific choice depends on the profitability. By comparing the two scenarios of higher and lower thresholds, it is evident that the merchant generates greater profit in the case of a higher threshold. Therefore, even in the intermediate threshold range, the merchant tends to control the price below the threshold.

Hence, Lemma 3 is obtained.

Lemma 3: Under the reform of transparent delivery fee rates on the platform and the scenario where the merchant chooses platform delivery (GK), two different equilibrium solutions can arise.

i) When $pa_0 \geq \frac{3+c_R+3h_K-2t(1+h_K)}{4-2t}$, the equilibrium solution is: $f_{GK} = \frac{1-2c_0+c_R+h_K}{2}$, $pa_{GK} = \frac{3+c_R+3h_K}{4}$, $d_{GK} = \frac{1-c_R+h_K}{4}$, $\Pi_b = \frac{(1-c_R+h_K)^2}{16}$, $\Pi_p = \frac{(1-c_R+h_K)^2}{8}$;

ii) When $pa_0 < \frac{3+c_R+3h_K-2t(1+h_K)}{4-2t}$, the equilibrium solution is: $f_{GK} = \frac{(1-t)^2-(2-t)c_0+(1-t)c_R+(1-t)^2h_K+t(2-t)pa_0}{2(1-t)}$, $pa_{GK} = \frac{c_R+(3-2t)(1+h_K)}{2(2-t)}$, $d_{GK} = \frac{1-c_R+h_K}{4-2t}$, $\Pi_b = \frac{(1-t)(1-c_R+h_K)^2}{4(2-t)^2}$, $\Pi_P = \frac{(1-c_R+h_K)^2}{4(2-t)}$.

Lemma 3 indicates that after the reform of the delivery fee rates for food delivery, two different equilibrium states can occur depending on the threshold price (pa_0).

When pa_0 is relatively high, in the equilibrium state, the platform, which has a first-mover advantage, continues to earn profits that are twice the equilibrium profits of the merchants. In this case, the optimal selling price for merchants and the optimal commission for the platform both increase with the strengthening of real-time delivery tracking effects and rider delivery costs. The results obtained when the price threshold is high are consistent with the pre-reform results. This is because if the price threshold is set too high, few merchants can reach the threshold, and the delivery costs remain fixed, similar to the pre-reform scenario.

When the price threshold (pa_0) is relatively low, the platform with a first-mover advantage still earns significantly higher profits than the merchants. However, compared to the pre-reform scenario, the equilibrium profits of the merchants are now less than half of the equilibrium profits of the platform. This indicates that the transparency reform of delivery rates benefits the platform more. Compared to the high price threshold, the negative impact of rider delivery costs on the optimal commission is stronger, while the positive impact of real-time delivery tracking effects on the optimal commission is weaker, and the positive effect of the price threshold is further enhanced. The optimal selling price for merchants is not affected by the price threshold but increases with the strengthening of real-time delivery tracking effects and rider delivery costs. This is because when the price threshold is low, merchants tend to set prices higher than the threshold to maximize their profits. As the price threshold increases, merchants' delivery costs decrease, and the platform tends to set higher commission fees to maximize its own profits.

3.2 Equilibrium Analysis of Merchant and Platform Profit

In the previous section, we obtained the optimal selling price for merchants, the optimal service fee for the platform, and the optimal profits for both the platform and the merchants in three different scenarios, as shown in Table 2. Building on this, we further discuss the choice of food delivery methods for merchants.

Table 2. Comparison of merchants and platforms in three modes.

	Self-delivery	Pre-reform platform delivery	Post-reform platform delivery	
			High price threshold	Low price threshold
Commission	$\frac{1-c_S}{2}$	$\frac{1+c_R+h_K}{2}$	$\frac{1-2c_0+c_R+h_K}{2}$	##
Online selling price	$\frac{3+c_S}{4}$	$\frac{3+c_R+3h_K}{4}$	$\frac{3+c_R+3h_K}{4}$	$\frac{c_R+(3-2t)(1+h_K)}{2(2-t)}$
The platform's profit	$\frac{(1-c_S)^2}{8}$	$\frac{(1-c_R+h_K)^2}{8}$	$\frac{(1-c_R+h_K)^2}{8}$	$\frac{(1-c_R+h_K)^2}{4(2-t)}$
Merchant's profit	$\frac{(1-c_S)^2}{16}$	$\frac{(1-c_R+h_K)^2}{16}$	$\frac{(1-c_R+h_K)^2}{16}$	$\frac{(1-t)(1-c_R+h_K)^2}{4(2-t)^2}$

Note: "##" represents $\frac{(1-t)^2-(2-t)c_0+(1-t)c_R+(1-t)^2h_K+t(2-t)pa_0}{2(1-t)}$

When $pa_0 \geq \frac{3+c_R+3h_K-2t(1+h_K)}{4-2t}$, that is, after the rate reform, when the price threshold for the tiered changes in delivery fees is set to a high value, the profits of both the merchants and the platform remain the same under the pre- and post-reform delivery models.

1) If $h_K < c_R - c_S$, $\max\{(\pi_b)_S, (\pi_b)_{NK}, (\pi_b)_{GK}\} = (\pi_b)_S$, merchants maximize their profits when they handle the delivery themselves, so whether the platform reforms or not, merchants will always choose the self-delivery mode.

2) If $h_K > c_R - c_S$, $\max\{(\pi_b)_S, (\pi_b)_{NK}, (\pi_b)_{GK}\} = (\pi_b)_{NK} = (\pi_b)_{GK}$, The maximum profit for both the merchants and the platform is achieved when the platform handles the delivery. Therefore, whether the platform undergoes reform or not, merchants will always choose the platform delivery mode.

When $pa_0 < \frac{3+c_R+3h_K-2t(1+h_K)}{4-2t}$, When the price threshold for the tiered changes in delivery fees is relatively low, let $h_1 = \frac{(2-t)(1-c_S)}{2\sqrt{(1-t)}} + c_R - 1$, $h_2 = \frac{\sqrt{2-t}(1-c_S)}{\sqrt{2}} + c_R - 1$, where $h_1 > c_R - c_S > h_2$. Indeed, it is evident that under the GK scenario, the platform profit is higher than under the NK scenario, while under the NK scenario, the merchant profit is higher than under the GK scenario.

1) If $h_1 > h_K > c_R - c_S$, the relationship between platform and merchant profits in the three scenarios are as follows: $(\pi_p)_{GK} > (\pi_p)_{NK} > (\pi_p)_S$, $(\pi_b)_{NK} > (\pi_b)_S > (\pi_b)_{GK}$. The game process between merchants and the platform under these conditions is shown in Table 3. The final equilibrium point is that the platform does not undergo reform, and merchants choose the delivery mode.

2) If $h_K > h_1$, The relationship between platform and merchant profits in the three scenarios are as follows: $(\pi_p)_{GK} > (\pi_p)_{NK} > (\pi_p)_S$, $(\pi_b)_{NK} > (\pi_b)_{GK} > (\pi_b)_S$. The equilibrium strategy set is (G, K), If the platform undergoes reform or not, merchants will still choose the platform delivery mode.

Table 3. The game process between the platform and the merchants

	N	G
K	$(\frac{(1-c_R+h_K)^2}{8}, \frac{(1-c_R+h_K)^2}{16})$	$(\frac{(1-c_R+h_K)^2}{4(2-t)}, \frac{(1-t)(1-c_R+h_K)^2}{4(2-t)^2})$
S	$(\frac{(1-c_S)^2}{8}, \frac{(1-c_S)^2}{16})$	$(\frac{(1-c_S)^2}{8}, \frac{(1-c_S)^2}{16})$

Note: In the notation (a, b), 'a' represents platform profit, and 'b' represents merchant profit.

3) If $c_R - c_S > h_K > h_2$, The relationship between platform and merchant profits in the three scenarios are as follows: $(\pi_p)_{GK} > (\pi_p)_S > (\pi_p)_{NK}$, $(\pi_b)_S > (\pi_b)_{NK} > (\pi_b)_{GK}$. The equilibrium strategy set is (S). Whether the platform undergoes reform or not, the merchants will still choose self-delivery.

4) If $h_K < h_2$, The relationship between platform and merchant profits in the three scenarios are as follows: $(\pi_p)_S > (\pi_p)_{GK} > (\pi_p)_{NK}$, $(\pi_b)_S > (\pi_b)_{NK} > (\pi_b)_{GK}$.

The equilibrium strategy set remains as (S) in this case.

In conclusion, based on the above discussion, by combining scenarios (3) and (4) and defining $h_1 = \frac{(2-t)(1-c_S)}{2\sqrt{(1-t)}} + c_R - 1$, we can summarize the following proposition.

Proposition 1: when $c_R > c_S$;

i) When $h_K < c_R - c_S$, the platform's decision to reform or not doesn't matter, and the merchants will maintain the self-delivery mode (S);

ii) When $\{c_R - c_S < h_K < h_1, pa_0 < \frac{3+c_R+3h_K-2t(1+h_K)}{4-2t}\}$, the platform will not undergo reform, and the merchants will choose the platform delivery mode (NK);

iii) When $h_K > c_R - c_S$且$pa_0 \geq \frac{3+c_R+3h_K-2t(1+h_K)}{4-2t}$, the platform's decision to reform or not doesn't matter, and the merchants will choose the platform delivery mode (NK/GK);

iv) When $h_K > h_1$ and $pa_0 < \frac{3+c_R+3h_K-2t(1+h_K)}{4-2t}$, the platform will undergo reform, while the merchant's delivery mode remains the same as platform delivery (NK $\rightarrow$ GK).

When $c_R < c_S$, the S scenario will not exist, but the rest remain the same.

Propositions 1 provides specific conditions for the platform's decision to undergo reform or not, as well as the optimal delivery mode chosen by the merchants. Through numerical analysis, Fig. 2 vividly illustrates the results of Propositions 1 for the cases of $c_R > c_S$ and $c_R < c_S$. It is worth noting that when the parameter values change, the specific trends in the region divisions in Fig. 2 remain the same. It can be observed that the real-time delivery tracking effect on the consumers has a dominant influence on the choice between self-delivery and platform delivery modes for the merchants. Additionally, the real-time delivery tracking effect and the price threshold jointly impact the platform's decision on fee transparency reforms.

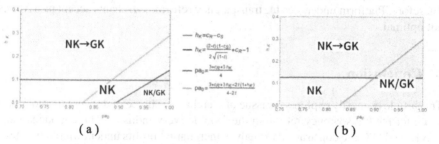

(a)   (b)

Fig. 2. Choice of Food Delivery Modes(a) $c_R > c_S$ (b) $c_R < c_S$.

By Proposition 1 and Fig. 2, we give the following specific explanations.

If consumers have little demand for real-time delivery tracking in food delivery, regardless of whether the platform undergoes reform or not, merchants will choose the self-delivery mode (S). If consumers have low demand for real-time delivery tracking and dynamic delivery routes, merchants tend to not choose platform delivery. Choosing platform delivery not only requires paying a certain commission to the platform but also incurs higher delivery costs compared to self-delivery. However, the limited improvement in consumer satisfaction from real-time delivery tracking has a limited impact on merchant demand. Additionally, the transparency reform of platform delivery fees has a minimal effect on self-delivery and does not significantly influence the choice of self-delivery mode for merchants. Therefore, merchants prefer the self-delivery mode due to relatively lower profits from choosing delivery.

If price threshold is small and real-time delivery tracking effect is moderate, platform won't undergo fee transparency reform, and merchants will choose platform delivery as the optimal choice for both parties (NK). Merchants prefer platform delivery as it leads to higher fees due to majority of orders exceeding threshold. Limited demand for real-time tracking restricts merchants from raising prices. Fee transparency reduces costs for small businesses, weakening platform's per-transaction profit. Despite attracting more merchants, platform prioritizes per-transaction profit and avoids reform.

If consumers demand real-time delivery tracking and there's a high price threshold, merchants will choose platform delivery mode (NK/GK) due to consumer satisfaction and increased demand, despite additional costs. Platform reform doesn't impact profits under this mode.

If consumers have a significant demand for real-time delivery tracking in food delivery, and the price threshold is low after reform, the platform undergoes fee transparency reform, and merchants insist on platform delivery mode (GK) as the optimal choice for both parties. Similar to the previous explanation, when there is a high demand for real-time delivery tracking, platform delivery mode is undoubtedly the better choice. When the price threshold is low, merchants need to balance delivery costs and the amount of goods sold, as the delivery fee becomes a function of the price. Reform seems to have no benefit for merchants. For the platform, the better the effect of real-time delivery tracking, the more efficient the order delivery will be, resulting in a better experience for both merchants and consumers. In this case, the platform is more inclined to reduce merchants' delivery costs to better promote real-time delivery services (platform delivery). Therefore, Platform undergoes fee transparency reform, merchants accept passively, but not optimal.

4   Conclusion

This article primarily explores the issue of merchants' choice of delivery methods before and after fee transparency reform in the food delivery industry. Three models, namely S, NK, and GK, are constructed to analyze merchants' profits under different modes. By comparing the profits in different modes, the specific conditions affecting their choice of optimal delivery methods in response to platform reform are analyzed.

Fee transparency reform in the food delivery industry has made the expenditure more transparent for merchants but has also reduced their profit margins, further widening the gap between platforms and merchants in terms of profits. The effects of real-time delivery tracking and price thresholds are key factors influencing the decisions of platforms and merchants. The specific conditions for merchants' delivery choices are as follows: If consumers have minimal demand for real-time delivery tracking, merchants are more likely to choose self-delivery to avoid high delivery costs and platform commissions. When the price threshold is small and there is moderate demand for real-time delivery tracking, merchants prioritize profits on each order and opt for platform delivery, while platforms are reluctant to undergo reform. When consumers have high demand for real-time delivery tracking and a low price threshold, merchants choose platform delivery, and fee transparency reforms can further increase their profits. Finally, if consumers have high demand for real-time delivery tracking and a high price threshold, the reform does not significantly impact merchants' choices. In conclusion, this study examines the impact of fee transparency reform on merchants in the food delivery industry. It emphasizes the need for merchants to consider consumer demand, price thresholds, and the pros and cons of self-delivery and platform delivery. The findings highlight the positive effect of fee transparency reform on merchants' profitability. These insights contribute to a better understanding of the challenges in the industry and can guide decision-makers and practitioners towards promoting its sustainable development.

However, there are limitations to this study. 1) Ignored minimum commission impact on low-value orders in platform revenue sharing. 2) Focused solely on individual merchant's delivery mode selection strategy. In a competitive environment, further research is needed on the delivery selection strategies of multiple merchants.

Acknowledgement. The authors gratefully acknowledge financial support from the National Social Science Foundation of China (Grant No. 21BGL033), Principal Scholar/Excellent Team of Instructors of Qinglan Project of Universities in Jiangsu, Postgraduate Research & Practice Innovation Program of Jiangsu Province and Innovation Team Project "Internet Platform Strategy and Governance (KYCTD202201)" sponsored by Nanjing University of Finance and Economics.

References

1. Choi, T.M., Guo, S., Liu, N., et al.: Optimal pricing in on-demand-service-platform-operations with hired agents and risk-sensitive customers in the blockchain era. Eur. J. Oper. Res. **284**(3), 1031–1042 (2020)
2. Ma, L., Jin, C., Huo, Y.: Selection of logistics service modes in e-commerce based on multi-oligopolies Cournot competition. Int. J. Ship. Transp. Logist. **11**(4), 354 (2019)
3. Liu, J., Guan, Z.: B2C E-commerce Logistic channel structure in China (2015)
4. Song, Y.Y., Maher, T.E., Nicholson, J.D., et al.: Strategic alliances in logistics outsourcing. Asia Pacific J. Market. Logist. **12**(4), 3–21 (2000)
5. Du, Z., Fan, Z.-P., Gao, G.-X.: Choice of O2O food delivery mode: self-built platform or third-party platform? Self-delivery or third-party delivery? IEEE Trans. Eng. Manag. **70**(6), 2206–2219 (2023)
6. Li, J., Shen, W., Liao, Y., et al.: The fulfillment service in online marketplaces. Eur. J. Oper. Res. (2024)
7. Tao, Z., Gou, Q., Zhang, J.: A local seller's app channel strategy concerning delivery. Int. J. Prod. Res. **58**(1), 220–255 (2020)
8. Du, Z., Fan, Z.P., Sun, F.H.: O2O dual-channel sales: choices of pricing policy and delivery mode for a restaurant. Int. J. Prod. Econ. **257**, 15 (2023)
9. ABN, AQL, AZM, et al.: Platform logistics or self-logistics? Restaurants' cooperation with online food-delivery platform considering profitability and sustainability. Int. J. Prod. Econ. (2021)
10. Sheryl, E.K., Laque, P.: Online, mobile, and text food ordering in the U.S. Restaurant Industry **11**(17), 6–18 (2011)
11. Liu, W., Florkowski, W.J.: Online meal delivery services: perception of service quality and delivery speed among Chinese consumers. In: Proceedings of the 2018 Annual Meeting, 2–6 February 2018, Jacksonville (2018)
12. Dao, Z.: Research on decision-making model of estimated delivery time in O2O food delivery. Indust. Eng. Manag. Sci. **23**(5), 8–14 (2018)
13. Wen, Y.: Research on Optimization of Two Types of Delivery Personnel Allocation in O2O Instant Food Delivery Platforms. Chongqing Jiaotong University (2023). (in Chinese)
14. Zhao, X.: Research on the Optimization of O2O Profit Model in Meituan Delivery. Qingdao University (2022). (in Chinese)
15. Xiaoyan, W., Kailing, P.: Current situation, problems and countermeasures of China's B2C logistics. In: Proceedings of the World Automation Congress (2012)

Research on the Influencing Factors and Efficiency of Digital Trade: Evidence from the Macro Level

Shiqian Xing[(⊠)]

School of Information, Central University of Finance and Economics, Beijing 102206, China
s.xing.bj@gmail.com

Abstract. Digital trade has become a crucial component of the digital economy and a significant area of focus in the field of commerce. However, there is still a need to investigate the factors and mechanisms that impact digital trade as well as evaluating its efficiency. Using national panel data, this paper employs various empirical research methods such as Difference in Differences (DID) and Data Envelopment Analysis (DEA), utilizes the United Nations Commodity Trade Statistics Database (UN Comtrade), and references international organizations' broad definition of digital trade including the Organization for Economic Cooperation and Development (OECD), World Trade Organization (WTO), and International Monetary Fund (IMF). The study measures the degree of digital trade while examining its factors and efficiency. Results indicate that China's digital trade efficiency ranks highly among major countries, with regional trade agreement significantly promoting its development. This study provides theoretical support and guidance for enhancing governance systems surrounding digital trade while clarifying its developmental positioning.

Keywords: Digital Trade · Difference in Differences · Data Envelopment Analysis · Regional Trade Agreement

1 Introduction

Digital Trade was proposed by the United States International Trade Commission (USITC) in Digital Trade in the U.S. and Global Economies, Part 1 in 2013, only ten years ago. Digital trade has brought significant benefits to the global economy [1]. In today's digitally enabled trade development, whether we can successfully make achievements in the field of digital trade is an important factor in national economic development, and also the key to the game of great powers. First of all, we must clearly position the problem. Some relevant scholars have done some research on the measurement and efficiency evaluation of digital trade. Gong Tong and Zhang Tianding used bilateral digital service value-added to measure the degree of digital trade, and selected the output input of four industries: publishing audio-visual and broadcasting activities, telecommunications, IT and other information services, and financial and insurance activities [2]. Wang Weiwei and Li Yuchen measured and evaluated the degree of digital trade in China from narrow and wide angles, and used the Stochastic Frontier Gravity Model to evaluate the efficiency and potential of digital trade in China [3]. In addition, Lan Qingxin and Dou Kai [4], Sun Yuqin and Wei Huini [5] examined the influencing factors and effects of digital trade from the perspectives of technological level and market foundation. It can be seen that the existing literature on digital trade mainly focuses on the influencing factors and effects, while the measurement and evaluation of digital trade efficiency in major economies in the world is still lacking. It is of far-reaching significance to clarify the input and output efficiency of China's digital trade for the formulation of relevant trade and digital economy policies. In view of this, according to the logic of measuring efficiency first and then clarifying factors, this paper uses Data Envelopment Analysis (DEA), Difference in Differences (DID) methods to carry out relevant research.

2   Literature Review

Regarding the measurement of digital trade efficiency, existing studies mainly measure it from a broad and narrow perspective. The narrow-angle measurement of digital trade mainly focuses on digital trade services enabled by information and communication technologies. This narrow-angle measurement method is mainly proposed by the United Nations Conference on Trade and Development (UNCTAD) and the United States International Trade Commission (USITC). Nowadays, the concept of potential ICT-enabled services proposed by UNCTAD is mainly adopted (UNCTAD, 2018).

The broad-based concept was proposed by international organizations such as the Organization for Economic Cooperation and Development (OECD), the World Trade Organization (WTO), and the International Monetary Fund (IMF), which defined digital trade as "all trade ordered and/or delivered through digital forms" (OECD, WTO, and IMF, 2020). The measurement framework of digital trade released in 2020 based on OECD, WTO, and IMF mainly divides digital trade into Digitally Ordered Trade, Digitally Delivered Trade, and Digital Intermediary Platform Enabled Trade. Digitally Ordered Trade mainly refers to trade activities ordered on online platforms and delivered in the form of services, taking into account TO B and TO C levels, such as online ordering of tourism accommodation products. Digitally Delivered Trade refers to trade activities ordered on online platforms and delivered in digital form, such as online ordering and delivery of transnational scientific research data. While Digital Intermediary Platform Enabled Trade refers to digital trade activities based on digital platforms that provide intermediary services for both parties.

By comparing the narrow and broad concept, it can be seen that the broad concept focuses more on trade brought about by digital empowerment, including trade enabled by digital platforms in the scope of digital trade.

Scholars have adopted a combination of broad and narrow concepts to measure digital trade [6]. Other studies have investigated the current state of digital trade measurement in China from the perspectives of enterprise surveys and customs statistics, and have also examined the advantages and disadvantages of different measurement methods by combining the concept of "ICT-enabled services trade" in digital delivery trade [7].

There is limited research on the efficiency of digital trade. Some scholars have used the Stochastic Frontier Gravity Model to measure China's digital trade potential and efficiency. According to their findings, China's digital trade efficiency is generally insufficient and the regional development is unbalanced, but there is great potential [3, 8]. Other scholars have used the Entropy Weight Method and Dagum Gini Coefficient to measure the efficiency of digital trade in Chinese urban agglomerations, and found that the Beijing-Tianjin-Hebei, Pearl River Delta, and Yangtze River Delta urban agglomerations have better digital trade development.

Regarding the factors that affect digital trade, some scholars have studied the impact of regional trade agreements on the trade in value-added digital services [2]. At the same time, other studies have focused on the impact of digital trade agreements on digital trade [9, 10]. The development level of the internet, population income, convenience of payment, and digital technology all have a positive impact on digital trade, while state intervention and the degree of dependence on foreign trade have a negative impact on it [11, 12]. From a national perspective, developing countries face greater barriers to digital trade, and RCEP represents an opportunity for China to enhance its governance capabilities in digital trade.

Overall, there is still limited research on measuring the efficiency of digital trade in major economies around the world. The research on factors affecting digital trade mainly focuses on relevant policies and agreements.

3 Research Hypothesis and Question Proposal

Given the overall lack of research on the efficiency of digital trade in major economies around the world, this study will focus on this topic. Referencing the studies of scholars such as Gong Tong, Tao, and Jeongmeen, and combining economic reality, this paper will focus on the role of digital trade agreements and regional trade agreements in promoting digital trade. As digital trade rules are becoming a key factor affecting the development of global value chain (GVC) service trade [13].

The Comprehensive and Progressive Agreement for Trans-Pacific Partnership (CPTPP) is a regional trade agreement signed by 12 Asia-Pacific countries, which includes provisions related to digital trade. Digital trade rules play a significant role in the agreement, with its framework continuing traditional e-commerce issues such as duty-free electronic transmission, personal information protection, and online consumer protection, while also introducing some controversial issues such as cross-border data flows, localization of computing facilities, and source code protection. Its rules on digital trade will inevitably regulate digital trade and reduce information asymmetry and barriers. The CPTPP agreement establishes an international framework for cross-border data flow, encompassing traditional e-commerce topics while also demonstrating inheritance, innovation, and foresight in the design of its digital trade framework [14]. Theoretically, the CPTPP agreement is expected to have a positive impact on regional digital trade integration [15]. In terms of the practical economic significance of CPTPP for digital trade, this paper selects the CPTPP agreement as a regional trade agreement that will affect digital trade, and studies the impact of the agreement on digital trade represented by CPTPP.

Based on the above analysis, the following hypothesis is proposed:

Assumption 1: Regional trade agreements related to digital trade represented by CPTPP will positively promote digital trade.

4   Model Construction and Variable Explanation

4.1   Data Envelopment Analysis (DEA) Model Design and Variable Description

Data Envelopment Analysis (DEA) is a quantitative method for evaluating the input-output efficiency of economic units or sectors with comparable indicators, proposed by American operations researcher A. Charnes and professor W.W. Cooper in 1978. It is primarily based on multiple input and output indicators. Regarding the inputs of digital trade and combining the approach of scholars Wang Weiwei and Li Yuchen (2023), the country's digital trade inputs are measured from six aspects: total economic scale, population size, cultural level, imports and exports, level of scientific and technological research and development, and government revenue. The outputs of digital trade are measured using the import and export trade volumes of typical digital service industries, including the communications services industry, computer and information services industry, and other commercial services industries. The classification standards are based on the United Nations Commodity Trade Statistics Database. The input indicators include the total population, GDP, public spending on education, research and development expenditures, tax revenue, and import and export of goods and services. The output indicator is the amount of digital trade. The data source is the World Bank. The research subjects are the top ten countries in the world GDP ranking in 2023, namely: the United States, China, Japan, Germany, India, the United Kingdom, France, Russia, Canada, and Italy. Due to missing data for some indicators in Japan, the final research subjects are the remaining nine countries excluding Japan.

The BCC model of Data Envelopment Analysis (DEA) is used to model the aforementioned indicators. Let x_{ij} represent the amount of the i input indicator for the j country, with $x_{ij} > 0$. Let y_{ir} represent the amount of the r output indicator for the j country, with $y_{ir} > 0$. The BCC model is constructed as follows:

$$
\begin{cases}
\min \theta \\
s.t. \ \sum_{i=1}^{n} \lambda_i x_{ij} \leq \theta x_{ij} \\
s.t. \ \sum_{i=1}^{n} \lambda_i y_{ir} \geq y_{kr} \\
s.t. \ \sum_{i=1}^{n} \lambda_i = 1 \\
\lambda_i \geq 0, j = 1, \ldots, m, k = 1, \ldots, n
\end{cases} \tag{1}
$$

The BCC model is adopted because it is suitable for variable returns to scale and can explain technical efficiency, pure technical efficiency, and scale efficiency. Considering the current economic situation and data availability, data from 2012–2021 were selected for analysis.

The results of the model solution are in Table 1:

From the results above, it can be seen that over the ten-year period from 2012 to 2021, China, the United Kingdom, and Canada were DEA effective. Among them, China and Canada were strongly DEA effective, while the United Kingdom was weakly DEA effective. The bar chart of the comprehensive benefits of each country is shown in Fig. **1**.

Table 1. Validity Analysis of the BCC Model Results

Country	Technical Efficiency	Scale Efficiency	Comprehensive Efficiency	S-	S+	Efficiency
China	1	1	1	−0.01	0	Strong DEA efficient
USA	0.578	0.75	0.433	6.72×10^{13}	0	Non-DEA efficient
UK	1	1	1	0.00	0	Weak DEA efficient
France	0.818	0.295	0.241	2.52×10^{11}	0	Non-DEA efficient
India	1	0	0	4.54×10^{9}	0	Non-DEA efficient
Germany	0.804	0.673	0.541	1.14×10^{13}	0	Non-DEA efficient
Italy	1	0.131	0.131	1.12×10^{12}	0	Non-DEA efficient
Russia	1	0.183	0.183	1.13×10^{12}	0	Non-DEA efficient
Canada	1	1	1	0.00	0	Strong DEA efficient

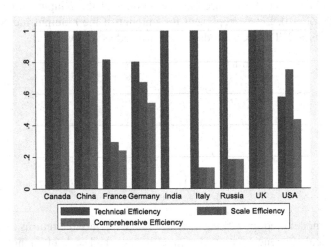

Fig. 1. Bar chart of the comprehensive efficiency of digital trade by country

The BCC model examines the digital trade efficiency of various countries under constant returns to scale. Here, the slack variable S- represents "how much input can be reduced to achieve target efficiency", while the slack variable S + signifies "how much output should be increased to reach the target efficiency".

4.2   Difference-In-Differences (DID) Model Design and Variable Description

Model Design.   Regional Trade Agreements (RTAs) are a significant factor affecting the extent of digital trade. This paper selects the Comprehensive and Progressive Agreement for Trans-Pacific Partnership (CPTPP) as an exogenous shock to study whether joining a particular RTA has an impact on a country's digital trade, hence conducting a quasi-natural experiment. The CPTPP, as a regional trade agreement composed of Asia-Pacific countries, is typically representative of the impact of RTAs. Countries that have joined the CPTPP are considered the treatment group, while those that have not are the control group. The following Difference-in-Differences (DID) model is constructed:

$$y_{it} = \beta \times cptpp\_after_{it} + X_{it}\gamma + \varphi_t + \alpha_t + \varepsilon_{it} \tag{2}$$

$$cptpp\_after_{it} = cptpp_i \times after_t \tag{3}$$

The Eq. (2) above represents a Difference-in-Differences (DID) estimation model that accounts for year and country fixed effects. In the model, y_{it} denotes the state of a country's digital trade, which, based on practical research considerations, is measured as the percentage of Information and Communication Technology (ICT) product imports and exports relative to the total volume of product imports and exports. $after_{it}$ is a dummy variable indicating the treatment effect period. The CPTPP agreement was signed into effect on December 30, 2018. Since the effective date was only one day away from 2019, this paper sets 2019 as the policy implementation year. Adjustments are also made in line with the actual circumstances of different countries. Specifically, the years 2019 and thereafter are assigned a value of 1, while previous years are assigned a value of 0. $cptpp_{it}$ is a dummy variable for the treatment group, indicating whether a country has joined the CPTPP agreement. A value of 1 is assigned if a country has joined the CPTPP, and 0 otherwise. $cptpp \times after_{it}$ is the interaction term for the DID, used to estimate the impact of joining the CPTPP on digital trade. X_{it} is a set of time-varying country characteristic variables, including basic macroeconomic indicators of the country. φ_t And α_i are used to control for annual fixed effects and country fixed effects, respectively, and ε_{it} is the random error term.

Variable and Data Description.   The data for this Difference-in-Differences model is all sourced from the World Bank Economic Database.

The core dependent variable. This paper constructs a Difference-in-Differences model at both the year and country levels. The core explanatory variable (y_{it}) is the percentage of Information and Communication Technology (ICT) in the total import and export volume of goods for a country. Here, drawing on the broad definition of digital trade by the OECD, WTO, and IMF, and considering practical research conducted by relevant scholars using digital trade intermediary platforms for empowerment measurement [3], we have selected the percentage of ICT in the total import and export volume of goods as the core dependent variable. ICT services, as the core hardware and software infrastructure supporting digital trade, empower it and can reflect the state of digital trade's infrastructure and support to a certain extent.

The core dependent variable. The core dependent variable ($cptpp\_after_{it}$) is obtained from multiplying $cptpp_i$ with $after_t$. $cptpp\_after_{it}$ Represents the interaction term for joining the CPTPP and the year of joining. When the core explanatory variable takes a value of 1, it indicates that the country has joined the CPTPP agreement and the year is after joining the CPTPP agreement. When the core explanatory variable takes a value of 0, it means that at least one of the above conditions is not met.

Control variables. Considering the close connection between the volume of a country's digital trade and its level of economic development, representative macroeconomic indicators of the country were selected as control variables. Specifically, this includes: national GDP (in US dollars) ($\ln gdp$), per capita GDP ($\ln per\_capita\_gdp$), the number of secure national internet servers($\ln server$), etc. All control variables are in logarithm.

5   Empirical Results and Analysis

5.1   Baseline Regressions

The results of the baseline regression are reported in Table 2, with fixed effects and control variables added to the model in sequence. The results show that, regardless of the addition of any control variables and the setting of fixed effects at different levels, the interaction term $cptpp\_after_{it}$ is significant at least at the 0.1 level, indicating that joining the CPTPP agreement has a significant promotional effect on a country's digital trade. This is consistent with the conclusions of existing research. As countries join the CPTPP agreement, the rules of digital trade are standardized and trade barriers are reduced, which promotes the country's digital trade, thus verifying the hypothesis of this paper. At the same time, after controlling for all fixed effects, the estimated coefficient of the number of secure internet servers is significantly positive, indicating that the more secure internet servers there are, the more obvious the promoting effect on digital trade.

Table 2. Difference-in-Differences Regression Results

variable	(1)	(2)	(3)	(4)
did	19.00^{***}	1.97^{**}	1.85^{*}	1.92^{*}
	(3.02)	(1.86)	(1.67)	(1.76)
$\ln gdp$		1.59	0.29	
		(1.23)	(0.29)	
$\ln server$		0.37^{*}	0.15^{*}	0.36^{*}
		(1.74)	(1.95)	(1.87)
$\ln per\_capita\_gdp$		-0.14	-0.11	
		(-0.07)	(-0.06)	
Control Variables	No	Yes	Yes	Yes
Country-Year Fixed Effects	No	Yes	No	Yes
Country Fixed Effects	No	No	Yes	No
Observation	1,177	1,170	1,170	1,170
R^2	0.10	0.97	0.97	0.97

*** $p < .01$, ** $p < .05$, * $p < .1$

5.2 Robustness Test

Parallel Trend Test.   To test the robustness of this Difference-in-Differences model and ensure that the prerequisites for treatment effects are met, this paper conducts a parallel trends test. Figure 2 presents the results of the parallel trends test.

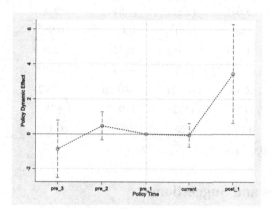

Fig. 2. Results of Parallel Trend Test

Figure 2 shows that, compared to the years before the shock began, the years after the shock started exhibit different differences, thus passing the parallel trends test.

PSM-DID Method.   To mitigate the endogeneity issues arising from sample selection bias, this paper follows the approach of Gong et al. (2023) and employs the Propensity Score Matching - Difference-in-Differences method (PSM-DID) for robustness checks. In the choice of matching methods, this paper opts for 1:1 nearest neighbor matching. Table 3 reports the results from pooled OLS, fixed effects models, samples using non-empty weights, samples satisfying the common support assumption, and regressions weighted by frequency. The results show that the coefficient of the Difference-in-Differences interaction term remains significantly positive and is largely consistent with the baseline regression. This indicates that the promotional effect of joining the CPTPP agreement on national digital trade is robust.

Table 3. Baseline Regression and PSM-DID Result

	(1)	(2)	(3)	(4)	(5)
	OLS	FE	Weight! =	On_Support	Weight_Reg
did	14.25^{**}	16.02^{**}	20.34^{**}	16.48^{**}	19.06^{**}
	(2.27)	(2.39)	(2.34)	(2.29)	(2.12)

(*continued*)

Table 3. (*continued*)

	(1)	(2)	(3)	(4)	(5)
	OLS	FE	Weight! =	On_Support	Weight_Reg
ln*gdp*	1.37***	1.29***	3.21*	2.18***	2.22
	(3.08)	(2.82)	(1.81)	(2.96)	(1.38)
ln*per_capita_gdp*	0.66*	0.70*	1.37	0.95**	1.08
	(1.67)	(1.76)	(0.82)	(2.09)	(0.84)
ln*server*	0.82***	1.02***	−0.41	0.89*	−0.21
	(2.86)	(2.92)	(−0.26)	(1.92)	(−0.17)
N	1172	1172	150	871	246
Adj. R^2	0.19	0.20	0.07	0.19	0.06

*** $p < .01$, ** $p < .05$, * $p < .1$

6 Conclusions and Suggestions

6.1 Research Conclusions

Based on the results of the DEA analysis, the aforementioned countries can be categorized into three types. The first type: countries with an early start in digital trade and have already achieved initial success. The United States is representative of this category. The second type: countries that are vigorously developing digital trade, where the digital economy is a key focus of the nation. China, the United Kingdom, and Canada are examples. The third type: countries with substantial technological strength but slower development and relatively lower efficiency in the field of digital trade. France, India, Germany, Italy, and Russia are representative of this group.

Looking at the comprehensive benefits of DEA for each country, China, the United Kingdom, and Canada have the highest overall efficiency, indicating that the comprehensive input in these countries yields a higher output in the field of digital trade. The input-output efficiency in digital trade is not very high for other countries, suggesting that there is considerable resource wastage or investment not targeted at digital trade. For the same macroeconomic input indicators, higher comprehensive benefits indicate that these countries pay more attention to digital trade or the digital economy, with China, the United Kingdom, and Canada being typical examples. The United States has a comprehensive benefit of only 0.433, indicating that the input-output efficiency in the field of digital trade is relatively low. Analyzing the reasons, as the world's largest economy, the United States started early in digital trade and currently has achieved higher effectiveness in this area. Therefore, it has allocated its overall input to other fields, resulting in lower comprehensive benefits. China's investment in the field of digital trade is sufficient, and the focus should be on how to better maximize the efficiency of the input resources in digital trade.

For countries that are not DEA-efficient and have lower comprehensive benefits, India, Russia, and Canada all have high technical efficiency, indicating that these countries are relatively rational and effective in the technical utilization, factor input, and resource allocation of digital trade. However, the lower scale efficiency and comprehensive benefits indicate that the main problem for these countries lies in scale efficiency. The next step for these countries should focus on improving the scale efficiency of digital trade to maximize its potential. At the same time, it is also necessary to strengthen the investment in digital trade to achieve the desired efficiency.

Analyzing the scale efficiency and comprehensive benefits of each country reveals that countries with lower scale efficiency often have lower comprehensive benefits, even though they possess higher technical efficiency. This indicates that for digital trade efficiency, leveraging the economic scale efficiency is key to enhancing the efficiency of digital trade.

Combining the results of the Difference-in-Differences analysis with the actual exogenous shocks selected in this paper, it is evident that joining the CPTPP agreement can have a positive impact on a country's digital trade. Generalizing this conclusion, it can be seen that Regional Trade Agreements (RTAs), represented by the CPTPP, play a significant role in promoting national digital trade. Therefore, while developing the domestic economy, countries should pay attention to the undeniable role of joining Regional Trade Agreements in their digital trade. Regional trade agreements standardize trade rules within the region, reduce trade barriers, and effectively promote the development of digital trade. The CPTPP agreement selected for study in this paper includes specific provisions on digital trade. Its framework for digital trade rules not only continues traditional e-commerce topics such as duty-free electronic transmission, personal information protection, and online consumer protection but also innovatively introduces issues like cross-border data flow, localization of computing facilities, and source code protection.

6.2 Research Limitations and Future Prospects

Due to data source limitations, this paper has limited construction of indicators in analyzing national digital trade efficiency using data envelopment analysis. Further research is needed to develop a more comprehensive set of indicators for digital trade output and input. It is also necessary to include a larger number of countries in the study. At the same time, a more in-depth investigation is required into how regional trade agreements affect the mechanisms of national digital trade.

From the data envelopment analysis of major countries' digital trade measurements, it can be seen that the United States started early and is relatively ahead in the field of digital trade. China is positioned just behind the United States in the second tier and has also achieved effective results, indicating that China's recent economic focus remains on digital trade and the digital economy. Among other major countries, there are also some whose digital trade has not yet reached an effective scale or considerable efficiency. Overall, as one of the world's major economies, China still needs to continue paying attention to digital trade and further develop it strategically and practically.

At the same time, joining Regional Trade Agreements represented by the CPTPP plays a significant role in promoting national digital trade. As one of the world's important economies, China needs to continuously strengthen international cooperation, actively play a major country role in regional trade agreements, reduce trade barriers, and promote the development of digital trade.

Acknowledgement. This work is supported by the Innovative Training Program for College Students of CUFE "The Path of Digital Transformation Driving Green Transformation: Empirical Study on Manufacturing Enterprises" (C2023112312).

References

1. Hao, S., Chen, Z., Wang, C.-C., Hung, C.-Y.: Impact of digital service trade barriers and cross-border digital service inputs on economic growth. Sustainability **15**(19), 14547 (2023). https://doi.org/10.3390/su151914547
2. Gong, T., Zhang, T.: How do digital trade rules in regional trade agreements affect the trade of digital service value-added - based on the study of rule network structural power. J. Int. Trade **11**, 40–56 (2023). (In Chinese)
3. Wang, W., Li, Y.: Calculation of China's digital trade efficiency and potential for digital trade. Stat. Decision **39**(21), 108–112 (2023). (In Chinese)
4. Lan, Q., Dou, K.: An empirical study on the international competitiveness of china's digital trade based on the "diamond model." Social Sci. **03**, 44–54 (2019). (In Chinese)
5. Sun, Y., Wei, H.: Reflections on China's development of digital trade with Central and Eastern European countries under the "belt and road" Initiative. Intertrade **01**, 76–87 (2022). (In Chinese)
6. Gao, X., Wang, M., Jia, H.: Research on digital trade measurement — from focusing on the actual delivery of digital services to full coverage of digital trade. Stat. Res. **40**(11), 17–28 (2023). (In Chinese)
7. Yue, Y., Zhang, C.: Statistical Measurement and Analysis of Digital Trade. Intertrade (2021) (In Chinese)
8. Ma, S., Guo, J., Zhang, H.: Policy analysis and development evaluation of digital trade: an international comparison. Chin. World. Econ. **27**(3), 49–75 (2019)
9. Suh, J., Roh, J.: The effects of digital trade policies on digital trade. World Econ. **46**(8), 2383–2407 (2023)
10. Jiang, T., Hu, Y., Haleem, F., et al.: Do digital trade rules matter? Empirical Evidence from TAPED. Sustainability. **15**(11), 9074 (2023)
11. Hu, Y., Zhou, H., Zou, Z.: An assessment of China's digital trade development and influencing factors. Front. Psychol. **13**, 837885 (2022)
12. Zhang, X., Wang, Y.: Research on the influence of digital technology and policy restrictions on the development of digital service trade. Sustainability. **14**(16), 10420 (2022)
13. Wu, J., Luo, Z., Wood, J.: How do digital trade rules affect global value chain trade in services? — analysis of preferential trade agreements. The World Economy. **46**(10), 3026–3047 (2023)
14. Xie, Z., Yang, S.: Cross-border data flow regulation in global governance and China's participation — a comparative analysis based on WTO. CPTPP and RCEP. Int. Rev.. **5**, 98–126 (2021). (In Chinese)
15. Mishra, N., Valencia, A.M.P.: Digital services and digital trade in the Asia pacific: an alternative model for digital integration? Asia Pacific Law Rev. **31**(2), 489–513 (2023)

Author Index

Printed in the United States
by Baker & Taylor Publisher Services